ABR 8720

D

FEI

MW01062805

12/16/2002

DATE			
DEC 1 2003			
MAR 8 2004			
JUN 3 0 2004			
AUG 0 5 2005			

BAKER & TAYLOR

The Regions of Italy

The Regions of Italy:

A Reference Guide to History and Culture

Roy Palmer Domenico

Greenwood Press
Westport, Connecticut • London

Library of Congress Cataloging-in-Publication Data

Domenico, Roy Palmer.
    The regions of Italy : a reference guide to history and culture / Roy Domenico.
      p. cm.
    Includes bibliographical references and index.
    ISBN 0–313–30733–4 (alk. paper)
    1. Italy—Handbooks, manuals, etc.
√DG417.D65 2002
  945—dc21   00–052434

British Library Cataloguing in Publication Data is available.

Library of Congress Catalog Card Number: 00–052434
ISBN: 0–313–30733–4

First published in 2002

Greenwood Press, 88 Post Road West, Westport, CT 06881
An imprint of Greenwood Publishing Group, Inc.
www.greenwood.com

Printed in the United States of America

The paper used in this book complies with the
Permanent Paper Standard issued by the National
Information Standards Organization (Z39.48–1984).

10 9 8 7 6 5 4 3 2 1

CONTENTS

A photo essay follows page 219.

ACKNOWLEDGMENTS

I wish to thank a number of colleagues and friends at the University of Scranton whose generous help considerably lightened my load. Michael De Michele, Willis Conover, Robert Hueston, Robert Shaffern, William Parente, Carol Long, Joseph Dreisbach, Richard Passon, Robert Powell, Eileen Callahan, and Vito Del Vecchio all provided crucial assistance along with hearty doses of good cheer. Josephine Dunn and Virginia Picchietti, of the University of Scranton's Italian Studies Program performed a valuable service by reading and commenting on parts of the manuscript. The staff of the Henry and Jeanette Weinberg Memorial Library, particularly its interlibrary loan desk, deserve special thanks for going the extra mile in procuring some obscure Italian titles. At the library Betsey Moylan earned kudos for accompanying me on a delightful trip through Italian recipes. Thanks to students in my Modern Italy class and to student research assistants, Paul Habermas, Chris Budano, Sean St. Ledger, and Andres Rodriguez. At the University of Scranton's History Department office, Anne Marie Mulcahy, Elizabeth Scoblick, Linette Sandoval, Karen Swikata, Sandra Kase, and Ashley Graf all unflinchingly rendered on-call help under the wise and watchful guidance of Rosemarie Pryle. Beyond Scranton, Lynn Berrettoni, Helen Holmes, Jonathan Nashel, George Sirgiovanni, and Beverly Anderson contributed sound advice. My editors at Greenwood, Wendi Schnaufer and Rebecca Homiski, deserve medals for their great patience. Finally, my wife, Robin, provided enormous support in a million ways, and our children, Katie, John, Matthew, and Clare, helped a lot by not trying to help too much.

INTRODUCTION

From the time people first uttered the word "Italia," or some variation of it, until this century, Italians have identified more with their own locales than with what we now know as "Italy." Rarely, in fact, did one nation even bear the name of Italy after the fall of the Roman Empire. The centuries that followed the empire's collapse were full of foreign invaders who humbled Italy but never extinguished its spirit. The cities and regions of medieval and Renaissance Italy responded to war and strife with an extraordinary vitality. It was a vigor that fueled fierce local pride but worked against national unity, often excluding communities only a short distance down the road. The Italian wars that began in the 1490s, however, signaled the start of a long and debilitating wave of foreign invasions and subjugations that ended only with the defeat of Nazi Germany in 1945.

Comparing a fifteenth-century map of Italy and one from the twelfth or the eighteenth reveals a bewildering jumble of small states administered by myriad and ever-changing regional princes and foreign masters. Dukes ruled Milanesi and Florentines, Venetians owed allegiance to their doges, and Neapolitans had their kings, often French or Spanish. But those maps reveal a further truth: that few regions were immutable. By the early nineteenth century Prince Clemens von Metternich's characterization of Italy as a "mere geographical expression" may have enraged nationalists, but it was based on more than a grain of truth. In Metternich's time, furthermore, Italy had just endured Napoleon's invasions. The French had created a new "Kingdom of Italy," ended the Venetian Republic after a thousand-year existence, and dismantled the Papal States which had lasted, in one form or another, for the same stretch of time.

A single Italian state finally resurfaced between 1859 and 1870, when the Risorgimento united the country under the Piedmontese kings of the House of Savoy. Ironically, unification also completed the deterioration of the ancient Italian states by placing all of them under the control of a single master, the central government. Many Tuscans, Venetians, or Sicilians could not consider their new Savoy kings or their Roman servants and bureaucrats as cut from their own cloth. Rather, they saw the new monarchs as Piedmontese and the new state as indeed a foreign imposition. One of the key figures of the Risorgimento, the Modenese politician Luigi Farini, illustrated some of the dangers of unification when he boasted of his intention to remake Emilia Romagna so that "by the New Year from Piacenza to Cattolica the laws, the regulations, and the name will all be Piedmontese." Another zealous promoter of the new order was Urbano Rattazzi who, as Interior Minister, and as Prime Minister in 1862 and 1867, extended Piedmont's laws and systems to the states that joined Italy. This process was first termed "Piedmontization" although it was soon clear that Piedmont, too, would be a victim. In 1864, the people of Turin rioted on hearing the news that their city would not remain as Italy's capital.

The new state advanced its own authority by attempting to smother all rival local and ancient cultures. Its methods included taxation, national education, and mixing male populations via military duty. Another tactic was to redraw Italy's map, handing slices of one region or province over to another, or carving new regions out of old states, such as the Kingdom of the Two Sicilies or the papal lands. Between 1922 and 1943, Benito Mussolini's Fascist regime accelerated the process that submerged local beneath national identity.

Compared to France, Spain, or Britain, however, unification came so late that local identities enjoyed better chances to survive the catastrophe of modernization and the national impulse. Thanks to the Risorgimento, crowns might have shifted from Austrian or Bourbon heads to a single one from Turin, but resilient local cultures persisted. Since the Second World War these identities have re-emerged with new vitality.

The postwar Italian government recognized the importance of regional identities when it re-created and strengthened them beginning with the 1948 Constitution. Legislation in 1970 allowed for regional elections and created the basis of the system that exists today. Furthermore, Sicily, Trentino–Alto Adige, the Valle d'Aosta, and Sardinia became autonomous regions in 1948, a status that Friuli–Venezia Giulia also achieved in 1963, bringing the number to five. The revived regionalism received a grassroots boost in the late 1970s when the first "league" movement was formed in the Veneto. Calling for more autonomy and sometimes even for independence, the leagues proliferated mainly across the north and gathered steam in the 1980s and 1990s. Most have grouped under the leadership of the electric (or polarizing) personality of Umberto Bossi and his Lega Nord (Northern League).

With the exception of the Valle d'Aosta, each Italian region is subdivided into a number of provinces, smaller political units which command at least as much loyalty from the Italians as do the regions. Often, in fact, many provinces enjoy older and clearer identities than do their regions. Bologna and Modena, for instance, are arguably more vital concepts than is Emilia Romagna, whereas the relationship between Tuscany and Florence is a bit more equal. Since the creation of a united Italy, however, the number of provinces has fluctuated. In 1927 Mussolini created quite a few of them. Latina was born in the 1930s, and Pordenone became a province in 1968. Isernia and Oristano were established in the 1970s, and in the 1990s, Vibo Valentia, Crotone, Verbania, Biella, Prato, Rimini, and Lecco were created.

That Italy is built on the regions is reflected in this book's organization— the region forms the basis for each chapter. A section on "regional characteristics" inaugurates each discussion, presenting an overview of demography and geography. This is followed by short overviews of the region's economy, cuisine, and history. The remainder of each chapter is devoted to the individual provinces within the region, beginning with the capital. After a short provincial profile, the province's history and culture are outlined. Information on other significant towns concludes each provincial section.

A word on place names. Some Italian names have replaced the anglicized versions but others have not. I thus refer to "Livorno" and not "Leghorn," because most English-language atlases seem to have abandoned the use of "Leghorn." I debated the use of "Puglia" instead of "Apulia," although I retained the latter Anglicized term. On the other hand, I chose to employ "Lazio" instead of "Latium." Nevertheless, I acknowledge the persistence of our common use of "Rome," "Florence," "Naples," and "Venice" in place of the Italian equivalents, "Roma," "Firenze," "Napoli," and "Venezia."

The figures listed in the "Vital Statistics" and "Provincial Profiles" sections derive from those issued by Italy's National Statistics Institute (Istituto Nazionale di Statistica) in 1997 and 1998. "City" population figures correspond to what in Italy are called *comuni* (communes).

Chapter 1

ABRUZZO

REGIONAL CHARACTERISTICS. Area: 4,168 sq. mi. Population: 1,276,040. Capital: L'Aquila. Abruzzo is Italy's thirteenth-largest region in land area and fourteenth in population. It has three Catholic metropolitan sees: L'Aquila, Chieti/Vasto, and Pescara/Penne.

Abruzzo, sometimes referred to as "Abruzzi" or "the Abruzzi," is in the center of Italy. It is bordered on the east by the Adriatic Sea, on the north by the Marche, on the west and southwest by Lazio, and on the south by Molise. The University Gabriele D'Annunzio, named for one of the region's favorite sons, had four separate campuses in the provincial capitals that became separate institutions in the 1990s.

Abruzzo is a land of stunning natural beauty. In 1922–1923, one of the nation's first and most important national parks, the Parco Nazionale d'Abruzzo, was created in the region's southwest corner, along its borders with Lazio and Molise. Some of the reserve lies in those two regions as well, but the great bulk of it is in Abruzzo. Since then Abruzzo has been transformed from a poor and remote agricultural zone to a tourist mecca for snow skiers, aquasport enthusiasts, trekkers, and fisherfolk challenged by its rugged terrain. Mountains comprise 65.1 percent of the region, and 34.9 percent is hilly terrain. The Italian Statistical Institute does not classify any of the region's land as plain, although some flat spots can be found (e.g., in the Fucino basin in the southwest). The highest spots in the entire Apennine chain are found in Abruzzo. The Corno Grande of the Gran Sasso d'Italia (9,555 feet) is the tallest mountain between the Alps and Sicily. Other mountains and hills—the massive Maiella to the east of the

Gran Sasso, the Lagas, and the Simbruinis—are separated by plateaus and broad limestone valleys such as the Campo dell'Imperatore and the Cinquemiglia near Roccaraso. The Gran Sasso and the Laga form a second national park, the Parco nazionale del Gran Sasso e Monte della Laga. Abruzzo's principal rivers, the Vomano, the Pescara, and the Sangro, flow east from the mountains toward the Adriatic.

ECONOMY. Abruzzo's economy, long considered one of low profits and agriculture, has turned to industry and the service sector. Of its workforce, 32.6 percent are in industry, 8.1 percent in agriculture, and 59.3 percent in the teriary sector. Of Abruzzo's 445,000 employed workers, 288,000 are men and 157,000 are women. Farming is still important to the region. Vegetable cultivation is common throughout, along with olives at the higher altitudes and fruits along the coast. Tobacco is also a significant crop. The mountains have always been, and remain, important as livestock country, although too many grassy meadows now sit beneath asphalt, concrete, and resort homes. Tourism and industry have transformed this region, it has been argued, more than any other in Italy.

Since the 1960s Abruzzo has developed faster than any southern region, in a pattern more akin to that found in northeast Italy. But other aspects, such as persistent unemployment (10.1 percent in 1998), appear more typical of the troubled *mezzogiorno* (southern Italy) than the prosperous *settentrione* (northern Italy). And some observers lament that traditional social temperaments, such as familism and suspicion of women in commerce, have slowed the march of modernization and profit. Abruzzo's economic capital is Pescara, which anchors one end of an industrial corridor that extends to Chieti. But the metropolis has surrendered some of its status to the region's political center, L'Aquila.

CUISINE. The people of L'Aquila are noted for a particularly robust banquet called the *panarda*, which, tradition has it, no one can refuse. The feast begins with a bowl of *paniccio di Sant'Antonio Abate*, a millet flour polenta with ricotta or pecorino cheese mixed in. It is followed by local specialties such as smoked herring in milk, cheeses such as Scamorza and Cacciacavallo, sweet breads, beef, and so forth. *Le virtù* is one of Teramo's special dishes. It is usually served during May, when the first beans are picked from the fields. Various legumes are mixed into a stew of pork castoffs (the ears, feet, and so forth), garlic, onions, and tomatoes. It is finally added to pasta. *Maccheroni alla chitarra*, very thick, spaghetti-like pasta, is particularly popular among the Teramani and throughout the Abruzzo.

Historically, Abruzzo was not famous for its wines, and many of the grapes grown there were intended for the table rather than the bottle. The Peligna Valley, between the Gran Sasso and the Maiella, near Sulmona, was the area's most important winemaking center. Around the turn of the nineteenth century, however, Tuscan grapes were imported to stimulate wine production and, since 1950 especially, great advances have been made. The light red Montepulciano and the Trebbiano called, respectively, the Abruzzo red and the Abruzzo white, along with the recent Controguerra, are the local wines enjoyed most often.

SPAGHETTI ALLA PESCATORA

1 lb. ripe, firm tomatoes, peeled	1 c. dry white wine
½ c. olive oil	Salt and pepper, to taste
4 cloves of garlic, minced	1 lb. medium spaghetti
20 mussels, rinsed and de-bearded	Grated romano cheese

Briefly boil tomatoes in water, then remove from the pot and mince, discarding the seeds. Combine the oil and the minced garlic in a pan and heat the mixture until the garlic begins to brown. Add mussels and cook for one minute, then add the wine to the pan, bring the mixture to a boil, and allow most of the wine to evaporate. Add the tomatoes, salt, and pepper to the pan and bring the sauce to a simmer. Meanwhile, prepare the spaghetti, drain it, and place it in a bowl. Add the sauce to the pasta and sprinkle with grated cheese to taste.

HISTORY. Traces of prehistoric peoples prove that a human society thrived in Abruzzo at least as early as the middle Paleolithic age. By the first millennium B.C., the Piceni culture had taken hold of the coastal areas, and Abruzzo was settled by various Italic peoples: the Sabines, Samnites, Marsi, Praetutii, Equi, and Volsci, among others. Some of the tribes became subject allies with Rome against the fiercely independent Samnites at the battle of Sentinum (Sassoferrato in Marche) in 295 B.C. Within ten years of Rome's victory there, pacification and colonization efforts were evidenced by the extension of the Via Salaria from the capital to San Benedetto del Tronto and the construction of the Via Cecilia. Most of the tribes would unite again against Rome, and again without success, in the bloody Social War of 90 B.C. The new masters divided the Italic peoples into various districts, or *regii*. Neither the Romans nor the Italic peoples conceived of any unit that we might recognize today as Abruzzo until at least the rule of Hadrian (117–138), who created a province of Valeria which encompassed much of the region. Some of the reorganization might be explained by the fact that Hadrian's family hailed from Hatria (Atri). The first reference to "Abruzzo" was "Aprutium," in sixth-century letters of Pope Gregory the Great. (However, the origin of the name may stem from one of the Italic tribes, the Praetutii.)

The fall of the Roman Empire in 476 brought new invaders and masters for Abruzzo, from Lombards and Byzantines to Muslims and Hungarians. Parts of the region, such as the lands of the Counts of Marsi and the Dukes of Teate (Chieti), maintained a spotty or vague independence, but the pattern was one of repeated subjugation. The popes took much of the Abruzzo between the ninth and the twelfth centuries; then the Normans incorporated it into their Kingdom of Sicily, which was later transformed into the Kingdom of Naples. In turn, Spain's rule of Naples from the sixteenth to the eighteenth centuries had particularly devastating consequences for the Abruzzo. Absentee landlords often lived in Naples and had little interest in their estates beyond the collection of rents. An oppressed and frustrated population turned to banditry which became endemic. The eighteenth century witnessed a short period of more enlightened Austrian administration, then a return to the Spanish Bourbons in 1735 (although independent from Madrid). The French invasion of 1796 ended that.

The Bourbon monarchs of Naples returned to Abruzzo in 1815 and, until the Risorgimento in 1860, administered it in four units: Abruzzo Ulteriore

I, Abruzzo Ulteriore II, Abruzzo Citra (or Citeriore), and Molise. Near the Marche border, the fortress at Civitella del Tronto, built over an ancient Picene bastion, was one of the last Bourbon holdouts against unification with Italy. It surrendered to Italian forces on March 20, 1861, after a three-day bombardment. After the Risorgimento the whole area was reorganized as Abruzzi e Molise. The province of Campobasso was detached from Abruzzo in 1965 to form the new region of Molise. The few reforms engineered by the new liberal state failed to balance the oppressive taxation imposed on Abruzzese peasants, and many decided to leave the area for Argentina, the United States, and, later, Rome, where today, 100,000 inhabitants were born in Abruzzo. With that number, Rome ranks behind only Pescara as the largest "Abruzzese" city.

Thanks in part to the influence of Benito Mussolini's lieutenant Giacomo Acerbo, an Abruzzese who also lived in Rome, the Fascists left their mark by creating the province of Pescara and developing the coast, to the detriment of the inland regions and L'Aquila. Abruzzo suffered during the Second World War as the location of the Gustav Line, where Adolf Hitler's forces faced the British Eighth Army between September 1943 and June 1944.

After the war, reconstruction brought expressways, more industry, and a tourist boom. But with the construction of the E55, A25, and A24 autostradas, the region has begun to lose its reputation as a remote corner of the peninsula and to witness significant incorporation into the national economy and society. Construction of the A24, however, prompted controversy over its environmental impact, particularly its lengthy tunnel under the Gran Sasso d'Italia.

RECENT POLITICS. Politically, until the early 1990s Abruzzo was considered a stronghold of the Christian Democratic Party, which gained as much as 45.7 percent of the vote in 1979. The region votes as the seventeenth electoral district (*circoscrizione*). In the 1996 Chamber of Deputies election the Polo per le Libertà barely edged out the Ulivo coalition with 44.6 against 44.0 percent of the majoritarian vote. In the proportional vote, the right-wing Alleanza Nazionale took 21.2 percent, the PDS captured 20.7 percent, and the conservative Forza Italia gained 19.3 percent. In the Senate election, the Polo outpolled the Ulivo overall—46.4 percent against 38.1 percent. The latter won four out of the five Abruzzese seats, however, thanks to the results of the separate counts. The region swung from left to right in the April 2000 regional elections. With 49.3 percent of the vote, a Center-Right coalition took control of the regional assembly under Giovanni Pace. Although Abruzzo has the lowest street crime statistics in Italy, arrests there during the *mani pulite* ("clean hands") scandal were only slightly lower than Lombardy's (with three times the population).

L'AQUILA

PROVINCIAL PROFILE. Area: 1,944 sq. mi. Population: 304,221 (province), 69,233 (city). L'Aquila province contains 108 communes. The province is a long diagonal unit that borders all of the other Abruzzese provinces to its north and east. To its west and south it meets the regions of Umbria, Lazio, and Molise. It is the only landlocked province in Abruzzo. The national park lies mostly within its borders. Of particular note regarding its intermountain valleys is the enormous reclaimed marshland, the Fucino plain, near Avezzano.

HISTORY. The province of L'Aquila was settled by the Sabines before the rise of Rome, but the city of L'Aquila did not exist until Emperor Frederick II established it about 1240. He had designated Sulmona as the capital of the area in 1233, and left his son, Conrad IV, to build L'Aquila. As early as 1257 L'Aquila had aquired some status, because Pope Alexander IV transferred a see there from Forcona. But Sulmona remained the political center of Abruzzo until the Angevin monarchs of Naples accorded L'Aquila that honor. During the Franco-Spanish wars for the control of Italy, the people of L'Aquila chose the losing side and, to keep an eye on his rebellious new charges, the Spanish viceroy, Don Pedro of Toledo, ordered the construction of an imposing fort in 1543. This did not daunt the L'Aquilans, who joined Masaniello's revolt against the Spanish (1647).

In 1703 an earthquake left most of the city in rubble. During the Napoleonic Wars, L'Aquila was noted as a center of determined opposition to the revolutionary regimes set up by the French. After the defeat of Napoleon's lieutenant Joachim Murat, it returned to the Kingdom of Naples until its absorption into the Italian state after unification. During the Second World War, L'Aquila's mountains sheltered rebels again, and the Maiella Brigade was one of first partisan units to fight for Italy's liberation from the Third Reich.

ARTS AND CULTURE. The Basilica of Santa Maria Collemaggio, among Italy's finest examples of the Romanesque Gothic style, was built by an old Abruzzese priest, **Pietro da Morrone**, who had been ordered to do so by the Virgin Mother, who came to him in a dream. Shortly afterward, in 1294, da Morrone was elected pope in a grueling conclave that lasted more than a year; and his creation in white and rose stone was the site of his coronation as Celestine V. However, the new pontiff had been a simple, guileless hermit, and proved to be unsuited to the political demands of the Holy See. His detractors portrayed him as a puppet of King Charles II of Naples, who had promoted his election, and Celestine's pontificate is remembered chiefly because he voluntarily ended it less than six months after it began. The unfortunate ascetic ended his days as a prisoner in the fortress of the new pope, Boniface VIII, scion of the aristocratic and socially savvy Caetani family. In his *Divine Comedy* Dante placed Celestine in Hell for the abdication. L'Aquila remembers its pope every August 28 when it celebrates the *Gran Perdonanza* (Great Pardon). On that day Celestine granted a plenary indulgence to the people of the city who had gathered for the feast of the Beheading of St. John the Baptist. Every year L'Aquila's archbishop launches the festivities by a public reading of Celestine's bull. They conclude the next day when penitents climb the stairs of Santa Maria Collemaggio before the archbishop and relics of the pope.

Silvestro dell'Aquila was one of the region's best-known sculptors. Active in the late fifteenth century, he is remembered for his *Madonna d'Ancarano*, which he fashioned for the Church of Santa Maria del Lume in Civitella del Tronto; it served as a model for many subsequent wood and polychrome terra-cotta pieces. Between 1525 and 1542 **Cola d'Amatrice**, from Lazio (also known as Nicola Filotesio [1489–1559], erected in L'Aquila the greatest renaissance work in Abruzzo, the gleaming facade of the Church of San Bernardino, which contains the tomb of L'Aquila's patron saint, Bernardino of Siena. The church collapsed in the 1703 earthquake, but the facade remained intact. The church has since been rebuilt. Also in L'Aquila is the "Spanish Fort" built to intimidate the people of L'Aquila. The work of the Valencian architect **Pirro Luis Escribà**, who also designed the Castel Sant'Elmo at Naples, the impressive stronghold was constructed between 1543 and 1567. It boasts a magnificent entranceway beneath the coat of arms of Charles V, the Spanish king and Hapsburg emperor. Today the fort houses the Museo Nazionale d'Abruzzo (National Museum of Abruzzo). The city's most particular, and perhaps favorite, landmark is the Fountain of the Ninety-nine Taps (Fontana delle Novantanove Cannelle). Begun in 1272, it was completed in the eighteenth century; each spout represents one of L'Aquila's ninety-nine legendary castles.

Serafino de' Ciminelli (1466–1500), known as L'Aquilano, was a court poet from L'Aquila. He enjoyed a broad fame during his life for his poetry as well as for his singing and lute playing.

OTHER CENTERS. The cities of **Avezzano** and **Sulmona** are rivals of L'Aquila, and the question of carving separate provinces for them has been raised on occasion. Avezzano is an ancient place with evidence of Bronze Age settlement. Beginning in the fifteenth century, it changed hands between two aristocratic families from Rome, the Orsini and the Colonna, before it was absorbed by the Spanish and the Kingdom of Naples. Under Napoleon's lieutenant Joachim Murat, Avezzano became the seat of a district. But physical evidence of Avezzano's heritage was mostly destroyed in the catastrophic earthquake of 1915. Of 15,000 inhabitants, only 2,000 survived and, with a handful of exceptions like the Orsini Castle, the city was completely demolished. Avezzano received some help in its recovery in the 1950s by the distribution to peasants of the land reclaimed from the Fucino marshes in parcels of 2.5 to 10 acres.

Sulmona's origins are uncertain, although the Roman historian Livy mentioned that Hannibal passed by the city in 211 B.C. In A.D. 570 it was absorbed into the Duchy of Spoleto and survived, barely, sacking by Goths, Muslims, and Hungarians. In 1224, after it had endured the siege of John of Brienne, the Hohenstaufen emperor Frederick II bestowed favors on the city. The privileges ended, however, when the Angevins, enemies of the Swabian Hohenstaufens, took the region and heaped rewards on Sulmona's rival, L'Aquila. Nevertheless, the town remained important for the fame of its goldsmiths and the location there of a mint.

One of Rome's greatest poets, Publius Ovidius Naso (43 B.C.–c. A.D. 17), known as Ovid, was born in Sulmona. Famous as the author of the *Metamorphoses*, he was also known for works on love, the *Amores* (loves) and the *Ars Amatoria*. (Art of Love). These last compositions harmed his reputation in the prudish court of Caesar Augustus, who banished Ovid to the shores of the Black Sea. More recently, Sulmona produced a famous daughter, the film star Gina Lollobrigida. Born in 1927, she became a significant idol of the postwar popular Italian cinema, appearing in *Pane, Amore e Fantasia* (Bread, Love and Dreams, 1953), and in British, American, and French films.

The ruins of two deserted cities also hold a particular importance for the province of L'Aquila. One is Amiternum, now **San Vittorino**, on the banks of the Aterno River, which was one of the principal sites of the Sabine people. The other is Alba Fucens (now **Albe**), originally an Equi town which, like Hatria and Giulianova in Teramo province, was later used by the Romans to extend their cultural influence in the region. Ruins of a number of second- and third-century B.C. structures remain.

Southeast of L'Aquila is the hamlet of **Cocullo**, site of one of Italy's most unusual festivals. On the first Thursday in May, a procession of snake charmers honors San Domenico of Sora, who guards against snakebites. Accompanied by the charmers cloaked in live snakes is a statue of the saint, also covered by serpents. The celebration probably reaches (in altered form) back to a festival that honored the pre-Christian goddess Angizia, favored by the Marsi tribe. Like San Domenico, Angizia was thought to cure snakebites. **Capistrano** is the home of the Counter-Reformation saint John of Capistrano.

Italy's greatest modern philosopher, Benedetto Croce (1866–1952), was born to a family of large landholders at **Pescasseroli**. He later established himself at Naples, a city to which he became intensely attached. Croce was a central figure in the neo-idealist critique of positivism before the First World War, although he deeply believed in liberalism. This and his writings on the German philosopher Georg Hegel brought him an international prestige that helped protect him from Fascist censure. At first sympathetic to Mussolini's movement, Croce soon soured on it and, in 1925, issued his "Manifesto of Anti-Fascist Intellectuals," which was published in the Neapolitan anti-Fascist journal *Il Mondo* (The World). Though his famous histories of Italy and of European liberalism were thinly disguised critiques of Mussolini's regime, Croce maintained the life of a nonpolitical academic through the rest of the dictatorship. After 1943, however, he surfaced as the leader of the Liberal Party and was a major voice in the debates on the shape of postwar Italy until his death.

One of Italy's most acclaimed twentieth-century authors, Secondo Tranquilli (1900–1978), who wrote under the name Ignazio Silone, was born in **Pescina dei Marsi**, near L'Aquila. Silone studied with the Jesuits in Rome but returned to Abruzzo to work with peasant federations and the Socialist Party. He was present at the creation of the Italian Communist Party in 1921 and served on its central committee, but grew disillusioned with it. By 1930 Silone had returned to Socialism. His anti-Fascism was manifested in political action, but it is for his novels and other writings that Silone remains best remembered. His two most famous critiques of life under Mussolini, *Fontamara* (1930) and *Pane e Vino* (Bread and Wine, 1936), contrasted the humble lives of Abruzzese peasants with the cold brutality of the Fascists. After the Second World War, Silone returned to Italy from exile in Switzerland and assumed editorial command of the Socialist journal *Avanti!* (Forward!). His anti-Communist sentiments placed him in the moderate wing, and Silone broke with the Socialists after the 1947 schism between the factions of Pietro Nenni and Giuseppe Saragat. He retired from politics in 1950.

CHIETI

PROVINCIAL PROFILE. Area: 999 sq. mi. Population: 389,722 (province), 56,984 (city). The province contains 104 communes. Chieti is bordered on the northeast by the Adriatic, on the northwest by the province of Pescara, on the southwest by the province of L'Aquila, and on the south by the region of Molise. It is bounded in part on the north by the Pescara River and on the south by the Trigno. It is bisected by the Sangro, which flows into the Adriatic near Fossacesia.

HISTORY. Chieti is an ancient city. It began as an Oscan hill settlement overlooking the Pescara River and was taken by the Marsi and Marrucini in 1000 B.C. The Greeks were also in Chieti, and its ancient name, Teate, probably derives from them or from the Marrucini. In A.D. 1524 the old name was revived and was given to the Catholic Theatine Order, established in part by Gian Pietro Carafa, the bishop of Chieti who later became Pope Paul IV. Ancient scholars debated whether Teate was founded by

Hercules or Achilles. The Romans took it in 305 B.C. After the fall of the Roman Empire in A.D. 476, Theodoric resurrected the town and the Lombards used it as a fortress. Chieti passed to the Franks, Normans, Swabians, Angevins, and Aragonese until Emperor Charles V brought the city under his control. Under the Neapolitan Bourbons, Chieti became the capital of Abruzzo Citra, although their reign is not remembered as remarkably enlightened. On the other hand, Naples benefited from the efforts of Ferdinando Galiani (1728–1787), from Chieti, whose work on economics and money made him a principal figure in Neapolitan Enlightenment circles.

ARTS AND CULTURE. Chieti was an important Roman town with many structures that have partly survived. Impressive first-century baths and cisterns, for example, were carved out of volcanic rock. Three small connected temples, dedicated to Hercules and Diana Trivia, also remain. Chieti's cathedral dates from the ninth century, and was rebuilt in the thirteenth. It houses a silver bust of Chieti's patron saint, Giustino, the work of **Nicola da Guardiagrele** (also known as Nicola di Andrea Gallucci [1380/ c. 1395–c. 1462/1471]), probably a native of the city. Giustino's story is lost in legend, but he is believed to have lived in the third century. Lack of evidence caused his name to be removed from the list of saints in 1968. Chieti is also home to the National Antiquities Museum (Museo Nazionale di Antichità), which houses an extensive collection of pre-Roman items including the famous sixth-century B.C. *Warrior of Capistrano*. Chieti commemorates the death of Christ on Good Friday with a famous torchlit procession organized by the Confraternity of the Monte dei Morti.

OTHER CENTERS. The Adriatic coast is dotted with quite a few notable towns. **Ortona** was founded by the Frentani and used as a link to Greek trade; Ortonium later became an important Roman port on the Adriatic. The town received some notoriety in September 1943 as the place where King Victor Emmanuel III and his circle fled after the collapse of Italy. At Ortona they boarded a navy corvette which took them to Brindisi and safety behind the Allied lines. Three months later, however, Ortona was the site of a ferocious battle between the Germans and Allies, mainly British and Canadians, in which over 2,000 townsfolk were killed and most of the city was destroyed.

Vasto is Abruzzo's southernmost city on the Adriatic coast. It began as a Greek settlement, and legend attributes its founding to the Greek warrior-king Diomedes, who is more usually associated with Apulian places. Under the Romans, Vasto was known as Histonium. It later passed from one conqueror to the next, beginning with Pepin the Short and the Franks. The town suffered serious sacks by the Hungarians in 937 and by Crusaders waiting to leave for the Holy Land in 1194. In 1566 the Turks set fire to Vasto and destroyed its churches. From 1497 until 1798 Vasto was a feudal land of the D'Avalos family, which constituted it into a marquisate that, for a while, extended as far as Pescara.

Inland and south of Ortona is the ancient town of **Lanciano**. It began as Anxanum, a fortified Frentani settlement overlooking the Feltrino River valley. Lanciano's cathedral was dedicated to Saint Mary of the Bridge (Santa Maria del Ponte), because it was constructed over an ancient Roman bridge. It was begun in the fourteenth century and rebuilt in the eighteenth. Also in Lanciano is the Cistercian Church of Santa Maria Maggiore, begun in 1227. Near Lanciano is **Orsogna**, site of the impressive abbey of San Giovanni in Venere. Its roots extend to the eighth century, and it was rebuilt by the Cistercians in the eleventh and twelfth centuries.

Bomba, near Chieti, is the home of the Spaventa brothers, Bertrando (1817–1883) and Silvio (1822–1893). Silvio, an activist during the Risorgimento, was condemned to death after the Neapolitan revolution of 1848. (His sentence was commuted to life in prison.) Upon the unification of Italy, he became a government figure in various capacities and was nominated to the Senate. Bertrando, who began as a priest, later taught the history of philosophy at the University of Naples from 1861 until his death. His work on the German philosopher Georg Hegel prepared the way for later scholars, particularly Benedetto Croce.

PESCARA

PROVINCIAL PROFILE. Area: 473 sq. mi. Population: 293,097 (province), 117,957 (city). Pescara province has 46 communes. It touches the Adriatic on the northeast and is bordered by Teramo on the north, L'Aquila on the west, and Chieti on the south and southeast. The Pescara River rises in L'Aquila province, near Sulmona, then flows through the center of Pescara province until it forms part of the border with Chieti.

HISTORY. Pescara's roots still stir debate. Traces of early settlement reach to 1500 B.C., but there is disagreement concerning which Italic tribe was the first. The Romans called it Aternum and took it in 214 B.C. after it chose an alliance with the Carthaginian general Hannibal. Aternum became a center of trade and shipment between Rome and the Balkans, and was made the capital of Valeria. The city was nearly destroyed by barbarian raids, particularly at the hands of the Lombards, who martyred Aternum's bishop and patron saint, Ceteo. In the early Middle Ages it was revived as a fishing village, called Piscaria, but it frequently fell to marauders and was periodically abandoned. The Hapsburg Emperor Charles V developed Pescara as a military stronghold in 1510, and under his lieutenants Ferdinand D'Avalos and the Duke of Atri, the fortress repulsed repeated attacks by Turkish Muslims.

After a period of Austrian rule in the eighteenth century, Pescara passed to the control of the Neapolitan Bourbons, who incorporated it into

Abruzzo Citra. Pescara was still primarily a fortress when it was absorbed into the Italian Kingdom in 1860. At that time, the Pescara River formed the border between Chieti and Teramo provinces, with the town and its fortress on the southern (Chieti) bank, and the larger center of Castellamare on the northern (Teramo) side. The twin cities flourished quickly but independently, and in 1927, when the region of Abruzzo was reorganized, Pescara was united and made its capital. Pescara's new honor, however, was viewed as treachery by the people of Castellamare, who staged an unsuccessful revolt. Only a visit to the city by Gabriele D'Annunzio, its native son, calmed the hard feelings. From a seaplane, the poet littered both banks of the river with leaflets pleading for harmony. A key Adriatic port, modern Pescara was heavily damaged in the Second World War. Allied bombers destroyed 78 percent of the city and killed thousands in three raids during August and September 1943. Since the war Pescara has experienced great development at the expense of the environment. In 1988 a new railway station was opened.

ARTS AND CULTURE. Pescara's roots as a fishing village can still be appreciated in two major festivals: that of Sant'Andrea (St. Andrew) at the end of July and that of the Madonna of the Seven Sorrows. The feast of Pescara's patron saint, Ceteo, is celebrated at the river. A bishop of the city in about 600, he was martyred when a Lombard chief, Umbolo, ordered him thrown into the river with a rock tied around his neck.

Ennio Flaiano (1910–1972) was born in Pescara. His 1947 novel, *Tempo di uccidere* (Time to Kill), captured the Strega Literary Award, and he went on to write screenplays and other novels and diaries which often evoke memories, not always happy, of his childhood in Pescara.

Basilio Cascella (1860–1950) spent most of his life in Pescara and is considered one of the region's most important modern painters and lithographers. Among his works are many scenes of Abruzzese peasant life.

Gabriele D'Annunzio (1863–1938) was born in Pescara. Arguably Italy's most important poet since at least Giacomo Leopardi, D'Annunzio is remembered both for for his sensual and decadent creations and for his nationalist politics. The poet Eugenio Montale remarked that, to become truly modern, a poet had to come to terms with D'Annunzio. His fame was assured through his 1889 masterpiece *Il Piacere* (Pleasure), but by the early twentieth century, works such as *Canzoni del gesta d'oltremare* (Patriotic Songs from Overseas) established a space for him among the propagandists of national glory and imperialism. He rallied Italian crowds for war in 1915 and undertook a number of risky feats in combat against Austria. On one raid against the enemy, D'Annunzio lost an eye; but that did not curtail his 1918 flight to shower Vienna with propaganda leaflets.

After the war, he became Benito Mussolini's most important rival on the political right, a prominence magnified by his "conquest" of the city of Fiume on the Yugoslav border. D'Annunzio believed the city should have been awarded to the Italians after Austria's 1918 collapse, but had been denied to them by the other Allied powers. As a noisy dictator of the tiny state, he chided the liberal government in Rome for its supine policies. After Mussolini's seizure of power (and Italy's absorption of Fiume), the Fascists accorded highest honors to the poet. The Duce chaired a commission to publish a forty-nine-volume deluxe edition of D'Annunzio's works; he was named president of the Royal Academy; and he received the prow of a destroyer which he placed on the lawn of his Lake Garda estate, the Vittoriale degli Italiani.

OTHER CENTERS. On the Monday after Pentecost, the Festival of the Oxen is celebrated in **Loreto Aprutino**. The celebration derives from the transfer of relics from Rome to the town of a questionable—some might say fictitious—saint, Zopito, in 1711. The town already hosted an ancient ox festival, and the procession of the relics was simply merged with it. The central ritual of the feast takes place when a white ox kneels before the sacred relics. Loreto Aprutino's Palazzo Acerbo houses an important museum of ceramic arts.

Loreto Aprutino was the birthplace of Giacomo Acerbo (1888–1969), a professor of agriculture and an early follower of Benito Mussolini who organized Abruzzo's Fascist movement. In 1923 he drafted the legislation which enabled the Fascists to establish their dictatorship. Known as the Acerbo election law, it gave any political party that captured 25 percent of the popular vote a two-thirds majority of the seats in the Italian Parliament. Acerbo later served Mussolini as minister of agriculture and minister of finance.

TERAMO

PROVINCIAL PROFILE. Area: 752 sq. mi. Population: 289,000 (province), 52,212 (city). The province contains 47 communes. Teramo is bordered by the Adriatic on the east, by the provinces of L'Aquila on the southwest and Pescara on the south, the region of Lazio on the west, and the region of Marche on the north. The highest of the Apennines, Gran Sasso d'Italia, is on Teramo's border with L'Aquila. The Vomano, the province's principal river, flows to the Adriatic, as do the Vibrata, the Salinello, the Piomba, and the Tordino, which joins the Vezzano at Teramo city.

HISTORY. Teramo was founded by the Praetutii tribe and was first known as Interamna (from "between two rivers"). The Romans changed it to Teramne after they annexed it about 290 B.C. The Visigothic king Alaric burned down Teramne in the fifth century A.D., and the town experienced barbarian invasions following the fall of Rome in 476. In 1155 the Normans burned Teramo to the ground before it passed from their hands into those of the Duke of Apulia.

ARTS AND CULTURE. Some Roman remains can be found in Teramo, but its most significant historic treasure is its Cathedral of San Berardo. Born in the eleventh century into a noble Abruzzese family, Berardo joined the Benedictines at Montecassino and went to San Giovanni in Venere, near Lanciano, before he became the bishop of Teramo in 1116. A number of miracles have been attributed to him, particularly (an important Teramo legend) the "miracle of freedom and peace" (1521). In that year, visions of Berardo and of the Madonna appeared on the city's ramparts and frightened off the troops of the Duke of Atri. The cathedral, first built between 1158 and 1335 and later modified, is distinguished by a cosmatesque doorway designed by **Diodato Romano** (active 1320–1340). Inside is an *Assumption* by Chieti's **Nicola da Guardiagrele,** who is intimately associated with Teramo's Renaissance tradition. Teramo also boasts a proud tradition in majolica. The late sixteenth until the early nineteenth century was a golden age of this work associated with **Oratio** (active c. 1600) and **Tito Pompei** (active c. 1516), **Francesco Grue** (d. 1673), **Antonio Lolli** (1586–1619), and **Gesualdo Fuina** (1755–1827).

OTHER CENTERS. Atri and **Giulianova,** important towns in the province, began as Rome's colonies of Hatria and Castrum Novum, respectively, which were established on the Adriatic after the defeat of the Samnites. The Hatrians in particular were known as fiercely loyal to Rome, and the historian Livy credited them with securing the empire's safety. That Emperor Hadrian's family came from Hatria also strengthened the ties. Atri's cathedral is one of the province's most impressive structures. Dedicated to the Assumption of the Virgin Mary, it was consecrated in 1223 and rebuilt in the thirteenth and fourteenth centuries on a site above a Roman reservoir and a ninth-century church. It is considered one of the finest examples of the Abruzzese Gothic style. Another important church in Teramo province is **Castel Castagna's** twelfth-century Santa Maria di Ronzano, one of the region's finest Romanesque structures.

SELECT BIBLIOGRAPHY

Costantini, Massimo, and Felice Costantino, eds. *L'Abruzzo*. Turin: Einaudi, 2000.
Istituto Geografico De Agostini. *Abruzzi-Molise*. Novara: Istituto Geografico De Agostini, 1983.

Chapter 2

APULIA
(Puglia)

REGIONAL CHARACTERISTICS. Area: 7,469 sq. mi. Population: 4,090,068. Capital: Bari. Among Italy's regions, Apulia ranks seventh in both land area and population. It has four Catholic metropolitan sees: Bari/Bitonto, Foggia/Bovino, Lecce, and Taranto.

Apulia occupies the southeastern point of Italy, the "heel" of the "boot." Situated at an angle running lengthwise from the northwest to the southeast, all of Apulia's northeast side faces the Adriatic Sea. To the southeast, the coastline swings around to the west at Cape Santa Maria di Leuca and heads up along the shores of the Ionian Sea and the Gulf of Taranto to the border with Basilicata. There, Apulia turns inland and meets Campania and Molise in the northwest. Apulia is Italy's flattest region. Only 1.5 percent of it is mountainous; 45.3 percent is hilly; and 53.2 percent is plain. Northern Apulia is divided into the Gargano Peninsula, the "spur" of Italy's "boot" (most of which is included in a national park established in 1995), the Tavoliere tableland, and the Daunia, western hills that extend from the Apennines. The middle of Apulia is dominated by the Murge plateau, which slopes eastward to the Adriatic; and the southern zone is the low-lying Salentine Peninsula, which is mainly a collection of low plateaus (*murge*). Flat coastline can also be found particularly around Taranto. Important rivers include the Fortore, which forms part of the border with Molise, and the Ofanto, which empties into the Adriatic at the southern end of the Tavoliere.

ECONOMY. Of Apulia's 1,395,000 employed workers (1997), 947,000 are men and 448,000 are women; 12.9 percent are employed in agriculture,

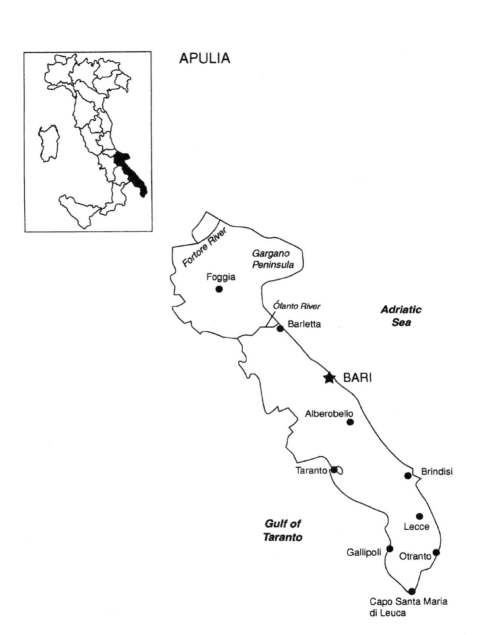

APULIA

Fortore River

Gargano
Peninsula

Foggia

Ofanto River

Barletta

Adriatic
Sea

★ BARI

Alberobello

Taranto

Brindisi

Lecce

Gulf of
Taranto

Gallipoli   Otranto

Capo Santa Maria
di Leuca

Ionian Sea

25.3 percent in industry, and 61.8 percent in the tertiary sector. Apulia's January 1998 unemployment rate was 20.4 percent. With Sicily and Calabria, Apulia is one of Italy's three regions where more agricultural workers are employed than are independent. Olives, grapes, tomatoes, fennel, lettuce, wheat, corn, peppers, cabbage, cherries, almonds, carrots, eggplant, and artichokes are important crops. The region's catch of fish ranks fourth in Italy. Natural gas is found in Apulia, and some bauxite is mined at Trani and in the Gargano Peninsula. The region's most important industrial concentrations are at Bari and Taranto.

CUISINE. The traditional Pugliese diet is heavy in pasta and bread. Naturally, seafood is important in Apulian kitchens, particularly lobsters from the Tremiti Islands. Oysters have blessed Taranto with a certain fame. And Gallipoli boasts of its fish soup *alla gallipolina*, which blends a variety of local catches, such as hogfish, *cernia* (a whitefish), cuttlefish, and prawns. It is seasoned with onions and hot spices. More than any other region, Apulia's culinary heritage owes a debt to Greece; and partisans claim that their fish soup *alla gallipolina* recipe has been handed down since the times of Magna Graecia. Gravina claims an ancient tradition of cooking lamb in milk, olive oil, onions, spices, and herbs. It is called *caldariello*, a name that stems from the *caldaia* (cauldron) in which it stews. Reminiscent of Spanish rule is *tiella*, which resembles paella (although the recipe varies from place to place). Rice is usually included, but Pugliese *tiella* must have a generous amount of potatoes. Apulia is one of Italy's most important sources of olive oil. Figs are popular, particularly the famous *fichi mandorlati* ("almondized" figs), which are heated and flavored with almonds, bay leaves, and fennel.

Apulia produces more wine than any other region, and many believe Pugliese wines to be the strongest in Italy. However, much of it is blended with other wines, and most of it is not well known. The southern slopes of the Gargano Peninsula, facing the Tavoliere, are noted for their production of a red wine.

ZUPPA ALLA GALLIPOLINA

4 lbs. fresh fish, such as pazza (ray), cernia (grouper), calamari, or gamberi (crawfish), cleaned and washed

1 Tbs. olive oil

½ large onion, chopped

3 hot peppers

1 clove garlic, minced

¾ c. white wine

4–5 tomatoes, peeled and chopped

4 c. water

Salt and pepper, to taste

Heat oil in a frying pan, and sauté onion, pepper and garlic. Add fish and cook briefly. Pour in the white wine and water and add the tomatoes. Bring to a boil and simmer 15 minutes over low heat.

HISTORY. Ample Neolithic remains can be seen in Coppa Avatra and Coppa Masselli in the southern Gargano Peninsula and in the Tavoliere. Iapygian peoples, from Illyria—particularly the Daunians in the north, the Massepicans, and the Peucetians—eventually settled in the area. The region takes its name from the Samnite Apuli nation. They were soon joined by Mycenaeans from Greece, whose pottery has been found at Coppa Nevigata, Leporano, and Taranto. Cretans founded Otranto and Spartans founded Taranto. Legend places King Diomedes in much of Apulia and the Tremiti Islands.

During the Second Punic War (218–201 B.C.) many Lucanian and Apulian cities gambled on the wrong side and opened their gates to the Carthaginian general Hannibal. Victorious Rome did not forget this, and exerted its dominion in earnest after his defeat. The new masters eventually joined Apulia to Calabria and administered them as Region II. Taranto lost prestige, and Romanized Apulia focused on Brundisium, which became the terminus of the Appian Way from Rome. The Romans also cultivated Apulian shipping, and the region prospered through its closeness to Greece and the East during the time of the *Pax Romana* (Roman Peace), circa the first century A.D. Because Sicily satisfied Roman demands for grain, Apulia's production shifted to livestock, olives, and wine. Furthermore, the Romans were attracted to the area's woodlands and, as they did in Sicily, deforested Apulia. The Gargano Peninsula was especially devastated.

As the Roman Empire crumbled in the fifth century, Goths first took much of interior but left the coastal cities largely in Byzantine hands. Greek influence was felt most in the Salento (Salentine Peninsula). In the eighth century an influx of Greek monks, refugees from Byzantium's controversy over the destruction of icons resulted in the construction of *laure*, caves for rest and prayer carved out of turf. Many walls around Apulia's towns were first built during the seventh and eighth centuries, when Saracen raids and conquests affected most of the region's coastline. The Frankish king Louis the German pushed the Muslims out of Apulia by 871 and brought the territory back under Christian rule. After another period under Byzantine rule, in 1056 the Normans launched their conquest of Apulia and, three years later, made Melfi (Basilicata) their capital. The Normans also permanently ended the broad influence of the Greek church in Apulia, replacing it with that of the Roman Catholic rite. In 1059 Pope Nicholas II sanctioned Norman rule by granting Apulia as a fief to Robert Guiscard. During this period, and particularly as a result of the Crusades, Bari became the chief port of the region.

In 1186 the marriage of Constance d'Hauteville (Altavilla) to Henry VI brought the Swabians to Apulia. Their son, Emperor Frederick II, inaugurated a number of building projects. After his death in 1250 and the death of his son, Manfred, at Benevento in 1266, the French Angevins took the region, launching a long period of bad government while Muslim raiders and slavers brought danger and misery. The fall of the Eastern Roman Empire in 1453 warned Apulia of a renewed Muslim threat, and in 1480 the Turks took Otranto.

Shortly afterward, Franco-Spanish struggle for dominance in the area ended with the French defeat at Cerignola in 1503. With some exceptions, such as Lecce, Apulia witnessed a general decline under Spanish rule. Discontent followed, and in 1647 the Masaniello Revolt in Naples spread into Apulia from Basilicata, under Matteo Cristiano of Casagrande. Spanish rule ended in 1700 and was formally replaced in 1713 by Austrian rule, then by the Neapolitan Bourbons in 1734. King Charles the Bourbon (who later became Charles III of Spain) and his minister Bernardo Tanucci extended some Enlightenment reforms into Apulia, working to end a system in which, of 2700 communes in the Kingdom of Naples, 1800 were still feudal holdings. The bottom line, however, was that the Neapolitan Bourbons paid little attention to the region. Taxes remained low, and the region languished in a general neglect.

Union with the Kingdom of Italy in 1860 brought skyrocketing taxes but continued the tradition of neglect. Between 1906 and 1939, however, to aid irrigation in Apulia, an enormous aqueduct was built from the Sele River in Campania. During the First World War, Apulia was an important base of naval operations against the Austrians. In the Second World War it was occupied by the Allies immediately after the armistice of September 8, 1943. After the war, Apulia received massive aid from the Cassa per il Mezzogiorno (Fund for the South), and the Land Reform Act of 1951 redistributed most of the region's latifundia.

RECENT POLITICS. The postwar Christian Democrats were strong in Apulia until the early 1990s. Apulia constitutes the twenty-first electoral district (*circoscrizione*). In the majoritarian part of the 1996 elections for Italy's Chamber of Deputies, the Center-Left Ulivo coalition narrowly won with 46.1 percent of the vote against 45.5 for the Polo per le Libertà. In the proportional count, Forza Italia took the highest number with 24.6 percent of the votes; the Democratic Party of the Left (PDS) captured 22.1 percent and the Alleanza Nazionale earned 17.9 percent. For the Senate, the Polo captured a 43.9 percent plurality, followed by 37.4 percent for the Ulivo. The Center-Right maintained its control in Apulia's April 2000 regional elections. Raffaele Fitto was elected president at the head of a Center-Right coalition which took 53.9 percent of the vote.

BARI

PROVINCIAL PROFILE. Area: 1,980 sq. mi. Population: 1,569,133 (province), 335,410 (city). The province of Bari has 48 communes. The

northern coast of Bari is on the Adriatic Sea. Down the coast to the southeast, Bari touches Brindisi, then Taranto on the southwest. West of Bari is
Basilicata, and Foggia meets it on the northwest.

HISTORY. Bari has been inhabited since at least 1500 B.C., and the
province is associated with Peucetian settlement and then a strong Greek
presence. The Romans called the town Barium and developed its port. Just
south of the border with Foggia, near the Ofanto River, is Cannae, site of
Republican Rome's most humiliating defeat on August 2, 216 B.C. It was
on the banks of the river, called the Aufidus in those days, that Hannibal
and his Carthaginians destroyed an entire Roman army of 70,000 men,
and killed one of the Republic's consuls (Lucius Aemilius Paulus) and 80
of its senators. Because the river has shifted its course frequently over the
centuries, the exact site of the battle cannot be located, although a cemetery
has been discovered that apparently holds the graves of many of the fallen.
After Cannae, Hannibal continued his efforts to conquer Italy, but he never
matched his victory on the Ofanto. Eventually he fled back to North Africa,
where the Romans defeated him at Zama in 202.

The first record of a Christian bishop in Bari names a Gervasio in 347.
After the fall of the Roman Empire in 476, Lombards and Byzantines struggled for control of Bari. Emperor Constans II sacked the city in 669, and
the Greeks eventually took it. Bari rebelled against Emperor Leo the Isaurian during the Iconoclast controversy in the 700s and established an autonomous rule. The Lombard Dukes of Benevento seized the opportunity
and made Bari a satellite. About 840 Bari was besieged by Muslim troops
from Calabria. The force had been employed by the Duke of Benevento to
fight the Prince of Salerno but, camped near Bari, they discerned an opportunity in the undefended city and forgot their obligations to the duke.
They took Bari and ruled it until the Carolingian Emperor Louis II liberated
it in 870 or 871.

Bari frequently changed hands during the next two centuries, although
Byzantine rule was reestablished by the eleventh century under a *catapano*
(administrator). From that title was derived Catipanata or Capitanata, a
term later employed by the Neapolitans and still sometimes used in place
of Apulia. Local revolts against the Greeks begun by Melus in 1009 and
continued by his son, Argirus, drew assistance from the Normans. In 1068
the Norman forces of Robert Guiscard laid siege to the Byzantine fortress.
Along with his land troops, Guiscard used his fleet to blockade Bari harbor;
three years later, in 1071, the Greeks submitted and yielded their last
stronghold in Italy. After Guiscard's death in 1085, Pope Urban II proclaimed his son, Bohemond, Duke of Bari. As he had at Taranto, Bohemond contributed to the prosperity of Bari by designating it an important
point of departure for Crusaders on their way to the Holy Land.

After suffering a terrible sack by William of Sicily in 1156, Bari revived
in the thirteenth century under the Swabians. Emperor Frederick II rebuilt

the castle and ordered the construction of a new port. Bari became an Angevin city, and then Aragonese. It passed to the Sforza family in 1464 and to the Spanish rulers of Naples in 1557. The Masaniello Revolt in Naples (1647) found echo in Bari under Paolo Ribecco, a sailor who led attacks on Church and noble property.

The Austrians' brief rule of Apulia and southern Italy ended outside of Bari, at Bitonto, when General José Carillo de Albornoz, the Duke of Montemar defeated them on May 25, 1734. The victorious Neapolitan Bourbons established a royal college in Bari, but their plan to expand the city beyond its walls was cut short by the revolutionary uprising in 1799. A French army restored order but sacked the treasure of Saint Nicholas.

In 1860 Bari became part of the Kingdom of Italy. Like the other Apulian ports, Bari's ties with the eastern Mediterranean have been strong. In 1924 Mussolini opened an "Adriatic" University in Bari. In 1930 he established the Fiera del Levante (Levant Fair), a Mediterranean trade fair which continues today. And in 1934 he launched Radio Bari there to transmit Fascist propaganda to the Middle East.

ARTS AND CULTURE. In 1087, when merchants translated his remains to Bari, Saint Nicholas (Bishop of Myra) replaced Sabino as the patron saint of the city. Nicholas also protects shepherds, children, sailors, and women in search of husbands. A Greek from what is now Turkey, he lived in the early fourth century; although details of his life are largely conjectural. When the relics of Nicholas reached Bari, work immediately commenced on a basilica dedicated to him. The Romanesque structure was built on top of the Byzantine governor's palace and was completed in the twelfth century. Bari honors St. Nicholas each May 7 with a Sagra, or historic procession. Because of his association with Christmas, Nicholas is one of Christianity's most popular saints, although he is particularly important for the Orthodox. Russia's last czar, Nicholas II, made a pilgrimage to Bari and constructed a church there to serve Eastern devotees of the saint.

Bari's cathedral, finished in the twelfth century and built on the remains of a Byzantine Duomo, honors its pre-Nicholas patron, Sabino. Bari boasts a significant collection of Daunian, Peucezian, and Massepican treasures in its Museo Archeologico (Archaeological Museum). It is home to the Laterza publishing house. Established by Vito Laterza in nearby Rutigliano, the company moved to Bari in 1889; **Giovanni Laterza** (1873–1943) took it over in 1901 and built it into one of Italy's leading publishers.

In September, Bari hosts an international trade fair. Throughout the year the city is a commercial center of southern Italy, hosting a number of other fairs. There are also exhibitions of farming and food equipment, automobile arts, and construction equipment. A food show, the Cibus Mediterraneo, is held in May, and a contemporary art fair, Expoarte, occurs in April. Tourism, sports, and leisure shows run concurrently in March.

OTHER CENTERS. Bari province is home to a number of other important towns, such as **Barletta**, a place the Romans knew as Baruli or Barduli. It was a significant Norman and Angevin stronghold. Barletta's fame rests in part on the work of the nineteenth-century statesman and novelist Massimo Taparelli, Marquis of Azeglio, who immortalized the town in his popular story of the dashing knight Ettore Fieramosca. In 1503 Fieramosca met the "challenge of Barletta" (*disfida di Barletta*) and defeated the Frenchman La Motte. Barletta is also home to the *Colosso* (Colossus) which stands next to the twelfth-century Basilica of the Holy Sepulchre (Santo Sepolcro). An enormous ancient statue, about 16 feet high, it probably depicts the Eastern Roman Emperor Valentinian I. Most of the statue, dated from the fourth century, was found on the beach in the thirteenth century, and its arms and legs were added in the fifteenth. Much local art is found in the Museo Civico Giuseppe de Nittis. The museum honors De Nittis (1846–1884), a local painter who achieved some success in Paris and London before his early death.

Bitonto, another ancient town with Peucenzian roots, was known to the Romans as Butontum or Butuntum. Its most famous structure is its magnificent twelfth-century cathedral, dedicated to Saint Valentine. Modeled in part on Bari's San Nicola, it is considered a masterpiece of the Apulian Romanesque style.

Inland from Barletta is **Canosa de Puglia**, whose Cathedral of San Sabino contains the tomb of Bohemond, the Crusader who ruled much of Apulia as Prince of Taranto and Duke of Bari. It is an old city, called Canusium or Canusion by the ancients, with fourth-century B.C. burial grounds, and a Roman arch and bridge. Nearby is the Basilica of San Leucio, a sixth-century structure built over a pagan temple. It was largely destroyed and rebuilt in the eleventh century, although important paleo-Christian pavements remain.

Emperor Frederick II's **Castel del Monte** occupies an isolated site, high on a hill over the Murge plateau. Some believe that the imposing octagonal structure, built between 1240 and 1250, was designed by the emperor himself.

The effects of Frederick II in the province can be seen in **Altamura**'s thirteenth-century cathedral, dedicated to the Assumption of the Virgin.

Apulia is quite famous among Italians for a distinct style of houses found there, the *trulli*. These simple white dwellings have cone-shaped roofs and are generally found in the Itria valley. The greatest concentration of them, over 1,000 is at **Alberobello**, near the border with Taranto.

Gravina in Puglia, the ancient Civitas Gravinae, was a Peucetian settlement before it was a Roman town. It contains some remarkable churches, including San Michele dei Grotti, carved from rock, and the fifteenth-century Santa Sofia, which contains the tomb of Angela Kastriota Skanderbeg.

Molfetta was known in the Middle Ages as Melphi and Melphicta. Its thirteenth-century "Old Duomo" (*Duomo vecchio*) is one of the best examples of the Apulian Romanesque style. Molfetta was the birthplace of the historian and anti-Fascist polemicist Gaetano Salvemini (1873–1957). As a member of Parliament, as a professor at the University of Messina— where he lost his wife and five children in the 1908 earthquake—and at the University of Florence, Salvemini applied his socialist principles to defend the working class and especially the *mezzogiorno* poor. He fled to France in 1925 and then emigrated to the United States, where he taught at Harvard University and worked to counter Fascist propaganda. After the Second World War, Salvemini returned to Florence to teach.

BRINDISI

PROVINCIAL PROFILE. Area: 709 sq. mi. Population: 414,906 (province), 94,732 (city). The province has 20 communes. The Adriatic bathes the north shore of Brindisi province. Lecce sits to its southeast, and Taranto is to its south and west. Bari touches the province on the northwest.

HISTORY. The Greeks called Brindisi Brentesion, and the Romans called it Brundisium, a name derived from the Greek *brenda* (deer's head), which may have resembled the shape of the port. Some accounts connect the foundation of the city with the legendary Diomedes, whereas others state that Cretans from Knossus were the founders. Under the Greeks, Brindisi rivaled Taranto as the primary city of the region. But Taranto's alliance with the Carthaginian general Hannibal in the third century B.C. canceled its status and brought Brindisi rewards from the victorious Romans. The city served as the terminus of the Appian Way, which stretched to Rome. Two ancient columns near the port marked what was then the end of the road. One of them toppled in an earthquake, but the other still stands.

After the fall of the Roman Empire in 476, Brindisi was sacked and destroyed by the Muslims and by Emperor Louis II, who captured it from them between 867 and 871. The city revived as a Crusader port between the eleventh century and the the end of the fourteenth. Brindisi was later controlled by the Swabian emperors, then the Angevins until 1385, when it became a feudal possession of Raimondo Orsini del Balzo. The Aragonese Neapolitans took Brindisi, and Ferrante of Aragon repaired much of the city after the earthquake of 1456. Naples placed Brindisi in the Lecce district.

Brindisi revived after union with the Kingdom of Italy in 1860 and with the opening of the Suez Canal in 1869. Its port facilities were expanded, and it became Italy's naval base of operations in the Adriatic during the First World War. The Fascists carved Brindisi province from Lecce in 1927.

During the Second World War the city briefly became the national capital. After the Allied forces and Italy declared an armistice on September 8, 1943, King Victor Emmanuel III and Prime Minister Pietro Badoglio fled Rome and reorganized the shreds of a government in Brindisi. The administration remained there until the king transferred it to Salerno the following February. Brindisi remains a busy port for the import of oil products and is well known for its convenient ferry connections to Greece.

ARTS AND CULTURE. Brindisi was the birthplace of the Roman tragic poet **Pacuvius**; and **Virgil**, the author of the *Aeneid*, died there in 19 B.C. upon his return from Greece.

Like Saint Nicholas of Bari, Brindisi's patron saint, **Leucio**, was from the Greek East and reflects Apulia's Byzantine heritage. Leucio was born in Alexandria and was Bishop of Antioch before coming to Brindisi. Brindisi's most singular church is the circular San Giovanni al Sepolcro, begun in the eleventh century, by the order of the Knights Templar, above an older paleo-Christian structure. On the outskirts of the city, near the airport, is another significant church, the thirteenth-century Santa Maria del Casale, a Romanesque-Gothic structure.

OTHER CENTERS. Oria was an ancient Massepican place before it passed to the Romans. It boasts a thirteenth-century imperial castle of Frederick II and holds an annual parade in his honor.

Ostuni was a Massepican town. It has an impressive medieval center and a late Gothic cathedral of the fifteenth century. Nearby **Marina di Ostuni** is a popular seaside resort.

FOGGIA

PROVINCIAL PROFILE. Area: 2,774 sq. mi. Population: 697,638 (province), 156,301 (city). The province of Foggia comprises 64 communes. Foggia caps Apulia on its northwest end. The Ofanto River runs along its southeastern border with Bari, the only other Apulian province that it touches. To Foggia's south is Basilicata, and Molise is to the west. The Adriatic and the Gulf of Manfredonia meet the province on its north. Offshore are the Tremiti Islands, principally San Domino, San Nicola, and Capraia. Foggia province is divided into three distinct zones, the rocky Gargano Peninsula, the flat Tavoliere or Capitanata, and the pre-Alpine Daunia.

HISTORY. A traditional but still-used term for the province of Foggia, particularly its western, hillier, regions, is Daunia. The name recalls King Daunus, who, according to legend, befriended Diomedes, the Homeric hero from the Trojan War, who reached the Apulian shore when his ship was blown off course. He stayed and married Euippe, the king's daughter. Some versions of the story place Diomedes's death on the Apulian mainland or the Tremiti Islands, where his companions were turned into herons. The Romans valued the Gargano for its heavy oak forests and cut them down, leaving only barren earth.

Although legend has the city of Foggia established in ancient times by people of nearby Arpi who fled a malaria outbreak, the first recorded reference to it, as Santa Maria de Fovea, is found in a bull, dated 1069, from Pope Alexander II to the Bishop of Troia. Later, Emperor Frederick II favored Foggia. He built a castle for himself and lived there for a time, and he made it a chief market town and transportation hub. The people, however, rebelled against him and suffered his ruthless retaliation. They rose again in 1250 against Frederick's illegitimate son, the troublesome Manfred. Nevertheless, at Foggia in December 1254, Manfred inflicted a crushing defeat on a papal army, less than one week before the death of Pope Innocent IV.

Under the Kingdom of Naples the city prospered as a leading grain market. The Tavoliere continued to be one of southern Italy's major producers of grains, supplying not only Naples but also other parts of Italy, particularly Venice. Foggia was a center of Carbonaro (a secret political society) activity after the fall of Napoleon and participated in the nationalist revolts of 1820, 1848, and 1860. During the Second World War, Foggia was captured in 1943 by the Allies, who used it as an important air base against Nazi Germany. The city's reputation remains linked to the land, and it hosts two agricultural festivals, in May and September.

ARTS AND CULTURE. An earthquake destroyed much of Foggia in 1731. Consequently, old structures such as the cathedral were renovated with new Baroque exteriors. Foggia's patron saints are the Madonna of the Seven Veils, San Guglielmo, and his son, San Pellegrino. Guglielmo and Pellegrino came to Foggia from Antioch, probably in the twelfth century, to live as hermits. The image of the Madonna of the Seven Veils, said to have been etched on the so-called "Holy Table" by Saint Luke the Evangelist, was brought to Apulia in the fifth century by Bishop Lorenzo Maiorano. The image was endangered in the eighth century when the Byzantine Emperor Leo the Isaurian launched his campaign against the worship of icons and ordered the destruction of icons throughout his realm. The people of nearby Arpi, Apulia's first see, buried it. After the town was sacked, the sacred treasure was largely forgotten. A flood uncovered the Madonna in 1062, when some shepherds found it under three flames. Foggia celebrates its Madonna from August 13 to August 16. Only a bit of Frederick II's castle remains in Foggia, its "doorway arch" (*arco del portale*).

The lyric composer **Umberto Giordano** (1867–1948) was born in Foggia. Associated with the *verismo* (realist) style, he is best known for *Andrea Chenier* (1896), the story of a poet during the French Revolution's Reign of Terror.

OTHER CENTERS. Little remains of Foggia's ancient neighbor, **Arpi,** called Argyripta by the Greeks. The last of the town was destroyed in an eleventh-century Muslim raid. Some excavations can be viewed at **Montarozzi,** and many of the discoveries were transferred to Foggia's archaeological museum.

Emperor Frederick II favored **Lucera** and lived there from 1224 until 1226. He transferred a population of his Muslim subjects there from Sicily and made the town the headquarters of his professional army. Frederick's palace was converted into a fortress by the Angevin rulers who followed him. An impressive fourteenth-century Duomo dedicated to the Assumption of the Virgin and a Roman amphitheater distinguish the town.

At the edge of the Gargano, **San Giovanni Rotondo** is one of Italy's most important religious centers. It is unusual, however, in that its significance stems not from early or medieval Christianity, but from the twentieth century, as the home of Padre Pio, a Franciscan Monk who attracted an enormous following until his death in 1968, who is buried in the crypt of the new church.

Monte Sant'Angelo is the center of the Gargano Peninsula. The Lombards built its commanding sanctuary of San Michele Arcangelo in the late sixth century. The Muslims destroyed it in the ninth century, but it was rebuilt and added to over many centuries. The town also contains the Giovanni Tancredi Museum of Arts and Popular Traditions of the Gargano.

Troia, near Foggia, was the birthplace of Antonio Salandra (1853–1931), Prime Minister from March 1914 until June 1916. Salandra guided Italian foreign policy through the May 1915 declaration of war against Austria-Hungary and the alliance with Britain, France, and Russia. In October 1922, Salandra was invited by King Victor Emmanuel III to form a government, but he refused, proposing that the monarch turn instead to the Fascist leader, Benito Mussolini. Salandra lived to regret his suggestion.

LECCE

PROVINCIAL PROFILE. Area: 1,065 sq. mi. Population: 818,033 (province), 99,763 (city). The province of Lecce comprises 97 communes. Lecce forms Apulia's (and Italy's) southeast corner. Except to the northwest, where it meets Taranto and Brindisi, Lecce faces water on all sides: the Ionian Sea on the west and the Adriatic on the east, until the two meet at Cape Santa Maria di Leuca.

HISTORY. Lecce grew from, first, an ancient Massepican town and, second, the third-century B.C. Roman settlement of Lupiae (later Licea or Litium). After the chaos of the fall of the Roman Empire in 476, Lecce was taken by the Byzantine Greeks. After Carolingian, Lombard, and Muslim interludes, the Normans captured Lecce and turned it into the seat of a county in the eleventh century. After a devastating twelfth-century sack by William I of Sicily and a period of Angevin rule, in 1353 Lecce became a feudal possession of the Enghien family, which merged with the Orsini del Balzo in 1385. In 1463 Lecce passed to the Kingdom of Naples. For most areas of Apulia, Spanish rule was an unfortunate development, but not in Lecce. Christendom's victory over the Turks at the Battle of Lepanto in 1571 lessened the danger of Lecce's proximity to the Muslim East and prompted a construction boom in the city. The University of Lecce was established in 1956.

ARTS AND CULTURE. Outside of Lecce are the ruins and excavations of Rudiae, a Massepican and Roman town. **Ennius**, author of the *Annales*, was born there. Lecce's patron saints are three martyrs: Giusto, Oronzo, and Fortunato. According to legend, Giusto was a follower of Saint Paul and accompanied him to Italy. He landed in the Salentino (Salentine Peninsula) and converted two pagans, Oronzo and Fortunato, both of whom became bishops of Lecce. After a series of dramatic events, such as the collapse of pagan temples during their trials, Giusto and Oronzo were killed during Nero's persecutions; it is said that flowers bloomed from their blood. A statue of Oronzo stands on an ancient column in Lecce's central square, which also bears his name.

Considerable evidence of Roman rule remains in the city. A second-century A.D. amphitheater shares a corner of the Piazza Sant'Oronzo with the sixteenth-century Palazzo del Seggio (or Sedile), which for a few centuries was Lecce's seat of government. An impressive Norman church dedicated to Saints Nicholas and Cataldo was built by King Tancred of Sicily in the twelfth century. Charles V, Holy Roman Emperor (1519–1556; also King Charles I of Spain), left his mark on Lecce with a triumphal arch (also called the Porta di Napoli). He also constructed the castle which stands in the middle of the city.

Lecce is best known throughout Italy as a Baroque city, thanks to the many structures built after Lepanto. A number of churches—particularly the Duomo, San Matteo, Santa Croce, Sant'Irene—and secular structures such as the seat of the government, the Palazzo del Governo, are outstanding examples of the style.

OTHER CENTERS. Gallipoli began as a Greek town, possibly as *Kalepolis* (beautiful city). Its older part sits on a small island in the Ionian Sea and is connected to the mainland by a seventeenth-century bridge. Its Baroque cathedral, dedicated to Saint Agatha, was constructed between 1629 and 1696. It contains paintings by a native of Gallipoli, Giovanni Andrea Coppola (c. 1597–1659). Gallipoli also boasts an unusual Hellenistic fountain a sixteenth-century structure with ancient bas-reliefs. One of Mussolini's most loyal lieutenants, Achille Starace (1889–1945), was born in Gallipoli. He served as secretary of the Fascist Party from 1931 until 1939 and followed the Duce north to his Salò puppet government in 1943. He was captured and executed with Mussolini, in April 1945.

Interior from coastal Gallipoli are **Galatone** and **Galatina**. The former is the site of the Crocifisso della Pietà, a rich Baroque structure completed in 1710. The latter is home to the fourteenth-century Franciscan church dedicated to Saint Catherine of Alexandria. Its early fifteenth-century frescoes depicting the Apocalypse and the saints, and the story of Saint Catherine are considered some of Apulia's most glorious.

Maglie is the birthplace of Aldo Moro (1916–1978), the Christian Democratic leader and prime minister of Italy. Moro was one of the principal figures in Italy's "opening to the Left," which admitted Socialists back into the ruling coalition in the early 1960s. He was preparing the way for a similar arrangement with the Communist Party when Red Brigade terrorists of the far Left kidnapped and murdered him in 1978.

Colonists from Taranto founded **Otranto** in ancient times. It endured occupations by all of the forces that came to Apulia through the ages, and one more. In August 1480 the Turks landed at Otranto and occupied it in what Sultan Muhammad planned as the start of an invasion of Italy. The sultan died the following year, however, and in September 1481 Neapolitan forces chased the Turks from Otranto. The Turks had imposed a harsh occupation. The castle survived, however, as did Otranto's twelfth-century cathedral dedication to the Annunciation. The eleventh-century Church of San Nicola di Casole was not so lucky, and only ruins mark its location today.

TARANTO

PROVINCIAL PROFILE. Area: 941 sq. mi. Population: 590,358 (province), 211,660 (city). The province of Taranto contains 29 communes. Taranto bends around the top of the Ionian Sea, which it faces to the south. To the west of Taranto is Basilicata; Bari is to its north; Brindisi is to its east; and Lecce is to its southeast.

HISTORY. Greeks from Sparta and Laconia took ancient Taras from the Massepicans in the eighth century B.C. By the fourth century the city had acquired central importance among the Greek cities of southern Italy (Magna Graecia). But Taras declined after it fell under Hannibal's control during the Second Punic War (218–202 B.C.). The victorious Romans sacked it, took it, and named it Tarentum. The city's position continued to deteriorate after the fall of the Roman Empire (476). The Byzantines occupied it more than once, and the Muslims did so between c. 840 and 880. They also destroyed it in 927. The Norman Robert Guiscard took what was left of the town in 1063, and his son, the Crusader Bohemond

I, assumed the title of Prince of Taranto. Bohemond, one of the leaders of the First Crusade, revived Taranto as a port. After Angevin control, the city was incorporated into the Kingdom of Naples. It remained a contested place, suffering repeated Turkish onslaughts, and Napoleon used it as a French base. As part of the Kingdom of Italy, Taranto became a major naval base and, in 1882, the site of an important shipyard. Another significant shipyard, the Cantieri Navali Tosi, opened in 1914. In November 1940, British torpedo fighters attacked the fleet anchored there, sending most of it to the bottom of the rather shallow harbor. Italy's postwar government designated Taranto as a major development zone and pumped enormous sums into it. The greatest project was the construction of enormous steelworks, the IV Centro, by the semiprivate Finsider Corporation.

ARTS AND CULTURE. One of Apulia's most important celebrations occurs between May 8 and 11, the feast of Taranto's patron saint, Cataldo. The statue of the saint is taken from a chapel in the Duomo, and then the mayor of the city leads a seaborne regatta through the harbor and a procession on foot up and down the main streets. Almost nothing about the saint is known with certainty. He was, perhaps, a seventh-century Irish bishop who died and was buried at Taranto while on a pilgrimage to the Holy Land. Saracens destroyed Taranto's cathedral, in which Cataldo was entombed, and upon its reconstruction, his corpse was discovered with a gold cross on it. The city's "Procession of the Mysteries" is one of Italy's most important Good Friday rituals. Taranto's National Museum is one of the most important in southern Italy.

Livius Andronicus, the third-century B.C. Roman poet who translated *The Odyssey* into Latin, was from Taranto, as were the composer **Giovanni Paisiello** (1740–1816) and the playwright **Giulio Cesare Viola** (1886–1958).

OTHER CENTERS. Northwest of Taranto is **Castellaneta**, a town with two well-preserved medieval quarters, Sacco and Muricello.

Martina Franca owes its existence to refugees from Taranto who settled there in the tenth century. Philip of Anjou, Prince of Taranto, added to the town and built its walls in the fourteenth century. It is noted today for a collection of seventeenth- and eighteenth-century structures, including the Palazzo Ducale, the collegiate Church of San Martino, and the churches of San Domenico and del Carmine.

SELECT BIBLIOGRAPHY

AAVV. *Puglia: Turismo, storia, arte, folklore.* Bari: Mario Adda Editore, 1991.
Masella, Luigi, and Biagio Salvemini, eds. *La Puglia.* Turin: Einaudi, 1989.
Rosa, Antonio. *La Terra del Silenzio: Proverbi contadini e tradizioni popolari della Daunia.* Bari: Mario Adda Editore, 1983.
Ventura, Antonio. *La guida della Puglia: Itinerario storico Artistico.* Lecce: Capone, 1998.

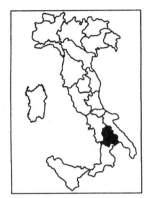

BASILICATA

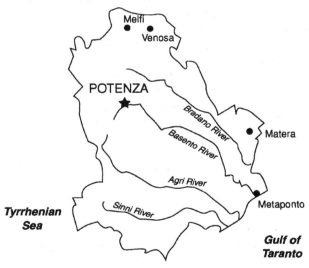

Melfi
Venosa

POTENZA

Bradano River

Basento River

Matera

Agri River

Metaponto

Tyrrhenian
Sea

Sinni River

Gulf of
Taranto

Ionian Sea

Chapter 3

BASILICATA

REGIONAL CHARACTERISTICS. Area: 3,857 sq. mi. Population: 610,330. Capital: Potenza. Among Italy's regions, Basilicata ranks fourteenth in land area and eighteenth in population. There is a Catholic metropolitan see at Potenza/Muro Lucano/Marsico Nuovo.

To the northwest of Basilicata is Campania, and to its northeast is Apulia. To the south is Calabria, which Basilicata cuts off from the rest of Italy by stretching from the Ionian Sea in the east to the Gulf of Policastro and the Tyrrhenian Sea in the west. Almost half (46.9 percent) of the region is mountainous, a good part of which has been set aside in the Pollino National Park along the southern border with Calabria; 45.1 percent of Basilicata is hilly, and 8 percent is flat. Along the Ionian shore the Metaponto plain, Basilicata's largest, spills into Apulia. Significant rivers flow east from the central and southern uplands. Along the coast between the borders with Apulia and Calabria, these rivers include the Bradano, the Basento, the Cavone, the Agri, and the Sinni. A large forest is preserved at the mouth of the Sinni near Policoro.

ECONOMY. In Basilicata 15.6 percent of active workers hold jobs in agriculture, 30.6 percent in industry, and 53.8 percent in the tertiary sector. Of the region's 173,000 employed workers, 119,000 are men and 54,000 are women. In January 1998 the unemployment rate was 16.9 percent. Basilicata's economy was long dismissed as backward and impoverished. In 1951 over 75 percent of its workers tilled the soil, but it has made some important recent advances. Agriculture and vineyards around Monte Vulture and in the Ofanto valley are distinguished by their high technology.

During the 1960s the discovery of methane gas deposits and the rise of the chemical industry transformed parts of the Basento valley. More recently, the new plant of the Italian automaker Fiat near Melfi has become famous for its use of advanced Japanese managerial techniques. Tourism is an important factor, particularly on the coast.

CUISINE. Some believe that Basilicata is the birthplace of pasta and note a reference to it in the *Satires* of Horace, a native son. It is ubiquitous in the region's cuisine, and can be said to possess a spiritual as well as a physical quality because across Basilicata lasagna is prepared for the poor in honor of Saint Joseph. Cheese is also very important, particularly a Lucanian pecorino made from a blend of 70 percent sheep's milk and 30 percent goat's milk that is aged for between three months and a year. Elaborate pork sausages, known throughout Italy as *lucanica* or *lucanega*, are produced in the area. *Soppressato* sausage, oval and flat and flavored with ginger, is popular in Basilicata. Sauces are well seasoned and hot. Ginger is a favorite seasoning, as are very hot pimientos. *Lampascioni* are local wild onions known for their distinctive flavor. Olive oil is another specialty of Basilicata. The region's most famous wine is Aglianico del Vulture, the only Basilicata wine to possess the DOC mark and perhaps the best red produced in southern Italy. Since before the Romans the grapes from which it is produced have been grown primarily on the slopes of Monte Vulture, an extinct volcano near Melfi and Venosa. Its name, Aglianico, recalls the *ellenico* (Greek) rule of the area. Grapes used to produce another Aglianico are cultivated around Matera.

PANE COTTO

1 hot pepper (peperoncini), chopped	4 eggs
2 oz. leeks, chopped	2 Tbs. fresh parsley
2 Tbs. olive oil	Salt to taste
4 c. water	1 loaf of hard crust bread (approx. ½ lb.), sliced

Fry hot pepper and leeks in olive oil for a few minutes, then add water and bring to a boil. Stir the eggs and parsley. Place the bread in a bowl and pour the hot mixture over it.

HISTORY. Historically Basilicata has frequently been referred to as Lucania, a name still preferred by many and derived either from the Latin term for woodlands, or from the ancient Lyki (or Liky) people, who came to Italy from Anatolia during the Iron Age. The name Basilicata stems from a twelfth-century document referring to a Byzantine administrator (*basili-*

kos). The Fascist regime resurrected the name Lucania in 1926, but the postwar state reverted to the use of Basilicata.

Greek settlers came to Basilicata in the eighth century B.C. and founded the cities of Metapontum, Siri, and Heraclea (today, Policoro). Oscan/Samnite peoples, including the Lucanians, came in the sixth and fifth centuries B.C. They were followed by the Romans, who established a military colony at Venusia (Venosa) in 291 B.C. The Lucanians first considered themselves allies of the Romans, but later turned against them in league with their Samnite cousins and the Greeks. Rome absorbed the area, crushed Lucanian resistance, and incorporated the land into Region II (Apulia) and Region III (Bruttium-Calabria). Diocletian's third-century A.D. reforms reunited the region and attached it to Bruttium. After the fall of the Roman Empire in 476 and the Gothic invasions, Lucania suffered the rivalry between Byzantines and Lombards for control of the area. At the end of the sixth century, however, most of the region came under the domination of the Lombard principality of Salerno and remained there for almost 300 years.

In 1059 the Normans made Melfi the capital of their south Italian holdings. Their dominion persisted until 1186, when the last of their rulers, Constance d'Hauteville (Altavilla) married the future Swabian emperor Henry VI. Norman resistance to Swabian rule erupted under Tancred, the brother of Constance. The rebellion collapsed in 1194, however, with Tancred's death and the incarceration of his son, William III. In 1197 Henry was succeeded by his brother Philip, who struggled for the imperial crown against Otto IV of Brunswick, and was followed in 1212 by Henry's son, Frederick II. The brilliant youth, known as Stupor Mundi (wonder of the world), established a splendid court and reorganized imperial administration throughout southern Italy in the Constitutions of Melfi (1231). The Holy See challenged the Swabians, and in c. 1264 Pope Urban IV invited Charles of Anjou (Charles I of Naples) into Italy to claim their lands. A civil war erupted, turning Basilicata into a battleground. Echoing the Sicilian Vespers (1282) uprising that challenged the French, a group of barons supporting the Swabians (Ghibellines), together with 2,000 Muslim troops, fortified themselves in the Lagonegrese, near the Noce River valley, and in the Crati valley. The house of Anjou and that of Aragon, which replaced it in 1442, left most of Basilicata as a fief to the Sanseverino family, which extended its rule as far as Salerno. In the sixteenth century, Spanish domination brought different barons and more bad government to Basilicata. In 1663 they made Matera the capital of their Lucanian province. Foreign rule continued during the wars of the French Revolution and the Napoleonic era, and reactionary Sanfedisti activity against it proved popular and strong. In the early nineteenth century, the Carbonari (a secret political society) caught on within segments of Basilicata's bourgeoisie, and the region witnessed some activity in favor of unification. The year 1848 also saw brief social revolutions in Matera and, especially, in Venosa.

However, the Risorgimento alienated many of Basilicata's poor and triggered widespread brigandage throughout the area during the 1860s. The most important band, loyal to the Neapolitan Bourbons, fought under Carmine Donatelli, known as "Crocco." Basilicata's image suffered further in 1868 through the publication of an influential book on the region by Enrico Pani Rossi. Italians were shocked by his reports on burial practices in the small town of Muro, where the dead were thrown over a cliff, and in Ripacandida, where they were left to be eaten by the vultures. Embarrassing as it was, the book and other reports awakened many Italians to Basilicata's desperate poverty. In 1905, over 30 years later, Parliament passed the Special Law for Basilicata, to alleviate some of the misery. Public works, land reclamation, reforestation, and other projects were envisioned. There were no funds to implement the reforms, however, and the law remained a dead letter. Nevertheless, the modern world began to creep into Basilicata via such innovations as the railroad that connected Naples, Potenza, and the Ionian coast in 1874. Between 1880 and 1900, 1,250 miles of roads were built, and illiteracy dropped from over 90 percent in 1860 to 75 percent in 1901. Still, between 1881 and 1921 Basilicata lost 10 percent of its population to out-migration.

The Fascists used Basilicata (and other regions as well) as a place of exile for enemies of the state. During the 1930s, the anti-Fascist writer Carlo Levi was banished to remote Basilicata; he immortalized the experience in his autobiographical work *Christ Stopped at Eboli* (1945). In the 1960s the harsh images of Pier Paolo Pasolini's film *The Gospel According to Saint Matthew*, achieved a certain reality thanks to the use of Basilicata as a location.

RECENT POLITICS. After the Second World War, Basilicata's political life was dominated by the Christian Democrats (DC) under the local leadership of the longtime Treasury Minister, Emilio Colombo. The Communists (and Democratic Party of the Left [PDS], later Democrats of the Left [DS]) and the neo-Fascists made strong gains through the 1970s and 1980s although the DC still gained 44.5 percent of the vote in 1992. Basilicata constitutes the twenty-second *circoscrizione* (electoral district). In the 1996 elections the Center-Left Ulivo coalition won the majoritarian counts with 43.2 percent, followed by the Center-Right Polo per la Libertà group with 42 percent. In the proportional vote the PDS took 23.6 percent of the vote, followed by Forza Italia with 18.2 percent and the Alleanza Nazionale with 14.4 percent. For the Senate the Ulivo took 52.2 percent of the vote and the Polo captured 37.7 percent. Basilicata stayed with the Center-Left in the April 2000 regional elections with a 63.1 percent victory versus 35.1 percent for the Center-Right. The regional president is Filippo Bubbico.

POTENZA

PROVINCIAL PROFILE. Area: 2,527 sq. mi. Population: 403,019 (province), 66,132 (city). The province of Potenza contains 100 communes. The province has a long north-south shape that occupies the western side of Basilicata. It borders Apulia on the north and northeast, Campania on the west, and Calabria on the south. The province of Matera lies to the east. Potenza has a short but rugged coastline on the Tyrrhenian Sea that separates Campania and Calabria. Most of the province is hilly or mountainous, and much of its southern area along the Calabrian frontier is part of Pollino National Park. Monte Pollino rises 7,375 feet on the border. In the north, Monte Vulture is an inactive volcano that rises to 4,350 feet. At 2,688 feet above sea level, Potenza is Italy's highest regional capital.

HISTORY. Evidence indicates an eleventh-century B.C. settlement near Potenza, at Serra di Vaglio. Roman control was established over Potentia around 200 B.C. It became a Norman stronghold in the Duchy of Benevento and experienced a terrible siege by Frederick II in 1231. The Sanseverino family acquired the city in the late fourteenth century. Potenza has been plagued by major earthquakes throughout its history. Their destructive force in 1273, 1694, 1851, 1857, and 1980, among other years, was rivaled only by the devastating Allied air bombardment in September 1943 and, perhaps, the urban renewal begun in 1966.

ARTS AND CULTURE. Every year on May 29 and 30, Potenza honors its patron bishop, Saint Gerardo, with its *sfilata* (or *cavalcata*) *dei turchi* (procession of the Turks). The festival recalls a Muslim attempt to sack the city that was thwarted by the appearance of a legion of angels. The miracle was attributed to the intercession of Potenza's holy bishop, Gerardo. He is also honored in Potenza's thirteenth-century Duomo, which has frequently been restored. Gerardo was born at Piacenza, and documents attest that he was a twelfth-century Bishop of Potenza. The University of Basilicata opened at Potenza in 1984.

OTHER CENTERS. Potenza province was off the beaten imperial path, but some of its few Roman structures can be appreciated in **Grumento Nova** and **Venosa**. The former, ancient Grumentum, a Samnite Lucanian town and then a Roman colony, has remnants of an aqueduct, a basilica, and a theater. Venosa's roots also are Samnite-Lucanian and Roman, and the poet Horace was born there in 65 B.C. Venosa's Norman heritage persists in the remains of the Benedictine abbey of the *Trinity*, built, but never finished, during the eleventh and twelfth centuries. Outside of Venosa are fourth- and fifth-century Jewish and Christian catacombs.

An important Lucanian Romanesque-Gothic structure is the cathedral dedicated to the Assumption of the Virgin and San Canio in **Acerenza**. This ancient Roman town of Acheruntia, strategically located on a hilltop, gained an importance that persisted under the Lombards and Normans. The cathedral was first built in the eleventh century, and was renovated and added to into the sixteenth.

Baragiano was the birthplace of a popular south Italian saint, Gerardo Maiella (1726–1755), a monk of the Redemptorist order. Soon after Maiella's death in 1755, a cult developed, based on the belief that he protected mothers.

The Norman capital of **Melfi** is another important town in Potenza province. The Norman castle, with Swabian, Angevin, and modern alterations, still stands. It hosted several medieval councils, and Emperor Frederick II lived there for a time. Today the castle houses the National Archaeological Museum.

The statesman and reformer Francesco Saverio Nitti was born at Melfi in 1868. A professor of economics at the University of Naples, he entered Parliament as a Radical deputy in 1904 and became prime minister in 1919. He was considered a progressive reformer but was caught in the political turmoil that preceded Fascism's seizure of power, and fell from power in 1920. The Fascists hounded Nitti out of Italy by 1924; he moved to France, where the Germans arrested him in 1943. Freed from prison in 1945, he returned to Italy and reentered politics to oppose Italian participation in the NATO alliance. He died in 1953.

Frederick II also began an impressive limestone castle at **Lagopesole**, about halfway between Melfi and Potenza, but he never finished it. It has recently been restored. In 1528 the Spanish briefly lost Melfi after a siege by French troops.

Montemurro was the birthplace of the poet Leonardo Sinisgalli (1908–1981). Although he worked as an engineer and a publicist in Milan and Rome, his works *Fiori pari fiori dispari* (Even Flowers, Uneven Flowers, 1945) and *Belliboschi* (Beautiful Woods, 1948) reflect his Lucanian roots.

The dialect poet Albino Pierro (1916–1995), born at **Tursi**, focused on Basilicata's eastern and coastal tongues; the publishing firm Laterza issued a collection of his works, *Metaponto*, in 1963. Other works reflect the local dialect in their titles: *I 'Nnammurète* (*Gli innamorati* in Italian; The Lovers, 1963) and *Curte'lle a lu sòue* (*Coltelle al Sole*; Knives at the Sun, 1973).

One of modern Italy's most significant voices for reform, Giustino Fortunato, was born in **Rionero in Vulture** in 1848. As a deputy between 1880 and 1909, and then as a senator until his death in 1932, Fortunato joined Benedetto Croce, Gaetano Salvemini, and other Southerners to speak against government repression and push for investigations into poverty and measures for its relief.

MATERA

PROVINCIAL PROFILE. Area: 1,330 sq. mi. Population: 207,311 (province), 56,204 (city). The province contains 31 communes. Matera is a roughly box-shaped province with Apulia on its north. Potenza lies to the west and wraps around Matera a bit on the south. Calabria completes the southern border, and the Ionian Sea is on the east. Its coastline is flatter and more sandy than Potenza's on the Tyrrhenian Sea, and Matera is generally less mountainous than Potenza. Its hills, furthermore, are broken at almost regular intervals by river valleys cascading into the Ionian Sea.

HISTORY. Settlement in Matera dates from the Paleolithic age. The Roman consul Metellus established the town of Matera in 251 B.C. and called it Matheola. Medieval Matera, known as Materia, was sacked by the Franks, by Emperor Louis II, and by the Muslims in the tenth century. The Angevin and Aragonese rulers of southern Italy frequently sold or awarded Matera as a feudal possession to such landed families as the Orsini del Balzo, the Sanseverino, and the Tramontano. Giancarlo Tramontano proved to be such an insufferable ruler that the people of Matera murdered him in 1514. In 1663 the Spanish made Matera the capital of Lucania and the seat of the Royal Provincial Court. It lost its status in 1806, under the Napoleonic regime, and again in 1860, when Potenza, not Matera, became the capital of a united Basilicata within the Kingdom of Italy. In 1927, the Fascists resurrected Matera as a provincial capital.

ARTS AND CULTURE. Extraordinary cave and rock dwellings collectively called *sassi* distinguish Matera. The area of these dwellings is divided by a deep gorge, the Gravina di Matera. The Matera city side is usually considered to be the *sassi* proper; the far side, in a zone stretching to Montescaglioso, forms part of the Murgia, most of which is now included in the Murgia Materana National Historical Park. As Italy modernized through the twentieth century, impoverished citizens living in the *sassi* became a source of national shame, and in 1952 the national government declared their dwellings to be health risks and ordered their evacuation. Such an exceptional and remarkable type of dwelling caused the state to reconsider, however, and in 1986 it ordered renovation of the *sassi* districts. By 1994 the United Nations declared them part of "the heritage of humanity to be handed down to future generations." An important part of the *sassi* district is the "rupestrian" (cliff dwelling) churches. These structures were hewn from rock for over a millennium, many beginning as refuges and hermitages for Byzantine or Benedictine monks. Some of the most recent date from the eighteenth century. Matera's Domenico Ridola National Museum contains an impressive collection of ancient and prehistoric items. Soon after the University of Basilicata was established at Potenza in 1984, a satellite campus opened in Matera.

The literary scholar and writer **Giuseppe de Robertis** (1888–1963) was born at Matera. He taught Italian literature at the University of Florence and worked on the review *La Voce* (The Voice).

Matera has two patron saints, Eustachio (Eustace) and the Madonna della Bruna (Brown Madonna). The major festival honors the latter. Her feast, July 2, is one of the most important celebrations in southern Italy. Formally launched in the fourteenth century to honor Matera's patron, it probably began as a shepherds' procession and also exhibits Spanish influence. The central event of the festival is the procession, escorted by knights on horseback, of a float (*carro*) that bears a statue of the Madonna. At the tour's end, the statue is returned to the cathedral and the float is demolished. Farmers plant its broken pieces in their fields to ensure fertility.

OTHER CENTERS. On the coast is **Metaponto**, founded as Metabos, then Metapontum, by Greeks from Sybaris and Crotone about 700 B.C. As a result of its alliance with Hannibal, the Romans took and annexed the city. In the Middle Ages, a particularly devastating Muslim raid destroyed the town. It is now a popular beach resort. Metaponto's impressive Greek ruins are found largely in an archaeological zone and include the Palatine Tables, Doric columns from a sixth-century temple to Hera, and a sanctuary of Apollo. Many treasures from the Greek era are in Policoro's National Museum "della Siritide."

SELECT BIBLIOGRAPHY

Buccaro, Alfredo. *Potenza*. Rome: Laterza, 1997.
Ranieri, Luigi. *Basilicata*. Turin: Unione Tipografico-Editrice Torinese, 1971.
Regione Basilicata. *Basilicata turistica*. Novara: Istituto Geografico De Agostini, 1990.

Chapter 4

CALABRIA

REGIONAL CHARACTERISTICS. Area: 5,822 sq. mi. Population: 2,070,992. Capital: Catanzaro. Calabria is squarely in the middle range of Italy's 20 regions. It ranks tenth in both area and population. Calabria is home to the Catholic metropolitan see of Reggio Calabria/Bova.

Frequently considered the "toe" of the Italian "boot," Calabria is a long peninsula separated from the rest of continental Italy to its north by Basilicata. On Calabria's eastern shore is the Ionian Sea, and on its western shore is the Tyrrhenian Sea. At the region's southern tip, the Strait of Messina separates Calabria from Sicily. The land is 42 percent mountainous, 49 pecent hilly, and 9 percent plains. The highest points in the region are in the Pollini range, which forms the border with Basilicata. Monte Pollini and Serra del Dolcedorme are Calabria's two tallest peaks, each about 1,383 feet. The large *Pollino* National Park straddles the border with Basilicata. Below the mountains stretches a string of plateaus, or *sile*. These highlands are surprisingly green (*sila* derives from the Latin *silva*, forest), and are noted for their wildlife, including wolves. The northernmost *sila* is Greca, followed to the south by Grande, and then Piccola. The two southern *sile* and much of the Aspromonte highlands at the southern end of the region are in two national parks, the Parco Nazionale dell' Aspromonte and the Parco Nazionale della Calabria established between 1968 and 1978. Calabria does not boast many large rivers. Its longest is the Crati, which cascades from Monte Botte Donato, near Cosenza, and runs northeast into the Gulf of Corigliano and the Ionian Sea. The mouth of the Crati contributes alluvial deposits to Calabria's largest coastal plain, the Piana

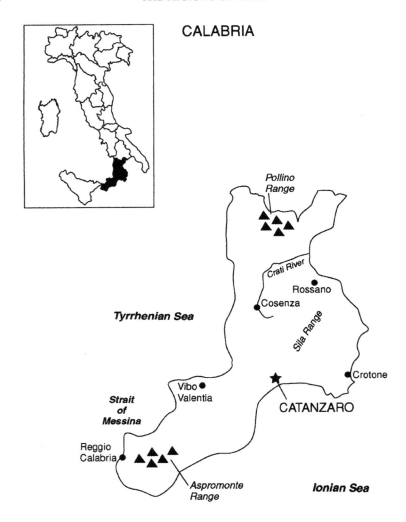

CALABRIA

di Sibari. Another large coastal plain, the Piana di Gioia, is situated toward the southern end of the region, where the Petrace and Mesima rivers empty into the Gulf of Gioia.

ECONOMY. Of the Calabrian labor force, 14.8 percent are in agriculture, 18.2 percent in industry, and 67 percent in the tertiary sector. In January 1998, 25 percent of Calabrians were unemployed. Of Calabria's 521,000 employed workers in 1997, 364,000 were men and 157,000 were women. The region's agriculture saw something of a renaissance as the countryside lost population in the twentieth century. Much of the land which might have been abandoned has been consolidated and devoted to high-technology agriculture. A concentration of heavy industry has formed on the west coast at Gioia Tauro. Olives, particularly around Rossano in the northeast, and citrus fruits are cultivated extensively. Tourism accounts for increasing revenues in Calabria, particularly since the 1970s, when the A-3 expressway connected Reggio with the north and an airport capable of handling jet traffic opened at Sant'Eufemia. Along with tourism in the *sile*, parts of the coast, such as the Costa Viola, north of the Strait of Messina, and the Costa Gelsomina, southeast of the Aspromonte highlands, have been developed.

CUISINE. Estimation of Calabrian cuisine has risen, thanks to a general appreciation of simple and healthy fare. Pasta is enjoyed with other foods, often mixed in soup. Calabresi cuisine highlights vegetables with spicy sauces, such as *alla carrettiera* (with ginger). Eggplant is used extensively and with great imagination. Fish is particularly popular in the coastal zones, and Cosenza is known for its heavily peppered snail sauce. A hash made from tripe and organ meats (*murzeddu* or *morsello*) and "small meats" (lamb and goat) is eaten in most areas; *fritula*, pig skin simmering at butchers' doorways, is seen mostly around Reggio. The *sila* area is home to a prized mushroom, the *porcino silano*. Sweet cakes are ubiquitous in Calabria. The traditional *sgute* or *aggute*, and the *cuddhuraci* or *cuzzupe*, which envelop hard-boiled eggs, are popular at Eastertime. *Mostaccioli*, *nzuddo*, and *mustazzoli* are sweet creations so elaborate that they are frequently given as wedding presents. Calabria's most distinctive cheese may be *buttiro*, a *caciocavallo* provolone with a butter center.

With a few exceptions, Calabrian wine is not well known in the rest of Italy. It is said that the heat there works against cultivation, and many Calabrese vines lie close to the ground, causing the plants to suffer the heat even more. Some have compared Calabrian wines to those of Algeria and Libya. Nevertheless, the region boasts a long tradition of viticulture which began at least in Greek times. Its red wines are robust and better than the whites, which often end up blended into other wines like vermouths. North of Crotone is one of the region's most important wine-producing areas, famous for Cirò.

MELANZANE ALL'OLIO

1 c. red wine vinegar	1 qt. olive oil
2 c. water	2 cloves garlic, finely chopped
Salt and pepper to taste	1 hot pepper (peperoncini), chopped
1 Tbs. sugar	
2 large eggplants, peeled and cut into thick slices	Oregano to taste

Place the vinegar, water, salt, pepper, and sugar in a pot and bring to a boil. Add eggplant slices and cook for 15 minutes.

Remove the eggplant slices and dry them with paper towels.
Cover the bottom of a 3-quart baking pan with oil, then top
with a layer of eggplant slices. Season the slices garlic, hot pepper, and oregano. Continue layering until all ingredients have
been used, then pour the remaining olive oil over the top. Mar-
inate, covered, in the refrigerator for a few days.

HISTORY. In Neolithic times tribes such as the Brutii populated Calabria. Some of Italy's earliest evidence of Greek civilization is also found
here, at Broglio di Trebisacce, Francavilla Marittima, and Torre Mordillo,
where Mycenaeans from the Greek Peloponnesus established colonies in
the second millennium B.C. Activity in these early locations, however, disappeared by the eleventh century B.C. Between the eighth and the sixth
centuries B.C., other Greeks crossed from Sicily into Calabria and founded
Reggio, which quickly became a preeminent town. It was soon rivaled,
however, by other centers, particularly Crotone, Locri, Sybaris, and, farther
east, Taranto. These territories, collectively called Magna Graecia, never
united except in the hands of conquerors such as the Syracusan tyrants
Dionysius the Elder and the Younger. In 280 B.C. Rome went to war
against Taranto, the largest Greek city in the area. Some towns, like Locri
and Reggio, allied themselves with Rome; some Italian nations, like the
Samnites, sided with Taranto. In 275 B.C., Rome defeated the Greeks at
Benevento and subsequently took possession of southern Italy, including
Calabria. The conquerors absorbed the area through the third century and
dubbed it Ager Bruttius. The Romans knew a "Calabria," but attached
that name to an area within modern Apulia. Only in the early Middle Ages
did "Calabria" come to signify the region that claims the name today.
Despite the victory of Latin Rome, much of Magna Graecia's culture and
tongue survived as a real presence well into the Middle Ages. The Romans
were mainly interested in the inland forests, and they established enormous
latifundia there to exploit those resources. Their neglect of Calabria's
coastal region was total, and that zone, particularly on the Ionian Sea,
became virtually depopulated.

In A.D. 60, Paul the Apostle reached Reggio. In 410 one of the first
barbarian invaders to humiliate Rome, King Alaric I of the Visigoths,
reached and sacked Reggio. Over the next century, others followed Alaric.
The armies of the Byzantine general Belisarius crossed from Sicily in 535
and destroyed much of the remaining Roman culture. The Byzantines attempted to revive and strengthen Greek culture by establishing Eastern
churches with gifts of large tracts of land. In 812 the Muslims devastated
the coast, slaughtering and placing much of the population in slavery. Muslim raids became more frequent after 843, when the Arabs subdued Messina and began to use it as a base against Christian Calabria. Even Reggio's
aged bishop was hauled away in chains in 902. The Franks became a

force in Calabria in 972 when the heir to the Imperial throne married a Greek princess and took as her dowry the few Byzantine territories left in southern Italy. Crowned as Otto II the following year, he dispatched a force to clear the area of the Muslims, which it did in 982 in the Stilo valley.

The Sicilian Normans under the d'Hautevilles (the Altavilla) were next to subjugate Calabria, taking it between 1058 and 1060 and proclaiming themselves Dukes of Calabria, Apulia, and Sicily with Mileto as their capital. Their reign was notable for promoting the Catholic Latin rite in Christian worship and rejecting the Greek rite once and for all. They also promoted monasteries, a policy that bore fruit in such places as Joachim of Fiore's abbey at San Giovanni in Fiore and Bruno of Cologne's at Serra San Bruno. Subsequent developments in Calabria mirrored those in much of the rest of southern Italy. The Swabians replaced the Normans, followed by the Angevins, and then the Aragonese and Spanish by the fifteenth and sixteenth centuries. Much of medieval Calabria was parceled out and exchanged, conquered, or surrendered among feudal lords. Only a few places, such as Cosenza, developed at least semi-independent communal status that mirrored developments in northern Italy.

Spain ruled Calabria from its base in Naples, despite frequent revolts against the viceroy. In 1599 Tomasso Campanella, a visionary member of Calabria's small Waldensian community, led an important but unsuccessful rebellion at Guardia. He was condemned to 27 years in prison.

Madrid's rule lasted until the War of the Spanish Succession; from 1707 until 1735, the area passed between Austria and the house of Savoy. The Neapolitan Bourbons returned to Calabria in 1735 under Charles IV (Charles III of Spain). Independent of the Spanish, they demonstrated more interest in Calabria's development with ambitious if disappointing attempts to modernize the economy after the massive earthquake of 1783. Beginning in 1798 and continuing into the nineteenth century, their projects included foundries at Mongiana and Ferdinandea, and spinning mills at San Giovanni and Cannitello. Nevertheless, most of Calabria remained a backward and neglected corner of Italy. Until 1838, for example, the only link between the outside world and Catanzaro was a single mule trail.

Although the Neapolitan Bourbons dominated nineteenth-century Calabria, a lively republican current distinguished regional affairs during the Risorgimento. In 1799, after Napoleon's troops chased the Bourbons from Naples for the first time, Cosenza raised its own flag as a republic. Bourbon authority returned to Calabria with Cardinal Fabrizio Ruffo and his peasant force, the Christian and Royal Army, which landed in February 1799 from Palermo, home of the exiled court. The French returned in 1806 and ruled Calabria from Naples until the defeat of Napoleon and his lieutenant, Joachim Murat, in 1815.

Later in the nineteenth century, the Venetian Bandiera brothers, Attilio and Emilio, and their friend Domenico Moro, tried to spark a revolt in

Calabria. In June 1844, shortly after yet another revolt at Cosenza, they landed near Crotone with insurrectionist hopes, but were captured and paid with their lives. Moro and the Bandiera brothers were avenged when Bourbon rule finally collapsed sixteen years later. Then, on August 19, 1860, Giuseppe Garibaldi landed at Melito Porto Salvo with 4,000 men and began his long and victorious march north through Calabria and on to Naples and the Papal States.

In August 1862, Garibaldi repeated his landing at Melito Porto Salvo with the intent of pressing on to Rome and completing the unfinished Risorgimento. He and his men marched along the beach toward Reggio, but this time clearly against the wishes of the new Italian government. After the force was shelled from an offshore naval vessel, the column moved inland toward the Aspromonte highlands, where Italian government soldiers engaged it in battle. The advance ended and Garibaldi was wounded during the skirmish.

The Kingdom of Italy absorbed Calabria, but it remained a neglected region under the Liberal governments which lasted through the First World War. Calabria's struggles were rendered more difficult by a number of earthquakes, particularly the disastrous tremors of 1894, 1905, and 1908. The 1908 quake, also felt in Sicily, claimed the lives of 120,000 people. The persistence of brigandage, poverty, and an unjust land tenure system convinced many Calabrians to emigrate from the region. According to official figures, between 1876 and 1913, 850,000 people abandoned Calabria for new lives in other nations; and the number of illegal emigrants may have brought the sum closer to 1 million.

After 1922 the Fascists developed some of the hydroelectric potential of the *sila* rivers and reclaimed some coastal lands. But more focused attention had to wait until after the Second World War, when Italy's Christian Democratic governments targeted the area for reform. Their "Sila" law of 1950 was a model for further measures: the *stralcio* (emergency) law of Antonio Segni, another law applied to Sicily, and more reforms across Italy's less developed zones. The "Sila" law broke up large estates and appropriated billions of lire for home and public works construction. Communist opponents enjoyed pointing out that resistance from landholders, both intense and subtle, worked against the proper function of the "Sila" law; they were quick and correct, furthermore, to focus on its uneven application. The problems were reflected in the continuing exodus from Calabria. Between 1946 and 1976 about 759,000 people left the region. Nevertheless, the Christian Democratic measure was the most far-reaching land reform that Italy, and particularly Calabria, had ever seen; 90 percent of the original beneficiaries were still on the land in 1969.

RECENT POLITICS. The Christian Democrats were Calabria's premier party until the 1990s, when they were replaced by the neo-Fascist Alleanza Nazionale and Silvio Berlusconi's Forza Italia. Many Catholic voters chose the Popular Party in alliance with the ex-Communist Democratic Party of the Left (PDS). Calabria votes as the twenty-third electoral district (*circoscrizione*). In the 1996 national elections for the Chamber of Deputies, the Center-Right Polo per le Libertà captured 46.0 percent of the majoritarian vote against 45.7 percent for the Ulivo coalition. In the proportional contest the Alleanza Nazionale took 23.4 percent of the ballots, ahead of the PDS with 21.0 percent and the Forza Italia with 18.2 percent. For the Senate, the Polo took 44.8 percent against the Ulivo's 36.7 percent. In the April 2000 regional elections the Center-Right won in Calabria with 49.8 percent of the votes against 48.7 for the Center-Left. Giuseppe Chiaravalloti was elected regional president.

CATANZARO

PROVINCIAL PROFILE. Area: 923 sq. mi. Population: 384,483 (province), 97,204 (city). Catanzaro contains 80 communes. Catanzaro cuts across the middle of Calabria from the Tyrrhenian Sea to the Ionian. Its west coast, at the Gulf of Sant'Eufemia, is not as long as its eastern shore, at the Gulf of Squillace. To its north are Cosenza and Crotone provinces, and Vibo Valentia and Reggio di Calabria border it on the south.

HISTORY. The Byzantines founded Catanzaro as Catasarion or Katantzarion in the tenth century. High on a hill overlooking the Gulf of Squillace, the name derives from the Greek for "under" and "terrace," and recalls the terrace farming on the nearby slopes. Robert Guiscard fortified the location with a castle in 1055. In 1528 Catanzaro's imposing location enabled it to resist a four-month siege by the French.

ARTS AND CULTURE. Catanzaro has perhaps Calabria's largest Good Friday procession, *La Naca*. A Holy Week tradition in many towns is the commemoration of the *pigghiata*, the arrest of Christ in the Garden of Gethsemane. Vitaliano of Capua and the Virgin Mary are Catanzaro's patron saints. A figure of uncertain origin, perhaps a martyr in Roman times, Vitaliano is also known as a Bishop of Capua who was challenged by enemies, stuffed into a sack, and thrown into the Garigliano River. He was miraculously saved, but subjected Capua to terrible calamities. Vitaliano is still invoked to protect against earthquakes. His tomb is in Catanzaro's Duomo, which is dedicated to the Assumption of the Virgin and to Saints Peter and Paul. His feast day is July 16. The University of Catanzaro was created out of Reggio Calabria's in 1997.

OTHER CENTERS. Squillace was the ancient town of Scyllentium. It was the birthplace of the Roman senator and scholar Cassiodorus, who founded the Vivarium monastery nearby, one of Italy's chief intellectual centers of the late sixth century.

COSENZA

PROVINCIAL PROFILE. Area: 2,567 sq. mi. Population: 751,918 (province), 77,238 (city). Cosenza province contains 155 communes. Cosenza is the northernmost province in Calabria. It is south of Basilicata and stretches from the Tyrrhenian to the Ionian Sea. To its southeast is the province of Crotone, and to the southwest is Catanzaro.

HISTORY. Situated in the Crati valley, early Cosenza was capital of the lands of the Brutii, a people who fought Rome and lost. Later the Brutii allied themselves with Hannibal and lost again. The Romans took Cosenza in 204 B.C. and called it Cosentia. The Visigothic king Alaric charged through the area at the Roman Empire's end in 476 and was buried, according to legend, in the Busento riverbed near where it joins the Crati at Cosenza. Neither his body nor his vast hoard of booty was ever recovered, and they are said to rest together somewhere beneath the waters. After a short Byzantine occupation, the Lombards took Cosenza and attached it to the Duchy of Benevento. Muslim raiders destroyed the city in 986 and 1009. King Roger II of Sicily (1130–1154) established Cosenza as a regional capital of the Terra Giordana (Jordan Land), and it has remained the principal city of northern Calabria ever since. Cosenza has suffered many earthquakes, the last major one in 1908.

ARTS AND CULTURE. Cosenza has maintained a historic center distinguished by a tenth-century castle and a Cistercian-Gothic cathedral. The Swabian Emperor Henry VII and Isabella of Aragon, wife of King Philip III, of France, are buried in the church. Near Cosenza on the Tyrrhenian shore is Paola, home of Saint **Francis of Paola** (1416–1507), founder of the Friars Minor and patron saint of both Cosenza and Calabria. Later in his life, Francis traveled to France, where he served King Louis XI and where he is buried. His feast is celebrated on April 2.

OTHER CENTERS. Sibari (Sybaris) is an ancient site on the Crati River. Achaean Greeks established it in the eighth century B.C., and it enjoyed an almost legendary prosperity and luxury which are the source of the modern word "sybaritic." The halcyon days ended when raiders from Kroton (Crotone) sacked and destroyed it in 510 B.C. The victors diverted the flow of the Crati to submerge the remains of Sibari. A subsequent Greek settlement (**Thurii** in Basilicata) and a Latin one (**Copia**) replaced Sybaris. Archaeological sites and the Museo della Sibaritide contain remains of the successive towns.

San Giovanni in Fiore is where the medieval mystic Joachim of Fiore founded a monastery in 1189. At **Guardia**, the Waldensian stronghold from which Tommaso Campanella staged his rebellion in 1599, the reactionary forces of Cardinal Ruffo slaughtered members of the religious minority in 1799. The Porta del Sangue (Gate of Blood) commemorates the event.

Altomonte, an important medieval center of Calabria, recalls its past in the fourteenth-century Church of Santa Maria della Consolazione, which was erected over an earlier Norman church dedicated to the Virgin Mary of the Franks.

Between the eighth and eleventh centuries **Rossano,** near the Gulf of Corigliano and on the Sila Greca's northern slope, was one of the most important Byzantine centers of Calabria. Its Diocesan Museum contains the sixth-century Gospel manuscript *Codex Purpureus* (or *Codex Rossanensis*), which was brought to Calabria by Basilian monks. Rossano's tenth-century Church of Saint Mark is considered, along with that of Santa Maria della Consolazione, the Cattolica (Catholic Church) of Stilo (in the province of Reggio Calabria), to be among the finest Byzantine structures in Italy. It houses the eighth- or ninth-century fresco of the *Madonna Achiropita*, which, according to tradition, was not painted with human hands.

Calabria's Albanian communities, descendants of refugees who fled the Turks in the fifteenth and sixteenth centuries, are concentrated mainly at **Lungro** and at **San Demetrio Corone.**

CROTONE

PROVINCIAL PROFILE. Area: 663 sq. mi. Population: 177,547 (province), 59,638 (city). There are 27 communes in Crotone province. Crotone is on Calabria's east coast, facing the Ionian Sea. To its southwest is Catanzaro, and Cosenza is to its west and northwest.

HISTORY. The Greek Kroton was settled by Achaeans from the Peloponnesus about 710 B.C. By the sixth century B.C. it had gained some fame as the home of a medical school, of the great Olympic wrestler Milo of Kroton, and of Pythagoras, the philosopher who moved there from Samos and became a political leader by opposing popular government. As the only real port between Taranto and Reggio, the town prospered, and in 510, Kroton's army, under Milo's command, defeated its hated neighbor Sybaris. Urged on by the vindictive Pythagoras, the Crotoni diverted a nearby river to cover what was left of the vanquished city. Pythagoras's followers were later driven out and Kroton embraced democracy. By the 270s, it had become a prize in the last Greco-Roman conflicts for dominion over southern Italy, passing from the control of King Pyrrhus to that of the Roman Republic. During the Second Punic War (218–201 B.C.), Crotone rebelled against the Romans, and it was there that Hannibal learned that he must return to Carthage. In 1993 Crotone province was carved out of Catanzaro.

ARTS AND CULTURE. Near Crotone, at the Cape Colonne, is the site of the temple of Hera Lacinia, which dates from the sixth century B.C. In 203 B.C. Hannibal departed there for Carthage after having left an account of his exploits in the temple. (A year later the Roman general Scipio Africanus defeated him at Zama.) Hardly anything remains of the sanctuary beyond a single pillar and its evocative location. It was largely intact until the sixteenth century. In its time, Hera Lacinia was considered one of the most beautiful Greek temples in Italy.

Many places reenact the *affruntata* which recalls the meeting between the risen Christ and the Virgin Mary. In Calabria many Carnival traditions, including slaughtering pigs for local feasts, precede Lent. In their festive parades, many towns, such as Crotone, feature the popular legend of the Calabrian woman kidnapped by the Turks for enslavement in the sultan's harem. She hurls herself into the sea, and sometimes gives birth to a sea siren.

OTHER CENTERS. Santa Severina was an important bastion of Greek culture in the Middle Ages. Its well-preserved historic center is dominated by a Norman castle constructed on Byzantine foundations. Next to the city's thirteenth-century cathedral, dedicated to Saint Anastasia, is an eighth-century Byzantine baptistery. Two other churches distinguish the town: Santa Maria del Pozzo, built on top of a cistern, and Santa Filomena, a Norman structure that displays strong Byzantine influence.

REGGIO DI CALABRIA

PROVINCIAL PROFILE. Area: 1,229 sq. mi. Population: 578,231 (province), 180,034 (city). Reggio di Calabria contains 97 communes. The province is the southern tip of continental Italy. It dangles between the Ionian Sea on the east and the Strait of Messina and the Gulf of Gioia on the west. Vibo Valentia and Catanzaro are to the north. Ferry service from Villa San Giovanni and Reggio di Calabria connects the region to Sicily. Plans for a bridge have languished for many years. Much of the province's middle stretches are taken up by the Aspromonte National Park.

HISTORY. Reggio was established as Reghion in the eighth century B.C. by Greeks from Chalcis. Reghion's strategic location at the Strait of Messina ensured that it would be the object of frequent struggles among factions bent on domination. After a period of misrule by the Calabrian Mamertini mercenaries and the threat of Brutii invasion, in 282 B.C. the city asked for protection from the Romans, who changed its name to Rhegium. They extended the Popilian way down to Rhegium and in 89 B.C., designated the city a Roman *municipium* (free town), Rhegium Iulium. After the fall of the Roman Empire in 476, Reggio experienced frequent earthquakes and Muslim incursions.

After Sicily fell to the Muslims in the ninth century, Reggio became the capital of what little was left of Byzantine Italy. The Muslims took the city in 950.

The last conquerors were the Allied forces, who landed on September 3, 1943, near Reggio di Calabria and began the long march north which ended in the defeat of the Axis in the spring of 1945.

Reggio di Calabria suffered extensive damage in the earthquake of 1908, the epicenter of which was in the Strait of Messina. Twelve thousand died in the city, and another 18,000 in the rest of the province. An earthquake of a different sort occurred after the 1970 elections, which established Catanzaro as the capital of the reorganized Calabrian region. Angry Reggiani took to the streets, and the riot was quelled only after a great deal of damage. A compromise was reached in which Reggio kept the Regional Assembly within the city limits.

ARTS AND CULTURE. George of Lydda is the patron saint of Reggio di Calabria (and also of Genoa and Ferrara). Little of the city's premodern past remains after the earthquakes early in the twentieth century. The National Museum in Reggio houses two of Calabria's most treasured masterpieces, the Riace bronzes. In 1972 the two remarkably well preserved statues of Greek athletes were found offshore near Riace. After some discussion of where the statues would find a permanent home, the Calabresi insisted that the Greek athletes remain in Reggio.

OTHER CENTERS. Locri was founded by the Greeks in the seventh century B.C.; the site had been inhabited by the Siculan peoples, who left tombs from as early as the ninth century. The Greeks established a successful port there, but it was soon contested by its larger neighbors: Kroton (Crotone), Sybaris (Sibari), and Rhegion (Reggio di Calabria). To survive, Locri found an ally in Syracuse and provided refuge for its deposed and debauched tyrant, Dionysius the Younger. Locri prospered and was known for its great sanctuary to Persephone. Remains of the sanctuary, as well as those of other temples, can still be seen. The Romans conquered Locri in their wars against Hannibal (third century B.C.), and its long decline commenced. The Muslims destroyed what little was left of the city, and it sank into the shadow of its offspring, Gerace. The place, in fact, came to be known as Gerace Marina until 1934, when it reclaimed its ancient name. Extensive ruins of the ancient town are still visible at Locri Epizeferi, on the outskirts of the modern city; and an archaeological museum, the Antiquarium Statale, houses many of the finds from these excavations.

Refugees from Locri moved inland and established **Gerace** in the ninth century. They called the place Hagia Kyriake (Santa Ciriaca), from which "Gerace" stemmed. One of Calabria's finest Norman structures is Gerace's eleventh-century cathedral, constructed in part with materials taken from older edifices, perhaps from Locri. The church is one of Calabria's largest.

Strong Greek identity persists at the southern end of the Aspromonte highlands, at **Condofuri, Roccaforte del Greco, Stilo,** and the ruins on the imposing summit of **Bova.** Despite the d'Hauteville interdict and a Norman castle there, Bova remained a Greek see until the mid-1500s. Turkish raids emphasized its importance as a place of refuge, including for the Archbishop of Reggio di Calabria and his court in 1586. Bova was attacked by the Turks as late as 1638, and the cathedral was rebuilt after an earthquake in 1783. Stilo's tenth-century Cattolica is one of Calabria's best examples of Byzantine influence. Today Bova hosts an annual festival of local Greek culture. The Greek communities have become known particularly for wood carving.

Calabria's Catholic patrimony is displayed across the region in vivid and varied Holy Week and Easter commemorations. Good Friday processions are ubiquitous, with one of the most famous at **Polistena.** There, in other towns, such as **Palmi,** and, in Cosenza province, Nocera Tirinese and Terranova di Sibari, flagellant traditions are maintained. A museum of folklore, the Museo Calabrese di Etnografia e Folklore (Calabrian Museum of Ethnography and Folklore) is located in Palmi.

The journalist and author Corrado Alvaro (1895–1956) was born near Reggio di Calabria in **San Luca.** He served as editor of the important newspapers *Il Resto del Carlino* (Change from the Carlino; the name is based on the price of the paper—the change you'd receive from using an old coin, the Carlino), *Corriere della Sera* (Evening Post), and *Il Mondo* (The World). Alvaro is best remembered for his sympathetic portrayals of Calabrese peasants in *Gente in Aspromonte* (People in Aspromonte, 1930) and *L'età Breve* (The Brief Time, 1946). His birthplace has been developed as a "literary park."

VIBO VALENTIA

PROVINCIAL PROFILE. Area: 440 sq. mi. Population: 178,813 (province), 35,405 (city). Vibo Valentia province contains 50 communes. To its west the province faces the Tyrrhenian Sea at the Gulf of Sant'Eufemia and the Gulf of Gioia. To its north and east is Catanzaro, and to its south is Reggio di Calabria.

HISTORY. Vibo Valentia is the capital of one of Italy's newest provinces, created out of Catanzaro in 1993. It is, nevertheless, an ancient city. Initially settled by the Siculans, the city was formally founded as Hipponion in the seventh or sixth century B.C., first by Greeks from Reggio and Messina and then recolonized by people from Locri. Dionysius the Elder of Syracuse destroyed Hipponion, and it was later conquered by Carthaginians, Brutii, Agathocles of Syracuse, and the Locrians, who held it before the Romans took it about 230 B.C. Hipponion enjoyed some prosperity under its new masters, but after the imperial security evaporated in the fifth century A.D., it suffered repeated attacks from the sea. The Muslims later destroyed what was left of the town, which was rebuilt in the thirteenth century by Emperor Frederick II, who sojourned there briefly. Charles of Anjou awarded the city to the Ruffo family in 1284. Ferdinand I, the Aragonese King of Naples, built a fortress at Pizzo in 1486. There, in 1815, Joachim Murat, Napoleon's general and brother-in-law, was put to death.

ARTS AND CULTURE. Fifth- and fourth-century B.C. walls recall the era of Hipponion, and Vibo Valentia's medieval past is revealed in a Norman castle that looms above the city. Some of the fortress was constructed with material taken from the town's ancient acropolis. Two of Calabria's Baroque showpieces are in Vibo Valentia's cathedral and in the Church of San Giorgio Martire in Pizzo.

OTHER CENTERS. Under Norman patronage, Bruno of Cologne established the monastery of Santo Stefano del Bosco at **Serra San Bruno** in 1090. Much of the complex was rebuilt after the earthquake of 1783. The monks there still produce a famous cheese.

Tropea sits on dramatic cliffs above the Tyrrhenian Sea. An ancient place, Pliny the Elder referred to it as Portus Herculis. Its eleventh-century cathedral has been damaged by earthquakes but rebuilt well, with an eye for its original design. One of Italy's most popular film stars, Raf Vallone, was born in Tropea in 1916. He appeared in important postwar films, particularly *Riso Amaro* (Bitter Rice, 1948) and *Il Cammino della Speranza* (The Road of Hope, 1950). Vallone has appeared in American and French films as well.

SELECT BIBLIOGRAPHY

Bevilacqua, Piero, and Augusto Placanica, eds. *La Calabria*. Turin: Einaudi, 1985.
Currù, G., and Giuseppe Restifo. *Reggio Calabria*. Rome: Laterza, 1991.
Istituto Geografico De Agostini. *Calabria Tourist Guide*. Novara: Regione Calabria and Istituto Geografico De Agostini, 1997.
Placanica, Augusto. *Storia della Calabria dall'antichità ai nostri giorni*. Catanzaro: Meridiana Libri, 1993.
———. *Storia della Calabria moderna e contemporanea: Il lungo periodo*. Reggio di Calabria: Gangemi, 1992.
Zappone, Bruno. *Reggio Calabria e la sua provincia: Storia—Arte—Monumenti—Tradizioni*. Cosenza: Pellegrini Editore, n.d. (c. 1988).

CAMPANIA

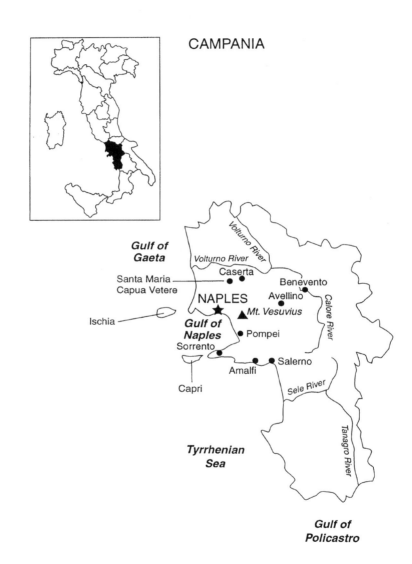

Gulf of Gaeta

Volturno River

Caserta

Santa Maria Capua Vetere

Benevento

NAPLES

Avellino

Ischia

▲ *Mt. Vesuvius*

Calore River

Gulf of Naples

● Pompei

Sorrento

Salerno

Amalfi

Capri

Sele River

Tyrrhenian Sea

Tanagro River

Gulf of Policastro

Chapter 5

CAMPANIA

REGIONAL CHARACTERISTICS: Area: 5,250 sq. mi. Population: 5,796,899. Capital: Naples (Napoli). Campania is Italy's twelfth largest region in land and ranks second in population. Campania has three Catholic metropolitan sees: Naples, Benevento, and Salerno/Campagna/Acerno.

Naples is home to a major center of NATO (North Atlantic Treaty Organization) operations. In 1951 it was designated the headquarters for Allied forces in southern Europe. Under an American four-star admiral, the Naples command covers Italy, Greece, Turkey, the Mediterranean Sea, and the Black Sea.

Campania lies south of Lazio and Molise. To its east and south are Apulia and Basilicata. It faces the Tyrrhenian Sea on its west. Along the coast is a series of gulfs, from Gaeta to Naples to Salerno and Policastro. Campania takes its name from the Latin *campus* (field), which described the agricultural plain around the ancient city of Capua (now Santa Maria Capua Vetere). A large plain, the Piana di Sele, also occupies a stretch of the coast in the province of Salerno. Still, only 14.7 percent of the whole region is flat. Most of Campania is either hilly (50.7 percent) or mountainous (34.6 percent). Some of the highest peaks in the southern Apennines are found in Campania, as is Italy's most famous mountain, the volcano Vesuvius, which, since 1995, has been the home of a national park. At 6,726 feet, the region's highest peak is Monte Miletto, in the Matesian group along the Molise border. Campania's most important rivers are the Volturno, flowing into the Gulf of Gaeta, and the Sele, which reaches the Gulf of Policastro near Paestum.

ECONOMY. Of the region's 1,494,000 employed labor force, 1,054,000 are men and 440,000 are women. Of Campania's active labor force, 10.6 percent work in agriculture, 23.4 percent in industry, and 66 percent in other fields. Campania has long been considered a land of agricultural bounty, and it still produces a great deal of wheat, fruit, wine, and tobacco. It is also the most industrialized part of southern Italy, with heavy concentrations around Naples and Salerno. Artisan industries and tourism are of particular importance and value for the economies of Capri, Ischia, Sorrento, and the Amalfi coast. Pollution from heavy industry has scarred the cities. Smoke from factories in Naples often obscures the sight of Capri from the shore, and their waste has polluted the bay. The tourist industry, traditionally centered around the sights of Naples, its still-beautiful bay, and the Sorrento Peninsula, has made recent inroads in the largely unspoiled Cilento of Salerno province.

CUISINE. Many Campanian grapes are grown to produce wines that are blended with others. Greek settlers brought with them their knowledge of winemaking, and Cumae became the center of a Falernian variety which the Romans came to compare with those from Chios and Lesbos. The grapes were grown on the slopes of the hills near present-day Mondragone. Today, the Falernian's descendant may be the Falerno, which yields a dry, full-bodied wine. One of Campania's most widely grown grapes is the Aglianico, which grows well in volcanic soil and yields a lusty red table wine. It is particularly common around Salerno and in the Avellino and Benevento areas. Its name may derive from *ellenico*, raising the possibility that the Greeks brought the grape from their homeland. Benevento is well known among Italians as the home of one of their most popular liquors, Strega.

Pizza is probably the most widely known Campanian dish. The Neapolitans have turned it into a high art form, although it has not reached the outlandish manifestations found in the United States. In Naples pizza is still identifiably pizza. Its basic form is *alla napolitana*, with a fairly thin crust spread with olive oil under some mozzarella cheese, pieces of tomato, and one or two herbs, perhaps oregano and basil. *Margherita* is also a popular style, dedicated by the city to Italy's queen who devoted much of her energy to earthquake relief there. Mozzarella and provolone are Campanian cheeses.

PASTA ALLA PEPPINO

¾ c. olive oil

1 medium eggplant, diced

1 large chili pepper, diced

½ onion, chopped

1 lb. peeled tomatoes

Salt and pepper to taste

3 sweet basil leaves, rolled and chopped

½ lb. mozzarella cheese, diced

Grated parmesan cheese to taste

1 lb. penne pasta

Heat olive oil in a small pan, then add eggplant, chili pepper, and onion. Sauté for about ten minutes on medium heat. Add tomatoes to mixture and cook for 10 minutes more, slowly adding salt, pepper, and basil. Then add the mozzarella and parmesan cheese. Meanwhile, prepare the pasta according to the package instructions. Drain the pasta and add the sauce.

HISTORY. Campania has been inhabited since Paleolithic times. Opici (Oscan) culture existed there before the Etruscans and the Greeks arrived. The latter were followed in the fifth century B.C. by Samnites, particularly the Caudini and the Irpini, who conquered much of the area and whose Oscan tongue persisted well into the Roman period.

The Samnites notwithstanding, the Greeks targeted Campania for colonization. Their first settlements appeared in the eighth century B.C. on Ischia at Lacco Ameno (Pithecusa) and at Cuma, which the Greeks called Kyme. Another ancient city is Paestum, which was established at the mouth of the Sele as Poseidonia by colonists from Sybaris, an earlier Greek settlement in Calabria.

Roman penetration began in earnest after the First Samnite War of 343–341 B.C. Samnite Capua soon allied itself with the new conquerors, who dominated most of the area by the end of the fourth century. The political bonds strengthened with the construction of the Appian Way and the Latin Way, parallel roads from Rome that joined north of Capua, then diverged again south of the city. The Appian Way continued down to Brindisi, and another road, the Popilian Way ran south to Reggio di Calabria. Caesar Augustus later fused Campania to Latium (Lazio) to form the administrative unit Region I. In the fourth century, Emperor Diocletian redrew those lines and merged Campania with Samnium, breaking Naples's link to Rome and artificially orienting the region toward Adriatic ports. The Goths occupied Campania in the fifth century. In the sixth, the area was divided between the Byzantines, who annexed part of the coast, and the Lombards, who established three duchies to comprise what came to be considered "Lesser Lombardy" (Lombardia minore). Thus, Campania maintained itself while the rest of Italy succumbed to barbarian and Byzantine plunder. Muslim pirates, however, found this prosperity attractive, and inflicted frequent raids and pillage on the Campanian littoral. To aid their ships sailing along the coast and to facilitate raids into the interior, the Muslims established bases such as one at the mouth of the Garigliano. On the Sorrento Peninsula, Amalfi became the chief trading city in the area and possessed the only local fleet strong enough to challenge the Muslims.

By the eleventh century the Normans had taken most of the area except for small areas around Benevento and Pontecorvo which were held by the Pope. The pontiff, Gregory VII, countered their incursions by excommunicating them in 1078. For administrative purposes the Normans divided Campania into four zones—Naples, the Terra di Lavoro (Working Land), the Principato Citra (Near Principate), and the Principato Ultra (Far Principate)—while consolidating the whole area with the Kingdom of Sicily.

The Normans were swept aside by other foreign masters who continued to control Campania. The Holy Roman Emperors were first, in the twelfth century, followed in the 1260s by the Pope's French Angevin allies, then the Aragonese in 1442, and finally the Spanish, who maintained their control from the early sixteenth century until 1713, when the Treaty of Utrecht awarded the region to the Austrians. Vienna's brief rule ended in 1734, when the Bourbon Charles (later Charles III of Spain) led an army of conquest into Campania. After he entered Naples and defeated the remainder of the Austrian force at Bitonto in Apulia, the warring powers agreed that Charles would wear the crown, but he was obligated to keep his lands independent from Madrid. Charles then took the throne and ruled the Kingdom of the Two Sicilies with its capital at Naples. Except for the Napoleonic interlude, his Bourbon descendants ruled the entire area until it entered into union with the Kingdom of Italy in 1860.

The forty-five years between 1815 and 1860 were a time of crisis. After the Bourbon restoration, Naples faced an unsettled situation, and sentiment for a constitution remained strong. Unsuccessful revolutions exploded across the kingdom in 1820–1821 and in the Cilento in 1828. More serious revolutions broke out in January 1848, first in Sicily, then Salerno, and later in Naples, when King Ferdinand II of the Two Sicilies fled to Caserta. He retaliated on May 15 with Swiss mercenaries and artillery. The revolution was crushed, and Ferdinand disgraced his throne by shelling the homes of his own subjects. Italians still remember him as "King Bomba."

Campania had to wait until 1860 for union with Italy. In that year the forces of the last Bourbon monarch, Francis II, collapsed in the final battle of the Volturno before the triumphant revolutionary Giuseppe Garibaldi and his Red Shirts. The new situation was validated in an 1861 plebiscite, and Campania appeared on the map as the "Neapolitan Provinces." Today's five provinces were largely in place by 1870, although outside of Naples, the names of four were different: Avellino was the capital of Irpinia; Benevento, of Sannio; Caserta, of Terra di Lavoro; and Salerno, of Principato. The Fascist government took Campania's northern frontier, much of the Terra di Lavoro north of Caserta, and gave it to Lazio to create the provinces of Frosinone (1926) and Littoria (1934).

Campania became a battleground in the Second World War when a massive Allied invasion was launched at Salerno on the night of September 8–9, 1943. Soon afterward, King Victor Emmanuel III and the royal family relocated to Salerno until the liberation of Rome in June 1944. Sympathy for the Crown remained strong in Campania; the region voted overwhelmingly and unsuccessfully to retain it in 1946, and the monarchists scored some of their highest electoral totals there after the war. The Christian Democrats

(PDC) maintained alliances with the monarchists until the 1960s, when they began to overtake them.

RECENT POLITICS. In 1992 the PDC gained over 40 percent of the vote. The neo-Fascist National Alliance subsequently became the largest party by earning 20.4 percent of the vote in 1994. In the 1996 "majoritarian" elections for the Chamber of Deputies, the nineteenth electoral district (*circoscrizione*) leaned Center-Left, with 47.7 perecent of its votes to the Ulivo coalition and 44.1 percent to the more conservative Polo per la Libertà. The more outlying parts of the region that comprise the twentieth electoral district voted 46.2 percent for the Polo and 39 percent for the Ulivo. In the nineteenth district's proportional vote, the conservative Forza Italia took 24.7 percent against 22.9 percent for the ex-Communist Democratic Party of the Left and 18.1 percent for the ex-Fascist National Alliance. In the voting (as one region) for the Senate, the Ulivo coalition won a razor-thin victory of 43 percent over the Polo's 42.9 percent. The Center-Left retained its hold on the regional government in the April 2000 elections. President Antonio Bassolino's coalition enjoyed a greater victory than the 1996 national totals: 54.2 percent versus 44.2 for the Center-Right.

NAPLES (NAPOLI)

PROVINCIAL PROFILE. Area: 452 sq. mi. Population: 3,117,095 (province), 1,045,874 (city). Naples province contains 92 communes. The province faces the southwest to embrace the Bay of Naples, swinging around from the islands of Ischia and Procida to that of Capri. To the north is Caserta. Naples province briefly touches Benevento to the northeast and Avellino on its eastern border. Salerno is on the southeast.

Naples sits on restless land between two areas of volcanic activity. Most recently, the region suffered a destructive earthquake in 1980. On one side of the city are the Campi Flegrei (the Phlegraean Fields), near Pozzuoli and Cuma. On the other is Italy's most famous volcano, Vesuvius, which looms over the city and the Bay of Naples. Due to its many eruptions—the last major one in 1944—it is no longer a cone-shaped mountain but looks more like a saddle. The remarkable excavations of the dead cities of Pompeii and Herculaneum near Vesuvius's base bear witness to its deadly power. Nevertheless, Neapolitans have displayed a sentimental attachment to Vesuvius in landscape paintings and in their popular songs such as "Funiculì Funiculà," which concerns an ascent up its side on the funicular railroad.

HISTORY. Naples began as the conglomeration of three towns, one founded by Hellenic settlers from Rhodes, one by immigrants from the established colony of Cumae (Kyme), and one by Greeks from Chalcis on Euobea. Along the northern shore of the Bay of Naples, colonists from

Cumae formed a settlement called Parthenope, named for the mythic siren. It expanded in about 470 B.C. into the "new city," or Neapolis, leaving Parthenope behind as a smaller, suburban *palaiopolis* (old city). The Romans displayed an early interest in the Bay of Naples and proposed a protectorate there in 328 B.C. to challenge the Samnites. Much of the local population was still Samnite, however, so the offer was rejected. The ambitious Romans thereupon dispatched an army of conquest and took the area in 327–326. Although Greek culture and language remained vibrant, the bay's beautiful location and pleasant climate attracted prominent Roman figures, who lined the waterfront with their sumptuous villas. Emperor Tiberius incorporated Capri into his possessions and built one of the ancient world's most magnificent palaces there. Naples became famous throughout the Roman world as the center of perfume production.

After the fall of the Roman Empire (476), Naples changed masters in quick succession. A brief period under the Goths ended in 536, when after a spirited defense, Naples succumbed to the vengeful Byzantines, who severely punished the population. Totila the Ostrogoth took Naples in 543, but in 553 the Byzantines recaptured it after they defeated his successor, Teias, at the foot of Mount Vesuvius. In 661 the Byzantines made the city the capital of one of their Campanian duchies under the nominal control of the Exarchate of Ravenna. The last figure dependent on the Byzantines was Duke Stefano II, who ruled from 755 to 800 and moved Naples closer to the papacy.

In the tumultuous ninth century, however, the city threw off its foreign masters and established its own duchy while braving attacks from all sides. The Dukes of Benevento waged a perpetual war against Naples, and the city suffered an attack by the Duke of Salerno. Naples briefly allied itself with the Muslims against Benevento but soon turned on them. The Emir of Palermo occupied Ischia and marched through the area to the slopes of Vesuvius. But his ambitions ended when the Neapolitans dealt him impressive seaborne defeats in 846 and 849.

The Neapolitan duchy survived until a long history of foreign subjugation was launched with Norman conquest in the 1130s. Roger II, Norman King of Sicily, entered Naples in 1140 but allowed the city to retain nearly total autonomy. Domination by the Holy Roman Empire followed that of the Normans. That power broke in 1266, at the Battle of Benevento, and in 1268, when the young Conradin succumbed to the executioner's axe in Naples's Piazza del Mercato. The victorious Angevins, allied to the papacy, established Naples as a capital and ruled it until the fifteenth century.

The Neapolitan Angevins launched many building and public works projects through the city: walls, streets, a new port, and, as papal allies, a number of new churches. When Joanna II, the last Angevin queen of Naples, died childless in 1435, the kingdom became contested between René (or Renato) of Anjou, backed by the pope, and Alfonso of Aragon, who enjoyed the support of the Visconti of Milan. René's, wife, Isabella of Lorraine, arrived first at Naples, followed in 1438 by her husband, who had been held captive by the Duke of Burgundy. Alfonso then reached the city with a military force. René was clearly the more popular, but Alfonso took the city in 1442 after a dreadful siege. He further endeared himself to his new subjects by conducting a ruthless sack of their city.

The invasion of Italy by the King Charles VIII of France triggered the beginning of the end of Aragonese rule. Alfonso's son, Ferdinand (Ferrante) I ruled Naples from 1458 to January 1494. His son, Alfonso II, succeeded him but, widely despised, soon abdicated in favor of his son, Ferdinand II, known as Ferrantino. When Charles entered Naples on February 22, 1495, the young Aragonese king fled to Ischia and then to Messina. French ambitions were curtailed, however, by a hostile alliance which formed in March and forced Charles to cancel his adventures in southern Italy. He fled north, and his troops remaining in Naples were defeated by Ferdinand II, aided by a Spanish force under Gonzalo Fernández de Córdoba. In 1496 the young and childless king died, and the throne fell to his uncle, Frederick, (Federigo), the last Aragonese ruler of Naples. The city's fate was decided in 1500 by the Treaty of Granada, which awarded Calabria and Apulia to Spain and Naples to Louis XII of France who succeeded Charles VIII in 1498. To facilitate application of its provisions, Pope Alexander VI ordered Frederick deposed. But the king was not prepared to surrender so easily. He allowed Spanish troops to occupy some forts in his territory, and fighting soon erupted between them and the soldiers of King Louis. Spain was the rising star in southern Italy and in 1503, flush with triumphs over the French, King Ferdinand the Catholic, of Spain, considered his cousin Frederick too smart for his own good and deposed him as well. Spanish rule began in Naples, which had become Europe's largest city.

Like the Aragonese, the Spanish were never very popular in Naples, and their administration of the city, and of southern Italy, was a model neither of probity nor of generosity. Removal of art treasures to Spain, heavy taxes, and corruption led to discontent. The last straw was a duty on fresh fruit announced on July 7, 1647, which triggered a massive popular insurrection led by Tommaso Aniello, known as Masaniello. The young and illiterate fisherman rose to take charge of a revolutionary situation that was as much an attack on the Neapolitan elite as it was on the Spanish. Masaniello's behind-the-scenes mentor was the octagenarian social and political reformer Giulio Genoino, whose attempt to democratize the Neapolitan government a quarter-century earlier had earned him eighteen years in prison. The Spanish viceroy plotted to assassinate Masaniello and the murder took place in the Naples cathedral, despite the attempts of Cardinal Ascanio Filomarino to save the fisherman. But the viceroy had miscalculated. His brutal act fanned the rebellion beyond Campania to the rest of southern Italy, and a revolutionary junta in Naples declared the city a republic and independent from Spain. It was hoped that France would come to the aid of the republic, but Paris did not respond; instead, a Spanish fleet bombed Naples, forcing the insurgents to call a truce. The settlement of April 6, 1648, was nevertheless a negotiated one that called for reforms and even compensation for losses suffered during the naval bombardment. Naples remained tied to the Spanish Empire, but the rope that held it had become frayed.

Spain's hold on Naples ended with the War of the Spanish Succession. The conflict enabled Naples to rise in revolt on July 7, 1707, and Austria took possession of the city the following month. In 1735 Austria ceded Naples to an independent branch of the Spanish Bourbons, on the condition that it never be united to Spain. Charles the Bourbon took control of Naples as the seat of its new kingdom. Under him the city became a center of the Enlightenment. Charles embarked on an ambitious program of reforms which reorganized state administration, promoted trade, and aimed to curtail ecclesiatical power. He did so with the aid of key Spanish and Tuscan advisers, particularly the Marquis of Salas Montealegre and Bernardo Tanucci, a professor at the University of Pisa.

One of the many other efforts undertaken under the Bourbons was the excavation of the buried city of Herculaneum, begun in 1738. A key figure of the Neapolitan Enlightenment, and one of Italy's most important philosophers, was Giambattista Vico (1668–1744). His *Principles of New Science* (1725) advanced the cause of the social sciences in that humanity best understands its own creations, such as history and culture. The Bourbons appointed Vico court historian. Other leading lights of the Neapolitan Enlightenment were Pietro Giannone (1676–1748), whose views on Church and state provoked his exile to Vienna; Antonio Genovesi (1712–1769), a priest who became Europe's first professor of political economy, at the University of Naples; and Ferdinando Galiani (1728–1787), who served as a crucial link to the French philosophes as secretary to the Neapolitan embassy in Paris.

Charles the Bourbon abdicated in 1759 to assume the Spanish throne as Charles III. His successor, Ferdinand I, however, was a minor, and Bernardo Tanucci administered Naples as regent. With him, the reformist impulse reached its apex. However, a devastating famine and epidemic in 1764 took the wind from the Neapolitan Enlightenment. Forty thousand died in the city, and perhaps as many as 200,000 throughout the kingdom. Aided by Queen Maria Carolina, the Church and nobles engineered a formidable comeback of the anti-reformist forces. The daughter of the Austrian Hapsburg Empress Maria Teresa, Maria Carolina challenged Bourbon power and its champion, Tanucci, forcing his resignation in 1776.

Faced with invasion by Napoleon's troops, the royal family fled to Palermo in 1798. Less a year later, on June 13, 1799, Cardinal Fabrizio Ruffo's Christian and Royal Army took Naples from the French and launched one of the most vengeful bloodbaths in the city's history. Ruffo promised safety for the last republicans who held out in the Castel Nuovo and the Castel dell'Ovo; but upon his return on June 8, King Ferdinand agreed with his English allies, who insisted that the resisters must be put to the sword. Consequently, more than one hundred were hanged or beheaded. In 1805 the Bourbons again fled and Napoleon's brother, Joseph, was proclaimed king on March 30, 1806. In 1808 Joseph was called to rule Spain and was succeeded by Joachim Murat. With help from the Austrians, Ferdinand and Maria Carolina returned for good on June 17, 1815.

After Napoleon, Naples was the base of a reactionary government under the restored Bourbons as well as a hotbed of Risorgimento sentiment. The first clash occurred in 1820, when a group of Carbonari (a secret society) and soldiers who had served Murat launched a revolt in Nola and Avellino. Inspired by the Spanish Constitution of 1812, the tumult spread to Naples under the command of General Guglielmo Pepe. King Ferdinand accepted a charter but had no intention of living up to it. The reform became a dead letter in 1821, when the Austrian army invaded and ended the revolution. In 1848, Naples erupted again. Ferdinand II granted a constitution and an assembly formed at the monastery of San Lorenzo. Also, an expeditionary force under General Pepe left to battle the Austrians. In May, however, Ferdinand felt strong enough to act against the revolutionaries, and reassumed control with the help of Swiss mercenaries. A native son, Luigi Settembrini (1813–1877), was a central figure in the revolutionary movement until his arrest after the Revolutions of 1848. He escaped from prison, however, and did not return to the city until the unification. The Bourbon monarchy finally fell in 1860 before the troops of the nationalist Giuseppe Garibaldi, who landed in Sicily in May and entered Naples on September 7.

The new Italian government neglected Naples until a cholera epidemic killed 7,000 people in 1883. Two years later, Prime Minister Agostino Depretis launched an agenda of urban renewal including housing and programs to ensure proper sewage treatment and healthy drinking water. The Fascists established a High Commission to administer Naples, although this body continued the same type of urban renewal projects that the Liberals had begun in the nineteenth century.

Naples suffered heavy Allied bombardments in the Second World War. After the collapse of the Italian government on September 8–9, 1943, the Germans occupied Naples. They evacuated after the city rose in a stiff popular resistance, known as the "Four Glorious Days," (September 26–30). The retreating Germans added to the city's trouble by mining many of its downtown buildings and destroying most of its water filtration plants. Consequently the city suffered a devastating cholera epidemic. Postwar Naples has been distinguished by very conservative politics. In the 1946 referendum on the monarchy, 79 percent of its citizens voted for the Savoyard

Crown and monarchism remained a powerful force in the city. Through the 1950s, Neapolitan politics was dominated by Achille Lauro (1887–1982), the monarchist shipping magnate and (sometimes) mayor.

Naples contributed other significant personalities to Italian public life. The reformist Socialist Arturo Labriola (1873–1959) was from Naples, as was Armando Diaz (1861–1928), commander of the Italian army during the First World War. Diaz succeeded the disgraced Luigi Cadorna in 1917, after the military disaster of Caporetto. Naples is also the home of one of Italy's Christian Democratic presidents, Giovanni Leone (b. 1908). One of the founders of that party in Naples, he was elected to the Constituent Assembly in 1946 and to the Italian Parliament in 1948. He served as prime minister twice (1963, 1968), and was elected president in 1971. His term was cut short in 1978 when he resigned amid accusations of complicity in the Lockheed payoff scandals and illegal speculations.

ARTS AND CULTURE. Naples has built over most of its ancient past; many structures were constructed over Roman foundations. The Baroque Church of San Gennaro Estra Moenia, for example, dates to the fifth century and contains significant paleo-Christian catacombs. The first-century A.D. Temple of the Dioscuri is still visible within the Church of San Paolo Maggiore, and parts of the fourth-century Basilica of Santa Restituta remain within the cathedral.

Construction began in the twelfth century on the Castel dell'Ovo, on a small island in the Bay of Naples that has been joined to the mainland. It was finished in the thirteenth century by Frederick II but was subsequently rebuilt and became the seat of the Neapolitan treasury. The Angevin King Charles I began the Castel Nuovo (or Maschio Angioino) in 1279, and the Aragonese later enlarged it as a royal residence. It was decorated by the Florentine **Giotto** (1266/1267 or 1276–1337), although almost nothing of his frescoes remains. In the seventeenth century the Spanish employed the Swiss architect **Domenico Fontana** (1543–1607) to build the Royal Palace around the corner from the Castel Nuovo, and Joachim Murat renovated parts of it while he lived there with Caroline (formerly Marie-Annonciade) Bonaparte, his wife and Napoleon's sister. Away from the port area is the Castel Capuano, known as the Vicaria. The Norman King William I of Sicily launched its construction in 1165, and Frederick II completed it as a fortress and prison. Since 1540 it has served as a courthouse. Nearby is the impressive Renaissance Porta Capuana (Capuan Gate).

Turbulent seventeenth-century Naples hosted an important generation of painters who took inspiration from the work of **Caravaggio**, who visited there in 1606–1607 and 1609–1610. Among the leaders of this new spirit were the Spaniard **Jusepe de Ribera** (called "Lo Spagnoletto," 1591–1652), who painted for the viceregal court, and the Neapolitans **Gian Battista Caracciolo** (called "il Battistello," c. 1570–1637) and **Luca Giordano** (1634–1705). The paintings and frescoes of Giordano, of **Francesco Soli-**

mena (Canale di Serino, 1657–1747), and of a transplanted Bolognese, **Domenico Zampieri** (called "il Domenichino," 1581–1641), are associated with the outburst of Neapolitan Baroque.

In the mid-eighteenth century Charles the Bourbon employed a number of architects to undertake a significant neoclassical construction project. Above the city is the royal palace of Capodimonte, built for the king by **Giovanni Battista Medrano** (b. 1703). It was used as a royal palace until the monarchy was voted out in 1946. Charles lured the Neapolitan **Luigi Vanvitelli** (1700–1773) back to his native city to work on the royal palace at Caserta and other projects. The son of a Dutch artist and a Roman mother, Vanvitelli also designed the Foro Carolino of 1758, which was later renamed the Piazza Dante. He rebuilt the Church of the Annunciation in the 1760s as well. Charles also induced the Florentine **Ferdinando Fuga** (1699–1782) to come to Naples. Fuga had built a very successful career in Rome, and among his duties was architect for Charles' Roman possessions. Like Vanvitelli, Fuga concluded his career in Naples.

Murat continued Charles's tradition when he brought a Tuscan, **Antonio Niccolini** (San Miniato al Monte, 1772–1850) to redesign Medrano's Teatro San Carlo, one of Italy's premier opera houses. The last major manifestation of the neoclassical building boom, and one of the most distinctive structures in the city, was begun as a project under Ferdinand I. The church of San Francesco di Paola, by the Swiss **Pietro Bianchi** (1787–1849), reminds the observer of Rome's Pantheon. It faces onto the impressive colonnaded Piazza del Plebiscito, which Bianchi designed and helped him secure the position of court architect for the Bourbons.

The Capodimonte Palace is today one of Italy's most noteworthy art museums, with works by Caravaggio, Simone Martini, and Masaccio. The other outstanding gallery in Naples is the National Archaeological Museum, which contains many of the objects recovered from the excavations at Pompeii as well as a significant Egyptian collection.

Naples claims over 50 saintly protectors, but above all others it venerates San Gennaro (Januarius), and the cathedral is dedicated to him. First built in the French Gothic style at the end of the fourteenth century, it underwent a major renovation following an earthquake in 1456, and craftsmen finished its facade in the twentieth century. The Chapel of San Gennaro is a richly decorated triumph of the Baroque. Gennaro was martyred during the late Roman Empire, and a church stands near Pozzuoli where he is believed to have been decapitated for his faith. Neapolitans have implored his protection since an eruption of Vesuvius in 685, and his image appeared on the seal of the city's bishop by the 700s.

One of Italy's most remarkable manifestations of popular Catholicism occurs each May 8 in the Church of Santa Lucia when dried powder, thought to be the blood of San Gennaro, becomes a healthy red liquid. This marvel, considered a sign of the saint's love for the Neapolitans, is repeated at other times as well; in the cathedral on September 19, the feast of the patron, and occasionally on December 16 to commemorate Vesuvius's eruption in 1631, when the city was spared destruction. The Catholic faithful and many others, motivated by a trace of curiosity, follow this miracle closely, especially in troubled times.

San Gennaro's great popularity has withstood efforts to discredit him. In the seventeenth century the Spanish tried to replace Gennaro with their Saint Domingo de Guzman, an effort thwarted by Pope Alexander VII. Another challenge came in 1799 when the Bourbon monarchy was restored following a brief occupation by French revolutionary troops. The Crown attempted to replace Gennaro with Sant'Antonio Abate because the blood of the patron had liquefied for the French and, therefore, indicated approval of their revolutionary regime. Even the 1964 Vatican decision to declassify Gennaro as a saint, for lack of historical proof of his existence, served only to rally the Neapolitans behind him. But perhaps the greatest challenges were overcome in 1902 and 1989, when scientists tested the mysterious substance in the vial and declared it to be real blood.

Other important churches of the city include the ninth-century Santa Restituta and the Franciscan Basilica of San Lorenzo Maggiore, begun in the thirteenth century and said to be Naples's greatest Gothic structure. The Dominican Church of San Domenico Maggiore, built between 1283 and 1324, has been renovated and repaired many times after fires and earthquakes. A number of Naples's Angevin rulers are buried there. Nearby is the popular *guglia* of San Domenico, an obelisk created in 1737 and topped by a statue of the saint. Also close by is the Sansevero Chapel, a Baroque masterpiece. Baroque additions were placed over the fourteenth-century Church of Santa Chiara, but after a Second World War bombardment, the structure's Gothic essence was restored. The remains of many Angevins rest in Santa Chiara, particularly those of Charles I.

Naples boasts a profound literary heritage. Two of Italy's most important poets, the Roman **Virgil**, who owned a villa on the waterfront, and the nineteenth-century **Giacomo Leopardi** (1798–1837) are buried in the Crypta Neapolitana. The University of Naples began as the *studium generale* founded by Frederick II in 1224. Its faculty claims important figures from **Thomas Aquinas** to **Luigi Settembrini, Francesco De Sanctis,** and **Benedetto Croce**, a native of Abruzzo who spent most of his life in Naples. The brilliant fourteenth-century court of **Robert of Anjou** welcomed **Petrarch, Boccaccio,** and **Giotto. Giovanni Pontano** (c. 1426–1503), one of the best Latin poets of the Quattrocento, helped the Aragonese monarchs to establish a humanist academy. After its initial period of medieval glory, the university grew moribund until the Jesuits resurrected it in the eighteenth century. Upon the annexation of Naples to the Kingdom of Italy, the university came under state control.

Naples has been a center of music since at least the seventeenth century.

Some of Europe's first music schools started there, many to serve orphans. Its San Carlo Theater ranks among Italy's most prestigious opera houses. **Domenico Scarlatti** (1685–1757) was born in Naples. He began his career under his father, Alessandro, at the viceroy's court, then moved on to Rome, Venice, Palermo, Portugal, and Spain, where he became a musician for the royal court. Scarlatti wrote sacred vocal music and operas, but is best remembered for his more than 500 innovative keyboard sonatas. The composer **Giovanni Paisiello** (1740–1816) was trained in Naples and, besides holding positions in the courts of Catherine the Great of Russia and Napoleon Bonaparte, spent the bulk of his time in Campania. He is best remembered for his production of engaging comic operas, composed largely in the first half of his career. **Ruggero Leoncavallo** (1858–1919) was born in Naples. His greatest fame rests on *I Pagliacci* (The Clowns), his one-act opera which premiered at Milan in 1892. Another Neapolitan composer was **Nicola D'Arienzo** (1842–1914). Like Leoncavallo, he wrote in in the style of *verismo* (realism) although his works were generally light and comic. His greatest success was *Il Cuoco* (The Cook, 1873). **Franco Alfano** (1875–1954) was born outside of Naples at Posilippo. He composed operas in Giacomo Puccini's style and, in fact, completed the latter's unfinished work *Turandot*. Perhaps the greatest lyric tenor of the twentieth century, **Enrico Caruso** (1873–1921), was born in Naples. He debuted at San Carlo, although his first success was in a Palermo production of *La Giocanda* (The Ballad Singer) in 1897.

Matilde Serrao (1856–1927), the founder of *Il Giorno* (The Day), was one of Italy's best-known writers and one of its first female journalists. She was born in Greece of a Neapolitan father and spent much of her life and energies in Naples, writing about its society. Her progressive views, it has been said, caused Benito Mussolini to veto her chance to receive the Nobel Prize.

The anti-Fascist journalist and martyr **Giorgio Amendola** (1882–1926) was born in Naples. A student of philosophy as a young man, he developed a nationalist critique of positivism and Giolittian liberalism. But service in the First World War converted him to more left-wing positions, and he was elected to Parliament and served as undersecretary of finance in the Nitti government in 1920. He opposed Mussolini's government in the pages of his newspaper, *Il Mondo* (The World), and in 1924 he was instrumental in a parliamentary boycott, the "Aventine Secession." After repeated beatings by Mussolini's Blackshirts, Amendola escaped to France, where he died of his wounds.

Another anti-Fascist Neapolitan was **Guido De Ruggiero** (1888–1948) a student of Benedetto Croce whose belief in liberalism was shaken by the First World War. His classic study, *The History of European Liberalism* (1925), called for the transformation of liberalism into a more activist and socially responsible philosophy. De Ruggiero was one of the founding fathers of the anti-Fascist Action Party during the Second World War.

Naples is home to a vibrant culture of dialect literature. An early such classic was **Giambattista Basile**'s (1575–1632) *Cunto de li cunti* (Song of Songs). Posthumously published in 1634–1636, it collected fifty tales told by ten old women and is sometimes called the *Pentamerone*. In the 1700s a dialect and folk form of opera, the *commedeja pe musica* ("comedy and music"), developed in Naples. A notable example of the art was **Antonio Orefice**'s *Patrò Calienno de la Costa* (1709). A later writer in Neapolitan dialect was **Salvatore Di Giacomo** (1860–1934), who composed some of the best examples of the art in poetry, novellas, and plays. The dialect also persists in a tradition of popular music by such figures as Di Giacomo and **Armando Gill** (1878–1945). Two famous examples of the form are "Santa Lucia" (1850) by **Teodoro Cottrau** (1827–1879) and "Funiculì Funiculà" (1880) by **Peppino Turco** (1846–1903) and **Luigi Denza** (1846–1922). Another noteworthy representation is "Malafemmena" (Evil Woman, 1952), by the Neapolitan **Antonio De Curtis** (1898–1967). Known professionally as **Totò**, De Curtis was probably Italy's most popular comic actor of the twentieth century.

The Neapolitan stage is distinguished most by the work of **Eduardo De Filippo** (1900–1984). Between the two world wars, with his siblings, **Peppino** and **Titina**, De Filippo established a number of troupes. His Teatro di Eduardo opened in 1945 with his great success *Napoli millionaria!* (Neapolitan Millionaire!). In their portrayals of Neapolitan life, De Filippo's plays are considered Italy's finest works of dialect theater.

OTHER CENTERS. The Sorrento Peninsula runs south of Naples, which shares it with the province of Salerno. South of Naples, before the point where it juts into the Mediterranean, is Mount Vesuvius. Its eruption of A.D. 79 wreaked most of its devastation in the direction of the peninsula, destroying **Pompei** (Pompeii), **Ercolano** (Herculaneum), and **Stabiae** (now **Castellamare di Stabia**). One of the most famous archaeological sites in the world, Pompeii has yielded magnificent remains of an ancient Roman city frozen in its surprise by a cataclysm. Houses, baths, gymnasiums, temples, theaters, and a forum remain; much of the city is still to be unearthed. Unlike Pompeii, Herculaneum and Castellamare were rebuilt after the eruption. In the former, an extraordinary archaeological zone has revealed superb remains, whereas only a few notable excavations in the latter remind the observer of what was lost. One of Italy's most popular shrines is located in Pompeii, the sanctuary of the Madonna of the Rosary, built in 1891.

Toward the western tip of the peninsula is **Sorrento**, a resort town since the days of the Roman Empire. Its most famous son is the poet **Torquato Tasso** (1544–1595). He attended school at Bologna and Padua before becoming a poet for the Este court at Ferrara, where he lived a sad and lonely life that led to bouts of vagrancy, insanity, and imprisonment. While incarcerated, Tasso composed much of his greatest work, *Gerusalemme liberata* (Jerusalem Liberated), which was published in 1581. Although a classic in its own right, Tasso's opus is often compared, usually unfavorably, to that of Ferrara's other court poet, **Ludovico Ariosto**. Sorrento is remembered in the song "Torna a Surriento" (Return to Sorrento, 1902), written in the popular Neapolitan tradition by the brothers Ernesto (1875–1937) and Giambattista (1860–1926) De Curtis. Giambattista came to Sorrento as an interior designer for hotels and the two brothers wrote the song to honor Prime Minister Giuseppe Zanardelli when he visited the city on his way to a fact-finding tour of Basilicata.

Off Sorrento is the island of **Capri**, a magnet for tourists and globetrotters. Ever since the Greeks built an acropolis on Capri in the sixth century and Emperor Tiberius sojourned there at the start of the first millennium, Capri's awesome beauty has weathered the onslaught of sightseers. Beyond the magnificent views, grottoes, and trails across the island, Capri's chief historical site is the Palace of Tiberius, known also as the Villa Jovis.

On the other side of the Bay of Naples is **Ischia**, the largest island in the bay. It was the site of a prehistoric settlement, and later of the Greek Pithacusa. The Aragonese built a fortress on the island in the fifteenth century.

Ancient Puteoli (or Dicearchia, modern-day **Pozzuoli**) was the chief commercial port for Rome and the location of the volcanic Phlegraean Fields. In A.D. 61 Saint Paul landed at Pozzuoli, and Christianity gained some of its first converts, evidenced north of the city, where extensive catacombs remain. Nearby are the remains of the great Roman port of Misenum, one of the most important installations under the empire. Under Caesar Augustus extensive improvements were made on what had been the old port of Cuma. Perhaps the most remarkable undertaking was *piscina mirabilis*, a cistern carved from an extinct volcanic crater, which served as a fresh water supply for the fleet. Impressive Roman ruins there include the Temple of Serapide, now thought to have been a marketplace, and a Flavian amphitheater. Close by is **Baia**, an ancient resort and the location of some of the most prestigious Roman villas.

Near Pozzuoli is **Cuma**, one of the oldest cities in Italy and perhaps its first Greek settlement. Founded in the eighth century B.C., the town enjoys literary fame as the site of the cave of the Cumaean Sibyl. In the *Aeneid*, Aeneas entered the cave to visit his dead father in the underworld. Cuma retains an extensive Greco-Roman heritage, including a fifth-century B.C. acropolis; the remains of an arch that marked the Via Domiziana (Domitian Way), which ran between Rome and Pozzuoli, and a temple of Apollo. The latter, begun by the Greeks and Samnites, it became a Christian basilica in the sixth century.

—————————— *AVELLINO* ——————————

PROVINCIAL PROFILE. Area: 1,082 sq. mi. Population: 441,499 (province), 55,998 (city). Avellino contains 119 communes. Present-day Avellino corresponds reasonably to the old province of Principato Ulteriore in the Kingdom of Naples. The province meets Apulia and Basilicata on its east, Salerno on its south, Naples on its west, and Benevento on its north. The western quarter of Avellino is an agricultural plain where 55 percent of its people live. Its eastern three-quarters is hilly and somewhat mountainous. The highest peaks in this area, referred often to as Irpinia, are Cervialto (5,935 feet), Terminio (5,850 feet), Acellica (4,554 feet), and San Michele (4,281 feet).

HISTORY. Avellino's roots are a few miles east of the present city, in the pre-Roman town of Abellinum. In 82 B.C. the Roman consul Lucius Cornelius refounded it as Veneria Abellinatium to honor the goddess Venus. Destroyed in the barbarian wars after the fall of the Roman Empire (476), Avellino was reestablished by the Lombards. The city later came under the control of Benevento and then the Normans. After 1581, under Spanish Neapolitan rule, Avellino became a feudal possession of the Caracciolo family, who became princes of Avellino in 1589. Napoleon ended Caracciolo power and feudalism in the area in 1806. After returning to the Kingdom of Naples, Avellino was the center of some Carbonaro activity in 1820 but was fairly quiet in 1848 and 1860.

The city has suffered repeated seismic activity; the earthquake of 1915 destroyed most of Avellino. After the Second World War, Avellino's population began to decrease because of an out-migration to Italy's and Europe's industrial North. The province lost 67,586 people, about 13 percent, between 1951 and 1971. This hemorrhage largely ceased in the 1970s, due in part to easy connections to the Italian expressway system. The growth rate over the past few decades has been between 1 and 2 percent.

ARTS AND CULTURE. Avellino's patron saint is Modestino, a Bishop of Antioch who suffered persecution under Emperor Diocletian in the early fourth century. He and two companions fled Syria to Calabria and then, according to legend, to the area around Avellino, where he died. His feast day is February 14. Avellino's Duomo has often been rebuilt over its twelfth-century foundation, but the original crypt remains.

OTHER CENTERS. In 1817 Francesco De Sanctis, the father of Italian literary criticism, was born in Morra (now **Morra De Sanctis**), he moved to Naples at age nine. He became Naples' and Italy's most noteworthy nineteenth-century literary scholar and critic. Active in the Risorgimento, he was imprisoned in Naples's Castel dell'Ovo after the revolutions of 1848. In 1853 De Sanctis was released and subsequently lived in Turin,

Florence, and Rome, as well as in Naples, where he returned after Garibaldi's conquest. He served as Minister of Education and occupied the chair of comparative literature at the University of Naples. De Sanctis died in 1883.

BENEVENTO

PROVINCIAL PROFILE. Area: 796 sq. mi. Population: 294,941 (province), 63,587 (city). The province of Benevento contains 78 communes. The province lies south of Molise and west of Apulia. To its south is Avellino and, very briefly, Naples. To the west is Caserta.

HISTORY. Benevento began as Maloenton, a Samnite settlement also referred to as Malies, Maleventum, or Malventum. The Romans took the area in the fourth century B.C., renamed it Beneventum, and later placed it on the Appian Way as the spearhead of their penetration into southern Italy. In 275 B.C. they defeated the Greek general Pyrrhus at Beneventum and secured their southward path of conquest. The city became one of the chief centers of southern Italy and an episcopal see in the fourth century. The Ostrogoth king Totila destroyed much of the city in 552, and in 571 the Lombards made it the seat of one of the area's most powerful duchies, an act by which Benevento acquired semi-independence. In the mid-700s Duke Arichis II proclaimed himself a prince after the death of the Lombard King Desiderius, his father-in-law. Benevento therefore became a *principatus* (principality), a title which continued for over a thousand years in the administrative names the Principato Citra and the Principato Ultra. Benevento reached its greatest power during this period, when it controlled most of present-day Campania and Molise, and much of Apulia. By the 800s, however, Muslim raids and internal rivalries weakened the principality. After a short period under the Byzantines and then under the Duke of Spoleto, Benevento came to be contested by the Normans and the papacy.

The Holy See won Benevento in the eleventh century and held it on and off for the next 800 years. An interval as a semi-independent commune in the thirteenth century ended when Benevento was taken by the Angevins. Their leader, Charles of Anjou, came into Italy at the invitation of his fellow Frenchman, Pope Clement IV, with the hope of crushing the Swabian successors of Frederick II. On January 6, 1266, in Rome, Clement crowned Charles King of Sicily. At Benevento, on February 26, Charles clashed with Frederick's illegitimate son, Manfred. Deserted by his Italian allies, Manfred fought only with his German and Muslim troops before he fell on the field. Two years later, Manfred's half brother, Conradin, was beheaded in Naples, and with the last brother, Enzo, captive in a castle in Bologna, Swabian ambitions in Italy ended.

In 1530, two years after a sack by imperial troops, Benevento passed again to the papacy, which ruled it, for the most part, until its union with the Kingdom of Italy in 1860. Papal representatives in Benevento were first called "rectors" and then "apostolic delegates." Papal control was interrupted between 1806 and 1815 when Benevento was presented to Napoleon's foreign minister, Tallyrand, the apostate Bishop of Autun. Revolutionary fervor remained high in Benevento after the French collapse and the Carbonari (a clandestine political group) engineered revolts in 1820 and 1825. In 1860 a committee of notables formed to petition a fusion with Naples, on the stipulation that Benevento would become seat of a province. On September 3 the last apostolic delegate left the city, and Benevento was formally established as a provincial capital on February 17, 1861. During the Second World War, Benevento suffered ferocious bombardments, with the loss of over 2,000 lives, from August through its liberation in October 1943.

ARTS AND CULTURE. Benevento's patron saint is Bartholomew. According to tradition, the bones of the apostle were transported to Lipari in the 500s. From there, in 838, they were rescued from the danger of Muslim attacks by the Duke of Benevento. He brought the remains to Benevento, where they rested, first in the Duomo and then in the Basilica of San Bartolomeo. This story was disputed by members of the Church of San Bartolomeo all'Isola in Rome, who claimed that the saint's remains were deposited there in the tenth century by Emperor Otto III. In 1740 a compromise was reached between the two cities, which now share the holy relics.

CASERTA

PROVINCIAL PROFILE. Area: 1,019 sq. mi. Population: 852,221 (province), 73,059 (city). Caserta contains 104 communes. Caserta borders the Tyrrhenian Sea on the west. To the north are Lazio and Molise, Benevento is on the east, and Naples is to the south.

HISTORY. Since the Middle Ages the fertile area around Caserta has been known as the Terra di Lavoro. The old city of Caserta was founded on a slope of Monte Virgo as Casa Hirta, a Lombard town, in the eighth century A.D. Most of present-day Caserta is the "new town" which sprang from a low-lying village called Torre. The veneration of Caserta's patron, Saint Anne, mother of the Virgin Mary, dates from the old town, now known as Caserta Vecchia. Because the Bourbons chose Caserta as the site of their palace, the town grew in importance and, in 1818, was designated capital of the Terra di Lavoro.

In 1926 and 1927 Mussolini's government cut the province of Caserta in half and put its northern portion into the new province of Frosinone in Lazio. The southern part was incorporated into the province of Naples. In 1934, Rome detached part of the old Terra di Lavoro, the coastal zone from Terracina to the current Campanian border and the offshore islands of Ponza and Ventotene, and awarded it to the new province of Littoria, also in Lazio. The post-Fascist Italian state resurrected Caserta province from Naples in 1945.

ARTS AND CULTURE. Caserta's most distinguished cultural patrimony is the Royal Palace, or Reggia, the occasional home of the Neapolitan Bourbons during the eighteenth and nineteenth centuries.

Luigi Vanvitelli, from Naples (1700–1773) began its construction in 1752 and his son, **Carlo,** continued the project. Among Europe's largest and most gracious palaces, it acquired new importance in 1943 as Allied Mediterranean headquarters. The palace hosted the surrender of German forces in Italy on April 29, 1945. Today, although it belongs to the Italian military, some of its rooms and the enormous gardens are open to the public. The old town, Caserta Vecchia, still boasts a medieval quarter and an impressive twelfth-century cathedral dedicated to Saint Michael, built with material from an earlier temple to Jupiter.

OTHER CENTERS. For most of its history, the major city of the area was Capua, now **Santa Maria Capua Vetere.** An old Etruscan town, Capua developed as a metalworking site and acquired importance as the leading slave market in Italy. It was from Capua that the Thracian slave Spartacus launched his rebellion in 73 B.C. After his defeat at the hands of Crassus, 6,000 followers were crucified along the Appian Way between Capua and Rome. After the fall of Rome in 476, Capua became a Lombard principality, and in 1062 the Normans took it. The town retains some impressive Roman ruins, remains of an amphitheater, and a triumphal arch honoring Emperor Hadrian. The Duomo of Santa Maria Capua Vetere, dedicated to Saints Stephen and Agatha, dates from the eleventh century and has often been reconstructed. It contains sculptor Matteo Bottiglieri's marble masterpiece representing the dead Christ (1724). Santa Maria Capua Vetere was the birthplace in 1853 of the anarchist Errico Malatesta. A follower of the Russian anarchist Mikhail Bakunin, Malatesta took part in a peasant revolt in Benevento in 1877. He lived abroad in exile but eventually returned to Italy, where he died under house arrest in 1932.

Sessa Aurunca's impressive thirteenth-century cathedral was constructed in part with materials taken from Roman temples to Mercury and Hercules. Medieval craftsmen added impressive pavements and bas-reliefs of biblical scenes and the life of Saint Peter. Another notable church is found at **Aversa.** The Normans took the town in 1029 and established its Duomo. Although the church retains some of its Arabic-Norman charm, particularly in its cupola, the structure was rebuilt through the eighteenth century. Aversa was the birthplace of the composer Domenico Cimarosa (1749–1801).

A very popular artist of his day, Cimarosa held positions in Italy, Russia, and Austria, where he scored his greatest triumph with *Il matrimonio segreto* (The Secret Marriage, 1792). He was imprisoned at Naples in 1799, during the Bourbon reaction to the first French occupation and died—some have claimed poisoned—in Venice two years later.

SALERNO

PROVINCIAL PROFILE. Area: 1,901 sq. mi. Population: 1,091,143 (province), 143,751 (city). Salerno contains 158 communes. The borders of present-day Salerno province closely follow the old lines of the Principato Citeriore. Naples and the Tyrrhenian Sea are to Salerno's west, Avellino is to its north, and Basilicata is to its east and south. The bulk of the southern end of the province, comprising perhaps a third of the entire region of Campania, is the sparsely populated Cilento, reserved as a national park.

HISTORY. The Romans established their colony of Salernum in 197 B.C. at the site of Irnthi, an earlier Etruscan town. The southern part of the province was first settled by the Lucanians. The Lombards absorbed Salerno very early and, after a period under the Duchy of Benevento, in 839 Salerno became the seat of its own principality. In 1076–1077 Robert Guiscard, the Norman Duke of Apulia and Calabria, took Salerno, the last Lombard stronghold, and made it his capital. Imperial forces sacked Salerno in 1194. Its independence was reestablished in the late thirteenth century under Giovanni da Procida, who expanded the port and established an annual trade fair in the city. The city passed to the Kingdom of Naples in 1419 as the seat of its Principato Citeriore, and much of the area was held in the feudal domains of the Sanseverino family. As a coastal capital, Salerno suffered repeated attacks and sacks by Muslim pirates; one of the last major ones took place in 1578.

During the Second World War, in the early morning hours of September 9, 1943, the Fifth American Army landed at Salerno as part of the invasion of Italy. The city suffered extensive damage. Nevertheless, the post-Fascist government transferred most of its operations to Salerno from Brindisi and kept them there until the liberation of Rome in June 1944. Salerno was the place from which the Communist leader, Palmiro Togliatti, announced his Party's *svolta*, or about-face, in April 1944, that advocated cooperation with the Italian government and sacrificed its commitment to revolution. Most doubted his sincerity. In the 1950s Salerno was designated as one of Italy's principal development zones (*poli di sviluppo*) in the government's efforts to relieve economic distress in the *mezzogiorno*. Port facilities were extensively upgraded, for example, and the city was placed on the E-45 expressway that extends south to Reggio Calabria.

ARTS AND CULTURE. Salerno's cultural reputation has long been identified with its medical school. Founded in the twelfth century, its roots extend back to Roman times. In 1252 the Swabian emperor Conrad IV attempted unsuccessfully to transfer the University of Naples to Salerno and join it to the medical school. The current University of Salerno was founded as a state institution in 1970.

Salerno was the birthplace of the twentieth-century poet **Alfonso Gatto** (1909–1976). A committed anti-Fascist who suffered in prison for his resistance to the regime, Gatto soured on his early communism but his writing maintained a social awareness in such pieces as *Il capo sulla neve* (The Head of the Snow, 1949) and *Storia delle vittime* (The History of the Victims, 1966).

Salerno claims San Antonino Abate as its principal patron and Saint Matthew as its protector. Antonino was a sixth-century monk from Monte Cassino who, after the monastery was destroyed by the Lombard Duke of Benevento, made his way to the Sorrento Peninsula. The remains of Matthew, who, depending on the tradition, died in either Iran or Ethiopia, were translated to Paestum in the tenth century and then to Salerno. In 1080 his remains were entombed in a church consecrated by Pope Gregory VII, and then in a crypt in the reconstructed Norman cathedral. The feast day of Saint Matthew, also the patron of tax collectors, is September 21. The Salernitani commemorate the translation of the saint from, they claim, Ethiopia on May 6.

OTHER CENTERS. In the Cilento, south along the coast from Salerno, is the ancient Greek settlement of Poseidonia, which the Romans took in 273 B.C. and renamed **Paestum**. Founded on an earlier Lucanian site as a fortified place near the mouth of the Sele River, it declined when the waterway silted. As a result, Paestum died in the early Middle Ages, after it found itself inland and endangered by malarial marshland. Its heritage remains, however, in striking remains of the Greek and Roman settlements. Within the bounds of its massive fourth-century walls are three large temples: the basilica, or first Temple of Hera; the Temple of Poseidon, or the second Temple of Hera; and the Temple of Ceres or Athena. These are considered some of the best-preserved structures of this kind in the Mediterranean. Much of the art and artifacts taken from the excavations is housed nearby in the Archaeological Museum.

West of Salerno is the mountainous Sorrento Peninsula, which is shared with Naples. One of Italy's most stunningly beautiful places and a location of remarkable historic and artistic importance, its coastline is dotted with many towns. The glamorous resort of **Positano** joins **Ravello** and **Amalfi**, the early medieval trading power and seat of a Byzantine duchy, to form part of Salerno province. Ravello has maintained a lovely historic center with an eleventh- and twelfth-century Duomo, still remarkable despite an unfortunate nineteenth-century restoration. Amalfi boasts a history as one of Italy's first trading powers after the fall of Rome. Tied to Naples, it sided with the Arabs and became a separate republic in 839, launching its period of greatest prestige as a mercantile power. A tenth-century Muslim traveler, Ibn Hawqal, put Amalfi ahead of Naples as a trading center. By the time of the Crusades, Amalfi was still a chief source of sea transport to the Middle East, although a sack by the Pisans in 1137 started the city on a slow decline. It passed as a feudal possession to the Sanseverino family in 1398 and then changed hands frequently until it passed to Spanish control in 1598. Amalfitan merchants founded the Knights of St. John, the Hospitallers, at Jerusalem in 1170.

Amalfi claims an apostle, Andrew, as its patron. Like Matthew, Andrew came to Italy on a roundabout journey. He was first entombed in Patras, then much of his body was brought to Constantinople in 357, remaining there until the beginning of the thirteenth century. Then, warriors of the Fourth Crusade (1202–1204) sacked the Byzantine capital against the wishes of Pope Innocent III and of his representative on the venture, Cardinal Pietro Capuano of Amalfi. Capuano, however, secured the remains of Saint Andrew and shipped them to Italy, where they remain in Amalfi's Duomo. The church was rebuilt at the start of the thirteenth century in an impressive Norman-Sicilian-Arab style over a ninth-century foundation.

SELECT BIBLIOGRAPHY

Barbagallo, Francesco, ed. *Storia della Campania*. 2 vols. Naples: Guida Editori, 1978.

Carratelli, Giovanni Pugliese, ed. *Storia e civiltà della Campania*. 3 vols. Naples: Electa, 1991.

Galasso, Giuseppe, ed. *Napoli*. Rome: Laterza, 1987.

Istituto Geografico De Agostini. *Campania*. 2 vols. Novara: Istituto Geografico De Agostini, 1980.

Macry, Paolo, and Pasquale Villani, eds. *Campania*. Turin: Einaudi, 1990.

Matassa, Angela. *Leggende e racconti popolari di Napoli*. Rome: Newton and Compton, 1997.

Chapter 6

EMILIA ROMAGNA

REGIONAL CHARACTERISTICS. Area: 8,543 sq. mi. Population: 3,947,102. Capital: Bologna. Emilia Romagna is Italy's sixth largest region in land area and its eighth in population. There are 341 communes in Emilia Romagna. Its three metropolitan sees are Bologna, Modena/Nonantola, and Ravenna/Cervia.

As its double name indicates, Emilia Romagna is the union of two regions, Emilia in the west and Romagna in the east. The region, created in 1948, is the nation's transition from the Italy of the Po and the Alps to that of the peninsula: 47.8 percent is plains and flatlands, 25.1 percent is mountainous, and 27.1 percent is hilly. Emilia Romagna shares its northern border with Lombardy and Veneto. Piedmont and Liguria touch it on the west. Tuscany, the Marche, and the Republic of San Marino face its southern side, and Emilia Romagna has the Adriatic Sea to its east. The region is generally framed by the Po River on the north and the Apennines on the south. The Foreste Casentinesi Monte Felterona, Campigna National Park straddles Tuscany's border with Forlì/Cesena province. The Panaro, Secchia, Trebbia, and Taro rivers flow from the mountains into the Po, and the Reno and Ronco are channeled toward the Adriatic. Between the mountains and the Po, much of Emilia Romagna is very flat with large fields of wheat and corn.

ECONOMY. Emilia Romagna's labor force is divided between agriculture (7.1 percent), industry (34.9 percent), and the tertiary sector (58 percent). Of its 1,694,000 employed workers, 993,000 are men and 701,000 are women. Emilia Romagna's unemployment rate stood at 6.1 percent in January 1998. The region has long been known as a manufacturing center,

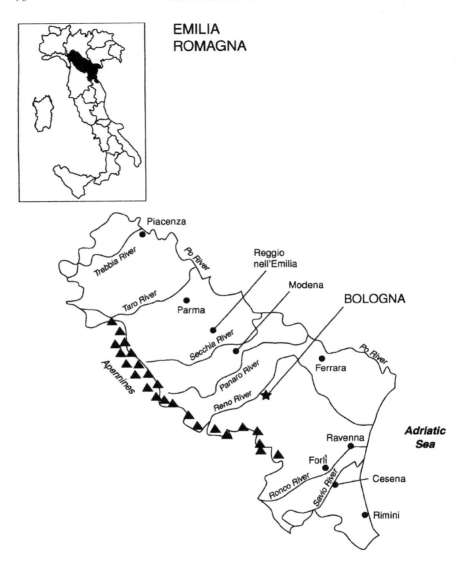

but it is also one of Italy's most productive agricultural areas. The two combine in large food processing and packing concerns. Italy's largest cattle market is in Modena. Some coastal towns, particularly Cervia, have long been known for their salt production. Emilia Romagna is also noted for its automotive, farm machinery, chemical, pharmaceutical, and clothing industries. In the province of Modena, Ferrari, Maserati, De Tomaso, and Bugatti autos are produced. There are natural gas deposits near Piacenza and Ravenna. The region has had its share of environmental problems, however—for example, on the coast near Ravenna, where industrial pollutants have taken their toll on the Pineta di Classe, the woods extolled by Dante Alighieri and Lord Byron. Emilia Romagna is one of Italy's most important tourist regions. More Italians visit here than any other region.

CUISINE. Emilia Romagna's boast as home to the best Italian cuisine may be disputed, but there is no doubt that it is rich in local dishes. The regional capital, Bologna, is often nicknamed *la grassa* (the fat). Parma is the home of Parmesan (*parmigiano*) cheese, a variant of which in nearby Reggio nell'Emilia is known as *parmigiano-reggiano*. Modena is famous for its balsamic vinegar; for its hams, cured in special Apennine places said to benefit from salt-water breezes; and for its stuffed pig's feet, *zampone*. Minced pork is jammed into "bags" made from pig intestines to make *coppa, coppa di testa, ciccioli*, and the almost universal *mortadella*. Tortellini, tagliatelle, and lasagna are pasta specialties in many Emilian cities, and debates rage over where the best can be procured. The tagliatelle and the lasagna are often green due to spinach mixed into the pasta. In Emilia Romagna tortellini is most typically served in a broth (*tortellini in brodo*), whereas tagliatelle are often enjoyed with Bolognese meat sauce.

Lambrusco is the wine most consumed throughout the region. It is a light, sparkling, red wine made from the grape of the same name, which grows throughout the area but is considered best around Modena. One of the premier types, Lambrusco di Sorbara, must be consumed soon after being opened and, it is said, does not travel well. Since 1975 the people of Sorbara (Modena) have dedicated September's third weekend to a wine festival.

The heavier red Sangiovese is produced around Ravenna and Forlì. The people of Faenza (Ravenna) celebrate Sangiovese in a winter *palio* (race) for a prize on "Bisò Night," January 5. Essential to the festivities is the *bisò*, boiled Sangiovese wine, which must be consumed in an *e gott*, a local ceramic container. *Bisò* is local dialect for "drink up" (*bevete su*). Predappio Alta (Forlì) also devotes a special day to Sangiovese, which is consumed with a very long *bruschetta*, toasted bread topped with garlic, tomatoes, olive oil, and often other flavors. The giant *bruschetta* sits on attached tables that wind up and down the town's streets. Emilia Romagna also hosts a number of festivals dedicated to mushrooms and chestnuts.

VALIGINI ALL'EMILIANA

2 c. breadcrumbs	4 oz. prosciutto crudo
1 large egg, beaten	1 c. water
2 cloves garlic, finely chopped	3 Tbs. tomato paste
1 Tbs. fresh parsley, chopped	1 small onion, chopped
5 Tbs. butter	2 Tbs. olive oil
Spices (oregano, basil, etc.), salt, pepper to taste	1 c. dry white wine
12 thin slices of veal (about 1½ lbs.)	

Preheat oven to 350°. In a bowl, combine breadcrumbs, egg, 1 Tbs. garlic, parsley, 3 Tbs. melted butter, salt, pepper, and spices. If the mixture is too dry add some water, chicken broth, or milk. Dip a veal slice into the breadcrumb mixture, then layer with a slice of prosciutto. Sprinkle some more of the breadcrumb mixture on top, then roll the two slices of meat together and secure with one or two toothpicks. Continue this process until all the veal and prosciutto has been used. Combine the water and tomato paste in a small bowl and set aside. In a small pan, sauté the onion and remaining garlic in 2 Tbs. each of butter and olive oil. Pour the onion mixture into a roasting pan, then place in the oven and roast the mixture for a few minutes. Add the meat rolls, salt, pepper, and water–tomato paste mixture. Cook, covered, for about an hour, periodically basting with the white wine.

HISTORY. Ancient Emilia Romagna possessed an Iron Age Villanovan culture and was later settled by Etruscans and the Boii Gauls before it was absorbed by Rome around 200 B.C. The Romans termed the area Cispadane Gaul and included it in their administrative Region VIII. Emilia takes its name from the Aemilian Way, which was built in the 180s B.C. by Marcus Aemelius Lepidus as a military road from the Adriatic shore at Rimini northwest along the Apennine foothills to Tortona and Piacenza. Piacenza, the Roman Placentia, became the chief city of the region. By the third century A.D., the eastern zone around Ravenna and along the coast came to be considered separate from the rest of Emilia, a situation reinforced in the sixth century when the Byzantines annexed it and chose the city as capital of their Exarchate of Italy. The Exarchate fell in 751 to the Lombards, who held the region until its capture by the Frankish King Pepin, who in turn awarded it in 756–757 to the pope as Romania or Romagna. Papal rule over Romagna, however, was weak until the sixteenth century, when Cesare Borgia and Pope Julius II eliminated the independent-minded local princes and brought it, along with Bologna and Ferrara, squarely under papal administration.

Most of the Emilian cities in the west remained freer of foreign control, developing as prosperous medieval communes, sometimes under tenuous papal control and later as part of the duchies of Parma and Piacenza or Modena. Upon the French invasion of Italy in 1796, Napoleon united much of the area in a succession of governments. The Cispadane Republic was followed by the Cisalpine Republic, and then, after a brief Austro-Russian conquest, the Kingdom of Italy under French control. During the Restoration, Emilia Romagna was again carved into the Duchy of Parma and Piacenza; the Duchy of Modena, which was awarded to the Hapsburg

Duke Francis; and the lands around Bologna and Romagna, which were returned to the Holy See.

Nineteenth- and twentieth-century Emilia and Romagna were characterized by volatile politics. The Risorgimento was particularly popular in the region, and Emilian and Romagnole cities frequently staged uprisings. Those of 1831 were particularly widespread, and in 1848, Reggio nell'Emilia, Parma, and Piacenza voted for annexation to Piedmont, eleven years before the fact. Many key leaders, furthermore, came from the area, including Marco Minghetti and the martyred priest Ugo Bassi. Perhaps Italy's greatest composer, Giuseppe Verdi, whose operas frequently dealt with national themes, was born in Roncole, outside of Parma.

Between the unification and the First World War, Emilia Romagna was distinguished by its high level of working-class consciousness and unrest, particularly among agricultural laborers, who inspired the development of sophisticated Socialist and Catholic unions and cooperative societies. Romagna, especially, came to be one of Italy's principal radical strongholds. To combat this, anxious landownwers and employers employed a virulent form of Fascism that eventually spun from their control and captured the region in the 1920s. Many important Fascists, starting with Mussolini himself, came from Emilia Romagna. The region suffered heavily in the Second World War, mostly through the winter of 1944–1945, when the Gothic Front, separating German and Allied forces, ran through the region from the Futa Pass in the Apennines, south of Bologna, to the Adriatic north of Rimini. After the war and Fascism's defeat, the Left resurfaced in Emilia Romagna and established Italy's "Red Belt," linking it to Tuscany, Umbria, and the Marche.

RECENT POLITICS. The Communist Party (PCI) earned 47.3 percent of the region's ballots in 1979 and 47.5 percent in 1983. Most of Emilia Romagna's major cities, beginning with Bologna, were led by Communist administrations throughout the Cold War and were considered models of efficiency. In the 1970s, for instance, Bolognese buses were abundant and free during rush hours for most of the population. During Italy's political reorganization, the Democratic Party of the Left (mostly ex-Communists) took 32 percent of the votes, and the more intransigent Communists of the "Refoundation" took 9 percent in the legislative elections of 1992. In 1995 Forza Italia took 18.2 percent, and 10.3 percent went to the neo-Fascists. In the 1996 elections, Emilia Romagna formed the eleventh *circoscrizione* (electoral district). In the 1996 majoritarian vote for the Chamber of Deputies, 54.2 percent of the region's votes went to the leftist Ulivo coalition, 33.5 percent to the Center-Right Polo per la Libertà, 6.8 percent to the Northern Leagues, and 5.1 percent to the old Left Progressisti. In the proportional vote, the Democratic Party of the Left led with 35.6 percent, followed by Forza Italia with 15.1 percent, and the National Alliance with 11.5. Of the region's 15 contested senatorial seats, the Ulivo captured 51.8

percent to 31.3 percent for the Polo. In the April 2000 regional elections, the Center-Left coalition, led by Vasco Errani, claimed a majority with 56.5 percent of the votes, against 40.3 percent for the Center-Right.

BOLOGNA

PROVINCIAL PROFILE. Area: 1,429 sq. mi. Population: 910,593 (province), 385,136 (city). The province contains 60 communes. Bologna lies on the northern side of the Apennines. Modena is on its west, Ferrara on its north, Ravenna on its east, and Tuscany on the south. The city is between the Reno and Savena rivers.

HISTORY. Some of the earliest remains of the Iron Age Villanovan culture were discovered near Bologna in 1853. The Etruscans later settled the site now occupied by Bologna and called it Velzna and then Felsina. By the sixth century B.C., Felsina was an important trading center that commanded the route from Spina on the Adriatic to the Etruscan centers on the other side of the Apennines. The Boii Gauls invaded the area in the sixth century and developed a healthy agricultural production while weakening the urban centers. Rome launched its conquest in the 220s B.C. and, by the 180s, had taken Felsina from the Gauls, renamed it Bononia, and linked it to the Aemilian Way.

After the fall of Rome (A.D. 476) and the barbarian invasions, the city became a fortress on the fringe of the Byzantine Exarchate. Charlemagne gave it to the papacy in 774, and the Holy Roman Empire later controlled it. The twelfth century witnessed important changes in Bologna. By 1114 it had become a commune within the Empire and had begun to lurch toward independence. Records indicate that consuls served in the city by 1156. Bologna participated in the Lombard League and defeated the imperial forces in 1176. This forced Emperor Frederick I Barbarossa to recognize Bologna's special privileges along with particular ones for its university scholars. Bologna's status was further enhanced after it joined the Second Lombard League that defeated Emperor Frederick II at Fossalta, near Modena, in 1249. The victory is recalled in the Palace of King Enzo (Palazzo di Re Enzo) in the city center, where the Emperor's captured son was held until his death 23 years later. Although the pope enjoyed authority after 1274, it was vague enough in the fourteenth century to permit the commune a de facto independence under the Pepoli and Visconti families.

The Bentivoglio family extended its challenge in the prosperous Bologna of the fifteenth century. The family first took power in 1401 but lost it to Gian Galeazzo Visconti the next year. They returned in 1435 and held the city until the turn of the sixteenth century, when Pope Alexander VI sent his son, Cesare Borgia, to extend papal control throughout the area. But the prince's northward march ended after Forlì and Imola, his last conquests. Alexander was succeeded by Julius II who arrested Cesare and in 1506 brought Bologna into the Papal States, which controlled it for the most part until Italy's unification. In 1530, Pope Clement VII crowned Charles V as Holy Roman Emperor in Bologna.

In modern times Bologna enhanced its status as one of Italy's chief cities. It led a federation of Romagnole cities as capital of the "United Provinces" during the revolutions of 1831. A key figure in the Bolognese Risorgimento was Marco Minghetti (1818–1886), who worked closely with Piedmont's Prime Minister Cavour (Camillo Benso) to bring much of central Italy into the united Kingdom. Minghetti served as prime minister in 1863 and 1864. His later career was something of an about-face, fighting for regional rights against the central government. Bologna experienced the start of an industrial revolution in the mid- and late nineteenth century. The opening of its railroad station in 1858 emphasized the city's importance as Italy's chief rail hub.

A stronghold of socialism before and after the First World War, Bologna became the site of an active and virulent Fascist reaction. The city was home to a number of important Fascists, such as Luigi Federzoni (1878–1967) and Foreign Minister and Ambassador to Britain, Dino Grandi (1895–1991). Born outside of the city at Mordana, Grandi was considered a moderate and eventually broke with Mussolini during the war. He led the opposition during the July 24–25, 1943, meeting of the Grand Council of Fascism which deposed the dictator. Working-class Bologna also produced the Fascist maverick Leandro Arpinati (1892–1945). As the Fascist provincial secretary there, and then as undersecretary of the interior in Rome (Mussolini was minister of the interior), Arpinati acquired a reputation as a leader of the party's left wing and a scrupulous investigator of corruption whose position was guarateed by the Duce's respect for and trust in him. But Arpinati's inquiries ultimately probed into too many dark corners, and his zeal landed him in prison as a subversive. He returned to Bologna a bitter man, and during the Second World War, he hid escaped prisoners of war and Resistance friends in his farmhouse at Malacappa.

Bologna suffered heavy damage during the War from Allied bombardments which were directed, sometimes inaccurately, at the city's important rail installations. In 1943 anti-Fascist partisans launched an intense resistance in and around Bologna. In November 1944 a number of Bolognesi rose against the Germans and fought them at the Porta Lama and in the working-class suburb of Bolognina.

Postwar Bologna was considered, somewhat incongruously, both a prosperous bourgeois city and a stronghold of Italian communism. Party leaders held the mayor's office from 1945 until 1999, when a former butcher, Giorgio Guazzaloca, won as a renegade centrist on his own ticket, La Tua Bologna (Your Bologna).

ARTS AND CULTURE. Bologna's Basilica of San Petronio, begun in 1390, is an important example of Italian Gothic. Facing the Piazza Maggiore in the heart of the city, it honors Bologna's patron saint, a Roman administrator who bolstered its defenses against marauding barbarians at the end of the imperial era. His feast day is October 4. Less than half of the church's marble facade was completed, and most of it remains severe brick. The Piazza Maggiore also contains the Palazzo Comunale (or Pubblico or d'Accursio), which houses the city art museum; the Palazzo di Re Enzo and its attached neighbor, the Palazzo del Podestà; the Palazzo dei Banchi; and the famous statue of Neptune, created between 1563 and 1566 by **Giambologna** (Jean Boulogne, 1529–1608). Bologna boasts a number of medieval churches, including San Giacomo Maggiore, begun in 1315 and finished in the fifteenth century, Santa Maria dei Servi, and the Basilica of San Domenico. Bologna's oldest and most distinctive church is Santo Stefano, which more precisely is a number of churches grouped in one complex. Built above what was probably an ancient temple to Isis, the Christian churches date primarily from the tenth to the thirteenth century. The bones of San Petronio rest in Santo Stefano.

Like most medieval Italian cities, Bologna was distinguished by fortress towers built by leading families. Some of these structures remain, most notably the twelfth-century Asinelli and the fourteenth-century Garisenda towers. Side by side and both leaning, they constitute one of the most familiar symbols of Bologna. Another characteristic of the city is the network of porticos that line 22 miles of its streets.

Sixteenth- and seventeenth-century Bologna was home to members of the Carracci family of painters, remembered mostly for their challenge to the Mannerist movement. **Ludovico Carracci** (1555–1619) was trained in the Mannerist style but rejected it for earlier forms identified more with the the Emilian Correggio and the Venetians Titian and Veronese. He worked closely with his cousins, the brothers **Agostino** (1557–1602) and **Annibale Carracci** (1560–1609), also of Bologna. Their influence was magnified when Ludovico established the Carracci Academy. Ludovico remained in Bologna, whereas Agostino left for Parma and Annibale ended his career in Rome, where he is perhaps best remembered for his ceiling frescoes at the Palazzo Farnese. The influence of the Carracci (and of Caravaggio) persisted in the "Bologna School" of painting, particularly **Guido Reni** (Calvenzano, 1575–1642). Upon the death of Reni, **Giovanni Francesco Barbieri,** known as "Il Guercino" (1591–1666), moved to Bologna from his native Cento, near Ferrara, and assumed the mantle of the Bolognese style until his death in 1666.

Bologna is home to one of Europe's oldest universities, its roots extending to a Roman medical school established there in ancient times. In the eleventh century the school was chartered as a university and quickly became the cultural center of Emilia and one of Europe's leading seats of learning. One sign of Bologna's cultural prestige in the thirteenth century was the greatest concentration there of manuscript illumination in Mediterranean Europe. Furthermore, through the accomplishments of such scholars as **Irnerius** (c. 1055–1125) and **Gratian** (d. pre 1159), Bologna became the center of canon law studies. One thirteenth-century Bolognese jurist, **Guido Guizinelli**, was a great influence on Dante Alighieri, who referred to him as "my father."

The modern university was home to **Giosuè Carducci** (1835–1907), who held the chair of Italian eloquence and received the 1906 Nobel Prize for literature. The philosopher **Benedetto Croce** considered Carducci, born in Val di Castello in Tuscany, to be Italy's greatest modern poet. His early works are neoclassical, or perhaps positivist, volleys against romanticism, exalting modernity and rationalism, whereas his later pieces, such as the *Rime nuove* (New Lyrics, 1861–1887) and the three *Odi barbare* (Barbarian Odes, 1877, 1882, 1889) are more conservative and intimate.

The University of Bologna has long been an important center of research and industry. The inventor of the wireless radio, **Guglielmo Marconi** (1874–1937), was born outside of Bologna. He received the Nobel Prize for physics in 1909 and served as president of the Royal Italian Academy from 1933 until his death.

Riccardo Bacchelli (1891–1985), known mainly for his historical novels, was born in Bologna. His first novel, *Il Filo Meraviglioso di Lodovico Clò* (The Wonderful Thread of Ludovico Clò) was published in serial form in 1911. As a young man he was associated with the circle around the Florentine review *La Voce* (The Voice), for which he wrote historical and political pieces. He also wrote for the stage. But Bacchelli is best remembered for his later historical novels, particularly *Il Diavolo al Pontelungo* (The Devil at the Long Bridge, 1927), on Bologna's anarchist uprising of 1874, and *Il Mulino del Po* (The Mill on the Po, 1938), the story of a family between the Napoleonic wars and the First World War. Sentimental accounts of life in the Piazza Santo Stefano were written by the Bolognese native **Giuseppe Raimondi** (1898–1985).

The painter **Giorgio Morandi** (1890–1964) was born in Bologna. Trained in his native city, he embraced the Futurist movement after encounters with **Umberto Boccioni** and others. Known as a meticulous painter, he was loosely associated with the metaphysical school of **Giorgio De Chirico** and maintained his interest in Paul Cézanne through most of his work.

Bologna was the birthplace of one of Italy's premier twentieth-century composers, **Ottorino Respighi** (1879–1936). After studies in his native city, Respighi left for Russia to work with Nikolai Rimsky-Korsakov. He returned to Italy to teach at, and later to head, the Santa Cecilia Academy in Rome. Ancient music fascinated Respighi, and he resurrected many pieces in order to orchestrate them. The most famous of these is his suite for small orchestra, *Gli Uccelli* (The Birds), of 1927. His best-remembered works, however, deal with his adopted city of Rome. His orchestral poems *The Fountains of Rome* (1917), *Roman Festivals* (1929), and especially *The Pines of Rome* (1924) still frequently surface in concerts. Respighi visited his Bolognese roots in his 1905 opera, *Re Enzo* (King Enzo).

One of the central figures of postwar Italian culture, the writer and film-maker **Pier Paolo Pasolini** (1922–1975), was born in Bologna. His first significant work was *Poesie a Casarsa* (1942), a collection of poems written in the Friulian tongue of his mother, and dialect literature intrigued him for most of his career. In 1943, after completing his studies at the University of Bologna, Pasolini relocated to Friuli, where he taught for the next six years. He also joined the Communist Party, even though his brother, Guido, had been murdered by Yugoslav Communist partisans. In 1949 he was fired from his teaching position and expelled from the Communist Party for sexual immorality, and moved to Rome. There, his fascination with life in the city's working-class suburbs surfaced in his novels *Ragazzi di vita* (The Ragazzi, 1955) and *Una vita violenta* (A Violent Life, 1959). The theme continued in the 1960s and 1970s as he turned to film in such works as *Accattone* (1961) and *Mamma Roma* (Mother Rome, 1962). Pasolini's connection with Bologna, however, continued; he was a founder of the neo-Marxist review *Officina* (workshop) there in 1955. With the collaboration of Franco Fortini, Roberto Roversi, and Francesco Leonetti, *Officina* lasted until 1959. Bologna was also the birthplace, in 1943, of the pop and rock star **Lucio Dalla**.

Along with the museum of the Palazzo Comunale, Bologna boasts an important art gallery, the Pinacoteca Nazionale, a significant medieval museum, an industrial heritage museum, and a number of university museums.

OTHER CENTERS. The second city of Bologna province is **Imola**, a place of prehistoric origins that became the Roman colony of Forum Cornelii. Destroyed by the Lombards in the sixth century, Imola was reconstituted by the tenth. Its cathedral, first built between 1187 and 1271, honors its patron, Saint Cassian, a Roman teacher who lived and was martyred there. Cassian taught a method of speed writing in an abbreviated script, and therefore he is recognized as the patron of stenographers. Imola was also the birthplace of Andrea Costa (1851–1910), one of the founders of the Italian Socialist movement.

South of Bologna is **Marzabotto** and its remains of the pre-Roman Etruscan town of Misa, founded in the sixth century B.C. and destroyed by the Gauls in the fourth. Many of the discoveries have been preserved in the Pompeo Aria Etruscan Museum. Marzabotto is also remembered for a tragic moment during the Second World War. There, in September and October 1944, two German regiments slaughtered over 1,800 men, women, and children. Also near Bologna is a monument to the anti-Fascist partisans at **Sabbiuno di Monte**, commemorating the site to which the Nazis transported 100 prisoners and massacred them in December 1944.

FERRARA

PROVINCIAL PROFILE. Area: 1,016 sq. mi. Population: 351,856 (province), 134,297 (city). There are 26 communes in Ferrara province. The province resembles a wedge that is wide to its east, where it faces the Adriatic and comes to a point in the west, with the Po River and the Veneto to its north, Ravenna and Bologna to its south, and Modena at its point. Much of its eastern half is reclaimed delta land, the Grande Bonifica Ferrarese and the area around the Comacchio basin. The city of Ferrara sits in the heart of Romagna on the Po di Volano, a branch of the Po.

HISTORY. Little is known of Ferrara's origins. It may have grown from the Roman site of Forum Alieni. Near Comacchio archaeologists have found the remains of Spina, an important Etruscan coastal port. But the provincial capital, Ferrara, was first chronicled in its capture by the Lombards from the Byzantine Exarchate in A.D. 753. The Franks presented the city to the papacy in 754 or 756, and the Bishops of Ravenna administered it. Beginning in the ninth century, the great Benedictine, and later Cistercian, monasteries began to reclaim much of the marshy lands of the Po delta, a project that lasted into the twentieth century. The semi-independent commune of Ferrara received imperial privileges in 1055 but was subjected to a host of overlords, beginning in 1101 with Countess Matilda of Tuscany and Emperor Frederick I Barbarossa in 1158. In the thirteenth century, through marriage with the Adelardi clan of local notables, the Este dukes took possession of the city and established a brilliant Renaissance court there along with, in 1391, a university. At the end of the fifteenth century Ercole I d'Este and his Bolognese architect Biagio Rossetti (active 1465–1516) planned and constructed a modern quarter that transformed the city. Its broad streets and palaces contrast with Ferrara's older, more medieval and chaotic south side. The new section was included within the massive walls constructed around the city in the fifteenth and sixteenth centuries, which remain largely intact.

Ferrara's Renaissance reputation as a cultural mecca and the reputation of Nicolò III d'Este brought an Ecumenical Council to the city (shared with Florence) that succeeded in the brief reunion of the Greek and Roman churches between 1438 and 1445. In 1471 the city received the grant of a duchy. Ferrara's incorporation into the Papal States in 1598 launched a long period of neglect and decline during which the Estes moved their court to Modena and the river began to silt. During the Risorgimento, the Austrians questioned Ferrara's loyalty to the Holy See and occupied the city's citadel after the 1831 declaration of the United Provinces in Bologna, and the entire city in 1847. The second occupation, which lasted for 12 years, was undertaken against international agreement and outraged Pope Pius IX. It became a point of contention as Italian unification grew near. On June 21, 1859, the Austrians evacuated Ferrara and the city joined its Romagnole neighbors in union with Piedmont and the new Italian Kingdom.

In the 1920s and 1930s, Fascism in Ferrara is identified with one of Mussolini's most important and popular lieutenants, Italo Balbo (1896–1940), who served as head of the Blackshirt militia, minister of aviation, and governor of Libya. Some feared that Balbo was too popular for the tastes of the jealous Duce. The problem was resolved during the Second World War when Italian gunners mistakenly shot down Balbo's plane as it approached for a landing at a Tobruk airstrip. Ferrara suffered extensive bombing damage during the war. After the conflict the Italian government accellerated its commitment to develop the eastern marshlands, and the ambitious national land reform bill of 1951 included provisions for the Agency for the Settlement of the Po Delta (Ente per la colonizzazione del delta padano). Since the 1980s, however, some caution on the side of preserving the wetlands has replaced the zeal to reclaim them.

ARTS AND CULTURE. The Castello Estese, seat of the ruling house of Este, was constructed between 1385 and 1570, and remains in the center of Ferrara. The Este court was known as one of Italy's intellectual centers. The family established a university in 1391 and brought from Venice the acclaimed Greek scholar **Guarino Veronese** (1370/1374–1460) and his son, **Battista,** to establish a school and serve as tutor, particularly to Isabella and Beatrice d'Este. The court attracted other writers, such as **Matteo Maria Boiardo** (c. 1441–1494), cousin of Pico della Mirandola and author of the unfinished *Orlando innamorato* (Orlando in Love, 1487). Painters, too, came to work for the Este family. Most important were the Tuscan **Piero della Francesca** (c. 1420–1492) and the Venetian **Jacopo Bellini** (c. 1400– c. 1470); the Ferrara native **Cosmè Tura** (c. 1430–1495) devoted much of his professional life to serving the family. Duke Borso appointed him court painter in 1458. Borso's death in 1471, however, meant that Tura fell from favor, and although he continued to receive commissions, he died in poverty. The Este family also launched important tapestry manufactures in the mid-1400s.

One of the few important structures in Ferrara not associated with the Este family is the cathedral, which honors Saint George (consecrated in 1185). Its remarkable facade is the most famous example of the Romanesque style in the Po valley. Members of the Este court built palaces which still distinguish Ferrara. Among these are the Palazzo Schifanoia, Palazzo di Ludovico il Moro, and Palazzo dei Diamanti. The last includes the National Art Gallery, which contains works by **Giovanni Luteri,** known as Dosso Dossi (c. 1479–1542), who was born in Ferrara. The house of the

Renaissance poet **Ludovico Ariosto** (born in Reggio nell'Emilia in 1474) has been preserved. Ariosto worked at the Este court and there completed his greatest work, *Orlando furioso* (1516, 1532), as well as a number of plays for Duke Ercole. His *Cassaria* (1508) is considered the first important Italian comedy. Ariosto died at Ferrara in 1533. The composer **Girolamo Frescobaldi** (1583–1643) was born in Ferrara. He became the organist of Santa Maria Maggiore and then of Saint Peter's in Rome, as well as for the courts of Mantua and Florence. He composed 12 volumes of keyboard works.

Modern Ferrara is distinguished by a great deal of cultural activity. The painter **Giovanni Boldini** was born there in 1842. As a young man he left to study in Florence, where the *macchiaioli* movement attracted him, and later he worked in Paris, where he was in great demand as a portrait artist. He died there in 1931. During the First World War, Ferrara became the scene of a concentration of artists including the Greek-born **Giorgio De Chirico** (1888–1978) and the Piedmontese **Carlo Carrà** (1881–1966). **Corrado Govoni** (1884–1965), a poet associated with the *Crepuscolare* (Crepuscular) and Futurist movements, was born outside of Ferrara. The Futurist painter **Achille Funi** (or Virgilio Socrate, 1890–1972) was born in Ferrara. After the First World War, Funi was one of the original *Sette Pittore* (Seven Painters) movement that developed into the broader *Novecento* (Twentieth Century) group, which was sanctioned by the Fascist regime. His *Myth of Ferrara* was commissioned in 1934 by Italo Balbo as a huge mural for the Palazzo Comunale. The Blackshirts appointed Funi to head Milan's Brera Academy in the waning days of the Second World War, and he was purged after the peace. He stayed to work and teach there, however, and returned to the director's position from 1957 until 1960.

Another Ferrara native was the novelist **Giorgio Bassani** (1916–2000), whose *The Garden of the Finzi Contini* (1962) told of the struggles of the city's Jewish community under the Fascists. Vittorio De Sica translated the novel into an important film in 1971. Another of Bassani's works, *Cinque storie ferraresi* (translated into English in 1971 as *Five Stories of Ferrara*), won the 1956 Strega Prize. Ferrara was the birthplace as well of the filmmaker **Michelangelo Antonioni** (1912–1999). He began as a scriptwriter but turned to directing in the 1950s. His films *L'Avventura* (The Adventure, 1960), *La Notte* (The Night, 1960), *L'Eclisse* (Eclipse, 1962), and *Deserto rosso* (Red Desert, 1964) made Antonioni among the most controversial artists of the *dolce vita* (sweet life) epoch.

OTHER CENTERS. Cento was the birthplace of the artist Giovanni Francesco Barbieri, known as "Il Guercino" (1591–1666), who is more associated with Bologna. Its civic art museum contains a good collection of his works; further examples of his work are in the Casa Provenzali and in the Church of the Rosary. Another native of Cento was Isaac Israeli, an ancestor of the nineteenth-century British Prime Minister Benjamin Disraeli.

In the eastern part of Ferrara province, on the flat, marshy Po delta, is the Benedictine abbey of **Pomposa**. It was built in the eighth and ninth centuries on what was then an island but was later joined to the mainland by silt deposits. Malaria forced the evacuation of the place in the seventeenth century. The abbey contains important Byzantine decorations and fourteenth-century frescoes.

The coastal zone also contains **Porto Garibaldi**, whose name was changed from Magnavacca to honor the liberator. There, Austrian forces captured what remained of Giuseppe Garibaldi's followers who had joined his flight from Rome after the failed Revolution of 1849. Garibaldi, his wife, Anita, and his comrade Leggero dodged the Austrians and made it to Mandriole on the shores of Lake Comacchio. There, the pregnant Anita died and was buried by her husband before he escaped to America.

FORLÌ/CESENA

PROVINCIAL PROFILE. Area: 918 sq. mi. Population: 351,604 (province), 107,827 (combined cities). The province contains 30 communes. Ravenna province is to the northeast and northwest of Forlì. To its southeast is the province of Rimini; the Marche lie to its south, and Tuscany is on its southwest. The Adriatic Sea, where there is a short string of coastal resorts, faces Forlì/Cesena on its east.

HISTORY. The Roman consul Livius Salinator established Forlì as Forum Livii and joined it to the Aemilian Way in 188 B.C. Later it was closely tied to the Byzantine Exarchate, but by the twelfth century, Forlì had become a commune, a Ghibelline stronghold in the largely Guelph Romagna. The papacy inaugurated a loose rule in 1278, although between 1315 and 1480 it was effectively ruled by the Ordelaffi family. Rome periodically reexerted its authority, however, as in the mid-fourteenth century under the indefatigable Cardinal Egidio (Gil) Albornoz. Later, Pope Alexander VI dispatched his son, Cesare Borgia, to take Forlì and other Romagnole towns, which he did in 1500. The city remained in the papal domains for the most part until the unification of Italy.

Cesena's origins are prehistoric. After the fall of the Roman Empire, the city passed to the Byzantine Exarchate and the archbishop of Ravenna. The city was torn by the struggles between Guelphs and Ghibellines. The popes took it from the Ordelaffi family, and Cesena suffered near total destruction in 1377 at the hands of mercenary troops under Cardinal Robert of Geneva. The Holy See then awarded what little was left of the town to the Malatestas of Rimini, who ruled from 1378 until 1465. The popes assumed power quickly thereafter, and Cesare Borgia commissioned Leonardo da Vinci to design its port, now known as Cesenatico. Papal rule lasted until the nineteenth-century Risorgimento. The city was the home of two consecutive popes. Giovanni Angelo Braschi (1717–1799) became Pope Pius VI in 1775. He was thrust into the Napoleonic Wars when the French took the papal territory of Avignon in France in 1790 and when they invaded the Papal States in 1796. Napoleon occupied Rome and declared a republic in 1798. Pius was arrested and sent to prison in France, where he died. He was succeeded by another native of Cesena, Barnaba Chiaramonti (1740–1823), who became Pius VII. He reached a concordat with the French, although Napoleon's persecution of the Church and occupation of Rome brought his excommunication in 1809. Napoleon retaliated by imprisoning the Pope. Pius survived the incarceration and the Napoleonic regime.

ARTS AND CULTURE. The principal patron saint of Forlì is Mercuriale, its bishop in the 400s. On April 30, his feast day, the saint's remains are transferred from the Church of the Most Holy Trinity to the cathedral, which bears his name. Forlì also celebrates the feast day of Mercuriale's successor, San Grato, and of San Marcello, who, according to legend, served as subdeacon to both bishops. **Melozzo da Forlì** (Melozzo degli Ambrogi, 1438–1494) and his pupil **Marco Palmezzano** (c. 1456–1539) came from Forlì. (Melozzo's chief works are found in museums elsewhere.) The playwright **Diego Fabbri** (1911–1980) was a native of Forlì. He was noted as one of Italy's most significant Catholic artists, and his most important works include *Processo a Gesù* (translated as *Between Two Thieves*, 1955). Forlì is also home to an important archaeological museum.

Rimini's domination of Cesena is recalled in the fourteenth-century Malatesta fortress (*rocca*) and in the Malatesta Library. Built in the fifteenth century by **Matteo Nuti** (Fano, d. 1470), it is considered the best-preserved example of a Renaissance study.

Cesena was the home of **Renato Serra** (1884–1915). A student of Giosuè Carducci's at Bologna, Serra joined the literary circle around the Florentine journal *La Voce* (The Voice) and later directed the Malatesta Library in Cesena. He died on the Podgora River shortly after Italy's entry into the First World War.

OTHER CENTERS. Near Forlì is the small town of **Predappio**, the home of Benito Mussolini. The Fascist dictator was born there in 1883 to a blacksmith/innkeeper and a schoolteacher mother. In 1919 he established the Fascist movement in Milan, and became Italy's prime minister in 1922. By 1925, Mussolini had taken the reins of power as Duce and dictator of Italy. He allied Italy to Nazi Germany and entered the Second World War in June 1940. His regime collapsed in 1943 and was resurrected as a puppet state under German overlords until 1945, when he was shot by partisans on the banks of Lake Como. Mussolini's remains rest in a cemetery on the outskirts of Predappio, and a small industry of souvenir shops flourishes in the town. Not surprisingly, Predappio's architecture shows pronounced Fascist influence in, for example, the city hall (Palazzo Varano) and the church, constructed in 1934. Forlì also contains a memorial to Bruno, the Duce's son, who died in an air crash in 1942.

The poet Giovanni Pascoli (1855–1912) was born in San Mauro, now **San Mauro Pascoli**. He taught Greek, Latin, and Italian literature at the University of Bologna and was one of Italy's premier writers of the late nineteenth and early twentieth centuries. His goal was to portray the simple and humble side of life, and in doing so, he departed from Italian lyric tradition in his use of images and of language. Pascoli also wrote extensively in Latin, and Gabriele D'Annunzio described him as the greatest Latin poet since the ancients. Marino Moretti (1885–1979) was born on the Adriatic shore at **Cesenatico**. Originally known as a poet of the *Crepuscolare* (Crespuscular) movement, he turned to novels in 1916 with *Il Sole di Sabato* (Saturday's Sun) and, later, to memoirs.

MODENA

PROVINCIAL PROFILE. Area: 1,039 sq. mi. Population: 616,668 (province), 175,124 (city). Modena comprises 47 communes. It is a long, north-south province which borders Bologna on its east, Tuscany to the south, Reggio nell'Emilia on the west, Lombardy on the north, and Ferrara on the northeast. The city of Modena lies on the northern side of the Apennines between the Secchia and Panaro rivers. About 35 percent of the province is mountainous, with many peaks above 3,000 feet. The summit of Monte Cimone, near the Tuscan frontier, stands the tallest at 7,103 feet.

HISTORY. The Etruscans established Modena, which was later taken by the Boii Gauls and, in 183 B.C., by the Romans, who connected the place to the Aemilian Way and called it Mutina, a name which may derive from *mut*, an Etruscan term for a rise in the ground. A parallel but distinct culture of the Friniati, a tribe of the Liguri Gauls, developed in the southern, Apennine, zone of the province. The Friniati land was conquered by the Romans about 189 B.C., and its legacy continues in the name of that particular zone, Frignano. Modena was destroyed by the Huns and the Lombards in the fifth and sixth centuries but revived between the sixth and the ninth, first under the name of *Cittanova* (New City) or *Città Geminiana*. Geminiano was a Roman Bishop of Modena who died around 396, and is the patron saint of the city.

Under the lordship of Catholic bishops and archbishops, Modena fell to the County of Canossa around 1000 and then, by 1135, became a free commune. It allied with other Emilian cities against the Holy Roman Empire in the Lombard Leagues. The key victory over Frederick II took place at the bridge at Fossalta in 1249, outside of Modena. Between 1288 and 1336 Modena was controlled by the Este family, the lords of Ferrara. It became a duchy in 1452 and was the home of the Este after the family lost Ferrara in 1598.

The Modenese Age of Reason was distinguished by the Jesuit historian of letters and reformer of education Ludovico Antonio Muratori (born in nearby Vignola, 1672–1750). His works, particularly the *Primi disegni di una repubblica Letteraria d'Italia* (First Plans for a Literary Republic of Italy, (1704), aimed at the organization of Italian intellectuals and the future unity of the nation in what he termed a "literary republic" led by intellectuals. After the fall of Napoleon's empire, the Congress of Vienna awarded Modena to Duke Francis IV of the Austro-Italian Hapsburg-Lorraine dynasty. His oppressive reign bred a revolutionary opposition which fed the Risorgimento during the uprisings of 1821, 1831, and 1848, the last of which was aimed at Duke Francis V. In 1859 the duchy dissolved and the area was incorporated into Piedmont and, the next year, into Italy.

ARTS AND CULTURE. In 1099 Countess Matilda of Tuscany employed **Lanfranco** to start work on Modena's Romanesque-Lombard cathedral, dedicated to San Geminiano. Its distinctive Romanesque-Gothic bell tower, known as La Ghirlandina, was built later, between 1224 and 1319. Modena is also the site of a university, established in 1175. Much of it was rebuilt around 1750. Modena's most important Renaissance artists were **Francesco Bianchi Ferrari** (c. 1460–1510), **Guido Mazzoni** ("Il Modanino," c. 1450–1518), and **Antonio Begarelli** (1499–1565). A number of Bianchi Ferrari's works, strongly influenced by French and Flemish styles, can be viewed throughout the city, including his *Crucifixion* at the Este Gallery. Mazzoni, who was very active throughout Emilia, painted and also created terra-cotta statues such as *The Holy Family* (also known as the *Madonna della Pappa*), which is in the cathedral. Most of Begarelli's works were intended for the Benedictines of Modena and the surrounding area. One of Italy's most important twentieth-century Futurist artists, **Enrico Prampolini** (1894–1956), was a Modenese. The Este Gallery is located in the Palazzo dei Musei, which houses other important museums as well as the Este Library.

Modena is home to one of Italy's officer training schools, the Accademia Militare, housed in the old Ducal Palace. The opera celebrities **Luciano Pavarotti** (b. 1936) and **Mirella Freni** (b. 1935) are Modenesi, as was the Bononcini family of musicians. **Giovanni Bononcini** (1642–1678) played the violin for the Este family, was *maestro di capella* (choirmaster) at the Modena cathedral, and composed highly regarded sonatas. His sons were also accomplished. **Giovanni** (1670–1747) composed over 40 operas, about 90 instrumental pieces, and over 200 choral works. **Antonio Maria** (1677–1726) wrote cantatas and choral works, and followed his father as the cathdral's *maestro di capella*.

OTHER CENTERS. Some 9 miles outside of Modena is **Maranello,**

home to the Ferrari auto works. The enterprise was established by the former race car driver Enzo Ferrari (1898–1988), and the first model, number 125, appeared in 1947.

Carpi is an important town with roots in the seventh century. Under the Pio family, which ruled from 1327 until 1525, particularly Alberto "il Dotto" (the Wise), and then under the Este family, the town attained some note as a Renaissance cultural hub. The fourteenth- and fifteenth-century Pio Castle dominates the center of Carpi and houses the Giulio Ferrari Civic Museum. Behind the castle is the "Sagra," or church of Santa Maria in Castello. It dates from the eighth century, and was restored in the twelfth and sixteenth centuries. It has a Renaissance facade by the Sienese artist Baldassare Peruzzi (1481–1536).

Mirandola was the birthplace and ancestral home of one of the greatest Christian humanists of the Renaissance, Giovanni Pico della Mirandola (1463–1494). He was mostly associated with the Medici court of Lorenzo "the Magnificent" in Florence, where he wrote his *Oration on the Dignity of Man* (1486).

An important cultural bastion northeast of Modena was the Benedictine monastery of **Nonantola**. It was founded in 753 on a gift of what was then marshland from the Lombard king Aistulf to his brother-in-law, Anselm, Duke of Friuli. Anselm had grown weary of ruling and longed for the contemplative life in the Church. Aistulf's successor, Desiderio, removed Anselm as abbot and banished him to Monte Cassino until Charlemagne defeated the Lombards and brought Anselm back to Nonantola, where the old man died in 803. The monastery was sacked by the Magyars in 899, but it rebounded quickly. Its successful renaissance meant that it was soon coveted by the Bishops of Bologna and Modena. In 1083 Nonantola was taken by Matilda of Tuscany and, in 1121, pressured by the Modenesi. The monks instead opted for submission to Bologna. In 1514 the Cistercians replaced the Benedictines and, after the disruptions of Napoleon's invasion, Pope Pius VII entrusted the monastery to the Archbishop of Modena.

PARMA

PROVINCIAL PROFILE. Area: 1,332 sq. mi. Population: 393,971 (province), 167,504 (city). The province contains 47 communes. The Po River separates Parma from Lombardy to the north. Reggio nell'Emilia faces Parma on the east, Tuscany and Liguria are to its south, and Piacenza is on its west.

HISTORY. The Romans founded Parma in 183 B.C. at the junction of the river which bears its name and the Aemilian Way. The origin of

"Parma" is debated; it may have stemmed from the Latin word for "shield." It was also called Iulia and Iulia Augusta by the Romans. The town prospered thanks to its location and became an episcopal see in the fourth century. Attila the Hun put Parma to the torch in 452, as did Totila the Ostrogoth in the mid-500s. It was rebuilt a number of times as a Lombard capital, the site of a Byzantine treasury, and, from the ninth century, a bishopric. One of the ruling bishops, the twelfth-century reformer Saint Bernardo of Parma, became the patron of the city along with Saint Hilary of Poitiers.

As an independent commune in the twelfth and thirteenth centuries, Parma was a frequent site of battles between Guelph and Ghibelline forces until it was subjugated by a successon of secular lords. The Visconti bought Parma for 70,000 gold florins in the fourteenth century. In the fifteenth, the Este family briefly acquired the city, which later passed to the Sforza. After a brief but brutal French occupation, Parma became a possession of the Holy See. In 1545 Paul III, a Farnese pope, detached Parma from the Papal States and reorganized it into the Duchy of Parma and Piacenza. He awarded it to his son, Pier Luigi Farnese (1503–1547) and his descendants. Duke Alessandro Farnese (1545–1592) served Spain's King Philip II during the Wars of the Reformation and entrusted the duchy to his 17-year-old son, Ranuccio I (1569–1622). Ranuccio proved to be an energetic ruler who reformed Parma's legal and judicial systems as well as its eleventh-century university. When the family died out in 1731, the duchy was transferred to the Bourbons.

The marriage of Duke Philip of Bourbon to Elizabeth-Louise, a daughter of King Louis XV of France, brought the influence of the French Enlightenment to Parma. As his chief minister the duke imported a Frenchman, Guillaume Du Tillot, who, during his tenure from 1756 until 1771 became perhaps Italy's principal reformer. Du Tillot promoted industry, particularly textiles, reformed education and the state apparatus, expelled the Jesuits, and ended the Inquisition. He also established the Academy of Fine Arts and imported French philosophes such as Etienne Bonnot de Condillac (1715–1780), a tutor who cultivated the little heir, Ferdinand, as an enlightened "philosopher king." The experiment ended, however, when the "philosopher king" reached maturity. The Bourbons held Parma until Napoleon annexed it in 1808 as the Kingdom of Italy's department of Taro. In 1814 the Congress of Vienna extended the Duchy to Napoleon's second wife, Maria Louisa. Although she briefly fled the city in the revolution of 1831, she was reinstated and held Parma until her death in 1847. The Bourbons returned then under Charles II and his son Charles III, who proved to be very unpopular and were maintained on the throne only by Austrian arms. The father fled Parma during the revolution of 1848, and the son was assassinated in 1854. The last Bourbons were expelled in 1859, and the duchy was absorbed into Piedmont (and, in 1861, into the new

Kingdom of Italy). A powerful socialist movement bloomed in Parma as industrialization came to it in the late nineteenth century. Parma suffered extensive damage in the Second World War air bombardments.

ARTS AND CULTURE. Parma's Piazza del Duomo is one of Italy's most renowned. The Bishop's Palace; the eleventh-century Duomo, dedicated to the Assumption of the Virgin; and the baptistery face the square. The Duomo is considered one of the Po valley's finest examples of the Romanesque style. Next to it sits the remarkable octoganal baptistery, built between 1196 and 1216. Parmigian art developed its own style in the eleventh and twelfth centuries, but remained in Lombardy's shadow until the Sienese painter **Michelangelo Anselmi** (1491–1555) and **Correggio** (born Antonio Allegri in the nearby town of Correggio (1494–1534) evolved a distinct and separate school. The works of Correggio and of his followers, like **Parmigianino** (Girolamo Francesco Mazzola, 1503–1540), can be appreciated in the city museums at the Palazzo della Pilotta, a strange, unfinished, and partly destroyed building intended as a Farnese palace and as a court for the Basque ball game *pelota*. The National Gallery, housed in the palace and across the street in the convent of San Paolo; the Duomo; and the churches of the Madonna della Steccata and San Giovanni Evangelista are particularly important for Correggio. The Duomo contains his *Assumption*, and his famous *Vision of St. John at Patmos* adorns the dome of the church honoring Saint John the Evangelist. Parma's artistic tradition continued through Parmigianino to **Girolamo Mazzola Bedoli** (1500–1569) and **Il Bertoja** (Jacopo Zanguidi, 1544–1574). Outside of the city is the Charterhouse of Parma, dating from 1282, which was made famous in the novel *The Charterhouse of Parma*, by **Stendhal** (Marie-Henri Beyle, 1839).

In the eighteenth century, Bourbons infused French ideas and styles into Parma's art, particularly through the sculptors **Jean-Baptiste Boudard, Jean-Baptiste Cousinet,** and **Laurent Guyard,** and the architects **Ennemond-Alexandre Petitot** and **Pierre Constant d'Ivry.** The French influence is also apparent in the works of the writer **Tommaso Traetta** (1727–1779) and the librettist **Carlo Innocenzo Frugoni** (1692–1768).

Parma is closely identified with opera. The Teatro Reale, built between 1821 and 1829, has long been considered one of Italy's premier houses and has a notoriously demanding audience. Among the native sons and daughters of Parma province was Italy's greatest opera composer, **Giuseppe Verdi.** Born in 1813 outside of Parma at Roncole, he studied for a time in Milan before returning to nearby Busseto. His first opera, *Oberto* (1839), brought him back to Milan and the La Scala opera house. He earned his reputation with *Nabucco*, his third opera. Premiered in 1842, its "Va Pensiero" chorus has become one of the most beloved melodies in Italy and an unofficial national anthem. Verdi's potboiling nationalistic works of the 1840s and 1850s meshed perfectly with the unfolding political drama of the Risorgimento. His last, most mature phase was marked by his greatest critical triumphs, *Aida* (1871), the *Manzoni Requiem* (1874), *Otello* (1887), and *Falstaff* (1893). Verdi died at Milan in 1901.

The conductor and director of Milan's La Scala opera house, **Arturo Toscanini** (1867–1957), was a Parmigiano. After a brief attraction to early Fascism, he broke with Mussolini. His frequent refusal to conduct the Fascist anthem, "Giovinezza," courted the wrath of the Blackshirts, who confronted the sixty-four-year-old Toscanini outside Bologna's Teatro Comunale in 1931 and brutally beat him. He soon abandoned Italy for New York, to conduct at the Metropolitan Opera and the National Broadcasting Company Symphony Orchestra. Toscanini participated in anti-Fascist activity until the collapse of Mussolini's regime and his return to Italy.

Parma is also the home of the filmmaker **Bernardo Bertolucci** (b. 1940). He worked with Pier Paolo Pasolini and others until he premiered his own films, such as *Il Conformista* (The Conformist, 1971) and *Novecento* (1900, 1976), followed by a number of international works including *The Last Emperor* (1987).

OTHER CENTERS. The summer residence of both the Farnese and the Bourbons, the Ducal Palace at **Colorno** was transformed in the seventeenth century from an old fortress into a luxurious estate. The metamorphosis was the work of Ferdinando Galli da Bibiena (Bologna, 1657–1743), the court artist of Ranuccio II before he went on to work in Barcelona and Vienna. Galli da Bibiena's son Giuseppe (Parma, 1696–1756) and grandson Carlo (Vienna, 1728–1787) carried on the family tradition as artists.

Northwest of Parma is **Fidenza,** founded as the Roman colony of Fidentia along the Aemilian Way. After the barbarian invasions the town resurfaced as Borgo San Donnino. Its impressive Duomo, built between the eleventh and thirteenth centuries, honors San Donnino (Domninus), fourth-century Christian martyr. The town became a semi-independent commune, with privileges granted by Conrad III (r. 1138–1152). In 1108 its people chose to break from Parma but, urged on by Bishop Bernardo, the Parmigiani brutally defeated Borgo San Donnino. In 1927 the Fascists dropped the town's medieval name and reverted to the more Roman-sounding Fidenza.

PIACENZA

PROVINCIAL PROFILE. Area: 1,000 sq. mi. Population: 265,899 (province), 99,665 (city). The province contains 48 communes. To Piacenza's east and southeast is Parma, Liguria is on its south, Piedmont faces it on the west, and the Po forms its northern border with Lombardy.

HISTORY. The Romans founded Piacenza on the south bank of the Po as their military colony of Placentia in 218 B.C. It was besieged by the Carthaginians under Hasdrubal in 207 and sacked by the Gauls in 200. As terminus of the Aemilian Way, the junction of other Roman roads, and a river port, Placentia became the chief city in the region. The barbarians destroyed it, but Piacenza revived by the 900s under the local bishops. It became a free commune by the twelfth century and engaged in the Lombard League's successful struggle against Emperor Frederick I Barbarossa. During the Renaissance, the city was frequently exchanged among the French, the papacy, the Viscontis, and the Sforzas until Pope Paul III created the Duchy of Parma and Piacenza for his son, Pier Luigi Farnese.

Risorgimento activity for unity and liberation was more intense in Piacenza than that in its sister city of Parma. Early nationalist thinkers Gian Domenico Romagnosi (1761–1833) and Melchiorre Gioia (1767–1829) came from Piacenza, and the city was involved in the revolutions of 1821 and 1831. On May 10, 1848, Piacenza was the first Italian city to vote for union with Piedmont. A provisional Piacentino government under Giuseppe Manfredi finally joined with Piedmont in 1859, a decision sanctioned by plebiscite on March 11, 1860.

ARTS AND CULTURE. Some of Piacenza's most important buildings are located at either end of the Via Venti Settembre. At its northwest end is the Piazza dei Cavalli, so called because of two bronze equestrian statues of Alessandro and Ranuccio Farnese by the Tuscan **Francesco Mochi** (1580–1654). The Palazzo del Comune, the thirteenth-century city hall (also called "Il Gotico"), faces the piazza. At the southeast terminus of the street is the Duomo, dedicated to the Assumption of the Virgin and built between 1122 and 1233 in the Lombard Romanesque style. Piacenza's earlier cathedral, begun in the fourth century, was dedicated to its patron saint, Antonino, a martyred Roman centurion. There, negotiations between the Lombard League and Emperor Frederick I Barbarossa led to the Treaty of Constance in 1183. Sant'Antonino was rebuilt in the eleventh century. Piacenza's first bishop, canonized as San Vittore, also is a patron saint. The film director **Marco Bellocchio** was born at Piacenza in 1939.

OTHER CENTERS. Near Piacenza is the old town of **Castell'Arquato**, which dates at least from the sixth century A.D. and probably earlier than that. Its central Piazza del Municipio is framed on three sides by the twelfth-century Palazzo Pretorio (now the town hall), a fourteenth-century Visconti fortress (or *rocca*), and the apse of the twelfth-century collegiate church.

One of Europe's most important monasteries, **Bobbio**, was established in the 600s near Piacenza by the Irish saint Columban. It later became a Visconti possession and passed to the house of Savoy in 1748. The monastic complex dates from the ninth century.

RAVENNA

PROVINCIAL PROFILE. Area: 718 sq. mi. Population: 350,019 (province), 137,337 (city). Ravenna province contains 18 communes. Ravenna faces the Adriatic on its east. Its southern border is an arc which curves around Forlì and reaches Tuscany on its southwest. Bologna sits to the west. In ancient times the city of Ravenna was a port that faced a group of lagoons which joined the Adriatic Sea. Since then the coast has silted up and left the city about six miles inland. A canal now links it to the sea.

HISTORY. Ravenna was one of the most important cities of late antiquity. Originally inhabited by Italic peoples who migrated from the north, the area was taken by the Romans in 191 B.C. They cultivated the area's potential, Augustus developed port facilities at nearby Classis (Classe), and Ravenna became the home of Rome's Adriatic fleet. Emperor Honorius transferred the capital of the Western Empire to Ravenna in 402, and it remained the seat of the goverment until the final collapse in 476. The succeeding barbarian kings Odoacer (476–493) and Theodoric (493–526) continued to rule from Ravenna until the Byzantines took it in 540 and made it the capital of their Italian holdings, the Exarchate. The Byzantines held Ravenna until 751, when the Lombards briefly took it. The Frankish King Pepin the Short annexed it and transferred it to the papacy in 756–757.

The Holy See ruled Ravenna until it became an independent commune in the twelfth century. It resumed loose control in 1278 through the Da Polenta family, which administered Ravenna as papal vicars until 1441, when Venice took it. The papacy returned in 1509, after he joined the League of Cambrai with King Louis XII of France. In 1511, however, with Venice and Spain, Pope Julius II organized the Holy League against France and went to war. His forces were defeated at Ravenna in April 1512, in one of the bloodiest battles fought in Italy during those bloody centuries. The victor, Gaston de Foix, who had just sacked Brescia, was killed in the battle. But the French forces were so depleted that they were pushed from the area, and papal rule was secured with few interruptions until the Italian unification.

ARTS AND CULTURE. Late Roman and Byzantine art distinguishes Ravenna as one of Italy's and Europe's cultural treasures. The Basilica of Sant'Apollinare Nuovo, erected by Theodoric as an Arian church, became a Catholic church in 560. Its mosaics representing the life of Christ are some of the earliest extant. More Byzantine mosaics are found in the Neonine Baptistery, built in the early 400s by Ravenna's Bishop Neon. Originally a Roman bath, and located in a state-run archaeological zone, is the Church of San Vitale, considered one of the chief masterpieces of Byzantine art anywhere. It was conceived, and its construction was launched, however, by Bishop Ecclesius and the Ostrogoth Queen Amalusuntha, before the Greek conquest. It was finished in 547, seven years after the arrival of General Belisarius and his Greek troops. Along with biblical themes, the spectacular mosaics of San Vitale depict Emperor Justinian, his wife, Theodora, and members of the imperial court in Constantinople. The important National Museum of Antiquities is located in the cloisters of San Vitale.

In the same archaeological park is the fifth-century tomb of Galla Placidia, the sister of Emperor Honorius. She rests in an unimposing brick structure formed in an early Latin cross. The interior mosaics are exquisite. The King Theodoric of the Goths built a daunting tomb for himself in Ravenna. Finished in 520, it is distinguished by its impressive Istrian limestone dome. The tomb was used as a church until the eighteenth century. **Dante Alighieri** is buried in Ravenna at the Church of San Giovanni Evangelista. The poet, banished from his beloved Florence, was accepted by the Da Polenta family and by the Ravennesi who buried him, a centuries-old source of frustration and embarrassment for repentant Tuscans. Outside Ravenna is Classe, the old Roman port of Classis. Now considerably inland, nothing remains of its ancient glory except a Byzantine masterpiece, the sixth-century Church of Sant'Apollinare in Classe, named for an early martyred bishop who has become the patron of Ravenna and of Emilia Romagna.

Late Roman and Byzantine Ravenna produced important literary figures. Its first archbishop, **Pietro Crisologo** (Peter Chrysologus), wrote tracts on sacred subjects, and a school of writers developed which included the poets **Aratore** (Arator, sixth century) and **Venanzio Fortunato** (Venantius Fortunatus, c. 540–c. 600), and the writer of prose **Anonymous Valesian**. The Catholic reformer and cardinal who preached against the sins of the clergy, **Peter Damian** (Pier Damiani, 1007–1072), was born in Ravenna.

OTHER CENTERS. The second city of the province of Ravenna is **Faenza**. Known as Faventia by the Romans after 173 B.C., the city attained a reputation as a minor power under the Manfredi in the fourteenth and fifteenth centuries. It later developed a successful trade in majolica, or faience, ware.

Faenza is known for its adjacent central squares, the Piazza del Popolo, with its twelfth- and thirteenth-century Palazzo Comunale and Palazzo del Municipio, and the Piazza della Libertà, with its Renaissance Duomo, begun by Giuliano da Maiano (1432–1490), on top of an eighth-century structure, and with its Baroque fountain by the Faenza native Domenico Paganelli (1545–1624). The Duomo contains the relics of Faenza's martyred patron, San Savino, which were brought to the city in the middle of the fifteenth century. A native of Faenza was Pietro Nenni (1891–1980), the head of the Italian Socialist Party and one of the leaders of post-Fascist Italy until his party was excluded from the cabinet in 1947. Under him, the Socialists reentered the government in the ruling coalition with the Christian Democrats in 1962.

Faenza boasts the National Museum of the Neoclassical Era (Museo Nazionale dell'Età Neoclassica), situated in the remarkable Palazzo Milzetti of Giuseppe Pistocchi (1744–1814), a native son. It contains frescoes by Felice Giani (1758–1823). The International Museum of Ceramics (Museo Internazionale delle Ceramiche) is housed in a former Servite convent.

Quite a few artists came from some of the small towns in Ravenna province. **Cotignola** is the home of the Zaganelli brothers, Bernardino (b. c. 1470) and Francesco (c. 1470–1532), who worked mainly in Ravenna and Ferrara. **Bagnacavallo** was the birthplace of Bartolomeo Ramenghi (1484–1542), who is known as Il Bagnacavallo. His *Redentore e Santi* (Redeemer and Saints) is in the collegiate Church of San Michele Arcangelo (Rimini province) and in other places, mainly Bologna.

REGGIO NELL'EMILIA

PROVINCIAL PROFILE. Area: 885 sq. mi. Population: 438,613 (province), 137,242 (city). Reggio nell'Emilia province has 45 communes. Like Parma, Modena, and Bologna, Reggio nell'Emilia is a long north-south province that leans to the northeast. Modena faces its eastern, and Parma its western, boundary, the Po and Lombardy sit to its north, and Tuscany is on its south.

HISTORY. The city of Reggio nell'Emilia was founded in the second century B.C. by Marcus Aemilius Lepidus at the point where the Crostolo River crosses the Aemilian Way. It was known by the Romans as Regium Lepidum. As the Roman Empire collapsed, the Goths devastated the city A.D. in 409; it was later ruled by Lombards, Franks, and then bishops. The Magyars sacked Reggio nell'Emilia in 899 and 924. In the tenth century it was made a protectorate of the Counts of Canossa; in the twelfth it became an independent commune; and between 1409 and 1796 it was under the control of the Este family.

Most of the province was included in the Cispadane Republic after the French invasion of 1796, and on January 7, 1797, in Reggio nell'Emilia's city hall (Palazzo Comunale), the red, white, and green tricolor was first proclaimed as an Italian flag. Between 1808 and the collapse of Napoleon's empire, the city was the capital of the department of Crostolo in the French puppet Kingdom of Italy. During the Risorgimento, Reggio nell'Emilia was incorporated into Piedmont in 1859 and, in 1861, into the Italian Kingdom. The province became one of the centers of the cooperative move-

ment during the late nineteenth century, and the city hosted a number of
national meetings on the subject between 1901 and 1905. Many of its
industrial and rail zones were heavily bombed during the Second World
War.

ARTS AND CULTURE. Reggio nell'Emilia's cathedral, which honors
its fifth-century bishop and patron, San Prospero, was begun in the ninth
century and has been renovated a number of times. The ruins of the Castle
of Canossa are southwest of the city. The Counts of Canossa ruled much
of medieval Emilia and parts of Tuscany until Countess Matilda died without heirs in 1115 and willed her lands to the Roman Church. During the
eleventh-century power struggle between the papacy and the Holy Roman
Empire Investiture Controversy, Emperor Henry IV came to Canossa to
beg the forgiveness of Pope Gregory VII. Gregory, as the guest of Countess
Matilda, it is said, watched from the ramparts while Henry, humiliated and
in rags, stood outside the fortress for three days and begged for papal
compassion. He received it, and promptly left to resume his assault on
Church authority. The foundations of the ruined castle date from the time
of the humiliation, although most of the structure is from the thirteenth
century. The *perdono di Canossa* (pardon of Canossa) is recalled every year
in a celebration that takes place the first weekend in September. The Spal-
lanzani Museum in the enormous Piazza Cavour contains a number of
smaller galleries, including one devoted to the Risorgimento and the anti-
Fascist resistance. The poet **Ludovico Ariosto** (1474–1533) was born in
Reggio nell'Emilia, although he is mostly associated with the Este court at
Ferrara; and the artist **Correggio** (Antonio Allegri, 1494–1534) took his
working name from his hometown northeast of the city.

OTHER CENTERS. Brescello, one of the oldest towns in the province
of Reggio nell'Emilia, is in its northwest corner. It was founded by the
Gauls and was known as Brixellum before the Romans arrived. The Romans used the town as a bridgehead on the Po and built a road from there
to Cremona. After being burned and destroyed twice, in 586 and 603, the
town was abandoned for a few centuries. Brescello contains ancient ruins,
and its Church of Santa Maria Maggiore is thought to have been the model
for the parish in Giovanni Guareschi's popular Don Camillo novels of the
1950s.

North of Reggio nell'Emilia is **Novellara,** home to the Museum of Peasant Culture and Work (Museo della Cultura e del Lavoro Contadino). Also
north of Reggio nell'Emilia is **Guastalla.** Founded by the Lombards, it
achieved importance from the sixteenth to the eighteenth centuries as a
possession of Mantua's Gonzaga family.

RIMINI

PROVINCIAL PROFILE. Area: 206 sq. mi. Population: 267,879 (province), 129,526 (city). The province has 20 communes. Rimini occupies Emilia Romagna's southeast corner and shares a border with only one of the region's other provinces, Forlì/Cesena, which sits to the northwest and to which it belonged until 1993. Northeast of Rimini is the Adriatic Sea, and the city of Rimini is Emilia Romagna's largest coastal resort. The Marche curve around the province from the southeast to the southwest, where they reach Forlì/Cesena. Wedged between Rimini and the Marche is the tiny Republic of San Marino.

HISTORY. The Roman Ariminum, Rimini was established as a Latin colony in 268 B.C. and became the eastern terminus of the Aemilian Way and, in turn, connected to the Flaminian Way that ran to Rome. The city was accorded the status of an Augustan colony. After the fall of the Roman Empire in 476, Rimini joined the Byzantine Pentapolis confederation of Adriatic cities which was centered mainly along the Marche coast. A long period of vague papal rule followed, although a commune developed by the eleventh century and the Guelph Malatesta family usurped power by the middle of the thirteenth. They ruled, eventually as papal vicars, into the early sixteenth century. After a brief Venetian occupation, Rimini was absorbed into the Papal States from 1509 until 1528 where it remained until the Risorgimento.

During the Second World War, Rimini was at the eastern end of the Gothic Line and suffered heavy damage. It was liberated in September 1944 by Polish troops attached to the British Eighth Army.

ARTS AND CULTURE. Rimini's Roman past is visible in the Arch of Augustus (27 B.C.), the oldest such structure in Italy; in the Ponte Tiberio, (A.D. 20); and in a second-century amphitheater. Rimini's Renaissance past is best exemplified in the Church of San Francesco, better known as the Malatesta Temple (Tempio Malatesta). Named for the family which ruled Rimini as papal vicars until the sixteenth century, the temple was built in the 1200s and renovated in the 1400s with a new facade by **Leon Battista Alberti** (Genoa, 1404–1472), inspired by the Arch of Augustus in Rimini and the Arch of Constantine in Rome. Its interior is graced with frescoes by a Tuscan, **Piero della Francesca**. Rimini is the birthplace of the film director **Federico Fellini** (1920–1993). His works, such as *La Strada* (The Road), *Nights of Cabiria, La Dolce Vita* (The Sweet Life), *Otto e mezzo* (8½), and *Amarcord* (I Remember), are among the most distinctive, important, and, in some ways, emblematic of Italy's cinema and society.

OTHER CENTERS. The poet Antonio (Tonino) Guerra was born at **Sant'Arcangelo di Romagna** in 1920. He is known for his verse, often in

dialect, and for work in films. Another poet, Elio Pagliarini, was born at
Vaserba in 1927.

Riccione and **Cattolica** are important beach resorts; the latter also boasts
an archaeological zone.

SELECT BIBLIOGRAPHY

Citroni, Maria Cristina. *Leggende e racconti dell'Emilia Romagna.* Rome: Newton
    and Compton, 1997.
Finzi, Roberto, ed. *L'Emilia-Romagna.* Turin: Einaudi, 1997.
Istituto Geografico De Agostini. *Emilia-Romagna.* 2 vols. Novara: Istituto Geo-
    grafico De Agostini, 1979.
Nicoli, Ottavia, et al. *Per una storia dell'Emilia Romagna.* Ancona: Società Editrice
    Il Lavoro Editoriale, 1985.
Zangheri, Renato, ed. *Bologna.* Rome and Bari: Laterza, 1986.

Chapter 7

FRIULI–VENEZIA GIULIA

REGIONAL CHARACTERISTICS. Area: 3,028 sq. mi. Population: 1,184,654. Capital: Trieste. Friuli–Venezia Giulia, an autonomous region, ranks seventeenth among Italy's regions in land area and fifteenth in population. Friuli-Venezia Giulia contains 219 communes. Gorizia and Udine are designated as metropolitan sees.

The region forms the northeastern corner of Italy. It shares its western border with the Veneto, Austria sits to its north, and Slovenia is on its east. The region is one of sharp contrasts within short distances. Friuli–Venezia Giulia is 42.6 percent mountainous, 19.3 percent hilly, and 38.1 plains. The Adriatic shore and coastal plain form the region's southern and southwestern features; much of its north and northeast is Alpine or pre-Alpine. The highest mountains are the Carnic Alps along the Austrian border, with Monte Coglians the tallest peak (9, 120 feet). In the northeast, along the Slovene border, are the Julian Alps, with Monte Mangart at (8,787 feet) and the Iof di Montasio (9,033 feet). Another important peak is the Cima dei Preti (8,868 feet) on the Veneto border. It lies within a regional nature reserve that encompasses much of the Friulan Dolomites. Friuli–Venezia Giulia's most important river is the Tagliamento, which flows from the northern mountains into the Adriatic. It forms the border between Pordenone and Udine provinces and, closer to the sea, it separates Friuli–Venezia Giulia and the Veneto. Other significant rivers are the Meduna, which flows mainly in Pordenone province until it reaches the Veneto in the southwest, and the Isonzo, which rises in Slovenia, enters Italy in Gorizia province, and empties into the Gulf of Trieste.

FRIULI-VENEZIA GIULIA

ECONOMY. Of Friuli–Venezia Giulia's 467,000 employed workers, 284,000 are men and 183,000 are women; 34.7 percent are engaged in industry, 4.9 in agriculture, and 60.4 in the tertiary sector and other pursuits. In January 1998, Friuli–Venezia Giulia had a 6 percent unemployment rate. Friuli–Venezia Giulia is Italy's wettest region, and the town of Musi on the Torre River records, on average, the nation's greatest annual rainfall. Much of the midland low areas are devoted to wheat farming; fruits and tobacco are grown along the coast. Dairy and meat products are also important. Some lead and zinc mining occurs in the northeast of Udine province near Trevisio.

CUISINE. The region's cooking often surprises, with local specialties ranging from goulash (*golas*) in the east to the prosciutto of San Daniele del Friuli in the west, which, some claim, is the finest in Italy. *Brovada*, which has been described as a Friulan sauerkraut made with turnips, is served with a native sausage, *muset*. Trieste is noted for *granzevola alla triestina*, breaded spider crab cooked with garlic and other seasonings. Friuli produces its own version of strudel, *strucolo*, often made with ricotta cheese.

Friuli–Venezia Giulia's eastern regions near Gorizia and Cividale del Friuli, the Colli Orientali del Friuli and the Collio, produce some of the region's favorite wines, the dessert wine Picolit and, most important, some of Italy's best whites, such as Tocai Friulano, Pinot Grigio, and Pinot Bianco. The Ribolla Gialla (yellow) is very popular, as are its less well-known cousins, the lemony *verde* (green) and the *nera* (red), also called *schioppettino*. The Grave del Friuli zone on the Tagliamento between Udine and Pordenone yields a wide variety of wines, although it is mostly known for its voluminous production of merlot. The red *refosco* is found farther south in the Latisana zone, where the Tagliamento rolls toward the sea, as well as in the Carso hills near Trieste.

POLENTA

5 c. water	1¾ c. yellow cornmeal
Salt	

Bring water to a boil in a heavy-bottomed 3 qt. pot and add salt. Slowly sprinkle in the cornmeal and cook for 50–60 minutes, stirring constantly. After the mixture solidifies, remove it from the pot and knead it on a wooden carving board. Form the dough into a flattened round and slice into serving sizes.

HISTORY. Friuli–Venezia Giulia was home to the Iron Age Veneti peoples until the Gauls conquered them in the fourth century B.C. Rome absorbed the zone around 200 B.C. and established Aquileia as a Latin colony in 181. Aquileia quickly assumed central importance as the chief city in the zone. In 27 B.C., Augustus reorganized the region as Region X, Venetia et Histria, with its capital at Aquileia. Christianity spread quickly through the area, and Aquileia had become a metropolitan see by the fifth century. After Attila the Hun sacked and destroyed that city in 452, the capital was transferred to Forum Iulii (or Julii), called Cividale del Friuli today (and the origin of the name "Friuli").

Friuli's location on a plain connecting Italy with the East meant that it was particularly devastated by the barbarian hordes which destroyed the Western Roman Empire in the fifth century A.D. Alaric passed through in 401–402 and returned in 408. Attila led his Huns in sacks of Aquileia and other centers. In 476 Odoacer, and in 489 the Ostrogoths of Theodoric, took their turns. As was so often the case elsewhere in Italy, the Byzantine conquest between 535 and 553 destroyed most of what was left. More invaders, Alboin and the Lombards, crossed the Julian Alps into Italy at Cividale del Friuli, on their way to establish a kingdom with its capital at Pavia. By the end of the sixth century, then, the region was divided between Byzantium, which controlled Istria, Tergeste, and the coastal lagoons, and the Lombard Kingdom, which ruled the inland area as the Duchy of Friuli. The Byzantines promoted orthodox Christianity and anchored it at Grado, whereas heretical Arianism was advanced by the Lombards before they embraced Latin Catholicism under Aquileia's metropolitan archbishop (later patriarch). In the mid-eighth century Ratchis of Udine was preeminent among the Lombard kings until 749, when his brother, Aistulf, deposed him and placed him in the Benedictine monastery of Monte Cassino. Shortly afterward, in the late eighth century, Charlemagne united most of the area as the Duchy of Istria and Friuli, and joined it with a frontier county (*marca*) that extended from Tarviso to the Drava River. Forum Iulii remained the capital, but under the new name of Civitas Austriae.

Hungarian tribes inflicted devastation on Friuli again between 899 and 951. Through the first centuries of the new millennium, Friuli was contested by the Patriarchs of Aquileia, who concentrated on the coastal areas and Istria, and by northern figures such as the Dukes of Bavaria and Carinthia, and the Babenberg Dukes of Austria. Northern Friuli consequently was affected more than most of Italy by central European feudal practices and institutions. In the south, furthermore, the expansion of Venetian power ended local freedoms for most of the area by 1420, after Venetian forces under the Udinese Tristano Savorgnan repelled a Hungarian invasion. The commander of the Hungarian force was none other than Ludwig of Teck, the Patriarch of Aquileia, who, with the Counts of Gorizia, had allied with Hungary's King Sigismund. The Venetian rule over Friuli was established, but it was not always secure. The Turks invaded Friuli from the east between 1472 and 1499. They devastated Friuli as far west as Livenza before turning back.

Soon after the Turks left, Friuli suffered again when Count Leonardo of Gorizia died. Because he was without an heir, Venice and the Hapsburgs quarreled over his lands and in 1508 went to war over them, part of the larger conflict associated with the League of Cambrai. Venice was saved through its Holy League alliance with the Pope and in 1515, the conflict ended with the defeat of the imperial forces at Pordenone. As a result, Austria held the eastern cities of Gorizia, Gradisca, and Trieste, and the Venetians retained most of Friuli, an arrangement that endured until the French invasions at the end of the eighteenth century. In 1797 Napoleon conquered the entire area, but he delivered it in January of the following year to the Austrian Hapsburgs, according to the terms of the Treaty of Campoformio. Napoleon returned in 1805 and incorporated the territory into the Kingdom of Italy, except for Trieste and Gorizia, which he included in France's Illyrian provinces. Austria reconquered the territories in

1813, and in June 1814 incorporated nearly all of northeast Italy into the Lombard-Venetian Kingdom ruled by a viceroy on behalf of the emperor. A large slice of land, roughly east of the Ausa River and including Trieste, Gorizia, Palmanova, Cividale del Friuli, and Tarvisio in the far north, remained directly dependent on the Austria Empire. Most of that territory was split into two districts, Gorizia in the center-north and Litorale in the south, with its capital at Trieste.

Italian nationalist sentiment against Vienna's presence was growing, and revolts flared across the region in 1848, although some, such as those in Udine and Cividale del Friuli, were more intense than others. In 1859 the Piedmontese and French invaded Austrian Lombardy, but their advance was halted at the Lombard-Veneto border, leaving Friuli in Vienna's grip. Shortly afterward, Italy's participation on Prussia's side in the Seven Weeks War of 1866 led to Italy's annexation of the bulk of the region. The new province of Udine, however, did not include Trieste and Gorizia, which remained on the other side of the Austrian frontier and, along with Istria and Trentino–Alto Adige, constituted part of "Unredeemed Italy," dear to nationalists as *Italia irredenta*.

Those areas were finally taken by Italy during the First World War, when Rome directed its full attention to northeast Italy, once again subject to invasion and military convulsion. The Italians used Udine city as their base of operations and took Gorizia in 1916. But in October 1917 the Italian line cracked at Caporetto, a military catastrophe that opened virtually all of Friuli to conquest by the Austrians. One year later, however, Rome inflicted a crippling blow on the enemy at Vittorio Veneto and conducted a seaborne landing at Trieste. Friuli was liberated, Austria collapsed, and the Italian national border was extended to include not only Gorizia and Trieste, but also Istria and parts of Dalmatia on the Adriatic coast. Between 1924 and 1927 Mussolini's government organized the new territories into the region of Venezia Giulia, which was separated from Friuli by the Isonzo River. Recognizing that Italy had absorbed a sizable Slovene and Croat population in the border areas, Mussolini launched a program of Italianization similar to the ones carried out in the Alto Adige and the Valle d'Aosta. Opponents were imprisoned, and some were executed. Slavic teachers were fired, civil servants were transferred out of the area, and Italian was made the only language of instruction.

The situation changed in the Second World War when, in September 1943, Italy and the Allies declared an armistice. Hitler retaliated by annexing Friuli–Venezia Giulia as Adriatisches Kustenland and launched a process of Germanization there. A powerful Italo-Slav resistance soon challenged the Nazis with guerrilla warfare. But the resistance soon split. By the end of the war the Slavic Communist movement of Josip Broz (Tito), often supported by sympathetic Italian Communist partisans, had begun to compete with the rest of the Italian resistance, and fighting broke out between the two factions. Tito's forces occupied Gorizia and Trieste after Germany's collapse in April 1945 but pulled back when the Allies secured those cities, along with Monfalcone and Pola in Istria, as a neutral zone under their occupation. They returned Gorizia to Italy and divided the Free Territory of Trieste into two zones, A and B. The former, under Anglo-American rule, extended from Monfalcone to Muggia, and the latter covered the northwest corner of Istria under Yugloslav administration. Belgrade annexed the rest of Istria, Fiume, and the former Italian holdings in Dalmatia.

Venezia Giulia remained a heated issue until the present boundary was imposed on the area in 1954. Italy and Yugoslavia cemented the arrangement in 1975 with the Osimo Accords. The region acquired autonomous status in January 1963, and a Friulan separatist movement has assumed some importance, particularly since 1990. Friuli–Venezia Giulia was integrated further into the Italian economy. Formally reintegrated into Italy, Gorizia and Trieste were grafted onto Friuli in the new region of Friuli–Venezia Giulia. Their truncated forms created an imbalance in the region, however, which gave Udine 91 percent of the land and 64 percent of the region's population. In 1968 this was addressed to some extent with the creation of Pordenone province out of Udine's southwestern territory.

RECENT POLITICS. Due to its being a volatile border area, nationalist and "irredentist" feelings that call for a return of lost territories run high in the politics of Friuli–Venezia Giulia. The List for Trieste (Lista per Trieste) has done well in local campaigns, and the neo-Fascist MSI (Movimento Sociale Italiano) traditionally has done well. Friuli–Venezia Giulia comprises Italy's ninth electoral district (*circoscrizione*). In the 1996 elections for the Chamber of Deputies, the Polo per le Libertà captured 37.3 percent of the majoritarian vote, 32.2 percent went to the Ulivo coalition, and 24.5 to the Northern League. In the proportional vote the Center-Right captured more than half the votes: the Northern League took 23.2 percent, Forza Italia gained 21.1 percent, 15.2 percent went to the National Alliance, and 13 percent to the Partito Democratico della Sinistra (Democratic Party of the Left). In the Senate vote, the Polo took 38.5 percent, followed by 37 percent for the Ulivo and 24.2 percent for the Northern League. As an autonomous region, Friuli–Venezia Giulia did not participate in the Italian regional vote of April 2000.

TRIESTE

PROVINCIAL PROFILE. Area: 81 sq. mi. Population: 250,829 (province), 221,551 (city). Six communes are in the province. Trieste is a small province which incorporates a sliver of territory jutting into the northwest corner of the Istrian Peninsula. To its northwest, the province of Trieste touches only Gorizia. The Republic of Slovenia engulfs Trieste to its north, northeast, and southeast, and the Gulf of Trieste borders the province to the west.

HISTORY. Trieste began as a group of prehistoric villages clustered around Monte Giusto. Not without resistance the Romans took Trieste during the second century B.C. and adopted the name Tergeste, perhaps from a Veneti word. The city became a Roman colony in either 100 or 56 B.C., and the Romans constructed its walls about A.D. 30. Christianity spread into the area under the Roman Empire, and by the fifth century the local bishop seems to have enjoyed great authority in what had become one of the easternmost outposts of Latin and Roman influence in the face of conquests and sacks by the Goths in 484, the Byzantines in 549 and 752, and the Lombards in 568.

Charlemagne absorbed Trieste into his holdings in 788. He earned Triestine resentment by replacing vital Latin legal traditions with Germanic ones and adopting a policy of settling Slavs in the city's hinterland. The Empire reciprocated by allowing Trieste a certain autonomy and restoring the older laws. It was a semi-independent commune briefly in the twelfth century, a status that was extinguished when the Venetians under Doge Enrico Dandolo conquered Trieste in 1202. With assistance from the patriarch in Aquileia, Trieste resisted Venice's domination, but the city finally succumbed with the humiliating Peace of Treviso in 1291, and in 1304 Aquileia renounced its claims to the territory. This did not end the rebellions, however, which continued until Venice surrendered its hold to the Hapsburg dukes in 1382. A jealous Venice repeatedly blocked Hapsburg attempts to develop Trieste as a major Adriatic port. Trieste briefly pulled away from the Hapsburg Frederick III in the 1460s, and Venice saw its opportunity. It launched a devastating blockade and siege until the intervention of Trieste's former bishop, who had become Pope Pius II. The Hapsburgs then returned with a vengeance and replied to the hapless townsfolk with the "destruction of Trieste" in 1469. To complete the misery, the Turks threatened Trieste in 1471.

In 1719 the Hapsburg Emperor Charles VI made Trieste a free port and the city rivaled, but did not replace, Venice as the chief hub of Adriatic trade. Its success warranted the opening of a stock market in 1755. Charles's daughter, Maria Theresa, added much of the city's infrastructure and launched new road connections to the Istrian hinterland and to Vienna. The city consequently took on a different shape, extending from its older quarters on Monte Giusto to fill out the lowlands and salt marshes near the port. The Triestini dubbed this new zone the Borgo Teresiano, after the Empress. Expansions continued under Emperor Joseph II in the 1780s, and the reclaimed additions became known appropriately as the Borgo Giuseppino after him. After the French occupations of 1797–1798 and 1805–

1813, Trieste had grown into the principal port of the Austrian Empire, a status further enhanced in 1869 when the Suez Canal opened and facilitated links to India and East Asia. Perhaps the city's prosperity, so tied to the Austrians, subdued the urge for union with Italy.

But Trieste remained ethnically Italian, and in the nationalist fever of the times its pro-Italian voice was ultimately heard in the literary review *La Favilla*, begun in 1836, and in the Minerva Society (Società della Minerva) of Domenico Rossetti. Rail connections to Milan were completed in 1859, but the Risorgimento wars of 1859–1860 and 1866 failed to bring Trieste into Italy's fold. The conflicts nevertheless served to intensify feelings for union on both sides of the border. The nationalist martyr Guglielmo Oberdan came to represent this sentiment. Born in Trieste in 1858, he fled to Rome and joined the Italian army. In 1882 he returned to his native city, where he planned to kill Emperor Franz Josef during a state visit. The plot failed, and the Austrians hanged Oberdan, who proclaimed from the gallows, "Long live Italy! Long live a free Trieste!" The growing irredentist sentiment persisted, however, in cultural associations and the journals *Il Piccolo* (The Little One) and *L'Indipendente* (The Independent). It soon captured the communal administration and dominated the political life of the city. In 1915, when Italy entered the First World War against Austria, Trieste's open political life was extinguished, newspapers were shut, and many irredentists were put in prison. After the Austrian collapse at the battle of Vittorio Veneto, however, the Triestini overthrew the Hapsburg administration and welcomed the seaborne Italian forces which reached the city on November 4, 1918.

Trieste became part of Italy, but the war and liberation produced a disquieting jolt for the city and its economy. Trade froze during the war, and the city's population declined from 230,000 to less than 150,000. The postwar border separated Trieste from most of its eastern hinterland customers when the nation of Yugoslavia was created from the old Slovene and Croat domains of the Hapsburgs. The decline continued into the mid-1930s, when port business fell two-thirds, a contraction offset somewhat by Italy's development of ship construction, oil refining, and pipeline traffic. Rome launched a number of construction projects as well, including a new university complex in 1940. Trieste did not suffer much physical damage in the Second World War before the collapse of Fascism in July 1943. Shortly thereafter, Allied air raids targeted the city when the Germans occupied Trieste, annexed it, and selected the city as capital of their reorganized *Adriatisches Kustenland*.

Tito's Yugoslav troops liberated and occupied Trieste on May 1, 1945, and, after a great deal of bloodshed, handed it over to the Allies on June 12. After its time in political limbo as occupation Zone A, Trieste with some of its surrounding land was returned to Italy in 1954, and the truncated province, with only six communes, was restored in 1956. After the

Second World War, Trieste was further integrated into the Italian economy with the inauguration of the Trieste-Udine expressway in 1963 and its connection to Venice in 1970. Also in 1963 Trieste was designated the capital of the newly autonomous Friuli–Venezia Giulia. In 1961 an international airport (Ronchi) opened nearby in Gorizia province; a major oil pipeline to Ingolstadt, Germany, was inaugurated in 1967; and Trieste's port facilities were expanded with Molo VII in 1970. Since the fall of communism and the independence of neighboring Slovenia and Croatia, Trieste's economy has enjoyed something of a renaissance.

ARTS AND CULTURE. The best-preserved Roman remain is the Riccardo Arch, built in 33 B.C., perhaps as part of the city walls. The name comes from the suspicion that England's King Richard the Lionhearted was held captive there in the twelfth century as he returned home from the Third Crusade. There are remains of a theater and an ancient basilica as well.

Trieste's basilica, dedicated to its patron, San Giusto, stems from the fifth century. Much of the Giusto legend is lost in history, although it is believed that he was an Egyptian who lived in Aquileia. After he refused to acknowledge pagan gods, the Romans martyred him in 303 by attaching lead weights to his hands and feet, then throwing him into the Adriatic. The basilica was built mostly in the eleventh and twelfth centuries, on top of two earlier churches, which were in turn constructed over the site of a Roman temple dedicated to Jupiter, Juno, and Minerva. It connects to the fourteenth-century baptistery of San Giovanni. Close by are the ruins of a Roman *basilica*; both it and San Giusto sit below the castle of San Giusto, which today houses a civic museum. Trieste still reflects the heterogeneous heritage of the Austrian Empire and boasts important Greek, Serbian, and Lutheran churches, as well as one of Europe's largest Jewish synagogues (built in 1910–1912).

A masterpiece of Baroque Trieste is the seventeenth-century Church of Santa Maria Maggiore, the work of the Jesuit **Giacomo Brinani** and later enlarged by another Jesuit, **Andrea Pozzo**. In the prosperous eighteenth and nineteenth centuries a number of neoclassical structures were built, such as the Church of Sant'Antonio, which sits in the center of the port area at the head of the Canal Grande, a large inlet or slip built in 1756. Trieste hosts a sailing race, the Barcolana, every October.

Still part of the Austrian Empire, Belle Epoque Trieste witnessed a flowering of literary expression manifested in the work of **Italo Svevo** (Ettore Schmitz, 1861–1928), **Scipio Slataper** (1888–1915), and **Umberto Saba** (Umberto Poli, 1883–1957). The widespread criticism of Svevo's daring 1898 novel *Senilità* (Old Age) caused him to abandon his writing career. His friend, the Irish novelist James Joyce, convinced Svevo to take up the pen again; the result was his 1923 masterpiece, *La coscienza di Zeno* (The Confessions of Zeno). For most of his life the self-taught Saba ran a bookstore in Trieste. His embrace of the classics is seen in such works as the *Canzoniere* (Collection of Lyrics, 1921, 1945). Because Saba's mother was Jewish, during the Second World War he fled Trieste for Florence, where the poet Eugenio Montale provided a place of refuge. After the war, Saba returned to Trieste. Slataper wrote in the *vociani* school (based at the Florentine review, *La Voce*) and is best remembered for his *Il Mio Carso* (My Carso). He was killed in the fighting at Gorizia in 1916. Early twentieth-century Trieste was also home to foreign artists such as James Joyce, the novelist D. H. Lawrence, and the German poet Rainer Maria Rilke, who composed his *Duino Elegies* at the castle at Duino, a resort town north of the city.

Trieste is the home of a vibrant tradition of dialect literature and theater. **Alberto Catalan, Antonio Pittani**, and **Angelo Cecchelin** founded the Triestissima theater company in 1929. One of twentieth-century Italy's most important stage directors, **Giorgio Strehler** (1921–1997), was born at Barcola, a suburb of Trieste. As a youngster, he moved to Milan, where, with **Paolo Grassi**, he founded the Piccolo Teatro (Little Theater) in 1947; presented his own plays and those of others; and directed operas at La Scala. One of Italy's chief twentieth-century composers, **Luigi Dallapiccola** (1904–1975), was born outside of Trieste at Pisino d'Istria. After studies in Trieste and Florence, his music, particularly three operas and a number of choral works, reflected the influence of Arnold Schoenberg, Alban Berg, and Anton Webern.

The *palio* (race) of San Giusto is run every September in Trieste, and the city hosts an annual trade fair in June. One of Italy's chief collections of nineteenth- and twentieth-century art is in the Pasquale Rivoltella Civic Museum. Another of Trieste's chief museums is the Arte e Orto Lapidario (Lapidary Garden), with many prehistoric and ancient artifacts as well as more recent works. In the 1850s the Hapsburg emperors constructed a palace just north of the city at Miramare, which today is a museum and a nature reserve.

OTHER CENTERS. In the tiny provincial district beyond Trieste, **Muggia** is an industrial town that boasts a distinctive Duomo. The structure dates from the 1200s and was rebuilt between 1444 and 1467 with a Gothic-Venetian facade. Muggia also hosts a principal Carnival of the region. Nearby, at **Muggia Vecchia**, are Roman ruins and a ninth-century basilica.

GORIZIA

PROVINCIAL PROFILE. Area: 180 sq. mi. Population: 137,799 (province), 37,609 (city). Gorizia province contains 25 communes. It is wedged between Slovenia to its north and east and Udine province to its west. On the southeast, at the town of Monfalcone, Gorizia touches Trieste province. Beyond the Gulf of Panzano and the Grado Lagoon, and the Gulf of Trieste to the south, Gorizia faces the Adriatic. The city of Gorizia is in the northeast corner of the province and straddles the Slovene border. It is there that the Isonzo River enters Italy. Its mouth, at the Gulf of Panzano, has been set aside as a nature reserve.

HISTORY. Gorizia's story before A.D. 1001 is largely a matter of conjecture. A record from that year indicates that part of Goriza ("little mountain" in the local Slavic tongue) was given to Aquileia and noble families, mainly Germans who were nominal vassals of the patriarch. However, they soon enjoyed authentic independent status. By the end of the fourteenth century, the counts of Gorizia requested Hapsburg protection and dissolved the last ties to Aquileia's shrinking power. They looked upon their new protectors as allies against Venice's encroachments into the hinterland. The counts failed, however, in their identification with the cause of Hungary's King Sigismund, and by the 1420s submitted to victorious Venice. The Austrians took Gorizia in 1509 and held it, with few exceptions, until the end of the First World War. In 1815 the Hapsburgs accorded Gorizia and nearby Gradisca the status of Crown lands in their empire and developed their economies. In the nineteenth-century age of nationalism, however, they launched a policy of Germanization against Italian culture and language. Perhaps the policy and Gorizia's strong attachment to the Hapsburgs caused the city to remain calm during most of the Risorgimento, although some sentiment for union with Italy could be found in the local organ, the *Giornale di Gorizia*.

In 1850 the railroad linked Gorizia to Trieste, then Milan, and finally, in 1907, to Vienna. When Italy declared war in 1915, the Austrians viewed Gorizia as their first line of defense and ordered its civilians evacuated. The Austro-Italian struggle fluctuated back and forth, and at least twelve battles were fought on the Isonzo. Although Gorizia had been reduced to a hollow shell, Italy took it for the last time in 1918 and formally annexed the city in 1921. New ethnic difficulties presented themselves at the end of the war. Although the predominantly Italian population of Gorizia welcomed the liberation, Rome also absorbed significant rural districts inhabited by Slavic populations who were not as enthusiastic. Consequently, during the 1920s and 1930s Mussolini's Fascist regime made Gorizia a focus of often brutal Italianization measures.

After the fall of Mussolini's dictatorship in 1943, Germany annexed Gorizia. A fierce resistance emerged, comprised of both Italian and Slav elements which were sometimes allied and sometimes at odds. Marshal Tito's Yugoslav forces and local partisans liberated the city at the beginning of May 1945, and ruled in an atmosphere of ethnic tension and retribution before Anglo-American soldiers undertook the occupation on May 12. In 1947 Italy formally surrendered the territory east of Gorizia to Yugoslavia, and today the border between Italy and the Slovene Republic runs just beyond the city limits. A Slovene suburb, Novi Gorica, has blossomed since the war; but the loss of Gorizia's eastern hinterland has adversely affected its economy.

ARTS AND CULTURE. An old castle on a hill dominates Gorizia. It was the fortress of the Counts of Gorizia, and the Venetians made additions to it before the Austrians took it in 1509. The city's fourteenth-century Duomo was completely rebuilt between 1682 and 1707, and again in the 1920s. Its main significance rests in its treasury, which was transferred from Aquileia when the patriarchate merged with Udine and Gorizia in 1751. Gorizia, Udine, and Aquileia share the same patron saints, Ermagora and Fortunato. Ermagora probably lived around the middle of the third century and may have been Aquileia's first bishop. An eighth-century legend contradicts this by claiming that Ermagora was baptized by Saint Mark in Rome, where Saint Peter designated him the bishop. He and a deacon, Fortunato, were martyred under Emperor Nero. Regardless of the authentic story, the two are acknowledged as the patrons of travelers, and their feast day, July 12, has been traditionally marked at Udine with a blessing of automobiles.

OTHER CENTERS. Grado was the Roman Gradus (which referred to its position as an outlying port, or "step," toward Aquileia). During the barbarian attacks at the end of the Roman Empire in the fifth century, Grado became an key place of refuge for those in flight from the interior. In the sixth century the patriarch of Aquileia transferred his see to Grado. This situation was only temporary, however, and the two cities eventually each had a patriarch, Aquileia's with close ties to the Lombards and Grado's under the protection of the Byzantines, a situation resolved at the start of the eighth century. Grado grew and prospered until Patriarch Poppone (Poppo) of Aquileia sacked and torched it in 1024 and 1042. The Venetians absorbed Grado in the fifteenth century and took its patriarchal title as their own in 1451.

Grado retains an impressive historic quarter built around the basilicas of Santa Maria delle Grazie and Sant'Eufemia. The former structure was rebuilt in the sixth century over earlier foundations, and renovated in the seventeenth. The Baroque additions, however, were removed in another renovation of 1929. Sant'Eufemia is Grado's cathedral and was established as the chief church by Patriarch Elias in 579, when Grado was still known as Nova Aquileia. Betraying the influence of Byzantium and Ravenna, the basilica boasts important sixth-century mosaic pavements, a baptistery (between the two churches), and a treasury.

Grado became one of Italy's first popular beaches and resort centers in 1873, when its healthy air was recommended by a Florentine doctor, Giuseppe Barellai. After official sanction as a health resort by the Austro-Hungarian government in 1892 and rail connections in 1910, the town evolved into one of Europe's best-known resorts. Tourist villages have since multiplied throughout the area and stretch west to the beaches of Udine province.

Monfalcone was a prehistoric settlement and then the Roman town of Puciolis before the barbarian raids under Alaric and Attila devastated it in the fifth century A.D. Lombard and Avar incursions reduced it to a small fishing village before its recovery in the Middle Ages, when the patriarchs of Aquileia developed it as a fortress. Under the Austrians, Monfalcone developed as a military port and an important shipbuilding center which continued to exist after the Italians took the city at the end of the First World War.

Across the Isonzo from Gorizia, at **Oslavia**, is an enormous cemetery and monument to those who fell in the First World War battles fought there. Another mass cemetery from the First World War and a museum dedicated to events in the conflict are southwest of Gorizia at **Redipuglia**.

PORDENONE

PROVINCIAL PROFILE. Area: 889 sq. mi. Population: 277,174 (province), 48,584 (city). The province contains 51 communes. Pordenone has a fairly regular rectangular shape. To its north and east Udine province wraps around Pordenone. On its west and south is the Veneto.

Pordenone is the capital of the westernmost province in Friuli–Venezia Giulia. Its name derives from its situation on the Noncello River, which the Romans called the Naonis. Pordenone, thus, was their Portus Naonis.

HISTORY. The Pordenone area was first settled in the second millennium B.C. and later served as a crossroads between the Villanovan/Etruscan and the Alpine Halstatt/La Tène cultures. By the Middle Ages, Pordenone belonged to Treviso, and soldiers from Aquileia sacked it in 1233. From 1278 until 1508 Pordenone was ruled directly by the Hapsburgs, although after 1420 it was an enclave surrounded by Venetian territory. The city prospered, attracting more than a few Tuscan merchants, and in the fifteenth century established itself as a production center for wool and silk textiles, paper, and ceramics. This activity accentuated problems between the city's rising pro-Venetian Guelph bourgeois class and its pro-Hapsburg Ghibelline nobles. Venice occupied Pordenone in 1508, in part at the request of the faction that supported it. But the occupation was contested, and for some time the city was ruled by the condottiere Bartolomeo d'Alviano and his family. In 1537, however, Venice took Pordenone and held it until Napoleon's invasion in 1797. Austria controlled Pordenone from 1813 until 1866, when the Kingdom of Italy annexed it.

The city developed as Friuli's first important industrial center and was the third community in Italy (after Milan and Tivoli) to harness hydroelectric power in 1888. Thanks to its location on a plain, Pordenone became the first center of Italian aviation. The nation's first flying school opened in 1910, in the Comina valley north of the city, and the nearby Aviano airstrip was inaugurated the following year. It is still used by the Italian air force and its NATO partners. On November 5, 1917, the Austrians occupied Pordenone and held it until the Italians liberated it on November 1, 1918. During the Second World War the city suffered 43 bombardments. It was liberated by anti-Fascist partisans on April 30, 1945. In 1968 Pordenone became Italy's ninety-third province when it was carved from Udine.

ARTS AND CULTURE. From the fifteenth century Pordenone was heavily influenced by Venetian styles which can be recognized in the work of Friuli's most significant artist of the Renaissance, **Giovanni Antonio de' Sacchis**, or "Pordenone" (c. 1484–1539). Some of his work can be seen in the civic museum located in the fifteenth-century Palazzo Ricchieri. Pordenone's *Madonna della Misericordia* is in the city's Duomo. Dedicated to Mark the Evangelist, the city's patron, that church was first built in the thirteenth century; major renovations extended into the nineteenth with the partial construction of the facade. The film director **Damiano Damiani** was born outside Pordenone at Pasiano in 1922. One of the principal employers around Pordenone is the Zanussi Company, manufacturer of small appliances founded by Antonio Zanussi in 1916. In the 1960s and 1970s the corporation commissioned **Gino Valle** (Udine, b. 1923) to design a number of structures throughout the city, from the Calcolo Zanussi Center to corporate offices at nearby Porcia.

OTHER CENTERS. The eighth-century Benedictine monastery of Santa Maria in Sylvis is found at **Sesto al Reghena**. Much of the complex was built between the eleventh and the fourteenth centuries, and an abbey museum contains Lombard frescoes.

North of Sesto al Reghena is **Casarsa della Delizia**, home to the Little Academy of the Friulan Language (Academiuta di Lenga Furlana). The filmmaker and poet Pier Paolo Pasolini is buried there. Although he was born in Bologna, his mother came from Casarsa della Delizia and Pasolini considered this his spiritual home, composing a number of works in Friulan.

UDINE

PROVINCIAL PROFILE. Area: 1,878 sq. mi. Population: 518,852 (province), 95,098 (city). Udine province contains 137 communes. Udine is a longish north-south province that occupies the center of Friuli–Venezia

Giulia. To its east are Slovenia and the province of Gorizia. North of Udine is Austria, and the province juts to the northwest to connect with the Veneto. To its west is Pordenone. In the south, Udine faces the Marano Lagoon and the Adriatic. Udine city was near the epicenter of a destructive earthquake in 1976.

HISTORY. Little is known of Udine before 983, when it became part of the Patriarch of Aquileia's territories. After the thirteenth century the patriarchs lived in Udine, first at the castle and then at the archiepiscopal palace. Austrian rulers intervened in 1350 and triggered a long period of internal factional struggle. The Venetians annexed Udine in 1420 and placed it in the hands of Tristano Savorgnan, the head of a local family that had suffered execution and exile under the Austrians but had allied itself with the Venetians and returned in triumph. After 1420, however, Udine experienced a long decline, the result of neglect by its new masters. Venetian rule lasted until Napoleon's conquest; a brief time under the French was followed by Austrian administration in 1814. After a revolutionary explosion and a brief independence in 1848 which ended in an Austrian artillery assault, sentiment for union with Italy increased until its achievement in 1866. During the First World War, Udine served as headquarters for the Italian forces until October 1917, when, in their march of conquest after Caporetto, the Austrians overran the city. Italy liberated Udine in November 1918.

ARTS AND CULTURE. Udine's artistic flowering of the fifteenth and sixteenth centuries did not mirror its decline under the Venetians. Construction on Udine's Duomo began in 1335 and continued until the sixteenth century. Facing onto the city's attractive central square, the Piazza della Libertà (formerly the Piazza Contarena), is the Palazzo del Comune, built between 1448 and 1456 by **Bartolomeo delle Cisterne** in typical Venetian design. Elsewhere on the piazza, in 1533 **Bernardino da Morcorte** added his *porticato* (arcade) *di San Giovanni* to a 1527 clock tower by **Giovanni da Udine** (1487–1564) and a chapel, now converted into a monument to the dead of the First World War. The clock recalls the more famous one in Venice's Piazza San Marco; the two Moors on top of the structure were added in the nineteenth century. Along with other structures, fountains, and statues in the piazza is an arch, the Arco Bollani, that the Veneto architect **Andrea Palladio** constructed in 1556.

On a hill above Udine is a Renaissance castle by Giovanni da Udine, after an earlier design by the Swiss **Giovanni Fontana** (1540–1614). The current structure replaced an earlier one, and was built for Udine's Venetian overlords after they had expelled the Patriarch to the archbishop's palace. The castle today houses the civic museum and art gallery that holds a variety of collections, among them works of the Veneto artist **Giovanni Battista Tiepolo** (1696–1770), who is well represented around Udine. His work can be seen at the Duomo, in an *Assumption* painted for the Oratorio della Purità, and in some magnificent frescoes at the archiepiscopal palace, which serves as the diocesan museum. Udine contains a natural history museum and a modern art gallery with a strong collection of local artists of the nineteenth and twentieth centuries.

Udine is the capital of Friuli's rich and lively dialect heritage of poetry, stories, and theater. **Pietro del Zocol** (1427–1504) and **Ermes di Colloredo** (1622–1692) were among the first and most popular authors in the vernacular. In the nineteenth century, Friulan musical productions by **Pietro Zorutti** (1792–1867) and **Pacifico Valussi** (1813–1893) were performed at Udine's Teatro Sociale. After union with Italy the Dramatic Institute (Istituto Filodrammatico Udinese) and other societies promoted a flowering of dialect works, such as those of **Giuseppe Edgardo Lazzarini** (1832–1883). Among painters, Udine produced **Sebastiano Bombelli** (1635–1719), one of Italy's foremost portrait painters of the late seventeenth and early eighteenth centuries. Much of his production is connected to Venice, where he went as a young man. Udine's university was inaugurated in 1978 to replace a satellite campus of the University of Trieste.

An Epiphany tradition in Udine is to light fires during the night across the plain and into the pre-Alpine hills. It is a custom shared with most of the Veneto. Higher in the mountains, fires commemorate the feast day of Saint John the Baptist. Udine's patron saints are Ermagora and Fortunato, who it shares with Gorizia and Aquileia.

OTHER CENTERS. In the southeast corner of Udine province is **Aquileia**, which the Romans founded in 181 B.C. Udine's most important city for over 1,000 years, Aquileia became one of the chief military and commercial centers of Italy, Rome's most significant port on the Adriatic, capital of Augustus's Region X, (Venetia et Histria), and later the seat of a key Christian patriarchate.

According to tradition, the episcopal see of Aquileia was established by Saint Mark. The bishop exercised authority from what is today Venice to Croatia and north into Austria; and in the sixth century he took the title of patriarch. In the last days of the Roman Empire, however, Aquileia was sacked by the Huns in 452, and in 568 the Lombards incorporated the town into their Duchy of Friuli. Byzantine power, however, moved up the Adriatic coast and forced the bishop to flee the Lombards and transfer the see to nearby Grado. The Lombards then installed their own patriarch on the mainland. Pope Sergius I resolved the schism about 700 when he established two patriarchates, at Aquileia and Grado. By the 800s Aquileia had recovered as a power that controlled the southern part of the current region as well as lands that extended into Croatia. In 1077 Emperor Henry IV confirmed Aquileia's renaissance by awarding most of Friuli to the patriarchs. The glory lasted only until the thirteenth and fourteenth centuries, however, when the patriarchs slowly began to relocate to Udine, a move that accelerated after an earthquake devastated Aquileia in 1342. Venice's conquest of 1420 ended Aquileia's independence, and eventually all of the patriarchs were Venetians. In 1751 Pope Benedict XIV suppressed the patriarchate and replaced it with the archiepiscopal sees of Udine and Gorizia.

Although its port silted and malaria conquered much of the area, Aquileia has not lost its memories of Roman and medieval splendor. Ancient houses, many with impressive mosaics, a forum, and the old port on the Natissa River constitute some of the most significant remains in its archaeological zone. Aquileia's basilica was built in the 300s by Theodore, Aquileia's first patriarch, and was reconstructed by Patriarch Poppone in the early eleventh century. Early in the twentieth century, enormous and brilliant paleo-Christian mosaics was uncovered, and others that predate the basilica were discovered in the "Scavi's" crypt.

On the banks of the Natisone River, **Cividale del Friuli** served Rome as the capital of Venetia et Histria and as an episcopal see at the end of the Roman Empire. Its privileged status continued under the Lombards, who made the city their capital in 568, and later as a free commune in the twelfth century. During the Middle Ages the city was frequently the seat of the Patriarch of Aquileia. Venice annexed Cividale in 1420. It retains parts of an old Roman wall and boasts the beautiful oratory of Santa Maria in Valle. Perhaps inspired by Sant'Apollinare in Classe outside of Ravenna, it was built in part by Byzantine artists in the eighth and ninth centuries. Cividale's cathedral, dedicated to the Assumption of the Virgin, was built in 1457, then reconstructed by the Swiss **Pietro Lombardo** (c. 1435– c. 1515) and his son **Tullio** (1455–1532). The city also boasts two important museums, the *Museo Archeologico Nazionale* (National Archaeological Museum) and the Museo Cristiano e Tesoro del Duomo, which contains the eighth-century altar of the Lombard King Ratchis and a patriarchal throne from the eleventh century. The 1976 earthquake caused extensive damage in Cividale del Friuli.

Some of the worst damage from the 1976 earthquake occurred along the Tagliamento at **Gemona del Friuli**, near **Osoppo** and **Venzone**. A prehistoric settlement, Roman town, and feudal possession of the patriarchs of Aquileia, Gemona lost some treasures forever but has rebuilt much of its cathedral, which dates from the late thirteenth century. The medieval fortress of Osoppo was one of the last holdouts to fall to the Austrians in the Revolutions of 1848. The earthquake, however, completely destroyed the structure. Another victim was Venzone, which lost its medieval walls and fourteenth-century Duomo.

The Venetians built **Palmanova**, originally **Palma**, at the end of the sixteenth century as a fortress town to defend their eastern border. As a fort it served its purpose. Though it never witnessed any important battles, Palmanova was Venice's greatest inland bastion and one of Europe's most formidable. But as a town it failed, never attaining the population intended for it. Although Palmanova was planned by Giulio Savorgnan (1510–

1595), much of the construction was undertaken by Vincenzo Scamozzi (1552–c. 1616). In 1993 Palmanova underwent a major restoration to commemorate the 400th anniversary of its foundation.

San Daniele del Friuli was heavily damaged by the 1976 earthquake, although the splendid Renaissance frescoes in the Church of Sant'Antonio Abate were saved. They are the work of a local artist, Pellegrino da San Daniele (1467–1547).

Zuglio sits in the Carnic Alps not far from the Austrian border. It was the Roman settlement of Julium Carnium and was an episcopal see until 737. Remains of an early basilica have been discovered. The area's most outstanding monument is the church of San Pietro di Carnia, which dates from the beginning of the fourteenth century.

SELECT BIBLIOGRAPHY

Annuario di Friuli–Venezia Giulia. Venice: Marsilio.
Apih, Elio. *Trieste*. Rome: Laterza, 1988.
Godoli, Ezio. *Trieste*. Rome: Laterza, 1989.
Goi, Paolo, ed. *Pordenone, una città*. Pordenone: Savioprint, 1991.
Istituto Geografico De Agostini. *Trentino–Alto Adige, Friuli–Venezia Giulia*. Novara: Istituto Geografico De Agostini, 1979.
Regione Autonoma Friuli–Venezia Giulia. *Friuli–Venezia Giulia: Compendio statistico*. Pasian de Prato: Regione Autonoma Friuli–Venezia Giulia, 1997.
Tentori, Francesco. *Udine*. Rome: Laterza, 1988.
Valdevit, Giampaolo, et al. *Friuli e Venezia Giulia: Storia del '900*. Gorizia: Libreria Editrice Goriziana, 1997.

Chapter 8

LAZIO

REGIONAL CHARACTERISTICS. Area: 6,642 sq. mi. Population: 5,242,709. Capital: Rome. Lazio is Italy's ninth largest region in land area and its third in population. The Holy See of the Catholic Church is in Rome.

Lazio is a rough rectangle that leans to the northwest. Its western coast-line faces the Tyrrhenian Sea. To its northwest is Tuscany. Umbria sits north of the region, and Marche touches it briefly on the northeast. To the east are Abruzzo and Molise, and Campania shares Lazio's southeastern border. Most of the region is hilly (54 percent) or mountainous (26.1 percent), and its eastern reaches form ranges of the central Apennines. Stretches of the coast are plains or reclaimed marshland, from the Agro Pontino and the Roman *campagna* (countryside) in the south to the Maccarese and the Maremma in the north. Plains comprise 19.9 percent of Lazio. Lakes of volcanic origin dot western Lazio, the largest being Bracciano, between Rome and Viterbo, and Bolsena, near the Tuscan border. About fifteen miles inland from the coast, the city of Rome sits on the Tiber (Tevere) River, the region's major waterway, which snakes along the Umbrian border until it fully enters Lazio and continues south to the Tyrrhenian Sea. Lazio's string of coastal beach resorts is interrupted by the important ports of Gaeta and Civitavecchia.

ECONOMY. Only 4.4 percent of Lazio's labor force is engaged in agriculture, 19.9 percent are in industry, and 75.7 percent work in the tertiary sector. Of the region's 1,817,000 employed workers, 1,173,000 are men and 644,000 are women. The region's January 1998 unemployment rate

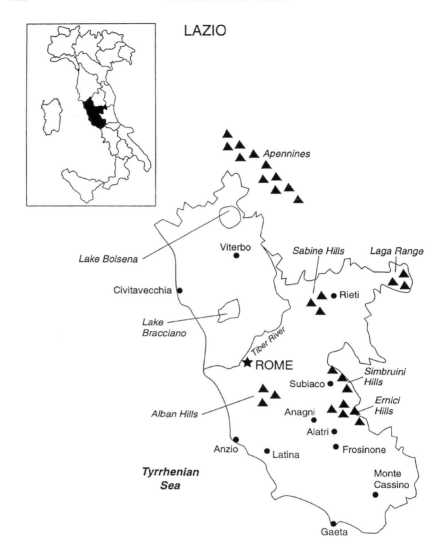

was 12.1 percent. Tourism and the government are the largest sources of employment, and Rome is Italy's premier center for both. The region is not noted as an industrial zone, although some food-processing, chemical, and pharmaceutical concerns, and paper manufacturing exist there. Lazio is also a traditional center of Italy's film industry.

   CUISINE. Lazio is an important wine-producing area, although critics believe that its production is merely a bland reminder of a bygone and better era. On some of the higher hills near the Agro Pontino the ancient Romans developed a Setine wine, named from the town of Setia (Sezze), which was said to have been the favorite of Emperor Caesar Augustus. Today the two primary wine zones are the Castelli Romani, southeast of the city in the Alban hills, and Lake Bolsena, in the province of Viterbo. The best and most famous of the Castelli Romani wines are Frascati and its sweet cousin, Cannellino. Some claim, however, that better reds, such as Fiorano or Colle Picchioni, are produced there. The Lake Bolsena area is home to a light white wine with the unsual name of Est! Est! Est! The story of the beverage is well known in Italy. A twelfth-century German bishop, Johann Fugger, passed through Montefiascone, near the lake, on his way to Rome. Throughout the trip he had ordered his servant, Martin, to precede him by a few days and sample the local wines. If one pleased the servant, he was to alert the bishop by chalking "Est!" on the inn's door. The product he found at Montefiascone was better than anything he had ever tasted, and there the ecstatic Martin scrawled *"Est! Est! Est!"* Consequently the happy bishop never made it to Rome and tippled out his remaining days on the shores of Lake Bolseno. His body rests at Monte-fiascone in the twelfth-century church of San Flaviano.

Porchetta, spit-roasted suckling pig, is very popular, as is milk-fed lamb, *abbacchio*. Roman-style tripe, *trippa alla romana*, has long been a popular staple. It is simmered in a tomato sauce with ham, garlic, parsley, and mint. Simple country dishes associated with the Rieti area include *stracciatelle*, a broth with egg and cheese, and *maccheroni a fezze*, egg pasta with meat sauce and cheese. Artichokes are Roman specialties *alla giudia*, deep-fried in olive oil and, according to tradition, introduced to Rome by its Jewish community. Artichokes also are served *alla romana*, with a touch of mint. Lazio is famous for many cheeses, especially the sharp pecorino romano made from sheep milk. Popular among the Romans is the city's version of *spaghetti all'amatriciana*, which may add hot pepper or mint to the usual bacon, onion, oil, and tomato sauce.

SPAGHETTI ALL'AMATRICIANA

2 Tbs. olive oil

¼ lb. guanciale, chopped (may substitute Canadian bacon)

¼ large onion, chopped

1 small hot pepper (peperon-cino), chopped

6 small tomatoes, peeled and chopped

½ tsp. salt (or to taste)

1 lb. spaghetti

Grated pecorino cheese

Heat oil in a pan and brown the guanciale. Remove the guan-ciale from the pan, blotting dry between paper towels. Set the guanciale aside and keep warm. Sauté onions, hot pepper, to-matoes, and salt in the leftover oil, then add the guanciale to the mixture. Prepare pasta and place in a bowl, add the sauce, and sprinkle with grated cheese.

HISTORY. In prehistoric and ancient times the Tiber was an important cultural boundary between the Etruscans, generally to the north and west of the river, and the Latins to its east and south. The early Latin peoples of the lower Tiber valley probably fashioned the name "Latium" (Lazio) from some word that they used to describe flatland. The Romans used *Latium vetus* to refer to the area around Rome proper along with the Laziali and Tiburtine hills. They called the territory stretching from there down the coast to Gaeta and the Garigliano *Latium novum* or *Latium adiectum*. Caesar Augustus considered today's Lazio as three regions: Latium, which extended south from Rome and which he joined to Campania; Etruria, in the north; and the separate zone of Sabina to the northeast.

After the fall of the Roman Empire in A.D. 476, the name of Latium was replaced by various names, such as the Marittima for the coastline between the Tiber and the Circeo promontory, and, by the sixteenth century, the Campagna di Roma for the old core area around Rome. Gaeta and the southern end of Latium Novum were incorporated into the Kingdom of Naples by the twelfth century. In the north, the zone around Viterbo and Orvieto (today a city in Umbria) was eventually referred to as Tuscia Romana.

Byzantine control over the Duchy of Rome in the sixth century was followed by alternating periods of temporal rule by the popes and by foreign powers. The close alliance with Pepin the Short and Charlemagne against the Lombards in the 700s, for example, entailed placing and protecting Rome within the bounds of the Frankish Empire. At the same time the pontiffs retained their spiritual authority. The twelfth- and thirteenth-century popes exerted their authority over the *patrimonium S. Petri*, a "papal state" comprised of what are today Lazio, southern Tuscany, Umbria, the Marche, and parts of the Romagna. The idea was to join the old duchy with the Byzantine Exarchate of Ravenna. This configuration persisted with few modifications until the Kingdom of Italy absorbed it in the nineteenth century. The papal reins, however, were rarely taut, and outlying cities achieved broad measures of de facto self-rule.

During the fourteenth century, furthermore, when the Holy See was moved to Avignon in France, the popes lost control of the whole area. The mission of the Spanish Cardinal Gil Albornoz to reconsolidate the popes' authority after 1353 succeeded in facilitating their return in 1378. Albornoz's "Egidian Constitutions" of 1357 consolidated the state and formed its basis until Napoleon's conquest over 400 years later.

The French Revolution brought Napoleon Bonaparte's invading army into the pope's domains. He invaded the Papal States in 1796 and quickly dictated the punitive Treaty of Tolentino in February 1797. In February 1798 Napoleon took Rome itself, evicting the pope and declaring a republic. The first French occupation ended within a year, however, although

Napoleon returned in 1808 and incorporated all of Lazio into France from 1809 until 1814.

With the Italian conquest of 1870, Lazio was molded into one province with its capital at Rome. The Fascists launched a reorganization of Lazio in 1923 by annexing to it the area around Rieti from Umbria. In 1927 they took more land from northern Campania, gave it to Lazio, and divided the enlarged region into four provinces: Rome, Rieti, Viterbo, and Frosinone. Mussolini set Lazio's final contours in 1934 by establishing the province of Littoria, which was renamed Latina in 1945.

RECENT POLITICS. After the Second World War, the Christian Democrats were Lazio's largest party. However, their plurality of about 35 percent of the vote, depending on the election, eroded until 1976, when the Communists replaced them. After the collapse of communism, some of its strength was transferred to the Democratic Party of the Left (PDS) with 27.3 percent of the ballots, followed by the right-wing National Alliance with 24.6 percent.

Lazio votes in two electoral districts (circoscrizioni): the fifteenth, which covers Rome, some suburbs, and Civitavecchia, and the sixteenth, which embraces the rest of the region. In the 1996 majoritarian elections to the Chamber of Deputies, the Center-Right Polo per le Libertà defeated its Ulivo rival in both—47.5 percent to 45.9 percent in the fifteenth, and 48.5 to 44.9 percent in the sixteenth. In the fifteenth district's proportional vote, the Alleanza Nazionale captured 30.9 percent against the PDS's 24.9 percent and Forza Italia's 13.4 percent. Forza Italia won in the sixteenth district with 23.9 percent, followed by the Alleanza with 23.5 percent and the PDS with 19.6 percent. Lazio votes as one unit in the Senate race. In it, the Ulivo won 46.8 percent of the votes and the Polo took 44.7 percent. In the April 2000 regional elections the Center-Left government took 46.0 percent of the votes and a Center-Right coalition led by Francesco Storace received 51.3 percent.

ROME (ROMA)

PROVINCIAL PROFILE. Area: 2,066 sq. mi. Population: 3,802,868 (province), 2,645,322 (city). The province of Rome has 120 communes. The province of Rome cuts across Lazio from west to east. Viterbo and Rieti border it on the north, and Latina and Frosinone face it on the south. The Tyrrhenian coast forms Rome's western border and Abruzzo is on the east. Much of the province is urban, with the city of Rome at its core. Within the city limits is Vatican City, an independent country of 0.15 square miles that contains the Basilica of Saint Peter and the central administration of the Catholic Church. Suburban Rome reaches at least to Tivoli in the east and to the coast in the west. At the north end of Rome's coastline is the important regional port of Civitavecchia. The central coast is crowned by the mouth of the Tiber River, which empties into the Tyrrhenian Sea at the ancient Roman port of Ostia Antica, the modern beach resort of Lido di Ostia, and near the Leonardo da Vinci airport complex at Fiumicino. Except for the Tiber valley, a thin littoral plain quickly merges into the gentle slopes of the Roman *campagna* which surrounds the city and is bordered by the Alban Hills in the Castelli Romani district southeast of the city, the Prenestini hills near Tivoli, the Sabini to the northeast, and the Sabatini to the north. Farther east the terrain acquires a more rugged character in the Sabini and the Simbruini near the Abruzzo border.

HISTORY. Rome's history is among the most profound of any city of Western civilization. In ancient times it evolved from a farming village into the capital of an enormous empire that bore its name. As the residence of the bishops of Rome, for almost 2,000 years Rome has been the seat of the papacy (the Holy See), the oldest functioning institution of the Western world. Moreover, the city was a center of the Renaissance, and for more than a century, it has been the capital of modern Italy.

Rome began in the ninth and eighth centuries B.C. as a cluster of small agricultural hamlets and vaguely in the orbit of nearby Alba Longa. Two of the villages on the Palatine hill merged to become Rome. Romans later calculated the founding date at 753 B.C., a year which is probably not far off the mark. The nascent village was ruled by kings; the first was the legendary Romulus, who plowed its original boundary, the *pomerium*. Rome still takes as its symbol the image of the brothers Romulus and Remus nursing from a she-wolf. Virgil's mythic epic, *The Aeneid*, traced Rome's roots even further back, to Romulus's ancestor Aeneas. After a voyage from Troy that took seven years, Aeneas reached Italy, married the daughter of King Latinus, and established the town. Whether Romulus or Aeneas was the first, those who followed constituted a line of Latin kings until the Etruscan people dominated Rome through the Tarquins, a dynasty begun about 600 B.C.

The Romans rose in revolt against the Tarquins and expelled them, according to tradition, in 509 B.C. But the elimination of Etruscan rule seems to have been more the result of a Latin-Greek alliance of about 475; and Rome quickly fell under the brief sway of another Latin town, Tusculum. During the fifth century, however, Rome began to conquer its neighbors. One of the first rivals to fall was Alba Longa, founded in legend by Ascanius, son of Aeneas and Creusa and, tradition says, an ancestor of the noble Julia family of the Caesars. Fifth-century Rome's greatest contribution to Western history, however, was its development of republican institutions grounded in the rule of law. It was a rigid society, divided among aristocratic patricians, plebeian commoners, and slaves. But the Romans accepted a certain human dignity as just, and codified safeguards to protect it in the Law of the Twelve Tables in 451–450 B.C. Step by step through the fifth and fourth centuries, furthermore, the plebeians accumulated privileges and status, even the ability to marry patricians, until they achieved a parallel state within a state.

A horrible sack by the Gauls almost destroyed Rome in 386, but the city soon revived, and dominated its Latin neighbors after a war that lasted from 340 until 338. By the third century B.C. Rome had mastered central Italy, and turned to secure the south against the Greeks and the Carthaginians. The former were expelled from southern Italy in the 270s, and the latter were beaten in three Punic Wars (264–146). Victory, however, came at great cost. The armies of the Carthaginian general Hannibal had devastated the Italian countryside for over a decade before his own defeat in Africa in 202. Consequently, small farmers who were the bedrock of society found themselves ruined. Wealthy Romans rubbed salt in the wounds by buying up the land from the exhausted farmers and staffing it with slaves imported from the newly conquered territories. The repercussions for republican Rome were catastrophic. Dispossessed families moved into crowded urban tenements and changed the nature of politics. Rome's society spun out of control and the Republic's last decades were marred by nearly constant civil war.

The Roman Republic died when Julius Caesar's ambitions were cut short as he entered the Senate chambers on March 15, 44 B.C. Thirteen years after Caesar's assassination his nephew and heir, Octavian, avenged his uncle's death by defeating Marc Antony at the naval battle of Actium. Octavian took the name of Caesar Augustus and ruled what was, from then on, known as an empire. The seat of vast territories, Rome considered itself the capital of the world, or *caput mundi* as the Romans are still fond of saying. Octavian's instincts were conservative and he tried to preserve as many of the old Republican ways as possible. Instead of "King" he took the title "Princeps," or "first man" of the Empire. He maintained the Senate and took seriously his responsibilities as *pontifex maximus*, the chief priest of the land. Augustus also maintained a Republican fiction when he decided that the throne would not be hereditary but handed to some chosen worthy.

The Roman state functioned reasonably well, and the empire continued to expand almost until the middle of the second century A.D. But the political instability of civil wars and abruptly deposed emperors weakened Rome while it battled foreign enemies—old ones, such as the Persians, and new ones, barbarian invaders from northern and eastern Europe. In the chaos of this disintegration, Rome's place as center of the world eroded until it came to pass that many emperors were no longer Romans. The city finally lost its formal status in A.D. 293 when Diocletian relocated the empire's Western capital to Milan. The selection of Constantinople as the Eastern hub in the 300s was just another step in this transition. The Senate, however, generally remained in Rome.

As imperial authority dissolved, the Christian church emerged to fill the void and administer the city. According to tradition, Rome's patron saints, Peter and Paul, brought Christianity to the city in the first century. Peter became Rome's first bishop before he was martyred on the cross, and Paul was executed by decapitation. They met their fates at the beginning of a history of persecutions, the worst of which came at the end of the third century and the beginning of the fourth under Emperors Diocletian and Galerius. Many Romans had grown attached to the old gods that had served their city well, and they resisted Christian evangelization. Christian ranks nevertheless swelled until Emperor Constantine's Edict of Milan legalized the religion in 313. Roman bishops even took the emperor's old title of *pontifex maximus* as they assumed the leadership of the Christian church. In 381 Emperor Theodosius I sanctioned papal supremacy over Constantinople's patriarch, and in 445 Valentinian III recognized the primacy of Pope Leo the Great (440–461) over all Christendom. When the West finally fell to the barbarians in 476, Italy's new Ostrogoth king, Odoacer, did not contest papal authority. In fact, although he identified with the Arian heresy, in 484 Odoacer defended Rome, in arguments that had arisen, against the Eastern patriarch and emperor in Constantinople.

Late and post imperial Rome suffered much of the pillage endured by the rest of Italy at the time. Alaric's sack of 410 was followed in 455 by Vandal plunder. The Lombard King Aistulf besieged the city in the 750s. In 846 the Muslims sacked Saint Peter's Basilica, then in the suburbs, but failed to penetrate the the rest of city. Three years later, however, another Muslim attempt at Rome was beaten offshore near Ostia by a combined fleet from Naples, Amalfi, and Gaeta. In 1084 the Normans took their turn at destruction. Population figures gauged Rome's decline. During the age of Augustus the city peaked at about 1 million people, an apex not again achieved until the twentieth century. Rome and the Western Empire then deteriorated together, and by the middle of the fourth century the city held about 250,000 people.

A former capital of a defunct empire, sixth-century Rome nevertheless maintained some dignity until the Byzantines humiliated it in their wars to take Italy from the Goths. Marauding Greeks nearly completed the city's abasement, and shortly after their conquest in 554 its population had shrunk to 50,000. They turned Rome into a Byzantine duchy, although most power remained in papal hands. That most of the late seventh- and early eighth-century popes were transplanted Greeks or Syrians further testifies to Byzantium's influence. As Greek power in the West dwindled, however, the Italians retook the papacy, beginning with the reign of the Roman Saint Gregory II (715–731). They preferred a Western champion and found him in the Frankish King Pepin the Short. He and Pope Stephen III (752–757) pledged mutual support, an alliance sealed when the Franks defeated the Lombards in northern Italy. Pope Leo III (795–816) crowned Pepin's son, Charlemagne, as head of a restored Western Empire in 800.

But Frankish power also withered, and by the late 800s local gangsters and warlords struggled for control of Rome. Duke Lamberto of Spoleto, for example, a claimant to the Imperial throne, was crowned by Pope Formosus (891–896). When the legal Emperor, the Frankish Arnaulf, took Rome in 896 Formosus duly crowned him as well. Arnaulf then died on his way to punish Lamberto at Spoleto and Lamberto returned to Rome, bent on revenge. Formosus had died in the meantime, an event that did not deter the Duke from exhuming his corpse and judging it guilty of collusion with the enemy. The decomposing fingers that he had employed to give benediction were chopped off, and the rest of his remains were flung into the Tiber.

Duke Lamberto was but one of many foreign conquerors who inflicted indignities on the pontiffs throughout history. In 1084 Pope Gregory VII (1073–1085) sought refuge in the Castel Sant'Angelo when Emperor Henry IV entered the city and crowned his own pope, Archbishop Guibert of Ravenna. Guibert became known as the antipope Clement III (1084–1100). The Normans came to Gregory's rescue, but in doing so undertook their own sack of Rome. The pope died in 1085 at Salerno, the guest of the Norman King Robert Guiscard. Another intervention occurred in 1303. As Pope Boniface VIII (1294–1303) prepared to excommunicate King Philip IV, of France, the monarch arranged with Roman aristocrats to dispatch a company of troops to arrest Boniface at his castle in Anagni. Liberated after his brief incarceration, Boniface died a month later and the papacy was soon moved to Avignon, in France, where it remained until 1378.

Local families and the Roman people also seized control of the city from the popes. Nobles wrested control of the papacy through the tenth and eleventh centuries and, despite arguments with imperial power and long stretches of astonishing corruption, maintained it—even reforming the Holy See on occasion. Below the papal level a popular element existed in medieval Rome's government. At various times the city was administered by senators or a podestà whom the pontiff appointed, or even one who was popularly elected. Sometimes these local governments came to loggerheads with the popes. In 1145, for instance, on the death of Pope Lucius II, the revived Roman Senate, dominated by Arnold of Brescia, insisted that the new pope submit to its temporal power. Eugenius III (1145–1153), the Pisan nobleman who had just been elected, fled the city and twice required foreign assistance to force his return. In 1347, moreover, during the Avignon period, a semi-independent state was established under Cola di Rienzo, the son of an innkeeper. The popes continued to claim authority while alternately blessing and condemning the revolutionary government. After an alliance of nobles expelled Cola from the city, he returned with Cardinal Gil Albornoz and a papal force determined to reassert papal authority over Rome and central Italy. Reinstated, Cola adopted more dictatorial methods, and in 1354 was murdered by a mob while trying to escape the city in disguise.

By the early fifteenth century the papacy was firmly reestablished in Rome and the city became a magnet of Renaissance culture, aided in part by its historic treasures that beckoned artists and in part by the financial resources of the popes and members of the Curia who supported the arts as patrons. The Ottoman conquest of Constantinople in 1453 triggered a migration of Greek scholars to Rome led by Cardinal Bessarion, who established an important school and library. Papal and episcopal commissions led to the creation of some of Europe's greatest works of art, such as Michelangelo's frescoes in the Sistine Chapel and the building of Saint Peter's Basilica.

The cultural excitement was dampened but not extinguished by the wars of the sixteenth century. The old Roman factionalism added to the mix in such embarrassing incidents as the 1526 sack of Saint Peter's by 5,000 troops commanded by no less a figure than Cardinal Pompeo Colonna. The following year the Medici Pope Clement VII (1523–1534) laid the ground for a far greater catastrophe by forming an alliance of Italian states with France against the Hapsburg Emperor Charles V. In May 1527 an imperial German-Spanish army under the Duke of Bourbon retaliated by plundering Rome. Three years later, in Bologna, a humbled Clement crowned Charles King of Italy and Holy Roman Emperor.

Rome survived, however, and rebounded as the capital of the Catholic Reformation (or Counter-Reformation) of the sixteenth and seventeenth centuries. A monumental Baroque reconstruction of the city occurred, most importantly under Popes Sixtus V (1585–1590), Paul V (1605–1621), Urban VIII (1623–1644), Innocent X (1644–1655), and Alexander VII (1655–1667).

Eighteenth-century Rome was an active center of the Enlightenment. In the spirit of the age, Pope Pius VI (1775–1799) undertook extensive land reclamation projects in the Roman countryside. Alessandro Verri (1741–1816) moved to Rome from Lombardy and published the progressive review *Le notti romane* (Roman Nights) from 1782 until 1790. France's Revolutionary government, however, offended Pius, and his administration turned more conservative and particularly anti-Jacobin. The murder of Hugou de Bassville, a French spy in Rome, brought matters to a head in 1793, although Napoleon did not invade the Papal States until the end of 1796.

No match for the invaders, the troops of Pope Pius VI suffered defeat and the indignity of the Treaty of Tolentino (February 1797), which surrendered lands in the Romagna and Avignon to the French. Tolentino's monetary indemnities, furthermore, crushed the papal finances, and patriotic resentment of Napoleon's domination ended in the assassination of the French general Leonard Duphot on December 28. France retaliated by invading the city of Rome and proclaiming a republic on February 15, 1798, when a tree of liberty was planted on the Capitoline Hill. In the long tradition of the northern barbarians, Napoleon's revolutionary troops sacked the city. When the octagenarian Pius opposed the French usurpation, Napoleon's forces kidnapped him and hauled him across the Alps. Finally, weakened by age and illness, his heart stopped at Valence in southern France. Local resistance hampered French consolidation, however, in places such as Trastevere, and at Castelgandolfo 900 men of Velletri made a stand. The brief French occupation ended on June 18, 1799, when soldiers of the King of Naples liberated Rome. A new pope, Pius VII (1800–1823), arrived in the city in June 1800.

Napoleon's forces occupied Rome again in February 1808, although Pius VII remained on the throne until he, too, was arrested in July 1809. The emperor incorporated Rome directly into his own territories, and proclaimed his infant son as its new king.

After the collapse of Napoleon's empire, Pius returned to power in May 1814, determined to squelch liberalism and the new nationalism sparked by the French wars. Dismayed by the nationalist and liberal politics of the day, the pontiff and his successors stood foursquare against the Risorgimento, although Giovanni Maria Mastai-Ferretti's election as Pius IX (1846–1878) raised hopes of a liberal pope who might favor national unity. Such hopes were soon exposed as groundless. The revolutions of 1848 and Piedmont's war against Austria terrified Pius. In November of that year he fled Rome, where a republic was declared on February 9, 1849 a triumvirate consisting of Giuseppe Mazzini and two others and defended by Giuseppe Garibaldi. Soldiers from France, Spain, and Naples soon chased the revolutionaries from Rome and put Pius back on the throne in 1850, more intransigent than ever and protected by a French guard. The days of the Patrimony of Saint Peter, however, were numbered. In 1859 and 1860 the pope lost all of his territories beyond Lazio to the new Italian Kingdom, which delivered its final blow on September 20, 1870. The Franco-Prussian War had required Emperor Louis Napoleon to withdraw his soldiers from Rome, leaving the city almost defenseless. Under General Raffaele Cadorna, the Italian army attacked and breached the city walls near the Porta Pia. The troops charged to the papal palace on the Quirinal Hill, where Pius surrendered. Pius proclaimed himself the "prisoner of the Vatican" and urged Catholics not to participate in the new government or support it with their votes.

The cold war, or "Roman Question," between the Italian state and the Holy See was resolved by the Lateran Accords of 1929. With the signatures of the Fascist Prime Minister Benito Mussolini and Pope Pius XI's Secretary of State, Pietro Gasparri, Catholicism was acknowledged as Italy's official religion and Vatican City was established as an independent state. The basilicas of San Paolo Fuori le Mura (Saint Paul Outside the Walls), Santa

Maria Maggiore, San Pietro in Vincoli (Saint Peter in Chains), San Giovanni in Laterano, and some other spots throughout the city were accepted as Vatican territory.

Mussolini assumed the prime minister's chair in October 1922 when King Victor Emmanuel III invited him to form a government. He assembled his Fascist dictatorship over the next few years. The top ranks of the regime tended to be filled by northerners, although Rome was the birthplace of at least one of Mussolini's chief lieutenants, Giuseppe Bottai (1895–1959). A partisan of the Futurist movement, Bottai joined the Fascists as a young man and became known as an intellectual and an architect of the regime's "corporate state." From 1936 until 1943 he served as minister of national education. Carlo Rosselli, born at Rome in 1899, opposed Mussolini's government, fled Italy, and organized the significant anti-Fascist organization Justice and Liberty in France. He and his brother, Nello, were murdered by French Fascists in 1937.

Rome was spared most of the physical destruction of the Second World War, although other areas in the province suffered. Velletri and Frascati were heavily damaged by Allied bombardments in 1943 and 1944, and Anzio on the coast became a major battlefield when Allied forces landed there. On June 4, 1944, the U.S. Fifth Army under General Mark Clark entered Rome and liberated it from the Germans.

The pope at the time was Pius XII (1876–1958), who was born in Rome as Eugenio Pacelli. In 1939 he was elected to the Throne of Saint Peter and took the name of Pius XII. As pope, he guided the Catholic Church through the Second World War and the Cold War that followed. Rome is also the birthplace of the conservative Christian Democratic leader Giulio Andreotti (b. 1919). Andreotti became prime minister for the first time in 1972; the end of his career in the 1990s was marred by criminal allegations that could not be proved in court. Another Roman is Massimo D'Alema (b. 1949) who served as prime minister from 1998 until 2000. He rose through the ranks of the Italian Communist Party and reached its Central Committee in 1986. After the party dissolved, D'Alema continued as a leader of the reformed Party of the Democratic Left (later Democrats of the Left) and was elected to Parliament as a deputy from Apulia.

ARTS AND CULTURE. Although Rome contains many hills, of its fabled seven, the Capitoline, or Campidoglio, stands at the old center of the city. Atop it is the city hall, or Palazzo dei Conservatori, and the Capitoline Museums. In ancient times Rome's principal temple stood there, dedicated to Jupiter and first built in 509 B.C. The hill slopes down to the southeast into ancient Rome's main forum, the Foro Romano (or Foro Repubblicano). Still visible near the bottom is the Tarpeian Rock, where the Romans executed traitors, as are parts of the Tabularium, the state records office, which was largely the work of the republican dictator Sulla. The forum extends out from the third-century A.D. Arch of Septimius Severus at the base of the Capitoline, along the Via Sacra, which passes the temples of Saturn, Castor and Pollux (or the Dioscuri), and Vesta, and the fourth-century Basilica of Constantine (or of Maxentius) until it reaches the Arch of Titus (first century A.D.), near the fourth-century Arch of Constantine and the Flavian Amphitheater, or Colosseum. The Colosseum stood next to a great statue of Emperor Nero, the *Colossus*, which has vanished. Over the centuries, construction crews picked the edifice clean of its marble facade, and bits of the Colosseum appear across the city in structures such as the Palazzo Venezia. Pope Pius VII began the job of restoration in the nineteenth century.

Looking down on the Forum from Palatine Hill are the remains of the Palatium, the rambling palace of the emperors, partly the work of Augustus and Tiberius and partly built for Domitian at the end of the first century A.D. The Roman Forum formed the most important part of a network of imperial fora (*fori imperiali*), most of which have been paved and built over. Part of the Forum of Nerva and its spectacular column survive, as do sections of those built under Julius Caesar, Augustus, and Trajan. A forum of Claudius has been lost.

Ancient Rome's physical legacy remains in other places throughout the city. Among the more important is the reconstructed Ara Pacis Augustae, the altar of peace next to the remains of the tomb of Caesar Augustus. A glass structure protects the work from automobile exhaust fumes. In the Middle Ages, the second-century tomb of Emperor Hadrian was stripped of its marble exterior and converted into a papal fortress, Castel Sant'Angelo. The great pile sits on the banks of the Tiber, and a long wall and enclosed passageway connect it to the Vatican Palace, a getaway to the safety of the fortress that serves as a reminder of the violent medieval papacy and of Clement VII's sojourn there during the 1527 sack of Rome.

The Pantheon was built in 27–25 B.C. by Marcus Agrippa and rebuilt during the reign of Hadrian as a temple to all gods. In 608 the Byzantine Emperor Phocas gave it to Pope Boniface IV, who in 609 consecrated the structure as a church dedicated to Mary and all the saints and martyrs. To honor Phocas, a commemorative pillar was raised in the Roman Forum, the last monument built there. In the 660s the Byzantine Emperor Constans II was not as gracious. Upon reaching Rome, he looked upon the Pantheon as a source of loot, and ordered his soldiers to rip the copper off of its dome.

The third-century remains of gigantic Roman baths (*terme*) of Caracalla (206–215) and of Diocletian (298–306) recall the Roman Empire, as does the impressive Theater of Marcellus. Built in the time of Augustus with a capacity of 20,000 people, its strategic proximity to the Tiber caused its conversion into a medieval fortress before the architect and artist **Baldassare Peruzzi** (Siena, 1481–1536) turned it into a Renaissance palace.

Early Christian Rome is easily imagined in many churches. Some of the most significant are the fifth-century Santa Sabina, on the Aventine Hill, and Santo Stefano Rotondo. The latter was built with material from earlier structures and in a circular design modeled on the Church of the Holy Sepulchre in Jerusalem. Other early churches include the sixth-century San Giorgio in Velabro, built on the *Velabrum*, the plain between the Capitoline Hill and the Tiber, and San Clemente, constructed in two phases over an ancient temple of Mithras. At the end of the Roman Empire the Christians built a basilica over it, and in the twelfth century yet another church rose on top of that. Santa Maria in Trastevere dates from the third and fourth centuries, and may be the oldest public Christian church in Rome. Important mosaics were added in the ninth and tenth centuries, and the structure was renovated in the twelfth.

Special status as patriarchal churches is accorded to the great fifth-century Basilica of Santa Maria Maggiore, Saint Peter in Chains (with Michelangelo's famous statue of Moses intended for the tomb of Pope Julius II), Saint Paul Outside the Walls, and Saint John Lateran, both of the fourth and fifth centuries. As the cathedral of Rome, Saint John Lateran has been the city's principal church for much of its Christian history. Across the street from the basilica is the *scala santa*, the "Holy Staircase" which Constantine's mother, Saint Helen, located in Jerusalem and transported to Rome. According to tradition, it is the set of steps that Christ descended after hearing the judgment of Pontius Pilate. Pilgrims still climb the stairs on their knees, pausing in prayer on each step.

Outside of the historic central city are catacombs, burial places for early Christians. That the long underground passages carved from soft tufa rock were hideouts is a misconception. The most extensive are those of San Callisto (Calixtus) and Santa Domitilla on the Appian Way (the Via Appia Antica). Other catacombs are found in the Via Nomentana under the fourth-century church of Sant'Agnese fuori le Mura (Saint Agnes Outside the Walls). Next to it is a church dedicated to Santa Costanza, the daughter of Constantine.

Rome lacks a strong Gothic element in its medieval art. The most noteworthy representative of the style is the church of Santa Maria sopra Minerva. Commissioned by the Dominicans in 1280 over the remains of an ancient temple to Minerva, the church was partly the work of the Tuscan **Arnolfo di Cambio** (Colle di Val d'Elsa, (c. 1245–1302). Works of the fifteenth century include the papal Chancery (Palazzo della Cancelleria) and the Palazzo Venezia in the center of the city. The Chancery was first called the Palazzo Riario and was built by a nephew of the della Rovere Pope Sixtus IV (1471–1484). It has been attributed to the Lombard **Andrea Bregno** (1418–1503) or to **Antonio da Montecavallo** (active in Rome c. 1490). **Bramante** (1444–1514) may also have worked for a time on revisions to the structure. The Medici Pope Leo X (1513–1521) confiscated it and turned it into an office building.

The Venetian Cardinal Pietro Barbo built the Palazzo Venezia between 1455 and 1467. It sits next to his "titular" church of San Marco, perhaps the oldest parish in Rome. In the sixteenth century it became the residence of the ambassadors from the Republic of Venice to the Holy See; later the Austrian Embassy moved there. The Italian government took the palace during the First World War and, from 1929 until 1943, the building seared a place in Italy's collective memory as the site of Benito Mussolini's office. From the palace's lone balcony facing onto the Piazza Venezia, the Duce proclaimed the Italian Empire in 1936, declared war on Britain and France in 1940, and harangued enormous crowds of Romans.

Sixteenth- and seventeenth-century Rome exploded in a new vigor as Italy's chief cultural center. Led by **Raphael** (Raffaello Sanzio, Urbino, 1483–1520), whom Pope Julius II (1503–1513) employed in 1508, Roman painting triumphed over the Tuscan schools. Influenced by Perugino and Leonardo Da Vinci, Raphael enjoyed enormous success in Rome. Above all, he and his workshop produced the magnificent frescoes in the *stanze*, or apartments, in the Vatican Palace. **Michelangelo**'s enormous frescoes on the Sistine Chapel's barrel-vaulted ceiling took from 1508 until 1512 to complete. He returned 24 years later, at the behest of Pope Paul III, to create the *Last Judgment* on the wall behind the chapel's altar. He finished the work in 1541.

Roman and Italian painting was changed by the arrival in the city, around 1595, of the Lombard Michelangelo Merisi, known by the name of his home town, **Caravaggio** (1573–1610). He achieved his greatest triumph in his three episodes from the life of Saint Matthew in the Contarelli Chapel of the Church of San Luigi dei Francesi. Caravaggio's employment of "naturalistic," almost pedestrian, depictions of biblical scenes (which offended the clergy at San Luigi) and his use of light and dark (chiaroscuro) for dramatic purposes influenced painting for the next hundred years. Caravaggio killed a man during a fight and fled Rome in 1606.

Two of Caravaggio's early followers were the Roman **Artemesia Gentileschi** (c. 1597–c. 1652) and her father, **Orazio Gentileschi** (Pisa, 1563–c. 1647). The most prominent woman artist of the Italian Renaissance, Artemesia was trained by her father and a hired teacher, Agostino Tassi. Tassi, however, attempted to rape her and, after a trial that condemned him to prison, Artemesia in 1612 left Rome for Florence with her new husband. Shortly afterward she painted her most famous work, the ghastly image of the biblical Judith beheading Holofernes (c. 1618). She later spent some time in London with her father and, after his death, returned to Italy and died in Naples.

Pope Julius II launched various practical urban projects, such as wall and road repair, which he entrusted to the Marchigian artist **Bramante** (Donato di Agnolo, Fermignano, 1444–1514). Bramante's most important challenge, however, was the reconstruction of Saint Peter's Basilica. Emperor

Constantine's original Saint Peter's dated from the 300s and suffered fire damage and general disrepair before Pope Nicholas V (1447–1455) undertook to replace it in the mid-1400s, although little was accomplished under him. Pope Julius began real activity, and the first stone was laid in 1506. Bramante's designs, however, were liberally interpreted, if not altogether abandoned, by later architects. Among other artists, Raphael, **Antonio Sangallo "the younger"** (1483–1546), and Baldassare Peruzzi directed the construction before Michelangelo turned to it in 1546. Work continued into the seventeenth century under the Swiss **Carlo Maderno** (1556–1629), who finished the facade in 1612.

Appointed architect of Saint Peter's following Maderno's death, **Gianlorenzo Bernini** (Naples, 1598–1680) is most associated with the final stages of its construction. Inside the basilica, over the traditional spot of Peter's grave, he built the soaring baldacchino with its twisting pillars reminiscent of the Temple of Solomon in Jerusalem. Bernini also created the nearby statue of Longinus, the tombs of Popes Alexander VII and Urban VIII, the *scala regia* (royal staircase) entrance to the papal palace, the gigantic piazza in front of the basilica, and, in the apse, the glorious explosion of the *cattedra* (throne) of Saint Peter. The Vatican City state which today contains Saint Peter's is also home to a complex of papal palaces and offices. Much of the complex has been converted into the Vatican Museums, which, taken in toto, probably form the greatest collection in Italy and the world of the art of Western civilization.

The artists of Saint Peter's joined others to adorn sixteenth- and seventeenth-century Rome with new monuments. Bramante was responsible for one of the singular Roman masterpieces of the age, the small, round Tempietto on the Janiculum Hill. It was completed in 1502 to commemorate the execution of Saint Peter, which, at the time, was believed to have taken place on that spot. Bramante's work sits in a courtyard next to the Church of San Pietro in Montorio (1481), which was commissioned by Spain's King Ferdinand and Queen Isabella to commemorate Peter's death. The church is mostly the work of the Florentine **Baccio Pontelli** (1450–c. 1492), although many other artists worked on chapels inside.

Michelangelo designed the Piazza del Campidoglio on the Capitoline Hill. Its current appearance is not too far from his vision, which was completed by two native Romans, **Giacomo della Porta** (c. 1537–1602) and **Girolamo Rainaldi** (1570–1655). Michelangelo also converted part of the cavernous tepidarium from the ancient baths of Diocletian into the Church of Santa Maria degli Angeli. Although the Neapolitan **Luigi Vanvitelli** (1700–1773) modified Michelangelo's work in the eighteenth century, the church remains one of the most striking in Rome.

Powered by his endless energy, Bernini worked in all facets of Roman artistic life. His bust of his patron, Cardinal Scipione Borghese, statues of Apollo and Daphne and David in the Borghese Gallery, and his *Saint Teresa in Ecstasy* in the unassuming Church of Santa Maria della Vittoria are among the finest works of the age. Bernini also built or collaborated on countless other churches throughout the city. His favorite was the oval Sant'Andrea al Quirinale, across the street from the Palazzo Quirinale. Bernini and many others worked on the palace, which was a papal residence before the Italian royal family took it for their use in 1870. Since 1946 the Quirinale has served as the official home of the presidents of Italy.

Antonio Sangallo "the Younger," Michelangelo, and Giacomo della Porta all worked on the Palazzo Farnese, one of Italy's outstanding Renaissance achievements. The building passed from the Farnese family to the Spanish ruling house and later became the Roman residence of the Neapolitan Bourbons. It is today the French Embassy. Sangallo created the nearby Farnesina Palace as well. Another exceptional Renaissance palace was the Villa Giulia, built for Pope Julius III (1550–1555). Its principal architect was the Emilian **Giacomo Barozzi**, or **"Vignola"** (Vignola, 1507–1573), while della Porta and the Tuscans **Giorgio Vasari** (Arezzo, 1511–1574) and **Bartolommeo Ammannati** (Settignano, 1511–1592) also worked on the structure. Today the villa houses one of Rome's largest museums specializing in Etruscan art.

Nearby is another museum, the Villa (or Galleria) Borghese, built by **Flaminio Ponzio** (c. 1559–1613) and the Dutch artist **Ivan van Santen** (called **Vasanzio**; 1550–1621) and expanded in the eighteenth century. Its Borghese family art collection, purchased by the Italian government in 1902, includes Bernini's sculptures *Apollo and Daphne* and *David* mentioned earlier, and the famous reclining figure of Napoleon's sister Paulina Borghese by the Veneto artist **Antonio Canova** (1757–1822). Canova served in both the papal and the French courts, a testament to his artistic ability if not to his political scruples. The villa's picture gallery also boasts an impressive collection of Caravaggio's works. Another noteworthy museum converted from a palace is the Galleria nazionale d'Arte Antica (National Gallery of Ancient Art), in the seventeenth-century Palazzo Barberini, built for members of the papal family by, among others, Maderno, Borromini, and Bernini.

Vignola launched the construction of a key symbol of the Catholic Reformation, the Jesuit Church of the Gesù. A follower of Leon Battista Alberti and a student of the ancients, Vignola composed an influential treatise, *The Five Orders of Architecture*, which revived the classical ideas of Vitruvius. After Vignola's death, Giacomo della Porta finished the Gesù. Its severity was later softened by the delightful frescoes of **Giovanni Battista Gaulli,** known as **"Baciccia"** (Genoa, 1639–1709) and by the spectacular tomb of Saint Ignatius Loyola, the founder of the Jesuit order. The Jesuit artist **Andrea Pozzo** (Trent, 1642–1709) is credited with the tomb.

Alexander VII commissioned the artist **Francesco Borromini** (Francesco Castelli, (1599–1667) to complete the Church of Sant'Agnese al Circo

Agonale, or in Agone, in the Piazza Navona. Pope Innocent X is buried in the crypt. The piazza began in ancient times as a stadium, the Emperor Domitian's Circus Agonalis, and the contours of the track remain plainly visible. Bernini's magnificent Fountain of the Four Rivers dominates the middle of the square. Among Borromini's other works is the Church of San Carlino alle Quattro Fontane, one of his finest, and his last creation before he committed suicide.

A central figure in eighteenth century Roman building was the Florentine **Ferdinando Fuga** (1699–1781). His career in Rome benefited when a fellow Tuscan, Lorenzo Corsini, was elected as Pope Clement XII. In 1731 Fuga was appointed architect to the papal palaces and worked on the expansion of the Palazzo Quirinale, now Italy's presidential residence. He was also responsible for the Palazzo Consulta, across the piazza from the Quirinale. Among his most acclaimed works was the facade of the ancient Basilica of Santa Maria Maggiore. Fuga ended his career in Naples. Another key eighteenth-century figure was a native Roman, **Nicola Salvi** (1697–1751), best remembered for one of the city's signature sites, the Trevi Fountain. Unfortunately, the artist did not live to see his project's conclusion.

The end of papal rule in Rome and its new status as national capital in 1870 launched a construction boom tied to the city's expansion and the erection of government buildings and monuments. One of the grandest, or most garish, is the Palazzo di Giustizia, begun in 1889 and finished in 1910 by the Perugian **Guglielmo Calderini** (1837–1916). To commemorate King Victor Emmanuel II and Italy's nationhood, the government chose a location next to the Capitoline Hill for the construction of Rome's chief modern monument, the Altare della Patria (Altar of the Fatherland) or Vittoriale (of Victor Emmanuel II). Designed and begun in 1885 by the Marchigian **Giuseppe Sacconi** (1854–1905) and finished in 1911, Romans affectionately refer to the gigantic pile as the "Typewriter" or the "Wedding Cake," a sobriquet attributed to British occupation troops during the Second World War.

Along with new structures, the new Italian Kingdom acquired a number of old Roman palaces for its use. The Montecitorio Palace became the site of the Chamber of Deputies. A seventeenth-century structure that replaced an earlier Colonna palace, the Montecitorio was expanded to make room for government business by the Sicilian **Ernesto Basile** (1857–1932). Next to the Chamber of Deputies is the Palazzo Chigi, a seventeenth-century edifice built for the Aldobrandini family before another papal family, the Odescalchi, acquired it. It became the Ministry of Foreign Affairs in the 1920s, and Mussolini used it as well before he moved his offices to the Palazzo Venezia. Today it houses the prime minister's complex. The Renaissance Palazzo Madama was built in the sixteenth century for the Medici, and since 1871 has been the home of the Italian Senate.

Mussolini changed the city's face by means of his construction of usually colossal structures and projects intended to recall Rome's imperial heritage and to remind everyone of his own regime. His chief architect, **Marcello Piacentini** (Rome, 1881–1960) was responsible in whole or in part for many of the most grandiose endeavors. Among his achievements are the Via della Conciliazione, a monumental avenue running from the Tiber to the Vatican, opened in 1937 to commemorate the reconciliation of Italy and the Catholic Church through the 1929 Lateran Treaty. Piacentini also led in the creation of the University of Rome's relocated campus and in the Esposizione Universale di Roma (or EUR), south of the city. Intended as a world's fair for 1942, a collection of stark and defiant structures were built there before the Second World War cancelled the celebration. Today they form the nucleus of an upscale suburb, and Piacentini's buildings sit, sometimes incongruously, next to modern skyscrapers. One of Piacentini's chief collaborators at the University and on EUR was **Giuseppe Pagano** (Trieste, 1896–1945). His disillusion and later opposition to the Fascist regime led to his arrest and death in the German camp of Mauthausen.

Fascism is recalled in a small museum in the Via Tasso near Saint John Lateran. There, in 1943 and 1944 Mussolini's henchmen and their Nazi overlords transformed a nondescript apartment house into torture chambers for use against the regime's enemies. The grisly quarters remain almost unaltered to remind everyone of one of the saddest chapters in Italy's history.

In the 1990s alteration began on another of Mussolini's projects, the Via dei Fori Imperiali, a triumphant boulevard connecting the Colosseum and the Piazza Venezia. Underneath the street are the remains of Rome's ancient forums and the government has embarked a gigantic project of excavation and preservation.

One of the chief figures of Roman painting in the twentieth century was the Greek-born **Giorgio De Chirico** (1888–1978), who lived there primarily from 1918 until 1924 and from 1947 until his death. The works of this son of Italian Levantines who had fled the Ottoman Empire reveal his study of the world of myth and the philosophy of Friedrich Nietzsche.

Rome's literary heritage is distinguished by authors and writers who came to the city and others who were born there. The city's intelligentsia achieved an institutional structure in the seventeenth century with Prince **Federico Cesi**'s *Accademia dei Lincei* (Academy of the Lynxes, 1603) and the "Arcadian" school under the patronage of Sweden's exiled **Queen Christina**. She arrived in Rome in 1655 and operated the city's most glittering salon until her death in 1689. The Arcadia, however, survived her and united writers and poets across Italy. Rome's first newspaper, the *Diario Ordinario* (Workday Diary), began publication in 1716.

The University of Rome's roots reach back to the endeavors of Pope Boniface VIII at the end of the thirteenth century and to Renaissance figures such as **Leonardo Bruni** in the fifteenth. The old Palace of the Archiginnasio (or Sapienza) was renovated by della Porta, and Borromini added the Church of Sant'Ivo with its distinctive dome said to have presaged the Rococo style. In the 1930s Benito Mussolini moved the university to its present location near the San Lorenzo quarter. Among the university's scholars was the humanist **Lorenzo Valla** (1407–1457), a native of Rome and a student of Latin. His 1444 six-part work on the beauty of the language (*Elegantiae Linguae Latinae*) was an influential text on the subject. His interest in the history of Latin led to his discovery that the "Donation of Constantine," a document that justified papal claims to temporal power, was a forgery.

Among modern writers, **Giuseppe Gioacchino Belli** (1791–1863) holds a special place as Rome's greatest dialect poet. His sonnets, often gritty and despairing, nevertheless ring as tributes to the common people. A statue of him stands at the entrance to the popular Trastevere quarter. The *crepuscolare* poet **Sergio Corazzini** (1886–1907) was also a Roman. His works reflect the despair of a sickly youth who found small pleasures in the immediate world around him.

One of Italy's chief twentieth-century poets, **Giuseppe Ungaretti**, was born in Egypt in 1888 but spent most of his career in Rome as a journalist and an official in the Foreign Ministry. In 1942 he secured a position as professor of modern literature at the University of Rome. Ungaretti was purged after the fall of Fascism, but the faculty voted to retain him as a colleague. He died in 1970 and is buried in Rome.

The writer **Elsa Morante** (1918–1985) was a native of Rome. Her first novel, *Menzogna e sortilegio* (House of Liars), won critical acclaim and the 1948 Viareggio Prize. Fame eluded Morante, however, until her *L'Isola di Arturo* (Arthur's Island) won the Strega Prize in 1957. Her 1974 work *Storia* (History) was an international success set in war-torn Italy. In 1941 Morante married the novelist **Alberto Moravia**, from whom she later separated. Moravia (1907–1990) was also a Roman. Born Alberto Pincherle, he produced works that often dealt with psychological and sexual themes, beginning with *Gli indifferenti* (The Indifferent, 1929), perhaps his greatest work, and with social ideas, such as the acclaimed *La Ciociara* (1957), which director Vittorio De Sica made into the Academy Award-winning film *Two Women* (1961).

Rome's theatrical tradition has given Italy important actors, many of whom are closely identified with the city. **Aldo Fabrizi** (1906–1990), born in Rome, is best remembered for his portrayal of the priest in Roberto Rossellini's neorealist classic *Roma, città aperta* (Open City, 1945). **Alberto Sordi** (b. 1920) is a native of Rome. One of the most recognized Italian comic actors, Sordi started in variety shows and radio after winning a competition to dub Stan Laurel's voice for Italian films. His subsequent cinema career is distinguished by work with Federico Fellini and his own directorial ventures. The actress **Sophia Loren** was born in Rome in 1934, but spent most of her youth in the Naples area. Early cinema success in such films as Vittorio De Sica's *L'Oro di Napoli* (The Gold of Naples, 1954) established her as one of Italy's top stars and later an artist of global renown.

Rome is the birthplace of a number of significant film directors. The early filmmakers **Augusto Genina** (1892–1957) and his cousin **Mario Camerini** (1895–1981) were born in Rome. **Alessandro Blasetti** was born there in 1900. His first film, *Sole* (Sunshine, 1929) was a critical success, and some of his works of the 1930s prefigured the postwar neorealist style. Roberto Rossellini (1906–1977), told a story of his native city in *Roma, Città Aperta* (1945), a film that established neorealism as a major current in the Italian cinema.

Early Roman music is distinguished by figures such as **Pietro Trapassi** (1698–1782). The adopted son of the writer **Gian Vincenzo Gravina** (1664–1718), Trapassi is better known as "Metastasio." His librettos were used by the composers George Frederick Handel and Wolfgang Amadeus Mozart, among others, and constitute important treatises on the meeting of drama and music that influenced the foundations of opera.

OTHER CENTERS. Many towns and centers of historic importance dot the countryside around Rome. Abundant evidence of the Etruscans remains throughout the city and province. **Palestrina**, for instance, east of the city, began as the Etruscan town of Praeneste. To the northwest, toward the Tyrrhenian coast, is **Cerveteri**, the early Etruscan site of Kysrj (or Kysry) which the Romans later knew as Caere. An ally of Carthage, it extended its control as far as Corsica around 540 B.C. but was sacked by Greek Syracusans in 384 and ultimately absorbed into the Roman dominion. An enormous network of necropolises in Cerveteri testifies to its Etruscan past. On the nearby coastline are more tombs at Kysrj's port, Pyrgi. Many of the treasures unearthed at Cerveteri are in a museum housed in a castle of the Ruspoli family, and other items have been transferred to the Villa Giulia at Rome and the Vatican.

Another area of Etruscan rule is the Castelli Romani to the city's south, where **Castel Gandolfo, Frascati, Albano Laziale, Velletri**, and **Grottaferrata** are some of the major towns. The area and its famous wines have attracted Romans since ancient times. Iron Age settlements there date from the ninth century B.C., and the Etruscans took the area and its imposing hilltop positions which dominated the Sacco River valley and the route to the Greek settlements in Campania. In 431 B.C. the Romans extended their authority into the area and heavily fortified it. After the civil wars at the end of the Republic, (44–31 B.C.) the area lost its military significance and acquired a more pleasant reputation. Tusculum, near Frascati, was the birthplace of Cato the Censor; Emperor Antoninus Pius was from Lanuvio; and Velletri was the ancestral home of the Octavia, the family of Augustus. At Grottaferrata is the Greek monastery of Saint Basil. It was established in 1004 by Saints Nilo and Bartholomew of Rossano, on the ruins of an ancient villa. Cardinal Giuliano della Rovere, the future "warrior pope" Julius II, fortified the monastery in the 1470s.

Renaissance princes, both secular and ecclesiastical, constructed villas throughout the Castelli Romani. Among the most noteworthy are the Villa Mondragone, begun in 1570 and expanded in the early seventeenth century by Cardinal Scipione Borghese, and the palace of Cardinal Pietro Aldobrandini, built between 1598 and 1604 by Giacomo Della Porta and two Swiss architects, Carlo Maderno and Giovanni Fontana (c. 1634–1714). Maderno also worked on Castel Gandolfo, which Urban VIII established as the papal summer retreat in 1629. It was extensively rebuilt in the twentieth century under Pope Pius XI (1922–1939). Castel Gandolfo is also the site of the seventeenth-century Church of San Tommaso di Villanova by Gianlorenzo Bernini.

Another significant concentration of villas and castles is found around **Lake Bracciano**. There the structures tend to be slightly older than their cousins in the Castelli Romani. But perhaps the most famous of all the villas are not in the Castelli Romani nor on the shores of Lake Bracciano, but east of Rome, at **Tivoli**, in the Tiburtini Mountains. Many leading personalities of ancient Rome—Julius Caesar, Augustus, Horace, and Sallust, among others—maintained residences there. The grandest belonged to Emperor Hadrian and was built on the banks of the Aniene River and waterfalls. The remains of the palace and a number of temples are considered by many to be among the most magnificent in Italy. Not far from Hadrian's palace is the equally famous Villa d'Este. Established as a Benedictine convent, it was taken over in 1550 by Cardinal Ippolito II d'Este. His architects, principally the Neapolitan Pirro Ligorio (c. 1500–1583), constructed stupendous gardens with a spectacular collection of fountains.

Farther up the Aniene, at the eastern end of the province of Rome, is **Subiaco**. Originally the site of one of Nero's villas, Subiaco became a place of refuge and penance for Saint Benedict. Born around 480 of an aristocratic family at Norcia (Nursia), he settled in a small grotto, the *sacro speco* (holy cave), located on a hill outside of Subiaco. After arguments with a local priest, Benedict left and went on to found other monasteries, most notably Monte Cassino, which is today in the province of Frosinone. After Benedict's departure from Subiaco, an enormous monastery was built on top of the cave, although the *sacro speco* still exists within it. A bit lower down the mountain is a monastery, first dedicated to Saint Sylvester but now honoring Benedict's sister, Saint Scholastica. The entire slope is dotted with the huts of Benedict's followers.

Along the coast, Rome's beaches are dotted with many notable places. One of them is **Civitavecchia**, a port that Emperor Trajan built along the Aurelian Way. Situated at the northern end of the province, where the Tolfa Mountains reach the sea, it was intended as a harbor more defensible than Ostia and one unhampered by the Tiber's floods. First known as Centum

Cellae (later Centocelle), it was also popular as a thermal spa. The fall of the Roman Empire signaled the end of Roman naval protection, and the city endured frequent attacks from Ostrogoths, Byzantines, and Saracens. A particularly furious assault by Muslim pirates in 828 left the port ruined and the city almost deserted. At the end of the ninth century, however, some refugees returned, although their reconstruction amounted to a few hovels around the old port. Anything resembling a true revival had to wait. Papal control of Civitavecchia, nonetheless, had already begun to be felt in the seventh century, and continued until the nineteenth.

By the sixteenth century the revitalized Civitavecchia became home both to the papal fleet and to an imposing fortress, begun by Bramante about 1502 and continued by the Florentine Antonio da Sangallo "the Younger." Michelangelo also worked briefly on it. The city attained its greatest prosperity in the seventeenth century, when it rivaled the ports of Livorno and Genoa. Bernini built a shipyard (*arsenale*) in Civitavecchia, but it was destroyed during the Second World War along with much of the port area. Civitavecchia became part of Italy on September 16, 1870, when detachments of the Royal Navy, the *Regia Marina*, docked there in the takeover of the Papal States. It remains a lively regional port noted for its connections to Sardinia and Corsica.

Rome's urban sprawl extends to the Tyrrhenian coast. Close to the mouth of the Tiber is the city's major airport, Leonardo Da Vinci, in the town of **Fiumicino**. Nearby is the old port of Rome, **Ostia**, or Ostia Antica. Begun in 338 B.C., it protected the Tiber's entrance into Rome and quickly grew into an important city. After the fall of the Empire, however, the port slipped into decay, the harbor silted, and it reverted to a nearly deserted malarial swamp. Today, much of Ostia's Roman plan can still be appreciated, and the extent of its excavations is surpassed only by Pompeii. The resurfaced city runs for about three-quarters of a mile on either side of a Roman artery, the Decumanus Maximus. The Ostiense Museum houses many of the town's unearthed artifacts and artworks.

At the southern end of Rome's coastline are **Anzio** and **Nettuno**. Anzio was developed by the Romans as a port but it fell into disuse by the Middle Ages. It was revived in the sixteenth and seventeenth centuries by the pontiffs and the current structures were built under Innocent XII in 1695. Nettuno may have been established by the Saracens. It is home to the Torre Astura, a waterfront stronghold constructed in 1193 over the ruins of an ancient villa. Even grander is Nettuno's *forte*, the largest fortress between Gaeta and Civitavecchia. Built at the end of the fifteenth century for the Borgia Pope Alexander VI (1492–1503), it is presumed to be the work of Antonio da Sangallo the Elder. Both towns suffered extensive damage from the Allied seaborne landing there and subsequent battle which began on January 22, 1944. German forces of Field Marshal Albert Kesselring trapped General John Lucas's Allied units on the beach. The area is now home to large cemeteries which commemorate the battle and those who fell there.

Palestrina's sixth-century B.C.. roots recall the Etruscans, although it is for the gigantic Roman temple, or sanctuary, of Fortuna Primigenia that the town is best known. Built in the second and first centuries on four hillside terraces, the ancient pile was the home to a principal Roman oracle. On top of everything is the imposing palace of the Colonna and Barberini. A National Archeological Museum preserves many of the temple's treasures, particularly the magnificent mosaic depicting a flood of the Nile River. The Counter-Reformation musician and composer, Giovanni Pierluigi da Palestrina, was born there about 1525. Thanks to the election of the bishop of Palestrina as Pope Julius III, the composer was appointed choirmaster of Rome's prestigious Capella Giulia (1551). He moved on to San Giovanni in Laterano (1555) and Santa Maria Maggiore (1561), and ended his career at Saint Peter's Basilica. He is remembered for his sacred music.

FROSINONE

PROVINCIAL PROFILE. Area: 1,251 sq. mi. Population: 492,184 (province), 46,243 (city). Frosinone province contains 91 communes. It sits diagonally at the southeastern end of Lazio. Along its south-southwest is Latina. Its northwest border is shared with Rome. To Frosinone's southeast are the regions of Campania and Molise, and Abruzzo faces it on the northnortheast. The province is generally hilly and is mountainous in some spots. The Simbruini and Ernici ranges separate it from Abruzzo, and the more gentle Ausoni and Aurunci lead into Latina. There are a few river valleys, particularly that of the Sacco, which cuts across the territory from Rome, then flows into the Liri toward Campania. Part of a nature reserve, the Parco Nazionale d'Abruzzo lies in Frosinone province.

HISTORY. Frosinone sits on a hill overlooking the Cosa River and takes its name from Frusino, a town of the Volscian people. The Romans annexed it in 386 B.C. and connected it to the capital along the Casiline Way. Frosinone is traditionally known as the center of the Ciociaria, an agricultural zone immortalized in Alberto Moravia's 1957 novel *Two Women* (*La ciociara*) and Vittorio De Sica's Academy Award–winning film of the same title. This reputation changed during the Second World War, when it suffered extensive damage, and during the 1970s, when it became more industrial. As a result of the 1927 Fascist administrative reform, Frosinone city remains a *primus inter pares* among such older regional centers as Sora, Alatri, Anagni, and Monte Cassino.

ARTS AND CULTURE. A long list of sacks and destructions by barbarians from the fall of the Roman Empire until the Second World War have taken a sad toll on Frosinone's patrimony. Almost nothing is left of its past except for some remains of a Roman amphitheater, a Gothic gate, and parts of its Duomo, dedicated to the Assumption of the Virgin.

OTHER CENTERS. Frosinone province is home to some of Italy's most important religious centers. The eleventh-century abbey of Casamari, outside of **Veroli,** mirrors that of Fossanova. Begun by the Benedictines in 1035, it was given to the Cistercians, who totally rebuilt it after 1140 in a Gothic style recalling their Burgundian roots.

Carpineo is the birthplace of Pope Leo XIII (1810–1903). Born Gioacchino Pecci, he led the Holy See from his election in 1878 until his death. He is best remembered for his encyclical *Rerum Novarum* (1891), which sympathized with the plight of modern workers in their struggle against capitalist exploitation.

The Lombard policy of promoting monasticism bore early fruit in the establishment of **Monte Cassino** at the southeast end of Frosinone province. An Umbrian and then a Samnite settlement before it became known as a center of Western Christendom, the monastery was established in 529 by Benedict of Norcia, the patron saint of Europe. At Cassino, Benedict composed his "Rule," which became the basis for much of Latin monasticism. The complex suffered devastation through frequent sacks and has been patched together and rebuilt often. Napoleon's troops plundered it in 1799. But Cassino's most wrenching days came in the Second World War, when its magnificent location as a hilltop fortress made it a prime target on the Gustav Line. In the winter of 1943–1944, when its German defenders refused to surrender the monastery, Anglo-American bombers pulverized it. The Benedictines rescued some of Monte Cassino's treasures before the apocalypse and, after the war, rebuilt the place.

Not far from Frosinone is the ancient city of **Alatri,** a well-preserved place on the slopes of the Ernici chain of mountains. Alatri boasts ancient walls and an acropolis whose temple provided the foundation for the Duomo. A substantial medieval development is evidenced in the city's Le Piagge quarter. The Church of Santa Maria Maggiore reflects Alatri's medieval character as well. Last renovated in the thirteenth century, the church houses the wooden *Madonna of Constantinople*, a masterpiece of Romanesque sculpture.

Anagni is another notable city in the province. Traces of cylopean, Roman, and Byzantine cultures survive there, and the town was the religious center of an alliance of cities, the Nomen Hernicum, at the beginning of Rome's history. But it is for its papal administration that Anagni is best remembered. By the twelfth century it was a key place for transacting papal affairs. Much of the politics behind the Lombard League and victory over the German Emperor Frederick I Barbarossa in 1176 was conducted there. Part of the town's importance stemmed from its status as base for the noble

Caetani clan, one of whose sons, Benedetto, who became Pope Boniface VIII (1294–1303). Known for his insufferable vanity as well as for his promotion of the concept of papal power in both the temporal and spiritual domains, he issued a bull, *Unam Sanctam* (1302), that claimed authority over all Christian rulers and prompted political trouble with France. In 1303 Guillaume de Nogaret and the Roman aristocrat Sciarra Colonna were sent to Anagni as envoys of King Philip IV of France. They roused Pope Boniface from his bed, slapped him (or so the story goes), and briefly imprisoned him. Soon after the fracas Boniface died, it is said, of humiliation, as did pontifical claims to supremacy on earth.

Much remains of Anagni's medieval past. Its Cathedral of Santa Maria was built on the ruins of an earlier church and an even earlier temple, perhaps to Ceres. Bishop Peter launched the current edifice in the eleventh century, and it is the work of Lombard architects. With its crypt of San Magno and rich Cosmatesque decorations, the cathedral is one of the finest Romanic Gothic buildings in Italy. Nearby are the twelfth-century Palazzo Comunale and the thirteenth century Papal Palace, the scene of Pope Boniface's disgrace.

Northeast of Frosinone, near the Abruzzo border, is **Sora**, another old regional center which occupies a strategic spot above the Liri River at Monte San Casto. A medieval castle there was rebuilt by Lombard engineers in the sixteenth century. In the adjacent countryside stands the Church of San Domenico. It was built over the remains of a Roman villa, the birthplace of Cicero (106–43 B.C.), a senator, writer, and orator, and one of the chief figures of late Republican Rome. The film director and actor Vittorio De Sica (1901–1974) was born at Sora. He bridged the gulf between popular comedic and romantic fare, starring in "Cary Grant" roles and directing serious projects, often in collaboration with Cesare Zavattini. His *Ladri di biciclette* (The Bicycle Thief, 1947) and *Umberto D* (1952) are classics of the Italian cinema.

The film star Marcello Mastroianni (1923–1996) was a native of **Fontana Liri**. His career began on the stage under Luchino Visconti, and his first film was Alessandro Blasetti's 1941 *La Corona di Ferro* (The Iron Crown). Mastroianni's appearances in Federico Fellini's *La Dolce Vita* (The Sweet Life, 1960) and *Otto e Mezzo* (8½, 1963) guaranteed for him a secure place in the history of the art.

Southeast of Frosinone is **Aquino**, the Roman Aquinum, where the poet Juvenal (c. 60–after A.D. 127) was born, as was one of the most important philosophers of medieval Christianity, Saint Thomas Aquinas (1226–1274). Born of a noble family outside the town at the fortress of Roccasecca, Aquinas studied at nearby Monte Cassino, beginning his spiritual and intellectual journey toward the reconciliation of reason and faith, of Aristotle and Christianity. He explored these issues in his *Summa contra Gentiles* and the *Summa Theologiae*. Thomas's *De Regimine Principum*, another of his major works, dealt with medieval Christian politics. If Thomas walked the streets of Aquino today, he still might recognize a few buildings. The Church of Santa Maria della Libera, for example, was built by his ancestors partly, from the remains of a Roman temple to Hercules the Liberator.

LATINA

PROVINCIAL PROFILE. Area: 869 sq. mi. Population: 505,846 (province), 111,679 (city). The province contains 33 communes. Latina is a long, diagonal province that hugs the Tyrrhenian shoreline from the Roman border near Nettuno and Anzio all the way down to Campania, where the Garigliano River forms a natural border. To Latina's north and east are Rome and Frosinone provinces. Much of the northern half of Latina consists of the reclaimed Pontine Marshes (Agro Pontino). More hilly terrain is found in the southern part. The coastline is dotted with villas and resorts, and is broken by two rocky promontories at San Felice Circeo and Gaeta.

Part of the shore around Mount Circeo comprises a national park established in 1934. Many feel that San Felice Circeo, with its cliffs and grottoes, is the best beach in the area. It forms part of Circeo National Park, the only one entirely in Lazio. It is also an ancient site. Seventy-thousand-year-old Neanderthal remains have been discovered there, and parts of walls and a fourth-century acropolis remain. In legend, it was the spot from which Circe enticed Ulysses. The shoreline, now advertised as the "Ulysses Riviera," recalls that seduction. Included in the province is the offshore Pontine archipelago, which consists of two groups of islands, one centered around Ponza and the other around Ventotene.

HISTORY. Throughout history, much of what is now the province of Latina was sparsely inhabited because of its malarial marshlands. The healthier uplands allowed some towns to survive, such as Sezze, which, legend says, was founded by Hercules. Another upland town is Sermoneta, where, it was said, Rome's god of the harvest, Saturnus, escaped the wrath of Jupiter by hiding in a pleasant villa. Many other attempts at settlement, however, failed. The medieval town of Ninfa, one of the Caetani domains, was abandoned to the mosquitoes in the fourteenth century. Papal efforts to drain the swamps failed, and reclamation waited until the successful endeavors of Benito Mussolini's regime in the 1920s. The Fascists built a number of towns—Littoria (later Latina, 1932), Saubadia (1934), Pontinia (1935), Aprilia (1937), and Pomezia (1940)—and distinguished them with their stark and monumental style of building. Mussolini also undertook administrative reform of the area between 1927 and 1934, creating the province of Littoria by taking land from Campania and the province of Rome. In 1947 the names of the province and the city were changed to Latina.

ARTS AND CULTURE. Latina was a planned city, conceived and built by Mussolini's regime. It has since spread past the original boundaries. Many of Latina's first Fascist buildings were the work of the Bolognese architect **Angiolo Mazzoni** (1894–1979).

OTHER CENTERS. West of Latina city, the ancient port and fortress of **Gaeta** sits on a promontory of the Aurunci Mountains that juts into the Tyrrhenian. Gaeta, along with **Formia**, a popular resort since Roman times; **Fondi**, another well-preserved city said to house the tomb of Cicero; and the islands formed the northern reaches of the Kingdom of Naples from the Middle Ages and, after union with Italy in 1861, remained a part of Campania's Caserta province until the 1927 administrative reorganization placed them in Lazio. In legend Gaeta was named for Caieta, Aeneas's wet nurse, who died on the voyage to Lazio. Gaeta probably derives its appellation from the "cave" shape (*kaiadas* in Greek) of its port. The Romans developed the town as a port for the then larger city of Formia. After the fall of of the Roman Empire (476), Gaeta emerged as a Byzantine duchy, and an imposing eighth-century castle from that era still dominates the city. As a fortress, Gaeta endured frequent sieges. The Muslims devastated much of the coastline in the ninth century and raided nearby Minturno as recently as 1552, when they torched the town and kidnapped about 200 Christians.

Gaeta's massive walls were rebuilt in the sixteenth century by the Hapsburg Emperor Charles V, but they have since been largely removed. From November 1848 until April 1850, Gaeta became the Holy See-in-exile when Pope Pius IX fled Rome at a time of revolution and took refuge there. After the French General Nicolas Oudinot forced Giuseppe Garibaldi's revolutionary forces from the Eternal City, Pius returned from Gaeta. During the later wars of the Risorgimento, the Neapolitan Bourbons made their last stand there, surrendering to the Italians on February 13, 1861, after a 93-day siege.

Gaeta's first Cathedral of Santa Maria del Parco was founded in 681 by the bishop of Formia, who had taken refuge in the town to escape Muslim raids. It was rebuilt in the eleventh century and rededicated to Saints Erasmus and Marziano. Gaeta also boasts an exceptional fourteenth-century church dedicated to the Annunciation. In the seventeenth century it was reconstructed with a Baroque facade although much of the earlier church remains in the interior.

The area around Gaeta was the scene of significant resistance to the Napoleonic invasions, particularly by Michele Pezza, who took the *nom de guerre* Fra Diavolo. Born at nearby **Itri** in 1771, Pezza led a series of audacious raids against the French until he was captured and hanged at Naples in 1806. The King of Naples, and later the Italian state, used Lazio's offshore Pontine Islands as prisons and places of confinement. In 1795 a Bourbon prison was opened on **Santo Stefano**, an islet next to **Ventotene**.

It operated until 1964. On **Ponza**, Mussolini was briefly held after his fall from power in July 1943.

Up the coast, between Gaeta and San Felice Circeo, is **Terracina**, said to have been established by Spartan refugees. It was the Volscian town of Anxur and home to an important ancient temple to Jupiter, the Giove Anxur. Also known as Giove Fanciullo, it sits atop Monte Sant'Angelo, which looms over the town. Terracina has been a resort since the Romans took it in the fourth century B.C. and located it along the Appian Way. There, Emperor Trajan (98–117) built a dramatic stretch of the road hugging a mountain, the Pisco Montano, much of which remains. Terracina contains a number of pagan temples, a republican forum, and a medieval quarter with an impressive Duomo, built in the eleventh and twelfth centuries over the remains of a Roman temple.

Inland, southeast of Sezze is the abbey of **Fossanova**. Founded by Benedictines in the ninth century, it was awarded to the Cistercians in 1135 by Pope Innocent II. The new owners rebuilt the Church of Santa Maria between 1171 and 1208 and drained some of the surrounding swamp with a large new ditch, the *fossa nova*. Saint Thomas Aquinas died at Fossanova in 1274.

RIETI

PROVINCIAL PROFILE. Area: 1,061 sq. mi. Population: 150,534 (province), 45,890 (city). Rieti province contains 73 communes. The province is situated in Lazio's northeast corner. Viterbo is to its west and Rome to its south, and it is wedged between Umbria on the north, Marche on the northeast, and Abruzzo to the east. Jutting out from the rest of Lazio, the province follows the ancient Salarian Way, along which the Roman legions traveled on their path of conquest. The Velino plain northwest of Rieti city, along with the Turano and Salto valleys in the Cicolano to the southeast, are some of the province's few flatlands. Most of Rieti is hilly and mountainous. The Carseolani and the Reatini ranges form part of the high central Apennines; Mount Terminillo, in the Reatini, reaching 7,260 feet. Farther to the northeast, the Laga range, which spills over into Abruzzo, is home to Mount Gorzano, which, at 8,064 feet is the highest point in Lazio. The Gran Sasso e Monti della Laga National Park touches the northeast corner of the province. Consequently, road and rail connections are not well developed and many sections of Rieti are quite remote.

HISTORY. Mount Terminillo looms over the city of **Rieti**. As Reate it was the capital of the Sabine lands before the Roman conquest was completed by 288 B.C. Within twenty years the Sabines received the citizenship and voting rights, and remained loyal to Rome when the Social War erupted with other Italian peoples in 91 B.C. As Sabina, the region was incorporated into Caesar Augustus' Regio IV and later into Constantine's revised Tuscia. The fall of Rome in 476 resulted in the division of Sabina between the Lombard Duchy of Spoleto and the nominally Byzantine Duchy of Rome. After devastating ninth-century Muslim raids and tenth-century Magyar incursions, much of the area became the domain of important families such as the Roman Colonnas and Orsinis. Rieti became an independent commune by the late 1100s with nominal allegience to the pope. By the fifteenth century, it had been securely absorbed into the territories of the Church in Rome, although the lands east of Mount Terminillo were controlled by the Kingdom of Naples. After a period of French occupation, in 1816 Rieti was again made the capital of Sabina. In 1860 the area was absorbed into the Kingdom of Italy and Rieti was joined to the other papal districts of Perugia, Spoleto, and Orvieto to constitute the province of Umbria. The Fascists resurrected Rieti as capital of its own province in 1927.

ARTS AND CULTURE. Parts of Rieti's thirteenth-century walls evoke the city's medieval past. A Duomo dedicated to the Assumption of the Virgin was built in 1109 and restored in 1639. An impressive bell tower remains. Rieti's episcopal palace, however, may be its premier historical treasure. The Roman historian **Marcus Terentius Varro** was born at Rieti in 116 B.C.

OTHER CENTERS. Farfa, in the Sabini Mountains, shares its name with an important abbey. Founded in the sixth century by the Bishop of Spoleto, Saint Lawrence Siro (the Syrian), it was destroyed by the Lombards and reestablished in the seventh century by the Benedictine Thomas of Moriana (Maurienne). The new abbey enjoyed the protection of both the Duke of Spoleto and the pope. By the ninth century it was said to have rivaled Nonantola as the richest in Italy. This fame reached the ears of the Muslims, who sacked Farfa along with Rieti and many other Sabine towns about 890. By the Middle Ages the abbey had revived, again becoming one of the wealthiest in Italy. Along with fourteen villages, the abbey controlled the cities of Alatri and Civitavecchia.

Rieti is also closely connected to the story of Italy's patron saint, Francis of Assisi, who frequently visited the nearby convents at Fonte Colombo and Greccio, and those of San Giacomo and La Foresta, near **Poggio Bustone**. Students of Francis believe that he composed his "Canticle to Brother Sun" at La Foresta in 1225 and made the first Christmas nativity scene, or *presepio*, at the convent of Greccio in 1223.

VITERBO

PROVINCIAL PROFILE. Area: 1,395 sq. mi. Population: 291,277 (province) 60,486 (city). Viterbo contains 60 communes. Viterbo province, generally the Tuscia Romana, forms the northwestern spur of Lazio. Rome faces it on the south, and Rieti touches it for a short stretch on the southeast. On its north, Viterbo wedges between Tuscany and Umbria. To its west is the Tyrrhenian Sea. The eastern part of the province is distinguished by modest Apennines, such as the Volsini range, which faces the northern shore of Lake Bolsena; the Cimini, south of Viterbo city; and the Sabatini, which extend into Rome province. The coast forms part of the Maremma lowlands which extend down the coast from Tuscany.

HISTORY. Before the rise of Rome, the land that is now the province of Viterbo was home to many of the most important Etruscan cities, such as Tarquinia, Tuscania, Vetralla, and Viterbo itself. Although Rome took Viterbo in 310 B.C., little is known of the early town until the Lombard King Desiderius chose it as a base for his operations against Rome in 773. Countess Matilda of Tuscany gave Viterbo to the Holy See at the end of the eleventh century, and it became so important to the popes that Eugenius III took refuge there in 1145 after the revolutionary commune of Rome expelled him. From Viterbo he arranged with Frederick Barbarossa an invasion of the Eternal City in 1153. Seven years later Barbarossa took Viterbo in preparation for another attack on Rome. Although the city became home to a papal court by the second half of the 1200s, it was contested by the Holy Roman Emperors until the popes established definitive control following their return from Avignon in the late fourteenth century.

In the sixteenth century the Knights of Saint John were granted refuge in Viterbo after the Turks had expelled them from Rhodes and until they could move on to Malta. Pope Paul III, who called the Council of Trent in 1545, was particularly attached to Viterbo, and referred to himself as a citizen of the city. He enacted many agricultural and civic reforms there, including the establishment of a university. On September 12, 1870, Viterbo was taken from the Papal States and became part of the Kingdom of Italy. During the Second World War the city suffered heavy Allied bombardments.

ARTS AND CULTURE. Viterbo is noted mostly for its medieval quality. Its San Pellegrino quarter, which dates from the 1200s, is one of Italy's best-preserved districts. The papal palace, built between 1255 and 1266, sits next to the impressive Romanesque Cathedral of San Lorenzo, a twelfth-century structure. Viterbo's Renaissance heritage often mirrors those of its larger neighbors, Rome and Florence. A native figure who merits special note is **Lorenzo da Viterbo** (c. 1437–after 1476), whose frescoes can be seen in the twelfth-century Church of Santa Maria della Verità.

OTHER CENTERS. Viterbo province is the home of important traces of Etruscan culture. Near the border with Rome province, for instance, **Nepi** is the old Nepet; some of its fifth-century B.C. walls survive. Near the ancient town of **Tarquinia** is an extensive necropolis distinguished by vivid paintings from the sixth to the second centuries B.C. In the early Middle Ages the people of old Tarquinia moved to a more defensible position at nearby Corneto. There, where the name of Tarquinia was later reapplied, the town enjoyed a revival as a Guelph stronghold. Two of the most important signs of this power are the twelfth-century Church of Santa Maria del Castello, built next to a castle of Matilda of Tuscany (of which little remains), and the fifteenth-century palace of Cardinal Giovanni Vitelleschi. The palace houses the Tarquinian National Museum.

Tuscania contains Etruscan tombs as well an an impressive medieval quarter rebuilt after a terrible earthquake hit the town in 1971. On a hill east of Tuscania is the Church of San Pietro. It is surrounded by the remains of Etruscan, Roman, and medieval structures, and much of the church retains its eighth-century character. It was rebuilt in the twelfth century with many Cosmatesque additions. Santa Maria Maggiore, another eighth-century church, is nearby.

Another town in Viterbo province with an Etruscan necropolis is **Civita Castellana**. Nearby are many remains from the Roman town, known then as Falerii Novi, which was built after the Iron Age settlement of Falerii Veteres, or Halesus, was plundered. After the fall of the Roman Empire, in A.D. 476, the people of Falerii Novi moved back to the original site. Civita Castellana contains two impressive twelfth- and thirteenth-century Gothic and Cosmatesque structures, the Church of Santa Maria di Falleri and the Duomo. Both display influence of the Roman Cosmati decorators. Popes Alexander VI (1492–1503) and Julius II (1503–1513) commissioned Antonio da Sangallo the Elder to build an impressive fortress there, the Rocca, which still stands.

One of Viterbo's most important and splendid churches is the Cistercian monastery of Saint Martin at **San Martino al Cimino**. Along with Fossanova and Casamari, it was part of the Cistercian explosion of the twelfth and thirteenth centuries.

Northeast of Viterbo is **Bomarzo**, site of one of Italy's oddest treasures, the "Monster Park" (*Parco dei Mostri*), also known as the "Sacred Wood" (*Bosco Sacro*). Created between 1552 and 1580 by the Orsini family, who also built an impressive palace in Bomarzo, the park is a collection of bizarre stone carvings, rocks and boulders assembled in fantastic shapes, and a leaning house.

The spectacular star-shaped Palazzo Farnese at **Caprarola**, built by Giacomo Vignola for Cardinal Alessandro Farnese on top of an earlier fortress, includes famous gardens and a circular courtyard. Some of the structure is decorated with frescoes by the Umbrian artists Federico Zuccari (c. 1540–1609) and Taddeo Zuccari (1529–1566).

SELECT BIBLIOGRAPHY

Caracciolo, Alberto, ed. *Il Lazio*. Turin: Einaudi, 1991.
Hibbert, Christopher. *Rome: The Biography of a City*. London: The Folio Society, 1997.
Istituto Geografico De Agostini. *Lazio*. 2 vols. Novara: Istituto Geografico De Agostini, 1979.

LIGURIA

Ligurian Apennines

Maritime Alps

Savona

San Remo

Imperia

Albegna

GENOA

Gulf of Genoa

Ligurian Sea

La Spezia

Chapter 9

LIGURIA

REGIONAL CHARACTERISTICS. Area: 2,089 sq. mi. Population: 1,641,835. Capital: Genoa (Genova). Liguria ranks eighteenth among Italy's regions in land area and eleventh in population. The Catholic Church designates Genoa as a metropolitan see.

Liguria is a long coastal region that stretches along the Ligurian Sea from the French border to Tuscany. It is thin, squeezed between the sea and the Maritime Alps and the Ligurian Apennines. Sixty-five percent of its terrain is mountainous and 35 percent is hilly. The Italian Statistical Institute classifies none of Liguria as plain. Nevertheless, a few river valleys spread out a bit when they reach the sea. The Centa, for example, meets a tiny flatland when it reaches the sea at Albegna, and in the east the Magra valley cuts between La Spezia and Sarzana. Nevertheless, the cities on Liguria's shoreline have never been fully linked by a coastal plain. The region's mountains, rather, continue right to the shore, where they often tumble dramatically into the sea.

Liguria borders France on its west, Piedmont on its north, Emilia Romagna and Tuscany on its east, and the Gulf of Genoa and the Ligurian Sea on its south. Its coastline divides in two, the Riviera di Ponente to the west of Genoa and the Riviera di Levante to the east. The Levante catches the winds coming from across the Mediterranean and receives more rain than does its leeward twin, the Ponente.

ECONOMY. Of Liguria's active workers, agriculture employs 4.2 percent, industry 22 percent, and the tertiary sector 73.8 percent. As of January 1998, 10.9 percent of the labor force was unemployed. Of the region's

577,000-member active labor force, 362,000 are men and 215,000 are women. Although Genoa and La Spezia are traditionally important centers of ship construction, it and heavy industry have suffered precipitous declines since about the 1970s. Liguria's industrial workforce, now 22 percent of the total, was over 54 percent in 1951. Oil refining is a major industry, however, and La Spezia is a terminus for natural gas from Libya. The region lacks significant mineral deposits, although Capo Fari, Carignano, Albaro, and Passano yield some high-quality marble. The island of Palmaria, near Portovenere, is famous for its *portoro* black and gold marble. As the Italian Riviera, Liguria has an important tourist industry.

CUISINE. Liguria does not produce much wine for public distribution. Most of its slopes, rather, are devoted to the cultivation of olives and flowers, particularly carnations. One of the most famous Ligurian wines is a *bianco* from the Cinqueterre, a charming collection of coastal villages near La Spezia. Sciacchetrà, a sweet dessert Cinqueterre, is also popular. Another favorite is the Dolceacqua, made mostly from the Rossese grape, in the area near Bordighiera and Ventimiglia on the French border.

Liguria is closely associated with pesto, a blend of basil leaves (without stems or veins), garlic, pecorino and Parmesan cheeses, olive oil, and pine nuts (and, in some places, cream). It can flavor pasta (particularly Liguria's *trenette*), gnocchi, or soup. La Spezia is noted for its *trenette a stuffo*, which is made with a bean sauce; and ravioli is said to have originated in Liguria. *Farinata*, a paste made from chickpeas and fried in oil, is another local favorite. Adding onions to *farinata* makes it *panissa*. Ligurians cheat a bit during Lent by consuming *cappon magro*, a rich fish-based "salad" that is put together layer by layer, an act which can create a meal of monumental dimensions. Liguria's *torta pasqualina* is a pie of vegetables, eggs, and curd (*quagliata*) made at Easter.

PANIZZA (PANICCIA) CON OLIO, LIMONE, E TARTUFFI

3½ c. water	Juice of 1 lemon
1⅓ c. chickpea flour	4 Tbs. olive oil
1 tsp. salt	Pepper to taste
½ c. minced truffles	

Heat water in a 3 qt. heavy-bottomed pan. Slowly add flour into water, mixing as you go to avoid lumps. Add salt and cook over medium heat for 1 hour, stirring constantly. Remove from heat and add truffles, lemon juice, oil, and pepper.

HISTORY. Paleolithic peoples inhabited Liguria and their cave and grotto dwellings can still be seen at Balzi Rossi, in the region's western end. Liguria takes its name from the Neolithic Ligurians (or Liguri), a people who lived along the European coast of the western Mediterranean, from the Ebro River in Spain to the Arno in Tuscany. Most of the Ligurians allied themselves with Carthage in the Punic Wars against the Romans (264–146 B.C.) and later suffered the consequences. Rome subdued Liguria between the late 200s and 155 B.C. It opened roads into the area and launched the process of Romanization. The Liguria of Augustus, Region IX, was a much larger entity than today's region, stretching from the seacoast on the south all the way north to the Po River. Christianity penetrated Liguria during the imperial period, and the region's first dioceses were established at Luni, Ventimiglia, and Genoa in the fourth century. The fall of the Roman Empire in 476 was not as traumatic in Liguria, still primarily an agricultural zone, as it was in some of the more sophisticated parts of Italy. Liguria nevertheless witnessed a long list of invaders. The Byzantines launched an invasion under Belisarius, who landed at Genoa in 538. Lombards followed in the 560s, and the sporadic havoc wreaked by the Arabs reached its height toward the end of the first millennium.

Genoa recovered by the eleventh century, when it became a leading commercial power. Its domination of the region slowly made itself felt along the coast, and by the thirteenth century Genoa's merchant aristocracy established their city as the capital of a republic whose borders roughly corresponded to the current region's. Liguria had thus attained a true regional identity by the Middle Ages. The capital, Genoa, was not an oppressive master, and it did not exert its power over other Ligurian towns much past matters of taxation. An exception, however, might be made for Savona, the old local rival of Genoa. Challenge after challenge was made, and they left their marks on sixteenth- and seventeenth-century Liguria. A general decline in Mediterranean trade combined with civil war in 1575 and a plague in the 1650s to darken the horizon. The actions of other states also affected the Genoese Republic. Tuscany's development of the free port of Livorno in 1575 increased competition, as did Piedmont's annexation of Oneglia in 1576, and French aggression brought a destructive naval bombardment of Genoa in 1684. Other Ligurian cities, La Spezia in particular, shared the blows to Genoa's pride.

Still, the Republic of Genoa lasted, albeit under occasional foreign masters, until French revolutionary armies extinguished it once and for all with their invasions of the 1790s. Napoleon Bonaparte established a satellite Ligurian Republic in 1797 and allowed it considerable freedoms, but a Russo-Austrian army cleared Liguria and the rest of northwestern Italy of French armies in 1799. The following year Napoleon returned in victory, and in 1805 he incorporated Liguria directly into his empire. After the final collapse of French power, the victorious nations at the Congress of Vienna in 1815 chose not to resurrect the old republic but to award Liguria to Piedmont. The unpopularity of this decision was widely acknowledged, and the new masters agreed to establish provincial and advisory councils, to limit taxation so that the new territory paid no more than did Piedmont, and to maintain existing internal tariffs. Liguria's economy nevertheless continued its downward slide until industrialization revived it. In the later nineteenth and early twentieth centuries, developments in shipbuilding and other industries enabled the region to join Piedmont and Lombardy as part of Italy's "industrial triangle." During the Second World War the mountainous areas of Liguria were largely controlled by anti-Fascist partisans.

RECENT POLITICS. After the fall of Mussolini's collaborationist Salò regime in 1945, the Communist Party dominated the region's politics. Despite, or perhaps because of, the region's industrial hardships, the Left still controls most of Liguria's politics. Liguria votes as the tenth electoral district (*circoscrizione*). In the 1996 elections to the Chamber of Deputies, the Ulivo coalition captured 46.3 percent of Liguria's majoritarian vote, the Polo per le Libertà took 38.1 percent, and the Lega Nord registered 11.9 percent. In the proportional vote the post-Communist Party, Democrats of the Left, took 25.6 percent of the ballots, followed by the Forza Italia with 19.3 percent, the Communist Rifondazione with 10.3 percent, and the Northern League with 10.2 percent. In the Senate vote the Ulivo coalition received 41.4 percent against 38.1 percent for the Polo per le Libertà. In the April 2000 regional elections, Liguria swung rightward. Sandro Biasotti was elected president as head of the Center-Right coalition, which collected 50.8 percent of the votes, against the Center-Left's 46 percent.

GENOA (GENOVA)

PROVINCIAL PROFILE. Area: 707 sq. mi. Population: 920,549 (province), 653,529 (city). The province has 67 communes. Genoa province wedges between Savona on the west and La Spezia on the east. It sits to the south of the Piedmont region and faces onto the Gulf of Genoa. It is linked to the upper Po valley through the Giovi Pass. Genoa is one of Italy's largest cities and is a key port for the nation and for Europe.

HISTORY. Traders in the third century B.C. probably established Genoa as a permanent town set precariously on steep hills overlooking the sea. Evidence exists, however, of commerce in the area as early as the sixth century. The Punic Wars (264–146 B.C.) divided the people of the region, and though many neighbors sided with the Carthaginians, Genoa did not. It consequently suffered a devastating sack at their hands. Genoa therefore received some preferential treatment when Rome annexed it in 205 B.C., although the city never attained much status as a port or administrative center. Ventimiglia, Albegna, and Vado were more important at the time. Rather, Genoa sat as a *castrum* (fortress) along Rome's key road to Spain. Genoa perhaps was noted chiefly for its place at the head of the Postumian

Way, which ran into Venetia, built with the intent of penetrating north-eastern Italy and establishing a Roman presence there.

After the fall of the Empire, Genoa was reduced to barely a fishing village, subjugated first by the Ostrogoths and, from 539 until about 642, by the Byzantines. It was later incorporated into Lombard and then Carolingian territories. Moreover, incessant Muslim raids weakened Genoa. The cruelest sack occurred in 934–935 and left the place uninhabited for some years. By the eleventh century, however, the town could fight back, and it supported the Normans in their Sicilian and North African campaigns against the Arabs. By the 1070s, furthermore, the Genoese and Pisans had chased the Muslims from Sardinia and Corsica. In 1099 Genoa became an independent commune, an archiepiscopal see in 1133, and by 1162 it had achieved virtual independence from the Holy Roman Empire. After brief intervals of imperial and Angevin rule in the early fourteenth century, Simone Boccanegra became Genoa's first doge in 1339. Genoa was a port from which Crusaders sailed to the Middle East after the eleventh century. As a result the city's merchants obtained lucrative trading concessions at Constantinople and Alexandria.

Genoa emerged as one of Italy's richest and most successful powers with possessions in the Greek islands, outposts in the Crimea, and subject towns along the North African coast. Emblematic of Genoa's financial power was the Bank of Saint George, founded at the beginning of the fifteenth century and soon one of Europe's most powerful institutions. Another part of Genoa's prosperity came from the slave trade. Between 2 and 4 percent of the city's late medieval population was slave, one of the highest such figures in Europe. Saracens comprised most of the number early on, but were later replaced by Russians and Circassians. One important study on the subject estimated that 86.4 percent of the slaves were women, the bulk of whom were in domestic servitude.

By 1290 Genoa had vanquished its immediate competitor, Pisa, and in 1299 annexed Corsica; but it never overcame its greatest rival, Venice. In the late fourteenth century the two engaged in their decisive struggle. Genoa's victories in the late 1370s brought its forces to Chioggia, at the watery gates of Venice. But in 1380 the Venetians turned the tide and Genoa never again challenged their supremacy. Instead, Genoa (and Venice) soon faced new demands from another quarter: the Ottoman Turks, whose expansion throughout the eastern Mediterranean led to a contraction and then the loss of the city's possessions there. The last Genoese territory to fall to the Turks was the Aegean island of Chios in 1566. In the west, Genoa's last overseas possession was Corsica, which it sold to the French in 1768.

The decline continued through the sixteenth century, when the city became a pawn in the struggles among France, Spain, Austria, Milan, and Piedmont. The aristocratic Admiral Andrea Doria helped France take

Genoa in 1527, but he switched sides the next year and paved the way for a Spanish hegemony that lasted until the early eighteenth century. Genoa maintained a vague independence, however, and Doria even wrote a new constitution for the city. This course, however, was more political than economic, and while Spain held Genoa in a sphere of influence, certain institutions went on as before with handsome profits. After 1575 the Bank of San Giorgio, for instance, assumed the interests and the hefty deposits of the Hapsburgs, and Genoa remained a financial power well into the seventeenth century.

France attempted to lure Genoa from Madrid's orbit, but in 1684, when that policy appeared to have failed, King Louis XIV dispatched a fleet to shell Genoa for five days. The Treaty of Utrecht in 1713 established the rule of the Austrians, which lasted until 1746, when the people of Genoa revolted in the Balilla uprising and expelled them from the city. "Balilla" was the nickname given to Giambattista Perasso, a boy who launched the tumult when he threw stones at Austrian soldiers. The revolt was as much a strike against the old aristocratic clans who seemed to have betrayed their city to foreign oppressors as it was against the foreign oppressors themselves. Consequently, during the Balilla events the nobles either kept a terrified silence or fled the city. When the Austrians left, however, the nobles regained control of Genoa, and extinguished hopes of reform. Genoa's finances declined, furthermore, when the Grand Dukes of Tuscany challenged its supremacy by developing Livorno as a free port in 1593. Although port tonnage figures continued to rise through the sixteenth century, a decline followed. Receipts dropped by half between 1667 and 1700, and Genoa surrendered the honor of being Italy's premier western harbor to the Tuscans. In 1669 and 1751 the city scrambled to alter its laws to compete with Livorno by also becoming a free port, although the reform was very limited and largely unsuccessful.

Genoa reacted more mildly than most Italian cities to the French Revolution and extended recognition to its newborn sister republic. Nevertheless, the city suffered Napoleon's conquest and became the capital of the Ligurian Republic in June 1797, one month after a local uprising against the privileged classes. In 1805 the Doge of Genoa and a civic commission petitioned Napoleon to incorporate the republic into the French Empire. In 1815, upon the collapse of Napoleon's empire, the Congress of Vienna incorporated Genoa and the rest of Liguria into the Kingdom of Sardinia.

Genoa became a hotbed of intrigue and activity during the Risorgimento. It was the birthplace of the "prophet" of national union, Giuseppe Mazzini (1805–1872). As a youth Mazzini witnessed the flight of failed Carbonari from the country and concluded that their conspiratorial approach to revolution and national unity were doomed to failure. He opted instead to promote more popular revolutionary groups, beginning with his own Giovine Italia (Young Italy). Mazzini's leadership in the movement for a united and democratic Italy resulted in his exile from Genoa. Another figure central to the Risorgimento, Giuseppe Garibaldi (1807–1882), was born down the coast at French Nice, which at the time was the Piedmontese Nizza. Also active in Genoa, Garibaldi and his force of 1,000, the *Mille*, sailed in 1860 from the suburban port of Quarto (now Quarto dei Mille) on their way to launch the invasion of Sicily. One of his chief lieutenants and the commander of one of the two ships, the *Lombardo*, was the *genovese* Nino Bixio (1821–1873). He led forces through southern Italy and was wounded at Palermo. Bixio went on to become a general in the new Italian army and later died of cholera in Sumatra, scouting imperialist ventures.

After the national unification, Genoa surfaced as one point on Italy's industrial triangle (the other two are Milan and Turin). The city was connected to Turin by rail in 1854 and industrialized at the end of the nineteenth century. As a city with a large working-class population, Genoa hosted the 1892 meeting which gave birth to the Italian Socialist Party. Later, labor agitation there contributed to the downfall of Fascism. Riots in Genoa in 1960 led to the collapse of Fernando Tambroni's Christian Democratic government when it accepted neo-Fascist support. Genoese and Triestino shipyard workers launched an intense series of strikes in 1967.

Many working-class leaders have come from Genoa. The head of the Italian Communist Party, Palmiro Togliatti (1893–1964), was born in Genoa. A close associate of the Sardinian Antonio Gramsci, Togliatti was among the founders of the party in 1921. He spent most of the Fascist period outside of Italy—in Moscow, Spain, and other places. He returned in 1944 to lead the resurrected Communists and joined the Italian government in a number of capacities, including minister of justice. Togliatti's conciliatory policy through the mid-1940s ended when the Communists and their Socialist allies were ejected from the Christian Democrat-led governing coalition in 1947. Genoa's working-class politics also produced two left-wing Christian Democratic leaders, the labor organizer Giulio Pastore (1902–1969) and a chief ideologue, Giuseppe Dossetti (1913–1996), who abandoned party politics and became an activist cleric. Among modern popes, Benedict XV (1854–1922) was a *genovese*. Born Giacomo Della Chiesa, he reigned from 1914 until 1922.

Genoa was heavily damaged by Allied bombardments during the Second World War. Partisan action against the Nazis and Fascists was intense in the city and the surrounding hills, and the resistance fighters have been credited with saving the port facilities and much of the central city from destruction at the hands of the retreating Germans in 1945. After the war Genoa faced new challenges: expanding population and poor city planning. An elevated expressway has marred much of the central city and, as an old industrial site nestled between mountains and the sea, Genoa was plagued by some of Italy's worst pollution. Like other manufacturing centers, moreover, Genoa became a postindustrial city with an economy more and more geared toward the tertiary sector. In 1951 industry accounted for 54.47 percent of the city's employment; in 1991 that figure had declined to 25.12 percent.

ARTS AND CULTURE. Modern times have taken a toll on central Genoa. Much of the old city has been bulldozed and paved over in the rush of industrialization. Construction of an eyesore expressway through the middle of the port area was only one of the mistakes inflicted on the city. Miraculously, however, Genoa has retained something of its historic core and ancient treasures have been spared; thus the city can boast of quite a few exquisite structures. Memories of Genoa's struggle for independence are recalled by the remains of its walls built in 1155 to withstand Frederick Barbarossa's assault. A part of the defenses that is still intact is the impressive Porta Soprana or Porta Sant'Andrea. Genoa's cathedral is a Romanesque-Gothic masterpiece, consecrated in 1118 and dedicated to San Lorenzo. Much of the early work on the structure, indebted to the Pisan style, was undertaken by the workshop of **Nicola Pisano**. Later additions include the magnificent Chapel of John the Baptist, mostly the work of **Domenico Gagini** (Palermo, active 1456–1492) and **Giovanni de Aria** (or D'Aria, active 1480–1508), from the Lake District in northern Italy. The chapel also contains a statue of the saint by the Tuscan **Andrea Sansovino** (c. 1467–1529). Another addition, from 1556, is an impressive cupola by the Perugian **Galeazzo Alessi** (c. 1512–1572). The patron of Genoa is Saint George (San Giorgio), who is venerated in many west Mediterranean cities. He was probably introduced to the Genoese by the Normans and was popularized during the Crusades.

In spite of economic or political crises, sixteenth- and seventeenth-century Genoa gained in importance as an artistic center. Like Venice, Genoa's strong merchant past is reflected in its many palaces. Work began in 1528 on Andrea Doria's villa in suburban Fassolo. An international project that brought artists from Florence and Rome and served as a model of Renaissance construction, the palace was badly damaged in the Second World War. In the mid-1500s the city cleared a run-down section of brothels to construct its "New" or "Main" Street (*Strada Nuova* or *Strada Maggiore*), which came to be lined with some of the most imposing palazzi of some of the city's most imposing families. Today it is the Via Garibaldi, and two of the structures, the Palazzo Bianco and the Palazzo Rosso, have been converted into major art museums. The Lombard architect **Pier Antonio Corradi** (Como, 1613–1683) built the Rosso between 1672 and 1677. Along with works by Italian masters, both museums contain important collections of Dutch artists such as Peter Paul Rubens and Anthony Van Dyck, in particular, who spent long sojourns in the city.

Genoa began the nineteenth century by undertaking a major project of urban renewal with a native architect, **Carlo Barabino** (1768–1835). His work includes a number of wide boulevards and civic buildings, particularly the opera house, the Teatro Carlo Felice (1826–1827). Industry also began to make its mark on Genoa, notably in its western districts. The Ansaldo railway works became Italy's largest factory when it opened in 1852. At the beginning of the twentieth century, a nostalgic Genoa undertook Romanesque and Gothic revivals in the Castello Mackenzie, the Palazzo Pastorino, and other works of the Florentine **Gino Coppedè** (1866–1927). The Romans **Marcello Piacentini** (1881–1960) and **Luigi Carlo Daneri** (1900–1972) later added a Fascist presence in the Piazza della Vittoria and in the residential Foce quarter. After the Second World War the problem of reconstruction was compounded by immigration from the South and misguided urban planning.

In modern times, Genoa was the birthplace of Italian soccer. The game was imported in 1893 by English residents who founded the Genoa Cricket and Football Club. Four years later the organization admitted its first Italian members, and a national institution was born. Today the city is home to two national teams, Genoa and Sampdoria.

The explorer **Christopher Colombus** (Cristoforo Colombo) was born at Genoa in 1451 or 1452. A typical merchant of the Renaissance, he traveled for his business from Chios to the Azores before he reached Spain and secured financing for his voyage of discovery to the New World. To commemorate his feat, Genoa hosted a world's fair in 1992, and portions of the port area were redesigned by the *genovese* architect **Renzo Piano** (b. 1937). Attendance levels disappointed the organizers, but the celebration helped to transform much of the aged industrial harbor into something of a tourist attraction with Europe's most impressive aquarium. In 1990 Genoa inaugurated its subway system.

Genoa was the birthplace and home of many important writers. An early history of the city, the *Chronicon Januense*, was written by **Jacopo da Varazze** (c. 1230–1298). Renaissance Genoa was the birthplace of **Leon Battista Alberti** (1404/6–1472), one of the key figures of his age. The son of exiled Florentine parents, he became a humanist scholar, artist, mathematician, and social critic. He returned to Florence as an assistant to Pope Eugenius IV and subsequently traveled to Mantua and Rimini, where his genius as an architect can still be seen. Alberti's works on painting (*Della pittura*, 1436) and architecture (*De re aedificatoria*, 1452) were seminal to the study of those subjects. His *Della famiglia* (On the Family, 1435–1444) delved into social issues and he was also known for his musical abilities and athletic prowess.

Giovan Ambrogio Marini (c. 1594–1650) was a Genoese priest who wrote an important early novel, *Calloandro Fedele*, in 1653. Another innovative author was the cleric **Francesco Fulvio Frugoni** (c. 1620–1686), whose individual and baroque style was best expressed in his *Cane di Diogene* (Diogenes's Dog). **Piero Jahier** (1884–1966) was a Genoese who translated into Italian the works of a number of foreign authors and also wrote his own works, often social criticisms. His *Resultanze in Merito alla Vita e al Carattere di Gino Bianchi* (The Outcome Concerning the Life and Character of Gino Bianchi) of 1915 was an assault on the cold world of bureaucracy. **Eugenio Montale** (1896–1981), one of Italy's chief poets, won the 1975 Nobel Prize for literature. He was born and raised in Genoa, and spent much time at his family's villa at Monterosso in La Spezia's Cinqueterre, although he moved to Florence in 1927 and then to Milan, where he died. His first book, *Ossia di Seppia* (Cuttlefish Bones), established his reputation as a major author in 1925. Another native of Genoa is the maverick poet **Edoardo Sanguinetti** (b. 1930). A Marxist, he joined the *Gruppo 63* (Group 63) movement in Milan and insisted that his work was more akin to Jackson Pollock's painting than it was to conventional poetry. The internationally recognized architect Renzo Piano was born in Genoa in 1937. Among his most significant works is Paris' Centre Pompidieu which Piano designed with the British partner, Richard Rogers.

The motion picture director **Pietro Germi** (1914–1974) was born in nearby Colombo. He was considered one of the better directors in the neorealist style; his productions include *Gioventù perduta* (Lost Youth, 1949) and *Il cammino della speranza* (Road of Hope, 1950). His most popular output came later, with such films as *Divorzio all'Italiana* (Divorce Italian Style, 1961).

Genoa's most important musician was **Nicolò Paganini** (1782–1840). His virtuoso ability as a violinist led to his reputation across Europe. As a freelance performer, Paganini also became one of the continent's first modern celebrities. His compositions, such as *Le Streghe* (The Witches, 1813), were showcases for his stage brilliance.

OTHER CENTERS. East of Genoa is **Chiavari**, a Genoese fortress town until commercial concerns became paramount in the fifteenth century. Nearby is **Cogorno** with its thirteenth-century Fieschi Basilica and Palazzo dei Fieschi (a noble Genoese clan). Two Fieschi occupied the papal throne: Sinibaldo, as Innocent IV (1243–1254) and Ottobono, as Adrian V (1276).

Farther east, the coastline juts out into a peninsula separating two small gulfs, the Golfo Paradiso and the Golfo di Tigullio. Much of the land is reserved for the Portofino Regional Park, although the towns of **Camogli, Portofino, Santa Margherita Ligure**, and **Rapallo** share the space. Camogli was a fishing village in the Middle Ages and now boasts an attractive waterfront, the colorful *porticciolo*. In a nearby dramatic location is the abbey of Nostra Signora del Monte, at San Fruttuoso di Capodimonte. Built by the Franciscans in 1444 over an earlier structure, much of it was renovated in the seventeenth century. Santa Margherita Ligure was the birthplace of the *crepuscolare* poet Camillo Sbarbaro (1888–1967). Rapallo is perhaps the chief victim of the Italian Riviera's success. Its lovely location has been ruined since the 1960s by overbuilding of vacation homes and a new port.

IMPERIA

PROVINCIAL PROFILE. Area: 446 sq. mi. Population: 216,789 (province), 40,567 (city). Imperia province is home to 67 communes. It is the westernmost of Liguria's provinces, located south of Piedmont, east of France, north of the Ligurian Sea, and west of the province of Savona. Imperia's coastline on the Riviera Ponente is distinguished by lush vegetation and an extensive cultivation of flowers. In fact, the province bills itself as the "Flower Riviera" (Riviera dei fiori) and is home to some of Italy's most famous resorts, such as Ventimiglia, Bordighera, Alassio, and the most important holiday spot on the Italian Riviera, San Remo. The province maintains many links to France's Provence, and its economy has on the whole been healthier than that in the rest of Liguria.

HISTORY. The old towns of Oneglia, Porto Maurizio, and some smaller villages united in 1923 to form the city of Imperia. It took its name from the Torrente Impero, a river that runs through the town. In early times the Romans used Imperia as a port. The Lombards gave Oneglia to the popes in the eighth century and, after a devastating Muslim raid, the town prospered as Ripa Uneliae under the authority of the bishop of Albegna. The Genoese Doria family purchased Oneglia and Porto Maurizio in 1298 and ruled them, with brief interruptions, until the sixteenth century. The famous Admiral Andrea Doria was born in Oneglia in 1466. Doria aided France's conquest of Genoa in 1527–1528, then defected to Emperor Charles V and secured the city's independence. In 1576 Oneglia and Porto Maurizio became possessions of the Piedmontese Savoys, who developed Oneglia as a rival port to Genoa. Its valiant but doomed resistance against Napoleon's army prompted the Savoys to name Oneglia seat of a province when Piedmontese rule resumed in 1814. In 1860, however, it was placed within a reorganized province of Porto Maurizio until the two cities were united in 1923.

ARTS AND CULTURE. Porto Maurizio's historic center is the more important of the two old towns that comprise Imperia. Its Church of San Pietro, which dates from the twelfth century, was often altered through the eighteenth. The patron of Imperia is Saint John the Baptist.

The writer and publisher **Gian Pietro Vieusseux** (1779–1863) was born in Oneglia of Swiss parents. He moved to Florence and established the influential review *Antologia* (Anthology), which called for a national Italian culture. It was published between 1821 and 1833, when it was closed by the Tuscan government for its nationalistic and progressive ideas. One of nineteenth-century Italy's most popular writers, **Edmondo De Amicis** (1846–1908), was born in Oneglia. He wrote about military life and travel, although his best-remembered work is the 1886 *Cuore* (Heart), a "school-boy's journal."

OTHER CENTERS. San Remo is a center of modern tourism. Since 1951 it has hosted an annual pop music festival which has become an Italian institution. The center of the city is anchored in the Art Nouveau Casino Municipale, built in 1904–1906 by Eugenio Ferret. The port has been expanded recently to accommodate more yachts. Overlooking the newer waterfront city is Pigna, the old town, with its thirteenth-century Duomo dedicated to San Siro. The writer Italo Calvino (1923–1985) was born in Cuba but moved to San Remo as an infant and always considered it his home. Calvino's participation in the anti-Fascist resistance was reflected in many of his early works. Their neorealist aspects, however, were blended with a fondness for fables. Fantasy and folktales then came to distinguish much of his work, such as the stories collected in his 1960 anthology, *I nostri antenati* (Our Ancestors). His later works tested the novel form and resulted in more complex works, particularly the 1979 *Se una notte d'inverno un viaggiatore* (If on a Winter's Night a Traveler) and *Palmomar* (1983).

The Romans called **Ventimiglia** Albium Intemelium (or Albintimilium); it was well established as a Ligurian settlement before they arrived. Allied with Carthage during the Punic Wars (264–146 B.C.), the town was occupied by the Romans in 181 B.C. Evidence of Christianity's arrival in the early 300s A.D. is the martyrdom of San Secondo, the patron of Ventimiglia. Records from 373 demonstrate that a diocese existed there under the jurisdiction of the metropolitan see of Milan. Beginning in the fifth century, Ventimiglia endured a succession of barbarian raids. It became the seat of a Lombard duchy and a Frankish county. This status is reflected in its eleventh-century baptistery and cathedral (finished in the thirteenth) and in the Church of San Michele, built about 1100. Genoa first took Ventimiglia in 1251, but the city soon changed hands, beginning with Charles VI of France, followed by the Visconti of Milan, the Lomellini family of Genoa, the Grimaldi of Monaco, the Milanese Sforzas, Louis XII of France, and the Bank of San Giorgio before the city returned to Genoa's rule. After Napoleon's invasion of 1797 introduced a brief period of incorporation into France, Piedmont (the Kingdom of Sardinia) annexed the city in 1814; it transferred it to the new Kingdom of Italy in 1861. As a frontier station, the city suffered damage in the Second World War, and was almost annexed to France after the conflict. Ventimiglia has recovered as a tourist center with an important trade in flowers.

Alassio is a popular resort town of uncertain origin, although a Benedictine feudal village existed there by 1100. The monks, based on the offshore island of **Gallinara**, dedicated a small church to Saint Anne there. The monastery acquired feudal possessions along the coast all the way into Catalonia. In 360 A.D. Gallinara was the home of Saint Martin of Tours. In the late nineteenth century English tourists followed the Hanbury family and popularized Alassio. It hosts an international yacht race, a bicycle rally with Monte Carlo, and the Italian veterans' tennis championships.

The Ingauni, a Ligurian people, founded **Albegna** between the sixth and fourth centuries B.C. The Romans knew it as Albium Ingaunum when they took it in 181 B.C. Albegna then developed into a prosperous city until the barbarian Alaric destroyed it and slaughtered the inhabitants in A.D. 409. The Romans rebuilt the town in 414, and it became a diocesan see. Albegna's cathedral and magnificent baptistery, considered Liguria's finest paleo-Christian monument, date from that time. It contains a sixth-century mosaic of symbols representing Christ and the apostles, as well as eighth-century tombs. The Byzantines took Albegna in 568. Lombards followed, then Franks, along with incessant Muslim raids. Albegna revived as a free commune of seagoing merchants, was a port from which Crusaders departed and secured trading concessions in the Middle East. It may have overextended itself, however, which prompted its greater rival, Pisa, to sack the city in 1165. (Albegna achieved some measure of revenge by joining the alliance that defeated Pisa at the Battle of Meloria in 1284.)

Struggles between Guelphs and Ghibellines and the silting of its harbor set Albegna on a less ambitious path. It submitted to a series of foreign lords, including the Genoese, who took it for the first time in 1251, the Visconti after 1335, and the French under Charles VI between 1396 and 1413. Piedmont annexed Albegna after the fall of Napoleon in 1814 and transferred it to the Kingdom of Italy in 1860. Albegna endured Allied bombing raids in the Second World War and was the site of ferocious battles between the anti-Fascist partisans and the Nazis. The Germans inflicted a terrible massacre there on the banks of the Centa River.

Along with its baptistery, Albegna boasts impressive Roman ruins and the Cathedral of San Michele, built between the eleventh and thirteenth centuries. The town is the site of the Ingaunno Civic Museum, devoted to items from the early Ligurian tribes through the Middle Ages. There is also a Roman Naval Museum with objects rescued from ancient sunken ships.

LA SPEZIA

PROVINCIAL PROFILE. Area: 340 sq. mi. Population: 223,400 (province), 97,712 (city). The province of La Spezia has 32 communes. It borders Genoa to the north, the regions of Emilia Romagna to its northeast and Tuscany to its east, and the the Ligurian Sea to its west and south. The Magra River, which rises in Tuscany, flows through the province and reaches the sea southeast of the city of La Spezia. Much of its course has been protected by the Ligurian Regional Park of Montemarcello-Magra. The picturesque coastline west of the city, the Cinqueterre, is a collection

of five villages—Monterosso, Riomaggiore, Vernazza, Manarola, and Cor-
niglia—that cling to the hilly and rocky shoreline and form much of a
national park. La Spezia, the capital of the province, sits at the head of the
Gulf of La Spezia. It possesses a well-protected harbor, serves as Italy's
major naval base, and is home to one of its two naval academies.

HISTORY. La Spezia's origins are sketchy. Through the Roman period
it was not a well-traveled area, and the dominant town was nearby Luni.
The Obertenghi, Pisan feudal lords in eastern Liguria, held La Spezia in the
eleventh century, and the Fieschi family ruled it until they sold it to Genoa
in 1276. The city subsequently and often became a prize in the constant
struggles among Genoa's ruling families. When Napoleon conquered the
area in 1797, he absorbed La Spezia first into the Ligurian Republic and
then into France itself. In 1808 the emperor created La Spezia and its gulf
as a "maritime *arrondissement*" in anticipation of a large naval base that
never materialized under his rule. In 1857, however, Piedmont's Parliament
voted to transfer its (and subsequently Italy's) fleet to La Spezia from
Genoa. Work began on the base in 1861, and it was dedicated eight years
later. Shipyards joined the military plant, and La Spezia became an important industrial center. Consequently, between 1861 and 1901 the city's
population climbed from 11,556 to 66,263. In 1923 Mussolini's government designated La Spezia as the capital of its own province.

ARTS AND CULTURE. The patron saint of the city of La Spezia, of its
gulf, and of lighthouse keepers, is San Venerio, a seventh-century holy man
who rejected the self-indulgence of his fellow monks at Luni and lived as
a hermit on the island of Palmaria. He was buried on the nearby island of
Tino, and Muslim raids threatened his remains there until they were transferred for safekeeping to Reggio nell'Emilia. The Benedictines returned Venerio to his first tomb, and then to La Spezia's Basilica of San Prospero, at
the start of the seventeenth century. La Spezia's naval and military importance is recalled in the Castle of San Giorgio, which dates from the thirteenth century and was rebuilt periodically until the beginning of the
seventeenth. The nineteenth-century arsenal, built by **Domenico Chiodo**
(1823–1870), still stands. The city also boasts the Ubaldo Formentini Civic
Museum with many relics of ancient Luni, an important naval museum,
and the recently opened Amedeo Lia Museum, devoted mainly to medieval
and Renaissance art. La Spezia's artisanal boatmaking tradition is displayed
offshore on the first or second Sunday of August in its *Palio del Golfo* race,
part of its *Festa del Mare*.

OTHER CENTERS. Portovenere is an ancient town at the end of a short
peninsula that extends from the provincial capital. In A.D. 594 Pope Gregory the Great referred in his letters to the town's Church of San Pietro, a
structure that still stands, jutting out on a rocky promontory. (It is unstable
and has been closed to the public.) Portovenere fell under the control of
the lords of Vezzano, who sold it to Genoa in 1113. In the sixteenth century

the *genovesi* rebuilt an imposing coastal fortress atop ruins of earlier Roman and medieval fortifications.

Across the Gulf of La Spezia from Portovenere is **Lerici**, an old port dominated by a massive thirteenth-century castle. Lerici's picturesque location attracted the English Romantics Percy Bysshe Shelley and Mary Shelley.

Inland from Lerici are the remains of the ancient Roman settlement of **Luni**. Founded in 177 B.C. as a port near the mouth of the Magra River, Luni was the chief city of the area (called the Lunigiana). During the Middle Ages the port area silted up, and the city was abandoned. Luni's archaeological park contains some of northern Italy's best-preserved Roman ruins, including an amphitheater and an early Christian basilica. The Lunese National Museum contains objects uncovered in the excavations.

The ruins of Luni sit just outside of **Sarzana**, a city whose medieval quarter reflects its importance as center of the Lunigiana. Sarzana sits on the historically contested ground where at various times Genoa, Florence, and Pisa met. In 1322 the adventurer and tyrant Castruccio Castracani built a fortress, the Sarzanello, outside of town; his son, Guarnierio degli Antelminelli, is buried in the thirteenth-century Church of San Francesco. The Florentine ruler Lorenzo the Magnificent de' Medici took Sarzana in 1487 and established another fort there, the Cittadella. Construction on the city's cathedral, dedicated to the Assumption of the Virgin, began in 1204, when the see of Luni was transferred to Sarzana. Work on the structure continued into the fifteenth century.

SAVONA

PROVINCIAL PROFILE. Area: 596 sq. mi. Population: 281,097 (province), 64,205 (city). Savona province has 69 communes. Savona province fits between Genoa to its northeast and Imperia to its southwest. Northwest is Piedmont, and the Ligurian Sea washes Savona's beaches on the southeast.

HISTORY. Savona's ancient roots are linked to the Sabazi, a Ligurian tribe noted for its fierce independent spirit. Their support of the Carthaginians during the Punic Wars (264–146 B.C.) led to a long period of Roman pacification and control. Vado Ligure became the area's chief port, and almost nothing is known of Savona again until the Middle Ages, when, along the Riviera Ponente, it and Albegna led an alliance against Genoa that put them on the side of the Emperor Frederick II (1212–1250). After his death they carried the Ghibelline banner against Guelph Genoa until Savona capitulated in 1372. In 1440 Savona took advantage of Genoa's war against the Milanese Visconti and again rebelled. The Genoese entered the city through an act of treachery and sacked the town, destroying port fortifications and sinking ships in the harbor. Savona made another bid for independence in the early sixteenth century, when it aligned itself with French invaders. But the campaign failed and Genoa reoccupied Savona in 1525, destroyed its port again, and sank three boats heavy with stone cargoes in the harbor. The vengeful *genovesi* built the Priamar fortress, and Savona at this point accepted, or at least sadly recognized, its destiny.

During the Napoleonic occupation at the beginning of the nineteenth century, the Priamar fortress held Pope Pius VII. When the Kingdom of Sardinia annexed Liguria after the fall of Napoleon, the port of Savona enjoyed something of a revival and ironworks were later established there. Giuseppe Mazzini spent 1831 in the Priamar, and while there he formed his ideas for an association, the Giovine Italia (Young Italy), dedicated to the unity of Italy. Prime Minister Paolo Boselli (1838–1932) was born in Savona. A middle-of-the-road figure, he is best remembered for the military disaster of Caporetto during the First World War. Left holding the political bag, Boselli and his cabinet resigned immediately after the catastrophe.

ARTS AND CULTURE. Savona has retained an old city center with Renaissance and Baroque structures. Among the most notable is the Palazzo della Rovere, built for the papal family that came from the area. Cardinal Giuliano della Rovere, later Pope Julius II, commissioned the Florentine **Giuliano da Sangallo** (c. 1445–1516) to build the palace, which remains uncompleted and serves today as a courthouse. Across from the palace is the cathedral, built mostly between 1589 and 1605; its facade was redone in the nineteenth century. Next to the cathedral is the Sistine Chapel (*Capella Sistina*), less known than the one in the Vatican but ordered by the same figure, the other della Rovere pope, Sixtus IV, as the tomb of his parents. It is the work of the Genoese **Michele de Aria** (active 1466–1502) and the Lombard **Giovanni de Aria**. Much of the structure was rebuilt in the eighteenth century. On Savona's outskirts is the sanctuary of Santa Maria della Misericordia, the city's patron. Her appearance there in 1536 to a peasant, Antonio Botta, inspired its construction. The work was entrusted to the Lombard architect **Pace Sormano** who had just finished the Priamar fortress at the harbor. By 1540 the basilica was completed; another Lombard, **Taddeo Carlone** (1543–1613), added its facade in 1610–1611.

OTHER CENTERS. Down the coast, near the border with Imperia, is **Finale Ligure**, an ancient town distinguished by its distinct zones. Its Varigotti quarter forms the medieval center of the city, and its castle contains traces of Byzantine and Lombard occupations. The abbey Church of Santa Maria di Pia is found in the Finale Pia quarter. Built between 1170 and 1729, it reflects every architectural style from the Romanesque to the Rococo. Another important church is the nearby Nostra Signora di Loreto, a Renaissance masterpiece built at the end of the fifteenth century.

Now known as a vacation spot, **Noli** was a significant Ligurian port established by the Byzantines. Medieval Noli prospered and developed as a rival to its more powerful neighbor, Savona. Consequently Noli allied itself to Genoa in 1202 and remained in its orbit until the Napoleonic conquest. The city retains an exceptional medieval quarter and the recently restored Church of San Paragorio. The eleventh-century structure is decorated in part with Islamic ceramic pieces.

Stella is the birthplace of Sandro Pertini (1896–1990), who served as president of Italy from 1978 until 1985. In the 1920s the Fascists jailed him as a Socialist subversive, and he later fled to France, where he joined other opponents of Mussolini's regime. Pertini was recaptured and imprisoned until he joined the resistance during the war. As a member of the anti-Fascist coalition of leaders in Milan, Pertini issued the order to execute Mussolini in 1945. He served in Italy's Constituent Assembly after the war and was elected to the Senate and the Chamber of Deputies.

The Socialist leader Lelio Basso (1903–1978) was born in **Verazze**. A major organizer of the party, he was arrested by the Fascists in 1928 and remained their prisoner until 1931. During the Second World War, despite another short prison term, Basso worked to reorganize the Socialists, and when the conflict ended, he served as a member of the Constituent Assembly.

SELECT BIBLIOGRAPHY

Epstein, Steven A. *Genoa and the Genoese, 958–1528.* Chapel Hill: University of North Carolina Press, 1996.

Fara, Amelio. *La Spezia.* Rome: Laterza, 1983.

Gibelli, Antonio, and Paride Rugafiori, eds. *La Liguria.* Turin: Einaudi, 1994.

Istituto Geografico De Agostini. *Liguria.* Novara: Istituto Geografico De Agostini, 1981.

Poleggi, Ennio. *Genova.* Rome: Laterza, 1998.

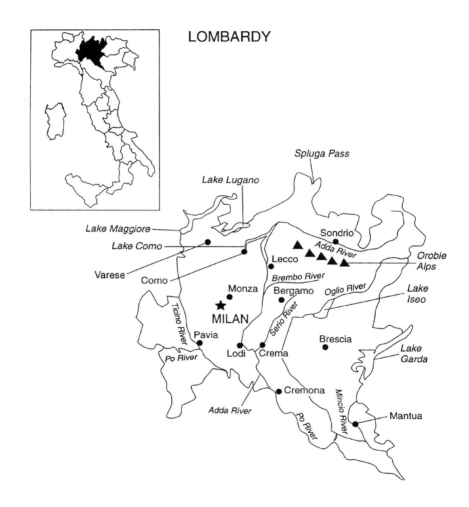

LOMBARDY

Chapter 10

LOMBARDY
(Lombardia)

REGIONAL CHARACTERISTICS. Area: 9,202 sq. mi. Population: 8,988,951. Capital: Milan (Milano). Lombardy is Italy's fourth largest region in land area and its first in population. Lombardy has 1,546 communes. The Catholic Church maintains a metropolitan see at Milan.

To the west of Lombardy is Piedmont, to its south is Emilia Romagna, to its east are Trentino/Alto Adige and the Veneto, and to its north is Switzerland. Lombardy's topography moves quickly from the Alps to the Po plain: 40.5 percent of the region is mountainous and 47.1 percent is plain; only 12.4 percent is regarded as hilly. The northern tier of Lombardy is Alpine or pre-Alpine mountains, from the Lepontine Alps on the Piedmont border through the Orobic Alps and the Rhaetian Alps on the Trentino–Alto Adige side, with most of its highest peaks are in the province of Sondrio. Lombardy is distinguished by a string of fjord-like lakes, long the favorites of tourists. Italy's largest lake, Lago di Garda, forms part of Lombardy's eastern border, and in the west Lago Maggiore separates the region from Piedmont. It also lies partly in Switzerland, as does Lago di Lugano. Lago di Como is the largest lake entirely within Lombardy. Also wholly within the regional borders, Lago Iseo is the smallest of the major lakes. Most rivers that flow from the mountains and lakes eventually reach the Po, which serves as most of Lombardy's southern border. An exception to the Po tributaries is the Adda, which runs east to west in Sondrio, from the San Giacomo and Cancano lakes near the Spluga Pass until it empties into Lake Como. Other important rivers are the Oglio, Serio, Brembo, Mincio, and Ticino. From and beyond these waters Lombardy has enormous stretches of canals through the rich agricultural flatlands of the Po valley.

ECONOMY. Of the region's 3,674,000 employed workers, 2,253,000 are men and 1,421,000 are women; 2.8 percent of Lombard workers labor in agriculture, 41.8 percent in industry, and 55.4 percent in the tertiary sector. Six percent were unemployed as of January 1998.

Lombard factories produce iron and steel, automobiles, furniture, and leather goods. Chemicals, food, graphic arts, and the clothing industries are important to the area; and Milan is considered one of the world's fashion centers. Milan is the capital of Italian commerce and industry, and the nation's principal stock exchange, or *borsa*, is located there, as are many of the nation's largest banks. An unfortunate consequence of this industrial and commercial success has been a high incidence of industrial pollution which plagues the area. An ecological catastrophe occurred northwest of Milan at Seveso's Icmesa plant in July 1976, when a carcinogenic gas escaped into the atmosphere.

CUISINE. Much of the Lombard diet is based on polenta and rice. Saffron-flavored rice, *risotto alla milanese*, is said to have been a consequence of Spanish presence in Lombardy. *Ris con la luganega* is a dialect term for rice served in a soup with a lean sausage made at Monza. *Ris e rav* is rice with browned turnips. *Cotoletta alla milanese*, breaded veal chop, and can be found almost anywhere in Italy. Milan's panettone has become a Christmas favorite across Italy. At Easter it is formed into a dove, then crowned with sugar and almonds to become the *colomba pasquale*. Lombardy is also a significant cheese region. Lecco is noted for its production of Gorgonzola (although the cheese was named for a small town northeast of Milan). Lodi makes a *grana* cheese similar to Parmesan. Creamy *Bel paese* also comes from Lombardy, particularly the Melzo area east of the capital.

Lombardy's more important wine country is located largely in three zones: in the region's northern hills of the Valtellina along the Adda, in Pavia's Oltrepò zone, south of the Po and reaching into the Ligurian Apennines, and in the east near Lake Garda, down to the Po. The *nebbiolo* grape is grown extensively in Lombardy, as it is in Piedmont (in Lombardy it is called the *chiavennasca*). About half of Lombardy's wine is produced in Pavia province, particularly the Oltrepò Pavese. More distinctive is the Valtellina in Sondrio, a quality red wine made from the *nebbiolo* grape. Near Brescia, around Franciacorta, is the home of one of Italy's best sparking red wines. A Mantuan Lambrusco is also produced in Lombardy's southeast corner.

RISOTTO ALLA MILANESE

3½ c. beef broth	1¾ c. Arborio rice
¼ c. olive oil	½ c. white wine
½ large onion, finely chopped	1 tsp. saffron
½ tsp. salt	1½ Tbs. grated Parmesan cheese
¼ c. beef marrow	

Bring broth to a boil, set aside, and keep warm. In a 3-qt. pot, heat the olive oil and sauté the onion with the salt and beef marrow until onion is brown. Add rice and continue sautéing until the rice begins to crackle. Add the white wine and stir until the liquid is absorbed. Mix the saffron with the broth and add the liquid in half-cup increments, stirring constantly. Wait for each portion of broth to be absorbed before adding the next. After all of the liquid has been absorbed, add the cheese and serve hot.

HISTORY. Evidences of Neolithic villages, perhaps related to the lake dwellings found at Zurich, have been located near Como, Varese, and Cremona. Bronze Age remains have been discovered near Como and Varese as well as Brescia and Mantua. The early Iron Age Golasecca culture was named for its most important site, a town in Varese province on the border with Piedmont. Veneti and Celts also appeared in Lombardy toward the end of the prehistoric period. The people of Golasecca mingled with, and were absorbed by, the Etruscans who ruled the area, for the most part, from the fifth century B.C. until the Roman conquest in the third. The new rulers first favored Cremona, but after Caesar Augustus, who ended the period of military rule and conferred Roman citizenship on the population, they turned more and more to Milan (Mediolanum).

Christian practices existed in Lombardy before Constantine, but his Edict of Milan in 313 marked the beginning of widespread acceptance of the religion. The Edict also indicated the importance of Milan as the imperial capital for a time during Rome's turbulent late era. Fifth-century Lombardy became a battlefield for successive waves of barbarian invaders from Alaric and the Visigoths in 402 to Attila and the Huns in 452, the Alans in 463–464, and finally Odoacer and the Ostrogoths, who defeated the last army of the Western Empire, commanded by the Romanized barbarian Orestes, at Pavia in 476.

During the sixth century the Byzantines and Lombards invaded Lombardy and much of the rest of northern Italy. Although the Greeks held Como until 588 and Cremona until 603, the Lombards triumphed here, gave their name to the region, and ruled it from Pavia as a kingdom from 569 until 774. In that year Charlemagne, King of the Franks, responded to Pope Adrian I's clarion for aid and defeated the Lombard Kingdom. Frankish control continued until the forced abdication of Charles the Fat in 887 revealed trouble at the top that allowed the Lombard cities more options for local control. The area suffered barbarian invasions again at the end of the ninth century, this time by the Magyars.

The second millennium began as a time of unprecedented prosperity for Lombardy's growing towns, provoking the Holy Roman Empire in Germany to reexert its authority over them. With papal support, however, the Lombard League was formed in 1167, and successfully resisted imperial power at the Battle of Legnano in 1176. The Peace of Constance in 1183, between Frederick Barbarossa and the Italians, recognized the Lombard League and the special rights of its members, which included permission to elect magistrates, although the emperor maintained his power of validating their mandates.

In the thirteenth century, the Holy Roman Empire again attempted to control northern Italy, this time under Frederick II. A second Lombard League was formed, although victory seemed distant when Verona's tyrant, Ezzelino III da Romano, joined Frederick to deal a devastating blow to the League at Cortenuova in 1237. Only Milan, Brescia, Piacenza, Bologna, Faenza, and Alessandria remained in the League, and it appeared that Frederick had avenged Barbarossa. But he failed to take Brescia, and the tide turned against him. Frederick suffered defeat at Parma in 1248, and his son, Enzo, was captured a year later at Fossalta, near Modena.

After the defeat of the Holy Roman Empire, the Lombard cities faced a new challenge from within their own ranks, the Visconti clan of Milan. In 1277 the Visconti secured control of Milan and embarked on an expansionist policy, particularly under Gian Galeazzo, which extended the city's power across Lombardy and throughout northern Italy. After the Visconti came the Sforza, who ruled Milan mainly in the second half of the fifteenth century. While keeping Lombardy at war, the Sforza, especially Ludovico "the Moor," energized the Renaissance in Lombardy.

The foreign invasions which plagued all of Italy at the end of the fifteenth century held particularly crucial consequences for Lombardy. The League of Cambrai (1508), for example, although directed against Venice, determined the fate of the eastern part of the region. During the tumultuous sixteenth century, Sondrio and the Valtellina were lost to Swiss cantons. And Milan itself was held by the Spanish between 1535 and 1706, when the Austrians replaced them by force. Vienna's rule was ratified by the Treaty of Utrecht in 1713. In 1786 the Hapsburg Emperor Joseph II reorganized the administration of Lombardy into intendancies. After the period of Napoleonic rule, during which the region was transformed into the Cisalpine Republic and then the Kingdom of Italy, the Austrians returned in 1814 and held Lombardy, together with Venetia, until Italy's unification, the Risorgimento.

In the first half of the nineteenth century, Lombardy was a hotbed of activity directed toward liberation and attachment to the Kingdom of Piedmont (Sardinia) to form a united Italy. In 1848 and 1849 Piedmont attempted to invade Lombardy without success. In 1859 Franco-Piedmontese forces again crossed the border into Lombardy and liberated the region from the Austrians. Most of Lombardy was brought into the Kingdom of Italy in 1859 and the rest, the eastern parts of the region, followed in 1866, after the war that led to the annexation of the Veneto.

Lombardy's reputation as a manufacturing center stems from its production of silk and other textiles in the Middle Ages. By the mid-nineteenth century, however, the region had joined the massive industrial revolution that had begun in Britain a century before. In 1857, for example, the railroad linked Milan to Venice, and by the 1870s, to most of the Lombard centers. In 1883 Giuseppe Colombo harnassed Lombardy's water resources and inaugurated Milan's, and Europe's, first hydroelectric power station.

RECENT POLITICS. After the Second World War and the end of Fascism, Lombard politics were led by the Christian Democrats, who took 52.5 percent of the vote in 1948 and 39.4 percent in 1979. The Communists in the same period grew from 17.8 percent to 28.4 percent. The 1980s and 1990s, however, were distinguished by the rise of Silvio Berlusconi's Forza Italia and by the Lombard League and its umbrella, the Northern League of Umberto Bossi. Lombardy votes in the third, fourth, and fifth electoral districts (*circoscrizioni*). In the majoritarian contests, the third district, mainly Milan and its suburbs, voted for the Center-Right Polo per le Libertà (41.9 percent) over the Ulivo coalition (38.8 percent) and the Lega Nord (18.4 percent). In the fourth district, generally the region's northern and eastern reaches, the Lega Nord won with 37.2 percent of the vote, followed by the Ulivo with 31 percent and the Polo with 30.3 percent. The fifth district, which covers the south and west, gave 40.2 percent to the Ulivo, 36.3 percent to the Polo, and 23.5 percent to the Lega Nord.

In the third district's proportional election, 27.6 percent of the votes went to Forza Italia, 18.2 percent to the Democratic Party of the Left (PDS), 16.8 percent to the Lega Nord, and 9.7 percent to the Alleanza Nazionale. In the fourth district, the Lega Nord took 35.8 percent of the votes, followed by Forza Italia with 20.0 percent and the PDS with 10.5 percent. The fifth district gave 22.6 percent of its votes to Forza Italia, 21.1 percent to the Lega Nord, 19.0 percent to the PDS, and 10.6 percent to the Alleanza Nazionale.

In the Senate elections Lombardy votes as one unit. There, the Ulivo coalition took 34.1 percent of the valid ballots, 32.8 percent went to the Polo, and 24.4 percent to the Lega Nord. In the April 2000 regional elections, Lombardy reaffirmed the endorsement of the Center-Right that it made in the 1995 regional vote. Roberto Formigoni was reelected president of the region, at the helm of a coalition that captured 62.4 percent. The Center-Left took 31.5 percent of the votes.

———————————— MILAN (MILANO) ————————————

PROVINCIAL PROFILE. Area: 765 sq. mi. Population: 3,737,246 (province), 1,303,925 (city). The province contains 188 communes. It shares its northern border with Varese, Como, and Lecco. To its east Milan faces Bergamo, then Cremona and Lodi, a new province detached from Milan in the 1990s. To Milan's southwest is Pavia, and it faces Piedmont across the Ticino River to the west.

HISTORY. Milan's roots extend to prehistory. The place was contested in the sixth century B.C. between the Etruscans and the Insubri Gauls. After Rome repelled two invasions by the Boii Gauls, at Rimini in 236 and at Cape Telamon on the Tyrrhenian Sea in 225, the Republic launched a counterattack, an offensive that brought it to Milan. In 222 the Insubri surrendered Milan to the Consuls Gnaeus Cornelius Scipio and Marcus Claudius Marcellus. Hannibal's victories over the Romans spurred a brief but doomed rebellion. From then on, Milan, the Roman Mediolanum, remained loyal. It became a colony in 89 B.C. and served as Julius Caesar's base for attacks north of the Alps.

By the second century A.D. Milan had become one of the leading cities of the Roman Empire, and its importance continued to grow in relation to the increasing trouble with barbarians along the northern frontier. In 293 Emperor Diocletian confirmed Milan's status when his administrative reforms made it capital of the Western Empire. Religious activity mirrored Milan's political status. In 313 Emperor Constantine issued the Edict of Milan, which sanctioned the popularity of Christianity through official toleration and restoration of Church properties that had been confiscated during the Great Persecutions. Also at Milan, Emperor Constantius II, son of Constantine the Great, attempted in 355 to impose his own Eastern Christianity upon the Western, or Latin, bishops. His gambit failed in the face of their determined opposition. Consequently, in 381 Emperor Theodosius I recognized the primacy of the Roman pope over Constantinople's patriarch, and the centrality of the Nicene Creed to the Christian faith.

One of Theodosius's councillors was Ambrose (Ambrogio), a Roman governor of Emilia and Liguria who in 374 had been elected bishop by Milan's Christian community. He became one of the most powerful men in the Roman Empire, and the voice of Latin Christianity during his life. Theodosius died at Milan in 395 and was eulogized by Ambrose, who died two years later. Ambrose has since been recognized as a saint and a Doctor of the Church whose stamp on his city has remained for seventeen centuries. It is still commonplace in Italy to refer to Milan as the *città ambrogiana* (the Ambrosian City).

Milan's status slipped after Theodosius and Ambrose died. Thanks to the German-Roman General Stilicho, the city survived a siege by Alaric in 401–402. But the capital then moved to Ravenna. Milan's cultural life remained important—Saint Augustine went there to study in the 400s—although it fell victim to more barbarian incursions. The Huns sacked it in 452. Nevertheless, Milan fared better than other north Italian towns. Theodoric the Goth entered the city without great trauma and was welcomed as a guest. In 535 the Byzantines in Ravenna challenged the Goths for supremacy in the area. Milan's bishop, San Dazio, pledged his support to the Greeks, but their strength in Lombardy proved inadequate. Instead, in 538 the Burgundian Goths laid siege to Milan, which surrendered three years later. They destroyed the city and massacred the people or carried them off as slaves. In 555 the Greeks won an empty victory, such was the destruction, and were forced out just over a decade later by the Lombards.

The Lombards inherited a depopulated and squalid Milan in 568 and chose other places, such as Monza and Pavia, for their headquarters. Frankish rule followed the Lombards in 774. Charlemagne wanted to secure northern Italy by making Milan more of a Frankish city. He developed a close relationship with Archbishop Thomas, who baptized his daughter, Gisela. Thomas died in 783 and was succeeded by Peter, a Frank who was a friend of Charlemagne's spiritual guide, Alcuin. The Franks retained control until Charles the Fat's abdication in 887 gave more power to local bishops. One was Ansperto da Biassono (or Biasono), bishop from 868 until 881, who repaired the city walls. An age of powerful prelates followed which culminated in the rule of Bishop Ariberto da Antimiano from 1018 until 1045. By the lime of his death, Milan had become a strong and free commune seeking hegemony over other Lombard towns.

To exert his imperial authority over Lombardy, Frederick Barbarossa targeted Milan and laid siege to the city. Upon its unconditional surrender in 1162, the emperor destroyed Milan's fortifications and torched the rest of the city, sparing only the churches. Barbarossa's larger ambitions to exert his control over northern Italy, nevertheless, were dashed when the Lombard League dealt him a defeat at Legnano in 1176. Milan's fortunes quickly revived, although its politics became torn between the Guelphs, led by the Torriani family, and the Ghibellines under the Visconti.

In 1277 Archbishop Ottone Visconti defeated the Della Torre at the Battle of Desio and secured his family's authority over Milan. The city prospered, and at the end of the fourteenth century Gian Galeazzo Visconti was the most successful of his family, extending his reach past Lombardy, into Bologna, Pisa, Lucca, and Siena. He demonstrated his strength when Emperor-elect Rupert descended into Italy in 1402 for his coronation in Rome. On his way, Rupert opted to stop in Lombardy and deal with Gian Galeazzo; however, he completely underestimated the strength of his vassal and received a stinging defeat. There seemed no stopping Gian Galeazzo until, on August 13 of that year, he succumbed to a fever. A Florentine-Venetian alliance then chipped away at Milan's territories until they embraced not much than Lombardy, Novara, Alessandria, and parts of Emilia. The last Visconti, Duke Filippo Maria was a miserable ruler, universally detested by the Milanesi for his wars, taxes, and pederasty. He died without an heir in 1447, and Milanese politics fell into chaos.

For a brief time a Republic of Saint Ambrose was proclaimed and twenty-four "captains and defenders of liberty" administered the city. But the end of the Visconti rule created an international chaos which thrust Milan into war with Florence and Venice. Besieged and starving, the people of the city opened their gates to Francesco Sforza, condottiere and husband of Filippo Maria's only (illegitimate) child, Bianca Maria.

Francesco usurped the Republic's authority, slaughtered his enemies, and proclaimed himself Duke of Milan in 1450. Francesco concluded a pact with Florence against Venice and fought to the inconclusive Peace of Lodi in 1454 and the formation of a tenuous Holy League the next year that united all the warring states. Francesco's son, Galeazzo Maria, succeeded him in 1466. But Galeazzo Maria, not as able a ruler as his father, was murdered in 1476. His son, Gian Galeazzo (b. 1469), was too young to rule, and power was entrusted to the dowager duchess Bona of Savoy. Galeazzo Maria's brother, Ludovico, called "the Moor" (*il Moro*), pushed her aside in 1480 and took over as regent until his nephew died (or perhaps was murdered) in 1494, and he assumed the throne for himself. Ludovico married Beatrice d'Este, and his tenure as regent and duke brought prosperity to Milan until the French invasions ended his reign. He lost Milan to Louis XII of France in 1499, returned the next year, and was again defeated by Louis although this time he was captured. Ludovico died in captivity in 1508.

The Sforza briefly returned after the Holy League of the pope and Italian states defeated the French in 1513, and again in 1522 when Holy Roman Emperor Charles V made Francesco II governor. But Francesco's death in 1535 ended the Sforza period, and Charles gave the duchy to his son, Philip, introducing an era of Spanish control and Milanese decline that lasted until 1706. Although the Spanish dominated northern Italy, late sixteenth-century Milan identified just as much with its cardinal archbishop, Saint Charles Borromeo. The nephew of Pope Pius IV, who was also a Milanese, the tireless Borromeo occupied the see from 1565 until 1584. He reformed the local Church from top to bottom in the spirit of the Council of Trent, restoring Church lands, expanding charity and welfare work, and establishing the Jesuit order in Milan. His revival of the cult of Saint Ambrose, it has been claimed, also sparked a sense of pride in the tired city. His work was continued by his nephew, Federigo, who became archbishop in 1595. Seventeenth-century Milan experienced economic decline and a serious outbreak of plague.

In September 1706, during the War of the Spanish Succession, Prince Eugene of Savoy entered Milan at the head of an Austrian army and secured the city. Ruled by the Hapsburg emperors in Vienna, Milan entered a new era of commercial prosperity, good government, and enlightened reformers. In 1737 Austria's Italian possessions were reorganized with Milan as the capital under the Count of Traun. Later figures such as the Genovese aristocrat Gian Luca Pallavicini, who became governor in 1748, and the Trentino Count Carlo di Firmian, who did likewise in 1759, were noted for their enlightened administrations and reforms.

On May 15, 1796, French troops under Napoleon entered Milan and in 1797 established the Cisalpine Republic. The French were quickly chased out, but they returned to Milan in 1800 and established another republic until Napoleon proclaimed himself King of Italy in 1805. In his honor the Milanese artist Luigi Cagnola (1762–1833) was commissioned to build the Peace Arch (Arco della Pace), a neoclassical monument in the Sempione Park. Austrian rule resumed in 1814 when Lombardy was consolidated with the Veneto. The Risorgimento sentiment for independence and union with the rest of Italy ran high in the first half of nineteenth-century Milan. A central figure was Carlo Cattaneo (1801–1869). A liberal and a democrat, he founded the review *Il Politecnico* (The Polytechnic) in 1839. As mayor and chief of the Revolutionary Council, Cattaneo led the city when it rebelled against the Austrians and liberated itself during the "Five Glorious Days" of March 18–22, 1848. The revolutions of 1848 failed, however, and Cattaneo fled to exile in Switzerland. In 1860 he was invited back to take a seat in Italy's Parliament; he declined, and died in Lugano, north of the border.

Milan developed into an modern industrial concentration at the end of the nineteenth and the beginning of the twentieth centuries. Pirelli, Falck, Breda, and Alfa Romeo, among other firms, established large plants there. Heavy manufacturing and working-class districts grew hand in hand in quarters such as Sesto San Giovanni. The city undertook major urban renewal projects in the 1880s, 1912, 1914, and 1926.

In April 1919 Benito Mussolini founded the Fascist movement at Milan's Piazza San Sepolcro. Those who attended that first meeting became known as "Sansepolcristi," after the piazza. During the Second World War, Milan suffered extensive damage. When the Nazis resurrected Mussolini's fallen regime as the Italian Social Republic in 1943, Milan became its effective center. The Duce's penultimate public appearances took place there in December 1944, primarily a speech given at the Teatro Lirico. His last public appearance took place there as well, in April of the following year, when his corpse was hung upside down next to that of his mistress, Claretta Petacci, and other Fascists before a jeering crowd in the Piazza San Loreto.

After the war the Socialist and Christian Democratic parties struggled for control of Milan. By the 1970s, the Socialist Bettino Craxi (1934–2000) had risen to the leadership of that party there before going to Rome as prime minister in August 1983. Improprieties among his lieutenants in Milan, however, surfaced in February 1992 and exploded into the "clean hands" (*mani pulite*) scandal that ruined Craxi, devastated the Italian government, and triggered a reinvention of Italy's politics by the middle of the decade.

ARTS AND CULTURE. Milan is so identified with modern commerce and industry that its artistic heritage might be dismissed, except that it is so extensive and profound. The city keeps some of its Roman heritage in the remains of a theater, an arena, and baths. Most significant, however is a colonnade of 16 Corinthian pillars next to the Basilica of San Lorenzo Maggiore.

More important, however, are the paleo-Christian remains in the city. Milan is home to a number of important very old Christian basilicas, including San Simpliciano, built between the fourth and seventh centuries with bits and pieces of Roman edifices, and two basilicas founded by Saint Ambrose: San Nazaro Maggiore and, above all, the ancient San Lorenzo Maggiore. The last is a fourth-century structure rebuilt over the years after fires and collapses while retaining its original layout and much of its stonework. The heart of Lombard Christianity, however, is the Church of Sant'Ambrogio where the body of Milan's fourth-century bishop rests next to the martyred saints Protasio and Gervasio. A fifth-century mosaic depicts the three in the Chapel of San Vittore. Its ninth-century "golden altar" by Maestro Vuolvinio, depicting scenes from the lives of Christ and Sant'Ambrogio, is perhaps the apex of goldwork in Carolingian Europe. Later, the Umbrian **Donato Bramante** (1444–1514), the Piedmontese **Bernardino Lanino** (1512–c. 1583), and the Venetian **Giovanni Battista Tiepolo** (1696–1770) labored on the basilica. Other important Romanesque structures include the twelfth-century Basilica of Sant'Eustorgio, with its nineteenth-century facade, and parts of the Church of San Marco.

Milan's Duomo is perhaps the city's most famous emblem and is Italy's second largest church, surpassed only by Saint Peter's Basilica in Rome. The Duomo rose over an earlier church by order of Gian Galeazzo Visconti about 1386. It remained unfinished until the nineteenth century, when work on the upper part of the facade ended. Across the piazza from the Duomo are the Villa Reale with its modern and contemporary art museums and, on the other side of the cathedral, the Galleria Vittorio Emmanuele, a covered shopping area built between 1865 and 1878 by the Emilian artist **Giuseppe Mengoni** (1829–1877).

Francesco Sforza ordered construction of the distinctive and imposing Castello Sforzesco in 1450. It sits on the site of an earlier Visconti fortress, and today, in the middle of the large Sempione Park, it remains one of the most important buildings in Milan. Many artists collaborated on it, including Bramante and the Florentine **Benedetto Ferrini** (active 1456–1479). It houses a group of museums, the *Musei del Castello* that deal primarily with ancient and Renaissance works. Other important Renaissance structures include Santa Maria Incoronata, which was the union in 1468 of two separate churches, and the Dominican sanctuary of Santa Maria delle Grazie. Bramante worked on the structure, and **Leonardo Da Vinci's** *Last Supper* is found in the adjoining *cenacolo* (refectory). The work, commissioned by Ludovico il Moro in the 1490s, was damaged in a Second World War bombardment and has been restored.

Saint Charles Borromeo's tenure as Milan's archbishop and that of his nephew, **Federigo**, left their mark on Milan's culture and art. A burst of Baroque optimism distinguishes many structures built during this period, such as the Jesuit Church of San Fedele and the Barnabite Church of Sant'Alessandro. In 1609 Federigo established in the Palazzo Ambrosiana his famous library (Biblioteca Ambrosiana). In 1618 the cardinal added a museum to the library which today houses one of Milan's best art collections.

Under Austrian rule in the eighteenth century, Milan's construction boom continued, often with secular structures such as the Palazzo Clerici, which contains a magnificent ceiling fresco by Giovanni Battista Tiepolo, and the Villa Reale of the Viennese **Leopoldo Pollack** (1751–1806). Perhaps the most famous structure from this period is the La Scala Theater, begun in 1776 by the Umbrian **Giuseppe Piermarini** (Foligno, 1734–1808), where the Church of Santa Maria della Scala had stood.

As one of Italy's greatest manufacturing centers, nineteenth- and twentieth-century Milan acquired fame as the nation's most important concentration of modern and industrial architecture. One of Milan's chief construction projects was its ponderous central train station, designed by the Florentine **Ulisse Stacchini** (1871–1947) for a 1912 competition. Construction took so long, however, that when the station opened in 1931, it was considered hopelessly outdated. A school of avant-garde architects, the "Gruppo 7," which grew from the Futurist movement, contributed innovative designs to the Milan scene during the 1930s and early 1940s. After the Second World War, the city witnessed an explosion of experimental and controlled housing developments, beginning in 1947 with the "QT8" of **Pietro Bottoni** (1903–1973). A general building boom was partially tempered by an urban plan adopted in 1953. A major figure in the boom was the Milanese native **Gio Ponti** (1891–1979). His ideas reached a wide audience through the review *Domus*, which he founded in 1928 and edited for most of the rest of his life. With Sondrio's **Pier Luigi Nervi** (1891–1979), Ponti designed Milan's Pirelli tower (1958), the first real skyscraper in Italy. The city's first subway line opened in 1964.

Modern Milan also remained one of Italy's intellectual capitals. The Politecnico University was established in 1859, followed by the Bocconi School of Business in 1902, the State University in 1920, and the Catholic University of the Sacred Heart, founded by Milan's **Agostino Gemelli** (1878–1959), in 1924. A Franciscan and a leader of Italy's Catholic community, Gemelli nevertheless supported the Fascists; in the 1950s, embarrassed, he turned more to his professional interests in psychology. A close friend of Gemelli, who also worked at Sacred Heart University and was a leading figure in Italy's lay Catholic movement, was **Armida Barelli** (1882–1952). Under her guidance from the end of the First World War until 1946, the young women's wing of the Catholic Action society mobilized as a major national organization.

Between the eighteenth and twentieth centuries Milan developed a lively literary culture. Enlightenment Milan was spurred by the work of **Count Pietro Verri** (1728–1797), who hosted the meetings of the Accademia dei pugni (Academy of Fists) in his home. Among its members was Italy's principal intellectual of the age, **Cesare Beccaria** (1738–1794), whose work on crime and punishment prompted Grand Duke Leopold of Tuscany to end capital penalties in his lands. Another figure in Enlightenment Milan was **Giuseppe Parini** (1729–1799), who came from the Brianza area north of the city. Called the greatest poet of the age, Parini was a priest who challenged greed and ostentation as editor of the *Gazzetta* of Milan. His greatest work of poetry was the unfinished four-part opus *Il Giorno* (The Day).

In the nineteenth century, **Alessandro Manzoni** (1785–1873) was Milan's and Italy's greatest romantic novelist. His *I promessi sposi* (The Betrothed) told the story of young lovers negotiating their difficult path through a corrupt, Spanish-dominated Lombardy and the plague of 1630. One of Manzoni's chief followers was **Emilio De Marchi** (1851–1901), who discussed the travails of good people in bad societies in such works as *Demetrio Pianeli* (1889). The *Scapigliatura* (Bohemianism) movement began in Milan in the 1860s and 1870s. Attempting to capture an anti-bourgeois bohemian style, it included **Giovanni Rovani** (1818–1874), **Carlo Dossi** (1849–1910), and the opera composer and librettist **Arrigo Boito** (1842–1918). Milan's **Anna Radius Zuccari** (1846–1918), known as "Neera," was one of Italy's first modern feminist writers. She wrote of the disappointments of married life and the challenge of achieving happiness in a male society in such works as *Teresa* (1886), *Lydia* (1887), and *Anima sola* (Lonely Soul, 1894).

Pre–World War One Milan is identified with the work of the Futurists, although their movement knew other centers as well. Their work glorified the modern beauty of mechanical speed and action, and rejected what they felt was Italy's stodgy artistic tradition. Many of them became Fascists. Milan's first Futurist exhibition, the "Exhibition of Free Art [*arte libera*]" took place in 1911. The painter and sculptor **Umberto Boccioni** (1882–

1916) left his native Reggio Calabria and in 1907 arrived in Milan. His work and that of other Futurists, such as Turin's **Giacomo Balla** (1871–1958), the Tuscan **Gino Severini** (Cortona, 1883–1966), the Veneto's **Luigi Russolo** (Portogruaro, 1885–1947), and the Piedmontese **Carlo Carrà** (1881–1966) is found in Milan's important Civic Museum of Contemporary Art. With the exception of an innovative offshoot, "Aeropittura" (Air Picture, 1929), much of Futurism had run its course by 1930. A reaction, however, appeared at Milan's Pesaro Gallery in 1922, the "Novecento" (Twentieth Century) movement, which promoted a nationalistic return to traditional Italian principles and a portrayal of historic themes. The movement frequently enjoyed the blessings of the Fascist regime, and Mussolini opened the Pesaro exhibition with an inaugural address.

In the 1950s and 1960s avant-garde schools attracted poets from across Italy. The "Linea Lombarda" (Lombard Line) broke from the hermetic tradition and gathered around **Carlo Bo** (b. 1911), **Nelo Risi** (b. 1920) and **Luciano Erba** (b. 1922). The "Gruppo 63" continued this rebellion in the pages of **Luciano Anceschi**'s (1911–1995) *Il Verri* and the *Quindici* "Fifteen" of **Alfredo Giuliani** (b. 1924) and **Nanni Balestrini** (b. 1935). Three of the central figures in Milan's theatrical world were the Marchigian **Ugo Betti** (1892–1953), the Triestino **Giorgio Strehler** (1921–1997), and the Nobel Prize-winning playwright **Dario Fo** (b. 1926), a native of San Giano in Varese province.

Milan is the birthplace of the film directors **Luchino Visconti** (1906–1976), **Alberto Lattuada** (b. 1914), and **Ermanno Olmi** (b. 1931). Visconti first worked as a set designer with British and French teams before he made the path-breaking *Ossessione* (Obsession) in 1942 and later what may have been the best example of neorealist film, *La Terra Trema* (The Earth Trembles) in 1947. Beginning as a scriptwriter under Mario Soldati, Lattuada graduated to making his own films during the neorealist era. Olmi's first venture was *Il Tempo si è fermato* (Time Stopped, 1959). He went on to direct such critical successes as *Il Posto* (translated both as "The Job" and "The Sound of Trumpets," 1961). Two important pop-music idols were born in Milan: **Johnny Dorelli** (Giorgio Guidi, 1937) and **Adriano Celentano** (1938).

Milan boasts some of the finest museums in Europe. Along with those mentioned above, especially noteworthy are the Poldi Pezzoli and the Brera, which contains outstanding collections of Lombard and north Italian masterpieces.

Throughout the year Milan hosts many conventions, including one of Europe's greatest trade shows, the International Sample Trade Fair (the Fiera Campionaria di Milano), in April. Important fashion exhibitions are held at the end of February and at the beginning of October, and leather, footware, fabrics, and accessories shows occur in September and March. One of Europe's largest media fairs, MIFED, takes place in October.

OTHER CENTERS. Monza sits northeast of Milan on the Lambro River. It was the Roman Modicia and a small town until the Lombard Queen Theodolinda chose it as a residence and the site of a monastery. Inside Monza's Duomo, the chapel of Theodolinda contains the "Iron Crown." Said to have been forged from one of the Crucifixion nails, it was the crown of the Lombard kings, of the Holy Roman Emperors, and of Napoleon when he became King of Italy in 1805. The Duomo's Serpero Museum is particularly strong in Lombard and high medieval art. The Villa Reale was built on the city's outskirts in 1777–1780 by Giuseppe Piermarini. In 1900 King Umberto I was assassinated at a Monza gymnastics meet by Gaetano Bresci, an anarchist who had lived as an immigrant in Paterson, New Jersey. Today Monza is an industrial center and annually hosts the Grand Prix d'Italia auto race.

Outside of Monza is the industrial town of **Desio**, where in 1277 Archbishop Ottone Visconti triumphed over his enemies and established his family's rule. It is also the home of Achille Ratti (1857–1939), who became Pope Pius XI in 1922. In 1929 Pius resolved the "Roman Question," the estrangement between the Holy See and the Italian government that stemmed from Italy's capture of Rome from papal control in 1870. The Lateran Accords of 1929 between Pius and Benito Mussolini established the Vatican City as an independent state. Pius's relations with the Fascists soon soured, however, over turf battles between the Catholic and Fascist youth organizations and over Mussolini's embrace of Nazi racist policies in 1938.

Legnano, site of the battle against Frederick Barbarossa in 1176, was also the birthplace of the composer Antonio Salieri (1750–1825). Salieri moved to Vienna, where he was a student and protégé of Christoph Gluck. His greatest work was the opera *Tarare* (1787). But it is for his rivalry in Vienna with Mozart that Salieri is now, unfortunately, remembered.

Cistercian monks who settled in Lombardy named **Morimondo** after the French town of Morimond. They built an abbey and the Church of Santa Maria there in the twelfth century. It fell into disuse but has recently been restored.

BERGAMO

PROVINCIAL PROFILE. Area: 1,065 sq. mi. Population: 949,862 (province), 117,193 (city). Bergamo province contains 244 communes. It lies in the center of Lombardy and entirely within it. Sondrio is to its north, Brescia to its east, Cremona to its south, and Milan and Lecco to its west. The northern three-fourths of the province is either hilly or mountainous, and the lower quarter forms part of the Po valley. Lying between the

Brembo and Serio rivers, Bergamo is sometimes called the "split city" (*città sdoppiata*) because it is built on two levels; the older one is high on a hill and surrounded by sixteenth-century Venetian walls, whereas the newer, larger town sits below.

HISTORY. First settled by the Orobi tribe, Bergamo became the Roman possession of Bergomum in 196 B.C. Attila destroyed Bergamo in the fifth century A.D., as did the Magyars in the tenth. The Lombards made Bergamo the seat of a duchy, the Franks took it in 816, and the city became a free commune in the 1100s. After a period of fierce conflict between guelphs and ghibellines, it passed to Milan's Visconti family in 1332 and to the Venetian Republic in 1428.

The French took Bergamo and Brescia from the Venetians in 1509, but the two cities rebelled in order to rejoin their former masters. In retaliation, France ordered that Gaston de Foix, Duke of Nemours and commander of the army, punish the rebellious towns as he saw fit. Brescia, the first victim, was crushed with a ferocity astonishing even for that age. Bergamo witnessed the horror and wisely paid 60,000 ducats to turn Gaston in other directions. The Venetians returned and held Bergamo until Napoleon's invasion in December 1796. As in 1509, the French occupation was unpopular, particularly when Bergamo was detached from Venice and incorporated as a satellite state of the Cisalpine Republic. After Napoleon's defeat, Bergamo became part of Austrian Lombardy in 1814 and witnessed much activity during the Risorgimento. Like other Lombard cities which followed Milan's lead, Bergamo rose in revolt during the "Five Glorious Days" of March 18–22, 1848. Giuseppe Garibaldi added fuel to the flames when he arrived with a force on July 30. But the defeat of the Revolutions of 1848 meant that Bergamo had to wait until 1859, when it was finally liberated, again by Garibaldi, on June 9.

ARTS AND CULTURE. The Cathedral of Santa Maria Maggiore and the Colleoni Chapel occupy the center of Bergamo's old, or upper, town. Santa Maria Maggiore, which dates from the twelfth century, has been restored often, and the richly decorated chapel dates from the 1470s. The home of Bergamo's famous condottiere **Bartolomeo Colleoni** remains as the Luogo Pio della Pietà. Some believe that **Lorenzo Lotto** (c. 1480–1556) was born in Bergamo, although his birthplace is often listed as Venice. In Bergamo's Church of San Michele al Pozzo Bianco, Lotto painted a series of frescoes based on the life of the Madonna. The city's art museum at the Accademia Carrara is one of the finest in northern Italy.

Many of the lower town's broad streets and spacious piazzas were designed between 1914 and 1935 by the Roman architect **Marcello Piacentini** (1881–1960).

Gaetano Donizetti was born of humble roots at Bergamo in 1797. One of Italy's most popular opera composers, Donizetti first wrote in the manner of Rossini. But he later developed his own spirit and earned international fame for such frothy delights as *L'Elisir d' Amore* (The Elixir of Love, 1832), *Don Pasquale* (1843), and one of the greatest serious works of the lyric stage, *Lucia di Lammermoor* (1835). An ardent nationalist during the Risorgimento, he allowed his home in Paris to be used as a clearinghouse for information to and from Giuseppe Mazzini's base there. The composer returned to Bergamo, where he died in 1848. The explorer **Costantino Beltrami** (1779–1855), who investigated the sources of the Mississippi River, was born in Bergamo.

OTHER CENTERS. Angelo Roncalli, who became Pope John XXIII, was born in 1881 to a peasant family at **Sotto il Monte**. Ordained in 1904, he served as secretary to Bergamo's bishop before moving on to diplomatic posts in Bulgaria, Turkey, and France. He was elected pope in 1958 and announced his decision to launch the Second Vatican Council. The reforming council had just begun its deliberations when John died in 1963.

BRESCIA

PROVINCIAL PROFILE. Area: 1,837 sq. mi. Population: 1,080,212 (province), 189,767 (city). The province contains 206 communes. Brescia is divided between high mountains in the north and the Po plain in the south. Its capital, Brescia city, sits in the foothills between the two. To its northeast Brescia faces the Trentino-Alto Adige, to its east is Veneto across Lake Garda, and to its southeast is Mantua. Brescia's northern border with Sondrio is formed by the southern ridge of the Valtellina. Brescia faces Bergamo to the west, in part across the Lago d'Iseo, and Cremona to the south. Brescia city sits in the Val Trompea on a high plateau in the middle of the province.

HISTORY. The first Brescia was probably a settlement of the Liguri peoples before it was taken by the Etruscans. The Romans knew it as Brixia, a name derived from the Cenomani Celts, who took it from the Etruscans about 350 B.C. The Romans occupied the area around 200 B.C. and, under Augustus, Brescia was placed in Region X, Venetia et Histria. Brescia became the seat of the Roman colony in 27 B.C. After the fall of the Roman Empire in A.D. 476 and a brief Byzantine interregnum, Brescia became the seat of a Lombard duchy. Charlemagne took the area in 774. It became an independent commune in the eleventh century and was a member of the Lombard League (1167).

Beginning in 1258, Brescia succumbed again and again to foreign invaders and overlords, starting with Ezzelino da Romano, the Milanese Visconti, and the Veronese Scaligeri dynasty until it was absorbed by Venice in 1426. But Brescia's new lord was a victim of the French and Spanish wars which plagued the rest of Italy in the sixteenth centuries. In 1509, shortly after formation of the League of Cambrai, King Louis XII attacked Venice. Brescia and Bergamo were promised to France and were taken from the Most Serene Republic, but rebelled in 1512 to rejoin Venice. Gaston de Foix, Duke of Nemours (nicknamed "The Thunderbolt of Italy") was dispatched to end the trouble, and brutally sacked Brescia in February 1512. Two months later the count was killed at Ravenna and the Venetians, with Spanish help, returned to Brescia.

The French took Brescia in 1797, and Austria incorporated it into its Lombard possessions in 1814. *Bresciani* made important contributions to the Risorgimento. They were active in the 1821 revolutions and took to the streets in March 1848. The Austrians withdrew, and a provisional government voted to join Milan in revolution. On May 13 a plebiscite called for annexation to Piedmont. But these efforts were ill-fated. King Carlo Alberto of Sardinia-Piedmont and his Piedmontese forces suffered defeat at Custoza, and the Austrians returned on August 16. In 1849 the scene was repeated. After the Austrians had withdrawn to fight Carlo Alberto a second time, the Bresciani revolted again. Consequently, the emperor's troops returned only after a bombardment of the city. Ten years later a Franco-Piedmontese army pushed the Austrians out of Lombardy, and on June 13, 1859, Giuseppe Garibaldi entered Brescia at the head of his famous unit, the *cacciatori delle Alpi* (hunters of the Alps). The city was then joined to Italy.

ARTS AND CULTURE. Rome's rule of Brescia is best recalled in extensive remains of a forum, the most significant such archaeological complex in Lombardy. It includes a theater, a civic basilica, and the Tempio Capitolino, built by **Vespasian** in A.D. 73 and home today to Brescia's municipal archaeological museum. Medieval Brescia is well represented in the eleventh-century "old" Duomo, or Rotonda, and the thirteenth-century Palazzo del Broletto. Among Brescia's most important cultural treasures is the complex of structures that is anchored by the ninth-century Church of Santa Giulia and its convent, and that also contains the convent of Santa Maria in Solario and the Museum of the Christian Era. Part of the legacy of Renaissance Brescia is the fifteenth-century Church of Santa Maria del Carmine and the Piazza della Loggia. The Loggia, which was the work, in part, of the Tuscan **Jacopo Sansovino** (1486–1570) and **Andrea Palladio** (1508–1580) from the Veneto, is now used as the Palazzo del Comune. The Church of Santi Nazaro e Celso contains the works of many artists, including the *Gesù risorto*, *Gabriele*, and *Annunziata e santi* (The Risen Christ, Gabriel, Annunciation and Saints), a masterpiece of the young **Titian** (1488/1490–1576).

Marcello Piacentini rebuilt Brescia's Piazza della Vittoria between 1926 and 1932 in the Fascist style. The Tosio Martinengo Art Gallery contains works by **Lorenzo Lotto, Raphael** (1483–1520), **Girolamo Romani** (c.

1485–c. 1562, known as Romanino), and **Alessandro Bonvicino** (c. 1498–1554, known as Moretto da Brescia). Other works by the last two, natives of the city, are housed in the episcopal palace (Palazzo Vescovile)

OTHER CENTERS. **Concesio,** near Brescia, was the birthplace of Giovanni Battista Montini (1897–1978), who became Pope Paul VI in 1963, following the death of John XXIII. After serving in the Vatican Secretariat of State and as cardinal archbishop of Milan under Pope Pius XII, Paul completed the work of the Second Vatican Council and led the Catholic Church through the turbulent 1960s and 1970s.

On the shore of Lake Garda is **Gardone Riviera,** a resort town that is home to the enormous Vittoriale degli Italiani, the villa of the Abruzzese writer Gabriele D'Annunzio (1863–1938). The villa is largely the work of a local artist, Gian Carlo Maroni (1893–1952). A supporter and early rival of Benito Mussolini, D'Annunzio added to his gardens the prow of the Italian destroyer *Puglia,* a gift from the Duce. The complex is today a museum.

COMO

PROVINCIAL PROFILE. Area: 497 sq. mi. Population: 535,471 (province), 84,207 (city). Como province contains 163 communes. The city sits at the southwest end of Lake Como. Across Como's northwest border is Switzerland, and the frontier crossing is a few minutes' drive from the city of Como. Lake Lugano bends up from the Swiss canton of Ticino into Como province until it ends at the Italian city of Porlezza. Campione d'Italia, a small part of the province, faces the lake and is surrounded on three landward sides by Switzerland. Across Lake Como to the east is the province of Lecco, to the south is Milan, Varese sits to the southwest, and at its northeast point Como touches Sondrio.

HISTORY. Como, ancient Comum, was probably established by the Orobi; the Etruscans and Insubri Gauls also lived there before the Romans took it in 196 B.C. Como is among the few cities that benefited, at least for a while, from the barbarian invasions at the end of the Roman Empire. The Lombards chose it and revived it as a key city of their rule. It achieved the status as a free commune in the eleventh century but sided with the Holy Roman Empire against the Lombard League. For this the Milanesi conquered and razed the city in 1127. Nevertheless, imperial support helped Como flourish through the twelfth and thirteenth centuries. During this period, in 1215, Como erected its communal palace (City hall), the Broletto, next to the Duomo.

Struggles between Guelphs and Ghibellines, however, embroiled the city and drew Milan into Como's politics. The Visconti bought the city in 1355 from its ruler (and their ally), Franchino Rusca. Como achieved its independence again from 1408 until 1416, when its ruler, Lotterio Rusca, sold it a second time to the Visconti. After the fall of the Visconti, Como followed Milan's lead and briefly declared a satellite Republic of Sant'Abbondio until Francesco Sforza seized power in 1450. As a silk and wool center, and later as a headquarters of the printing industry, Como was integrated into Milan's economy. Silk is still an important industry in Como, and Italy's National Silk Institute is located there.

Como came under Spanish rule in 1535 and Austrian rule in 1706. Napoleon's troops entered Como for the first time in May 1796. On June 17, 1797, Napoleon himself visited the city, and was welcomed by a delegation of citizens which included the scientist Alessandro Volta (1745–1827), a native of Como. After the collapse of French rule and the Austrian resoration, Como became active in Carbonaro agitation for the liberation of Italy. Inspired by Milan, in 1848 the city rose in its own ill-fated rebellion of "Five Glorious Days." Como was finally joined to Italy when the victorious troops of Giuseppe Garibaldi entered it on May 27, 1859. After the Risorgimento the city further developed as an industrial center, and with the opening of the Saint Gotthard (San Gottardo) Pass in 1882, it was linked by rail to northern Europe.

ARTS AND CULTURE. Como's Cathedral of Santa Maria Maggiore, begun in 1396, is an impressive late Gothic structure. Its interior displays nine sixteenth-century tapestries made in Ferrara, Florence, and Antwerp. The Sicilian **Filippo Juvara** designed the cupola which was completed in 1744, eight years after his death. On the outskirts of town, parts of the Church of San Carpoforo date from the fourth century; the structure was built over a Roman temple of Mercury. Other important churches include San Fedele, built between the tenth and twelfth centuries over a fifth-century Church of Sant'Eufemia, and the eleventh-century Sant'Abbondio, which honors Como's patron. A native of Thessalonica in Greece, he was consecrated as the city's fourth bishop in 449.

Behind the Duomo is the Casa del Fascio, the Como headquarters of the Fascist Party. It was built between 1932 and 1936 by **Giuseppe Terragni** (1904–1942), who came from Meda, near Milan. The building was one of the most daring and famous "rationalist" structures of Mussolini's regime. The architect served as a captain in the Second World War and suffered a nervous collapse at the Battle of Stalingrad (1942). He died shortly thereafter in a Pavia hospital, perhaps as a suicide.

Another artist from Como was **Antonio Sant'Elia** (1888–1916). Inspired by industrial designs and American skyscrapers, in 1912 Sant'Elia founded the Nuove Tendenze (New Trends) group of Milanese designers, many of whom later found a home in the Futurist movement. In 1914, for the first exhibition of the works of the Nuove Tendenze, Sant'Elia published the "Futurist Manifesto on Architecture." He died two years later on the front near Monfalcone, during the First World War. Giuseppe Terragni built a monument to Como's war dead based on a design by Sant'Elia.

Pliny the Elder. (A.D. 23–79) and **Pliny the Younger** (A.D. 61/62–c. 113) were both born in Como. Como was also the place where Pope Innocent XI was born as Benedetto Odescalchi in 1611. He rose through the ranks of papal administration in Macerata and Ferrara before becoming Bishop of Novara. As pope (1676–1689) he was instrumental in forming a Hapsburg, Polish, Russian, and Venetian alliance against the Turks which came to the rescue of Vienna and then liberated Budapest.

OTHER CENTERS. North of the tourist towns of **Tremezzo** and **Cadenabbia, Bellagio** sits on a beautiful point that juts into Lake Como. Its picturesque location attracted Milanese and other European aristocrats who built villas there in the eighteenth and nineteenth centuries. Most famous is the Villa Melzi, constructed between 1808 and 1810 for Francesco Melzi d'Edril (1753–1816), Napoleon's vice president of his brief Italian Republic. When Napoleon transformed the area into the Kingdom of Italy, Melzi became the Duke of Lodi. The villa is the work of the Italo-Swiss artist Giocondo Albertolli (1742–1839).

Northwest of Como along the lakeshore is **Cernobbio**, the site of many villas belonging to nobles or wealthy families. The most famous is the Villa d'Este, built between 1565 and 1570 by the local architect Pellegrino Tibaldi (1527–1596), for Cardinal Tolomeo Gallio. The town has become a host for trade fairs, mainly concerned with textiles.

The founder of the Italian Socialist Party, Filippo Turati, was born at **Canzo** in 1857. A lawyer and writer in the Milanese Scapigliatura (Bohemianism) movement, he turned to politics in the 1880s. With the Russian exile Anna Kuliscioff, he founded the Socialist League of Milan in 1889, the review, *Critica Sociale* (Social Criticism) in 1890, and the Socialist Party in 1892, at a congress in Genoa. A moderate who was increasingly at odds with the party's radical wing, Turati was expelled in 1922 and went on to form another organization, the Unitary Socialist Party, with Giacomo Matteotti. Persecuted by the Fascists, Turati fled Italy in 1926 and worked toward a united anti-Fascist front until he died at Paris in 1932.

As the Second World War drew to an end in April 1945, the Fascist dictator Benito Mussolini, his mistress, Claretta Pettacci, and an entourage of Blackshirt officials were captured and shot by partisans at **Dongo** and nearby **Giulino di Mezzegra** at the northern end of Lake Como.

CREMONA

PROVINCIAL PROFILE. Area: 684 sq. mi. Population: 332,040 (province), 72,337 (city). Cremona province contains 115 communes. Cremona is a long, diagonal province that runs from northwest to southeast. On its western side Cremona faces Emilia Romagna across the Po and, in Lombardy, Milan and Lodi. Cremona touches Bergamo on the north, and on the east, it faces Brescia and Mantua. The Oglio River forms most of Cremona's northeastern boundary, and the Adda runs along most of its western border with Milan and Lodi. Cremona city sits at the southern end of the province, and Crema serves as an anchor for the northern zone.

HISTORY. The Second Punic War (218–201 B.C.) and the challenge of the Carthaginian general Hannibal brought the Romans to the area around Cremona. In 218 B.C. they absorbed Cremona, which had begun as a village of the Gauls and developed it into a major center. After the fall of the Roman Empire in 476, Goths and Huns destroyed the city, and then the Byzantines ruled it as Cataulada from 550 until the Lombards took it in 603 and apparently burned it. Little more is known of Cataulada until around 753, when monks from nearby Nonantola dedicated a church there to Saint Silvester. In 774 the area was added to Charlemagne's empire. In the ninth century Cremona's administration was entrusted to a count-bishop, and at the end of the eleventh the beginnings of an independent commune took root with the support of Countess Matilda of Tuscany. Cremona's ruling bishops, who had close ties to the Holy Roman Empire, posed difficulties as the commune developed; one of them, Arnolfo, was removed by Pope Gregory VII in the late eleventh century, during the Investiture Controversy. In the subsequent struggles between the Empire and the Italian cities, Cremona preferred to ally itself against its Lombard sisters, particularly its detested rival, Milan; but the city turned about and joined the Lombard League in 1167.

Except for a brief Venetian domination, Cremona was ruled by the Milanese Visconti and Sforza families from 1334 until Spain's subjugation began in 1535. The city passed to Austrian rule in 1707 and, except for Napoleon's occupation, remained under it until the unification of Italy in 1859. During the Risorgimento the subversive Carbonari movement was particularly strong in Cremona, and the city rose up with Milan during the "Five Glorious Days" at the beginning of the Revolutions of 1848.

Spurred by a close attachment to the activist Antonio Rosmini-Serbati (1787–1855), Cremonese Catholicism developed a strong progressive tradition in the nineteenth and twentieth centuries, and is particularly identified with the work of Guido Miglioli (Pozzaglio, 1879–1954). Some have claimed that Cremona's Catholic currents influenced the humanitarian socialism of Leonida Bissolati who was born there in 1857. Bissolati was close to Turati's moderate faction within the Socialist Party. His support for Italy's war efforts against the Ottoman Empire in 1912, however, resulted in his expulsion from the party. He later advocated Italy's entry into the First World War and served as a cabinet minister. He died at Rome in 1920. Another Socialist leader, Costantino Lazzari, was born at Cremona in 1857. A head of the party's intransigent wing, Lazzari refused to follow the far Left in its break with the Socialists in 1921. He died in 1927, a sick and broken man.

Under the Fascists, Cremona was the stronghold of Roberto Farinacci (Isernia, 1892–1945), a transplanted Southerner who was one of the regime's most important figures.

ARTS AND CULTURE. Roman Cremona was known as a productive artistic center. The Roman poet **Virgil** studied there, and Cremona was the home of the poet **Furio Bibaculo,** the philosopher **Quintilio Varo,** and the jurist **Alfeno Varo.** It was discussed in the works of **Livy** and **Tacitus.** In its Piazza del Comune, Cremona boasts one of Italy's finest Romanesque cathedrals. Consecrated in 1190 in the presence of the Emperor Henry VI and his wife, Constance d'Hauteville, its medieval character has remained intact despite later additions. Next to the cathedral is the enormous Torrazzo, a 303-foot tower built in the thirteenth century and frequently cited as the symbol of the city. Also in the piazza is the twelfth-century baptistery and the thirteenth-century city hall, the Palazzo del Comune.

A distinctive Cremonese manner of painting, in the late Gothic style, developed under the **Bembo** brothers, **Bonifacio** (active 1440–1478) and **Benedetto** (c. 1425–1495), both of Brescia, and **Cristoforo Moretti** of Cremona (Active 1450–1485). Renaissance painting was heavily influenced by the Venetian style, particularly in the works of **Boccaccio Boccaccino** perhaps born in Cremona, c. 1465–c. 1524), and later those of **Altobello Melone** (active 1497–1517) and **Gian Francesco Bembo** in the early sixteenth century. Cremonese mannerism was expressed in the work of the **Campi** family, beginning with **Giulio** (1502–c. 1572) and including **Antonio** (1536–c. 1591), **Bernardino** (1522–c. 1591), and **Vincenzo** (1536–1591). After the Campi, in the late sixteenth century, Milan's influence replaced Venice's in Cremona's art. Cremona hosts an international cattle fair in September.

Cremona is world famous for its production of stringed instruments and pianos. It was the home of the **Amati** family of craftsmen: **Andrea** (c. 1510–c. 1578) and his sons **Antonio** (c. 1540–1638) and **Girolamo** (1561–1630). Girolamo's son **Nicolò** (1596–1684), in turn, taught **Antonio Stradivari** (c. 1644–1737) and **Andrea Guarneri** (c. 1626–1698) who both launched dynasties of their own. The School of Violin and Viola Makers, located in Cremona, operates a museum in the Palazzo dell'Arte. Cremona's musical heritage is further distinguished in that one of the fathers of opera, **Claudio Monteverdi,** was born there in 1567. He went to Mantua to work in the Gonzaga court, where he wrote and produced *Orfeo,* the first important and, perhaps, the first great opera. Later, after more time in Cremona, Monteverdi obtained a position in Venice as the *maestro di cappella* at the basilica of San Marco. He wrote sacred and secular music including eight books of madrigals. But his finest work may be his *L'incoronazione di Poppea* of 1642. Monteverdi died in Venice in 1643.

OTHER CENTERS: Crema sits on the Serio River in the northern zone of Cremona province. It possesses some vague pre-Roman roots but the city first rose to prominence as a possession of the Bishop of Piacenza in the tenth century. But Crema was contested between Piacenza, Pavia, Milan, and Cremona, and it was fought over in three wars during the eleventh and twelfth centuries. During the third war, in 1159–1160, and despite help from Milan and Brescia, Crema suffered a vicious siege and sack at the hands of Emperor Frederick Barbarossa. The inhabitants were scattered and the town was completely destroyed. Twenty-five years passed before it was rebuilt in 1185. In 1338 Crema fell under Milan's influence at the hands of the Visconti family but subsequently changed hands often between France and Venice, which ruled Crema, for the most part, between 1454 and Napoleon's conquest in 1797. Austria succeeded Napoleon in 1814 and ruled Crema until the Risorgimento and its absorption into Italy in 1859. Crema has a Gothic-Lombard cathedral completed between 1284 and 1341. Its most famous structure, however, is the sanctuary of Santa Maria della Croce, a richy decorated circular temple built in the 1490s by Giovanni Battagio, a native of Lodi (active 1465–1499). The composer Francesco Cavalli (1602–1676) was born in Crema. He changed his name from Caletti to Cavalli to honor his patron, Crema's governor, Francesco Cavalli, who launched the young man on a career in Venice, the capital at the time. He served as the organist of the Basilica of San Marco and wrote many pieces of sacred music, although he is best remembered for his operas.

LECCO

PROVINCIAL PROFILE. Area: 315 sq. mi. Population: 305,964 (province), 45,381 (city). Lecco province contains 90 communes. Lecco is a bifurcated province; its northern end embraces Lake Como's eastern shore, and its southern end bulges out below the lake. To the west of the province is Como, to its north is Sondrio, to its east is Bergamo, and to its south is Milan.

HISTORY. After the fall of Rome, Lecco became a Goth stronghold that later passed to the Byzantines and Lombards. The Bishops of Como then ruled Lecco before it passed to Milan in the twelfth century. Seventeenth-century Lecco province is familiar to Italians as the setting for much of Alessandro Manzoni's novel *The Betrothed* (*I promessi sposi*, 1825–1827). The province of Lecco was carved from Como in 1993.

ARTS AND CULTURE. The Ponte Vecchio, or Ponte Grande, is a fourteenth-century bridge. A fourteenth-century tower of the Visconti fortress also distinguishes the city. Lecco's Civic Museum in the Villa Manzoni dedicated to the life and works of the author.

OTHER CENTERS. An eleventh-century baptistery distinguishes **Oggiono**, one of the major centers of the Brianza district on the small Lago di Annone at the southern end of the province.

LODI

PROVINCIAL PROFILE. Area: 302 sq. mi. Population: 193,036 (province), 42,159 (city). Lodi province contains 61 communes. Lodi province was a finger-shaped part of Milan until the 1990s. It reaches toward the southeast until it touches the Po. Cremona province sits to its east, Pavia to its west, and Milan to its north.

HISTORY. Lodi was settled by the fifth century B.C. at a site slightly east of the present city. The Romans took the village in 222, and it became the *municipium* of Laus Pompeia in 89 B.C. Its first bishop, San Bassiano, served from 373 until 409.

As an independent commune and an ally of the Holy Roman Emperor, Laus found itself at war with the Milanesi, who destroyed the city in 1111 and 1158. Frederick Barbarossa granted the request to rebuild the city on another location. The new city of Lodi was then erected on a spur of Monte Guzzone over the Adda River. Lodi failed to show Frederick much gratitude, however, and joined the Lombard League in 1167. Lodigiani then fought against him at Legnano in 1176. The about-face did not end Lodi's troubles with Milan, which persisted until Azzo Visconti took the city in 1335.

The Peace of Lodi, concluded in 1454, guaranteed Sforza rule in Milan and Venetian holdings on the mainland. It gave Renaissance Italy a general peace which lasted until the foreign invasions of the 1490s. Napoleon's first great victory in Italy was at Lodi, on May 10, 1796. There, at the bridge over the Adda River, his force of 5,000 men defeated an Austrian army twice its size.

The Risorgimento did not inspire Lodi as much as it did other Lombard cities. It did not rise in revolt in 1848, and in 1859 the Austrians deserted the city before it was occupied by a French force under General Marie MacMahon on June 10. It joined Italy as part of the province of Milan.

ARTS AND CULTURE. Lodi's Duomo dates from the late twelfth century. The structure was modified during the Renaissance, and a restoration in the 1960s restored some of its Romanesque qualities. Renaissance Lodi, nevertheless, is well represented in the sanctuary of the Incoronata. Built between 1488 and 1494 by the Milanese **Gian Giacomo Dolcebuono** (1440–c. 1506) and **Giovanni Battagio** (active 1465–1499), a son of Lodi, the church is considered to be among the masterpieces of the Lombard Renaissance.

The poet **Ada Negri** (1870–1945) was born in Lodi. Her working-class roots echoed in her works that called for social justice. She became a member of the Royal Italian Academy in 1940.

OTHER CENTERS. Lodi Vecchio is the site of the first city. It was demolished by the Milanesi in 1158; the only building in the town left (and still) standing was the eighth-century Basilica of San Bassiano. Additions were made and frescoes were added in the fourteenth and sixteenth centuries.

MANTUA (MANTOVA)

PROVINCIAL PROFILE. Area: 903 sq. mi. Population: 370,638 (province), 49,564 (city). Mantua province contains 70 communes. Mantua extends fingerlike southeast from Lombardy. Its western border touches the provinces of Brescia and Cremona. From there it wedges eastward into two other regions, Veneto to its north and Emilia Romagna to its south. Most of the province sits flat on the Po plain. The Mincio River widens briefly as it curves around the city of Mantua on three sides.

HISTORY. Mantua began as an Etruscan town and, after a period under the Cenomanni Gauls, was taken by the Romans in the third century B.C. Little is known of post-Roman Mantua until 781, when Charlemagne reorganized the territory, and 977, when it was annexed by the Canossa dynasty. The Canossa ruled Mantua until the death of Countess Matilda of Tuscany in 1115, when it gained status as a quasi-independent commune. Although the city was frequently at war with its neighbors, it joined most of them in the victorious Lombard League against Emperor Frederick Barbarossa in 1167. Mantua's communal period came to an end when the Bonaccolsi family took control and ruled it between 1272 and 1328, when it passed to the Gonzagas. Mantua expanded between 1382 and 1478, during the reigns of Francesco I Gonzaga, his son, Gianfrancesco, and his grandson, Ludovico.

The city maintained a tricky independence between Milan and Venice. But the visit to Mantua in 1530 by Emperor Charles V indicated that it had been reined into the growing Spanish orbit. At the same time Charles elevated Mantua to a duchy and added the marquisate of Monferrato in the bargain. The grateful Gonzagas soon joined the Hapsburgs in marriage. Upon the death of Duke Ferdinando in 1626, and his brother Vincenzo II in 1627, however, a civil war erupted between two branches of the family, one behind Carlo Gonzaga-Nevers, who enjoyed French support, and the other behind Spain's and Piedmont's ally, Cesare, Duke of Guastalla. This

War of the Mantuan Succession devastated the Gonzaga capital, which suffered a three-day sack of stunning ferocity at the hands of Hapsburg troops who intervened to preserve their interests and block French ambitions. The Treaty of Cherasco in 1631 allowed the Gonzaga-Nevers to remain on the Mantuan throne, but as vassals of Vienna. The terrible conflict, moreover, crippled the Lombard economy, particularly its agriculture, for decades to come.

In 1708 Mantua came under Austrian rule, and in 1737 it was joined to Lombardy. A vice governor ruled in Mantua until Emperor Joseph II's reforms of 1786 made it one of the Lombard intendancies. French Revolutionary armies entered Lombardy in 1796, and on February 2, 1797, after a stiff resistance, the Austrians surrendered Mantua to Napoleon's troops. By November the city had become the capital of the Mincio department in Napoleon's puppet Cisalpine Republic. France held Mantua, later as part of its Kingdom of Italy, until the Austrian Hapsburgs reestablished themselves.

The Risorgimento proved popular in Mantua, particularly when union with Italy was endorsed by the popular bishop Giovanni Corti. A number of Mantuan priests gave their lives in the cause. Nevertheless, in 1859, when Piedmont and its French ally went to war with the Austrians, the latter stood their ground along the Mincio, and Mantua remained in Hapsburg hands. The western part of the Mantovano was split between Brescia and Cremona provinces in the new Italian Kingdom while Mantua and Venetia stayed under Vienna's jurisdiction. Italy's alliance with Prussia in 1866, however, forced the Austrians to cede those territories to Rome. Shortly after the transfer of power, Ivanoe Bonomi (1873–1951) was born in Mantua. Italy's prime minister before and after Mussolini's Fascist regime, Bonomi began as a moderate Socialist who was expelled from the party in 1912. He led a small following, but nevertheless took the prime minister's office in 1921–1922 and 1944–1945.

ARTS AND CULTURE. The Roman poet **Virgil**, author of the *Aeneid*, was born in 70 B.C. at **Andes**, near Mantua. Mantua retains little of its Roman and medieval past, in part because scarce resources for construction resulted in the use of brick rather than stone. A number of important Renaissance structures remain, however, the most important being the Basilica of Sant'Andrea. The structure illustrates the heavy Florentine influence on Mantua's art of the time. Designed by the Florentine artist **Leon Battista Alberti** (1404–1472), one of the premier artists of the age, and finished by the Tuscan **Luca Fancelli** (1430–1495), the bulk of the church was completed in the 1490s, although the cupola, designed by the Sicilian **Filippo Juvara** (1678–1736), waited until 1763. Alberti also designed the classical Church of San Sebastiano, and Fancelli built it.

Along with Alberti's influence, Renaissance Mantua was fortunate in the presence of **Andrea Mantegna** (1431–1506). In 1457 Ludovico Gonzaga secured Mantegna's transfer from Padua as court painter. Although much of his work is now in museums around the world, Mantegna's series of frescoes still adorns the walls of the Camera degli sposi (wedding chamber) in the Gonzaga fortress, the severe Palazzo Ducale. More pervasive was the influence of **Giulio Romano** (c. 1499–1546), who built and decorated many palaces in the 1520s and 1530s, and that of the Mantua native **Giovanni Battista Bertani** (1516–1576), who directed the Gonzaga projects after 1549.

In 1748 the Austrians established the Colonia Virgiliana, which flourished as a learned academy. In 1768 it merged with three other academies (the Timidi, the Filarmonici, and the Teresiana) to form the Royal Academy of Sciences, Letters, and Arts. The reorganization demanded the energies of the architects, the Umbrian **Giuseppe Piermarini** (1734–1808), who designed the overall structure, and the Parmigian **Antonio Galli da Bibiena** (1700–1774), responsible for the exceptional Scientific Theater. Italy's oldest newspaper, the *Gazzetta del Mantova*, was founded there in 1664; and one of Italy's first opera performances, *Orfeo* (Claudio Monteverdi, 1567–1643), occurred in Mantua in 1607.

OTHER CENTERS. San Benedetto Po is the birthplace of the Socialist leader Enrico Ferri (1856–1929). Party chairman and editor of its newspaper *Avanti!* (Forward!) from 1903 until 1907, his policy was to please both wings of the organization. His eventual move to the far Left ended his career. San Benedetto Po is also the site of the eleventh-century monastery of Polirone.

Sabbioneta was a lesser Mantua, ruled as a small principality by a cadet branch of the Gonzaga. It contains a number of noteworthy late sixteenth-century structures, such as the Palazzo Ducale, the Church of the Incoronata, and the Olympic Theater of Vicenza's Vincenzo Scamozzi (1552–c. 1616).

PAVIA

PROVINCIAL PROFILE. Area: 1,240 sq. mi. Population: 495,406 (province), 74,699 (city). Pavia province contains 190 communes. The Po is navigable up to the Ticino River southeast of Pavia. The province forms Lombardy's southwest corner, wedged between Emilia Romagna to its east and Piedmont to its west. Milan and Lodi provinces occupy Pavia's northern border.

HISTORY. Pavia, first a Liguri settlement and then home to Gaulish tribes, was taken by the Romans about 220 B.C. and named Ticinum. They reinforced the town and made it a hinge of their north Italian defenses. Such precautions, however, did not stop Attila and his Huns, who sacked

Pavia in A.D. 452, nor the repetition of the deed by Odoacre and his Goths in 476. Theodoric the Great cultivated Pavia as a regional capital after Ravenna and undertook a construction program there. But Pavia's greatest status as one of Italy's most important cities came under the Lombards, who made it capital of their kingdom in the sixth century. As such, by the mid-700s Pavia became a target of Frankish penetration into northern Italy. Charlemagne laid siege to it and, for a year, the Lombard King Desiderius (Charlemagne's father-in-law) held. But he surrendered in 774 and spent the rest of his days at a convent in France. His son, Adelchis, rallied for a while at Verona, then fled to Constantinople. The Lombard Kingdom was then absorbed into the Frankish Empire.

After Frankish rule dissolved, Pavia evolved into a commune by the early twelfth century. Emperor Frederick Barbarossa used Pavia as a base, was crowned there in 1155, and accorded the city special rights. Galeazzo II Visconti of Milan subdued Pavia in 1359. In 1525 Pavia became the battleground of the Franco-Imperial struggle for hegemony in Italy. The forces of Emperor Charles V, supported by the Pavesi, defeated and captured King Francis I of France. Pavia's fortunes continued to follow Milan's as a Spanish and then an Austrian possession, with the Napoleonic interlude between 1796 and 1814.

ARTS AND CULTURE. The Visconti were responsible for many of Pavia's historic structures. Their Castello was built by **Bernardo da Venezia** (active 1360–1400) between 1360 and 1365. Today it houses the civic museums. Gian Galeazzo Visconti established the University of Pavia in 1361, although its roots extend to a ninth-century law school. Lanfranc, Archbishop of Canterbury, was born at Pavia about 1005.

OTHER CENTERS. Outside of Pavia is a Carthusian monastery, the **Certosa di Pavia**, a singular achievement. Constructed between 1396 and 1542, according to the desires of Gian Galeazzo Visconti, as a place to bury members of his family, much of the complex was completed by the Swiss artist Giovanni Solari (1400–c. 1484) and his son, the Milanese Guiniforte Solari (1429–1481). Guiniforte began work on the church's extraordinary facade in 1473, and the task was continued by a number of artists, including Pavia's Giovanni Antonio Amadeo (1447–c. 1552); the Mantegazza brothers, Antonio (active 1464–1495) and Cristoforo (active 1464–1482), also of Pavia; and the Milanese Gian Giacomo Dolcebuono (1440–c. 1506).

The northwestern stretch of the province is flat agricultural land called the Lomellina, with its towns of **Mortara, Vigevano,** and **Lomella.** Remains of a castle in Lomella attest to its medieval importance, as do the tenth- and eleventh-century Church of Santa Maria Maggiore and the fifth-century baptistery of San Giovanni ad Fontes. A second level was added to the baptistery in the eighth century.

The political leader Agostino Depretis (1813–1887) was born in **Mez-**

zana Corti. After the first rightist era of the united Italian Parliament, Depretis brought the Left to power in 1876 and served as prime minister for most of the period until his death. Depretis's legacy, however, was not ideological rigor, but the system of *trasformismo* (transformism), vaguely corrupt alliances and coalitions with little regard to principle.

The area of Pavia province south of the Po is known as the Oltrepò. Its unofficial capital is **Voghera**, an industrial town. The Catholic activist and organizer Don Davide Albertario (1846–1902) was born in **Filighera**.

SONDRIO

PROVINCIAL PROFILE. Area: 1,240 sq. mi. Population: 177,298 (province), 22,179 (city). Sondrio province contains 78 communes. The province is a long, U-shaped entity. Its western upswing is dominated by the Liro River, which empties into the Mera, and the Chiavenna plain. The province ends there at Lago di Mezzola, which spills into Lago di Como. In the east are less populated Alpine valleys, particularly the Alta Valtellina. In between, Sondrio sits on the banks of the Mallero River and serves as the central city of the Valtellina. The Stelvio National Park covers the northeast end of the province, and the Delle Orobi Valtellinesi Regional Park stretches along its southern border. To Sondrio's east and southeast are the provinces of Como and Lecco. To its south is Bergamo, and to its southeast is Brescia. Trentino-Alto Adige faces Sondrio to the east, and Switzerland sits across its northern frontier. On the Swiss border is Sondrio's highest peak, the Bernina (13,287 feet).

HISTORY. Since prehistoric times, Sondrio's valleys, especially the Valtellina, have been important routes between northern and southern Europe. Founded by the Lombards, Sondrio city was governed by local feudal lords before it came under Milan's sway with the Visconti and the Sforza. North of Spanish Milan and connected to central Europe and the Rhineland by the Spluga Pass, during the religious wars of the late sixteenth and early seventeenth centuries, Sondrio and the Valtellina assumed strategic importance in European politics. The Swiss Grisons canton had taken it when the old Duchy of Milan disintegrated; but the Catholic King of Spain, whose sea routes to Protestant enemies were plagued by English and Dutch pirates, turned to the valley as an avenue to channel his troops to northern Europe. In 1622, therefore, the Spanish Governor of Milan invaded the Valtellina. He was helped by the fact that, in 1620, the Valtellina had begun a revolt against its Protestant Swiss masters. The zone became a battleground, suffering invasions by almost all the European powers, including papal troops, until the Treaty of Westphalia in 1648 allowed Grisons to keep it on the condition of guaranteed religious liberty. In 1797, inspired by Napoleon's conquests, an independent Republic of the Valtellina was declared and annexed by the French to the Cisalpine Republic based in Milan. In 1815 the Congress of Vienna placed Sondrio and the Valtellina in Austria's Lombard-Venetian holdings.

ARTS AND CULTURE. Each March, Sondrio hosts an annual festival of organ music. The architect **Pier Luigi Nervi** (1891–1979) was born in Sondrio. Identified with Fascist rationalism, Nervi nevertheless also was inspired by the International Style associated with Le Corbusier and Walter Gropius. Some of his more important designs were airplane hangers, which were all destroyed in the Second World War. After the war his principal works were exhibition halls in Turin (1947–1949) and the Palazzetto dello Sport, built outside of Rome for the 1960 Olympic Games.

OTHER CENTERS. Grosio was an significant bastion in the Valtellina. Remains of a fourteenth-century fortress, the Castello Nuovo, still stand. A park containing Neolithic remains, the Parco delle Incisioni Rupestre, attests to the place's ancient strategic importance.

VARESE

PROVINCIAL PROFILE. Area: 463 sq. mi. Population: 811,778 (province), 84,520 (city). Varese province contains 141 communes. The province occupies Lombardy's northwest corner. Lake Maggiore and Piedmont face it on the west, Milan is to its south, and Como is on its east. Northeast of Varese province is Switzerland.

HISTORY. Varese is largely a modern town, although remains of Hellenistic frescoes were discovered at nearby Santa Maria di Castelseprio in 1944. During the Roman era and the early Middle Ages, however, Castelseprio and Angera were settlements of greater importance. The Visconti conquered the area in the thirteenth century, reduced Castelseprio to ruin, and ruled the land as an agricultural zone of Milan's territories. Under the new masters, Varese developed as a small but prosperous commune based on artisanal trades. By the eighteenth century it had become the residence of the Hapsburg Prince Francis III before he took the throne of Modena.

During the Risorgimento, Varese's location near the Lombard-Piedmontese border brought it attention. In 1848 Giuseppe Garibaldi attempted in vain to anchor some anti-Austrian resistance there, to take heat off embattled Milan. In 1859 Varese was the site of a battle between the Austrians and Garibaldi's troops in their victorious march to Como. Umberto Bossi was born near Varese in 1941. In 1982, when he was a medical student, the autonomist model of the Valle d'Aosta inspired Bossi to form a political organization having the goal of a semi-independent Lombardy. His faction became the Lombard League in 1986, and as part of the Northern League, one of Italy's largest political organizations by the 1990s.

ARTS AND CULTURE. Varese is a manufacturing center, particularly famous for its production of shoes. Its Basilica of San Vittore was built between 1580 and 1615 from a design of **Pellegrino Tibaldi** (1527–1596). Its neoclassical facade is the work of the Austrian **Leopoldo Pollack** (1751–1806).

OTHER CENTERS. Golasecca is the site of a large archaeological zone and museum with important remains of an Iron Age culture. It sits outside of **Arsago Seprio**, which contains the Church of San Vittore and its baptistery, built in part with ancient Roman materials between the ninth and twelfth centuries. **Castelseprio** was an early Insubri settlement and later a local center of Roman strength. Ruins of an ancient *castrum* (fortress) recall its strategic past. The Lombards and Franks also used the town, building a castle there and a mint. Castelseprio was demolished by archbishop Ottone Visconti when he took the area in 1287. It also contains the remains of a late imperial basilica complex, San Giovanni Evangelista.

Busto Arsizio is a hub of Italy's textile industry. It is also home to the Renaissance sanctuary of Santa Maria in Piazza, the work of Tommaso Rodari (active 1484–1526) and, perhaps, the sixteenth-century artist Antonio Lonati.

The composer Gian Carlo Menotti was born in **Cadegliano** in 1911. He began his studies at the Milan Conservatory but transferred to Philadelphia's Curtis Institute. In the decade after the Second World War, he wrote his most celebrated operas, *The Medium* (1946), *The Telephone* (1947), *The Consul* (1950), and *Amahl and the Night Visitors* (1951). In the 1950s he devoted much of his energy to the Festival of Two Worlds in Spoleto.

Castiglione Olona was a Roman town and the site of a medieval fortress. In the fifteenth century, Cardinal Branda Castiglioni imported Tuscan sculptors to build a string of palaces along the main street of the town. The major showpieces, however, are the fifteenth-century collegiate Church of Santi Stefano e Lorenzo and its adjacent baptistery. Toward the center of the city is the Palazzo Branda Castiglioni, which houses a museum. The Florentine artist Tommaso di Cristoforo Fini, known as Masolino da Panicale (1383–c. 1440/1447), contributed frescoes to all three structures.

SELECT BIBLIOGRAPHY

Biffignandi, Silvia. *Il sistema industriale della Lombardia.* Bologna: Il Mulino, 1987.
Istituto Geografico De Agostini. *Lombardia.* 2 vols. Novara: Istituto Geografico De Agostini, 1979–1980.
Pirovano, Carlo, ed. *Lombardia: Ritratto di una terra.* Milan: Electa, 1997.
Scalvini, Maria Luisa. *Bergamo.* Rome: Laterza, 1987.
Vicini, Donata. *Pavia e Certosa: Guida storico-artista.* Pavia: Azienda di Promozione Turistica/Pavia, 1994.

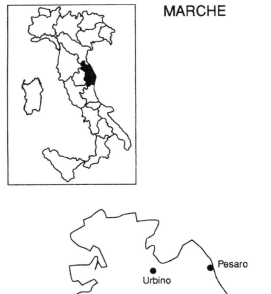

MARCHE

Pesaro

Urbino

Umbro-Marchigian
Apennines

Senigallia

Esino River

Jesi

★ ANCONA

Loreto

Macerata

Adriatic
Sea

Camerino

Sibillini
Range

Fermo

Ascoli Piceno

Chapter 11

MARCHE

REGIONAL CHARACTERISTICS. Area: 3,742 sq. mi. Population: 1,450,879. Capital: Ancona. The Marche rank fifteenth among Italian regions in land area and thirteenth in population. Marche is home to three Catholic metropolitan sees: Ancona/Osimo, Fermo, and Urbino/Urbania/Sant'Angelo in Vado.

The Marche are rugged lands; 68.8 percent of the territory is hilly and 31.2 percent is mountainous. The highest points are in the Umbro-Marchigian Apennines in the region's western districts, in the Montefeltro range at its northwest corner, at Monte Nerone below it, and in the Sibillini range west of Ascoli Piceno. The tallest mountain, at 8,124 feet, is Monte Vettore in the Sibillini range along the Umbrian frontier. By the time the land reaches the sea, the Marche landscape is rolling hills or dramatic cliffs cascading into the Adriatic, such as at the Conero Riviera, just south of Ancona and the coastline northwest of Pesaro. Rivers generally run northeast from the mountains toward the sea. In the north, the Metauro reaches the Adriatic at Fano, and in the south, the Tronto runs near the Abruzzo border. The most important river is the Esino, which rises at Monte Cafaggio and empties into the sea just north of Ancona. The Esino valley, or Vallesina, has often formed a cultural border between Marche's north and south.

ECONOMY. Of the Marchigiani, 6.9 percent are employed in agriculture, industry accounts for 39.2 percent, and 53.9 percent work in the tertiary sector. Of 563,000 employed in 1997, 342,000 were men and 221,000 were women. In January 1998 the Marche had an unemployment rate of 6.7 percent. Much of the farmland of the Marche is devoted to vineyards and olive groves. On the coast, fishing is a traditional occupation, and shipyards have employed large numbers in Ancona since they were established by Pope Gregory XVI in 1843. Some sulfur was mined in the northwest corner of the region.

CUISINE. Roast pig flavored with fennel and other spices is a traditional feast. Peculiar to Ascoli Piceno are breaded olives stuffed with meats and truffles, then fried or baked. Truffle sauce for pasta is also popular. The Esino valley around Iesi is the center of production for *verdicchio*, a strong white wine frequently judged as one of Italy's finest. *Bianchello* is a lighter white wine found around Fano and along the Metauro. In the southern part of the region, *rosso piceno* and *rosso piceno superiore* are popular, as is the white *falerio*. Near the Ancona coast, *rosso conero* is made from Montepulciano and Sangiovese grapes. A specialty across the Marche is the aged sweet *vin cotto* (cooked wine). Marchigiani drink more wine, per capita, than the citizens of any other Italian region.

BUCATINI ALLA MARCHIGIANA

¼ lb. pancetta, diced	½ c. red wine
1 medium onion, chopped	1 lb. ripe tomatoes, peeled
1 carrot, chopped	Salt and pepper to taste
1 stalk celery, chopped	1 lb. bucatini pasta
½ c. olive oil	Grated cheese

In a 3-qt. pot combine the pancetta, onion, carrot, and celery with the oil and cook over medium heat, then add wine and cook for a few more minutes. Meanwhile, place tomatoes briefly in boiling water, then remove tomatoes, mince, and remove seeds. Add the tomatoes to the pancetta mixture, add salt and pepper, and continue cooking. Prepare pasta according to package directions. Drain the pasta, then place it in a large bowl, add sauce and sprinkle with cheese.

HISTORY. After a period of proto-Villanovan settlements, the Piceni, an Iron Age people, arrived in the Marche. Their burial sites from as early as the ninth century B.C. can be seen near Iesi and Novilara. The Piceni were joined by their Umbri cousins and other Gauls. Some Greeks settled along the Adriatic coast and traded with the Piceni. The Romans penetrated the region toward the start of the third century B.C. and consolidated their rule in 295 when, allied with the Piceni, they defeated an alliance of Samnites, Galli Senoni, Umbrians, and Etruscans at Sentinum, near modern Sassoferrato. During the Second Punic War, Rome again relied on Piceni troops, whose aid was particularly crucial in 207 B.C. at the battle of the

Metauro (Metaurus) River, near present-day Cagli. There, the Romans and
the XX Legion of Piceni defeated and killed the Carthaginian general Hasdrubal, brother of Hannibal. The Marche retained some cohesion under
the Romans, although during the imperial epoch, the Marche were split
along the Esino River into a northern zone, Region VI (Umbria, which later
gravitated toward Ravenna and northern Italy—and a southern part, Region V (Picenum, which eventually looked toward Spoleto and central Italy).

Upon the collapse of the Roman Empire in 476, the Marche were
wrenched by the back-and-forth struggles involving Goths; then Byzantines,
who conquered and devastated most of the northern end of the region in
the 530s; and the Lombards, who arrived later in the sixth century to
control its southern parts. Under the Byzantines, Fano, Senigallia, Ancona,
and Pesaro joined with Rimini in Romagna to form a confederation of
trading ports, the Pentapolis, which acquired a semi-independent status.
The Carolingian conquest between 752 and 774 split the Marche yet again
into north and south; the lands above and including Ancona were designated for the Church, whereas the territory below it went to the Dukes of
Spoleto. By the 900s, Charlemagne's German successors called the region
Marka, a designation for frontier units of the empire and the origin of
today's Marche. The Italian *Marche* is plural and signifies a collection of
territories—the Marca Superiore, the Marca Guarneriana (later dubbed
Anconetana), and those of Fermo, Camerino, and so forth—that constituted this southern imperial outpost. Nevertheless, invasions and raids continued. The Muslims sacked the Marche through the ninth and tenth
centuries, followed by the Normans in the eleventh. By then, many of
Marche's cities had acquired autonomous communal status, led by the maritime republic of Ancona.

Despite vague papal control over much of the zone, in the thirteenth
century large expanses of Marche sympathized with Ghibelline factions.
The Ghibelline champion, Emperor Frederick II, was born at Iesi. Other
cities, however, such as Camerino and Ancona, identified more closely with
the Guelph cause. The papacy's transfer to Avignon in the fourteenth century further loosened its control, and Marchigian cities evolved further into
independent states that fell under regional families such as the Malatesta
from Rimini, the Ordelaffi of Forlì, and the Visconti of Milan. By the
1350s, however, the popes were intent on returning to Rome, and dispatched Cardinal Egidio (Gil) Albornoz through the Marche to reestablish
and consolidate their control. Rebellions flared by the 1360s, but the popes
succeeded in the end. Their rule, however, was not hegemonic, and noble
families maintained their influence over the Marche without too much in-
terruption. Between 1433 and 1444, for instance, Francesco Sforza ruled
nearly all of the region. During the Renaissance, Marche attained a measure
of prosperity based on trade and on local industries such as paper and silk

production. Evidence of an advanced economy can be seen in the estab-lishment at Ascoli Piceno of one of Italy's first banks, the Monte di Pietà, in 1458.

The Church's grip tightened in the next two centuries. Certain occasions, such as the proclamation of a republic of Ancona in 1532, required the pope's troops to restore his suzerainty. Camerino became a duchy under Ottavio Farnese, grandson of Pope Paul III, until 1545, when Rome took direct control. And when the Della Rovere line ended in Urbino, Pesaro, and Senigallia in 1631, those districts passed to Rome as well.

Between Napoleon's first invasion in 1796 and the defeat of his brother-in-law, Joachim Murat, at Tolentino in May 1815, the Marche were fre-quently exchanged between France, its satellites, and the papacy. Soon thereafter the restored papal administration detached Urbino-Pesaro and Camerino from the Marche, which were cut into four provinces: Ancona, Macerata, Fermo, and Ascoli Piceno. The defeat of Napoleon and of Mu-rat, however, did not extinguish revolutionary fervor in the Marche, and the region participated in many Risorgimento struggles. The revolts of 1831 had widespread support there, as did the uprisings of 1848. The firebrand revolutionary Giuseppe Garibaldi counted many Marchigiani among his followers in the ill-fated Roman Republic, and was elected to the Marche constituent assembly as a delegate from Macerata.

In 1860 the indefatigable Garibaldi poised to assail Rome from the south. Anxious not to provoke the pope's French defenders, the new Italian King-dom hoped to cut off the attack with a quick strike from the north. Royal forces thus crossed into the Marche, where they met and defeated a small papal force at Castelfidardo, south of Ancona, on September 18. From there the force proceeded to meet Garibaldi at Teano. The Marche were annexed to Italy after a plebiscite on November 4–5, 1860. When the Marche were incorporated into the new Kingdom, two of the pontifical provinces, Camerino and Fermo, were suppressed. After the Second World War, the Marche were a hotly contested area between the Christian Dem-ocrats and the Communists, with neither enjoying a clear-cut superiority. With the collapse of the former in the 1990s, however, the successors to the Communists in the Democratic Party of the Left (PDS) took the lead.

RECENT POLITICS. The Marche vote as the fourteenth electoral dis-trict (*circoscrizione*). In the 1996 majoritarian election to the Chamber of Deputies, the Center-Left Ulivo coalition captured 41.7 percent of the vote, followed by the more conservative Polo per le Libertà with 40.9 and a "Progressive" coalition with 12.5 percent. In the proportional vote the PDS took 28.7 percent, 17.4 went to Forza Italia, 16.3 percent to the Alleanza Nazionale, and 10.4 percent to the far Left Communist Rifondazione. In the Senate vote the Ulivo took 55.4 percent of the votes versus 40.6 percent for the Polo. The pattern continued in the April 2000 regional elections when Vito D'Ambrosio was reelected president of the region at the head of a Center-Left coalition that captured 49.9 percent of the vote over Center-Right's 44.2 percent.

ANCONA

PROVINCIAL PROFILE. Area: 748 sq. mi. Population: 441,815 (province), 99,453 (city). Capital: Ancona. The region contains 49 communes. Ancona is a diagonal province that tilts east-northeast toward the Adriatic coast. To its south is Macerata, to its north is Pesaro-Urbino, and to its west-southwest is Umbria.

HISTORY. With traces of prehistoric proto-Villanovan culture, Ancona was colonized in the sixth century B.C. by Greeks who named it Angkon (or Ankon or Dorica Ankon), for the elbow-shaped promontory that protects the harbor. Other sources date Ancona's foundation by exiles from Syracuse about 390 B.C. The city acquired some fame as an important Hellenic site, and the Roman poet Catullus and the Roman satirist Juvenal praised the city's temple to the Greek goddess Aphrodite. Ancona allied itself with the Piceni and the Romans in the 290s and was slowly brought under the Republic's sway as a naval base and commercial port. Ancona's links to the Eastern Roman Empire kept it safe for a while after the fall of the Western Empire in A.D. 476. It repulsed Gothic sieges in 539 and 551. As a coastal city, Ancona suffered Muslim raids; the worst one nearly destroyed it in 839. By the 700s the power of Constantinople grew more distant, and Ancona secured itself as a member of the Pentapolis confederation, then as a client state of the Dukes of Spoleto. Finally the city was given to the pope by Charlemagne in 774.

Tenth-century Ancona evolved into a free commune. It flourished as an Adriatic power with renewed, though vague, links to Constantinople while extending its presence in the eastern Mediterranean during the Second Crusade (1147–1149). For example, Anconans established merchant colonies in Constantinople and Alexandria. Ancona's success prompted anxiety among the Venetians, who reached a community of purpose with Emperor Frederick I Barbarossa, who also had grown apprehensive over Ancona's ties with the Byzantines. In the twelfth century Ancona had reached the apex of its power, and the Arab geographer al-Idrisi recorded it as one of the great cities of Christendom. As a consequence, between 1167 and 1174 Ancona suffered naval blockades by a jealous Venice and land sieges under Barbarossa and his chancellor, Archbishop Christian of Mainz. Rival Marchigian towns, happy to see their larger neighbor receive its comeuppance, joined in the attack. But Ancona held, and fought to a truce in 1177.

The city was then awarded to the Holy Roman Empire, but with the stipulation of papal control. It continued to engage the Venetians in sporadic battle until the fifteenth century. After a brief period of Malatesta rule, in 1355 the city, devastated by fire and by the Black Death, surrendered to Cardinal Gil Albornoz and returned to the papal fold. Above the town, on the hills of San Cataldo, Albornoz built a fortress that was demolished 28 years later during a popular uprising. Ancona nevertheless maintained itself as an autonomous commune until 1532, when Church control was finally secured when Cardinal Benedetto Accolti bought it from Pope Clement VII.

Two hundred years later, in 1732, Ancona revived when Pope Clement XII conferred on it the status of a free port. The city declared itself a republic upon the French invasion of 1797 and changed hands frequently during the subsequent wars until the defeat of Murat in 1815. But the revolutionary spirit remained strong in Ancona. It joined the revolutions of 1831, which required a French force to be garrisoned there from 1832 until 1839. Ancona declared itself part of Garibaldi and Mazzini's Roman Republic in 1849. On June 19 of that year the city surrendered to Austrian forces after a twenty-seven-day siege. Eleven years later, in September 1860, forces of the new Italian Kingdom, fresh from their victory over papal troops at Castelfidardo, laid siege to Ancona. The papal army had retreated into the city after Castelfidardo, and soon surrendered in the face of much larger Italian numbers and bombardments from naval contingents.

Unification with Italy brought some attention to Ancona, which was the home port of the Adriatic fleet until it was relocated to Venice in 1866. Although Ancona's industry suffered in competition with northern manufacturing after unification, the city prospered as a transportation hub. It was connected to a coastal railroad line in 1860 and linked directly to Rome over the mountains in 1866. Between 1899 and 1908 its port traffic more than doubled, and it ranked as Italy's eighth busiest. In June 1914 riots broke out in Ancona and discontent spread throughout Marche and into Romagna, launching the aborted revolution of "Red Week." Italy's entrance into the First World War had immediate repercussions for Ancona. On the first day of fighting, May 24, 1915, the Austrian fleet inflicted a heavy bombardment on the city.

Ancona suffered during the Second World War between November 1, 1943, and its liberation from Nazi occupation, by Polish troops, on June 18, 1944. The city endured terrific Allied bombardments that destroyed three-quarters of its homes and earned it the sobriquet "The Cassino of the Marche." A 1972 earthquake at the city center and a 1982 landslide transformed Ancona by launching an exodus of people and businesses to the suburbs. Nevertheless, restoration and reconstruction have proceeded steadily.

ARTS AND CULTURE. Ancona's Roman heritage can be examined in the impressive Arch of Trajan, which dates from A.D. 115. The structure commemorated extensive improvements to the harbor made by the emperor, who favored the city. Ancona's Duomo was begun in the ninth century over the ruins of a third-century temple and a sixth-century basilica. It is dedicated to Ancona's patron, San Ciriaco, who, according to one tradition, was an early bishop of Jerusalem martyred during the fourth-century persecutions of the Roman Emperor Julian the Apostate. His participation in Saint Helen's search for the Holy Cross brought him to Rome, where he was named Bishop of Ancona. Other accounts place Ciriaco as a second-century bishop who was killed in a revolt against the Romans. His feast day is May 4. Ciriaco's remains and those of Saints Liberio, Marcellino, and Palazia rest in the crypt. Next to the Duomo is an important diocesan museum.

Ancona's medieval glory as a mercantile power can be seen in the thirteenth-century Palazzo del Senato (or Pilastri), which was renovated in the fifteenth and twentieth-centuries. An important structure outside the city is the eleventh-century Church of Santa Maria di Portonovo, built by Lombard canons and considered the Marche's finest example of the Romanesque style. The Renaissance artist **Gentile da Fabriano** (c. 1370–1427) was born in Ancona, but the city is not associated with his work. The work of the eighteenth-century Neapolitan artist **Luigi Vanvitelli** (1700–1773) distinguishes Ancona, particularly the Duomo's Madonna Chapel (1738) and the marina (the lazzaretto or mole Vanvitelliana), which Pope Clement XII commissioned in 1733 as part of his free port project. Through the centuries the mole also served as a barracks and a prison. Ancona had a university, inaugurated by Pope Pius IV in 1562, but it ceased to exist by the end of the eighteenth century. In 1958 a branch of the University of Urbino opened at Ancona.

The important journalist and liberal historian **Luigi Albertini** (1871–1941), was born in Ancona. In 1900 he became the director and co-owner of Italy's most prestigious newspaper, Milan's *Corriere della Sera* (Evening Post), with the intent of using it to propagate his conservative liberalism. He opposed Mussolini's state and was stripped of his paper, which then became an organ of the Fascists. Albertini continued to speak against the regime as a senator until his retirement in 1929. The film actress **Virna Lisi** was born at Ancona in 1937. She achieved international fame in the 1950s and 1960s.

OTHER CENTERS. Southwest of Ancona is **Osimo** an ancient town that suffered for a mistaken choice taken in the fifteenth century when the Turkish threat worried many Italians. In 1480 the sultan's troops landed at Otranto in Apulia and menaced the rest of Italy's eastern shore. But the danger created opportunities, too, and Boccolino Guzzoni of Osimo struck a deal with Sultan Bayezid II, in 1486 to rule the Marche on behalf of Constantinople. Retaliation was swift. Cardinal Giuliano della Rovere marshaled papal and Marchigian forces in a siege of Osimo. The Turkish fleet came to Osimo's aid but without success. Guzzoni's gambit had failed.

Iesi (the Roman *Aesis*), on the banks of the Esino, predates Rome and flowered as a Roman colony after 247 B.C. After the Goths and Lombards sacked Iesi, it was awarded to the papacy in the eighth century by the Frankish King Pepin III. In the battles between Guelphs and Ghibellines, Iesi supported the Holy Roman Empire, and it was the birthplace of Emperor Frederick II in 1194. He added a lion and his crown to Iesi's coat of arms, designated it a royal city, and accorded it many privileges. In 1266, the city passed back into papal hands. Much of the city's thirteenth-century walls remain. Its Palazzo della Signoria is a Renaissance work of Siena's Francesco di Giorgio Martini (1439–1502). Iesi's cultural heritage is enhanced by its being the birthplace of one of Italy's finest composers, Giovanni Battista Pergolesi (1710–1736). His opera *La serva padrona* (The Servant Mistress) established his reputation as a composer of delicate wit.

Just southwest of Iesi is **Maiolati Spontini**, the former Maiolati which was renamed to honor a native son, the lyric composer Gaspare Spontini (1774–1851). After struggles producing his operas in Italy, Spontini (his nom de plume; he was baptized Gaspare Luigi Pacifico) moved to Paris in 1803 and had great success there under the patronage of Napoleon's wife, Josephine. His most acclaimed work was *La Vestale* (1807), and he directed the Théâtre Italien from 1810 until 1812. He later spent over twenty years in Berlin (1820–1842) but never matched his French successes.

The important Catholic shrine of **Loreto** is situated in the province of Ancona. According to tradition, the birthplace of the Virgin Mary was miraculously transported by angels to Loreto in the thirteenth century. In 1464 Pope Pius II ordered that a sanctuary and basilica be placed over and around the little house. Donato Bramante, Giuliano Sangallo, Jacopo Sansovino, and many others worked on the structures. Vanvitelli built the campanile between 1751 and 1754.

Senigallia was named for the Senoni Gauls who founded it in the fourth century B.C. After the fall of Rome in A.D. 476, it formed one of the five maritime cities of the Pentapolis confederation under loose Byzantine control. Senigallia became trapped in the medieval wars between the Guelphs and Ghibellines that left it in ruins. Its impressive fortress, the Rocca Roveresca, was built for Giovanni Della Rovere between 1479 and 1481 on the remains of an earlier stronghold of Cardinal Gil Albornoz. Giovanni Maria Mastai-Ferretti was born at Senigallia in 1792. In 1846 he was elected to the throne of Saint Peter and took the name of Pius IX. Known as one of the most reactionary popes of the nineteenth century, he opposed Italian unification and many modern currents in his 1864 *Syllabus of Errors* and *Quanta Cura*. Having lost the Papal States to Italian forces between 1860 and 1870, Pius condemned the new unified state and urged Italians not to participate in its politics. He died in 1878. Appropriately, his birthplace is today a gallery of sacred art.

The writer and novelist Alfredo Panzini (1863–1939) was born in Senigallia. A student of Giosuè Carducci at Bologna, he taught school in Milan and Rome while writing children's books and novels. His autobiographical account of a bicycle jaunt through Lombardy, *La Lanterna di Diogene* (1907), established his reputation.

Since the 1960s Senigallia has been one of Marche's chief shore resorts. Another important place in Ancona province is **Fabriano**. With roots going back to the Piceni, it established an international reputation during the late Middle Ages for production of quality paper. During the Renaissance it was home to the artist Antonio da Fabriano (active 1451–1489).

Chiaravalle was the birthplace in 1870 of the educator Maria Montessori. In 1894 she was the first woman to obtain a medical degree from the University of Rome and then lectured there in anthropology and pedagogy. She opened her first "children's house" (*casa dei bambini*) at Rome in 1907. In 1934 she left Italy for the Netherlands, where she died in 1952.

ASCOLI PICENO

PROVINCIAL PROFILE. Area: 806 sq. mi. Population: 368,027 (province), 52,320 (city). Ascoli Piceno contains 73 communes. Ascoli Piceno province forms the southern end of the Marche. To its east is the Adriatic Sea. Along its diagonal northern border sits Macerata. Its frontier to the west-southwest faces Umbria, and it faces Abruzzi across its southern border.

HISTORY. Ascoli Piceno was first settled along the banks of the Tronto River by the Piceni. By 268 B.C. the Romans had annexed it, naming it Asculum Picenum. Despite earlier alliances, the Piceni and other peoples of central and southern Italy revolted against Rome in the Social War of 91–88 B.C. The Roman general Pompey Strabo, father of Pompey the Great, crushed the revolt, besieged Ascoli Piceno, and destroyed it in a terrible sack. The town revived, however, and became a major center of the region. After the collapse of the Roman Empire in 476, Ascoli Piceno suffered repeated conquests, starting with that of Totila the Goth in 545. Lombard and Church control followed until in 1185, when it became a free commune. The bishop relinquished formal control in 1212. Embroiled in the thirteenth-century struggles between Guelphs and Ghibellines, Ascoli Piceno was sacked and conquered by Frederick II in 1242. The city's local nemesis was Fermo; the two engaged in a series of wars between 1256 and 1504. Many foreign lords, including the Malatesta, the Dukes of Atri, and the Kings of Naples ruled Ascoli Piceno until 1502, when the popes took definitive control and largely maintained it until 1860. Then, upon the defeat of the pontiff's forces at Castelfidardo, Ascoli Piceno voted overwhelmingly to join the new Kingdom of Italy. During the Second World

War, Pope Pius XII saved the city from bombardment by securing recognition of its status as a hospital center. After the war some industrial development occurred and, most important, tourism assumed central commercial importance.

The activist Romolo Murri (1870–1944) was born in nearby Montesampietrangeli. His populist Opere dei Congressi movement appeared too unwieldy for the conservative Pope Pius X, who supressed it in 1907. Italy's Prime Minister Fernando Tambroni (1901–1963), a Christian Democrat, was a native of Ascoli Piceno. His brief tenure, intended to get Italy through the summer and the 1960 Olympic Games at Rome, was marred by reliance on neo-Fascist support that triggered deadly riots across Italy. Tambroni resigned in disgrace and died shortly afterward.

ARTS AND CULTURE. Christianity came early to Ascoli Piceno, but a bishop was not appointed until Saint Emidio, the city's patron, arrived at the beginning of the fourth century. Emidio came from a noble German family and, after some time in Milan, was appointed bishop by Pope Marcellus. He was martyred in Diocletian's last great persecution of 303. His feast day is August 5, and his cult is particularly lively in the Marche and Abruzzo, where his intercession is implored for protection from earthquakes. Ascoli Piceno's thirteenth-century cathedral is dedicated to Saint Emidio. The structure boasts an unfinished Renaissance facade by **Cola d'Amatrice** (1480–1574) and a beautiful polyptych by **Carlo Crivelli** (c. 1430–1494). A significant collection of Marchigian art is housed in the Palazzo dell'Arrengo, the old city hall. On the first Sunday in August, Ascoli Piceno celebrates a medieval joust, the Giostra della Quintana, a joust and race that dates from 1613.

The architect **Giuseppe Sacconi** (1854–1905) was born at nearby Montalto delle Marche. He was superintendent of monuments in Ascoli Piceno; but it is for his design of Rome's monument to Victor Emmanuel II that he is best known, for better or worse. A civic museum in Ascoli Piceno is named for the painter **Adolfo De Carolis** (1874–1928) who was born in Montefiore dell'Aso and is identified with the Italian "Liberty" style.

OTHER CENTERS. Not far from Ascoli Piceno is its ancient rival, **Fermo**. It was called Firmum Picenum by the Romans, who colonized it in 264 B.C. and built massive cisterns which still survive. In 825 the Carolingian Emperor Lothair I chose Fermo as one of his nine *studi generali* (colleges). The cause of much of the troubles between the two cities stemmed from Ascoli Piceno's construction of a port, Porto d'Ascoli, at the mouth of the Tronto River. An early response from Fermo was to destroy the port in 1348. Fermo had a university between 1398 and 1850, when it was replaced by the Montani Technical Institute, one of the first in Italy. Not to be outdone by Ascoli Piceno's Giostra della Quintana, Fermo boasts an annual Palio dell 'Assunta (Race of the Assumption).

Offida is a town with prehistoric roots that lies about halfway between

Ascoli Piceno and the sea. It belonged to the abbey of Farfa before it became a free commune in the thirteenth century, and frequently allied itself with Fermo against Ascoli Piceno. Its distinctive Palazzo Comunale has a thirteenth-century tower and is the seat of the municipal museum. Outside of Offida is the dramatic Romanesque-Gothic church of Santa Maria della Rocca, which was rebuilt in the fourteenth century. Offida's "fake bullfight," or *corrida del bò finto*, is a popular celebration reminiscent of Pamploma's running of the bulls. Offida and the surrounding towns are known for lacework.

MACERATA

PROVINCIAL PROFILE. Area: 1,071 sq. mi. Population: 300,207 (province), 42,260 (city). Macerata contains 57 communes. Macerata province is roughly rectangular and leans from the southwest to the northeast. To its east is the Adriatic Sea. Ancona sits on its north, Umbria on its west, and Ascoli Piceno on its south.

HISTORY. Macerata sits atop a hill between the Potenza and Chienti rivers. An earlier Roman site, Helvia Recina, had been destroyed by King Alaric I and the Visigoths in A.D. 408, but the city reconstituted itself as a medieval commune by the early eleventh century. The Papal States annexed Macerata in 1445 and held it, with the exception of the Napoleonic years, until Italian unification in 1860. Macerata claims to have launched the first insurrection of the Risorgimento in 1817, and a vast Carbonaro conspiracy was uncovered there in 1821. Despite the setbacks, agitation for independence from the Papal States remained strong. In 1849 Giuseppe Garibaldi formed a legion at Macerata and became a deputy from Macerata to the Roman revolutionary assembly.

ARTS AND CULTURE. Macerata's patron is San Giuliano l'Ospedaliere (Julian the Hospitaller), the subject of a strange story according to which he murdered his parents but found redemption in his penance. It has been suggested that this is a Christian variation of the Oedipal story. The cult began in France and Belgium, and spread to Italy by the beginning of the second millennium. In 1188 Crusaders from Macerata adopted the banner of San Giuliano. His feast day is August 31. Also important to Macerata's religious life is the sanctuary of Macerata's co-patron, the Madonna della Misericordia, a basilica built in 1447 and restored during the eighteenth and nineteenth centuries. **Luigi Vanvitelli** (1700–1773) accomplished much of the later work on the sanctuary. On Good Friday, 1772, in the chapel of the Palazzo Compagnoni Marefoschi, Princess Louise of Stolberg-Gedern married Charles Edward Stuart, the pretender known as "Bonnie Prince Charlie."

The University of Macerata was founded in 1290 as a law school and became the University of the Piceno in 1540 through a bull issued by Pope Paul III. Macerata was the birthplace of Pietro Gasparri (1852–1934), the Holy See's secretary of state under Popes Benedict XV and Pius XI. He was instrumental in the compilation of the Codex of Canon Law in 1917 and the 1929 Lateran Accords between the Holy See and Mussolini's state. Macerata boasts an important museum of the Risorgimento.

OTHER CENTERS. Near Macerata is the city of **Camerino**, site of the important Roman town of Camerinum. In the Middle Ages, Guelph Camerino was caught in wars against the Ghibellines and, after repelling attacks by Emperor Frederick II and King Enzio of Sardinia, it was viciously plundered in 1259 by Percivalle Doria, lieutenant of Manfred, King of Naples and Sicily. Later, under the Varano family, Camerino became the home of a noted style of painting in the fifteenth century. It is the seat of a distinguished university, chartered in 1727, and boasts a well-preserved medieval quarter. Modern Camerino was the home of the poet and playwright Ugo Betti (1892–1953). Betti's early works were poems that drew from his experiences as a soldier in the First World War. His plays, however, written while he was a judge, constitute Betti's principal accomplishments. His first was *La Padrona* (The Mistress, 1927). Many of his later works, particularly *Frana allo Scalo Nord* (Landslide, 1932) and *Corruzione al Palazzo di Giustizia* (Corruption at the Palace of Justice, of 1949), were distinguished by a moral aspect which gave Betti his reputation as a Catholic writer.

Also near Macerata is the Roman town of Cingulum, today's **Cingoli**. The town has a particularly dramatic view of broad valleys which has earned it the nickname "The Balcony of the Marche." Another place, **Tolentino**, was a Roman town of some weight known as Tolentinum; but it achieved more fame as the birthplace in 1245 of San Nicola (Saint Nicholas of Tolentino) and as the site of an important fifteenth-century basilica dedicated to him. The church contains works by Il Guercino (1591–1666). In the Palazzo Parisani-Bezzi, Napoleon and Pope Pius VI concluded the Peace of Tolentino in 1797. Its first floor today houses the Napoleonic Museum, and the second floor contains another museum devoted to international caricature.

Recanati is the home of one of Italy's most beloved poets, Giacomo Leopardi (1798–1837). Although born into a comfortable situation, Leopardi was a sad and sickly youth who turned to books in his father's library. He mastered Latin and Greek so well that, at the age of fifteen, he had a respected and published reputation. In 1816 he turned to poetry and the current literary debates. He traveled throughout much of Italy until his premature death in Naples. His works are still admired for their simple sentiments as well as his call for a rebirth of Italy. The Palazzo Leopardi is now a museum dedicated to the poet, his works, and his family. Recanati was also the home of the twentieth-century lyric tenor Beniamino Gigli (1890–1957).

The film actor Massimo Girotti was born in **Mogliano** in 1918. Among his credits is his portrayal of Gino in Luchino Visconti's *Ossessione* (Obsession, 1942).

PESARO E URBINO

PROVINCIAL PROFILE. Area: 1,117 sq. mi. Population: 340,830 (province), 88,036 (combined cities). Pesaro-Urbino contains 67 communes. Pesaro e Urbino is the northern most of the Marche's four provinces. To its east is the Adriatic Sea. On its south is Ancona province. To its west are Umbria and Tuscany, and Emilia Romagna sits to its north. A small section of Pesaro e Urbino's northern frontier is broken by the tiny independent Republic of San Marino. The little country sits on top of Mount Titano and is known primarily for its gambling casino and commerce in postage stamps and souvenirs.

HISTORY. Located near the mouth of the Foglia River, Pesaro was established as a Roman colony in 184 B.C. The ancients knew the Foglia as the Pisaurus, hence the name of the town. Pesaro changed hands frequently after the fall of the Roman Empire in 476, from Goth to Byzantine to Frankish to papal. It submitted to Witigis the Ostrogoth in 536 but quickly rose to join the ranks of the Pentapolis confederation of coastal cities. Although the city was placed in papal hands by Pepin III, it evolved as a semi-independent commune and joined the Ghibelline cause in the Middle Ages. Pesaro later belonged to a succession of families, the Del Griffo, the Malatesta, and the Montefeltro. But it was under the Sforza, who bought it in 1445, and then the della Rovere, in the sixteenth century, that Pesaro achieved its greatest fame. In 1631 it passed once again into the hands of the popes and, except for the Napoleonic interludes of 1797–1799 and 1807–1813, remained in them until the Risorgimento.

Pesaro was active in the struggle for unity and liberation. It established a provisional government in the revolutions of 1831 and sent delegates to Bologna as part of the ill-fated United Italian Provinces. In that enlity the nationalist leader Terenzio Mamiani (1799–1885) of Pesaro occupied the Ministry of the Interior. Mamiani later achieved fame as a moderate voice in the tumultuous days before the Roman revolution of 1848–1849. Pesaro briefly joined the Roman Republic before it was occupied by Austrian troops in May 1849. Italian soldiers reached Pesaro in 1860, one week before the battle of Castelfidardo, and joined the city to their new Kingdom. During the Second World War, Pesaro and the Foglia River formed part of the eastern end of the Germans' Gothic Line of 1944–1945.

The Umbri first settled Urbino and were followed by Etruscans before it fell to the Romans in the third century B.C. They called the town Urbinum Hortense. After being under papal control, Urbino was ceded in the twelfth century to the Counts of Montefeltro. During the rules of Federigo da Montefeltro (1444–1482) and his son, Guidubaldo (1482–1508), Urbino gained the reputation of one of the most glittering Renaissance courts. Early on, the Montefeltro had been notorious Ghibellines and maintained bitter relations with the papacy. But by the fifteenth century, the family allied itself to Rome. Pope Sixtus IV honored Federigo in 1474 by elevating the Montefeltro from counts to dukes; it was a reward for permitting his daughter to marry a papal nephew.

The Della Rovere family succeeded Guidubaldo in 1508 and continued to foster Urbino's cultural tradition. Between 1513 and 1518, while ambassador to Urbino, Count Baldissare Castiglione wrote his Renaissance classic, *The Courtier*. Set in the court of Urbino, the book discussed the proper qualities of a prince's servant. Castiglione went on to take holy orders and became a bishop. In 1631, after the death of Francesco Maria II, the papacy retook control of Urbino and held it, except for the Napoleon's occupations (between 1797 and 1814), until September 1860.

ARTS AND CULTURE. According to tradition, Saint Terence brought Christianity to Pesaro as its first bishop. Imprisoned by the Romans, Terence escaped after the jail walls crumbled. He was guided by an angel to Rome and then to Pesaro, although brigands murdered him on the way. Saint Terence's feast day is September 24. Others record his martyrdom during the persecutions of Emperor Decius between 249 and 251. Historical record is sure, however, of a Bishop Germanus in the 300s. One of the greatest Roman authors, **Lucius Accius**, lived a long life in the Roman colony of Pesaro from 170 to 86 B.C.

Federigo da Montefeltro's court ranks as one of the premier hothouses of Renaissance Italian culture. Federigo, with his wife, Battista Sforza, were immortalized in two of the most famous portraits of the age by the Tuscan artist **Piero della Francesca** (c. 1420–1492), a frequent visitor to the Montefeltro court. The paintings are housed, side by side, in Florence's Uffizi Museum, each spouse gazing enigmatically, almost lazily, into the eyes of the other. Their Palazzo Ducale, begun in the mid-1400s by Arezzo's **Maso di Bartolomeo** (1406–1456) and the Dalmatian **Luciano da Laurana** (1420–c. 1479), dominates Urbino. Piero della Francesca worked on the palace as well. Some of its rooms now constitute the National Gallery of the Marche, considered the best collection of the region's figurative art.

Besides Piero della Francesca, artists such as **Paolo Uccello** (1397–1475) and **Melozzo da Forlì** (1438–1494) came to Urbino during this golden age. The painter **Raphael** (Raffaello Sanzio, 1483–1520) was born in Urbino, although as a youth he moved on to Florence and, later, to Rome, where he achieved his greatest success and where he died. His home in Urbino has been turned into a museum. Federigo gave the commission for Urbino's cathedral to the Sienese **Francesco di Giorgio Martini** (1439–1502), who also worked on the facade of the Ducal Palace. After a terrible earthquake in 1789, the cathedral received a neoclassical facelift from the Roman **Giuseppe Valadier**. Duke Guidubaldo established the University of Urbino in 1506.

Medieval Pesaro persists in its twelfth-century cathedral, built on the remains of a late Roman structure. The Sforzas built Pesaro's Palazzo Ducale in the fifteenth century. Its municipal museum also houses an important art gallery. Outside of Pesaro, in the San Bartolo hills, is Alessandro Sforza's Villa dell'Imperiale. Its name derives from a visit paid by Emperor Frederick III to Sforza in 1469. As an honored guest, Frederick was asked to place the first stone for the villa. Construction of the villa employed many artists, including Ferrara's **Dosso Dossi** (c. 1479–1542), Urbino's **Gerolamo Genga** (1476–1551), and the Florentine **Agnolo Allori**, known as "il Bronzino" (1503–1572).

Gioacchino Rossini (1792–1868), was born in Pesaro. Among Europe's most popular lyric composers during the first half of the nineteenth century, Rossini is remembered mainly for his light and frothy masterpieces. His only truly serious opera, *Guglielmo Tell* (William Tell, 1829), is important enough; but his greatest influence persists in such works as *Il Barbiere di Siviglia* (The Barber of Seville, (1816), *La Cenerentola* (Cinderella, 1817), and *L'Italiana in Algeri* (The Italian Girl in Algiers, 1813). Pesaro honors Rossini and his legacy in an annual opera festival, and preserves his boyhood home as a small museum. The artist **Gian Andrea Lazzarini** (1710–1801) was born in Pesaro.

OTHER CENTERS. Fano has Roman walls and an arch of Augustus. For many years the city was a possession of the Malatesta family, who undertook an extensive building program in the fifteenth century. Fano's Nolfi College (law and medicine) was established in 1680 and became a university in 1729, but by 1828 Fano had lost the institution through a papal reorganization. The town hosts one of the principal carnivals on the Adriatic shore. Fano was the birthplace of the writer Bruno Barilli (1880–1952). A music critic, journalist, and occasional composer for the lyric stage, Barilli collaborated in the founding the neoclassical review *Ronda*.

SELECT BIBLIOGRAPHY

Anselmi, Sergio, ed. *Le Marche*. Turin: Einaudi, 1987.
Istituto Geografico De Agostini. *Marche*. Novara: Istituto Geografico De Agostini, 1982.

Abruzzo: L'Aquila market.

Abruzzo: Spanish fort, L'Aquila.

Apulia: Castel Del Monte.

Basilicata.

Basilicata: Matera.

Campania: Paestum.

Campania: Capodimonte Palace, Naples.

Emilia Romagna: Mussolini's crypt.

Emilia Romagna: San Vitale, Ravenna.

Lazio: Forum, Rome.

Lazio: View from Spanish Steps, Rome

Lazio: Spanish Steps, Rome

Lazio: Palazzo Quirinale, residence of the presidents of Italy, Rome.

Lazio: Altare della Patria, Rome.

Lazio: Castel Sant'Angelo, Rome.

Lazio: Parking lot at the Italian Senate, Rome.

Lazio: Porta San Paolo, part of the third-century Aurelian wall network, and the "pyramid" tomb of the magistrate Gaius Castius, built in 12 B.C., Rome.

Lazio: Bramante's Tempietto, Rome.

Lazio: Game of bocce, Rome.

Lazio: Sant'Ivo, former site of the University of
Rome, now home of the city's archives, Rome.

Lombardy: Certosa di Pavia.

Lazio: Fossanova.

Lombardy: Sant'Ambrogio, Milan

Lombardy: Catholic University, Milan

Lombardy: Galleria, Milan.

Lombardy: Castello Sforzesco, Milan.

Marche: Numana beach.

Marche: Urbino.

Sicily: Cathedral, Syracuse.

Marche: Loreto.

Tuscany: Pisa.

Tuscany: Siena.

Umbria: Assisi.

Umbria: Church of San Damiano, Assisi.

Veneto: Venice.

Veneto: Grand Canal, Venice.

Veneto: San Rocco, Venice.

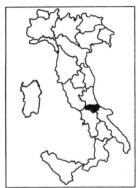

MOLISE

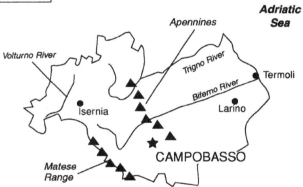

Chapter 12

MOLISE

REGIONAL CHARACTERISTICS. Area: 1,713 sq. mi. Population: 329,894. Capital: Campobasso. Molise ranks nineteenth among Italian regions in both area and population. Campobasso, Isernia, and Termoli are the only three towns in Molise with populations over 10,000. There is a Catholic metropolitan see at Campobasso/Boiano.

Molise borders Abruzzo to its north, Lazio on its west, Campania on its south, and Apulia on the east. On its northeast, the region occupies the Adriatic coast between Abruzzi and Apulia. Of Molise, 55.8 percent is mountainous and 44.2 percent is hilly. Italy's National Statistics Institute (ISTAT) does not classify any part of Molise as flatland. Its mountains form part of the southern Apennines, and the region generally slopes northeast down toward the sea. The highest ridges form a horseshoe around Molise, with the Adriatic as the open side. In the south, the Matese ridge faces Campania. The Mainarde ridge sits to the west along the Lazio line, and the Meta separates Molise, Abruzzo, and Lazio in the northwest corner of the region. Farther down the Abruzzese border toward the sea are the more gentle Frentanis. The Trigno and the Biferno rivers cascade from the eastern faces of mountains toward the Adriatic. In the west, the Volturno runs between the Mainarde and the Matese into Campania and the Tyrrhenian Sea.

ECONOMY. Agriculture employs 15.2 percent of Molise's active labor force; 27.6 percent work in industry; and 57.2 percent in the tertiary sector. Of the region's 105,000 employed workers, 69,000 are men and 36,000 are women. Molise's unemployment rate in January 1998 was 17.2 percent.

Much industrial activity, led by the establishment of a large Fiat plant and steelworks, has been concentrated in Termoli and the Biferno River valley. Tourism has been slow to develop.

CUISINE. Pasta is very important in the Molise diet, and *spaghetti con aglio e olio* (with garlic and oil) and *con baccalà* (with dried codfish) are widely popular. Potatos are frequently included in the diet. A common dish is *capuzelle e patane*, a mixture of lamb brains, potatoes, and bread crumbs. It is flavored with oregano, parsley, garlic, and the local hot pepper, the *diavolillo*. Another specialty is *a megliechelle*, greens and boiled pork in a pizza dough envelope. *Farro dei sanniti* a type of gruel and *baccalà con prugna e pomodoro* (dried cod with plums and tomatoes) are local favorites. The town of Ripalimosani has acquired fame as Molise's "capital of bread." Molise is not known for its wine, and what is produced resembles wines from Abruzzo. Most is either drunk as table wine or exported to other regions for blending.

ZUPPA DI ORTICHE (NETTLE SOUP)

30–40 nettle stems	¼ c. flour
4–5 small onions, sliced	2 c. vegetable broth
1½ Tbs. butter	Salt, sugar, and pepper to taste

Boil the nettle stems and onions for about 30 minutes. Drain, reserving the water. In another pan melt the butter and add flour, mixing to form a paste. Stir in vegetable broth. Add the nettle stems, onions, some of the drained nettle water, salt, sugar, and pepper. Bring it to a boil and serve hot.

HISTORY. The Sannio, a popular term for much of Molise, recalls the Samnite peoples, known for their ferocity and fighting prowess, who controlled much of the territory in ancient times. They successfully resisted Umbrian and Etruscan incursions, and had spread their influence as far as Cumae and Neapolis (Naples) in Campania by the late 400s B.C. By the 300s the Samnites came into contact with the Romans, and delivered them their worst defeat up to that time, at the Battle of the Forche Caudine in 321. But by the 270s the Samnites had succumbed to the Romans, who later savagely destroyed their culture, exterminated or enslaved most of them, and repopulated the region with colonists from Liguria. Caesar Augustus included the old Samnite lands in Region IV, Sabina et Samnium. In the third century A.D. the region was reorganized and divided between Region V, Flaminia et Picenum, and Region VIII, Campania et Samnium. After the fall of Rome in 476 and a brief Byzantine occupation, the Lombards invaded Molise and merged it in 570 with the Duchy of Benevento.

In 1053 the Norman Count Ugo I reorganized the area into the County of Molise, and in 1060 Robert Guiscard created another county, Loritello, and based it at Rotello in the east. The Counts of Molise enjoyed support from Emperor Frederick II (1212–1250) and ruled large expanses that reached well into Campania's Terra di Lavoro. In 1270 the Angevin King Charles I of Naples rewarded important clans with Molise's land. Loritello remained a feudal possession of various families until 1792, when it reverted to the Kingdom of Naples.

Between the fifteenth and eighteenth centuries, Molise received a number of runaway slaves from Dalmatia and Albania. Others came when the Aragonese King of Naples, Ferdinand (Ferrante) I awarded parts of Molise to the Albanian George Kastrioti Skanderbeg for his support against the Angevins. Some of their culture survives in places like Larino, Ururi, and Montemitro. The Spanish and the Kingdom of Naples controlled Molise for the most part from 1543 until the unification of Italy. In the eighteenth century enlightened Neapolitan Bourbon reformers drew on talents from Molise, in particular those of Francesco Longano (1729–1796) and Giuseppe Maria Galanti (1743–1806), who examined the conditions of Southern peasants and wrote a study of Sicily. The reforms, however, did not affect Molise itself, which remained a far-off and rarely thought-of part of the kingdom. Until 1817, in fact, only a medieval road connecting Monte Cassino and Barletta in Apulia crossed Molise through Campobasso and Boiano. The ancient Roman roads had fallen into disrepair, and nothing grander than mule tracks penetrated Molise. Even today, the coastal A-14 route is the only expressway through the region.

Until Napoleon's conquest, Spanish and Bourbon Naples administered Molise as part of its *capitanata* (administrative district) of Foggia. This anchored Molise into the South more securely than was its sometimes partner region, Abruzzo. Beginning in 1806, Napoleon's brother, Joseph, and brother-in-law, Joachim Murat, successive rulers of Naples, detached Campobasso from Foggia and made it capital of its own province that included the districts of Isernia and, in 1811, Larino. Although Civitacamporomano in Campobasso province was the birthplace of two Neapolitan revolutionaries, the general Guglielmo Pepe (1779–1849) and the historian Vincenzo Cuoco (1770–1823), Italian unification was not popular in the region. Participation in any of the early nineteenth century patriotic revolts was at best sporadic and, in fact, many revolted against the new order of the united Italian state as early as the autumn of 1860. Banditry with some politically reactionary ties plagued the region after the unification.

Another indication of discontent was massive migration out of the region toward the turn of the century. Between 1880 and 1900 Molise lost 40 percent of its population to migration. And of the 395,000 Molisani listed in the 1901 census, 130,000 left for America before 1910. Molise's population crested after World War Two at 406,000, but 260,000 left between 1946 and 1986. During the Second World War the area suffered intense bombardment after the September 1943 armistice. Allied forces landed at Termoli on October 13 and pushed the front up to the Sangro River, where it remained during the winter of 1943–1944.

In 1867 the new Kingdom of Italy joined Molise to Abruzzo, where it remained until it became its own region in 1963. Campobasso was Molise's only province until Isernia was carved from it in 1970.

RECENT POLITICS. Postwar Molise provided steadfast support for the Christian Democratic Party, which as late as 1992 registered a 51.8 percent majority there. Since the subsequent reorganization of Italian politics, much of that support has gone to the former neo-Fascist National Alliance (Alleanza Nazionale) and to the former Communist Party of the Democratic Left (PDS; later, Democrats of the Left). Molise votes as the eighteenth electoral district (*circoscrizione*). In the 1996 majoritarian election to the Chamber of Deputies, the Center-Right coalition, Polo per le Libertà, took 47.9 percent of the votes, against 37.2 percent for the Center-Left Ulivo alliance. In the proportional vote the Alleanza Nazionale took 18.7 percent, just ahead of the PDS (18.5 percent). Forza Italia took 16.9 percent, a moderate alliance around Romano Prodi captured 11.8 percent, and a Catholic group, the Christian Democratic Center and the Christian Democratic Union, earned 11 percent. For the Senate, the Ulivo received 50.1 percent and the *Polo* gained 39.4 percent. Molise maintained its Center-Left government in the April 2000 regional elections. Giovanni Di Stasi was elected president at the head of a coalition that earned 49.0 percent, just enough to defeat its Center-Right rivals, who took 48.7 percent.

—————————— *CAMPOBASSO* ——————————

PROVINCIAL PROFILE. Area: 1,123 sq. mi. Population: 237,878 (province), 51,833 (city). The province contains 84 communes. Campobasso is a rectangular province that leans to the northeast. Its northern limit is the Adriatic. To its northwest is Abruzzo; to its west is Isernia. On Campobasso's south is Campania, and Apulia borders it to the east.

HISTORY. After the Romans exterminated the Samnites in the third century B.C., they rebuilt some military colonies across the area and ruled it as a frontier region. Lombard and medieval Campobasso was the seat of a county that frequently changed hands among feudal lords. The Lombards evoked this situation when they christened the city Campus Vassorum, or "Vassals' Territory." Later, as part of the Kingdom of Naples, the County of Campobasso was merged into the *capitanata* of Foggia. The seventeenth-century Masaniello revolt in Naples triggered a rebellion in Campobasso. Under Nicola Mannara, a popular government took power and held it until the Neapolitan trouble ended. After the union of Molise to Italy in 1860, a group of 37 communes near Campobasso rose in revolt against the new government.

ARTS AND CULTURE. Campobasso grew down the slope from a fortified hill atop which sits the Castello Monforte. Built on Lombard foundations, the current castle was built in 1459 by **Count Cola di Monforte**. The twelfth-century Church of San Giorgio is considered one of Molise's best examples of the Romanesque style, and the sixteenth-century Sant'Antonio Abate is the region's outstanding Baroque structure. The Santissima Trinità (*Most Holy Trinity*) is the city's cathedral. It is a neoclassical structure by **Bernardino Musenga**, built in 1829. Campobasso's patron saint is San Leonardo di Nobiliacum. A figure whose story is obscured in legend, Leonardo was a sixth-century Frank from Nobiliacum (Limoges). He is also the patron of chain and buckle makers, prisoners, farmers, and the bedridden, and provides protection against brigands. The Crusader Count Bohemond I prayed to Leonardo while captive at Antioch. Upon his release by the Muslims, the count donated his chains and the amount of silver used to ransom him to the saint's sanctuary in France. Bohemond's fellow Normans brought the cult to southern Italy. A thirteenth-century church honoring San Leonardo remains among the most important in Campobasso. The city is home to a university and to museums dedicated to Samnite culture and Christmas creches.

Campobasso was the birthplace of **Alberto Bonucci** (1918–1969), an actor involved in Milan's Teatro Piccolo (Little Theater) and a founder, with **Franca Valeri** and **Vittorio Caprioli**, of the Teatro dei Gobbi (Hunchbacks' Theater). Molise's premier twentieth-century author was **Francesco Jovine** (1902–1950), whose neorealist novel, *Le Terre del Sacramento* (Lands of the Sacrament, 1950) told of Fascism's rise in the South of Italy.

OTHER CENTERS. An archaeological zone is at **Sepino**, one of the Samnite cities destroyed and then rebuilt by the Romans. A third-century A.D. theater, thermal baths, and older walls and turrets are among the significant remains of the city. Sepino was called Altilia when the Bulgar King Alczeco accepted it from the Duke of Benevento in 668. It was an episcopal see and enjoyed some measure of prosperity until a devastating Muslim attack in the ninth century.

Larino, was the important Roman town of Larinum, boasts an archaeological zone with second-century A.D. remains of an amphitheater. Larino contains a distinctive medieval quarter anchored by its cathedral, dedicated to the Assumption and San Pardo. It is a Gothic structure, built over ancient ruins, that was finished in 1319. In the central Biferno valley, **Petrella Tiferna** and adjacent **Matrice** are home to two significant twelfth-century churches, the Romanesque San Giorgio and the abbey church of Santa Maria della Strada, respectively.

At the Trigno River on the Abruzzo border is **Roccavivara**, site of the twelfth-century Church of Santa Maria di Canneto. Built by the Benedictines near a Roman villa, the church contains a remarkable pulpit from 1223.

Termoli is the second city of Campobasso province. Its industrial base has expanded since the 1970s and it has been acquiring a reputation as a seaside resort. Its cathedral honors San Basso and was built over a Roman temple. Emperor Frederick II erected a castle at Termoli in 1247. Many places in lower Molise host *corse dei carri* (ox races).

ISERNIA

PROVINCIAL PROFILE. Area: 590 sq. mi. Population: 92,016 (province), 21,094 (city). The province has 52 communes. East of Isernia is Campobasso, and to its north the province wedges into Abruzzo. Lazio faces Isernia on the west, and Campania sits to the south. It is the more rugged of Molise's two provinces. The city sits on a plateau above two torrents, the Carpino and the Sordo, which merge to form the Cavaliere, a tributary of the Volturno.

HISTORY. In 1979 archaeologists unearthed evidence of a Paleolithic settlement near Isernia that dates from over 736,000 years ago. In recorded history, Isernia was the Samnite Aesernia before it became a Roman colony in 263 B.C. In the seventh century A.D. the Dukes of Benevento awarded the territory to Alczeco and his Bulgar mercenaries who had been employed against the Byzantines. Much of this land evolved into part of the County of Molise. In the 800s Muslim sacks and a terrible earthquake (847) devastated both Isernia and the old city of Venafro. Nevertheless, during the turbulent ninth century, Isernia became an episcopal see, and by 964 it was a county. Isernia was the birthplace of Roberto Farinacci (1892–1945), one of the few Southerners to have a prominent position in the Fascist regime. As a youth, he moved to Cremona and ultimately established himself there as blackshirt *ras* (boss of the city). Farinacci was associated with the radical wing of the Fascist movement, and he remained loyal to Mussolini until the very end, when he was shot by partisans.

ARTS AND CULTURE. Earthquakes have taken a sad toll on Isernia's cultural heritage. Its cathedral was built in 1837 on the ruins of an earlier one destroyed in 1805. Below that was a pagan temple. The city's symbol of sorts is the Fraterna Fountain, built in part with Roman remains between the twelfth and the fourteenth centuries. On May 19 Isernia celebrates the feast day of its patron saint and native son, Pietro Angeleri da Morrone who became the canonized Pope Celestine V. A hermit who was elected to the throne of Saint Peter in 1294, he was born to an impoverished family of peasants about 1215 and is venerated throughout Molise, Abruzzo, and parts of Lazio. Another important festival honors Saint Peter on June 28 and 29. It is connected to a celebration of onions, a local specialty.

OTHER CENTERS. Late Samnite ruins can be seen near **Pietrabbondante.** The sacred city of Bovianum Vetus was the center of the Samnite civilization and is now the site of excavations of two temples and a well-preserved third-century B.C. theater. Samnite and Roman life is also recalled at **Venafro.** Imperial thermal baths and parts of a theater can be found in the area.

The Benedictines were active in Molise after the fall of Rome (476), and in 705 they established **San Vincenzo al Volturno,** one of southern Italy's most important monasteries. When the Muslims reached this monastery in 882, they decapitated most of the monks (between 500 and 900) and enslaved the rest. The place revived, however, and reached the apex of its glory in the eleventh and twelfth centuries. In 1669 it was united with the monastery of Monte Cassino in Lazio. Its ninth-century crypt of Saint Lawrence contains singular examples of Benedictine frescoes.

Once a important cultural center, **Agnone** is noted for its *ndocciata* Christmas procession. The "ndocce" are the enormous torches carried through the town on Christmas Eve.

SELECT BIBLIOGRAPHY

Istituto Geografico De Agostini. *Abruzzi e Molise.* Novara: Istituto Geografico De Agostini, 1983.
Quintano, Claudio. *Il sistema industrial del Molise.* Bologna: Il Mulino, 1986.

PIEDMONT

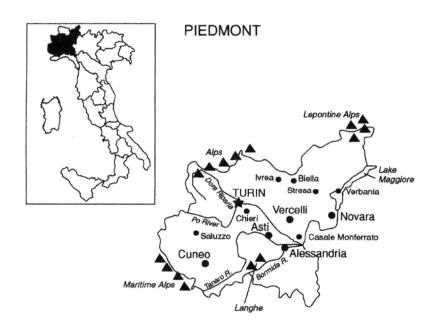

Chapter 13

PIEDMONT
(Piemonte)

REGIONAL CHARACTERISTICS. Area: 9,807 sq. mi. Population: 4,291,441. Capital: Turin (Torino). Piedmont is Italy's second largest region in land area (only Sicily is larger.) It ranks sixth in population. The region contains 1,209 communes. (Turin and Vercelli are Catholic metropolitan sees.)

In Piedmont 43.3 percent of the land is mountainous, 30.3 percent is hilly, and 26.4 percent is on the plain. It is a landlocked region that borders Liguria to the south, France to the west, the Valle d'Aosta to the northwest, Switzerland to the north, and Lombardy to the east. Piedmont briefly touches Emilia Romagna to its southeast. The Alps and the Apennines enclose Piedmont on the north, west, and south. The Mont Cenis Tunnel provides access to France on Piedmont's western border, and the Simplon Tunnel allows traffic between the region and Switzerland.

ECONOMY. The tertiary sector employs 55 percent of Piedmontese workers, 39.9 percent are occupied in industry, and 5.1 percent work in agriculture. Of Piedmont's 1,851,000-member work force, 1,089,000 are men and 762,000 are women. Piedmont's January 1998 unemployment rate was 8.1 percent. Its rivers provide good irrigation for its rich farmland, and hydroelectric power for much of northern Italy. Timber and dairy operations are important in the Alpine and pre-Alpine regions, and wheat, rice, fruits, and vegetables dominate the flatter parts of the Po valley. Of the industrial concentrations scattered across Piedmont, Turin's is the most important. It is the home of the giant Fiat automotive works. Textiles have also been important to Piedmont's economy, particularly around Biella.

CUISINE. Gourmets insist that there are two cuisines in Piedmont, one of the highlands, particularly in the north and west, and the other of the lowlands and cities. The former is considered the more authentically Piedmontese, whereas the latter owes much to Lombard and French cooking. Highland fare is heartier and more of what might be called peasant cuisine. *Viulin*, for example, is goat's leg cooked in spices, and is popular in the northern reaches of Piedmont. Fondue (*fonduta*), common in the mountains, is made with fontina cheese from the Valle d'Aosta. Polenta is popular there, and festivals celebrate it, particularly around Asti. Rice is eaten in large quantities; the region produces enormous amounts of it, although it is not as ubiquitous on Piedmontese tables as it is on Lombard ones. *Robiola* is a creamy goat cheese made at Roccaverano and Murazzano, and *paglierano* is made from cow's milk. Alba, in the Tanaro valley, is home to Piedmont's white truffle (*tartufo*), one of the region's most praised delicacies. The locals employ well-trained dogs to sniff them out. White truffles are the principal ingredient in one of Piedmont's most exceptional dishes, the *bagna calda* (hot bath), a dip, in which the fungi are mixed with with olive oil, salt, garlic, and chopped anchovies. Raw vegetables are dipped into it. Turin is also famous as the home of breadsticks. The Torinesi call these very thin pieces of bread *grissini*.

Many wine lovers agree that Italy's finest products come from Piedmont. The region produces the *nebbiolo* grape, from which comes the famous Barolo, honored by many as Italy's finest wine. The hills on either side of the Tanaro River valley—the Monferrati on the north and the Langhe on the south—in particular have the best claim of being home to Barolo. Made nearby and also from the *nebbiolo*, Barbaresco places second to Barolo. Some argue, however, that the Barolo of the Tanaro River region is surpassed by that of Gattinara, a town near Vercelli and Novara. Gattinara, however, has an uneven reputation. A list of other important grapes of the area would include the *barbera*, which is Piedmont's most common; the *freisa*; the *dolcetto*; and the *moscato* (muscat), which serves as the base for the vermouths made in Turin. Asti's most famous wine, the sweet, sparkling Asti Spumante, is made from the *moscato di Canelli* grape. *Loazzolo*, a golden *moscato*, is a recent development that has earned high marks. Asti (and Alessandria) is also noted for a light red wine, the Grignolino d'Asti.

BAGNA CALDA (OR CAUDA)

4 salted anchovies, finely chopped	½ pt. heavy cream (panna)
1 c. mushrooms, chopped	2 hot peppers, peeled and sliced
3 Tbs. butter	2 Tbs. vinegar
3 cloves of garlic, minced	½ tsp. salt (or to taste)
¼ c. olive oil	¼ tsp. sugar

Sauté the anchovies, mushrooms, butter, and garlic in a frying pan. Add the oil and fry slowly for 5 minutes. Remove from heat and let the mixture sit for about 5 minutes. Return to heat for another 5 minutes, adding the cream until the mixture thickens. Cook peppers in a mixture of vinegar, salt, and sugar for 15 minutes. Let the peppers cool for 10 minutes in a covered dish, then pour the cream sauce on top. Serve as a dip for vegetables or as a spread on Italian bread.

HISTORY. Ligurian tribes such as the Taurini and the Salassi settled prehistoric Piedmont. Rome penetrated the region after defeating the Liguri in 154 B.C., but did not recognize it as a single entity. "Piedmont" as a term did not appear until the twelfth century A.D., and then only to mean the upper Po tucked into the Alps. Not burdened with such definitions, Augustus (27 B.C.–A.D. 14) carved his territory into a number of administrative units. Much of what is today southern Piedmont merged into Region X (Liguria), and most of the region north of the Po became part of Transpadana. Its western edges spilled into Rome's three Alpine provinces: Alpes Maritimae, Alpes Cottiae, and Alpes Graiae. Toward the end of the imperial era Piedmont became a bit of a battleground, first between warring Romans and then between the Romans and their foreign enemies. In 312 Emperor Constantine I launched his conquest of Italy through the Mount Cenis Pass and defeated his first opponents at Campi Taurinati, near Rivoli. In 403 the Germano-Roman general Stilicho broke the siege of Milan by Alaric, King of the Visigoths. Stilicho chased the barbarian to Pollentia (Pollenza), where he defeated him. The Romans repeated the feat at Verona the following year; but Alaric regrouped, and sacked Rome in 410.

Piedmont was bitterly contested after the fall of the Roman Empire (476), and local bishops assumed a crucial role in preserving some continuity and civilization. Nevertheless, Vandals, Goths, and Byzantines battled for control until the mid-600s, when the Lombards established something like a hegemony over Piedmont. This lasted until the mid-700s, when a papal-Frankish alliance humbled the Lombards. Pepin the Short, the father of Charlemagne, defeated the Lombard King Aistulf in 754 and 756, both times in the Val di Susa. By the 770s the Franks had secured Piedmont and the rest of the Lombard Kingdom in northern Italy into their domains. The Franks organized the region into marches largely under the control of bishops and local lords. Power diffused further in the eleventh and twelfth centuries as towns became semi-independent communes, most of which joined the Lombard League against the Holy Roman Emperor. In opposition to this popular surge stood the power of the feudal chiefs, particularly the Marquis of Monferrato and the Counts of Savoy. The latter, who ultimately triumphed, were probably of Burgundian origin and began to move into Piedmont from Aosta in the early eleventh century. Their lands were only peripherally Italian, and extended west to the Rhone River in France and north to Lake Geneva in Switzerland.

Charles of Anjou, Count of Provence and brother of King Louis IX of France (Saint Louis), took much of Piedmont in the mid-thirteenth century; Asti led a successful alliance that prevented his conquest of the entire region. By the fourteenth century, the house of Savoys had launched a long struggle for control of Piedmont. Turin fell to them in 1380. Then Amedeus VI, Count of Savoy, prised much of the region from the tenuous grasp of the Angevin Queen Joan (Joanna) I of Naples. Amedeus VII, who ruled from 1383 until 1391, and his son, Amedeus VIII (ruled 1391–1434), consolidated this hold. Their success warranted the son's securing a new title for himself, Duke of Piedmont. Sixteenth- and seventeenth-century Savoy rulers, particularly Emmanuel Philibert (r. 1553–1580), continued to strengthen their state while attempting to remain neutral between the Spanish and French in their wars for control of Italy.

This did not, however, prevent sporadic territorial violations and wars within the borders of Piedmont. In 1703 Victor Amedeus II abandoned his alliance with the French to align against them (and with the Hapsburgs) in the War of Spanish Succession. This diplomatic gambit brought the French forces of Louis XIV to Piedmont. Valiant defenses of Chivasso and Turin kept Piedmont in the war and, at its end, on the winning side. Under the terms of the Treaty of Utrecht (1713), the Savoy holdings swelled with the Monferrato, Alessandria, the Langhe hills, and the districts between the Po and the Tanaro, much of what today constitutes the southern end of the region and also parts of Lombardy. The dynasty also acquired Sicily until 1718, when the Spanish took the island. The Treaty of London, however, later compensated Piedmont with Sardinia. The Savoy could then claim to be kings because Sardinia was an ancient kingdom.

French armies under Napoleon invaded Piedmont in 1796 and forced King Victor Amedeus III to sign the Armistice of Cherasco on April 28 and the Peace of Paris on May 15. His successor, Charles Emmanuel IV, abdicated in December 1798 and fled to Sardinia, where he enjoyed British protection. French annexations of Nice and of the ancestral Savoy homelands in the Alps were followed in February 1799 with a plebiscite for union with France. However, a Russian army and a popular uprising expelled Napoleon's forces by the spring. Napoleon returned through the Saint Bernard Pass in May 1800 and defeated Austrian forces at Marengo on June 14. Two years after this second invasion, in 1802, France annexed Piedmont. Subjected to Napoleon's Continental System, Piedmont's silk economy suffered, and the region was reduced to little more than an agricultural crutch for its masters.

Napoleon's defeat in 1814 brought King Victor Emmanuel I to the Congress of Vienna as a representative of a victorious power. There, his attempt to incorporate Lombardy into his territory failed; he was instead compensated with Liguria. The king's limited vision failed to appreciate that the middle classes and progressive nobles still favored reforms. Liberal and nationalist groups met clandestinely and surfaced in the botched revolution of 1821 when crowds in Turin, under the general leadership of Count Annibale Santorre di Santarosa called for a constitution and for Victor Emmanuel's abdication in favor of his nephew, Charles Albert. The young prince had grown up in France and was suspected of liberal sentiments. In Alessandria a Kingdom of Italy was proclaimed and war was declared on Austria. Victor Emmanuel abdicated, not in favor of his nephew but of his brother, the reactionary Charles Felix. Revolutionary chaos ensued until Austrian forces intervened to secure Charles Felix on the throne with the agreement that Charles Albert would succeed him, which he did in 1831.

After a series of revolutions across Italy in 1831, sentiment Italian unity reached a fever pitch in 1848. When Milan exploded in March and overthrew its Austrian masters, all eyes turned to Piedmont for leadership. Charles Albert granted a constitution, the *Statuto*, and led his forces across the border into Lombardy to liberate it from Austria. He enjoyed early successes against Vienna's troops, but failed to consolidate his victories and follow up on them. The Austrians rebounded and smashed Charles Albert's army at Custoza on July 25, forcing a cease-fire on August 9. Almost a year later, the king's quixotic last attempt to free Lombardy ended quickly and decisively at the Battle of Novara (or Bicocca) on March 23, 1849. Humiliated, Charles Albert abdicated and surrendered the throne to his son, Victor Emmanuel II, who concluded peace negotiations with the Austrians.

Despite the failures of 1821 and 1848–1849, Piedmont had become the leading Italian state in the fight for unity, the Risorgimento. Thinkers at the forefront included such Piemontesi as Vittorio Alfieri (1749–1803) of Asti; Turin's Vincenzo Gioberti (1801–1852), who published *On the Moral and Civil Primacy of the Italians* in 1843; and Turin's Cesare Balbo (1789–1853), whose *The Hopes of Italy* went to press in 1844. In 1847 the review *Il Risorgimento* was founded by Balbo and the leading statesman and architect of Italian unity, Count Camillo Benso di Cavour (1810–1861). Cavour became Piedmont's prime minister in 1852. He replaced Balbo's cousin, Massimo D'Azeglio (1798–1866), another activist for Italian unity and a writer known for his successful historical novel, *Ettore Fieramosca*.

Cognizant of Piedmont's need for foreign help against Austria, Cavour formed an alliance with Emperor Louis-Napoleon of France. For this assistance, Piedmont agreed by a treaty of January 1859 to give Nice and the Alpine territory of Savoy to France. To cement the deal, Victor Emmanuel's daughter, Princess Clotilde was to marry Prince Jerome Bonaparte, nephew of the emperor. The war with Austria began on April 29, 1859, and resulted in the conquest of Lombardy. It was the first crucial step in the unification of Italy. Lombardy and much of the rest of the country achieved union with Piedmont by 1860. Venice joined the kingdom after the Seven Weeks War of 1866 that pitted Italy (no longer just Piedmont) and its Prussian ally against Austria. The remaining parts of Italy's northeast were annexed after the First World War in 1918.

Piedmont industrialized in the late nineteenth century and developed large working-class populations in Turin, Biella, Ivrea, and other places. After the First World War, Piedmont was the center of labor agitation that brought Italy to the brink of revolution. Its factories exploded again in 1942 and 1943, trouble that hastened the downfall of Benito Mussolini's Fascist regime. When the Nazis occupied northern Italy between 1943 and 1945, they encountered their stiffest resistance from the partisans of Piedmont. Struggles to liberate their land were particularly fierce in the mountains and hills around the Po plain.

RECENT POLITICS. Immediately after the war, the Left parties controlled Piedmontese politics. Their status eroded through the 1950s and 1960s, however, as hundreds of thousands of Southern immigrants brought their Christian Democratic (DC) loyalties to the industrial suburbs. The situation changed again in the 1990s as the DC, the Socialists, and the Communists all fell apart. The Northern League (Lega Nord) increased in strength, and in 1994, with 25.6 percent of the vote, Silvio Berlusconi's Center-Right Forza Italia became Piedmont's largest party. Two electoral districts (*circoscrizioni*) comprise Piedmont: the first, centered on Turin and its suburbs, and the second, embracing the rest of the region.

In the 1996 "majoritarian" election for the Chamber of Deputies, 43.7 percent of the first district's votes were cast for the Ulivo coalition, 35.4 percent of the ballots supported the Polo per le Libertà, and 15.9 percent went to the Lega Nord. In the second district the Polo edged out the Ulivo, 37 percent to 36.8 percent, and the Lega captured 24.3 percent. In the first district's "proportional" vote, Forza Italia took 19.1 percent, with 18.9 percent for the Democratic Party of the Left, 13.8 percent for the Lega Nord, 12.8 for the Alleanza Nazionale, and 12.7 percent for the Communist Rifondazione.

In the 1996 Senate vote, Piedmont voted as a whole and gave 36.9 percent to the Ulivo, good for ten seats; the 34.2 percent for the Polo gave it five. The ruling coalition maintained its hold on Piedmont in the April 2000 regional elections. Enzo Ghigo was reelected president of the region; his Center-Right group was returned with 51.8 percent of the vote, against 39.5 percent for the opposition.

TURIN (TORINO)

PROVINCIAL PROFILE. Area: 2,637 sq. mi. Population: 2,222,265 (province), 919,612 (city). Torino contains 315 communes. The province of Turin faces the Valle d'Aosta to its north, Biella to its northeast, Vercelli to its east, Asti to its southeast, Cuneo to its south, and France to its west.

HISTORY. Turin was founded by the Taurini as Taurasia, where the Dora Riparia flows into the Po. In 218 B.C. Hannibal sacked the town; after his defeat it became a Roman military colony, known early on as Julia Taurinorum and then as Augusta Taurinorum. Caesar Augustus fortified the city and rebuilt it in a rectangle of seventy-two blocks. After the barbarian invasions and the fall of the Roman Empire in the 400s, the town fell victim to a particularly vicious Lombard sack. Pepin III and his Franks conquered the area in the mid-700s. By the 900s Turin became a county in the Carolingian march of Ivrea. The march was reorganized more than once, but Turin stayed in Frankish hands until Marchioness Adelaide married Oddone of Savoy, member of a family that had descended into Piedmont from the Alps. Adelaide outlived her husband and ruled until her death in 1091, after which the march fell apart. The city became a free commune in 1149. By the middle of the 1200s it was again in Savoy hands, although France made frequent attempts to exert its control over the area.

From the sixteenth until the nineteenth century, in particular, the dukes dealt frequently with French attacks. The French ruled the area from 1536 and transformed Turin into a heavily fortified town until the 1559 Treaty of Cateau-Cambrésis obligated them to return the city to the Savoy. Duke Emmanuel Philibert (Emanuele Filiberto) returned in 1562 and, a year later, transferred the capital of his family's Italian lands from Chambéry to Turin. He employed the Umbrian artist Ascanio Vitozzi (Orvieto, 1539–1615) to supervise a modernization and expansion of the city to befit its new status. The reconstruction of Turin continued into the seventeenth and eighteenth centuries under Emmanuel Philibert's successors. France besieged Turin in 1640 and in 1706, and ruled it during the Napoleonic era, largely from 1796 until 1814.

Acquisition of the title "King of Sardinia" by the dukes in 1720 made Turin the capital of the Kingdom of Sardinia. In 1861 Turin became united Italy's first capital, and a disproportionate number of the nation's first generation of leaders were Piemontesi and Torinesi. Turin's Benedetto Brin (1833–1898), for instance, who frequently served as minister of the navy, is remembered as the father of the Italian fleet. In 1865 the national capital was moved to Florence. Turin's anger over the transfer was expressed in riots in September and October 1864, and in the city council's refusal to attend the royal ball in honor of the new capital. A surly crowd stood outside the palace that cold January night and jeered the guests who had the nerve to show up. After a modest economic slump, however, the city made a quick transformation from a political to a manufacturing center.

Particularly in the years before the First World War, Turin witnessed one of Italy's most remarkable industrial expansions. Automotive manufacturing ranked first among large-scale concerns. Giovanni Agnelli (1866–1945), for example, founded Fiat at Turin in 1899. Lancia was established in 1906. This expansion paralleled similar developments in printing; tanning; production of airplanes, rubber, paper, and chocolate; and distilling. The number of industrial workers rose from 84,000 during the First World War to 190,000 in 1939. Consequently, Turin's working classes tended to be among the most organized and sophisticated in Italy. A major force in the city's Socialist movement was Antonio Gramsci (1891–1937), a Sardinian who came to the University of Turin in 1911. Gramsci went on in 1920 to become one of the principal leaders of the occupation of the factories, mainly in Turin and Milan, which brought Italy to the verge of revolution.

In 1921, Gramsci and Amedeo Bordiga (1889–1970) led a break with the Socialists and founded the Italian Communist Party. Turin's industrial success made it an Allied target during the Second World War, consequently it suffered terrible bombardments. Nevertheless, after the conflict, Turin continued to expand as an industrial center, particularly during the economic miracle of the 1950s and early 1960s. Its population grew from 700,000 in 1940 to crest at 1.2 million in 1974. More recently, Turin has faced the challenges of postindustrial society with the uneven success typical of such centers. One bright spot has been the choice of Turin to host the 2006 winter Olympic Games.

ARTS AND CULTURE. Turin's Roman past is recalled in its Porta Palatino (first century A.D.) and in the remains of an ancient theater. An important medieval structure is the Church of San Domenico, begun in the thirteenth century. But it is as a Baroque and modern city that Turin is best known. Named capital of the Savoy lands in 1563, the city experienced rapid growth and city planning. The central Piazza Castello was laid out in 1584 by **Ascanio Vitozzi** (1539–1615) as part of the rebuilding program ordered by Duke Emmanuel Philibert. It is dominated by the Palazzo Madama, more of a castle than a palace, that was begun in the 1270s by the Marquis of Monferrato. Another example of urban planning is the Piazza San Carlo, built between 1637 and 1640 by the Torinese native **Carlo di Castellammonte** (1560–1641).

Near the Piazza Castello are the seventeenth-century Savoy Royal Palace and the fifteenth-century Duomo dedicated to Saint John the Baptist, the work of the Tuscan **Meo del Caprina** (Settignano, 1430–1501) and one of Turin's few Renaissance structures. Its freestanding campanile was completed by a Sicilian, **Filippo Juvara**, in 1720. Inside the cathedral is the late seventeenth-century chapel of the *Sacra Sindone*. Known in English as "the Shroud of Turin," it has been kept in the cathedral since 1578, and is among the most treasured holy relics of Christendom. The shroud is said to be the cloth that wrapped Christ's body when it was taken down from the cross. It bears the faint outline of a human body and, many believe, the image of the face of Jesus Christ. The chapel was designed by a prolific mathematician, architect, and priest from Modena, **Guarino Guarini** (1624–1683).

In the hills overlooking the city Juvara built the enormous Basilica of Superga between 1717 and 1731 to recall Prince Eugene's 1706 victory over the French and as a monument to the Savoy dynasty. The edifice served as a tomb for the Savoy monarchs from 1730 until 1849. Another church associated with the Piedmontese state is the neoclassical Gran Madre di Dio, built by the Torinese artist **Ferdinando Bonsignore** (1760–1843), to commemorate the Savoy restoration after the Napoleonic Wars.

Novara's **Alessandro Antonelli** (1798–1888) exerted great influence on nineteenth-century Turin's landscape. His signature work was the Mole Antonelliana, an enormous pile 549 feet high that still looms over the center city and has become its symbol. Intended first as Turin's synagogue, it was later used as the city's exhibition center. As an industrial center, Turin was more open to innovative and modern design than were many other Italian cities. In 1928 the "Group of Six" was established by important architects there. Inspired by the work of **Edoardo Persico** (Naples, 1900–1936), they advocated a modern, rational, international style for Italy. Fiat's Lingotto plant (1919–1926) by **Mattè Trucco** (1864–1934), **Roberto Gabetti** (b. 1925) and **Aimaro d'Isola Oreglia's** (b. 1928) Bottega d'Erasmo (residential blocks, literally "Erasmus' workshop," 1953–1956), and the Lombard **Pier Luigi Nervi's** Palazzo del Lavoro (Palace of Labor, 1961) are some major achievements of twentieth-century Turin.

Many important museums are in Turin. The Museum of the Risorgimento is housed in the Palazzo Carignano. The structure is the work of Guarino Guarini, who settled in Turin in 1666 and, along with it and the chapel of the *Sacra Sindone*, is known for his Baroque masterpiece, the Church of San Lorenzo dei Teatini. The Sardinian Parliament met in the Carignano Palace from 1848 until 1861; then Italy's first national body deliberated there until 1864. On March 17, 1861, that Parliament declared the Savoy monarch Victor Emmanuel II "by the Grace of God and the will of the nation," the first King of a united Italy. Near the Palazzo Carignano, the Galleria Sabauda and the Museo Egizio are two of Italy's most important. The former contains the premier collection of Piedmontese painting, and the latter may have the best display of Egyptian antiquities in Europe.

Count Amedeus VIII founded the University of Turin in 1404. Erasmus studied there in 1506. Emmanuel Philibert revived it in the 1560s, and it was reorganized in 1713. Also in 1713 **Michelangelo Garove's** Palazzo dell'Università opened. A polytechnical university opened in 1862 as the Italian Industrial Museum (Museo Industriale Italiano).

Outside the city is Stupinigi, the Savoy hunting lodge. Built by Filippo Juvara in 1729–1730, it is considered a masterpiece of Italian Rococo.

The Socialist leader **Giuseppe Saragat** (1898–1988) was born at Turin. He fled Fascist Italy in 1926 and returned in 1943 to work with the resurrected Socialists. But the pro-Soviet platform of the party leaders alienated the more moderate Saragat, who broke with the Socialists in 1947 and formed the Italian Social-Democratic Party. Between 1965 and 1971 Saragat served as President of Italy.

Turin has a rich literary heritage. **Federico Della Valle** (c. 1560–1628), a figure in the Savoy court, is considered by some to have been the greatest Italian tragedian of his century. His most acclaimed work, *La Reina di Scotia* (1628), dealt with the last hours of Mary Queen of Scots. A leading *crepuscolare* poet, **Guido Gozzano** (1883–1916), wrote nostalgically of his aristocratic childhood in Turin and at his family's estate in the Canavese.

Fascism looms large in much of Turin's twentieth-century literature. **Piero Gobetti** (1901–1926) was an important liberal journalist who opposed the regime in his paper, *La Rivoluzione Liberale*, (The Liberal Revolution), from 1922 until 1925. The Blackshirts attacked Gobetti, and their severe beating destroyed his health. He died a year later in France. Gobetti's wife, **Ada Marchesini Prospero** (1902–1968), was a founder of the anti-Fascist organization Giustizia e libertà (Justice and Liberty) and of an international feminist alliance. She also became Turin's vice mayor. **Carlo Levi** (1902–1975) was a painter who opposed the Fascist regime. He was sent to *confino* in a remote Basilicata village, and told the story in his *Cristo si è fermato a Eboli* (Christ Stopped at Eboli, 1945). His sympathetic discussion of the people he found in his place of exile helped to call attention to the poverty of the South. Turin's **Primo Levi** (1919–1987) also suffered persecution at the hands of the Fascists and the Nazis, and he recorded his saga in *Se questo è un' uomo* (1947), which was released in English as *Death in Auschwitz*.

Turin was the home of **Mario Soldati** (1906–1999), whose varied career included periods as a screenwriter, mainly for Mario Camerini, and as a film director. As a journalist, he recorded his impressions of the United States in his book *America primo amore* (America, First Love) in 1945. One of Italy's best-known film comics, **Erminio Macario** (1902–1980), was born in Turin. A central figure in the world of Turin's dialect literature was the physician **Edoardo Ignazio Calvo** (1773–1804).

One of Italy's key figures in twentieth-century music, **Alfredo Cassella** (1883–1947), was born in Turin. After studying with Gabriel Fauré in Paris, Cassella went to Rome in 1915. His works reflected and embraced the modern influence of composers Igor Stravinski, Arnold Schoenberg, and Bela Bartok.

OTHER CENTERS. Chieri was a Liguri tribal town before the Romans arrived in the second century B.C. and dubbed it Carrea. It prospered as an agricultural center along the Fulvian Way. Knowledge of the city is slim after the fall of the Roman Empire (476), but by the eleventh century Chieri had emerged as a possession of the bishops of Turin and as a thorny rival to Asti. Frederick Barbarossa demolished the city in 1155 and then gave it back to the bishop, who in turn presented Chieri to the Di Biandrate family. The town rebelled, however, at the prospect of Di Biandrate rule and found an unexpected ally in Asti, which resented the rulers' restrictions on its merchants. The two cities remained frequent allies in the twelfth and thirteenth centuries. Chieri became a Savoy possession in 1418. It had many of the conquerors that Asti did, except for the brief subjugation by Swiss troops in 1515 under the Bishop of Sion. In 1586 the people of Chieri welcomed their Savoy ruler, Emmanuel Philibert, with a triumphal arch which remains today. Chieri's impressive early fifteenth-century Duomo and its thirteenth-century baptistery bear witness to the city's importance during the late Middle Ages.

Ivrea is the chief city of the Canavese, a sub-Alpine zone that extends into the Gran Paradiso National Park. The Romans founded Ivrea as Eporedia in the first century B.C. After the fall of the empire (476), the city was the capital of a Lombard duchy and then a Frankish march in 889. In 1170 Ivrea became a free commune, then a feudal possession of the Marquis of Monferrato in 1266; in 1356 it passed to the Savoy, who ordered Aymon de Challant to build a castle there that remains today. Early Ivrea is revealed in its Roman street grid and parts of an amphitheater, as well as in its Duomo, which has roots in the fourth century. It was extensively rebuilt in the tenth and seventeenth centuries. In the twentieth century Ivrea achieved fame as home (since 1908) of the Olivetti Corporation, whose complex, built by Luigi Figini and Gino Pollini between 1938 and 1942, together with Ignazio Gardella's *mensa* (dining hall), are showcases of modern industrial design. Ivrea's Carnival is famous for its raucous battle in which oranges are used as missiles.

Pinerolo was first recorded in 996 as a possession of the Bishops of Turin. It passed to the Cistercians for a while and then emerged as a free commune before the Savoy took it, for the first time, in 1220. From 1295 until the fifteenth century it was generally ruled by the Acaja, a cadet branch of the Savoy family. Pinerolo was frequently contested and heavily fortified, traces of which can still be seen. Until the twentieth century the town housed the school for cavalry officers, and it boasts a museum dedicated to the cavalry. Ferruccio Parri (1890–1981) was born in Pinerolo. An anti-Fascist, he fought Mussolini's regime and was frequently imprisoned. Behind the lines in the Second World War, Parri represented the Action Party (Partito d'Azione) in the northern Italian Committee of National Liberation. After the war, from June until December 1945, Parri served as prime minister.

Susa was a Celtic stronghold before the Romans absorbed it in 63 B.C. and called it Segusio. Susa nevertheless retained considerable autonomy under its kings. An important point on the road to the Mont Cenis Pass, Susa retained its importance after the fall of the Roman Empire in 476. The Byzantines maintained a fortress there until the 570s. Frederick Barbarossa destroyed Susa in 1173, but it recovered, and frequently changed hands between the French and the Savoy. Much remains of Susa's Roman patrimony: a first-century A.D. arch of Augustus, for instance, erected by King Cottius to honor the emperor, and remains of a second-century amphitheater, walls, and baths. The impressive Porta Savoia also dates from the imperial period. Medieval Susa is recalled in its eleventh-century cathedral dedicated to San Giusto and its baptistery, built in the ninth and tenth centuries.

Torre Pellice is a principal site of the Waldensians, adherents of a Christian faith based on the twelfth-century teachings of Peter Waldo. Protected by their defensive positions high in the French and Italian Alps, they maintained their freedom from the Dukes of Savoy. The Waldensian Church operates a college and a museum at Torre Pellice.

Turin province contains a number of important Catholic monasteries and abbeys. The Benedictine abbey of **Novalesa** dates from the seventh century. It was an important cultural center of the early Middle Ages and hosted Charlemagne in 773. Much of it has been rebuilt, although some older chapels and frescoes remain. Napoleon closed it, but almost 200 years later, in 1973, the Benedictines were allowed to return. Outside **Villarbasse** is the abbey of Sant'Antonio di Ranverso. A twelfth-century structure begun by French monks, it contains later works by Giacomo Jaquerio (1375–1453). But the most important Torinese abbey is the **Sacra di San Michele**, a tenth-century fortress 1,647 feet up on the promontory of Monte Pirchiriano. Considered the masterpiece of Piedmont's Middle Ages, the abbey's twelfth-century church is reached via the *scalone dei morti* (staircase of the dead) and through the Romanesque *porta dello zodiaco* (gate of the zodiac).

ALESSANDRIA

PROVINCIAL PROFILE. Area: 1,375 sq. mi. Population: 434,572 (province), 91,080 (city). Alessandria contains 190 communes. Alessandria city lies near the junction of the Bormida and Tanaro rivers. Alessandria province forms Piedmont's southeast corner. Of Piedmont's provinces, Vercelli sits to the northwest of Alessandria, Asti to its west, and between them, Turin touches Alesssandria. North and east of Alessandria is Lombardy, at its southeast corner is Emilia Romagna, and south is Liguria.

HISTORY. In 1168 member cities of the Lombard League established Alessandria as a stronghold against Holy Roman Emperor Frederick Barbarossa and his chief ally in Piedmont, William V ("the Old"), Marquis of Monferrato. First named Civitas Nova, the town was renamed Alessandria in honor of Pope Alexander III (1159–1181). Despite defeat at the hands of Barbarossa and his Monferrato allies, Alessandria remained a predominantly Guelph town that sided with Charles of Anjou during his victorious march through Italy in the thirteenth century. William VII of Monferrato occupied the town, but was overthrown in 1290 and died in prison two years later. In 1316 Alessandria switched its allegiance to Milan's Visconti family, which ruled sporadically until the Sforza succeeded in 1450. Holy Roman Emperor Charles V took Alessandria in 1524 and ruled it as part of his Spanish possessions. The Spanish focused on Alessandria's military potential and developed its fortifications.

In 1706, during the War of the Spanish Succession, the city passed to the house of Savoy. After Napoleon's conquests in 1796 and 1800, Alessandria was the capital of a French department until 1814. Back in Savoy hands, the city became a hotbed of revolutionary and conspiratorial activity that led to the Risorgimento. It was at the forefront of the revolutions of 1821 until the Austrians under General Ferdinand von Bubna took the city and held it until 1823, when it was handed back to Piedmont. The Austrians returned to occupy Alessandria for a few months after the Piedmontese defeat at Novara in 1849.

The statesman Urbano Rattazzi (1808–1873) was born in Alessandria. As leader of the Center-Left in Piedmont's Parliament, his alliance with Prime Minister Camillo Cavour's Center-Right enabled a united legislature (*connubio*) in support of national unification. Rattazzi was Italy's prime minister in 1862 and 1867.

ARTS AND CULTURE. Alessandria's eighteenth-century Cittadella (citadel) that sits above the Tanaro attests to its having been a military stronghold. Alessandria is the home of the wide-brimmed felt or straw Borsalino hat. The factory, which also now houses part of the University of Alessandria, welcomes visitors to its display of headwear manufactured there since 1857. The Municipal Museum and Art Museum houses an important collection of Piedmontese art. Alessandria was the birthplace in 1932 of **Umberto Eco,** one of Italy's leading intellectuals of the late twentieth century. His early work concerned the problem of aesthetics in the writings of Saint Thomas Aquinas. He later moved into questions of culture and of semiotics, teaching at the universities of Turin, Milan, Florence, and Bologna. In 1974 he organized the first international congress on semiotics, and two years later published his *A Theory of Semiotics*. Eco has been a very public intellectual, writing frequently for mass periodicals and publishing novels. His first novel, *The Name of the Rose*, was released in 1980. **Milly** (Carla

Mignone, 1908–1980), one of Italy's most popular singers and actresses of the twentieth century, was born in Alessandria.

OTHER CENTERS. Acqui (Acqui Terme) is an ancient city, founded by the Liguri, that gained prominence as a medieval town when it was a center of the Monferrato domains. Acqui contains some mosaic remains of a Roman hot springs bath and an aqueduct. Its Basilica of San Pietro is built on paleo-Christian foundations that were first restored in the seventh century. The present structure dates mainly from the eleventh century.

Outside of **Bosco Marengo** is the sixteenth-century Basilica of Santa Croce. Pope Pius V (1566–1572) ordered it built to serve as his tomb. Giorgio Vasari contributed paintings and a mausoleum was completed. Pius, however, was not entombed in the basilica, but rather in Rome. Nearby is the battlefield of Marengo, where Napoleon defeated an Austrian army in July 1800.

Casale Monferrato was a Roman town and then a medieval commune often in the domains of the bishops of Asti or Vercelli. In the tenth century, while still tied to Vercelli, it evolved first into the seat of the the Aleramic march and later the Marquisate of Monferrato under the quasi-mythic Aleramo and his descendants, the Aleramici. The origin of the name is uncertain; it may come from *mons ferax* (fruitful mountain) because of its rich soil. Under William V ("the Old"), a Crusader and uncle of Frederick Barbarossa, the marquisate sided with the Holy Roman Empire against the Lombard League. The policy gained it few friends in Italy, and in 1215, with Savoy support, the forces of Milan, Alessandria, and Vercelli laid siege to Casale and utterly destroyed it.

The humiliation was brief, however, and Emperor Frederick II resurrected the city and restored its privileges in 1220. The bishops of Vercelli renounced their claims to the place and the Aleramici reassumed complete control of the city and territory. The Monferrato power extended across much of Piedmont until Marquis William VII confronted the extension of Angevin power. Defeated, he died in 1292 in an Alessandria prison. The last Aleramici died childless in 1305, and Casale passed through a succession of ruling families: first the Paleologo (Byzantine relatives of the Aleramici), then the Visconti in 1370, and the Sforza later. The Paleologo dynasty, however, frequently returned to rule until the last, Gian Giorgio, died in 1533. Casale and the Monferrato passed to the Holy Roman Empire and then to the Gonzaga family. Toward the end of the seventeenth century, Monferrato gravitated into an alliance with France against its Savoy rivals, who looked to Spain. The Treaty of Utrecht finally awarded Monferrato to the house of Savoy in 1713. The Risorgimento did not affect Casale Monferrato much until 1849, when the city endured a two-day siege by Austrian troops. Some fighting also occurred near the city in 1859. After unification, Casale Monferrato developed an important cement industry.

A well-preserved historic center distinguishes Casale Monferrato with an eleventh-century *torre civica* (municipal tower) and Duomo. The latter has been often and extensively restored. Casale Monferrato's synagogue hosts an exhibit on its Jewish community and heritage. The Civic Museum is housed in the remarkable eighteenth-century Palazzo Gozzani di Treville. The palace boasts a Baroque facade by the Vicentino artist Vincenzo Scamozzi (1552–c. 1616) and frescoes by a native son, Pier Francesco Guala (1698–1757).

Castelnuovo di Scrivia was the birthplace of the writer Matteo Bandello (1485–1561). A Dominican who rose to become the Bishop of Agen in France, Bandello is best remembered for his 214 *novelle* (stories), which influenced such later authors as William Shakespeare and Lord Byron.

Fubine Monferrato was the birthplace in 1900 of the Communist leader Luigi Longo. After he participated in the occupation of the factories in 1920, Longo joined the nascent Communist Party. He fled to Moscow following the establishment of Mussolini's dictatorship. He fought in the Spanish Civil War against the Fascists and returned to Italy in 1943 to head the Communist insurrectionaries in the Nazi-occupied North. Longo was the secretary-general of the Italian Communist Party from 1964 until 1972.

The artist Carlo Carrà (1881–1966) was born in **Quarguento**. Carrà was a major figure in the Futurist movement although he mostly remained committed to Cubism. Under the Fascists he received a number of state commissions for murals.

ASTI

PROVINCIAL PROFILE. Area: 583 sq. mi. Population: 210,134 (province), 73,552 (city). Asti province contains 120 communes. Asti city is at the junction of the Tanaro and the Borbera rivers. The province borders Alessandria on the east, and Turin and Cuneo on the west. Alessandria and Turin wrap around northern Asti, and to its south the province wedges between Cuneo and Alessandria until it touches Liguria.

HISTORY. In prehistoric times Asti was a Liguri village. The Romans knew the place as Hasta. At the end of the second century B.C. they connected it to their other domains along the Fulvian Way. Much of the city's importance, in fact, rested in its being at a crossroads. As the Roman Empire fell in the late fifth century, Asti suffered barbarian sacks, beginning with an assault by Alaric II. The Lombards took Asti in 569 and elevated it to a duchy. The Franks followed, and awarded the city to its bishops. During the ninth century the domains of the bishops of Asti suffered the assaults of Saracen raiders.

The first mention of independent communal status was recorded in 1095, and by the thirteenth century Asti had achieved a degree of regional power. It enjoyed fame across Europe as a manufacturing and banking center, and was probably Piedmont's premier city by the 1200s. Asti went to war with its rivals, particularly the Marquis of Monferrato and the house of Savoy. In 1155 Emperor Frederick Barbarossa sacked Asti and appointed a podesta for the city who piloted a brief pro-imperial policy. Asti joined the Lombard League in 1167 and suffered defeat again at Barbarossa's hands in 1174. In 1273 Asti allied itself with Pavia, Genoa, and the Monferrato domains against Charles of Anjou. The coalition defeated his forces two years later at Valle Vermenagna. In 1348 Asti passed to the Visconti family and then in 1387 endured sporadic possessions by the French Valois dynasty.

Savoy rule came in the sixteenth century via a circuitous route. The King of Spain and Holy Roman Emperor Charles V took Asti from the French and gave it in 1531 to his sister-in-law, Beatrice of Portugal, the wife of Charles III of Savoy. Upon her death, the city passed to Emmanuel Philibert. Asti slipped on occasion from the dynasty's hands: to the Spanish in the seventeenth century and to the French in the eighteenth. Still, the house of Savoy always returned, and after the fall of Napoleon (1814), the city remained in their realm until the unification of Italy in 1860. In 1927 the Italian government carved Asti province from that of Alessandria.

ARTS AND CULTURE. The base of a sixteen-sided Roman tower (*torre romana* or *rossa*) is all that remains of Asti's first-century A.D. walls. Medieval Asti is recalled in many towers and palaces around the city. Most important are the Palazzo Falletti-Montersino and the Casaforte dei Roerio di Cortanze, from the twelfth and thirteenth centuries. The city's foremost monuments are the thirteenth-century collegiate Church of San Secondo and the early fourteenth-century cathedral. San Secondo, Asti's patron, was a second-century martyr. His feast day, May 1, is celebrated with a procession around the city of a standard that recalls his miraculous ride on horseback above the waves of a river. Asti's most famous son is probably the poet **Vittorio Alfieri** (1749–1803), the son of a privileged family that preferred French language and culture to Italian. While a student at Turin's Royal Academy, however, he discovered Italy's literary tradition. From 1775 until 1787 he composed 19 tragedies in which his sense of nation and of liberty were developed along with his later rejection of things French. A museum dedicated to him and his works is in the Palazzo Alfieri. Asti hosts an annual wine fair in early September and complements it with a *palio* (horse race).

OTHER CENTERS. In the northwest corner of the province, near **Albugnano,** is the abbey of Santa Maria di Vezzolano, built between the eleventh and thirteenth centuries.

Saint John Bosco (1815–1888) was born in **Becchi** and lived in what is now called **Castelnuovo Don Bosco.** The founder of the Salesian order, he was a school reformer and a leader in the development of vocational education. **Castelnuovo Calcea** was the home of the dialect poet and politician Angelo Brofferio (1802–1866). His *Canzoni piemontesi* (Piedmontese Ballads) were composed between 1831 and 1859.

The man who succeeded Mussolini in 1943 as prime minister of Italy, Marshal Pietro Badoglio (1871–1956), was born in **Grazzano Monferrato**. A soldier who bore some responsibility for the Caporetto disaster when the Italian lire collapsed before the Austrians in the First World War, he opposed Fascism in 1922 but later directed Mussolini's forces in Ethiopia and became chief of the High Command in 1940. The Fascists scapegoated Badoglio for Italy's miserable showing in the wars against Greece and British Egypt, and dismissed him. He joined the opposition gathered around King Victor Emmanuel III, who chose him to replace the Duce after the July 1943 coup. Badoglio resigned as prime minister when the Allied armies reached Rome in June 1944.

BIELLA

PROVINCIAL PROFILE. Area: 353 sq. mi. Population: 190,460 (province), 48,061 (city). Biella contains 83 communes. Biella city sits in Alpine foothills on the Cervo River. The province is almost circular, tucked into Vercelli to its north, east, and south. On its west are Turin and the Valle d'Aosta.

HISTORY. Biella was a center of the Gauls before it passed to the Romans. The name first appears in a ninth-century document as Bugella. It was awarded to the bishops of Vercelli, who ruled Biella as a feudal possession until 1225, when they granted autonomous powers to a citizens' council. In 1348 Biella opposed the choice of a Genoese nobleman, Giovanni Fieschi, as Bishop of Vercelli, and launched a series of struggles that ended in 1379, when the city placed itself under the protection of Count Amedeus VI of Savoy. In 1555 force of arms brought French control, which was sanctioned by the Peace of Cateau-Cambrésis in 1559. But this rule was short and the house of Savoy returned to make Biella the capital of a province in 1626. The Spanish attacked Biella in 1647 and 1649, and the French occupied it in 1704 and after 1797.

After the Napoleonic interlude, the house of Savoy returned to power and restored Biella as a provincial capital in 1817. The leaders of the Risorgimento merged Biella into the province of Novara, and the Fascists placed it with Vercelli in their reorganization of 1927. In the nineteenth century the city was noted for its textile production and was among the first Italian cities of the modern industrial revolution. It supported the revolutions of 1821 and 1848, and in 1864 working-class strikes across the

Biellese brought the acceptance of Italy's first labor contract. The city had a Socialist administration after the First World War. During the Second World War, the province was the scene of some of the fiercest Resistance struggles in Nazi-occupied Italy. Biella became a separate province, carved from Vercelli, in 1993.

ARTS AND CULTURE. Biella is divided into an upper town (Biella Piazzo) and a lower town (Biella Piano). Among the city's principal treasures are its ninth-century baptistery and the thirteenth-century bell tower of the Church of Santo Stefano. (The church itself has been destroyed.) Biella's Cathedral of Santa Maria Maggiore e San Sebastiano is a fifteenth-century structure, renovated—some might say ruined—at the end of the eighteenth century and beginning of the nineteenth.

OTHER CENTERS. Near Biella is the sanctuary of **Oropa**, said to have been founded in 369 by Saint Eusebius. Dedicated to the Madonna, it is thought to be the oldest Marian sanctuary in Italy.

CUNEO

PROVINCIAL PROFILE. Area: 2,665 sq. mi. Population: 553,005 (province), 54,811 (city). Cuneo contains 250 communes. Cuneo is an almost circular province that occupies southwest Piedmont. To its north is Turin, and Asti is on its northeast border. Its west and southwest face France, and to its south is Liguria. The southern end of the province is distinguished by the western Langhe and its transition into the Alps. Among the highest peaks is Monte Mongioie (8,628 feet). The Alta Valle Pesio Natural Park occupies the part of Cuneo that meets France and Liguria. Cuneo city sits on a plateau above the junction of the Stura di Demonte and the Gesso rivers. The city's name, which means "wedge" in Italian, reflects its shape.

HISTORY. Cuneo was established in 1198 as a new town by representatives from Asti and by Milanese refugees after Frederick Barbarossa had sacked their city. After a period of Visconti rule, in 1259 Cuneo surrendered to the Angevins, whose rule was interrupted from 1281 until 1305 (when it was in the hands of the Marquis of Saluzzo). The house of Savoy acquired the city from the Angevins in 1374 and formally purchased it in 1382. The wars of the sixteenth century introduced a brief occupation of Cuneo by Saluzzo (1523–1524) and frequent sieges by foreign, mainly French, armies. But the city remained loyal to the house of Savoy. Cuneo endured its last siege in 1799, by the troops of Napoleon. After a second French conquest in 1800, Cuneo became the capital of the French department of Stura. Cuneo was returned to Piedmont after 1814 and was incorporated into the Kingdom of Italy. During the Second World War

Cuneo was near some of the harshest partisan fighting against the Nazis and Fascists.

ARTS AND CULTURE. Cuneo's San Francesco, now in secular use, is its main Gothic structure, built mostly in the thirteenth and fourteenth centuries. The city, however, is distinguished more by its Baroque flavor. The Mondovano **Francesco Gallo** (1672–1750) is an important figure who contributed to Cuneo in the churches of Sant'Ambrogio and Santa Croce and in the apse (1726) of the seventeenth-century Church of Santa Maria.

OTHER CENTERS. Alba is a commercial and agricultural center of the Langhe. After its birth as a Liguri settlement, the Romans took Alba around 100 B.C. and called it Alba Pompeia. It became an episcopal see in the fourth century A.D. and an independent commune in the eleventh. The house of Savoy acquired Alba in 1631. During the Second World War, Alba and the Langhe was one of the most tempestuous zones of the Italian anti-Fascist Resistance. In the summer and fall of 1944 the area around Alba achieved independence from the Nazi occupation, a short-lived freedom ruthlessly crushed in a German assault between November 12 and December 20. Beppe Fenoglio (1922–1963) recounted the Resistance in *I Ventitre Giorni della Città di Alba* (The Twenty-three Days of the City of Alba, 1952) and *Il partigiano Johnny* (Johnny the Partisan, 1968).

Cavallermaggiore was a feudal possession of the Marquis of Susa and then of Saluzzo before it passed to the house of Savoy in 1418. The town boasts a number of sixteenth- and seventeenth-century structures; most notable is its eighteenth-century Church of the Confraternity of Santa Croce and San Bernardino, an outstanding work of Francesco Gallo.

Luigi Einaudi (1874–1961), was born in **Carrù**, near Cuneo. Through his work for the newspapers *La Stampa* (The Press) and *Corriere della Sera* (Evening Courier), he established a reputation as one of Italy's premier economists. Although he did not work against Mussolini, neither did he support him. Rather, he toiled as a writer and cultivated some fame as an economist until, after the Second World War, he served as minister of finance and guided the first years of Italy's economic reconstruction. In 1948 Einaudi became Italy's first elected president.

Fossano sits on the Stura di Demonte River. Founded in 1236, it was an important free commune and a feudal possession of the Marquis of Saluzzo from 1265 until 1314 before it became a Savoy territory in 1418. Although it is today largely an industrial and agricultural center, Fossano's past glory is recalled in its fourteenth-century castle of the Princes of Acaja, its fifteenth-century Senate, and the eighteenth-century *L'Ospedale Maggiore della Santissima Trinità* (Great Hospital of the Most Holy Trinity), which contains Francesco Gallo's masterpiece, the Church of the Most Holy Trinity, completed in 1738.

One of Piedmont's finest castles is found at **Manta**. Recently restored, it is a fourteenth-century stronghold with frescoes added later (1418–1430) by the Torinese artist Giacomo Jaquerio.

Angelo Tasca (1892–1960) was born in **Moretta**. He left the Socialist Party to join the founders of the Italian Communist Party in 1921. Josef Stalin expelled him from the organization in 1929, however, for his crime of Bukharin deviation, a blanket charge for anti-Stalinist activity, and he returned to the Socialists in their fight against Mussolini's regime. Tasca became a French citizen and died in Paris.

Mondovì was founded in 1198 in the Ellero Valley and rebuilt by the Angevins in 1231. In 1290 it became a free commune, then a Visconti territory, and then a possession of Monferrato. The house of Savoy took it in 1407, when Mondovì was perhaps the largest city in Piedmont. The impressive seventeenth-century Jesuit Church of San Francesco Saverio (or "la Missione") sits in the city's central piazza. The Trentino artist Andrea Pozzo (1642–1709) was responsible for the trompe l'oeil ceiling. Francesco Gallo contributed much to the city, including its cathedral.

Mondovì was the birthplace of Giovanni Giolitti (1842–1928), Italy's prime minister in the era before the Fascist seizure of power. He was a liberal reformer who expanded suffrage to include all adult men in 1913 and worked to nationalize railroads and insurance. His last ministry, from June 1920 until July 1921, has been criticized for failing to realize the potential of the Fascist menace. But unlike some of his liberal colleagues, Giolitti regretted his mistake and did not succumb to Fascism. He publicly questioned the regime in Parliament until his death.

Racconigi belonged to the Marquis of Saluzzo before the house of Savoy took it in 1605. Between the seventeenth and nineteenth centuries the Savoy built their chief country residence there. Italy's last king, Umberto II, was born at the palace in 1904. He left the country in 1946, after a national vote ended the monarchy, and died in exile in 1983.

Santo Stefano Belbo was the birthplace in 1908 of the writer Cesare Pavese. His dissertation concerned the poet Walt Whitman, and his interest in American literature prompted him to move to Turin and translate works of William Faulkner and Herman Melville for the Einaudi publishing house. He was also one of Italy's principle translators of the works of James Joyce. Pavese was involved in anti-Fascist activity, and his novel, *La Casa in Collina* (The House on the Hill, 1949) dealt with the Resistance. He committed suicide in 1950.

First mentioned about A.D. 1000, **Saluzzo** was a powerful town. It was the seat of a marquisate, established in 1142 by Manfred I from the lands of his father, Boniface of Savona. Saluzzo often served as a foil to Piedmont, and the two frequently went to war. But Saluzzo also suffered invasions by the Holy Roman Empire and the French in the sixteenth century after the last marquis, Gian Gabriele, died, poisoned in 1548 while in a Pinerolo dungeon. The French annexed Saluzzo after the Peace of Cateau-Cambrésis in 1559 and held it until 1601, when the house of Savoy took it. Turin and Paris exchanged Saluzzo through the seventeenth and the beginning of the eighteenth centuries until Savoy finally kept it. Saluzzo boasts a well-preserved town center with a late fifteenth-century cathedral dedicated to the Assumption of the Virgin and the Church of San Giovanni, built between 1330 and 1504. A civic museum is housed in the fifteenth-century Casa Cavazza, a notable structure. The nationalist revolutionary Silvio Pellico (1789–1854) was born in Saluzzo. A revolutionary *carbonaro*, he was arrested and imprisoned after the revolutions of 1820–1821. His, *Le Mie Prigioni* (My Captivity, 1832) discussed his experiences while incarcerated through the lens of his profound Christian sensibilities.

NOVARA

PROVINCIAL PROFILE. Area: 1,517 sq. mi. Population: 340,544 (province), 102,408 (city). Novara contains 88 communes. The city of Novara sits on the Agogna River. Novara is a compact province bounded on the north by Verbano-Cuso-Ossola, on the west by Vercelli, and on the east and south by Lombardy.

HISTORY. Founded by the Liguri, Novara was reestablished by Julius Caesar in the first century B.C. and called Novaria. After the fall of the Roman Empire in 476, Novara was torched twice, in the 500s by barbarian invaders and by Emperor Henry V in 1110. Milan dominated Novarese life until 1535, when the Sforza Duke Francesco II died and the area was annexed by Emperor Charles V. He partially detached Novara from Milan (it gained autonomy but not liberty), and sold it as a marquisate to Pope Paul III, who awarded it to his son, Pier Luigi Farnese. The Spanish cancelled Novara's special status and merged it back into Milan in 1602. In 1706 the city passed to the Austrians, and then, in 1738, to the house of Savoy.

In the nineteenth century, Novara's geographic position, at the eastern end of the Savoy territories near the Austrian Lombard border, made it a twofold locus of important Risorgimento activity. In 1821 the liberal revolutionary forces of Santorre di Santarosa were defeated there by Austrian and Savoy troops. In 1849 the city was the site of the Battle of Novara (sometimes called the Battle of the Bicocca), Austria's victory over King Charles Albert's Piedmontese forces. Afterward, the shattered king abdicated in favor of his son, Victor Emmanuel II, who later became the first monarch of united Italy.

ARTS AND CULTURE. Novara's porticoed central Piazza della Repubblica is distinguished by the city's Duomo, dedicated to the Assumption. Extensively rebuilt in the 1860s by Novara's **Alessandro Antonelli** (1798–

1888), the church stands next to an important baptistery with roots going back to the fifth century. Novara's most remarkable structure, almost a symbol of the city, is the Basilica of San Gaudenzio. The sixteenth-century church was altered between 1844 and 1888 by Antonelli's gigantic neo-classical cupola. Crowned with a statue of Christ the Savior, it looms 333 feet above the city.

OTHER CENTERS. Near Novara is **Oleggio**, site of some significant medieval structures, particularly the tenth-century Church of San Michele, the twelfth-century Romanesque oratory of Santa Maria del Galgano, and, at nearby **Agrate Conturbia**, a baptistery begun in the ninth century and rebuilt in the twelfth.

Orta San Giulio is now a tourist center on the shore of Lake Orta. It was the capital of a Lombard duchy before it became a feudal possession of the bishops of Novara. In 1767 it passed to the house of Savoy. Besides many attractive palaces, it is home to the Sacro Monte, a church and complex of chapels built between 1591 and 1770 dedicated to Saint Francis of Assisi. Also notable is the Basilica of San Giulio, first built in the ninth century and renovated in the eighteenth. It sits on an island in Lake Orta.

VERBANO-CUSO-OSSOLA

PROVINCIAL PROFILE. Area: 871 sq. mi. Population: 161,329 (province), 30,209 (combined city). Verbano-Cusio-Ossola contains 77 communes. Lago Maggiore comprises most of Verbano-Cuso-Ossola's eastern border with Lombardy. (The lake is occasionally referred to as Lago Verbano.) To the south is the province of Novara, and then the border bends around Biella to the southwest. On its west and north Verbano-Cuso-Ossola faces Switzerland. The Lepontine Alps dominate the province's northern stretches. The Sempione (Simplon) Tunnel passes under Monte Leone (11,654 feet), and the highest point is Monte Rosa (15,203 feet), at the province's westernmost point.

HISTORY. The Count Amedeus VIII of Savoy exerted control over the Ossola Valley in 1411. In 1939 the towns of Intra and Pallanza merged to form Verbania. Pallanza (Verbania) was the home of the Cadorna, a family closely identified with the Italian army. Raffaele Cadorna (1815–1897) commanded the Italian forces that took Rome in 1870. His son, Luigi (1850–1928), directed the nation's land forces during the First World War. An arrogant man intolerant of advice and government interference in military affairs, he was responsible for the disaster at Caporetto (October 1917), when the Italian line collapsed before an Austrian assault. He was replaced by Marshal Armando Diaz. Luigi's son, Raffaele (1889–1973), was a general who in the Second World War served as liaison between liberated Italy and the Resistance fighters behind Nazi lines. After the war he became chief of staff of the Italian armed forces. During the Second World War, anti-Fascist resistance was particularly effective in the area, and an independent Republic of the Val Ossola was established in September 1944 until the Nazis defeated it. Verbano-Cuso-Ossola was carved from the northern half of the province of Novara in 1993.

ARTS AND CULTURE. Verbania's foremost artistic treasure is the sixteenth-century Church of the Madonna della Campagna. At the beginning of August the festival of the "traditional militias" (*milizie tradizionali*) occurs in the Anzasca valley.

OTHER CENTERS. The small agricultural town of **Gignese** is home to Italy's Umbrella Museum, and contains items from as early as the seventeenth century.

One of Italy's most famous resorts, **Stresa,** is on the shore of Lago Maggiore. Many of its eighteenth- and nineteenth-century palaces and villas have become modern hotels. Offshore are the Borromean Islands, the largest of which, Isola Bella, is the site of the Borromeo Palace, begun in 1632, with its eighteenth-century gardens. Stresa achieved political note in 1935 when Benito Mussolini met there with French and British leaders to deal with the rising menace of Adolf Hitler. The anti-German "Stresa Front" was short-lived.

VERCELLI

PROVINCIAL PROFILE. Area: 1,159 sq. mi. Population: 181,863 (province), 48,376 (city). Vercelli contains 86 communes. Vercelli city is on the Sesia River. Vercelli is a long north-south province that is very narrow in the middle and bulges on either end. To the north and northeast is Verbania, to the east is Novara, southwest is Lombardy, Alessandria is to the south, and Asti is on the southwest. Turin, Biella, and the Valle d'Aosta face Vercelli to the west, and Switzerland touches the province on its northwest. The Sesia valley comprises most of its northern part, and the thin middle slices between the provinces of Biella and Novara. The south balloons again into the Po plain with the city of Vercelli. At the northern end of the province are the mountains of the Valsesia Natural Park. At the northwest tip of the park, where Vercelli meets Switzerland, is Gnifetti Point of Monte Rosa (14,958 feet).

HISTORY. Vercelli was first settled by the Libici, a Liguri people. Hannibal chose the area as a step in his invasion route through Italy, and in 218 B.C. he first defeated Roman troops at Campi Raudii, at the southeast corner of the province, near the junction of the Sesia and Po rivers. Vercelli became one of Italy's most important medieval episcopal sees. Its communal government, however, replaced the bishop's authority by the middle of the eleventh century. As his political power declined within the city, however, the bishop still wielded feudal authority in other areas. The city enjoyed its greatest prosperity from the eleventh well into the thirteenth century. It fell to the Visconti family in 1335 and to the Dukes of Savoy in 1427. The French and Spanish subsequently laid siege to, and conquered, Vercelli.

These subjugations took their tolls. When the Spanish returned the city to the house of Savoy in 1659, for example, only 6,303 people were left alive there. The French Duke of Vendome destroyed the city walls and fortifications in 1704, during the War of the Spanish Succession. Vercelli was finally restored to the house of Savoy in 1713. When French troops returned under Napoleon at the turn of the next century, Vercelli became capital of the department of Sesia. The French were not popular in Vercelli, but their liberal ideas persisted after they evacuated the area. The city was active in the revolutions of 1821 and 1848, as well as during the 1859 war, when it was occupied by the Austrians. With unification, Vercelli merged with the province of Novara, where it remained until the Fascist administrative reorganization of 1927 reinstated it as a capital.

ARTS AND CULTURE. Vercelli's ancient status as a see is demonstrated in its impressive Romanesque-Gothic Basilica of Sant'Andrea. Built in the early thirteenth century, it was damaged and restored in the seventeenth. Vercelli's cathedral, dedicated to the city's patron, Sant'Eusebio, is a Renaissance structure begun by **Pellegrino Tibaldi** (1527–1596), an architect from Como. Eusebio was a Sardinian who became Bishop of Vercelli in 345. The city contained a large faction of Arians, followers of the heretical priest Arius. According to legend, the Arians locked all church doors in Vercelli to bar Eusebio from exercising his office. The bishop knelt before the entrance of largest church until the Virgin Mary descended from heaven and the doors swung open. The Church of San Cristoforo is a Renaissance building that contains frescoes and an altar painting by **Gaudenzio Ferrari** (1470–1546), from Valduggia.

Nearby Andorno was the home of a family of artists, the **Galliari**, which began with the local work of **Giovanni** (c. 1680–1720). His grandsons achieved reputations beyond Vercelli. **Bernardino** (1707–1794) worked in Turin and Germany; **Fabrizio** (1709–1790) painted the dome of the Vercelli cathedral and contributed to projects in Bologna and Bergamo. Vercelli is home to the Borgogna Civic Museum, which boasts the best collection of Piedmontese works outside of Turin. It includes works by Ferrari and the Vercelli native **Il Sodoma** (Giovanni Antonio Bazzi, 1477–1549).

OTHER CENTERS. Trino was a Roman city that became a possession of the Marquis of Monferrato in the twelfth century and of the house of Savoy in 1631. Outside the town is the ancient Basilica of San Michele in

Insula. Established as a Roman compound in the fourth century, the church was redesigned in the eighth. Nearby, in **Lucedio**, is a twelfth-century Cistercian abbey dedicated to the Virgin. It was later restored in the Baroque style.

The principal center of the Sesia valley (or Valsesia) is **Varallo Sesia**. A medieval town that suffered the ambitions of Milan, Spain, and the house of Savoy, it boasts some important artistic sites. One of Piedmont's chief artists, Gaudenzio Ferrari (1470–1546), came from nearby Valduggia and did a great deal of work in Varallo Sesia. His most important work, in frescoes and sculpture, are displayed at Sacro Monte, a pilgrimage center on a dramatic site overlooking Varallo Sesia. Sacro Monte is a complex conceived at the end of the fifteenth century by a Franciscan, the Blessed Bernardino Caimi (d. 1499). Caimi's ambition was to construct a "New Jerusalem" with, ultimately, forty-five chapels dedicated to significant places in the Holy Land. The project lacked cohesion, however, until the Umbrian Galeazzo Alessi (Perugia, c. 1512–1572) was commissioned to reorganize it in the 1560s. The first stop on the path up the mountain is the Church of Santa Maria delle Grazie (1501), in which Ferrari painted a series of 21 frescoes on the life and passion of Christ. Many consider his masterpiece to be the Calvary Chapel.

SELECT BIBLIOGRAPHY

Castronovo, Valerio, ed. *Il Piemonte*. Turin: Einaudi, 1977.
Istituto Geografico De Agostini. *Piemonte*. 2 vols. Novara: Istituto Geografico De Agostini, 1979.

SARDINIA

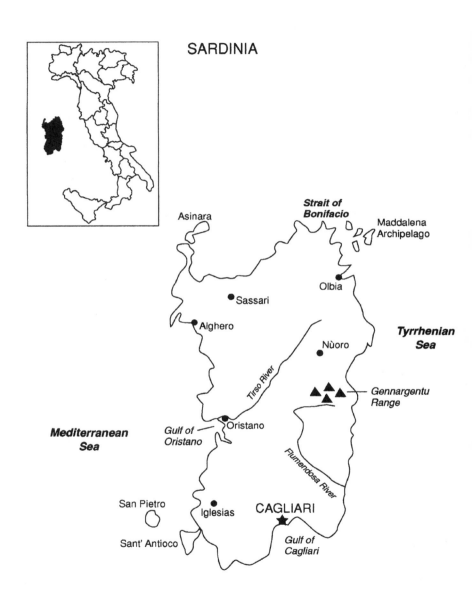

Chapter 14

SARDINIA
(Sardegna)

REGIONAL CHARACTERISTICS. Area: 9,301 sq. mi. Population: 1,661,429. Capital: Cagliari. Sardinia is Italy's third largest region in land area and twelfth in population. The region contains 377 communes. Sardinia has three Catholic metropolitan sees: Cagliari, Oristano, and Sassari.

With 1,125 miles of coastline, Sardinia is the second largest island in the Mediterranean. A number of smaller islands surround it, particularly Asinara, San Pietro, Sant'Antioco, and the Maddalena Archipelago. Asinara and the Maddalena Archipelago are both protected as national parks. Sardinia lies west of the Italian peninsula and northwest of Sicily. The Strait of Bonifacio separates it from its northern neighbor, the French island of Corsica. Sardinia is mostly rugged: 67.9 percent of the island is classified as hilly and 13.6 percent is mountainous; plains comprise 18.5 percent. The tallest peak is Punta La Marmora (6,018 feet) in the Gennargentu range of Nuoro province.

Sardinia is a dry island, and most rivers are torrents which have been dammed. The chief rivers are the Tirso, which empties into the Gulf of Oristano, and the Flumendosa, which spills into the Tyrrhenian. The island has many underground flows, karsts, and mineral springs. Sardinia's longest stretch of flatland is the Campidano, which cuts diagonally across the southern half of the island from the Gulf of Cagliari to the Gulf of Oristano.

ECONOMY. Of Sardinia's 491,000 employed workers, 342,000 are male and 149,000 are female; 12.4 percent of the Sardinian workforce is occupied in agriculture; 23.2 percent in industry, and 64.4 percent in the tertiary sector. The island's January 1998 unemployment rate was 21.8 percent. Sardinia is traditionally one of Italy's poorest regions. Mining (primarily lead and zinc), lumber, livestock farms, and fishing constitute the backbone of its traditional economy. Today 61 percent of the sales of Sardinian agricultural production comes from livestock. Sixteen percent of Italy's sea traffic is handled at Sardinia's five major ports. The tourist industry has become one of the economy's brightest areas. Much of Sardinia's terrain is wild and unspoiled, and its magnificent beaches and seaside resorts are being discovered by an ever-expanding number of tourists.

CUISINE. Sardinia has a long history of dairy farming and is noted for its pecorino (ewe's milk) cheeses: the *fiore sardo*, the *pecorino sardo*, and the *pecorino romano*. These have earned the D.O.P. (*denominazione di origine protetta*, a mark of authenticity and quality) label and make Sardinia Europe's only region to have three cheeses thus classified. The island also produces the hard *calcagno, pepato*, and *foggiano* cheeses, and the somewhat softer *crotonese*. *Ircano* and *biancospino* are two varieties of goat's milk cheeses produced in Sardinia. A gastronomic favorite around Oristano is *bottarga*, a type of caviar made from *muggine* (mullet eggs). The *muggine*, a fish native to the Gulf of Oristano, is also served as *mrecca*. Eel dishes are common to the area. One of Sardinia's more unusual breads is the paper-thin *pane carasau*. *Su farru* is a soup made with mint and barley. The suckling pig (*porceddu*), barbecued over an open fire, is a Sardinian tradition.

Phoenicians brought their winemaking skills to Sardinia by the eighth century B.C. The Spanish contributed to the island's wine production by introducing non-Italian grapes. The white Nuragus, Sardinia's most common wine, is made from grapes said to have been brought by the Phoenicians; Cannonau (and the better Cannonau di Sardegna), Malvasia Sarda, the dry Torbado, and the red Monica are made from Spanish grapes. West-central Sardinia produces the sweet Vernaccia di Oristano, one of Sardinia's premier wines.

BOTTARGA DI MUGGINE

2 medium tomatoes, sliced thin	Olive oil
1 small loaf of bread, preferably "carasau," sliced	Butter
½ c. bottarga (mullet roe)	2 lemons, cut into wedges

Place a slice of tomato on each slice of bread. Cover with bottarga, some olive oil, and butter, and serve with lemon wedges.

HISTORY. Sardinia has endured occupations by many foreign powers over the centuries, a fact reflected in the use of Genoese, Tuscan, Aragonese, and Arabic dialects along with native Sardo (or Sardu) and Italian. Sardinia was home to the prehistoric Nuraghi culture from about 1500 B.C. until about 400 B.C. The people of this little-known society used volcanic basalt boulders to construct cone- or mound-shaped structures called *nuraghe*, of which perhaps 7,000 remain today. Attracted by its mineral deposits and timber, Phoenicians landed on Sardinia around 800 B.C., followed in 509 by Carthaginians, who came from Africa, 120 miles to the south. The Carthaginians ruled most of the island except for the mountainous area called Barbaria or the Barbagie, which roughly corresponded to today's Nuoro province. After defeat in the First Punic War, Carthage ceded Sardinia to the Romans in 238 B.C. Although the Romans focused on the coastal cities, they penetrated into the Barbagie, which the Carthaginians had never been able to do, and crushed resistance there.

After a Vandal occupation upon the fall of the Roman Empire (A.D. 476), the Byzantines ruled Sardinia from 533/534 until about 900. During this period, particularly when incessant Arab raiding isolated Sardinia, the Barbagie asserted itself as a semi-independent pagan kingdom. In the 700s and 800s, as Muslim raids increased in frequency and ferocity, most of coastal Sardinia was abandoned and its Byzantine governor, the *judex provinciae*, reorganized the island into four administrative zones. Later, as the Sardinians shook off Byzantium's yoke, these four units evolved into independent kingdoms, known as the *giudicati*. The northeast became the *giudicato* of Gallura; the northwest was Logudoro or Torres; Cagliari was in the south, with its capital at Sant'Igea; and Arborea was in the west-central part of the island, corresponding roughly to today's province of Oristano. A medieval parliament, the *Corona de logu*, loosely united the four kingdoms. The political landscape was further distinguished at times by communal governments at Cagliari, Alghero, Iglesias, Sassari, and Bosa.

By the 1200s most of the *giudicati* lost their independence and came under Genoese or Pisan control. Only Arborea maintained a semi-sovereignty until the early fifteenth century. The Sicilian Vespers uprising against the French in 1282 changed Sardinia's fortunes. After the rebellion James II of Aragon renounced his claim to Sicily and in 1297, Pope Boniface VIII compensated him for the loss by hypothetically awarding him the newly created Kingdom of Sardinia and Corsica. In 1323 James, with aid from Arborea, took possession of his territory by defeating the remaining Pisan forces there. In 1353, however, Arborea went to war with the Aragonese and pushed them off the island except for two toeholds, at Calgiari and Alghero. Martin I the Young of Aragon finally triumphed over Arborea in 1409 and ended the last of the *giudicati*. His victory, however, was short-lived; he died of malaria later that year, and in 1412, Sardinia passed from the Aragonese to the Kingdom of Castile. In 1479 the crowns of Castile and Aragon were united through the marriage of Ferdinand of Aragon and Isabella of Castile, and the Kingdom of Spain was born. The Kingdom of

Sardinia, without Corsica, was incorporated into the Spanish dominions. For the Sardinians, the Aragonese and the Spanish left an enormous cultural legacy. Iberian rule was also distinguished by its imposition of feudalism and by a brutality that included the enslavement and deportation of men, women, and children from rebellious interior villages.

Between 1708 and 1718 Sardinia passed in rapid succession from Spanish hands to Austrian, back to Spanish, and, finally, with the Treaty of London, to the Dukes of Savoy. The latter took Sardinia's royal title as their own and permanently wed the island to Italy's fortunes. Sardinia thus became an extension of the wealthier and more European Savoyard possessions in Piedmont and the Franco-Italian borderlands. The Napoleonic invasion of northwest Italy drove the house of Savoy from Turin, and they took refuge at Cagliari between 1799 and 1814. They returned to Turin after the defeat of the French, and Sardinia was politically reunited with the mainland. Its increasingly vague royal status ended when it fused fully with Piedmont under a central government in 1847.

Transferred to the new Italian Kingdom in 1861, Sardinia was split into two provinces, Cagliari and Sassari. The pro-business liberal policies of the new Italy had debilitating consequences for the island's economy. An enclosure process had begun in 1820 with the Savoyard *chiudende* edict, and taxes more than doubled on Sardinia between 1850 and 1870. In the 1880s and 1890s a tariff war with France and the calamity in the wine industry from a phylloxera epidemic caused severe hardships. Between 1885 and 1897, for example, Sardinia witnessed as many confiscations of real estate due to tax evasion as did the rest of Italy combined. In 1897 the government in Rome passed its first "special law" to deal with Sardinian and Southern poverty, and a parliamentary investigation of 1905 found Sardinian per capita incomes to be the lowest in Italy. Returning veterans from the First World War constituted a force for change by forming the Sardinian Action Party; many others joined the young Fascist Party. Mussolini's regime attempted some land reclamation and public works projects on Sardinia.

The Sardininian wish for independence or at least autonomy from foreign masters has been an issue for centuries. Resentment against the Spanish was manifested in the assassination of Viceroy Camarassa in 1688. In 1794 Giovanni Maria Angioy led an ill-fated rebellion against the Piedmontese. In 1921, World War One veterans group led by Emilio Lussu (1890–1975) established the Sardinian Action Party (Partito Sardo d'Azione), which advocated autonomy for the island. Except for the Fascist era, when it was disbanded, the Sardinian Action Party has remained a powerful force in the island's politics. After the Second World War a special statute of 1948 finally awarded autonomous status to the island, followed by extensive government aid from Rome with the creation of the Cassa per il Mezzogiorno (Fund for the South) in 1950. An unsuccessful twelve-year plan of economic development was launched in 1962, followed by another in 1974 which focused more than its predecessor on decentralized growth, reforestation, and promotion of mining, cheesemaking, and grazing land. Tourist development has continued apace.

RECENT POLITICS. Sardinia forms the twenty-sixth electoral district (*circoscrizione*). In the 1996 majoritarian elections to Italy's Chamber of Deputies, the Center-Right Polo per le Libertà won 46.1 percent of the vote, compared to 27.2 percent for a coalition of Ulivo members and the Sardinian Action Party. A separate Ulivo coalition standing on its own received 15.8 percent. In the proportional count, Forza Italia won 22.8 percent, with 20.3 percent to the Party of the Democratic Left (PDS) and 18.4 percent to the Alleanza Nazionale. For the Senate, the Ulivo-Sardinian Action Party coalition won with 50.1 percent of the vote, against 44.6 for the Polo. As an autonomous region, Sardinia did not vote in the April 2000 regional elections.

CAGLIARI

PROVINCIAL PROFILE. Area: 2,662 sq. mi. Population: 770,101 (province), 174,175 (city). Cagliari province contains 109 communes. It occupies the southern end of the island, facing the the Tyrrhenian Sea to the east, the Mediterranean to the south, and the Sardinian Sea to the west. Cagliari city faces south onto the Gulf of Cagliari and is Sardinia's largest freight port. Northwest of the province is Oristano, and northeast is Nuoro. Most of the province is hilly; the major plain is the Campidano, which stretches northwest/southeast, mainly along the Mannu River. West of Cagliari are the woods of Gutturu Mannu, a protected reserve which is said to be the largest forest in the Mediterranean. Carbonia, Iglesias, and Sant'Antioco are other important towns in the province.

HISTORY. Cagliari has been the site of a human settlement since prehistoric times, although the city was probably founded in the sixth century B.C. by the Phoenicians. The Greeks knew it as Cardlis, and the Romans, as Caralis (or Karalis). The city was the chief Roman port on the island, and an anchorage for part of the Roman fleet based at Misenum (in Campania). The region also was important for its mining activity. After a period of Vandal occupation following the fall of the Roman Empire (476), the Byzantines landed at Cagliari and ruled until the tenth century. The *giudicato* of Cagliari, which replaced Greek power in the area, soon fell under Pisan influence. In 1326 the Aragonese took Cagliari and launched the long period of Spanish rule. In modern times labor discontent erupted in the mining districts of the southwest. Violence led to the death of three miners northwest of Iglesias at Buggerru, and triggered Italy's first general strike in 1904. The Fascists developed Cagliari as an air and naval base; both were neutralized in the Second World War by Allied aerial bombardments. **ARTS AND CULTURE.** A Phoenician necropolis and a number of Roman remains recall Cagliari's ancient past. The city's Basilica of San Saturnino (or San Saturno) dates from the fifth century. The Byzantines continued its construction, which had been interrupted by the Vandal conquest. The Duomo, Santa Maria di Castello, contains the tombs of the Aragonese King Martin I the Young, who took Sardinia from the *giudicato* of Arborea in 1409, and the unfortunate Savoyard King of Sardinia, Charles Albert, who led his troops to disaster in the first war of the Risorgimento. The latter abdicated in 1849 after humiliating defeats and retired to a monastery. Among Sardinia's most important Spanish-era structures is Cagliari's sanctuary of Bonaria, begun during the siege of the city in 1325. A significant collection of ancient and prehistoric artifacts is housed at the National Archaeological Museum.

The May 1 procession of Sant'Efisio through the streets of Cagliari recalls the Spanish occupation. Efisio is the patron of Sardinia and, with San Saturnino, co-patron of Cagliari. According to tradition, Efisio was a soldier in the Roman army who served for a time in the personal guard of Emperor Diocletian (284–315). He traveled to Gaeta, where a cross was made for him on which mysteriously appeared the names Gabriel, Michael, and Emmanuel. The miraculous cross led Efisio to victory over barbarous Sardinian tribes. But Efisio, in perhaps an excess of enthusiasm, reported the events to the pagan Diocletian, who promptly ordered his execution. According to tradition, Cagliari's Baroque Church of Sant'Efisio stands over the remains of the prison where the saint was martyred. Saturnino's legend is even more obscure. He was apparently a Bishop of Toulouse in the 200s who came from either Africa or the eastern Mediterranean.

Giuseppe Dessì (1909–1977) was a novelist and playwright from near Cagliari who portrayed a dark and oppressive side of Sardinian life through such works as *Paese d'ombre*, which won the 1972 Strega Prize and was translated into English as *The Forests of Norbio*. He has been compared to Sicily's Leonardo Sciascia. The popular Italian film actor **Amedeo Nazzari** (Salvatore Amedeo Buffa, 1907–1979) was born in Cagliari. After beginning as a stage actor, he transferred to film in the mid-1930s and acquired a reputation as a dashing and romantic leading man. Cagliari hosts an international trade fair every spring.

OTHER CENTERS. Sardinia's greatest concentration of Nuraghic structures is Su Nuraxi at **Barumini**, near the province's border with Nuoro. The site was partly revealed by floodwaters in 1949, and excavation began in 1954. Barumini's origins may stretch back to the fourth millennium B.C., but the central structure, an enormous pile of a fortress, can be traced to the fifteenth century B.C. The complex held between 1,500 and 2,000 people with a detachment of about 500 soldiers. Another important site in the province is the Genna Maria Nuraghic village at **Villanovaforru**.

Some of Sardinia's most important Phoenician and Roman excavations are at **Nora** on the Capo di Pula. Along with a forum, a theater, and a number of thermal baths, the place boasts a temple of Tanit which the Romans renovated. **Sant'Antioco** was the first Phoenician settlement on Sardinia, as Sulcis, and later an important Roman town. It contains an enormous Phoenician necropolis which served either as a children's cemetery or as a chilling site where children were sacrificed. Phoenician and Carthaginian remains, an acropolis and a necropolis, can also be observed at **Sirai**. At Sant'Antioco, **Uta**, and **Villaspeciosa** are three of Sardinia's most important Romanesque churches—Sant'Antioco, Santa Maria, and San Platano, respectively—all of the early twelfth century and all built by the Vittorini monks of Marseilles, France.

Dolianova boasts San Pantaleo, an important early Gothic structure of the twelfth century which reveals Pisan and a bit of Islamic influence.

Iglesias was long a mining and manufacturing center, although much of the mining has now ended. It was originally Villeclesia Argentaria, but a thirteenth-century document indicates its name had been changed to Villa di Chiesa before it finally became Iglesias. The town boasts two exceptional Pisan-Aragonese Gothic structures, the churches of Santa Chiara and San Francesco. Nearby are the remains of a Carthaginian temple of Antas, built around 500 B.C.

NUORO

PROVINCIAL PROFILE. Area: 2,720 sq. mi. Population: 271,870 (province), 38,003 (city). Nuoro province contains 100 communes. It faces the Tyrrhenian Sea to the east and borders Cagliari to the south, Oristano to the southwest, and Sassari to the northwest. Between the latter two provinces Nuoro extends a narrow arm west that reaches the Sardinian Sea at the town of Bosa. Large tracts of land have been set aside as two national parks, the Gennargentu, named for Sardinia's highest mountain range, and the Golfo di Orosei, after the gulf which occupies the central part of Nuoro's coastline. Nuoro city lies inland at the heart of Sardinia's most remote mountain area and in the poorest part of the island.

HISTORY. Nuoro was settled in prehistoric times. As Barbagie, it fiercely maintained its independence from the Carthaginians but succumbed to a brutal Roman occupation after a century of resistance. The first record of Nuoro city is a twelfth-century document which identifies it as Nugorus. Nuoro was a provincial capital from 1848 until 1860. Its loss of status and the harshness of the new Italian regime, particularly its sale of former feudal "commons" lands, begun by the Piedmontese before the unification, pushed Nuoro into the *su connottu* (recognition) riots of 1868. Rebellion and banditry persisted until Rome took military action in 1899. Nuoro's status was restored by Mussolini's administrative reforms of 1927, which carved its own province from Cagliari and Sassari. The province benefited after 1950 from government funds applied to road building and agricultural improvement. Mountain trekking has brought many tourists to Nuoro in recent years.

ARTS AND CULTURE. The nineteenth-century cathedral is dedicated to the Virgin of the Snow. The name recalls a dream of Pope Liberius in the fourth century, in which Mary dispatched the pontiff to construct her church on a snow-covered hill in Rome. The next morning, a day in August, Liberius woke to discover the Esquiline Hill topped with snow, and there built the Basilica of Saint Mary Major. The Marian cult is widespread in Nuoro, which has about eighty churches dedicated to the Madonna. The Procession of the Redeemer through Nuoro on August 29 recalls Spanish influence. The Museum of Sardinian Folk Culture and tradition is found here. The city also contains the Museo Deleddiano, honoring **Grazia Deledda** (1871–1936), the 1926 Nobel Prize-winning author from Nuoro. Influenced by Russian authors and Italian realists, her 1895 novel, *Anime oneste* (Honest Souls) was greeted with critical acclaim. Deledda moved to Rome and wrote other successful works, such as *Cenere* (Ashes, 1904), which became a famous film in 1916, and *La madre* (The Mother, 1920).

OTHER CENTERS. Important prehistoric tombs and one of the island's better Nuraghic villages are found, respectively, at **Traversa** and **Serra Orios**, in the area around **Dorgali**. Nuraghic remains are also found at **Macomer** (*nuraghe* Santa Barbara), **Orroli** (*nuraghe* Orrobiu or Arrobiu), **Orune** (*nuraghe* Noddule and the *temple at the well*), **Serri** (*nuraghe* Santa Vittoria) and **Silanus** (*nuraghe* Santa Sabina).

ORISTANO

PROVINCIAL PROFILE. Area: 1,016 sq. mi. Population: 158,567 (province) 32,891 (city). Oristano province has 78 communes. To its north and east, Oristano shares a border with Nuoro. To its south is Cagliari, and to its west is the Sardinian Sea. Much of the southern end of the province's coastline is on the Gulf of Oristano. The Tirso River, one of Sardinia's largest, flows from Nuoro province. It was dammed in the northeast part of Oristano in 1923 to form Italy's largest man-made lake, Lago Omodeo. The Tirso, however, continues past the dam and finally empties into the Gulf of Oristano on a coastal plain near Oristano city. This flat and sometimes marshy land forms the northwestern end of the Campidano, which runs southeast to Cagliari.

HISTORY. Oristano was founded as Maristanis or Aristanis by refugees from the nearby Phoenician town of Tharros. By the twelfth century A.D. it had become the principal city of the *giudicato* of Arborea, the most ambitious of the island's four. At Pavia in 1164, Emperor Frederick Barbarossa proclaimed Arborea's "judge" Barisone King of Sardinia. Arborea swelled to include most of the island under "judge" Eleonora, who extended a law code, the *Carta de lodu*, across her domains. In 1409, five years after her death, Arborea succumbed to the Aragonese and followed the Spanish, Austrian, French, Savoyard and Italian administration of the rest of the island. The Italian government radically altered Oristano's appearance by demolishing many of its old neighborhoods and replacing them with broad boulevards and piazzas, endeavors that persisted under the Fascists.

ARTS AND CULTURE. Oristano's Duomo was built by Lombard masters in the thirteenth century. An interior renovation in 1721 spared the impressive Gothic chapel dedicated to the Madonna "del rimedio" (of the remedy). Since 1942 the relics of Oristano's patron, Saint Archelao, have rested in the Duomo. Archelao was a young man of noble pagan birth from Fordongianus who converted to Christianity while a student at Cagliari. He returned to his hometown to preach, and was stoned to death in A.D. 100. Oristano province boasts many interesting festivals. The Sa Sartiglia is an elaborate popular ritual of horse racing and lancing with roots extending to the age of the Crusades. It occurs each year during Carnival, under the patronage of Saint John the Evangelist. Another horse race, the S'Ardia, occurs at Sedilo on July 6. It is repeated the next day at dawn. The S'Ardia honors the Roman Emperor Constantine, who is traditionally regarded as a saint, and takes place around a church dedicated to him.

OTHER CENTERS. Some of Oristano's most important concentrations of *nuraghe* are found in **Abbasanta** (*nuraghe* Losa), **Fertilia** (*nuraghe* Palmavera), **Paulilatino** (*nuraghe* Lugheras and Santa Cristina), and **San Vero Milis** (*nuraghe* S'Uraki)

Ancient Rome's military headquarters on Sardinia were at Forum Traiani, today's **Fordongianus**. Some of the city's thermal baths remain, still with very hot water. Outside of town is the beautiful Romanesque Church of San Lussorio, built by Vittorini monks from France, on top of an older structure in the twelfth century. Its fourth-century crypt survives.

One of Italy's principal political philosophers and a founder of the Communist Party, Antonio Gramsci, was born at **Ales** in 1891. In 1911 Gramsci went to study at the University of Turin, where he immersed himself in working-class politics. He was one of the founders of *L'Ordine Nuovo* (The New Order), which became a daily newspaper in 1921. After a period in Moscow, Gramsci was elected to the Italian Parliament in 1924. The Fascists arrested him in November 1926 and sent him to prison. This brutal experience drained most of the life from Gramsci, who had always been in delicate health, and in 1937 he died three days after his early release. Gramsci's work brought a cultural appreciation and a more human face to Marxism. His *Prison Notebooks*, posthumously published, brought him an international reputation as one of the twentieth century's key political thinkers of the Left.

Outside of Oristano are some towns of Carthaginian origin, **Santa Giusta** and **Tharros**. The twelfth-century Cathedral of Santa Giusta is one of Sardinia's most important structures. Tharros, the original metropolis in the area, is now an archaeological zone. By the time of the Punic Wars, it had become one of the principal centers of Carthaginian power in the western Mediterranean. Along with the remains of Roman baths, Tharros contains what is left of temples and a *thophet*, where Carthaginians sacrificed their children to the gods.

Cabras honors San Salvatore in its *corsa degli scalzi*, a barefoot race in which the statue of the saint is carried along a route to the nearby sanctuary, the *ipogeo* (underground chamber) *di San Salvatore*. The course commemorates the transfer of the statue to protect it from medieval Muslim raiders and is run twice, once in each direction, in September. The sanctuary was first a pagan holy place, and an underground cave inspired a cult of healing waters.

In 1928 Mussolini's regime founded the first of three experimental towns called Mussolinia and transplanted there a population of farming families from the Veneto and Emilia Romagna. Mussolinia was later renamed **Arborea**.

SASSARI

PROVINCIAL PROFILE. Area: 2,903 sq. mi. Population: 460,891 (province), 121,412 (city). Sassari province contains 90 communes. It occupies the northern quarter of the island. It faces the Tyrrhenian Sea to the east and the Sardinian Sea to the west. The only province with which it shares a border is Nuoro, to the south. Sassari's northern coastline mostly faces onto the Gulf of Asinara and the Strait of Bonifacio, which separates it from the French island of Corsica, twelve miles away at its closest point. Sassari, the provincial capital, sits somewhat inland; the chief coastal cities are Alghero on the west, Porto Torres on the north, and Olbia on the east. The most important river is the Coghinas, which flows north mainly from the Goceanu and Alà highlands near the Nuoro border into the Gulf of Asinara. Sardinia's northwest point, in Sassari province, is the island of Asinara, a national park.

Sassari is easily the chief tourist destination on Sardinia, serving almost twice as many visitors as second-place Cagliari. More ship passengers disembark at Olbia, on the east coast of the province, than at any of Sardinia's other ports. Porto Torres and La Maddalena, two of the province's other ports follow Olbia in the number of ship passengers. One of the area's chief attractions is Sardinia's northeast shore, which contains the Maddalena archipelago, named a national park, and the Costa smeralda, the glamorous resort area made famous in the 1950s and 1960s by the Aga Khan, a millionaire playboy.

HISTORY. In the ancient world the chief city in what is now Sassari province was the seaport of Torres, or Porto Torres. Muslim raids after the fall of the Roman Empire (476), however, caused the population to desert the coastal cities and Torres lost its status to the inland town of Thatari, later known as Sassari. It replaced Torres as the capital of the Logudoro *giudicato* and became an archiepiscopal see in 1441. Sassari enjoyed status as a free commune under the Pisans and the Genoese, and then passed to the Aragonese in 1323 to begin, along with most of Sardinia, its long age of subjugation under the Spanish. Sassari was heavily damaged during the Second World War.

Two of Italy's presidents came from Sassari. Antonio Segni (1891–1972) participated as a young man in the Catholic Popular Party. With the establishment of Mussolini's dictatorship, however, he turned to an academic career. He became the rector of the University of Sassari in 1943 and entered the Christian Democratic governments at the end of the Second World War, working for land reform. Segni became prime minister in 1955 and president in 1962; a severe stroke two years later ended his career. Francesco Cossiga (b. 1928) served as president from 1985 until 1992. He joined the Christian Democratic Party in 1945 and worked his way up to become minister of the interior during the 1970s. Unfortunately, his task was made difficult by the wave of terrorism at the time and the murder of former Prime Minister Aldo Moro in 1978. Since the collapse of the Christian Democratic Party, Cossiga has been attempting to create a new centrist organization.

Another native of Sassari was Enrico Berlinguer (1922–1984), the secretary-general of the Italian Communist Party from 1972 until his death. As leader of the party, he frequently found himself at odds with Moscow over such issues as support for NATO and the development of Eurocommunism.

ARTS AND CULTURE. Sassari's Duomo of San Nicolà is a twelfth-century structure heavily renovated along Spanish lines in the sixteenth century. It contains the relics of the patrons of Sassari (and Porto Torres), Saints Gavino, Proto, and Gianuario. Tradition says that Gavino was a noble Roman sent to Sardinia as an administrator. He found himself embroiled in the case of two Christians, Proto and Gianuario, who had been arrested and tortured by the pagan governor, Barbaro. At one point he banished Proto to Asinara Island, to be eaten by wild animals or to starve to death. Instead, the beasts befriended the Christian and brought him food. At wit's end, Barbaro entrusted Proto and Gianuario to the charge of his lieutenant, Gavino. The prisoners convinced their new captor to accept Christianity. Gavino allowed the two to escape, and asked Barbaro to inflict their punishments on him. Ultimately all three were decapitated and their heads thrown into the sea. The Church has since rejected the stories of the three.

The artist **Mario Sironi** (1885–1961) was a native of Sassari. He left the island as a baby, however, and grew up in Rome. Sironi was a Futurist early in his career, then joined the nascent *Novecento* (Nineteenth Century) movement in the early 1920s. Sassari's National Museum "Giovanni Antonio Sanna" contains a significant collection of ancient Sardinian works, including Nuraghic bronzes. The procession of the Cavalcata in Sassari, the penultimate Sunday in May, recalls the city's Spanish legacy.

OTHER CENTERS. The United States maintains naval support activity at **La Maddalena**. The most famous resident of the Maddalena archipelago was Giuseppe Garibaldi, the hero of the Risorgimento, who retired to his farm on **Caprera Island**, which forms part of the chain. His home there still stands as a national monument.

Perhaps because of its proximity to Iberian ports, **Alghero** is considered Sardinia's most Spanish city, and a form of Catalan dialect is still spoken there. An ancient city, it became moribund after the fall of Rome in 476. The Genoese Doria family revived it in the twelfth century and held it until the Aragonese took Alghero in 1353. The city has retained its medieval center and Spanish defenses, the Torre dell'Esperò Reial (or Torre di Sulis) and Magdalena fortress.

Andara was for a time the capital of the medieval Logudoro *giudicato* and retains some significant structures from that era. The twelfth-century Church of Santa Maria del Regno was model for Oristano's Santa Giusta. Outside of town is the Church of Sant'Antioco, built in the eleventh and twelfth centuries.

Enormous Neolithic tombs excavated from rock, collectively called *domus de janas*, are found at **Arzachena**, near **Bonorva**, at **Bosa**, and at **Sedini**. Nuraghic and other prehistoric remains are found at **Perfugas** and at **Torralba** (*nuraghe* Santu Antine). The "Sanctuary," which recalls a third millennium B.C. pre-Nuraghic culture with some similarities to Mesopotamian forms, is found at **Porto Torres**.

Pisa's influence on Sardinia's architecture can be examined in a number of churches across the province. Examples include San Pietro di Sorres in **Borutta**, San Pietro di Simbranos at **Bulzi**, and San Giorgio Martire at **Pozzomaggiore**, and a former Camaldolese structure, the delightful twelfth-century Santissima Trinità di Saccargia, at **Codrongianus**.

An early twelfth-century castle built by the Genoese Doria family is at

Castelsardo. Most of the remains of the current bastion date from the fourteenth century.

Sardinia's chief passenger port, **Olbia,** served Carthaginians. Although a fairly modern city, Olbia boasts an important Romanesque church from the eleventh century, San Simplicio.

Porto Torres has maintained something of its past glory as the area's chief city during ancient and medieval times. Roman ruins include thermal baths, and its Basilica of San Gavino is an outstanding example of the Pisan influence and the Romanesque style. In the fifteenth century Catalan additions were made to the doorways.

SELECT BIBLIOGRAPHY

Berlinguer, Luigi, and Antonello Mattone, eds. *La Sardegna.* Turin: Einaudi, 1998.

Day, John, Bruno Anatra, and Lucetta Scaraffia. *La Sardegna medioevale e moderna.* Turin: UTET, 1984.

Floris, Francesco. *La Sardegna del novecento.* Cagliari: Demos Editore, 1997.

Lilliu, Giovanni. *The Sardinia of the Nuraghi.* Novara: Istituto Geografico De Agostini, 1993.

Manconi, Lorenzo. *Breve storia di Oristano.* Cagliari: Edizioni della Torre, 1993.

Principe, Ilario. *Cagliari.* Rome: Laterza, 1988.

Sotgiu, Girolamo. *La Sardegna negli anni della repubblica: Storia critica dell'autonomia.* Rome: Laterza, 1996.

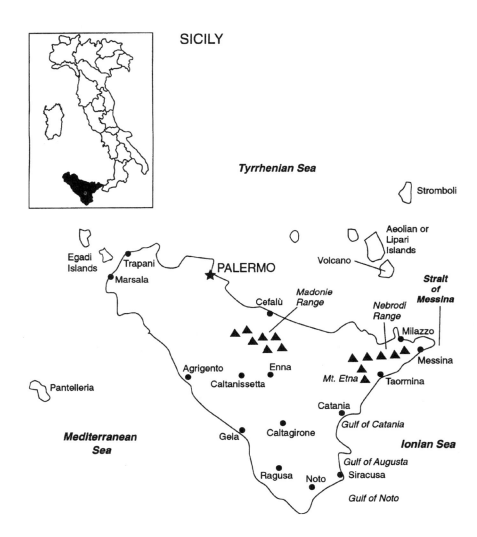

SICILY

Tyrrhenian Sea

Stromboli

Aeolian or
Lipari
Islands

Egadi
Islands

Trapani

PALERMO

Volcano

Marsala

Strait
of
Messina

Cefalù

Madonie
Range

Nebrodi
Range

Milazzo

Agrigento

Enna

Messina

Caltanissetta

Mt. Etna

Taormina

Pantelleria

Catania

Mediterranean
Sea

Gela

Caltagirone

Gulf of Catania

Ionian Sea

Ragusa

Noto

Gulf of Augusta

Siracusa

Gulf of Noto

Chapter 15

SICILY
(Sicilia)

REGIONAL CHARACTERISTICS. Area: 9,925 sq. mi. Population: 5,108,067. Capital: Palermo. The island of Sicily is an autonomous region of the Italian Republic. In land area it is Italy's largest region, and it ranks fourth in population. It is both the largest and the most populous island in the Mediterranean Sea. There are three Catholic metropolitan sees: Messina/Lipari/Santa Lucia del Mela, Palermo, and Syracuse.

Sicily is separated from Calabria and the rest of Italy by the 20-mile-long Strait of Messina, which is 2 miles wide at its northern point and 10 at its southern. Sicily is bounded on the north by the Tyrrhenian Sea, on the south and east by the Ionian Sea, and on the southwest by the Mediterranean. Hardly 100 miles separate the island from the North African coast at Tunisia, and barely half that distance from the island republic of Malta. Valleys occupy only a small part of Sicily. The largest one is around Catania in the east. Most of the island is made up of hills (61.3 percent) or mountains (24.5 percent). Plains account for 14.2 percent of Sicily. Some of the mountains are volcanic. Mount Etna, Europe's greatest volcano, and one of its deadliest, still erupts, releasing a never-ending supply of steam and smoke at its peak of 10,902 feet. Stromboli and Vulcano, two offshore islands in the Aeolian (or Lipari) chain, are also volcanic. Other islands off Sicily's coast include the Egadi Islands to its west and Pantelleria and the Pelagian Islands to the south. Most Sicilian hillsides are barren due to deforestation and soil erosion, the result of neglect and bad judgments by the Romans in ancient times. Only 4 percent of Sicily is forest. The garden over which Rome ruled 2,000 years ago is largely gone.

ECONOMY. Of Sicily's active workforce, 12.1 percent is in agriculture, 20 percent in industry, and 67.9 percent in the tertiary sector. Of the island's 1,294,000 active workers, 957,000 are men and 337,000 are women. Sicily's unemployment rate in January 1998 was 24.8 percent. Oil and sulfur are major sources of the island's income. Sulfur mines have dotted the Sicilian countryside since ancient times, and oil was discovered near Ragusa by the Gulf Oil Company in 1953. The Italian state-controlled ENI (Ente Nazionale Idrocarburanti) then located more under the sea off Gela. The area around Ragusa is noted for the production of asphalt and oil products. Food processing, winemaking, salt extraction, and shipbuilding are also important industries. Potassium deposits are mined near Enna.

CUISINE. Sicilian cuisine is strong in fruits, vegetables, olives, and, of course, fish. Swordfish is a favorite around Messina. *Cuscusu*, a couscous and fish stew popular in the Trapani area, recalls the island's Arab heritage. *Beccaficu* is sardines either stuffed and baked or breaded and fried. *Tonno alla siciliana* is tuna with white wine, anchovies, and a collection of spices. Anchovies and sardines are added to many pasta dishes; and the "fruit of the sea" is also found in *spaghetti al nero di seppi*, pasta tinted black with cuttlefish ink. Many of Sicily's sweets are derived from the Muslim occupation. The ubiquitous *cassata*, ricotta cheese, pieces of chocolate, and citrus peelings on a sponge cake base, stems from the *qasat*, while the *qubbayta*, a type of sesame cookie popular in the west, comes from the old *qubbayt*.

Sicily produces about 291 million gallons of wine a year, second only to Apulia. Marsala is the island's premier wine and Trapani province is the capital of marsala country. It makes more wine than any other Italian province. First developed in the eighteenth century to serve an English market, marsala was manifested in myriad ways until a recent D.O.C. reform simplified the rules. It usually comes as *oro* (gold), *ambro* (amber), or *rubino* (ruby). Sicily has recently enjoyed great success in the development of *moscato* grape varieties, particularly a *moscato di pantelleria*. Other favorites come from the Duke of Salaparuta's vineyards, the Corvo bianco and the Bianca di Valguarnera.

SARDE AL FORNO

2 lbs. fresh sarde (sardines)	1½ Tbs. fresh parsley, chopped
¾ c. breadcrumbs	Salt and pepper to taste
½ c. grated Pecorino cheese	Olive oil
2 cloves garlic, minced	Red wine vinegar

Preheat the oven to 375°. Remove the heads and scales from the sardines and dry them well. Combine the breadcrumbs, cheese, garlic, parsley, salt, and pepper in a bowl. Oil a baking pan and place a layer of sardines on the bottom. Cover the sardines with a layer of the breadcrumb mixture and pour some oil and vinegar over the breadcrumb layer. Continue layering in this order until all ingredients have been used. Bake for 25–30 minutes.

HISTORY. Sicily's history is extraordinarily rich. Remains of Paleolithic peoples have been discovered in the grotto of San Teodoro near Messina, and important cave grafitti have come to light on Levanzo, an island in the Egadi chain, and in the Addaura grotto near Palermo. Sicily's central location in the Mediterranean guaranteed that it would suffer often under the heels of invaders, from ancient warriors to Allied armies in the Second World War. Among Sicily's Neolithic settlers were the Sicani and the Siculi (or Sicels), who lived on the island by at least the thirteenth century B.C. Greeks then moved there; the earliest settlements were established around 730 B.C. on the east coast, at Syracuse and near Taormina. They were followed by Carthaginians, mainly in the west, and the Romans, who took the island from them in the First Punic War (264–241 B.C.).

Rome's Sicilian campaign took from 253 until 241 B.C., and its great victory came on the sea when the forces of Consul Gaius Lutatius Catulus defeated Carthage's ships off Favignana in the Egadi Islands in 242. The Romans viewed Sicily as a source of income, and milked its economy and people as much as they could. Their often brutal administration of labor in the Sicilian latifundia led in 135 B.C. to one of the worst slave revolts in history.

As the Roman Empire declined, Sicily enjoyed something of a revival with a repopulation of the countryside. This trend was not checked by Vandal invaders, who had taken much of North Africa from the Romans, and who launched an invasion of Sicily in A.D. 440 under King Gaiseric. Rome put up a stiff defense in a series of long wars. Gaiseric finally lost the struggle—not to the Romans, however, but to Odoacre and the Ostrogoths—in 476.

The Byzantines secured Sicily by 535 and ruled it for 300 years. Their reign, however, was soon contested by the Muslims, who launched raids along the coast as early as 652. By the end of the seventh century they were building shipyards in North Africa in preparation for attacks on Sicily and the rest of Christendom. In 827 the Aghlabids, Muslims based in Tunisia, launched their invasion in earnest. They first captured Mazara del Vallo and, later, aided by the treachery of Euphemius, the Byzantine commander of Messina, went on to conquer the entire island. By 860 most of it had fallen, with only a few holdouts lasting into the 900s. Sicilians remained for the part Christians, but the island also had a significant Jewish population; and all were required to wear distinctive clothing to identify their religious affiliations. They were permitted to repair their houses of worship but not to build new ones. Christians could not ring church bells or bear the cross in processions. Palermo surfaced as a brilliant capital of Sicily, a prosperous crossroads of the Muslim Mediterranean.

Quarrels between Arab and Berber Muslims isolated Sicily from its Tunisian metropole by the eleventh century, and Christian Europe targeted the island for reconquest. After a brief Byzantine attempt to retake the island failed in the 1030s, the Norman d'Hauteville (Altavilla) dynasty came next. Normans had participated in the earlier Byzantine campaign but returned to Sicily alone in 1060 to conquer it for themselves. Roger I "the Norman" took the island and ruled it until his death in 1101, while his brother, Robert Guiscard, occupied Calabria. Sicily's Muslim population reacted in a handful of ill-fated rebellions, particularly from their strongholds in the central and southwestern parts of the island, that lasted into the thirteenth century. The Norman conquest was also a blow to Byzantine hopes, because Latin Christianity would now be favored over Greek. The Normans presented gifts of land to Cluniacs and Cistercians, and constructed the great Benedictine abbey at Monreale. The papacy reciprocated by elevating Sicily to a kingdom. Roger's young son, Roger II, came to the throne in about 1105 and joined Sicily to Norman Calabria and Apulia in 1130 to form an expanded kingdom of Sicily. Although he preferred to rule from the mainland, Roger II forged an administration and court at Palermo that blended traditions of the Latin West, Islam, and the Greek East.

Roger II died in 1154 and was succeeded by his son, William I, who ruled until 1166, and then his grandson, William II, who lasted until 1189. Without issue, William was succeeded by his Aunt Constance, the daughter of Roger II. Constance survived a challenge from William's illegitimate nephew, Tancred, and married the young Henry of Swabia, the son of Frederick Barbarossa. He was crowned Holy Roman Emperor in 1191 as Henry VI and claimed the throne of Sicily for himself and his son, Frederick II. After Henry died in 1197, and Constance followed the next year, Pope Innocent III ruled Sicily as regent until the young king took the throne in 1211. Frederick, puritanical and pious to a fault, interfered in such matters as gambling and marriage; but he maintained the brilliance of the Palermo court. Although he crushed the last Muslim rebels, he still employed Islamic courtiers and soldiers.

Frederick's death in 1250 began a long period of decay. The defeat of his son, Manfred, at Benevento in 1266 led to the subjugation of southern Italy, including Sicily, by the French Angevins. Charles I of Anjou preferred to rule from Naples and relegated Sicily to an appendage of the mainland. In 1282 Sicily exploded in the revolt of the Sicilian Vespers, which expelled the Angevins from the island. However, the Sicilians accepted the rule and protection of Manfred's son-in-law, Peter III of Aragon, who arrived at Trapani on August 30 and was crowned at Palermo on September 4. Peter's ascendancy introduced a Spanish dominion over Sicily that would last, in one form or another, for over 400 years.

The Sicilians first accepted Spanish rule without much disturbance while their land sank further and further into colonial humiliation. A crisis of succession in Barcelona, for example, led to the election of the Castilian Ferdinand I as King of Sicily in 1412 without any consultation from the islanders. From their chambers in Naples or Spain, the Kings of Sicily ruled through their viceroys. In 1487 the Spanish Inquisition came to Sicily, and in 1492 the Spanish expelled the Jews from the island. Agricultural taxes increased, and some of the island's privileges were revoked. Consequently, the sixteenth and the seventeenth centuries witnessed more discontent and revolts. Violence plagued Sicily in 1516, 1523, and, as part of the Neapolitan Masaniello uprising, 1647.

Spanish rule lasted until 1713, when the Treaty of Utrecht ordered the transfer of the island to the Piedmontese house of Savoy. Five years later, Spain forced Piedmont to accept Sardinia in compensation. In 1720 Sicily became a possession of the Austrian Hapsburgs, and in 1735 the Spanish Bourbon King Charles (Carlo di Borbone) took possession of Sicily when he drove the Austrians from southern Italy and ruled from Naples. The new dynasty displayed little interest in, and less affection for, Sicilian affairs until Naples was conquered by the French Revolutionary armies and the Bourbons were forced to transfer to Sicily. The flight of King Ferdinand to Palermo in 1798, aboard the flagship of the British Admiral Horatio Nelson, was his first visit to the island in 40 years. Britain twice protected the spendthrift Ferdinand and his profligate wife, Maria Carolina, from 1798 until their return to Naples a year later, and again from 1806 to 1815. The queen was more interested in money than she was in the Sicilians, whom she detested, and even offered to sell the island to the British.

The Bourbons' second sojourn on Sicily was marked by something close to a British occupation. This emboldened some reformers to draw up a constitution in 1812 but, although parliaments subsequently convened and feudalism was formally abolished, little else was accomplished except to set an important precedent. When Napoleon's empire collapsed in 1815, Ferdinand returned to Naples and promptly rescinded the reforms that he had agreed to while in Sicily amid the "cannibals." He tightened his grip on the island, reinstituted censorship, and proclaimed himself no longer Ferdinand III of Sicily and Ferdinand IV of Naples, but Ferdinand I, King of the Two Sicilies.

The 50 years after Napoleon's fall were distinguished by attempts to liberate Sicily from the Neapolitan Bourbons. The first came in the revolution of 1820. Then, in 1848, Europe's first revolution broke out on Sicily, in the streets of Palermo. On January 9 rebels demanded a return to the abrogated 1812 Constitution and issued a call to arms. Fighting started on January 12. The troops of King Ferdinand II (grandson of the earlier Ferdinand) retreated into the fortress of Castellamare and bombarded Palermo but could not contain the revolution, which spread across the entire island.

In the countryside, peasants stormed villas and burned tax records. When Syracuse fell in mid-February, only the citadel at Messina remained in Neapolitan hands. On April 18 a revolutionary government under Ruggero Settimo, a retired naval commander, declared the island a free nation.

Hoping to end Bourbon rule in Sicily, Settimo's government searched for a different Italian prince to accept the throne. Facing revolution at home, Ferdinand had little choice but to accept the situation. But in September he felt strong enough to launch a reconquest. Stiff resistance prompted the intervention of Britain and France to find a settlement, and an armistice was reached on October 8. Fighting erupted again in the spring, however, and the Neapolitans finally pacified the island in May 1849.

Eleven years later, in his drive to bring the South into the new Italian Kingdom, Giuseppe Garibaldi sealed the Bourbons' fate. On May 11, 1860, with about 1,000 armed and red-shirted followers, he landed at Marsala. Twenty-five battalions of Neapolitan troops, along with cavalry and artillery, faced them. But Garibaldi's personal aura was enough to convince the islanders that his cause was just—and most of them were probably glad to see the Bourbons go. They rose in revolt almost immediately. As in 1848, the Neapolitans fell back to Messina, but not without delivering a costly blow to Garibaldi at Milazzo. Nevertheless, the Bourbon troops could not halt the Red Shirts' advance that ended on July 27 with the conquest of Messina. Garibaldi proclaimed himself dictator and ruled for five months before he pressed on to Naples. While in Sicily, he allowed some land reform, but not too much, and ruthlessly cracked down on those, like some at Bronte, who took to the project with too much zeal.

Prime Minister Camillo Cavour let it be known from Turin that Sicily would not gain regional autonomy. Piedmontese bureaucrats soon arrived and complained about the lazy and apathetic natives. Local resentment promptly surfaced, and the first anniversary of annexation was marked by riots. Attempts to draft poor peasants led to the desertion of half of the recruits. Tax collectors were met by lynch mobs. Brigandage became endemic. In 1866 Palermo exploded in riots which were largely led by criminal elements; 40,000 troops were required to extinguish them. In 1893 and 1894 most of the island erupted again in mass uprisings against the Italians, the *fasci siciliani* (Sicilian groups). Rioters had no central coordination and were often led on the local level by socialists, gentry, or mafiosi. Prime Minister Francesco Crispi, a Sicilian, completely misread the *fasci* as a Franco-Russian plot, with Vatican connivance, to detach the island from Italy; he dispatched an army and the fleet to crush the rebellion.

Italy's conquest of Ethiopia (1935–1936) and the Spanish Civil War (1936–1939) focused Rome's attention on Sicily as the Fascists' key to the Mediterranean, and in 1937 Mussolini announced major developments for the island. But Italy's empty coffers and the beginning of the Second World

War canceled those plans. A 1940 investigation showed that half of Sicily's peasants still lived in one-room hovels along with their animals.

In 1943, after the Axis collapse in North Africa during the Second World War, the Allies targeted Sicily as the first step in their invasion of Fascist Italy. After a landing on Pantelleria Island, British, Commonwealth, and U.S. troops launched the invasion on July 9. Resistance was minimal, and the island capitulated within a few weeks. The effect of the conquest combined with events in Rome to trigger the downfall of Mussolini's regime by July 25.

After a brief and sometimes violent flirtation with separatism at the end of the war, Sicily became an autonomous region in 1948, and its voters made the island a Christian Democratic stronghold. Mafia activity, which had submerged under the Fascist dictatorship, resurfaced after the Allied liberation in 1943. It has plagued the island, particularly its western half and the Catania area, ever since. Consequently, rural expanses in western Sicily were most resistant to Rome's land reform measures launched with the Milazzo Law in 1950. In the late 1970s and early 1980s, a flurry of assassinations pointed to a new struggle between the Mafia and the Italian government that resulted in a massive government crackdown with the aid of the United States.

RECENT POLITICS. Sicily votes in two electoral districts (*circoscrizioni*), the twenty-fourth, which corresponds to the western half of the island, and the twenty-fifth, in the east. In the middle of the island, Caltanissetta is placed in the west and Enna is in the east. In the 1996 majoritarian elections for the Chamber of Deputies, the Center-Right Polo per le Libertà won 52.6 percent of the twenty-fourth district votes, and the Center-Left Ulivo took 41.6 percent. The twenty-fifth district's figures were similar: 53.1 percent for the Polo and 39.1 percent for the Ulivo. In the twenty-fourth district's proportional vote, Forza Italia emerged on top with 32.6 percent, followed by the Party of the Democratic Left (PDS) with 15.9 percent and the Alleanza Nazionale with 14.4 percent. The twenty-fifth district gave Forza Italia 31.9 percent, 18.3 percent to the Alleanza Nazionale and 17.3 percent to the PDS. The island votes as one unit for the Senate, and gave 42.4 percent to the Polo and 40.4 to the Ulivo. As an autonomous region, Sicily did not vote in the April 2000 regional elections.

PALERMO

PROVINCIAL PROFILE. Area: 1,937 sq. mi. Population: 1,244,642 (province), 687,855 (city). Palermo province contains 82 communes. Palermo's fertile coastal plain, the *Conca d'Oro* (Horn of Plenty), is girdled by a cresent of short mountains. Higher peaks, found inland, culminate in the Rocca Busambra (5,292 feet). Palermo is a long east-west province with the Tyrrhenian Sea as its northern border. To its east is Messina; to its south are, from east to west, Enna, Caltanissetta, and Agrigento; Trapani is to its west.

The eastern part of the province is distinguished by the Madonie Mountains, Sicily's highest after Etna. Its tallest peak is Pizzo Carbonara (6,492 feet). In 1989 the Madonie Park was created from 98,800 acres; it is the habitat of the royal eagle. One of Italy's longest rivers, the Southern Imera or Salso, begins in the Madonie and flows south through Caltanissetta province to Licata on the southern coast.

HISTORY. The Phoenicians established Palermo in the eighth century B.C. It grew as an important trade link between North Africa and the Etruscan lands of the Italian mainland. Except for a brief Greek occupation in 276 B.C., the city remained in Phoenician hands or in those of their Carthaginian descendants, until 254 B.C., when the Romans conquered it during the First Punic War. They accorded the city special trading privileges that tied it to Campania. The fortunes of the Roman Panormus, however, declined over time. Following Vandal and Goth occupation after the fall of the Roman Empire (A.D. 476), the city passed to the Byzantines after a stiff resistance. It remained in their hands from 535 until 831, when Muslims from Tunisia took Palermo. The new rulers favored the city, expanding it with a new Arab quarter, the Kalsa, and making it the capital of the Emirate of Sicily in 948. The Normans took Palermo in January 1072.

When the Angevins defeated the Swabians in the 1260s, Palermo lost its status as a capital city and the island came to be ruled from Naples. Resentment of French brutality and cavalier attitudes toward the island's traditions led to the Sicilian Vespers revolt in the city on Easter Monday of 1282. Traditionally thought to have been sparked by an offense directed by a French soldier against a Palermitan maiden, the rebellion spread across the island.

Palermo's role in the two revolts of 1647 was also important. The first occurred in March in a city gripped by famine. The discontented followed Nino La Pelosa (or La Pilosa), a miller and escaped convict, in an attack on the city's administration and elite. La Pelosa was captured, and under torture confessed his intention to take the crown of Sicily for himself. He was then ripped apart with red-hot pincers. La Pelosa's revolt spread across the island, although it was not coordinated and other cities took action for their own local reasons which had nothing to do with Palermo. The second revolt in August was inspired by Naples's Masaniello tumult. In Palermo, a goldsmith named Giuseppe D'Alesi and a force led by tanners took charge of the city. In his success, however, D'Alesi distanced himself from his followers and they assassinated him. The revolt fizzled shortly afterward.

During the Napoleonic Wars, King Ferdinand fled from Naples to Palermo and used it as his capital. His sojourn is remembered mainly as a burden on the city.

Palermo was one of Italy's most active cities during the Risorgimento. Motivated in large measure by a desire for autonomy from Naples, it revolted in 1820, and it was Italy's (and Europe's) first city to explode in the revolutions of 1848. Palermo rose in revolt again on April 4, 1860, a month before Garibaldi landed at Marsala. He reached Palermo on May 27, and the last Bourbon troops evacuated on June 7.

Second World War bombardments caused a great deal of destruction in Palermo's residential neighborhoods and particularly of many of its Baroque churches. It was one of the first major Italian cities liberated during the war when Allied forces entered it on July 24, 1943.

Palermo was the home of Prime Minister Vittorio Emanuele Orlando (1860–1952). A professor of law, he was elected to Parliament in 1897. Orlando assumed the prime minister's chair in 1917, after Italy's cataclysmic defeat at Caporetto during the First World War, and he subsequently led the nation to victory over the Austrians and Germans in 1918. He headed the Italian delegation to the Paris peace conference (1919–1920) and soon found himself at the center of one of the most heated arguments at the talks. He railed against U.S. President Woodrow Wilson's obstinate refusal to accede to Italy's possession of much of the Dalmatian coast, across the Adriatic from Italy. Orlando's failure to secure possession led to a wave of nationalist furor and the fall of his government in June 1919. After some early support for Mussolini's government, he quickly grew disillusioned and resigned from Parliament in 1925 to protest Fascist electoral violence in Palermo. In 1931 he left his teaching position at the University of Rome rather than swear a loyalty oath to the regime. Orlando returned to politics as a liberal in 1944.

Ugo La Malfa (1903–1979) was born in Palermo. A leading anti-Fascist, he was one of the founders of the Action Party during the Second World War. When the party dissolved in the late 1940s, La Malfa joined the Italian Republican Party, which he served as secretary from 1965 until his death.

ARTS AND CULTURE. The Muslims expanded and fortified Palermo's port and built a castle for the emir which Roger II transformed into the Palazzo dei Normanni. The Spanish later demolished most of the towers and put an imposing Renaissance facade on it. Inside is the magnificent Palatine Chapel. Perhaps the finest example of the art of Norman Sicily, it was built for Roger II between 1132 and 1140. The palace is still a functioning government center, and Sicily's Regional Assembly convenes in the palace's Sala di Ercole (Hercules Room). Another important Norman work is the Zisa Castle, begun by William I in the 1160s. It reveals strong Islamic influence and boasts a mosaic of hunting scenes; its restoration has elicited some controversy. The Zisa contains the small Museum of Arab Civilization.

Palermo's Assunta cathedral was begun in 1184 over an older basilica that the Arabs had transformed into a mosque. The church has endured many renovations and additions, including a Catalan portico, a dome, and a neoclassical interior. The last two were the work of the Florentine architect **Ferdinando Fuga** (1699–1781). The cathedral contains the remains of some of Sicily's most important historic figures. Both Emperor Frederick II and his parents, Henry VI and Constance, are buried there, as is his first wife, Constance of Aragon. They rest near the bodies of Roger II and Odo of Bayeux, brother of William the Conqueror. A silver sarcophagus holds the remains of Palermo's patron, Saint Rosalia. Rosalia was born at Viterbo in the thirteenth century. She was a Third Order Franciscan and, legend has it, served in the court of King William I. Rosalia became a hermit and died at eighteen years of age. She was largely unknown until she revealed herself and her secret resting place to a woman of Palermo in the seventeenth century. The Palermitani have celebrated Saint Rosalia since 1625 with the *fistinu*, an elaborate procession conducted twice each year, on the second Sunday in July and in September.

Other examples of Norman art, with its Byzantine and Arab influences, are found in Palermo's streets and piazzas. San Cataldo, San Giovanni degli Eremiti, and the Greek Orthodox Church of the Martorana (or Santa Maria dell'Ammiraglio), all built in the twelfth century, are some of the best.

A Sicilian literary culture flourished in Norman Palermo. Important figures in this renaissance were Muslims: **Abu Daw**, who composed a long elegy upon the death of Simon, son of Roger II, and the court geographer, **al-Idrisi** (1100–1165), whose *Libro di re Ruggero* (Book of King Roger) is one of the premier geographic studies of the Middle Ages. Other prominent writers included the Greek **Neilos Doxapatres** (active early twelfth century) and the Normans **Peter** (c. 1135–1212) and **William of Blois**. The glittering court of Frederick II continued this tradition in the thirteenth century. The emperor surrounded himself with about 30 poets, of whom a third were Sicilians. Some were southern Italians and others were Tuscans. They were familiar with, and were influenced by, Provencal styles, and some experimented with early versions of the sonnet.

Notable late Gothic and Renaissance structures include the fourteenth-century Palazzo Chiaramonte, and the fifteenth-century Palazzo Abatellis and **Matteo Carnelivari**'s (active late fifteenth century) Church of Santa Maria della Catena. The Abatellis Palace contains the Sicilian Regional Gallery (Galleria Regionale della Sicilia), which has a fine collection of Italian and Flemish Renaissance art. Baroque Palermo can be appreciated in the Church of the Gesù, the colossal Church of San Domenico, the Piazza Vigliena (also known as the Quattro Canti or Four Corners), and what many consider to be the city's masterpiece in the style, the Church of Santa Teresa, built by **Giacomo Amato**

(Palermo, 1643–1742) between 1686 and 1706. In 1897 Palermo opened the Teatro Massimo. Built by **Giovanni Battista Filippo Basile** (Palermo, 1825–1891) and his son, **Ernesto** (Palermo, 1857–1932), it is one of Europe's great opera houses and its second in size, after Paris's Garnier Palace. The Massimo closed in 1974 for restorations which continue, although performances have resumed. Palermo's other great theater, the Politeama of the Campanian **Giuseppe Damiani Almeyda** (Capua, 1834–1911), opened in 1874. The city also boasts the exceptional Regional Archaeological Museum (Museo Regionale Archeologico).

The early opera composer **Alessandro Scarlatti** (1660–1725) was born in Palermo. After study and work in Naples and Rome, and a short and disappointing time in Venice, Scarlatti returned to Naples in 1708 as *maestro di capella* (choirmaster) for the Austrian viceroy. His son, **Giuseppe Domenico** (Naples, 1685–1757), was also an accomplished composer.

Giuseppe Tomasi di Lampedusa (1896–1957) was born in Palermo. His posthumously published novel *Il Gattopardo* (The Leopard) concerned the decline of a Sicilian aristocratic family during the Risorgimento. After an enormous success in Italy and in translation abroad, Luchino Visconti turned it into an acclaimed film.

Another writer born in Palermo was **Natalia Levi Ginzburg** (1916–1991). She moved to Turin as a young girl when her father took a teaching position there. She was married to the Russian activist Leone Ginzburg from 1938 until his death at Nazi hands in 1944. Natalia Ginzburg discussed resistance and the end of the Fascist regime in such works as *Tutti i nostri ieri* (All Our Yesterdays, 1952) and wrote the semiautobiographical *Lessico familiare* (Intimate Dictionary, 1963).

OTHER CENTERS. In 1174 the Norman King William II ("the Good") ordered the construction of a Benedictine abbey and cathedral at **Monreale** in what today are the outskirts of Palermo. The abbot controlled enormous expanses and was, after the king, the greatest landholder in Sicily. He possessed mills, a sugar refinery, and a fishery with a small fleet. Built by a Pisan, Bonanno Pisano (active late twelfth century), and others with Arab, Byzantine, and Norman touches, the abbey is one of the most beautiful structures in Italy. The bodies of William II and his father, William I ("the Bad"), are entombed in the church.

Norman fortresses and churches dot the Palermitan countryside. One of the most imposing castles is at **Caccamo. Cefalù** is traditionally the most important city on the coast between Palermo and Messina, although Palermo's industrial suburb of **Termini Imerese** may now be larger. Both are very old cities. Termini Imerese was built by the Carthaginians to replace nearby Himera, scene of the Greek victory over Carthage in the fifth century B.C. Ruins of the ancient town can still be viewed in an extensive archaeological park. Cefalù contains the remains of a prehistoric sanctuary, known as the Temple of Diana, that dates from the ninth century B.C. The

Romans took Cefalù in 254, and they followed the typical pattern of foreign masters. The Normans captured it from the Muslims in 1063 and developed the town as a cultural and economic center. In modern times Cefalù's dramatic location, with the sea on one side and the sheer cliffs of the Madonie range on the other, have made it a tourist mecca. Cefalù has prospered, but tourism has put great strains on its infrastructure and environment.

The city's greatest monument is its cathedral, begun by Roger II in the twelfth century. It was to serve two purposes: to carve a new diocese from Messina and anchor it at Cefalù, and to provide a burial vault for Roger and the Altavilla dynasty. The first objective materialized, but the second did not. The cathedral, however, remains one of the finest in Sicily, with beautiful mosaics depicting Christ Pantocrator (Ruler of the World) and other figures. A lovely cloister is adjacent to the cathedral. Cefalù's Mandralisca Civic Museum contains Antonello Da Messina's (c. 1430–1479) marvelous *Portrait of an Unknown* (*Ritratto d'Ignoto*), a figure with a charming but enigmatic smile.

The realist painter and anti-Fascist Renato Guttuso (1912–1987) was born in **Bargheria**, a beach resort on the coast near Palermo. His vivid paintings and drawings often carried themes critical of Mussolini's regime, and he joined the Resistance during the war. After the war Guttuso was influential in left-wing art movements, and his work displayed a strong social realism.

Giuseppe Antonio Borgese (1882–1952), one of Italy's most important literary scholars and critics, was born in **Polizzi Generosa**. He taught at the universities of Rome and Milan, and wrote criticism in the newspapers *La Stampa* (The Press) of Turin and *Corriere della Sera* (Evening Post) of Milan. Greatly inspired by Gabriele D'Annunzio, he fled the Fascists to teach in the United States.

AGRIGENTO

PROVINCIAL PROFILE. Area: 1,174 sq. mi. Population: 474,034 (province), 55,814 (city). Agrigento province contains 43 communes. Agrigento is a long diagonal province that dips to the southeast. It occupies most of Sicily's southwest coast. To its northwest is Trapani, to its north is Palermo, and Caltanissetta wraps around much of its eastern end. The Mediterranean is to the south.

HISTORY. Agrigento's Greek settlers first called the town Akragas. Colonists from Gela, and perhaps Rhodes, founded it in 581 B.C. Akragas quickly became a major Greek Sicilian center, particularly after the fifth-century B.C. victory over the Carthaginians at Himera. It was also proclaimed in a remarkable period of construction, much of which remains, particularly in the Valley of the Temples. Carthage returned, however, and subjugated Akragas and much of western Sicily. It targeted Akragas as the key to its possessions and established a military base there. The grip of Carthage ended during the First Punic War, when Rome took the city in 261 B.C. Its sack of Akragas was brutal and 25,000 of its inhabitants were sold into slavery. The Carthaginians, in their counterattack seven years later, unleashed even more misery by torching the city and ripping down its walls.

By 210 Rome's dominion was permanently established, and the city came to be called Agrigentum. It prospered under the expanding Republic, but during the Empire, Agrigentum was reduced more and more to a backwater port. The decline was hastened by Vandal, Goth, and Byzantine conquests, abuses, and neglect. In 877 the Muslims took what was left of Agrigentum and renamed it Girgenti. Because of its proximity to Africa, the Muslims turned Agrigento into the second city of Sicily by developing its military and economic potential. After the Normans broke their hold on Sicily, Muslim rebels remained active in the area and held Agrigento for a time. They used its cathedral as a barracks and held the bishop a prisoner for a year. Norman and Swabian arms won the day, however, and Agrigento evolved into a feudal possession within their domains. The Chiaramonte and Montaperto families ruled Agrigento for much of the Middle Ages.

The Fascist provincial reorganization in 1927 led to a change of name from Girgenti to the more Roman-sounding Agrigento. After the Second World War the city embarked on a disastrous urban renewal program, gutting many of the old neighborhoods and replacing them with ugly concrete slabs. But the problem was not only aesthetic; the construction was marked by corruption and the slipshod planning that often results from it. On July 19, 1966, the land gave way and Agrigento suffered a terrible landslide which might have been far worse had not a sharp-eyed street sweeper alerted the neighbors in time. Pollution from Agrigento's industrial suburb Porto Empedocle has not facilitated the preservation of the city's art treasures.

ARTS AND CULTURE. Some of the most important legacies of the ancient Greek world are found in Agrigento, particularly in the Valley of the Temples, a collection of structures situated on two hills with views of the sea. The largest temple was dedicated to Jupiter (Giove Olimpico) and dates from 480 B.C., immediately after the defeat of the Carthaginians at Himera. Never finished, it was constructed in part by prisoners of war and is the largest Greek temple anywhere in the Mediterranean. But the Temple of Concord is considered the gem of the group. Also built in the fifth century, it is a masterpiece in the Doric style and is one of the best-preserved Greek temples in the world. In the sixth century A.D. Belisarius converted it into a Christian church. The Temples of Hercules and of Hera Lacinia (or Giunone) are also superb evidence of the Greek patrimony.

Between the temples and the city are the thirteenth-century Cistercian Church of San Nicola and the ancient Ekklesiasterion, an amphitheater used by the Greeks for public meetings, to which the Romans added a small temple, the Oratorio di Falaride. The monks at San Nicola later used the oratorio. Close to San Nicola is the Regional Archaeological Museum (Museo Archeologico Regionale), one of the best in Sicily, which contains a rich collection of items from the province as well as from Caltanissetta. The city's cathedral was built by Saint Gerlando, a Norman bishop who dedicated the building to the Assumption of the Virgin. Since 1305 it has honored San Gerlando himself. In the nineteenth century Agrigento adopted the Neapolitan Saint Alfonso Liguori as its patron.

The author and playwright **Luigi Pirandello** (1867–1936) was born at Grigenti d'Agrigento. By the 1920s his novels, poems, and plays had brought him worldwide fame. His *Six Characters in Search of an Author*, *Henry IV*, and *To Each His Own* remain some of the most important theatrical works of the twentieth century. Although he signed the "Manifesto of Fascist Intellectuals," Pirandello's support for the regime was always ambiguous, and his international stature allowed him to dissociate himself from it and work in relative freedom. In 1934 Pirandello won the Nobel Prize for literature. He is buried beneath a pine tree near his home, which is today a museum and national monument.

OTHER CENTERS. Palma di Montechiaro was founded in 1637 by the Prince of Lampedusa, the ancestor of the Palermitan writer Giuseppe Di Lampedusa. The town is said to have been the model for Donnafugata, the setting of Lampedusa's important novel, *Il Gattopardo* (The Leopard).

Near Agrigento, at the mouth of the Salso River, is **Licata**, founded by the Syracusans in 284 B.C., and the site of a Roman defeat of the Carthaginian fleet in 256. Today it is an important fishing port. Also in the province of Agrigento is **Lampedusa;** it and its smaller neighbors, **Linosa** and **Lampione,** constitute the Pelagian Islands.

Racalmuto was the birthplace of the writer Leonardo Sciascia (1921–1989). Beginning with his earliest work of poetry, *Favole della dittatura* (Tales of the Dictatorship, 1950); and his novels, Sciascia's works often dealt with social issues, focusing on Sicily and the Mafia. In 1975 Sciascia was elected to Palermo's city council as a Communist, but resigned two years later and joined the Radical Party.

Italy's late nineteenth-century prime minister, Francesco Crispi (1819–1901), was born at **Ribera.** During the Risorgimento he was one of Garibaldi's chief lieutenants in Sicily. In Parliament, Crispi developed into an archnationalist, anticlerical imperialist, and as prime minister (1887–1891, 1893–1896) he advocated the German alliance and colonial expansion. In 1896, however, an Italian force met defeat in Ethiopia and the disgraced Crispi left office.

CALTANISSETTA

PROVINCIAL PROFILE. Area: 813 sq. mi. Population: 284,508 (province), 62,881 (city). The province contains 22 communes. Caltanissetta lies on the slopes Monte San Giuliano in the upper Salso valley. The Southern Imera, one of Sicily's longest rivers, begins in the Madonie in Palermo province and flows south through Caltanissetta to the Mediterranean at Licata. Caltanissetta borders Agrigento province on the south and west, Palermo on the north, and Enna, Ragusa, and Catania on the east. It touches the Mediterranean on its south at Gela.

HISTORY. Little is known of Caltanissetta's origins, although it is believed that the Greeks lived there and called it Nissa, a name that the Muslims changed to Calat or Qal'at (Castle) Nissa. The Normans developed Caltanissetta. From 1406 until the abolition of feudalism in 1812, Caltanissetta was a possession of the Moncada family. It became a center of the sulfur industry and a market town for the region's agriculture. In 1943 the city suffered heavy war damage.

ARTS AND CULTURE. Not much is left of the Castello di Pietrarossa, which dominated Norman Caltanissetta. Nearby is the twelfth-century abbey of Santo Spirito, which contains fourteenth-century frescoes. The city's cathedral is dedicated to its patron, Saint Michael the Archangel. Work began on the structure in the late 1500s; its facade was completed in the 1840s.

OTHER CENTERS. On the coastal plain, **Gela** remains important as a tourist destination despite the many petrochemical plants that mar its once beautiful coastline. It also possesses a long history as one of the most important of Sicily's Greek cities. Colonists from Rhodes and Crete founded Gela in 689 B.C., and its realm soon expanded across the southern coast at least to Syracuse. It was destroyed by the Carthaginians in 405 B.C. The city was rebuilt but was destroyed again in 282 B.C. after a devastating sack by Mamertine mercenaries. The people abandoned the city and relocated in Licata down the coast. Over 1,500 years passed before Emperor Frederick II founded a new town, Terranova, on the old site in A.D. 1230. In the Fascists' 1927 provincial reorganization, Terranova's name was changed back to Gela.

CATANIA

PROVINCIAL PROFILE. Area: 1,372 sq. mi. Population: 1,097,859 (province), 341,455 (city). The province of Catania is a long, thin entity that meets the Ionian Sea on its northeast and wedges into the interior to the southwest. Messina province sits on its north, Enna and Caltanissetta on its west, Ragusa on its south, and Syracuse on its southeast. The province's most prominent geographical feature is the active volcano Mount Etna. Etna has been protected since 1991, when the region of Sicily established a nature park there. Its top (10,902 feet) is often obscured in smoke and steam, and it has erupted frequently in modern times. The city of Catania has endured these eruptions; one in 1669 was particularly hard on the city, and many of its outlying neighborhoods are distinguished, and partly covered, by enormous mounds of hardened black lava. Most of the city, in fact, is built on top of hardened lava.

HISTORY. Sicily's second city, Catania was settled as a port in 729 B.C. by Greeks from Chalcis on the island of Euboea, who named it Katane. It was conquered by the Syracusans in the fifth century and renamed Aetna, or Aitna. The Romans took it in 263 B.C. and called it Catana or Catina. It was known as one of Sicily's more Roman cities, and by the time of Caesar Augustus most of the population was Roman. After a short period of Gothic rule, the Byzantines took the city in A.D. 535, and they favored Catania with the establishment there of a mint. Though the Muslim occupation came later to Catania than to most Sicilian towns, their rule was secure around 900. Roger I the Norman reestablished Christian rule when he entered the city in 1071. After the Normans, the Catanesi made a wrong choice by supporting Tancred rather than his victorious rival, Henry VI. Henry toyed with the idea of punishing the city but decided against it. Guelph sentiment in the area also tempted Frederick II to discipline the city, but he, too resisted. He nevertheless made a point to Catania when he built Ursino Castle there.

Later, the Aragonese kings annexed Catania, and established Sicily's first university there in 1434. By the late nineteenth century, Catania had benefited from a reputation for industriousness and openness to business interests, and had passed Palermo as Sicily's first port. The lessons of the popular *fasci siciliani* rebellions against Rome at the end of the nineteenth century fostered socialism among the middle class, and their leader, Mayor Giuseppe De Felice Giuffrida (1859–1920), was a popular and energizing, if largely unsuccessful, reformer in the city.

ARTS AND CULTURE. Etna's 1669 eruption and the catastrophic earthquake of 1693, which devastated much of eastern Sicily, ensured that little remained of premodern Catania. Nevertheless, the renovated Castello Ursino that Emperor Frederick II built between 1239 and 1250 still stands; today it houses the Civic Museum. Parts of the medieval cathedral, dedicated to Catania's patron, Saint Agatha, have survived, with a Baroque facade added after the earthquake. Three original apses of dark lava stone remain in the church, which was begun by Roger I the Norman in 1091. Many architects worked in Catania after the seventeenth-century catastrophes, and the city is dotted with important Baroque structures that they built. Foremost among the architects was the Palermitano **Giovan Battista**

Vaccarini (1702–1768), famous for Saint Agatha's facade and, in the adjacent piazza, the Fontana dell'Elefante (Elephant Fountain), long a symbol of the city. Later, **Antonio Amato** (Messina, active 1697–1717) helped rebuild the city, as did **Stefano Ittar** (active c. 1700), who worked on the gigantic eighteenth-century Church of San Nicolo. Its adjacent Benedictine monastery, the work of Vaccarini, was absorbed into the University of Catania in 1977.

The composer **Vincenzo Bellini** (1801–1835) was born in Catania, and his home has been converted into the Museo Belliniano. A master of the bel canto style of opera, he moved to Milan, where he premiered many works, particularly the popular *Norma* (1831) and *La Sonnambula* (The Sleepwalker, 1831), before his premature death in Paris at the debut of his *I Puritani* (The Puritans, 1835). He is buried in the Catania cathedral.

Catania is particularly devoted to its patron saint, Agatha, a beautiful young woman who lived there in the third century and fought the lecherous advances of the Roman proconsul, Quintianus. The frustrated and angry man ordered the amputation of Agatha's breasts, and she died shortly afterward in prison. According to tradition, Catania suffered an earthquake at the moment of the martyr's death, and she has come to be considered the city's protector against Etna's eruptions and seismic calamities. Agatha is also recognized as a vindicator of offenses. A warning of her influence was posted at the doorway of Catania's pre-earthquake medieval cathedral, and evidently caused Frederick II to change his mind about slaughtering the rebellious Catanesi in 1232–1233.

Catania was a center of the *verismo* (realism) movement in Italian literature at the turn of the twentieth century. **Giovanni Verga** (1840–1922) was a native of Catania, and **Luigi Capuana** (1839–1915) was born in nearby Mineo. Verga intended to portray peasant life in the countryside around Catania in a cycle of five novels called *I Vinti* (The Vanquished), but he finished only the first two, *I Malavoglia* (The Unwilling; published in English as *The House by the Medlar Tree*, 1881) and *Mastro Don Gesualdo* (1889). His *Cavalleria Rusticana* (Rustic Chivalry, 1884) was adapted for the opera by Pietro Mascagni. Capuana dedicated his first novel, *Giacinta* (1879), to the French naturalist Emile Zola. His later works are more concerned with character development than social criticism.

OTHER CENTERS. Beyond Catania, the province has developed an important tourist industry in the towns along the coast. **Acireale**, north of Catania, and other towns in the area, such as **Acitrezza** and **Aci Castello**, were named for Acis, mythical lover of the beautiful sea nymph Galatea. The jealous monster Polyphemus crushed Acis under a boulder and the distraught Galatea reconstructed her lover as the Aci River. Acireale's Piazza del Duomo is one of Sicily's finest showcases of Baroque architecture. Its cathedral, dedicated to the Annunciation and Saint Venera, was completed in 1618 and renovated in the eighteenth century. The Church of

Saints Peter and Paul and the city hall (Palazzo Comunale) are also clustered on the square. Nearby, in the Piazza Vigo, is one of Sicily's finest Baroque churches, San Sebastiano

Inland is Catania's second city, **Caltagirone**. The Muslims used it as a fort, and the Normans developed its regional commercial potential. Most of the old city was destroyed in the earthquake of 1693 and was rebuilt in the Baroque style. The cathedral of Caltagirone is remarkable in that its dilapidated facade was torn down in the nineteenth century and replaced with one in the "Liberty" style then in vogue. Caltagirone is famous for its ceramic products and boasts a museum dedicated to the art, the Museo della Ceramica, which is second, perhaps, only to that in Faenza.

Caltagirone was the birthplace of Don Luigi Sturzo (1871–1959), the founder, in 1919, of the Catholic Popolare Party. Educated in Sicilian seminaries and at the Gregorian University in Rome, Sturzo was an active reformer in Southern causes, peasant cooperatives. Between 1905 and 1920, he was the mayor of Caltagirone. After the First World War, Sturzo marshaled Catholic voters, and his Popolari were a key element in Italian politics before the rise of Mussolini. Sturzo opposed Fascism almost from the beginning, and was ordered by the Holy See to disband his organization in 1923. In 1924 he left Italy for London and, later, Jacksonville, Florida, and New York. In 1946 he returned to Italy and assumed an elder statesman role in the Catholic movement.

Caltagirone was also the birthplace of a significant Catholic politician of the postwar era, Mario Scelba (1901–1991). Scelba served as the Christian Democratic interior minister from 1947 until 1953, and prime minister in 1954 and 1955. He was known for his anti-Communist zeal and his commitment to traditional values in the struggles to define postwar Italy. Scelba later became president of the European Parliament from 1969 to 1971.

At the western side of the province is **Adrano**, a town founded around 400 B.C. by the Syracusan Greeks as Adranon. It was important to the Romans and then to the Normans. A twelfth century castle of Roger II and a church dedicated to the Assumption of the Virgin recall the Norman era. The church was enlarged in the seventeenth century and restored in the nineteenth. A beautiful Saracen-Gothic bridge connects Adrano with Centuripe in Enna province.

ENNA

PROVINCIAL PROFILE. Area: 989 sq. mi. Population: 183,642 (province), 28,427 (city). Enna province contains 20 communes. Enna is the region's only landlocked province and has been described as the center of the island, the *umbilicus Siciliae*. Messina province sits to its north, Catania to its east, Caltanissetta to its southwest, and Palermo to its northwest.

HISTORY. Originally Henna, Enna sits in the Erei Mountains at the island's center, with a command of the Dittaino valley. A natural fortress, Enna has a history that extends back beyond the Greeks to the ancient Sicani and Siculi tribes. It was a center of the worship of Demeter and Kore (Persephone). In myth, the Lake of Pergusa, outside of town, was the spot where Hades (Pluto) abducted Persephone into the underworld.

In the seventh century B.C. it was absorbed into the Greek world, and in 397 it was conquered by the Syracusans. After a short period of Carthaginian rule, in 259 or 258 the city passed to the Romans, who dubbed it Castrum Hennae. It was the center of Sicily's great slave revolt in the 130s, and briefly became the capital of a freemen's state. The Byzantines occupied Enna and used it as a fortress until 859, when it was conquered by the Muslims, who held it until 1087. They corrupted the old Roman name into Kasr-Yanni (or Oasr-Yani) which, in turn, was twisted into Enna's medieval name, Castrogiovanni.

In the modern era, Enna usually held second place after Piazza Armerina as chief city of the area, and the entire zone was part of Caltanissetta province. In 1927, the Fascists merged Piazza Armerina into a new province with its capital at Castrogiovanni, to which they restored the ancient name of Enna. Napoleone Colajanni (1847–1921), a republican and reformer for Southern causes in the Italian Parliament, was born in Enna.

ARTS AND CULTURE. Enna's strategic importance is recalled at the city's eastern edge in the well-preserved Lombard castle, a rambling pile begun after the Norman conquest. The octagonal tower of Frederick II is another outstanding medieval structure. Both were renovated by Frederick III of Aragon in the fourteenth century. The castle now hosts a number of civic events. Its Torre Pisana, the city's highest point, affords views of the entire island. The Jesuit missionary **Girolamo De Angelis** left his native Enna to die as a martyr in Japan in 1624. Enna's patron, Mary of the Visitation, is honored on July 2. An automobile Mediterranean Grand Prix is held each year at the Lake of Pergusa.

OTHER CENTERS. Southeast of Enna is **Piazza Armerina**, a resort town and one of Sicily's main archaeological attractions. Of chief interest is the Villa del Casale. Thought to have been the manor house of a Roman official in Sicily's late imperial revival, it was covered by a landslide in the twelfth century. The villa was rediscovered in the twentieth century, and excavation work continues. Of particular interest are extensive mosaics, many depicting hunting and mythological scenes.

MESSINA

PROVINCIAL PROFILE. Area: 1,253 sq. mi. Population: 681,843 (province), 262,224 (city). The province contains 108 communes. Messina occupies the northeast corner of Sicily. It shares its western border with Palermo and its southern with Enna and Catania. Messina's northern coast is washed by the Tyrrhenian Sea. Its eastern shore faces the Ionian Sea. Inland, Messina is dominated by two mountain ranges, the Nebrodi (or Caronie) in the west and the Peloritani in the east. The highest point in the Nebrodi is Monte Soro (6,060 feet) and the tallest of the Peloritani is Montagna Grande (4,419 feet). The Nebrodi Nature Park was established in 1993 and extends from Messina province into Catania and Enna. With about 212,400 acres, it is one of Europe's largest.

HISTORY. Messina sits at a strategic spot that commands the Strait of Messina between Sicily and Calabria. Greeks myths are recalled by the rock at the mainland side of the top of the strait, where violent currents gave rise to the story of the six-headed monster Scylla. Across the water, on the Sicilian side was the evil whirlpool Charybdis. To avoid one was to be captured by the other, and even the sea god Poseidon could offer no help. Mortal Greeks from Chalcis took Messina from the Siculi in 730 B.C. and named it Zankle (sickle), for the shape of its harbor. In the fifth century B.C. the town fell to Anaxilas, the tyrant of Reghium (Reggio Calabria). He changed the name to Messene, after his Peloponnesian homeland, Messenia. The Carthaginians sacked the town in 396 B.C., and it was rebuilt by the Syracusans. It became a Roman port in 264 B.C. and changed its name to Messana. The Byzantines annexed Messina in A.D. 535, and in 843 it fell to the Muslims who were aided by Neapolitan merchants eager for trading concessions. West of the Peloritani ridge, the Muslims subjugated Rometta. A small town, in 965 it was the last Sicilian town to fall.

Robert Guiscard liberated Messina from the Muslims in 1061, and it prospered. Messina changed hands many times in the next centuries, from Richard the Lion-Hearted, who briefly occupied it in 1190, to the Swabians, to the Angevins, to the Aragonese, and to the Spanish Bourbons. Against the Spanish, Messina rose in a short-lived and unsuccessful revolt in 1674. An earthquake almost destroyed the city in 1783. In 1860 Garibaldi completed his march across Sicily at Messina and incorporated the area into the Kingdom of Italy. In 1908 the city was again nearly leveled by a terrific earthquake, a catastrophe recalled by the extensive construction of low, reinforced concrete buildings and wide streets. In 1943 Allied bombs took their turn in damaging Messina.

ARTS AND CULTURE. Messina's church of the Santissima Annunziata dei Catalani dates from the twelfth and thirteenth centuries. In front of the church is a monument to the victory at Lepanto, where the ships of Christian Europe defeated the Turkish fleet in 1571. The combined flotilla assembled at Messina under its Hapsburg admiral, Don Juan, before it left to engage the Turks. Messina's monument to the event dates from 1572 and was the work of **Andrea Calamecca**. The city's medieval Duomo was frequently added to and renovated. Some work on it was accomplished by

Filippo Juvara (1678–1736), a native of Messina better known for his work in Piedmont. Messina's Regional Museum is one of the best in Sicily. Along with a large collection of Gothic works, it contains a room dedicated to the art of **Antonello Da Messina** (c. 1430–1479). It also has two works that **Caravaggio** (1573–1610) executed while living in Messina.

OTHER CENTERS. Along the northern coast from Messina is **Milazzo**, the second city of the province, a busy tourist center and the common embarkation point for the Lipari (Aeolian) Islands. Although founded by the Greeks as Mylae in the eighth century B.C., Milazzo's site has been inhabited since the fourth millennium. The Greeks built a fortress there, on a promontory that juts into the sea, and since then the city has been fortified most of the time. Its walls are still in good condition. Over Milazzo looms the Castello Normanno that Frederick II built in the thirteenth century and the Spanish later modified. Farther west, on the Gulf of Patti, are the ruins of **Tindari**, founded by the Syracusans as Tyndaris in 396 B.C. It flourished as a Greek and then a Roman city before the Muslims destroyed it; fortunately, impressive ruins are preserved in an archaeological zone. Many objects from Tyndaris have been transferred to the Excavations Museum (Museo degli Scavi). Classical dramas are performed on the stage of the Greek theater there.

The **Aeolian Islands** were settled in prehistoric times, at least by the fifth millennium B.C. In more recent times the islands were depopulated between the ninth and fifth centuries B.C., when the Greeks settled them. The Romans took them in 252 B.C., and Muslim raids caused their depopulation again in the seventh and eighth centuries A.D. The Normans devoted more energies to the development of the islands. A castle was built there that Mussolini used to house political prisoners. An important archaeological museum, the Museo Archeologico Eoliano, is on **Lipari**.

South of Messina, toward Etna, is **Taormina**, one of the world's premier resorts. Perched high on Mount Tauro, it was founded by Siculans in the fourth century B.C., they ruled it until Greeks from Gardini-Naxos took it in 358. The Romans joined it to their territories in 215. Taormina may have been the site of Christianity's first foothold in Sicily, for tradition says that Saints Berillo and Pancrazio (Pancras) established a church there in A.D. 39. When Syracuse fell to the Muslims in 878, Taormina became Byzantine Sicily's last capital and stronghold. When it finally fell in 902, the victors torched the city and slaughtered its people.

In the nineteenth century, Taormina became one of Europe's most exclusive resorts. Tourists, such as the German poet Johann Wolfgang von Goethe (1749–1832), had been visiting the city since at least the eighteenth century, but the Prussian aristocracy "discovered" Taormina in 1868, and it was soon frequented by the German kaisers. The town was linked to the Syracuse-Messina railroad line in 1870, and a hotel was built in 1874. In 1875 throngs of nobles from Palermo came to Taormina to escape a cholera epidemic. Winston Churchill liked to paint there. By the 1960s the local government adopted a conservative zoning policy and saved Taormina from some of the glut that plagues other tourist centers. Its center has maintained an interesting medieval quality and some ancient ruins survive, particularly a theater and a Roman cistern, the *naumachie*.

Outside Taormina on the coast, the older town of **Giardini-Naxos** is also a resort. It was first settled in the eighth century B.C. by Greek colonists from Naxos. When Dionysius the Elder of Syracuse destroyed the town in 403, its citizens fled, eventually settling at Taormina about 50 years later. Segments of the city's Greek walls and a temple of Aphrodite survive.

RAGUSA

PROVINCIAL PROFILE. Area: 623 sq. mi. Population: 300,761 (province), 69,389 (city). The province contains 12 communes. Ragusa province borders Caltanissetta on the northwest, Catania on the north, Syracuse on the east, and the Mediterranean Sea on the south.

HISTORY. Ragusa sits on the Iblei Hills above the Irminio River. It began as the Greek settlement of Hybla Heraea and became a Byzantine fortress in the sixth century A.D. It was was conquered by the Muslims in 848. Ragusa is divided into upper and lower towns; the difference was accentuated after an earthquake in 1693 destroyed the higher part, which was rebuilt largely in the eighteenth century, whereas the lower town, not as badly affected, preserved its medieval and Baroque qualities. The upper town came to be known as Ragusa and the lower as Ibla or Ragusa Ibla. The two were reunited by the Fascists in 1926 as the provincial capital.

ARTS AND CULTURE. According to tradition, St. George, the patron of Ragusa Ibla, rode next to Roger the Norman in his wars against the Muslims. The remains of a destroyed fifteenth-century cathedral named in his honor have been preserved in the lower town; a new structure was completed in 1755. John the Baptist, the patron saint of the upper town, is honored by an eighteenth-century Baroque cathedral.

OTHER CENTERS. One of Italy's greatest twentieth-century poets, Salvatore Quasimodo (1901–1968) was born in **Modica**. His collections, particularly *Acque e terre* (Waters and Lands, 1930) and *Oboe sommerso* (Sunken Oboe, 1932), brought him the 1959 Nobel Prize for literature. Modica has a long history dating back to the Bronze Age and boasts a necropolis from both Siculan and Christian times. A flood in 1902 damaged much of the city. A twelfth-century Byzantine church has been excavated in the old city and is open to the public. Modica's Church of Santa Maria di Betlem contains the impressive Chapel of the Sacrament, and the Church of San Giorgio is considered a masterpiece of the Sicilian Baroque.

On Ragusa's coastline is **Pozzallo**, the birthplace of Giorgio La Pira, the Christian Democratic mayor of Florence in the 1950s who earned fame for his application of Catholic thought to modern politics. He died in 1977 and has been beatified.

The roots of **Comiso**, located on the banks of the Ippari River, reach back to Rome. A prehistoric obsidian mine is nearby on Monte Tabuto. The Castello dei Naselli di Aragona, with its octagonal tower, was first built by the Byzantines. In 1983 and 1984 the town became an object of controversy when Pershing missiles were installed at Signonella, a U.S. naval air station outside of Comiso. A human chain linked Sigonella to Catania in protest, and Italy's Socialist President Sandro Pertini declared his solidarity with the protesters. His fellow Socialist, Prime Minister Bettino Craxi, however, ordered Italian compliance with America's intention to put the missiles at Sigonella.

SYRACUSE (SIRACUSA)

PROVINCIAL PROFILE. Area: 814 sq. mi. Population: 405,510 (province), 127,224 (city). The province of Syracuse contains 21 communes. It is bordered on the north by Catania, on the west by Ragusa, on the south by the Mediterranean, and on the east by the Ionian Sea. The east coast is divided by the city of Syracuse and the Maddalena peninsula. To the north is the Gulf of Augusta, and to the south is the Gulf of Noto.

HISTORY. Syracuse boasts one of the most glorious histories of the ancient Mediterranean. Greeks from Corinth established the city in the eighth century B.C. The first settlement was on Ortygia (Ortigia), an island in the harbor that a land bridge later connected to the mainland. Its early dominion over the immediate hinterland ended when rivals from Gela conquered the town in the fifth century B.C. Ultimately, the capital was transferred to Syracuse, and its defeat of the Carthaginians at Himera in 480 B.C. confirmed its status as the premier Greek city on Sicily. During the Peloponnesian War (431–404 B.C.), the Athenians attempted, but failed, to take Syracuse in a long siege (415–413), a campaign chronicled in the classic tale by the ancient historian Thucydides. Despite more encroachments by Carthage, the Syracusans constructed a small empire that extended onto mainland Italy by the 300s and 200s. Under the tyrant Dionysius the Elder, its fleet was the greatest of the time. However, Syracuse's subsequent alliance with Carthage during the Second Punic War (218–201 B.C.) resulted in Rome's conquest of the city in 212. Syracuse succumbed after the Romans used battering rams to pierce the city's defenses.

The Byzantines under General Belisarius launched their invasion of Sicily in A.D. 535, and designated Syracuse, which was still very much a Greek city, capital of the island.

After an aborted siege in 827, the Muslims finally took Syracuse in 878. They razed the city and slaughtered most of their prisoners. The archbishop survived by guiding the invaders to the fabulous cathedral treasure, which may have yielded the greatest amount of loot of any Muslim conquest to that date. The conquerors revived the city and allowed it to prosper. The Byzantines returned briefly in the eleventh century, and then the Normans in 1085. The Genoese held Syracuse for 15 years before the Swabians took it in 1221. Syracuse's history mirrored most of the rest of the island's from that date. During the Second World War the British Third Army launched its invasion of Italy from Syracuse in 1943.

ARTS AND CULTURE. At the northern end of the old city, Syracuse's sixth-century B.C. temple to Apollo is one of the oldest in Sicily. After their victory over Carthage at Himera, the Syracusans built another temple, to the goddess Athena. Its ancient columns still support a place of worship, the city's cathedral. In the 500s Belisarius ordered that the temple be used as a Christian church. Its ancient Doric pillars consequently merge into a later Baroque structure, particularly in the building's interior. Across the piazza from the cathedral is a pool of water that holds papyrus stalks. The nearby Cyane River is said to be the only place in Italy where such plants grow naturally.

Outside the old city is a large archaeological zone (*della Neapolis*). The old city (and much of the rest of Syracuse) retains a great deal of charm and has been spared many of the savage consequences inflicted by industrialization. It stands in contrast with the industrial port of Augusta north of city. Outside of Augusta are the important ruins of Megara Hyblaea, one of the earliest Greek settlements on Sicily.

The anti-Fascist writer **Elio Vittorini** (1908–1966) was born in Syracuse. He joined the Communist underground in 1941, the same year that *Conversation in Sicily*, his most famous work, was issued. In 1945 Vittorini founded and edited the respected left-wing cultural and political review *Il Politecnico* (The Polytechnic). By 1947, a disillusioned Vittorini resigned from the Communist Party after a public argument with its leader, Palmiro Togliatti. From 1959 until his death Vittorini edited the review *Il Menabò* (The Layout) with Italo Calvino.

OTHER CENTERS. Southwest of Syracuse city is **Noto**. The town was settled at the end of the seventeenth century when an earlier place at a different location, referred to as Noto Antica, was obliterated in the earthquake of 1693. Consequently, much of Noto was built in the Baroque style. Its impressive cathedral dominates the main square; however, its ceiling collapsed in 1996 and the building cannot be entered. **Palazzolo Acreide**, was also destroyed in 1693, was rebuilt largely on the old spot. It developed from the ancient Syracusan colony of Akrai, which is recalled in an impressive archaeological park nearby. Of particular note in the park is the collection of *santoni*, twelve rock carvings related to the cult of the goddess Cybele.

TRAPANI

PROVINCIAL PROFILE. Area: 950 sq. mi. Population: 435,268 (province), 69,664 (city). The province contains 24 communes. Trapani forms Sicily's northwestern bulge. It includes the Egadi Islands off its west coast, and its north coast is distinguished by Cape San Vito, much of which is set aside as the Zingaro National Reserve. The province of Trapani occupies Sicily's western point. To its north is the Tyrrhenian Sea and to its south is the Mediterranean. On its eastern side, Trapani faces Palermo and Agrigento.

HISTORY. The province of Trapani extends over what was in ancient times a contested area between Carthaginians, Greeks, and ultimately the Romans. In the north, Trapani city is a busy port that began as the Sicani and Elymi settlement of Drepana (later, Drepanon). By the eighth century B.C. it was a prosperous Phoenician trading town and naval base. The Carthaginians captured it in 260 B.C., and the Romans annexed it about 20 years later. It was a prosperous provincial *civitas romana* a city with broad freedoms until the Vandals sacked it in A.D. 440, followed by the Byzantines in 477 and Muslims about 830. The Muslims, and later the Normans, reestablished Trapani as a commercial center. Emperor Charles V granted it a number of privileges and strengthened the city walls in the sixteenth century. In 1817 Trapani became the seat of the province. It was severely bombed in the Second World War, and much of it has been rebuilt. A large part of the city is occupied by cultivated salt fields (*saline*).

ARTS AND CULTURE. The Madonna of the Annunciation is Trapani's patron, and a fourteenth-century sanctuary devoted to her constitutes the city's outstanding architectural treasure. It was largely reconstructed in the eighteenth century by **Giovanni Biagio Amico** (1684–1754), a local artist. The inner sanctuary houses a marble *Madonna and Child* by the Pisan **Ninno Pisano** (active 1349–1368), as well as works by **Antonino Gagini** (Bissone, 1425–1492) and his son **Giacomo** (Palermo, 1478–1536). Next to the sanctuary, in a former Carmelite monastery, is the Pepoli Regional Museum, a wide-ranging collection started in the eighteenth century by **Count Agostino Pepoli.**

OTHER CENTERS. The artistic patrimony of Trapani province is immense. Significant remains of ancient cultures are located throughout the province. East of Trapani is **Segesta**, with a lonely and evocative fifth-century B.C. Doric temple isolated at the foot of Monte Barbaro. Tucked on a slope of Barbaro is an ancient theater where plays are still performed.

In the south are the ruins of **Selinunte,** founded in the seventh century B.C. at the mouth of the Modione River by colonists from Rhodes. A mortal enemy of Segesta, during the Peloponnesian War, Selinunte joined with Syracuse against Segesta and its ally, Carthage. After an attack on Segesta, Carthage retaliated and destroyed Selinunte in 409 B.C. Some of the city's remains today contain Carthaginian elements. The historic site is distinguished by eight temples that were largely destroyed by earthquakes in the early Middle Ages. Some of the structures were reassembled in the twentieth century.

Some claim that Italy's largest fishing fleet anchors at **Mazara del Vallo.** The Muslims began their conquest of Sicily there in 827. The city's medieval church, San Nicolo Regale, was built in the Arab-Norman style in the twelfth century.

In the hills northeast of Trapani is **Erice,** a prehistoric settlement of the Elymi peoples who worshiped a now forgotten fertility goddess and built a temple to her atop a spectacular acropolis. The town's "chiesa Matrice," dedicated to the Assumption of the Virgin, was built in the fourteenth century by Frederick II of Aragon. The church's ceiling collapsed in the nineteenth century and was reconstructed according to an extraordinary neo-Gothic design.

Phoenicians first settled the area around **Marsala** in the eighth century B.C. at Mozia (or Motya), a location in the Stagnone lagoon. By the fifth century B.C. it was a Carthaginian town, and it submitted to a terrible sack by the Syracusans in 397. The Carthaginians rebuilt it in a slightly different location and called it Lilybaeum. The Romans took the city in 241 and developed it into an important naval base. The Muslims acquired Lilybaeum in 830 A.D. and redubbed it Marsa Ali (or Mars-el-Allah), a name that evolved into Marsala. Some Roman structures have been unearthed, but much of today's Marsala is Baroque. The Duomo, dedicated to St. Thomas of Canterbury, was built by the Normans and reconstructed in the eighteenth century. Marsala houses an important archaeological museum which contains the remains of a Carthaginian ship discovered in 1969. A tapestry museum, Museo degli Arazzi is in Marsala. It contains an impressive collection of Flemish tapestries that King Philip II of Spain gave to the Archbishop of Marsala in the sixteenth century. Outside of Marsala, in the Stagnone lagoon, the island of San Pantaleo contains the excavations of Mozia. Its protected wetlands and famous for their harvest of sea salt. Salt farming is a major industry along the coast between Trapani and Marsala. A salt museum is at **Nubia.**

Castelvetrano, near Trapani, was the birthplace of Giovanni Gentile (1875–1944), one of Italy's most prominent philosophers. A professor at Palermo, Pisa, and Rome, he collaborated with Benedetto Croce in the neo-idealist movement. The two parted over the issue of Fascism, and Gentile engineered the "Manifesto of Fascist Intellectuals" in support of Mussolini's regime. Gentile, who embraced the Duce's state and received honors as its major serious philosopher, was the ghostwriter of most of "Mussolini's" article "Fascism" in the *Italian Encyclopedia* (1932). He remained loyal to Mussolini and followed him north after the creation of the puppet Salò Republic in 1943. In 1944 he was assassinated in Florence by anti-Fascist partisans.

The boat (*traghetto*) from Trapani takes about an hour to reach the **Egadi Islands**. These have become popular vacation destinations, particularly for scuba and snorkeling aficionados. The largest island, **Favignana**, is famous for its communal tuna haul, the *mattanza*, a tradition whose days seem to be numbered. Favignana is one of the few places that has kept it alive at the turn of the twenty-first century. It is a rather grisly show, not for the faint-hearted, in which a large net connects a group of boats and snares the tuna between them. As the nets are pulled up, the fish surface and the fishermen bash them with clubs, hooks, and whatever else they have on hand.

SELECT BIBLIOGRAPHY

Aymard, Maurice, and Giuseppe Giarrizzo, eds. *La Sicilia*. Turin: Einaudi, 1987.

De Seta, Cesare, and Leonardo Di Mauro. *Palermo*. Rome: Laterza, 1988.

Duggan, Christopher, *Fascism and the Mafia*. New Haven, Conn.: Yale University Press, 1989.

Finley, M. I. *Ancient Sicily*. New York: Viking, 1968.

Finley, M. I., Denis Mack Smith, and Christopher Duggan. *A History of Sicily*. New York: Viking, 1987.

Giarrizzo, Giuseppe. *Catania*. Rome: Laterza, 1986.

Istituto Geografico De Agostini. *Sicilia*. 2 vols. Novara: Istituto Geografico De Agostini, 1983.

Mack Smith, Denis. *History of Sicily*. 2 vols. New York: Dorset Press, 1988.

Regione Sicilia, Assessorato Turismo, Comunicazioni, Trasporti. *Atlas of the Roads and Towns of Sicily*. Novara: Istituto Geografico De Agostini, 1997.

Runciman, Stephen. *Sicilian Vespers*. Cambridge: Cambridge University Press, 1992.

Stille, Alexander. *Excellent Cadavers: The Mafia and the Death of the First Italian Republic*. New York: Random House, 1995.

TRENTINO-ALTO ADIGE

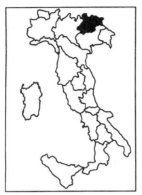

Chapter 16

TRENTINO–ALTO ADIGE

REGIONAL CHARACTERISTICS. Area: 5,256 sq. mi. Population: 924,281. Capitals: Trent and Bolzano (or Bozen). The region ranks as Italy's eleventh in land area and sixteenth in population. Trent is a Catholic metropolitan see.

The Trentino–Alto Adige (which German-speakers refer to as the Sud Tirol [South Tyrol]) was formed in 1948 as an autonomous region from the old Venetia Tridentina, which had been annexed from the Austro-Hungarian Empire after the First World War. The two provinces are largely independent of one another.

The Trentino–Alto Adige borders Austria to its north, Switzerland and Lombardy to its west, and Veneto to its south and east. In its south, the region's topography begins in gentle pre-Alpine forms and ascends northward to dramatic peaks cut by river valleys. The area is generally referred to as the Dolomites, although not all of the ranges fit the strict definition. The Dolomite range is found in the southeast corner of the Alto Adige along the border with Belluno province in the Veneto. The Italian Statistical Institute classifies both provinces in the Trentino–Alto Adige as entirely mountainous. The highest peaks include Monte Ortels (12,813 feet), near the Lombard border; the Pala Bianca (or Weisskugel) at 12,257 feet in the Ötztaler range, and the Gran Pilastro (or Hochfeiler) at 11,511 feet in the Zillertaler range, both along the Austrian frontier. The Stelvio National Park straddles the western end of the provincial line between the Trentino and the Alto Adige, and a number of "natural parks" dot the area.

The Adige (or Etsch) is the main river through the Trentino–Alto Adige. It rises in and around the Lago di Resia (or Reschensee) in the northwest corner. It flows east through Merano and joins with the Isarco (Eisack) near Bolzano, where it turns south through the Lagarina valley, Trent, and Verona until it reaches the Adriatic. The Isarco runs from near the Brenner Pass at the Austrian border south through Bressanone and finally to Bolzano, near which it joins the Adige. The E-45 autostrada parallels the Adige northward from Verona to Bolzano, where it follows the Isarco up to the Brenner Pass. It is the most recent manifestation of one of Europe's oldest roads.

ECONOMY. Of the 397,000-strong active workforce in the Trentino–Alto Adige, 240,000 are men and 157,000 are women; 64.9 percent of Trent's workers are occupied in the tertiary sector, 28.3 percent labor in industry, and 6.8 percent in agriculture. Bolzano's figures are, respectively, 61.2, 26.2, and 12.6 percent. In January 1998 the region's unemployment rate was 3.4 percent. Timber is important to the region, as are wine and fruit crops, particularly apples. Some claim that the potatoes of the Trentino are Italy's best. Dairy farming is conducted in the lower valleys. This is one of Italy's few important mining areas, and some of the deposits of zinc, lead, copper, and iron have been exploited since ancient times. Hydroelectric power is also well developed; the region provides 20 percent of Italy's total. Aluminum is produced at Bolzano and Mori, farm equipment and other mechanical industries are found at Bolzano and Trent, and beer is brewed at Merano. The tourist industry, however, provides the greatest source of income in the Trentino–Alto Adige.

CUISINE. Many German dishes, from *knödel* (dumplings) to *speck* (smoked bacon), are found throughout the region, particularly in the north; polenta and gnocchi are popular in the south. The Alto Adige is also famous for hearty German bread, such *Schuttelbrot* from Merano. Strudel and Viennese pastries are enjoyed throughout the region. Most wines of the Trentino–Alto Adige come from the Adige, Isarco, and adjacent valleys. In the north, the best wines are said to be the whites of the Isarco valley. Muller Thurgau and Sylvaner are known for their quality, as is Pacherhof, from the Novacella abbey near Bressanone. Vernatsch is the local favorite, particularly Caldaro (or *Kalteren*). Merano honors the region's wine production in a harvest festival, the *festa dell'uva* (grape festival), on the second Sunday of October. The Trentino produces more whites—Pinot Grigios and Chardonnays, for example—to compete with Friuli, although it is best known for Spumante. The province's special pride, however, may be Teroldego, a rich red wine produced in the Campo Rotaliano, north of Trent, where the Adige meets the Noce River.

BROBUSÀ

1 medium onion, finely chopped

1 Tbs. olive oil

1 Tbs. butter

2 Tbs. flour

½ lb. potatoes, peeled

¼ c. northern beans

½ lb. pancetta (or smoked bacon)

2 bay leaves

Salt and pepper to taste

Grated Grana Trentino cheese (or alternate such as pecorino)

In a large frying pan cook onion in oil and butter until golden brown. Mix in flour and set aside. In a saucepan, bring water to a boil and add potatoes, beans, pancetta, and bay leaves. When vegetables are tender, drain them. Chop potatoes and most of the beans and combine with onion mixture. Add salt, pepper, and cheese to taste. Cook for a few more minutes over low heat. Remove bay leaves before serving.

HISTORY. Despite their current separate identities, Trentino and the Alto Adige were united in prehistoric times. A Bronze Age society, the Lucans, flourished across most of the region between 1100 and 900 B.C., from Rovereto in the south to near the Brenner Pass in the north. The Fritzens-Sanzeno, or Rhaetian, culture followed the Lucan between about 500 and 100 B.C. Its southern frontier roughly corresponded to the Lucan, but in the north it extended to Austria's Inn River valley and Innsbruck. The Romans absorbed the Rhaetians and their land in fits and starts, completing the process by the time of Caesar Augustus (first century B.C.–first century A.D.). To consolidate their rule, the Romans built Trent into a real city and connected it to the Claudia Augustan Way, which ran north from the Adriatic. Instead of following the Isarco to the Brenner Pass, however, this road, built by Augustus's adopted son, Drusus, turned west into the Val Venosta and ran through the Resia Pass (or Reschenpass). Later, Emperor Septimius Severus (193–211) constructed a military road along the Isarco and through the Brenner Pass. The Romans divided the territory among three administrative units: Rezia (or Raetia), which occupied the northwest corner of today's Trentino–Alto Adige (or most of western Alto Adige); a small bit of Norico (or Noricum) in the northeast; and the southern part, generally Trentino province, was merged into Region X, Venetia et Histria.

The region suffered at the hands of the barbarian invaders. Attila, for instance, raided the mountain valleys from his base camp on the banks of Lake Garda. The Lombards and Bavarians contested the area in the 500s, the former in the south and the latter in the north. With the consolidation of the Frankish Empire in the 700s, Charlemagne parceled out the area as feudal lands to the Bishop of Trent, the Count of Bolzano, and the Bishop of Bressanone (Brixen). With the aid of the two bishops, Emperor Henry II invaded Italy in 1004. He and his successor, Conrad II, rewarded them by extending their possessions: Bolzano and the Venosta valley went to Trent, and Bressanone took the Isarco and Inn valleys. Later the Counts of Tyrol ruled much of the northern reaches of the region. The close ties maintained between the region and the Holy Roman Empire coincided with the persistence of feudal institutions there long after they had died out in most of the rest of Italy.

In 1363 the Austrian Hapsburgs acquired the Tyrolean lands, and in 1405 Venice took the Vallagarina at the southern end of the Trentino. By 1509 the Hapsburgs ruled the entire area. In 1525, however, they faced a widespread peasant rebellion, the Rural War, which began in Trent and Bressanone and was fueled by the excitement of the Reformation. The Prince-Bishop of Trent, Bernardo Clesio, fled to Riva del Garda, then returned in a vengeful and bloodstained triumph. An able administrator and a Renaissance patron, Clesio set the stage for the Council of Trent (1545–1563), but did not live to see it. The Council was hosted by his successor, Bishop Cristoforo Madruzzo.

The eighteenth-century Enlightenment reforms of Emperor Joseph II (1765–1790) were felt in the Trentino in such fields as reorganization of the confraternities and in education. An experimental school, for example, was established at Rovereto. Napoleon occupied Trent for the first time in September 1796. Austria returned, but in 1806 the French awarded the region to Bavaria, a regime not remembered with great fondness. When Austria took up arms against Napoleon and his Bavarian allies, a popular rebellion exploded under Andreas Hofer (1767–1810), a cattle merchant who remains the region's chief symbol of liberty. France sent 50,000 men to crush the uprising and granted amnesty to most of the rebels, although Hofer was executed at Mantua in 1810. Napoleon then divided the region, taking the southern districts for his Kingdom of Italy, awarding the far north to Bavaria, and placing parts of the east in France's Illyrian provinces. Austria returned in 1813 and reassembled the region in 1815 as the Princely County of Tyrol under a *gubernium* (Austrian government district) at Innsbruck. In 1849 Austria abolished the *gubernium* and ruled through a lieutenant appointed from Vienna.

Italy's victorious 1859 war of independence stopped short of an invasion of the Trentino–Alto Adige, and the area remained in the Austrian Empire. Italy's victories in the Valsugana and at Bezzecca during the Seven Weeks War of 1866 were not enough to change the situation. Irredentist hopes among Italian nationalists were channeled into the Pro Patria Society from its foundation in 1886 until the Austrians disbanded it four years later, and in the Lega Nazionale (National League) thereafter.

The region, known then as Venezia Tridentina, finally joined Italy after its World War One victory over the Austrians in 1918 and the Treaty of Saint-Germain (1919). In 1923 it was consolidated as the province of Trent except for Cortina d'Ampezzo in the northeast, which was awarded to Belluno province in the Veneto. By 1921, however, a separatist movement, the Autonomisten Partei (Autonomy Party), had evolved.

Nazi Germany invaded Italy in September 1943, and annexed Venetia Tridentina along with much of Belluno province in the Veneto to the Third Reich. The large number of German speakers who lived there, especially in the Alto Adige (Sud Tirol), prompted the Nazis to incorporate the territory into Germany as Alpenvorland.

RECENT POLITICS. After the war the Sudtiroler Volkspartei (SVP) usually captured the plurality of the Alto Adige vote, and in the Trentino the Christian Democrats scored well until the early 1990s. The region votes as the sixth *circoscrizione* (electoral district). In the 1996 majoritarian elections for the Chamber of Deputies, the Ulivo coalition led with 28 percent, followed by the SVP with 25.8 percent and the Polo per le Libertà coalition with 24.3 percent. In the proportional vote, a Catholic-SVP-Republican coalition connected with former Prime Minister Romano Prodi took first place with 17.7 percent. It was followed by Forza Italia with 14.3 percent and the Lega Nord with 13.2 percent. In the Senate vote, another coalition with the SVP earned 33.4 percent, the Ulivo captured 26.9 percent and the Polo per le Libertà took 23.8 percent. As an autonomous region, Trentino–Alto Adige did not participate in the regional elections of April 2000.

BOLZANO

PROVINCIAL PROFILE. Area: 2,857 sq. mi. Population: 457,370 (province), 96,949 (city). The province of Bolzano, or the Alto Adige, contains 116 communes. The Brenner Pass and a number of Alpine ranges, particularly the Ötztaler and the Zillertaler, separate the Alto Adige along its northern border from Austria. To its west is Switzerland. Lombardy touches the Alto Adige along the Ortles (Ortlergruppe) mountain chain on the southwest, Trentino faces its southern side, and the Veneto shares its eastern and southeastern borders. A strong German element distinguishes the province's culture and German-speakers outnumber the Italians throughout almost two to one, although the latter constitute the majorities in the cities of Bolzano, Merano, and Bressanone. Ladino speakers total 16,000, about 4 percent of the population. Its sister tongue, Romansch, is spoken in some pockets near the Swiss border.

HISTORY. Settlement was sparse in the high mountain areas of the Alto Adige during Roman rule. The imperial adjustments of the early eleventh century placed Bolzano and the Venosta valley in the hands of the Bishop of Trent, and the north and east parts of the province in those of the Bishop of Bressanone. In the twelfth century Trent surrendered control of its territories to the Counts of Morit-Greifenstein. The Counts of Gorizia soon intervened in the area, as did the Counts of the Tyrol, who ultimately dominated it. The last Countess of Tyrol, Margherita Maultasch, after the death of her husband, Ludwig of Bavaria and Brandenburg, and of her son, ceded her lands in 1363 to Rudolf IV, the Hapsburg Duke of Austria. With few exceptions, such as the Napoleonic interludes, the Sud Tirol remained in Austrian hands until the twentieth century.

Italy conquered the Alto Adige in 1918, at the end of the First World War, and made it part of Trent province in 1923. The Alto Adige, however, was still more of a German Sud Tirol, and the Deutscher Verband (German Alliance) formed to press for autonomy. The province's distinctive German character was still vibrant. The 1910 Austrian census, for instance, listed the population as 7,000 Italian speakers, 6,000 who spoke the local Ladino and Romansch tongues, and 221,000 Germans. By 1921, the Italian population had climbed to only 20,300. Despite a royal guarantee to "scrupulously" monitor the area's native traditions, however, Fascist nationalism reacted early to "foreign" elements in the mixed Italo-German population.

Upon taking power in 1922, Mussolini's government prohibited grammar school classes in the German language under penalty of imprisonment or banishment *in confino* to remote southern villages. In 1923 the government began to Italianize river, mountain, and valley names, those of towns, and even names on tombstones. Settlers from other parts of Italy, particularly industrial zones of Piedmont and Lombardy, were brought into the region to counter German culture. To appease his Fascist ally, Adolf Hitler abandoned his Sudtiroler (South Tyrol) cousins and in 1938 declared the Brenner Pass to be the inviolate border between the German and the Italian peoples. Mussolini allowed German residents of the area the option of "repatriation" to the Third Reich by December 31, 1939. About 75,000 left.

Germany's decision to annex the Alto Adige in September 1943 and merge it into *Alpenvorland* prompted a resistance force in the Andreas Hofer Bund and among some Catholic segments of the population.

After the Second World War, the establishment of a democratic government in Italy spurred hopes for an easing of tensions in the Alto Adige. But despite efforts to correct the "Italianized" corrections made before the war and, in December 1945, the official sanction of the German language in Bolzano, separatism gathered force. The pro-German Sudtiroler Volkspartei (SVP) formed in 1945, was first led in part by Nazi officials in the *Alpenvorland* administration. Consequently the party adopted more of a mainstream face and has been the chief voice of the province's German-speaking voters. A smaller group, the Movimento Autonomistico Regionale, was created by the Italian speakers. To meet these challenges, particularly the former, the Roman government granted autonomy to the Alto Adige in the September 1946 agreement reached at Paris between Prime Minister Alcide De Gasperi and Austria's Foreign Minister Karl Gruber (also known as the De Gasperi-Gruber Accords). The following February, however, Italy violated the arrangement when it merged the province with the predominantly Italian Trentino to form a region whose German identity was far less pronounced.

By the late 1950s the question reappeared as the SVP denounced the accords and German nationalists undertook occasional terrorist attacks; in 1960 the Austrian government sought the aid of the United Nations. Rome adopted a conciliatory attitude. Upon the agreement of the SVP at its congress in Merano, Italy granted the region extraordinary freedoms on November 30, 1969, the so-called *Pacchetto*. The reforms led to a new charter of autonomy in 1972. In 1992 Prime Minister Giulio Andreotti announced that Italy had fulfilled its application of the *Pacchetto* reforms and Austria subsequently withdrew its petition for United Nations mediation. Later in the 1990s, Vienna's admission to the European Union and the Schengen Accords of 1997–1998 ended border restrictions that had emphasized the Alto Adige's separation from Austria. In 1997 the University of the Alto Adige and the Free University of Bolzano were established.

ARTS AND CULTURE. The Alto Adige and Bolzano mix Italian and German cultures, creating an impression that can sometimes jar the observer. Bolzano's old city is gathered around the Romanesque Church of San Giovanni in Villa, which was built by an unknown German master trained in Padua. The modern city focuses on the twelfth- and fourteenth-century Gothic Duomo. The thirteenth-century Dominican church contains important frescoes in the style of Giotto. The Fascists added their stamp to Bolzano's architecture in their effort to Italianize it. Most impressive is **Marcello Piacentini**'s Victory Monument, built in 1928, with stone heads resembling Mussolini protruding around its top. Bolzano hosts an important folk festival on the last Sunday in May. In ancient garb, the **Schutzen**, medieval guards, march through the city, no longer to ward off enemies but to launch a day of fun.

OTHER CENTERS. Bressanone (or **Brixen**) is located at the junction of the Rienza and Isarco rivers. It was founded at the start of the tenth century and quickly became an episcopal see and, in 1027, that of a prince-bishop. The city's Duomo, begun in the tenth century, was rebuilt extensively and often through the eighteenth. North of Bressanone is **Varna**, home to the important twelfth-century abbey of Novacella. The frequent renovations of the abbey undertaken over the ages included fifteenth century fortifications prompted by fears of a Turkish invasion. Varna is also the home of the artist Friedrich Pacher (active 1474–1508), who contributed to many of the

Alto Adige's churches, including the Bolzano Duomo. (Kinship with the more famous Michael Pacher, however, remains unproven.) Close by, at **Velturno** (or **Feldthurns**), is the sixteenth-century castle which served as the summer retreat of the Bishops of Bressanone.

Northeast of Bressanone the Rienza River forms the center of the Pusteria zone, the geographically striking home of impressive castles such as the twelfth-century Castello Rodengo, quaint towns like **Brunico** (or **Bruneck**), and ski resorts. One of the area's most noteworthy artists, Michael Pacher (c. 1435–1498), was born in Brunico. Pacher's frescoes are found throughout the area. At the eastern end of the Pusteria, on the Drava River near the Austrian border, the town of **San Candido** (or **Innichen**) boasts an impressive collegiate Church of Saints Candido and Corbiniano. Dating from the twelfth century, it is perhaps the most important Romanesque structure of the province. The two saints are depicted in a fifteenth-century fresco by Pacher. Although German is the lingua franca of the zone, the Pusteria and the Cadore mountain range to its southeast remain among the few places where one enounters the ancient Ladino language.

North of Bolzano, near the Brenner Pass, is **Vipiteno** (or **Sterzing**), which began as a Roman outpost and achieved medieval importance as a mining area controlled by the German Fugger bankers and seat of a provincial council. A significant historic center remains, as well as two nearby fortresses, the twelfth-century Castel Tasso and the thirteenth-century Castel Pietra. Vipiteno also boasts a museum dedicated to local medieval works, particularly those of a Bavarian, Hans Multscher (1400–c. 1467).

Northwest of Bolzano, on the Passirio River near its junction with the Adige, is **Merano** (or **Meran**), seat of the Counts of Venosta, who in the twelfth century became the Counts of Tyrol. Their old Castel Tirolo, outside of town, was first built in the twelfth century; a landslide damaged it in the seventeenth century, and it has undergone frequent restorations since then. Merano has maintained its historic core along the porticoed Via dei Portici, which connects the city's fifteenth-century fortresslike Duomo and the Palazzo Principesco (today a museum), which was built at about the same time for the Hapsburg rulers. In the nineteenth century Merano's magnificent location and thermal baths made it a popular resort among well-to-do Austrians. Toward the end of Vienna's rule an elegant city of boulevards, promenades (*passeggiate*), hotels, and theaters was added to its medieval center.

At the western end of the province, the Adige flows south out of the Lago di Resia and the ancient Resia Pass, toward the town of **Malles Venosta** (or **Mals**). Its ninth-century church of San Benedetto contains some of the most significant Carolingian frescoes in Europe. Nearby, at **Burgusio**, is the Benedictine abbey of Monte Maria. It was established in the twelfth century and largely rebuilt through the nineteenth. In the crypt are frescoes from the original building, among the best in the region. South of Malles

Venosta, the Adige bends east and forms the **Val Venosta,** a zone of towns and castles evocative of German culture. Near **Sluderno** (or **Schluderns**), for example, is the thirteenth-century Castel Coira. San Procolo, a significant Carolingian church, is at **Naturno,** east on the Adige toward Merano.

——————————— *TRENT (TRENTO)* ———————————

PROVINCIAL PROFILE. Area: 2,399 sq. mi. Population: 466,911 (province), 103,474 (city). Trent province contains 223 communes. The province of Trent is to the south of Bolzano and the Alto Adige, east of Lombardy, and west and north of the Veneto.

HISTORY. Ancient chronicles of Pliny the Elder (A.D. 23–79) claim that the Rhaetian peoples first settled Trent. The Romans recognized the town's strategic value—lying along the Adige River and south of the Brenner Pass—and established a colony and military base there which they called Tridentum. Trent was the seat of a Lombard duchy in the late 500s. After 1027 the Bishop of Trent was accorded an additional, princely, title, that of Elector of the Holy Roman Empire. The adventurer Ezzelino da Romano wrested control of the lands from the ecclesiatical prince around 1250 and launched a period of feudal anarchy.

Trent's location served it again in the sixteenth century when the city was chosen by Pope Paul III as the site for a Catholic Church council (1545–1563). The general sessions of Council of Trent met at the Cathedral of San Vigilio to grapple with the dilemma of the Reformation that had begun in Germany in 1517. The reforms which were decided upon there launched the "Tridentine" era of the Catholic Church, which lasted until the Second Vatican Council in the 1960s.

Trent maintained its independence as the see of a prince bishop through the eighteenth century. The last ruler, Pietro Viglio Thun, who came to the throne in 1776, attempted without success to sell his lands to the Austrians. Napoleon solved the bishop's dilemma when, on September 5, 1796, he invaded the Trentino at the head of a French army. His attack launched a string of back-and-forth invasions until 1813, when Trent passed to Austrian hands. During the revolutions of 1848, Trent organized a national guard (the Corpi Franchi) and demanded separation from the rest of the Tyrol. Riots broke out on March 19, and the Austrians were forced to flee; but they reentered Trent by April 8. Italy had to wait until the First World War, when its victory over Austria allowed it to take the provincial capital on November 3, 1918. Rome formally annexed the area on September 26, 1920, although the act was never put to a vote by the Trentini. Any thoughts of autonomy were dashed when the Fascists took power in 1922.

Postwar Trentino politics were distinguished by Christian Democratic

hegemony, a fact perhaps fitting in that it was the home of Alcide De
Gasperi (Pieve di Trento, 1881–1954), Italy's prime minister from 1945
until 1953. From 1911 to 1918, De Gasperi served in the Austrian Parliament, where he lobbied for the creation of an Italian university at Trent, a
dream not fully realized until 1962. A leader in Italy's postwar Catholic
movement, De Gasperi was briefly imprisoned by the Fascists and then
secured a position in the safety of the Vatican Library. During the Second
World War he joined others in the clandestine task of resurrecting a Catholic political party. Under his leadership Christian Democracy triumphed
after the fall of Fascism and the crucial 1948 elections. De Gasperi also
secured Italian participation in the North Atlantic Treaty Organization
(NATO) and Rome's participation in the European Coal and Steel Community (ECSC), the forerunner of the Common Market and the European
Community.

Despite De Gasperi's prominence as a national leader, Trentino separatist
sentiments that the Fascists had quashed resurfaced in the Associazione
Studi Autonomistici Regionali (ASAR, Regional Autonomy Studies Association). Although distinct from parties and having a politically ecumenical
leadership, the ASAR became a major vehicle in achieving autonomous
status for the Trentino in 1948 and union with the Alto Adige.

ARTS AND CULTURE. In Trent's central Piazza del Duomo is the city's
cathedral, first built in the sixth century and reconstructed between the
thirteenth and the sixteenth. Some Baroque embellishments were added
later. Much of the first, ancient church was discovered and recovered
thanks to excavations in the late 1960s and 1970s. The diocesan museum
contains an impressive collection of Flemish tapestries.

The Duomo and about 20 other churches in the diocese of Trent are
dedicated to the city's third bishop, San Vigilio. According to tradition,
Vigilio was murdered while preaching in the Val Rendena. The date of his
martyrdom, June 26, 400, is celebrated across the Trentino. In 397 three
of Vigilio's missionaries, Sisinio, Martirio, and Alessandro, were martyred
by a pagan mob in the Val di Non. The pagans were outraged that the
three had convinced some locals to refuse to sacrifice before the statue of
Saturn. After the three evangelists were murdered, therefore, their bodies
were burned before the image of the Roman god.

For over 500 years the Prince-Bishops of Trent lived in the Castello del
Buonconsiglio, at the eastern edge of the old city. The bishops built their
residence in two stages. The north end is the medieval thirteenth-century
Castel Vecchio, and the sixteenth-century Magno Palazzo forms its south-
ern end. Today the palace houses the provincial art museum. A museum
of the Risorgimento, also in the castle, reminds the visitor of the patriot
Cesare Battisti (Trent, 1875–1916), who challenged Vienna's rule of the
Trentino. He represented Trent as a Socialist in the Austrian Parliament

before the First World War prompted him to cross to Italian lines and join the *Alpini* mountain troops. The Austrians, however, captured him and jailed him in the castle before they executed him and two comrades. In 1935 a monument to Battisti was erected on the Doss (or Dos) Trento, a huge rock on the other side of the Adige from the city center. A museum dedicated to Italy's Alpine troops (*Alpini*) also sits atop the hill.

The Baroque artist **Andrea Pozzo** (1642–1709) was born in Trent. A lay Jesuit, he won his reputation for a treatise on perspective and, above all, for his astonishing ceiling fresco of Rome's Church of Sant'Ignazio. Trent was also the home of **Carlantonio Pilati**, the Enlightenment thinker whose *Di una Riforma d'Italia* (A Reform of Italy, 1767) called for the end of Church privileges and increased state control over seminaries. He taught at the Trent *liceo* (secondary school) until he left for Chur, Switzerland, where for eighteen months he published the *Corriere Letterario* (Literary Post), a key link between French, German, and Italian Enlightenment circles.

OTHER CENTERS. North of Trent, near the Bolzano line, is **San Michele dell'Adige** (or **all'Adige**), the site of an important provincial folk museum, the Museo Provinciale degli Usi e Costumi della Gente Trentina. Northwest is the **Val di Non**, where, near **Sanzeno**, the sanctuary of San Romedio is an important pilgrimage church with six chapels built between the seventh and the sixteenth centuries. The valley contains important castles at **Taio** (Castel Bragher, which houses a museum) and at **Ton** (Castel Tono, or Thun).

The Venetians held **Rovereto**, situated in the Vallagarina at the southern end of the Trentino, for most of the fifteenth century; then the Austrians, aided by the locals, took it in 1509. The center of Rovereto is distinguished by the fourteenth-century castle built for the Castelbarco family, the city's medieval rulers. Rovereto was the birthplace of the Catholic philosopher Antonio Rosmini-Serbati (1797–1855). A priest, he was a liberal and a nationalist who believed in the cause of the Risorgimento until Pope Pius IX's reservations ended his hopes for a "Guelph" solution to unification in which the pontiff and the Church would play a central role. The composer Riccardo Zandonai (1883–1944) was born in nearby **Sacco di Rovereto**. His career began with opera (e.g., *Francesca da Rimini*, 1914) and the symphony, and concluded in the world of film, as a composer for the screen. Italy's principal museum of the First World War is at Rovereto, the Museo Storico Italiano della Guerra. The city's Fortunato Depero Museum is dedicated to the works of the futurist artist. Depero (1892–1960) was born at **Fondo** in the Val di Non.

At **Riva del Garda** the Trentino touches the northern point of Lake Garda. Protected by mountains on one side and a charming waterfront on the other, it became a popular Austrian resort in the late nineteenth century.

SELECT BIBLIOGRAPHY

De Finis, Lia, ed. *Storia del Trentino*. Trent: Associazione Culturale "Antonio Rosmini," 1996.

Giovannini, Augusto. *Trentino: The Signs of Time and Men*. Trent: Casa Editrice Publilux, 1997.

Istituto Geografico De Agostini. *Trentino–Alto Adige, Friuli–Venezia Giulia*. Novara: Istituto Geografico De Agostini, 1979.

Petri, Rolf. *Storia di Bolzano*. Padua: Il Poligrafo, 1989.

Provincia Autonoma Bolzano–Alto Adige. *Manuale dell'Alto Adige*. Bolzano: Giunta Provinciale di Bolzano, 1998.

Provincia Autonoma di Trento. *Otto Secoli di sovranità/Eight Centuries of Sovereignty*. Trent: Casa Editrice Panorama, n.d.

Chapter 17

TUSCANY
(Toscana)

REGIONAL CHARACTERISTICS. Area: 8,876 sq. mi. Population: 3,527,303. Capital: Florence (Firenze). Tuscany is Italy's fifth largest region in land and its ninth in population. The region embraces 287 communes. Catholic metropolitan sees are in Florence, Siena/Colle di Val d'Elsa/Montalcino, and Pisa.

Tuscany's shape is roughly triangular. On Italy's west coast, it faces the Ligurian and the Tyrrhenian seas. Its northwest tip touches Liguria. Northeast of Tuscany, across the Apennines, are Emilia Romagna and the Marche. The southeast border with Umbria and Latium is marked by gentler hills. Hills constitute 67 percent of the region, 8 percent is flatland, and about 25 percent is mountainous. The highest peaks are along the north of the region, from the Apuan Alps that jut into its northwest corner near Massa-Carrara, through the Succiso Alps and Mount Cusna (6,960 feet), and curving around Florence to the San Benedetto Alps. Much of the borderland with Emilia Romagna in Florence and Arezzo provinces is contained in a national park of the "Foreste Casentinesi, Monte Falterona, Campigna." High in the mountains and hills are important river valleys: the Lunigiana and Garfagnana in the northwest, the Mugello and the Conca di Firenze near the capital, and, going south, the Valdarno, the Casentino, the Val Tiberina, the Valdichiana south of Arezzo, and the Val d'Orcia, which forms part of the border between the provinces of Siena and Grosseto.

Tuscany's fertile valley farmlands take their water from rivers such as the Chiana, the Serchio, and the Orcia (which feeds into the Ombrone).

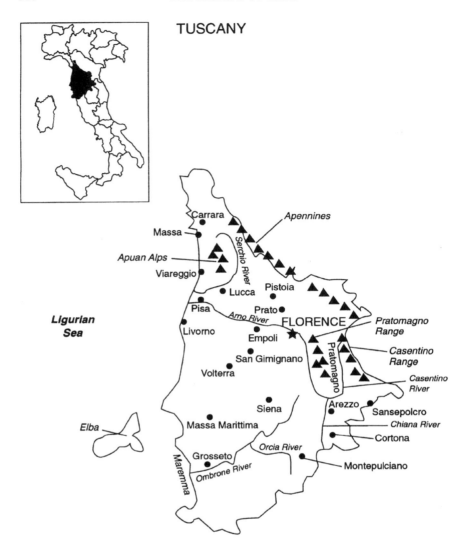

TUSCANY

The Tiber flows through Tuscany from Emilia Romagna. The region's most important river is the Arno, which rises in the Apennines, loops south near Arezzo, then up through Florence and west toward Pisa and the sea. Most of the southwestern coastal plains and the Maremma are reclaimed marshland.

ECONOMY. The Tuscan labor force is 4.2 percent in agriculture, 34.3 percent in industry, and 61.5 percent in the tertiary sector. Of Tuscany's 1,353,000 employed workers, 827,000 are men and 526,000 are women. Tuscany's January 1998 unemployment rate was 8.9 percent. Along with wine and olives, Tuscan farms produce grain, much of it used as fodder. The region ranks fifth in cattle population and third in hogs. Two thirds of Italy's iron is mined on the island of Elba. Tuscany produces some of the world's best marble; three-quarters of the nation's white variety comes from quarries in the Apuan Alps. Italy's large output of mercury is taken entirely from Monte Amiata in the southeast. The artisanal tradition remains in the manufacture of luxury items in shops throughout many of Tuscany's cities. A concentration of small and mid-sized workshops connected with the computer industry has surfaced in Tuscany, particularly in the area around Arezzo, the Aretino.

The Florence-Prato-Pistoia triangle is considered one of Italy's most industrialized areas. Much of Tuscany's economy also revolves around its cultural patrimony. The region boasts 5,787 archaeological sites, 2,300 religious structures of artistic and historic interest, and 319 museums and galleries. Such riches and a pleasant geography place it among Italy's top tourist destinations.

CUISINE. Tuscan cuisine is noted for its grilled meats, such as wild game, *arista* (pork loin with rosemary and garlic), and particularly *bistecca* (steak) *alla fiorentina*, preferably made with beef from the Valdichiana. Legumes constitute an important part of the region's diet, and are prepared in many ways; for instance, in Livorno chickpeas are made into a pie. Lucca and the Garfagnana are known for *farro*, a cereal grain which is used in thick soups or pies. The grain had become almost extinct until it was revived and cultivated by the farmers of the Garfagnana, who have sought to secure official protection for it. Lucca's olive oil is prized as one of Italy's best. Seafood distinguishes much of Livorno's and Grosseto's cooking: mullet, (*triglia alla livornese*) and *cacciucco*, a soup made with a selection of fish and mollusks. Also popular are *favolli*, large reef crabs. Siena's *panforte* is a hard, dark dessert cake famous across Italy.

Tuscany is one of Italy's most important wine-producing regions. Some families, like the Ricasoli, trace their endeavors as *vignaioli* back to the early Middle Ages. Above all, and for better or worse, Tuscany's Chianti has achieved global fame. Chianti officially comes from seven zones that stretch across the region, although its real home, the land of *chianti classico*, is in the hill country around Siena. Many other quality wines are found in the region, such as Brunello, Vino Nobile, Carmignano, and Pomino.

ARISTA DI MAIALE AL FORNO

3 cloves garlic, minced	1 tsp. dried parsley
1 tsp. rosemary	Salt and pepper to taste
½ tsp. sage	4 lb. pork roast
1 bay leaf	

Preheat oven to 350°. Combine garlic, sage, rosemary, bay leaf, parsley, salt, and pepper. Pierce the pork in a number of places and insert a portion of the mixture into each opening. Spread the remaining mixture over the top of the meat. Roast in an ungreased pan for about 2 hours, or until a meat thermometer reads the internal temperature as 185°. Baste periodically with water and white wine.

HISTORY. Tuscany's first civilization, the Etruscan (from which it took its name), clearly manifested itself by the eighth century B.C. and spread later into Emilia Romagna, Umbria, Lazio, and beyond. Etruscan settlements in Tuscany were often distinguished as prominent hill towns, many of which have endured into our times: Arezzo, Volterra, Fiesole, Cortona, and so on. By the 300s and 200s the Romans penetrated Tuscany and overcame the Etruscans. The conquerors included the area in what became known in Augustan times as Region VII, and, by the third century, as Tuscia et Umbria. After the fall of the Roman Empire (476), the region was vaguely united as a duchy with its capital at Lucca, and then as a Frankish county and marquisate after 774.

Although Tuscany was incorporated in the lands of the Counts of Canossa, by the eleventh and twelfth centuries many of its towns had begun to achieve quasi independence as communes. Through the first centuries of the second millennium, its towns gave Tuscany the right to claim to be Europe's first urbanized land. These new and prosperous cities soon suffered as battlegrounds in the fierce medieval struggles between Guelphs and Ghibellines. Although the alliances and commitments to causes were rarely clear, the Guelphs, supporters of the papal side, were generally concentrated in Florence, Prato, Lucca, Volterra, and Montepulciano; the Ghibellines, partisans of the Holy Roman Empire and Emperor Frederick II, led Pisa, Pistoia, Arezzo, and Siena. The principal local power, however, was Florence. It eventually extended its control over all of Tuscany, which by the middle of the sixteenth century had become a grand duchy under the Medici family. Florence's chief local rival, the Republic of Siena, succumbed to imperial troops and the Florentines of Duke Cosimo I de'Medici, first in 1555, when the capital surrendered, and then in 1559, when the last resistance was extinguished at Montalcino.

The lackluster Gian Gastone de'Medici was the last of his clan to rule Tuscany, and upon his death in 1737 the grand duchy was transferred to Francis Stephen of the house of Lorraine (later Emperor Francis I). The new grand duke married the Hapsburg Empress of Austria, Maria Theresa, and in 1745 relinquished Tuscany to his son, Leopold. The house of Lorraine imported foreign talent to reverse the last years of Medici neglect and to administer Tuscany until the young prince reached the age of majority in 1765. These regents, the Prince de Craon, the Count de Richecourt, and the Genoese Marshal Botta-Adorno, transformed the grand duchy into one of Europe's best-administered and most enlightened lands. Upon reaching his majority, Peter Leopold embraced their reforms and added some of his own. Under their government, and with the assistance of local figures such as Pompeo Neri and Giulio Rucellai, censorship was largely transferred from ecclesiastical to state control and then effectively curtailed. Church exemptions from taxes were greatly cut, opening underused land to more productive purposes. After the French invasion, Napoleon ended the grand duchy and created the Kingdom of Etruria in 1801 for Maria Luisa de Bourbon. He removed her in December 1807 and annexed Tuscany to France. The Lorraine dynasty returned after the defeat of Napoleon, maintaining many of his reforms and continuing its own progressive program.

Tuscany assumed an important place in the Italian Risorgimento. The spirit of 1848 reached the grand duchy, where a republic was proclaimed in February 1849. But the democratic experiment failed, and Grand Duke Leopold II was restored by the Austrians in an atmosphere devoid of the old reformist impulse. The 1859 Franco-Piedmontese war against Austria triggered another revolution that replaced Leopold with a provisional government under a Florentine aristocrat, Baron Bettino Ricasoli (1809–1880). Ricasoli guided Tuscany into the new Kingdom of Italy on February 18, 1861, and then succeeded Count Camillo Benso di Cavour as prime minister. Such was Tuscany's prestige that Florence was the capital of Italy from 1865 until 1871, before that honor was transferred to Rome.

RECENT POLITICS. After the Second World War, Tuscany formed part of Italy's Communist "Red Belt" that included Emilia Romagna, the Marche, and Umbria. Communist strength peaked at 50 percent in 1948 and continued until its collapse in 1989. Communist power was never all-encompassing in Tuscany, however, where strong anarchist traditions persisted among the working classes of Livorno and Massa-Carrara and other cities, such as Lucca, were known as "white," or Catholic.

Tuscany votes in national elections as the twelfth electoral district (*circoscrizione*). In the 1996 majoritarian contest for the Chamber of Deputies, the Center-Left Ulivo coalition achieved a 52 percent victory. The Center-Right Polo per le Libertà earned 36.4 percent. The Democratic Party of the Left took 34.7 percent of the proportional vote, followed by the Alleanza Nazionale with 15.8 percent, Forza Italia with 14.3 percent, and the Rifondazione Comunista with 12.5 percent. For the Senate the Ulivo took 50.8 percent of the vote, versus the Polo's 32.7 percent. Tuscany's Center-Left government was maintained in the April 2000 regional election. Claudia Martini was elected president with 49.2 percent of the vote for the ruling alliance, and the Center-Right received 40.0 percent.

FLORENCE (FIRENZE)

PROVINCIAL PROFILE. Area: 1,339 sq. mi. Population: 952,293 (province), 380,058 (city). Florence province contains 44 communes. To its west the province of Florence borders Prato, then juts further out to touch Pistoia and Lucca. Then it shares a longer frontier with Pisa. To its south is Siena, and Arezzo faces Florence to its east and southeast. On the northeast and north is the region of Emilia Romagna.

HISTORY. The Etruscan roots and Roman development of the city of Florence are obscure. The Roman Florentia acquired some small status as the seat of a *corrector* (provincial governor) during the age of Emperor Diocletian (284–305), but the city was insignificant and little survives of its ancient heritage beyond its street grid. Christian presence in Florence is first recorded in the third-century martyrdom of San Miniato, probably a merchant from the eastern Mediterranean. The earliest mention of a bishop, Felice, is found in accounts of a Roman synod in 313; Fiesole maintained a separate episcopal see. Florence later suffered at the hands of the barbarians but maintained some life as a Lombard *curtis regia* (fortress).

An early medieval reference to Florence dates from 825, when Emperor Lothair I, nephew of Charlemagne, decreed that a school be opened there for the education of young men intended for the priesthood. The city grew through the end of the first millennium, when Margrave Ugo of Tuscia transferred the seat of his holdings to Florence from Lucca. The town's economic strength was anchored in textile production, and by the end of the Middle Ages, Florence had become Italy's chief maker of woolen goods and the seat of a thriving silk industry transplanted from places like Calabria.

In 1115 the *popolus florentinus* (Florentines), residents of a vital trading center, achieved the beginnings of independence from the local bishop, and consuls are recorded in the city by 1138. By the 1180s guilds appeared and Florence became known as the chief Guelph stronghold in the area. In 1252 it was the first city to mint gold coins, "florins," which became one of Europe's major currencies. Florentine banks had achieved fame throughout the continent by this time, and were financing the military exploits of their victorious Guelph ally, Charles of Anjou. The Florentines eliminated their chief banking rival, Siena, at the Battle of the Colle Val d'Elsa in 1269. In 1289 the victory was repeated over an alliance of Ghibelline foes at Campaldino, a struggle in which Dante took part.

Quattrocento Florence, the city of the fifteenth century, was ruled by the Medici family, and in that era the city achieved its greatest fame. The first ruler of the Medicean "Golden Age" was Cosimo the Elder, the "Pater Patriae" (Father of His Country), who led Florence from 1434 until 1464.

He was followed by Piero (1464–1469) and then by the partnership of two brothers, Giuliano and Lorenzo "the Magnificent," beginning in 1469. The two challenged the expansionist policies of Pope Sixtus IV and became the objects of a plot that linked the Medicis' bitter rivals, the Pazzi family, with the pontiff in Rome. The "Pazzi Conspiracy" exploded on Easter Sunday, April 26, 1478, in the Duomo, where assassins fell upon Lorenzo and Giuliano, killing the latter. The wounded Lorenzo nevertheless triumphed, avenged his brother's death, and consolidated his rule, which lasted until 1492. Medici rule ended in the autumn of 1494, when King Charles VIII of France crossed into Florentine territory and took Fivizzano. Lorenzo's son, Piero, capitulated. To France he surrendered Pisa, Livorno, and frontier fortresses, and agreed to annual tributes. This enraged Florentine patriots, who expelled Piero from the city on November 9. The French king then agreed to milder terms after new negotiations with a citizens' committee.

A Grand Council was established to replace the Medici, but real power in Florence was linked to the heady rise and fall of the fundamentalist ascetic Girolamo Savonarola. The reformist Dominican monk became the dictator of Florence, and convinced or shamed wealthy Fiorentini to throw their luxury goods and untold pieces of art into the bonfire of the vanities. Savonarola's zeal earned him the enmity of many of his countrymen and of the pope. He was tortured and, on May 23, 1498, burned alive in the Piazza della Signoria.

Florence endured over three decades of struggle involving republicans; the Medici, ambitious to return to power; and foreign powers. The Medici took Florence again in 1512 and lost it in 1527. The soldiers of Emperor Charles V ultimately restored the ruling family, and Alessandro de'Medici assumed control of the city in 1531 with the ambiguous title Duke of the Florentine Republic. After his murder in 1537, Cosimo I became the Duke, and in 1569 the first Grand Duke, of Tuscany.

Battered and militarily humbled, Florence nevertheless continued its role as center of culture. The Accademia della Crusca (Bran), for instance, refined the Tuscan variant of Italian and in 1612 published the first dictionary of what would become the standard national tongue. When the academy was established in 1582 its members dubbed it the *crusca* (bran) and called themselves *crusconi* (bran flakes) as a joke. It remains Europe's oldest academy devoted to language. The most outstanding Florentine of the age in the field of learning was certainly Galileo Galilei (1564–1642), one of the first modern scientists.

Florence experienced the general decline that infected much of Italy in the sixteenth and seventeenth centuries. Medici rule ended in 1737, when Gian Gastone died without an heir and Francis Stephen of Lorraine (later Emperor Francis I) assumed control of the grand duchy. He surrendered the throne to his son Peter Leopold, who ruled from 1765 until 1790.

Under the two, Florence became a capital of the European Enlightenment through the patronage of such thinkers as Cesare Beccaria (1738–1794) and in the activities of such organizations as the Accademia dei Georgofili (Academy of the Friends of Farming).

Napoleon and the French army annexed Florence in 1799. The conqueror, himself of Tuscan descent, had visited the city in 1796 to pay his respects to his father's cousin, the canon of San Miniato.) After Napoleon, Florence enjoyed the relaxed rule of the restored Lorraine grand dukes, beginning in 1814 with Ferdinand III and continued in 1824 by his son, Leopold II. Under their benevolent administration the city's upper classes, led by such figures as Baron Bettino Ricasoli (1809–1880), embraced the principles of the Risorgimento. Such ideas were put forth in one of nineteenth-century Italy's most influential political and cultural reviews, Florence's *Antologia* (Anthology), published by Gian Pietro Vieusseux and Gino Capponi. It was issued from 1821 until 1833, when Vienna ordered the grand duke to suppress it.

Florence was quiet during the revolutions of 1821 and 1831 but exploded in 1848. A revolutionary government under Giuseppe Montanelli and Francesco Domenico Guerrazzi frightened Grand Duke Leopold, who fled at the end of January. Vienna restored him to the throne in April, and he instituted a more oppressive and vigilant regime burdened by the cost of Austrian occupation. By 1859 Baron Ricasoli had become the agent of Piedmont's prime minister and architect of the unification, Camillo Benso di Cavour. After Piedmont went to war with Austria in 1859, Leopold fled and the baron assumed the dictatorship of Tuscany, engineering its fusion with the new Italian Kingdom. From 1865 until 1871 Florence served as Italy's capital.

In the summer of 1944, after the liberation of Rome, the Germans retreated to the Apennines north of Florence. In August the city was liberated, although not before the Nazis had destroyed all of the bridges over the Arno with the exception of the Ponte Vecchio.

After the Second World War, Communist strength in Florence was challenged by a Christian Democrat, Giorgio La Pira. Elected mayor of the city in 1951, he held that office, except from 1958 through 1961, until 1964. La Pira was a Third Order Dominican who applied his Catholicism to Florence's modern problems by organizing international conferences on peace and Mediterranean civilization, and by championing the working class against private capital.

ARTS AND CULTURE. Florence ranks among the foremost centers of Italian and European culture; its artistic heritage is unsurpassed among the continent's cities. One of the earliest Florentine edifices that still survives may also be its most spendid, the Baptistery. It may date from a fifth-century construction, and was rebuilt perhaps with stones from ancient structures. It was consecrated in the eleventh century. Its distinctive green and white marble exterior (added in the twelfth century) is adorned with **Lorenzo Ghiberti**'s (Florence, c. 1378–1455) Quattrocento bronze doors. The eastern doors, which face the Duomo, are the most famous and have been dubbed the "Gates of Paradise" (the originals have been removed for safekeeping). The Baptistery's spectacular interior mosaics from the thirteenth century cause it to be ranked among the world's great buildings.

A few steps from the Baptistery is the Duomo, Santa Maria del Fiore. Florence's first cathedral was San Lorenzo, which by the end of the seventh century was transferred to the Duomo's present site, occupied in those days by the Basilica of Santa Reparata. The Fiorentini decided to construct a new church there and appointed **Arnolfo di Cambio** (Colle Val d'Elsa, c. 1245–1302) as the first architect in 1294. They assigned the bell tower to the city's official architect, **Giotto** (Giotto di Bondone, Colle di Vespignano, c. 1267/1276–1337), who undertook the task in 1334. **Nicola Pisano** (perhaps Apulian, c. 1220–1278/1284) and the Florentine artist **Francesco Talenti** (active 1325–1369) also worked on the tower until its completion in 1359. Florence's **Filippo Brunelleschi** (1377–1446) spent 16 years building the Duomo's magnificent dome. He is the only layman buried in the church. Pope Eugenius IV consecrated Santa Maria del Fiore in 1436, and Andrea di Francesco di Cione, known as **Verrocchio** (Florence, 1435–1488) placed the bronze ball and cross on top of it all. Verrocchio, a key figure in Quattrocento Florence, replaced **Donatello** (Donato de Betto di Bardi, Florence, c. 1386–1466) as the principal artist of the Medici court and taught Leonardo Da Vinci.

Other important early structures include the Basilica of San Miniato al Monte, built between the eleventh and thirteenth centuries on a hill across the Arno. It was built by the Clunaic order above an earlier shrine that honored the martyr who helped to bring Christianity to Roman Florence. The Olivetan order took over San Miniato in 1373. The superb Santa Maria Novella, a Dominican church built between 1246 and 1360, is considered Tuscany's masterpiece of the Gothic style and contains works by many of the city's chief artists, including Brunelleschi, **Domenico Ghirlandaio** (1449–1494), Giotto, and **Masaccio** (1401–1428/1429). The church also boasts a literary significance; in the *Decameron* it is the place where Boccaccio's characters gathered before they fled plague-ridden Florence. Santa Maria Novella is also familiar to many Italians and tourists in Italy because the central Florence train station, across the piazza directly behind the church, bears its name. The station was constructed in the 1930s by a Florentine group of architects led by **Giovanni Michelucci** (Pistoia, 1891–1991).

The Dominican church and monastery of San Marco has been called the heart of Renaissance Florence. A thirteenth-century complex renovated by **Michelozzo di Bartolommeo** (Florence, 1396–1472), its monastic cells were home to Savonarola and to **Fra Angelico** (1395–1455), who decorated 44 of these meager rooms with magnificent frescoes. Many of Italy's leading artistic figures are buried or honored in Florence's Pantheon, the Franciscan Basilica of Santa Croce. Reconstructed from an earlier edifice, the late thirteenth-century building may be the work of Arnolfo di Cambio. From Giotto to Brunelleschi to Donatello, the church, its tombs, and its monuments represent the labors of most of Florence's greatest artists of the Renaissance. The tomb of Michelangelo, for instance, is the work of **Giorgio Vasari** (1511–1574), a native of Arezzo.

Fifteenth-century Florence, the Florence of the Medici and center of the Renaissance, was the most dynamic spot on Europe's cultural map. Santa Maria del Carmine, on the other side of the Arno, holds a special significance in this period. Most of the austere church, established in the thirteenth century, was rebuilt after a fire in the eighteenth century. Only the exquisite fifteenth-century Brancacci Chapel and its frescoes survived the flames. Begun in 1424 by **Masolino** (1383–c. 1440/1447), the frescoes were continued by his student Masaccio. Masaccio, however, left them unfinished, and about 60 years passed before their completion by **Filippino Lippi** (Prato, 1457–1504). The frescoes mainly depict the stories of Adam and Eve and of Saint Peter, and broke ground for much of the Renaissance art that followed. Masolino and Masaccio were followed by other artists: Ghirlandaio, famous for his series of frescoes on Saint John the Baptist in Santa Maria Novella; **Sandro Botticelli** (Alessandro di Mariano Filipepi, Florence, 1445–1510), **Leonardo Da Vinci** (from Vinci, in the province of Florence, 1452–1519), and **Michelangelo Buonarroti** (Caprese [Arezzo], 1475–1564). All of them worked in Florence, often for the Medici.

Leonardo was a student of Verrocchio. A polymath in all artistic categories as well as science and mathematics, he may be the best-known artist in history. He lived in Milan from about 1481 until 1499, returned to Florence until 1503, then left again in 1506, ultimately for France. Botticelli replaced Leonardo as Florence's chief painter when the latter left the city. A student of Fra Filippo Lippi, his humanistic fascination with the ancients led to his groundbreaking and breathtaking paintings with mythological themes, *Primavera* (Spring, c. 1476/1478) and the *Birth of Venus* (1486). Michelangelo, the last of the great Renaissance artists, studied at Ghirlandaio's workshop before he left Florence for the first time in 1494. He returned frequently, living in the city from 1520 to 1534, when he moved to Rome for good.

Of the chief secular buildings in late medieval and Renaissance Florence, the most important is the Palazzo della Signoria, the seat of the government and now referred to as the Palazzo Vecchio. It was begun in 1299 by Arnolfo di Cambio and restored in the 1540s by Giorgio Vasari. Between 1865 and the 1871 transfer of the national government from Florence to Rome, the palace housed Italy's Chamber of Deputies.

Many of Florence's family palaces are also noteworthy. Cosimo the Elder commissioned Michelozzo di Bartolommeo to build the Medici-Riccardi Palace in 1444. The Medici lived there until they moved into the Palazzo Vecchio in 1540. The Medici-Riccardi is a chief example of the Renaissance style and now houses part of the city's prefectural administration. The chapel of the palace contains **Benozzo Gozzoli**'s (Florence, 1420–1497) wonderful *Corteo dei Magi* (1459–1460). Intended to portray the three Wise Men on their way to Bethlehem, the fresco more realistically depicts a Medici hunting party in the Tuscan hills. Other important palaces are the Palazzo Strozzi; the Palazzo Rucellai, which was built on a design of **Leon Battista Alberti** (Genoa, 1404–1472); and the gigantic Palazzo Pitti. The Pitti was purchased by the Medici in 1549. Between 1865 and 1871, when Florence was Italy's capital, it served as the residence of the royal family.

Despite the political convulsions that began in the 1490s, Florentine creativity continued through the sixteenth century. Among the masterpieces of the late Renaissance are Michelangelo's additions to the Church of San Lorenzo: the Laurenziana (Laurentian) Library and the Medici Chapels. The ancient San Lorenzo had been rebuilt in the fifteenth century by Brunelleschi and his pupil, **Antonio Manetti** (Florence, 1423–1497). In the sixteenth century the Medici popes, Leo X and Clement VII, commissioned Michelangelo to build the library and the chapels, which were intended as tombs. Two Medici dukes, Lorenzo II of Urbino and Giuliano of Nemours, are entombed in Michelangelo's masterpieces, which have immortalized them far more than did any of their own accomplishments in life. Another of Florence's chief sixteenth-century projects was Giorgio Vasari's construction of the Palazzo degli Uffizi, begun in 1560 as the offices of the Medici administration. To shelter the Medici on their way to work, an enclosed walkway linked the Uffizi with the Palazzo Pitti, via the Ponte Vecchio over the Arno. Today the palace no longer houses the Medici bureaucracy but, rather, the art museum that bears its name.

Late medieval and Renaissance Florence was home to a literary flowering that began in earnest with its native son **Dante Alighieri** (1265–1321). He began as a lyric poet but turned to the canzone after the death of his love, Beatrice Portinari, in 1290. Dante was influenced by **Guittone d'Arezzo** (c. 1235–1294) and the earlier Florentine poet **Guido Cavalcanti** (c. 1255–1300). Dante's *Vita Nuova* (New Life, 1293) was a collection of 31 poems dedicated to Beatrice. As a Guelph, Dante was tried and banished from Florence, and his property was confiscated after a Ghibelline administration took control of the city in 1301. He subsequently wandered across northern Italy. During his travels he wrote other important works: the *Convivio* (The Banquet, begun 1304), a discussion of philosophy; *De vulgari Eloquentia* (Eloquence in the Vernacular Tongue, begun 1304), on the Italian language; and, especially, *The Divine Comedy*, which he began in 1307. In 1318 Dante found his last home in Ravenna, where he died and is buried.

Another key figure in the early period was **Giovanni Boccaccio** (1313–1375), who was born in Paris to a Florentine merchant and his French wife. He was brought to Florence as a small child, and grew up there and in Naples, where he began to write, particularly of his love for Fiammetta. **Petrarch** (1303–1374) befriended Boccaccio and aroused his interest in the classics. Boccaccio wrote some commentaries on Latin works. But it is for his irreverent *Decameron* that Boccaccio is best remembered. Written about 1350, during the period of the Black Death, his "human comedy" ridicules pomposity and authority in late medieval Italy.

Most of Renaissance Italy's leading men of arts and letters spent some time, often a long time, in Florence and participated in the intellectual hothouse that the Medici built. Platonic thought, popularized by Petrarch in the fourteenth century, became enshrined in Florence by the work of Marsilio Ficino, Poliziano, and Giovanni Pico della Mirandola, who worked in the court of Lorenzo "the Magnificent." Born at Figline in the Valdarno, **Marsilio Ficino** (1433–1499) studied Plato. First under Cosimo, and later under Piero and Lorenzo Medici, Ficino became the glue in a union of scholars that became known as the Platonic Academy. His translations of and commentaries on Plato led to his own masterpiece, *Theologia Platonica* (Platonic Theology, 1482), on the immortality of the soul, and to his taking of Catholic orders in 1473.

Angelo Poliziano (1454–1494) was born Angelo Ambrogini in Montepulciano and took his nom de plume from his home town. One of the era's greatest humanists, he was a professor of Latin and Greek at the University of Florence and served as tutor to the sons of Lorenzo "the Magnificent." His poetry, particularly the *Stanze* (Stanzas, 1475–1478), had a great impact on subsequent Italian compositions. Poliziano fell from favor in 1479 and left for Mantua, where, the next year, he premiered Italy's first significant profane play, *Favola d'Orfeo* (The Tale of Orpheus).

Some have written that **Giovanni Pico della Mirandola** (1463–1494) was the most brilliant of the lot. A figure of broad intellect and learning, he came from a noble family in Emilia. He is best remembered for his *Oration on the Dignity of Man.*

Another literary figure of Renaissance Florence was **Niccolò Machiavelli** (1469–1527). A state functionary and ambassador, and a humanist scholar, Machiavelli was banished from his city during the convulsions of the early sixteenth century. His *Discourses* (1513–1517) were reflections on the state which posit the republic as the ideal government. Machiavelli is best remembered, however, for his shorter work, *The Prince* (1513), a guide for rulers and a call for the unity of Italy.

Francesco Guicciardini (1483–1540), another literary diplomat from Florence, wrote a *History of Italy* (published 1561–1564) and commentaries on Machiavelli and politics.

Perhaps because of the overwhelming impact of the Renaissance on Florence, the city's Baroque accomplishments are somewhat overshadowed. Its most noteworthy achievement may be the enormous and ornate Chapel of the Princes in the church of San Lorenzo. Intended as a sacristy for the church and a tomb for the Medici grand dukes, the chapel was the collaboration of many artists, beginning with **Matteo Nigetti** (1560–1649). It is inevitably and perhaps unfairly compared to Michelangelo's Medici tombs, although the Chapel of the Princes can, in a quirky way, stand on its own. The Baroque era also saw the birth of opera. Arguably Italy's first one was performed in Florence, where *Dafne* premiered in 1594. Its composer, **Jacopo Peri** (1561–1633), and librettist, **Ottavio Rinuccini** (1562–1621), staged the more ambitious *Euridice* at the Pitti Palace in 1600.

Napoleon's rule benefited Florentine art. Grand Duchess Maria Anna, called Elisa, promoted the work of the Accademia delle Belle Arti (Academy of Fine Arts), the Liceo Regio (Royal Secondary School), the Accademia della Crusca (Academy of Bran), and the Goldoni Theater. She also devoted herself to the renovation of her residence, the Palazzo Pitti. Napoleon's sister, Pauline, married the Roman Prince Camillo Borghese and lived in Florence for much of her life. She achieved immortality when she posed as Venus for **Antonio Canova**'s (1757–1822) celebrated statue. Two of Napoleon's brothers, Lucien and Joseph, retired to Florence; and his nephew lived there before becoming Emperor Napoleon III of France. Another relative, his niece Carolina, maintained one of Florence's most popular salons at the Palazzo Ognissanti until her death in 1839.

Modern Florence continued its tradition of artistic accomplishment. It was the home of the *macchiaioli* school of painters in the late nineteenth century. A Florentine critic dubbed the group, influenced by French schools and figures such as Camille Corot and Edgar Degas, *macchiaioli* after *macchia*, the Italian word for "spot," because of their pointillistic method. These artists who gathered at Florence's Caffè Michelangelo—figures such as the Florentine **Telemaco Signorini** (1835–1901), the Livornese **Giovanni Fattori** (1825–1908), the Neapolitan **Giuseppe Abbati** (1836–1868), and the Ferrarese **Giovanni Boldini** (1842–1931)—were led by the art critic **Diego Martelli** (Florence, 1839–1896).

At the same time Florence produced a number of important literary and political reviews. By the beginning of the twentieth century **Giuseppe Prezzolini**'s *La Voce* (The Voice, 1908), a renegade nationalist cultural organ that brought together leading figures of the Italian literary scene. Some of its contributors, particularly the Tuscans **Giovanni Papini** (Florence, 1881–1956) and **Ardegno Soffici** (Rignano sull'Arno, 1879–1964), left to found the Futurist *Lacerba* in 1913. **Enrico Corradini** (1865–1931) founded the nationalist *Il Regno* (The Kingdom) in 1903. A native of San Miniatello, near Florence, Corradini led the Italian Nationalist Association, which, as a party, allied itself to the Fascists. Another significant participant in this literary whirl was **Aldo Palazzeschi,** who was born Aldo Giurlani at Florence in 1885. Following a brief career in the theater, Palazzeschi produced an enormous and eclectic body of prose and poetry until his death in 1974. His first important novel, and perhaps his greatest work, was the revolutionary and imaginative *Il Codice di Perelà* (1911, translated as *The Man of Smoke*). The book attracted the attention of the Futurists; Palazzeschi flirted with that group but moved on to other experiences and cannot be considered part of any one movement.

After the Second World War, **Piero Calamandrei**'s *Il Ponte* (The Bridge) became one of Italy's most respected journals of public debate. Calamandrei (1889–1956) was one of the nation's principal jurists as well as the rector of the University of Florence.

The novelist **Vasco Pratolini** (1913–1991) was born in Florence. Although he worked under the Fascists, Pratolini joined the Resistance in 1943. After the war, he published a number of important neorealist novels, beginning with *Il quartiere* (A Tale of Santa Croce, 1945) and including *Cronaca Familiare* (Family Chronicle) and *Cronache di poveri amanti* (Tale of Poor Lovers) (both 1947). One of Italy's leading feminist writers, **Dacia Maraini** (b. 1936) was born in Florence. She lived in Japan as a child, part of the time in a prison camp during World War Two, and later in Rome. Her most significant works include *Donna in Guerra* (A Woman in War, 1975) and *La Lunga vita di Marianna Ucrià* (The Long Life of Marianna Ucrià, 1990). Florence was also the birthplace of the writer **Anna Banti** (1895–1985). She, too, examined the condition of women in society. *Artemisia*, her work of greatest renown, is a historical novel dealing with the life of the seventeenth-century Roman painter Artemisia Gentileschi, whose work *Judith Beheading Holofernes* (c. 1618) hangs in the Palazzo Pitti.

Florence's musical heritage includes the lyric composer **Antonio Sacchini** (1730–1786), whose greatest work, *Oedipe* (Oedipus, 1786), premiered in Paris. Another Florentine who moved to Paris was **Luigi Cherubini** (1760–1842). There, he established his reputation with such works as the powerful opera *Medea* (1797), and his Requiem in C minor (1816). The composer **Mario Castelnuovo-Tedesco** was born in Florence in 1895. He is remembered for his works for guitar and songs for the plays of William Shakespeare. Mussolini's anti-Semitic legislation forced Castelnuovo Tedesco to flee Italy in 1939. He moved to Los Angeles, California, and died there in 1968.

One of Italy's most popular entertainers, **Carlo Buti** (1902–1963), was a Florentine. He was famous in the 1930s and 1940s for his sweet renditions of songs on the radio and on stage. The **Taviani** brothers, **Paolo** (b. 1931) and **Emilio** (b. 1929) were born in San Miniato. Now known as directors, they began their careers in the theater and moved into films by the 1960s. The film director **Franco Zeffirelli** (b. 1923) was born in Florence. Through his treatments of William Shakespeare, Zeffirelli acquired an international status in film as well as on the legitimate and lyric stages.

A list of Florentine museums is almost endless. Among the most important are the Uffizi Gallery, the Bargello, the Pitti Palace, and the Accademia. Some have termed the Uffizi Gallery Italy's most important art museum, and it certainly must be placed in the elite first rank. The collection of early Renaissance masters and the hall dedicated to the works of Botticelli are incomparable. The fortress-like Bargello was Florence's Palazzo del Podestà and, later, police headquarters before it became famous for its collection of sculpture. Works of Donatello, Michelangelo, Giambologna and Benvenuto Cellini (Florence, 1500–1571) are featured. The Pitti Palace's Palatine Gallery contains an extraordinary collection of Tuscan, north Italian, Roman, and Neapolitan paintings from the fifteenth to the eighteenth centuries. The *Accademia* holds an exceptional collection of Renaissance works and is best known as the home of Michelangelo's enormous statue of David.

Florence hosts a number of festivals throughout the year. Its soccer (*calcio*) match, a medieval variant of the game, is played every June near the Basilica of Santa Croce. Another tradition is the explosion of the *carro* on Easter Sunday. The *carro*, a replica of the medieval cart which served as a symbol of the city during battle, is filled with fireworks and exploded in front of the Duomo. Florence's *Maggio Musicale* (Musical May) is a major international music festival with performances occurring throughout the city. Among the city's most treasured holidays is the feast of its patron, Saint John the Baptist. Florence hosts an international antiques fair every autumn.

OTHER CENTERS. The place in history of Florence's older neighbor, **Fiesole**, has been guaranteed by an exceptional Etruscan and Roman archaeological zone, its Cathedral of San Romolo, and the remarkable abbey, the Badia Fiesolana. An old Etruscan town situated on a high point above Florence and the Arno valley, Fiesole survived Roman conquest and the barbarian invasions until its younger neighbor in the valley captured it in 1125 and relegated it to a lesser status. The archaeological zone includes a first-century B.C. Roman temple, baths restored by Emperor Hadrian, and a theater that hosts an annual drama festival in July. The eleventh-century cathedral was enlarged in the thirteenth and fourteenth centuries. It contains work of the artist Mino da Fiesole (1430–c. 1484) who was born not in Fiesole but in Poppi. The site of the Badia served as Fiesole's cathedral until 1028, and Cosimo the Elder rebuilt the complex in the Quattrocento. In 1976 it became the seat of the European University Institute. The ancient art of bundling and working with straw is celebrated every October 4 in Fiesole's Feast of Saint Francis.

Outside of Florence is **Rifredi**. Now an industrial suburb, it is still home to the Medici villa of Careggi. The family acquired the place in 1417 and

Cosimo the Elder later commissioned Michelozzo di Bartolommeo to en-
large it. The villa was home to the group of Platonic scholars that Marsilio
Ficino led, and Lorenzo "the Magnificent" died there in 1492. Nearby are
two other impressive Medici estates, the Petraia and the Castello, which
was also the country residence of the Lorraine and is today the home of
the Accademia della Crusca.

At the western end of Florence province is **Empoli,** a city with an ancient
glassmaking industry. The roots of its collegiate church reach back to the
fifth century. It retains its medieval facade, but the interior was renovated
in the eighteenth century. The church museum contains an important Renaissance collection in which Fra Filippo Lippi and Tino da Camaino,
among others, are represented. Empoli was the birthplace of the painters
Jacopo Carrucci, known as Pontormo (1494–1557), and Jacopo Chimenti,
known as Empoli (1554–c. 1640). The composer and performer Ferruccio
Busoni (1866–1924) also was born in Empoli. At the age of ten he moved
to Austria, and in 1894 to Berlin, where he spent the rest of his life.

AREZZO

PROVINCIAL PROFILE. Area: 1,248 sq. mi. Population: 318,881 (province), 90,884 (city). Arezzo contains 39 communes. Arezzo faces Florence
on its northwest and Siena on its southwest. The regions of Emilia Romagna, Marche, and Umbria curve around Arezzo from its north to its
southeast. The Casentino and Pratomagno ranges occupy much of the
northern half of the province; the hills open somewhat in the south to the
more fertile Chiana and Tiber valleys.

HISTORY. Historians believe Arezzo, built on an Apennine slope, to
have been one of the twelve major urban centers of the Etruscan world.
Known as Arretium, in the fourth century the Etruscans circled it with a
wall. Later it became a Roman fortress and repelled an invasion by the
Gauls in 294 B.C. Livy recorded Arezzo's aid to Rome during the Punic
Wars (264–146 B.C.). Arezzo prospered and expanded downhill through
the Roman period. Although it almost disappeared after the barbarian invasions of the 400s, Lombard and other documents occasionally refer to
Arezzo's bishops. It clearly resurfaced as a city toward the end of the eleventh century, despite being hemmed in between the two Tuscan powers,
Florence and Siena. Consequently, Arezzo swung back and forth between
the Guelph and Ghibelline camps. Florence held Arezzo for a few years
after winning the Battle of Campaldino (1289), then lost it until, in 1384,
through legal and diplomatic maneuvers, it annexed Arezzo once and for
all. Despite rebellions in 1409 and 1529, and brief interludes of foreign
dominion (such as Napoleon's conquest), Florence ruled Arezzo until the
Risorgimento of 1859. A fortress, the Fortezza Medicea, ordered by Co-

simo I de'Medici in 1538, and much of a network of defensive walls remain as testimony to Florentine domination.

Arezzo entered the industrial age in the late nineteenth century with some ironworking concerns, wool mills, and, in 1907, a large factory (the Fabbricone) for railroad cars and other iron-based products, located south of the medieval neighborhood. Limited development, fortunately, did not ruin the quality of the city; the bombs of the Second World War did more to damage Arezzo. The province has benefited from new electronic technologies and has developed a reputation as an Italian Silicon Valley.

ARTS AND CULTURE. Beneath the few remains of the Fortezza Medicea, built by the Florentine artists **Antonio** (1483–1546) and **Giuliano Sangallo** (or Giamberti, c. 1445–1516), and razed in 1800, Arezzo spreads down the lower slopes of the hills somewhat ambitiously called the Poti Alps. One of Tuscany's finest examples of the Romanesque is Arezzo's oldest church, the Pieve di Santa Maria Assunta. Started in 1140 above an older building, its beautiful facade recalls works in Pisa and Lucca. Inside is a remarkable polyptych, the work of the Sienese artist **Pietro Lorenzetti** (c. 1280–c. 1348). It was commissioned by Bishop Guido Tarlati, who reestablished his city after its defeat at Campaldino in 1289. Work commenced on the city's Cathedral of San Donato in the thirteenth century and continued into the twentieth. It contains a monument to Bishop Tarlati. Donato, Arezzo's patron saint and bishop in the 360s, was martyred during the persecutions of Julian the Apostate.

Arezzo's Church of San Domenico was designed by **Nicola Pisano** (c. 1220–1278/1284) and houses the *Crucifixion* by the young **Cimabue** (c. 1240–c. 1302). Completed in 1275, the work influenced many other Italian *Crucifixions* that followed. Magnificent Renaissance frescoes by Sansepolcro's **Piero della Francesca** (c. 1420–1492), depicting the *Legend of the True Cross*, are preserved in the Basilica of San Francesco, a Franciscan church started in the late thirteenth century by Fra **Giovanni da Pistoia**. The basilica also contains works of **Spinello Spinelli** (active 1373–1410), known as Spinello Aretino after his birthplace. Arezzo boasts the Mecenate Archaeological Museum in the restored San Bernardo convent. A museum devoted to medieval and Renaissance art is housed in the fifteenth-century Palazzo Bruni-Ciocchi, also known as the Dogana.

Two houses in Arezzo hold particular cultural and historical significance, those of Petrarch and of Giorgio Vasari. **Petrarch** (Francesco Petrarca, 1304–1374) was born at Arezzo. He considered his works in Latin to be his most important, and he was among the founders of Renaissance humanism. But it is for his love poetry and his deeply personal musings, composed in Italian, that he is most remembered today. Petrarch was only nine years old when he left Arezzo; the house believed to have been his was reconstructed in 1948. (This is a question open to some debate.) The edifice is devoted to him and, along with a museum, houses an institute and library of Petrarch studies. The house of **Giorgio Vasari** (1511–1574) is a museum of social history as well as one that recalls the life of the artist.

Arezzo (or its adjacent territory) was the birthplace of the poet **Guittone d'Arezzo** (c. 1235–1294), who has been called the first significant Tuscan poet. His many love poems were influenced by Provencal styles. Later in life his work became more religious and he joined the knights of the Order of the Virgin Mary. The humanist scholar **Leonardo Bruni** (c. 1370–1444) was born in Arezzo but spent most of his life in Florence. He translated Aristotle from Greek into Latin and wrote a commentary on the Florentine constitution.

Arezzo was the birthplace of **Pietro Aretino** (1492–1556), who became one of the most popular writers of his day through his lewd and scandalous letters, lyrics, sonnets, plays, and other works. He spent much of his early life in Rome, and a Church official hired an assassin to kill him. Stabbed and left for dead, Aretino recovered, only to suffer another beating from agents of the English embassy to Venice, where he relocated in c. 1526. Titian immortalized Aretino in one of the most famous Renaissance portraits.

Music notation was invented in large measure by the Benedictine monk **Guido of Arezzo** (c. 991–after 1050). Guido was not a native of the city but was called there by Bishop Theodaldus to teach singers. His *Micrologus* was perhaps the most seminal work on music ever written.

Arezzo hosts two annual medieval spectacles, the "Saracen Jousts" (*giostre del Saracino*), which occur on the third Sunday in June and the first Sunday in September.

OTHER CENTERS. Near Arezzo in the higher Apennines is **Camaldoli,** the home of the Camaldolese monks. Camaldoli fostered a tradition of learning, and during the Renaissance it was the site of a humanistic academy associated with Leon Battista Alberti and under Medici patronage. During the Second World War, many leaders of the nascent Christian Democratic Party met at Camaldoli to devise one of their most important manifestos, the Camaldoli Code. The monastery subsequently came to be a major conference center for the party.

One of Italy's key Christian Democratic leaders, Amintore Fanfani (1908–1999), was born in **Pieve Santo Stefano**. A moderate leftist, Fanfani became prime minister for the first time in 1954, and the same year took charge as secretary-general of the party. He was instrumental in the 1962 "Opening to the Left" that brought the Socialist Party into the ruling coalition. In 1965 Fanfani served as president of the United Nations General Assembly. He occupied the prime minister's chair for the last time in 1987.

In the commune of **Chiusi della Verna** in the Casentino is an impressive Franciscan monastery, La Verna. In 1213 a local count presented the place to Saint Francis, and he lived there with some of his followers. At La Verna, Francis received the stigmata in 1224. The monastery is an important pilgrimage site, decorated with terra-cotta works by the Florentine Andrea della Robbia (1435–1525).

Sansepolcro is one of best-preserved towns in the province. It dates from an oratory and a Camaldolese monastery built there in the tenth and eleventh centuries. Sansepolcro's cathedral was built by the monks. The city was the home of the major Renaissance artist Piero della Francesca (c. 1420–1492). His interest in philosophy and mathematics aided his mastery of perspective in painting, particularly his masterpiece, *The Flagellation of Christ* (c. 1455). Piero lived in Sansepolcro, learning his craft, until about 1448, when he moved to Florence. Sansepolcro's civic museum, in the fourteenth-century Palazzo Comunale, contains Piero's first major work, the Misericordia Altarpiece, as well as his great *Resurrection* (1463). Works by Cortona's Luca Signorelli (1445/1450–1523), and Empoli's Pontormo (Jacopo Carrucci, 1494–1557) are also housed in the museum.

Near Sansepolcro is **Anghiari**, a well-preserved medieval fortress-town in the Tiber valley. It was recorded first as Castrum Angolare in the eleventh century, and the Florentines scored an important victory there over the Visconti in 1440. Its Palazzo Taglieschi houses a state museum of "popular traditions of the upper Tiber valley" and an art collection that includes works by Florence's Andrea della Robbia, Siena's Tino da Camaino, and others.

GROSSETO

PROVINCIAL PROFILE. Area: 1,736 sq. mi. Population: 216,207 (province), 72,161 (city). The province contains 28 communes. Along Grosseto's western border is the Tyrrhenian Sea. Three provinces are to the northwest: Livorno, Pisa, and Siena, the last of which extends across Grosseto's northeast and eastern border. The region of Lazio shares Grosseto's southeast frontier. The province's most important rivers are the Albegna and the Ombrone, both of which empty into the Tyrrhenian Sea. At its southern end, along the shore, Monte Argentario juts into the sea and would be an island were it not for two thin slices of land that connect it to the mainland. Offshore are a few islands, particularly Giglio and Montecristo. These are included in the Tuscan Archipelago National Park. Most of the low-lying Maremma coastal zone is in Grosseto province. It starts at the south of the province of Livorno, then extends down the coast past the city of Grosseto and on to Monte Argentario. Whether or not the Maremma proper continues over the border of Lazio is a matter of some dispute.

HISTORY. For centuries Grosseto and the Maremma were distinct from what is now the eastern part of the province. On the coast, the Roman settlement at Cosa (today Ansedonia) has been dated from 273 B.C. According to Livy, however, the Romans conquered the Etruscan settlement of Roselle in 294, and Cosa is thought to have replaced an earlier Etruscan site. Under the Romans the Maremma was a well-settled and productive farmland which was drained through subterranean canals. By the Middle Ages, however, the area had suffered a decline and the marshes had reconquered the zone. Tenth-century records reveal the origins of the city of Grosseto as a castle on the old Roman Maremannan Way, and the modest town was probably closer to the sea than it is now, the victim of silting at the mouth of the Ombrone River.

After a devastating war that cost the lives of a quarter of its 4,000 inhabitants, Grosseto fell to Siena in 1336. Its population continued to decline, chiefly from malaria, until the Florentines annexed it in the sixteenth century. Grosseto's fortunes rose under the Medici grand dukes, particularly Ferdinand I (1587–1609), who reclaimed some of the surrounding Maremma marshland and constructed important fortifications in the city. In the eighteenth century Peter Leopold (1765–1790) extended the reclamations, which, after the fall of Napoleon, continued under Vittorio Fossombroni (1754–1844), the most capable of the grand duke's ministers. The work continued into the twentieth century with the creation in 1951 of the Agency for the Settlement of the Tuscan-Latium Maremma (Ente per la Colonizzazione della Maremma Tosco-Laziale). Along with measures for the economic development of the marshland, Tuscany had the foresight to preserve some of it as a regional park in 1975.

ARTS AND CULTURE. Pisan architectural influence is clear in construction of the twelfth and thirteenth centuries throughout the province, particularly in Grosseto's Cathedral of San Lorenzo, a work of the little-known artist **Sozzo di Rustichino** (active 1294–1302). Its facade and parts of the interior were rebuilt in the 1840s, to the dismay of art historians. Grosseto's archaeological museum contains a significant collection of Etruscan objects taken from nearby excavations.

OTHER CENTERS. The upland parts of Grosseto province experienced histories different from the lowlands. To the south and southeast, Roman aristocratic families such as the Orsini and the Aldobrandeschi maintained a strong influence. The area around Monte Amiata to the east also developed more or less independently of the coastal zone. Northeast of Grosseto is another city of importance, **Massa Marittima**, a medieval town of substance which was the center of a thriving mining district; hence its old name, Massa Metallorum. Under its prince-bishop, Alberto, the town devised Europe's first mining codes in 1225. Massa Marittima fell under the Sienesi, who constructed a fortress in the fourteenth century and then, in 1555, to the Florentines. Massa Marittima is one of Grosseto's chief cities of art and has a noteworthy archaeological museum and municipal gallery, both in the thirteenth-century Palazzo Pretorio. It is thought to be the birthplace of Saint Bernardino of Siena (1380–1444) and boasts an important thirteenth-century cathedral which is dedicated to a sixth-century saint of north African origin, Cerbone, the patron of the city. The area's only medieval poet of note, Ugo da Massa, came from Massa Marittima.

The Etruscan presence is still visible at necropolises in **Rusellae** and **Vetulonia**. **Ansedonia** is the site of ancient Cosa, founded in 273 B.C. and maintained as an important port until the fourth century A.D. Extensive Roman ruins are still found there, including a forum, an acropolis, and a Capitolium, a type of temple devoted to Rome's principal gods. Also notable is the *tagliata etrusca*, a channel that the Romans cut through rock to protect the harbor from silt. A good archaeological museum, the Antiquarium di Ansedonia, contains relics unearthed at the excavation sites.

LIVORNO

PROVINCIAL PROFILE. Area: 471 sq. mi. Population: 335,555 (province), 163,950 (city). Livorno province contains 20 communes. Livorno is a long coastal province which runs alongside Pisa on its north and east until it reaches Grosseto toward its southeastern end. The Tyrrhenian Sea washes Livorno's western and southern shores. A few islands, notably Elba, Capraia, and Pianosa, belong to the province and are protected in the Tuscan Archipelago National Park.

HISTORY. Livorno was a fishing village called Livorna or Liberna when Countess Matilda of Tuscany presented it to the Church in Pisa (1103). It developed as a port but remained in Pisa's shadow during the Middle Ages. Livorno acquired greater status after the mouth of the Arno silted up and stranded its rival inland. In 1399 the Pisans sold Livorno to the Visconti family, which in turn sold it to the Genoese in 1407. Fourteen years later those overlords sold Livorno to the Florentines, who, with few interruptions, held it until the Risorgimento and union with the Kingdom of Italy. Grand Duke Cosimo I ordered the construction of modern port facilities in 1571. Livorno was subsequently declared a free port, and by the eighteenth century it had become the second city of the Grand Duchy of Tuscany.

Although Livorno declined after its free port status ended in 1868, its success as a trade and shipping center caught the attention of the Anglo-American forces in the Second World War, and the city suffered heavy bombardments in 1943 and 1944. Admiral Costanzo Ciano (1876–1939) of Livorno was among Benito Mussolini's chief collaborators. The Duce designated Ciano as his successor, but natural causes cut short the admiral's life before unnatural ones ended Mussolini's. Galeazzo Ciano (1903–1944), son of Costanzo, continued the collaboration and married Mussolini's daughter, Edda. This may have had something to do with his appointment as Italy's foreign minister in 1936. However, Ciano voted against his father-in-law during the crucial Fascist Grand Council meeting that deposed the dictator in July 1943. After the Germans rescued the imprisoned Mussolini and established him as head of the collaborationist Salò regime, the Duce ordered Ciano's execution by firing squad. Today one of Italy's naval academies is located in Livorno, and the city is the Mediterranean's largest container port.

Italy's current president, Carlo Azeglio Ciampi (b. 1920) was born in Livorno. Ciampi spent most of his career in the economic sector. He was governor of the Bank of Italy from 1979 until 1993 and served as prime minister in 1993 and 1994. He succeeded Oscar Scalfaro as President of Italy on May 13, 1999.

ARTS AND CULTURE. Livorno's most noteworthy historical monuments are two fortresses, the *fortezza vecchia* (old fortress) and the *fortezza nuova* (new fortress). The more significant *vecchia* was built in 1534 by **Antonio da Sangallo the Younger** (Florence, 1483–1546). It contains a tower, the Mastio di Matilde, that was part of the eleventh-century Pisan fort. Allied bombs destroyed Livorno's Cathedral of San Francesco in 1943, but the structure, first built in 1606 by the Florentine **Alessandro Pieroni** (1550–c. 1607), was totally reconstructed after the war. Livorno's patron saint is Giulia of Corsica, who, according to tradition, was a Carthaginian Christian enslaved by pagans and martyred. Near the old docks (the *darsena*) is the "Monument of the Four Moors" (*Monumento dei Quattro Mori*). Completed by **Giovanni Bandini** (Florence, 1540–c. 1598), the work honors Grand Duke Ferdinand I, who established Livorno as a free port. Frequently considered the city's symbol, the four bronze moors at its base were added in 1624 (or 1626) by **Pietro Tacca** (Carrara, 1577–1640) to commemorate Ferdinand's success in routing North African pirates.

The opera librettist **Raniero Calzabigi** (1714–1795) came from Livorno. He is most remembered for his work in Vienna with Christoph von Gluck, for whom he wrote the libretto for **Orfeo ed Euridice** (Orpheus and Eurydice, 1762). Calzabigi returned to Italy in 1773 and collaborated with Giovanni Paisiello. **Pietro Mascagni** (1863–1945), an opera composer of the *verismo* (realist) school also was born in Livorno. His greatest work is the one-act *Cavalleria Rusticana* (Rustic Chivalry). Based on a story of Sicilian peasants by Giovanni Verga, Mascagni's work premiered in Rome in 1890. The artist **Amedeo Modigliani** (1884–1920) was born to a Livornese Jewish family. After four years of study in Florence, he relocated in 1906 to Paris, where he befriended Pablo Picasso and other avant-garde figures. He is best remembered for his portraits and busts, often in a distinctive elongated style. Livorno was also the birthplace of the poet **Gino Caproni** (1912–1990).

OTHER CENTERS. The island of **Elba** is part of the province of Livorno. Its chief town is **Portoferraio**, the Roman Fabricia, which was sacked and destroyed by Saracen raiders in the eighth century. The Pisans built a fortress on the island at **Volterraio**, but the Florentines later chose to fortify Portoferraio instead, and made it the anchorage of the Tuscan fleet in 1751. From May 1814 until February 1815, Napoleon was exiled to Elba. He occupied a small house in Portoferraio and a larger summer place, the Villa di San Martino. On the coast opposite Elba is the port of **Piombino,** one of the centers of Italy's iron and steel production. It is also the site of the ancient Etruscan town of Populonia and boasts a very early necropolis.

LUCCA

PROVINCIAL PROFILE. Area: 684 sq. mi. Population: 375,496 (province), 85,717 (city). The province contains 35 communes. Much of the northern part of the territory embraces the Garfagnana, which in 1859 was joined to the province of Massa-Carrara until its union with Lucca in 1923. Now, Massa-Carrara and the shore of the Ligurian Sea are to Lucca's west, Pistoia is to its east, and the region of Emilia Romagna is to its north. Lucca shares its southern border with Pisa and, briefly, Florence. The Serchio River cuts through most of the province. From the top of the Garfagnana it runs to the city of Lucca and proceeds into Pisa province for a short distance until it flows into the sea.

HISTORY. On the banks of the Serchio River, the Liguri settled Lucca, a name that derives from *luk*, their term for a marshy place. Rome entered the area in the second century B.C., and although Lucca gained some importance as a regional and transportation center and, in the late Roman Empire, an episcopal see, it lived in the shadow of its larger neighbors, Pisa and Luni. It was taken by the Goths, Byzantines, and Lombards; then, in the ninth and tenth centuries, Lucca served as the capital of the Marquisate of Tuscany. The ducal palace outside of the city walls was said to have been the envy of Emperor Louis III (901–905). However, Florence, its more powerful neighbor to the east, overshadowed the town in the late tenth century when the Counts of Canossa absorbed Tuscany and moved their capital to Florence from Lucca. In the late Middle Ages, Lucca emerged as a major Tuscan commune, divided by Monte Pisano from its chief rival, Pisa. By the early twelfth century Lucca had acquired its independence from Florence as a commune. Consuls appear in its history by 1107, and the emperor allowed the establishment of a mint at Lucca in 1155.

As a Guelph city, Lucca often served as Florence's ally. In the early fourteenth century it suffered sacks by the Ghibelline adventurers Uguccione della Faggiuola and Castruccio Castracani. The Ghibellines at that time pinned their hopes on Louis of Bavaria, who in 1327 crowned himself king at Milan and rode into Italy intending to control the Roman papacy, use it against the "French" Avignon popes, and destroy Angevin power in Naples. On the way, he made Lucca a duchy and gave it to Castracani. But Louis's ambitions fizzled in Rome and he turned back northward. To detach himself from what was now a losing side, Castracani deserted his mentor. He died in 1328. Consequently, as Louis passed through Lucca on his way home, he dispossessed Castracani's sons and sold the city to their uncle, Francesco Castracani. Lucca subsequently fell to a long list of *signori* (lords), local clans such as the Guinigi, and foreigners such as the Visconti and the Sforza, until a republic evolved during the Renaissance.

A prosperous trading and silk center, Lucca maneuvered through Italian politics and successfully maintained its independence from Florence until 1799, when it submitted to Napoleon's armies. In 1805 Lucca became a principality dependent on the French Empire and Napoleon awarded the city, with Piombino, to his sister Elisa (Maria-Anna) and her husband, Felice Baciocchi. After France's defeat, Lucca became a geopolitical football. The Spanish Bourbon Maria Luisa, who had enjoyed a brief reign as Napoleon's Queen of Etruria, was to return to her throne in Parma. But she lost her claim there when the Congress of Vienna (1815) conferred that city on Napoleon's wife, the Hapsburg Maria Luisa. The Hapsburgs retained Parma until her death, when it would revert to the Bourbons. In compensation, the Bourbon Maria Luisa was given Lucca. After her death in 1824 her unbalanced son, Charles Louis, remained in Lucca until Napoleon's wife died in 1847. He then left for Parma, as Duke Charles II, and handed Lucca over to the Grand Duchy of Tuscany, ending forever the city's independence.

ARTS AND CULTURE. When arriving from any direction, visitors to Lucca encounter its distinctive sixteenth-century walls, massive fortifications which completely circle the city and today serve Lucchesi who wish to stroll or jog along their tree-lined walks. Within the walls, much of old Lucca has remained safe from the ravages of twentieth century urban reconstruction. The Roman street grid remains in the center of the city, and parts of a forum and an amphitheater have been uncovered. Along with well-preserved medieval quarters, Lucca contains a number of churches in the Pisan-Luccan style, many of which were built on Roman foundations. Chief among these are the Duomo, dedicated to Saint Martin, and the churches of San Michele in Foro and San Frediano. Lucca's principal Renaissance structure is its early sixteenth-century basilica that honors San Paolino, the city's patron. Many medieval and Renaissance palaces of Lucca's merchant families still survive. The Guinigi clan, in particular, left a fourteenth-century cluster of houses dominated by a tall tower, as well as a fifteenth-century villa which today houses a National Museum. Lucca also houses an impressive *Piacoteca Nazionale* (National Art Gallery) with works by Veronese, Tintoretto, Andrea Del Sarto, and Guido Reni, and another art museum outside Lucca at Villa Mansi.

An artisanal craft found in Lucca and nearby areas along the Serchio and in the Val di Lima is the working of small statues from chalk. When visiting Lucca in 1375, Saint Catherine of Siena is said to have been presented with such a piece by Dominican sisters who specialized in their manufacture.

Lucca was the birthplace of the lyric composer **Alfredo Catalani** (1854–1893), whose romantic and bohemian style was most successful in his opera *La Wally* (1892). More important were the works of another Lucca native, **Giacomo Puccini** (1858–1924). Considered Giuseppe Verdi's only rival as Italy's greatest opera composer, his first work, *Le Villi* (ghosts of young women who died for love), was a one-act opera entered in an 1882 competition. His subsequent accomplishments are some of the standards of the operatic repertoire: *Manon Lescaut* (1893), *La Boheme* (1896), *Tosca* (1900), *Madama Butterfly* (1904), and the unfinished *Turandot* (completed by **Franco Alfano** in 1925). Puccini is buried at his home near the Ligurian shore, at Torre del Lago.

OTHER CENTERS. Lucca is surrounded by smaller towns that have shared in the region's prosperity. **Barga** in the Serchio valley, was envied in the fourteenth century for its silk production and was fought over by Pisa, Lucca, and Florence. In 1352 it associated itself with the Florentines. Its impressive Duomo, dedicated to Saint Christopher, was built between the ninth and fourteenth centuries.

In the eighth century a Benedictine monastery stood at **Camaiore**. Its Church, the Badia of San Pietro, rebuilt in the eleventh century, still stands. A museum of sacred art is housed in the seventeenth-century Confraternity of the Blessed Sacrament (Confraternità del Santissimo Sacramento).

Viareggio is noteworthy as the center of a string of beach resorts and the home of one of Italy's most famous Carnival celebrations.

MASSA-CARRARA

PROVINCIAL PROFILE. Area: 446 sq. mi. Population: 200,267 (province), 68,082 (city). The province contains 17 communes. Massa-Carrara constitutes the northwest corner of Tuscany. The Apuan Alps form much of the province, and in the north the Lunigiana runs along its border with Liguria. Emilia Romagna lies to its north and northeast, and Lucca is on its east and southeast. To the southwest, Massa-Carrara is on the Ligurian Sea. South of the mountains, closer to the coast, is the Versilia, a fertile and prosperous agricultural zone.

HISTORY. At the foot of the Apuan Alps, Massa and Carrara are united as the capital of an area traditionally called the Lunigiana. At first they existed in the shadow of the important Roman city of Luna (also called Luni by the barbarians), which gave its name to the zone. Luni became deserted during the Middle Ages and, situated in Liguria's La Spezia province, it is today an archaeological site. The Romans knew the Massa and Carrara area as a source of excellent marble, and it still has the largest quarries in the world. The first post-Roman record of Massa dates from A.D. 822. Its sister city, Carrara, was a pre-Roman settlement. The root of the name Carrara may be *kar*, a Liguri word for "stone." No reference is made to the town until the record of a tenth-century donation from Emperor Otto I to the Bishops of Luni. Until then, Luni was the chief city of the area. The last bishop, Ceccardo, escaped Luni after it was destroyed by the Normans in 860. He was later martyred, and his remains were discovered in the fifteenth century near Carrara, where, it is said, he struggled for marble to rebuild his church. San Ceccardo of Luni was then accorded the status of patron of Carrara.

After struggles between Lucca and Pisa for control of the two towns, Massa and Carrara passed in 1422 to the Malaspina family, and in 1553 to its cadet branch, the Cybo Malaspina. Until 1790 the two cities formed part of the duchy of Massa and Carrara. After Napoleon's defeat they were transferred to the Dukes of Modena, and in 1859 they were annexed to the Kingdom of Sardinia. Carrara and Massa today are administratively linked.

ARTS AND CULTURE. A formidable fortress, the Rocca, dominates Massa's medieval quarter. Its cathedral, dedicated to Saint Peter and Saint Francis of Assisi (the patron of Massa-Carrara), was built in the fourteenth century. A facade was added in 1936. Massa's Church of San Rocco contains a crucifix that has been attributed to the young **Michelangelo**, who frequented the area to supervise his stone orders at the quarries. Carrara's eleventh-century Duomo was enlarged in the thirteenth and fourteenth centuries. As one might expect, Carrara has a civic museum dedicated to marble.

PISA

PROVINCIAL PROFILE. Area: 945 sq. mi. Population: 384,957 (province), 93,631 (city). The province contains 39 communes. The province of Pisa faces west onto the Ligurian Sea. From there it reaches east along the Arno valley and then bends south. The southern hook of the province is fairly hilly and is cut by the Era River, which flows north into the Arno, and the Cecina, which runs west into the Ligurian Sea. Below the Cecina the province ends in the Metallifere Hills. Across the hills to the south is

Grosseto Province. Pisa faces Siena on the southeast, Florence on the northeast, Lucca on the north, and Livorno to the southwest. Besides Pisa, the capital, one of Tuscany's most important cities, Volterra, is located in the province.

HISTORY. The origins of Pisa, situated in the flatlands at the mouth of the Arno River, have long been the object of some speculation. Myth places the establishment of the city by refugees in the aftermath of the Trojan Wars. Others believe it was an Etruscan town. Livy attributed it to the Liguri tribe. The Romans penetrated the area during their wars with the Liguri and conquered it by 155 B.C. Annexation led to the construction of the Aurelian Way through Pisa on its way to Luni. In 89 B.C. the Pisans were accorded Roman citizenship. The city had already acquired a reputation as an important port, and its fleet was placed at the disposal of the rebellious governor of Africa in A.D. 397, and in the fifth and sixth centuries, of Theodoric the Goth and the Lombards in their wars against the Byzantines. The Lombards annexed Pisa and used it as the point of embarcation for their invasions of Corsica and Sardinia.

In 812 Pisa entered Charlemagne's Marquisate of Tuscany. By the early eleventh century the independent commune of Pisa was one of Italy's chief maritime states. Its expansion into nearby Corsica and Sardinia, its defeat of Amalfi, its attack on Muslim Sicily in 1063, and its conquest of Muslim Majorca at the start of the twelfth century enhanced Pisa's reputation as a Mediterranean power. Pisa also played an important part, on sea and on land, in the First Crusade (1095–1099). But the city's fortunes turned after defeats at the hands of Florence in 1222, an imperial coalition in 1254, and Genoa (the Battle of Meloria) in 1284, which signaled the start of a slow decline. It lost Corsica to the Genoese in 1299, and most of Sardinia to the Aragonese by 1324. The silting of the Arno did not help Pisa's cause, placing it considerably upriver from the coast, and the city's fate was sealed. Although Pisa enjoyed important victories through the 1300s, particularly the annexation of its irksome neighbor, Lucca, in 1342, its days as a free city were numbered.

In 1406 the city fell to the Florentines, who entered the city after bribing a treacherous Pisan captain, Giovanni Gambacorta. Beyond a brief moment of liberty between 1494 and 1509, and other short conquests by foreigners, Pisa remained a Florentine and Tuscan possession until the Risorgimento. Florentine rule, however, brought some positive achievements to Pisa. Lorenzo "the Magnificent" reorganized the university in 1472 and made it the greatest in Tuscany. The sixteenth-century Medici also contributed a number of important building projects, including a much-needed aqueduct and a canal that connected the city to the rising port of Livorno. An important figure of the early Risorgimento, Filippo Buonarroti (1761–1837), was born in Pisa. He moved to Corsica and was involved in Gracchus Babeuf's Conspiracy of Equals in Revolutionary France (1796). His commitment to conspiracies and revolution influenced a generation of Risorgimento leaders, particularly the Carbonari and Giuseppe Mazzini. Pisa was the birthplace of Sidney Sonnino (1847–1922), Italy's prime minister in 1906 and 1909–1910. During the Second World War, Allied bombardments inflicted extensive damage on Pisa, and one of Italy's largest prison camps, Coltano, was located south of the city.

ARTS AND CULTURE. Pisa boasts a wealth of medieval and Renaissance churches and palaces, such as the tenth-century San Michele in Borgo and San Paolo a Ripa d'Arno. Its most famous contribution to Italy's cultural heritage is the *Campo dei Miracoli* (the Field of Miracles), which contains the Duomo, the Baptistery, and the Leaning Tower. The complex sits on the outskirts of the city because it was built alongside a cemetery, the *camposanto*. Construction of the existing structures began with the Duomo in 1064, then the Baptistery in 1152, the Leaning Tower in 1173, and the current cemetery buildings in 1278. In 1203 the Bishop of Pisa ordered that earth for interment be transported from Golgotha, the site of Christ's death. The cemetery was heavily damaged by an aerial bombardment in July 1944 but has been restored.

Pisa's university, officially founded as a *studio* by Pope Clement VI in 1343, has long been an important intellectual focus for the city. The seventeenth-century scientist and astronomer **Galileo Galilei** was born in Pisa, where he is said to have conducted his famous experiment concerning the velocity of foreign objects at the Leaning Tower. In the spirit of the Lorraine grand dukes, enlightened reforms of the university were conducted by its rector, Monsignor Gaspare Cerati. In 1801 the French transformed it into a satellite campus of the University of Paris, as an Imperial Academy with jurisdiction over all Tuscan schools. In 1851 the university was dissolved after a group of students and faculty had formed a battalion to fight in the revolutions of 1848. Under the command of **Ottaviano Fabrizio Mossotti,** who founded the university's physics institute, almost all the ill-fated band was massacred at Curtatone and Montanara. To punish the rebellious campus, the grand duke awarded the University of Siena the status of Tuscany's premier institution; only a few departments were located in Pisa. The university was resurrected, however, in 1859, after the region reorganized for annexation to Piedmont.

Pisa is the birthplace of the writer **Antonio Tabucchi** (b. 1943). His first novel was *Piazza d'Italia* (1975). Tabucchi teaches Portuguese literature at the University of Genoa, and some of his works are based on Portuguese themes.

Pisa celebrates June 17, the feast of its patron, San Ranieri, with an evening candlelight display along the Arno and a regatta the following day. The saint, a noble born in the early twelfth century, rejected the prestige of his family to live a rigorous life of penance.

OTHER CENTERS. Volterra dominates the Era and Cecina rivers from an imposing site. It displays traces of prehistoric Villanovan culture and as Velathri, was among the twelve cities of the Etruscan Confederation. Volterra was a Roman ally during the Second Punic War (218–201 B.C.), and its people were consequently accorded Roman citizenship in the reorganized city of Volaterrae. By the twelfth century Volterra was an independent commune, but it fell under Florentine control in 1361.

Volterra's ancient heritage is recalled throughout the city, particularly in a fourth-century B.C. arch and a Roman theater. Of medieval Volterra, the twelfth- and thirteenth-century Duomo and the austere and massive Palazzo dei Priori have survived impressively. An exceptional display of Etruscan art and artifacts can be seen in the city's Guarnacci Museum. Volterra was the home of the Renaissance artist Daniele Ricciarelli (known as Daniele da Volterra, 1509–1566), a pupil of Michelangelo who achieved success primarily in Rome. His most famous commission, unfortunately, was to paint garments over the nude figures that his master had portrayed in the Sistine Chapel. This forever earned him the unfortunate sobriquet "Il Braghetone" (the pants-maker).

Near Pisa are the religious centers of **San Piero a Grado** and **Calci**. Toward the shore is the Church of San Piero a Grado. Constructed in the eleventh century, it was built over a paleo-Christian structure and commemorates the traditional spot of Saint Peter's landing in Italy. Calci is the home of the charterhouse of Pisa, the Certosa di Pisa, founded in 1366. Much of it is now a seventeenth-century Baroque complex.

Pontedera was the birthplace of Giovanni Gronchi (1887–1978), the president of Italy from 1955 until 1962. Gronchi was a leader of the Catholic Popular Party after the First World War and served briefly in Mussolini's first coalition cabinet as undersecretary in the Ministry of Industry and Commerce. He was later associated with the labor wing of the Christian Democratic Party, and was the first president of the Chamber of Deputies after the Second World War.

PISTOIA

PROVINCIAL PROFILE. Area: 373 sq. mi. Population: 267,367 (province), 86,292 (city). Pistoia province contains 27 communes. The province extends southward from the border of Emilia Romagna and the foothills of the Apennines. To Pistoia's east is Prato, and south is the province of Florence. To its west is Lucca.

HISTORY. Pistoia's location, between the southern slopes of the Apennines and the Arno valley, placed it on important trade routes. The Romans knew it as Pistoria. Its foundation is unclear; the Liguri may have established it, although the Romans had definitely arrived in the area with the victory of the Consul Gaius Flaminius in 187 B.C. Little is known of Roman Pistoia. In the fourth century A.D. the town became an episcopal see, and after the fall of the Roman Empire, (A.D. 476), bishops administered Pistoia. By the early twelfth century the city had become a free commune with strong ties to the Ghibelline faction. Situated on a trade route and famous as an ironworking center, the city was perpetually at war. It was defeated by Lucca in 1177 and suffered horrific sacks in 1306 at the hands of the Florentines and in 1328 by the adventurer Castruccio Castracani. Guelph Florence finally took the city, so by 1401, Pistoia was secured permanently in its orbit.

The Risorgimento did not significantly alter this situation. Pistoia was placed in the prefecture of Florence, whereas the Valdinievole to its southwest was detached and administered with Lucca. The reforms of 1927 and 1928 carved out the new province of Pistoia. Pistoia has long been known as a manufacturing center. Its medieval ironworking plants were famous for a type of dagger named for the city. Industrial age Pistoia is noted as being the site of the gigantic Breda works, which produce railroad cars and other heavy items.

ARTS AND CULTURE. Pistoia's Duomo, dedicated to San Zeno, and the churches of San Giovanni Fuorcivitas and Sant'Andrea were constructed in the Pisan style, mostly during the twelfth and thirteenth centuries. The Duomo's baptistery was built in 1338 from a design by **Andrea** or **Nicola Pisano.** Pisan influence was also vividly expressed in the Church of San Bartolomeo in Pantano. The rise of Florentine dominion through the fourteenth century, however, placed Pistoia more and more under the artistic influence of Giotto and his school, beginning with **Maso di Banco** (Florence, active 1336–1350) and **Nardo di Cione** (Florence, active 1345–c. 1366). The Florentines **Benedetto Buglioni** (1461–1521) and **Giovanni della Robbia** (1469–c. 1529) added Renaissance touches to the medieval Ospedale del Ceppo in 1514; and the Church of the Madonna dell'Umiltà was begun in 1494 by **Giuliano da Sangallo** and **Ventura Vitoni** (1442–1522). The dome placed over it in 1561 was the work of **Giorgio Vasari.**

Among Pistoia's most important holidays is July 25, the feast day of its patron, Saint James the Great. Along with the procession of relics, brought to the city from Santiago de Compostela in Spain, a festive "Bear Joust" and a "Barbarians Race" mark the event. The Palazzo Rospigliosi, built largely in the sixteenth century, houses the Clemente Rospigliosi Museum, which focuses on paintings and the decorative arts, and the Diocesan Museum. Northwest of the city in the Apennine foothills is a network of sites collectively referred to as the "Ecomuseo." It includes a nature center, a restored iron foundry, an ice house, an agricultural museum, and a museum, dedicated to sacred art and popular religion.

OTHER CENTERS. Pescia lies in the center of the Valdinievole. It was contested between Lucca and Florence until it came under the domination of the latter in 1339. On the outskirts of Pescia is **Collodi**, home of Carlo Lorenzini (1826–1890), who, though a Florentine by birth, adopted the town and the name Carlo Collodi. He wrote the children's tale *The Adventures of Pinocchio* (published as a serial from 1881 to 1883, then in book form in 1883).

PRATO

PROVINCIAL PROFILE. Area: 141 sq. mi. Population: 224,388 (province), 168,892 (city). Prato province is one of Italy's smallest, with seven communes. The province extends fingerlike down from the border with Emilia Romagna. To Prato's east and south is Florence, and to its west is Pistoia. The city of Prato is on the shores of the Bisenzio River.

HISTORY. Long in Florence's shadow and under its jurisdiction, Prato became a separate province in 1992. In prehistoric times, the Liguri people visited the area, and the Etruscans penetrated it in the seventh century B.C. The Romans took the area, extending the Cassian-Clodian Way through it and, in the late Republic, dividing its land among army veterans. Whether or not the city of Prato existed under the Romans, however, is subject to some doubt. Some kind of settlement, called Pagus Cornius, existed on the higher ground over a meadow (*prato* in Italian). The Lombards instituted their rule in A.D. 570, followed by the Franks. By the eleventh century, documents note a fortified settlement at Prato which contained a church, a castle, and a populated quarter called the Borgo al Cornio (from Pagus Cornius).

A commune was established by 1142, when Prato was a feudal possession of the Alberti family. Although they were both Guelph cities, Prato nevertheless began to feel the domination of Florence and, in 1313, offered itself to the King of Naples. Nevertheless, Florence succeeded in ensuring that the Neapolitan envoys to Prato were Florentines. Finally, in 1350 Florence sent an army to Prato, and annexed it a year later.

Tied to the fortunes of Florence, Prato lost its Medici rulers in 1494. In 1512 Cardinal Giovanni de' Medici, soon to be Pope Leo X, supported by imperial troops, sacked Prato on his way to recapture Florence for his family. The town's status rose, and it technically became a city in 1653 when Pope Innocent X created the diocese of Prato, although it was a suffragan see under Pistoia.

Long established as a textile hub, nineteenth-century Prato developed as an industrial concentration earlier than most other Italian cities. The city's industry has weathered transformation successfully, and it remains a prosperous textile center.

ARTS AND CULTURE. A church has probably stood on the site of

Prato's Duomo since the fifth or sixth century, and certainly since the ninth. The current structure, the Cathedral of Saint Stephen, was begun in the tenth century and continued in the twelfth. It is a mixture of Romanesque and Gothic (from a fourteenth century remodeling project), and some of the key figures of Renaissance Tuscany contributed their labors to it. The pulpit is the work of Florentines, **Donatello** (c. 1386–1466) and **Michelozzo di Bartolommeo** (1396–1472). Florence's **Andrea della Robbia** (1435–1525) contributed a terra-cotta relief over the doorway, and there is stonework by **Giuliano da Maiano** (Florence, 1432–1490) and **Giovanni Pisano** (Pisa, c. 1250–after 1314).

The church also contains important frescoes by two more Florentines, **Agnolo Gaddi** (c. 1350–1396) and **Fra Filippo Lippi** (c. 1406–1469). Lippi's frescoes depicting the lives of Saint Stephen and Saint John the Baptist, in the choir chapel, are considered among his masterpieces. Much of the artistic attention devoted to the cathedral stems from its status as the home of the Holy Girdle (*sacro cingolo*), which is kept in a locked chapel. Legend states that the Madonna presented the girdle to the perpetually doubtful Saint Thomas. The church also has a museum with significant works by Fra Filippo Lippi, **Sandro Botticelli** (1445–1510), and, perhaps, the Florentine **Paolo Uccello** (Paolo di Dono, 1397–1475).

Prato's Church of Santa Maria delle Carceri is a Renaissance masterpiece of Florence's **Giuliano da Sangallo** (c. 1445–1516). It was built on the site of a former prison (*carceri*). Near the church is the imposing Emperor's Castle, built in the thirteenth century for Frederick II.

Kurt Suckert, known as **Curzio Malaparte** (1898–1957), was born in Prato. Malaparte was an early Fascist and a representative of its radical wing through his Florentine journal, *La Conquista dello Stato*, (Conquest of the State). His exhortations to push the regime were frequently interpreted as criticisms, and the government closed his review in 1925. He was imprisoned in the early 1930s.

In 1988 Prato opened the Luigi Pecci Museum of Contemporary Art, one of the most significant of such establishments in Italy. A civic museum houses the works of Cortona's **Luca Signorelli** and of Florence's Fra Filippo Lippi and his son, **Filippino** (c. 1457–1504), who was born in Prato. The city is, naturally, home to a textile museum.

OTHER CENTERS. At **Poggio a Caiano** is one of the most noteworthy Medici villas, built by Giuliano da Sangallo between 1480 and 1485. Filippo Mazzei (1730–1816) was born in Poggio a Caiano. A physician and merchant who was a friend of Thomas Jefferson and sympathetic to America's independence from Britain, he served during the American Revolution as Virginia's envoy in Europe.

—————————————— *SIENA* ——————————————

PROVINCIAL PROFILE. Area: 1,475 sq. mi. Population: 251,892 (province), 54,931 (city). The province contains 36 communes. Siena province shares its northern border with Florence. It faces Arezzo on its northeast and Umbria on its east and southeast. Siena touches Lazio on its south, and a long border with Grosseto runs along the southwest. It faces Pisa to the west. The city of Siena is on three large, and number of smaller, hills between the Elsa and Arbia rivers.

HISTORY. Siena was the Etruscan Sena, and the Romans referred to it as Sena Julia. Only a few references to the Roman town have survived. It was mentioned by Tacitus in the first/second century A.D., and various accounts chronicle the martyrdom in 303 of the young Ansano, a patron saint of the city who, according to tradition, brought Christianity to the place. Siena probably became an episcopal see during the next century. After periods of Lombard, Frankish, and episcopal rule, in the twelfth century the city became a free commune and turned fiercely Ghibelline. The townsfolk were frequently excommunicated. Siena was the home of one of Italy's most important saints, Catherine, a Doctor of the Church who is a patron saint of the city and, along with Francis of Assisi, of the entire nation. Except for a short period of Visconti rule (1399–1402), Siena remained independent until the sixteenth century. It became an important silk and banking center, with particularly lucrative ties to the papal financial administration.

Siena's prestige suffered, however, at the hands of the Florentines, anxious to dampen the fortunes of their rival to the south. Allied to the Swabian Manfred of Sicily, Siena drew first blood at Montaperti in 1260, a battle so traumatic for Florence that it led to the brief collapse of Guelph power there. By 1269, the Florentines recovered to deliver the Senesi a crippling blow in the Colle Val d'Elsa. Siena's Ghibelline leader, Provenzan Salvani, died in the battle, and the city turned briefly to the Guelph side. Beginning in 1309, furthermore, the city endured a string of bank collapses and long periods of internal strife. Nevertheless, Siena could still exert its influence over other Tuscan cities, maintaining control over much of the southern part of the region and even defeating Florence in the fifteenth century. The city was, moreover, host to a significant Renaissance culture at that time, fueled by aristocratic families such as the Piccolomini, the Sozzini, and the Tolomei. Then, in 1555, Siena was sacked by imperial forces in union with the Florentines. Four years later, the last vestiges of the republic surrendered at Montalcino. The Republic of Siena finally succumbed to Florence.

Medici rule may have been humiliating, but it was not oppressive. Florentine administration undertook road-building programs, alleviated economic distress, and established one of Italy's most important banks, the Monte dei Paschi. Under the last Medici and then under Lorraine rule, the Enlightenment flourished in Siena, where the abbot, Sallustio Bandini, devoted some of his vast energies to the reclamation of the Maremma marshlands. He also proposed radical economic measures to relieve poverty, measures which were partly applied in the free export of grain. Bandini's ideas were at first censored, but were later allowed to circulate under Grand Duke Peter Leopold and his Physiocrat circle (who believed government should not interfere with natural economic laws), in the late 1760s. Napoleon placed Siena in the Kingdom of Etruria, then in France itself, as the capital of the Ombrone department.

Industry in nineteenth-century Siena witnessed a healthy growth. Expansion in silk, other textiles, wood, and the manufacture of felt hats prompted the city to stage an industrial exposition as early as 1841. Sentiment for national unity developed gradually from the revolutions of 1821, which went unnoticed, to the popular uprisings of 1847–1848. In 1859, Siena was the first city of the region to vote for union with Piedmont.

After the collapse of Fascism, Siena witnessed some resistance action against the Germans. It was liberated on July 13, 1944, by Free-French colonial troops under General Alphonse Juin. The city survived the war without a great deal of damage, and has since enjoyed something of an economic renaissance based on artisanal work and tourism. Siena's Palio (race), run twice each summer, is one of Italy's most important public events.

ARTS AND CULTURE. Many towns in the province possess remarkable medieval quarters. Siena itself is a very well preserved city of steep hills and medieval streets. Its central square, the Piazza del Campo, onto which the Palazzo Pubblico (finished in the 1340s) and its tower, the Torre del Mangia, face, is considered one of Italy's most stunning city centers. The Palazzo Pubblico houses the civic museum and its famous frescoes depicting good and bad government by a Siena native, **Ambrogio Lorenzetti** (active 1319–1347). Also in the museum are works by the Piedmontese artist **il Sodoma** (Giovanni Antonio Bazzi, 1447–1549) and the Sienese **Simone Martini** (c. 1284–1344). Across the piazza from the Palazzo Pubblico is a copy of the original fountain by **Jacopo della Quercia** (c. 1374–1438), the Fonte Gaia.

Work on Siena's Italian Gothic Duomo and baptistery was begun in the twelfth century. White and black stripes reveal a Pisan influence that is also reflected in the work of **Giovanni Pisano** and in **Nicola Pisano**'s magnificent pulpit. Inside the Duomo, at the top of the nave walls, are terra-cotta busts of the first 171 popes, including the legendary Pope Joan disguised with a beard. Still inside, off to the side, is the beautiful Piccolomini Library with frescoes based on the life of Pope Pius II (1458–1464) by the Perugian artist

Pinturicchio (c. 1454–1513). Outside the Duomo, a single wall juts out to the right. It recalls the unfinished plan to greatly expand the structure, a venture cut short in 1348 by the Black Plague and the economic calamity that followed. Construction shifted at that point to the facade, a work in red, white, and green marble inspired by Orvieto's Duomo. Other treasures from the Duomo are kept at the Diocesan museum, the Museo dell'Opera Metropolitana.

Behind the Duomo is a Gothic fourteenth-century baptistery with a remarkable font by Jacopo della Quercia. Other important churches include San Domenico, where Saint Catherine's head and a finger are kept (the rest of her body is at the Church of Santa Maria sopra Minerva in Rome), the fourteenth-century Church of San Francesco, and the oratory of San Bernardino from the fifteenth. A national art gallery, the Pinacoteca Nazionale, is another important museum. Siena was the birthplace of many Renaissance artists, including **Tino da Camaino** (1285–c. 1337).

OTHER CENTERS. The province of Siena is particularly rich in its number of smaller but important urban centers. Such towns near Siena include **Chianciano**, famous as a thermal spa, and **Chiusi**, both in the southern Valdichiana. Both have remnants of the Umbri culture dating from the eighth and seventh centuries B.C. Much of Chianciano is given over to hotels and the mineral springs, although "old Chianciano" (*Chianciano vecchia*) sits high on a hill, the ancient Etruscan location. Chiusi is the site of the National Etruscan Museum.

Commanding a height above the Ombrone valley, **Asciano** is a medieval town with the eleventh-century collegiate Church of Sant'Agata and two important museums, one devoted to sacred art and the other, housed in an old Gothic church, dedicated to Etruscan works.

Near **Poggibonsi**, a regional transportation and manufacturing center, is **Colle Val d'Elsa**, a town with a lower, modern city and an older, upper one reached by stairs. Colle Val d'Elsa belonged to the bishops of Volterra and, after 1333, to Florence. It has a tenth-century fortress and the Church of Sant'Agostino with a thirteenth-century facade and late Renaissance interior. It is the birthplace of Arnolfo di Cambio (c. 1245–1302), the initial architect of Florence's Duomo, and the artist Cennino Cennini (active c. 1400).

Cortona, north of Lake Trasimeno, was an Umbri, and then an Etruscan, settlement before Rome ruled the area. In the Middle Ages it survived as a Lombard town, and was a free city by the twelfth century. An army from Arezzo sacked Cortona in 1258, and it was absorbed into Florentine territory in 1410. The artists Luca Signorelli (1445/1450–1523) and Pietro Berrettini, known as Pietro Da Cortona (1596–1669), were born in Cortona. The Diocesan Museum contains some of Signorelli's works, and his painting *Sacra Conversazione* (Sacred Conversation) is housed in the fourteenth-century church of San Domenico. Da Cortona's last, unfinished work, a depiction of the Annunciation, is in the Church of San Francesco, built between 1245 and the seventeenth century.

One of Italy's best examples of Renaissance architecture is Cortona's Church of the Madonna del Calcinaio, built on a design of the Sienese artist Francesco di Giorgio Martini (1285–1344). The collection of the city's Museum of the Etruscan Academy contains ancient pieces as well as works of a twentieth century Futurist painter from Cortona, Gino Severini (1883–1966).

San Gimignano began as a hilltop Etruscan settlement overlooking the Val d'Elsa. Although it was a free commune by the twelfth century, San Gimignano was torn apart in battles between Guelph and Ghibelline factions within its walls. Fifteen fortified medieval towers remain from that time. In 1300 in San Gimignano's thirteenth-century Palazzo del Popolo, built on Arnolfo di Cambio's plan in 1288, Dante Alighieri tried to persuade the city to join Florence. Forty-five years later it fell under Florentine rule. San Gimignano maintains an exceptional medieval center with its many old towers, the Piazza della Cisterna, and the adjacent Piazza del Podestà. In the latter is the twelfth-century cathedral, the Collegiata of Santa Maria Assunta, with frescoes by Il Sodoma and two Florentines, Benozzo Gozzoli (1420–1497) and Giuliano da Maiano (1432–1490). The life of San Gimignano's patron, Santa Fina, is celebrated in a number of places throughout the city, including Benozzo Gozzoli's representation in the Church of Sant'Agostino and in Giuliano da Maiano's acclaimed work in the Collegiata's chapel of Santa Fina.

Montepulciano occupies a high point between the Valdichiana and the Val d'Orcia. Its patron saint is the widely venerated Agnes of Montepulciano, who was born in the thirteenth century at nearby **Gracciano**. Although it probably was an Etruscan place, first mention of the town dates from a document of A.D. 715 that refers to Mons Politianus. Contested by Arezzo, Siena, and Florence, after 1390 the town usually gravitated toward the Florentine orbit. Montepulciano's historic center boasts quite a few notable structures, mainly Renaissance and Baroque. The focus of the city is the beautiful Piazza Grande, on which are the Palazzo Comunale, modeled on Florence's Palazzo Vecchio, and the late sixteenth-century Duomo, the work of Ippolito Scalza (Orvieto, 1531–1617). Outside of Montepulciano is a masterpiece of Renaissance architecture by Antonio da Sangallo "the Elder" (c. 1453–1534), the Church of the Madonna di San Biagio.

In the thick woods at **Monte Oliveto Maggiore** is the mother house of the Olivetan order. The abbey was founded by Giovanni Tolomei in 1313; something of a martial atmosphere recalls the period when it served as a fortress between 1393 and 1526. The complex contains frescoes by Cortona's Luca Signorelli that depict the life of Tolomei, who took the name of Bernardo and was canonized. They were finished by Il Sodoma, the Piedmontese Giovanni Antonio Bazzi (1477–1549).

Pienza is virtually a Renaissance town. In 1459 Pope Pius II employed Bernardo Rossellino (1409–1464) to reconstruct it entirely out of an older spot, Corsignano, on lands owned by his family. Popes Pius II (Enea Silvio Piccolomini) and Pius III (Francesco Todeschini Piccolomini) were members of the aristocratic Sienese Piccolomini family that claimed to have descended from the Etruscan King Lars Porsena.

Nearby is the great Romanesque collegiate church at **San Quirico d'Orcia**. A church since the eighth century, it was built mainly in the twelfth and thirteenth centuries. It may have partly been the work of Giovanni Pisano. The town hosts one of Italy's most important *Maggio Musicale* (Musical May) festivals at the end of April.

Abbadia San Salvatore was named for Tuscany's greatest medieval abbey. It was established on the southeast slope of Monte Amiata in 743 by the Lombard King Ratchis. Originally a Benedictine abbey, it became Camaldolese, and then Cistercian, before it was closed during the reforms of Grand Duke Peter Leopold in 1782. The Cistercians reoccupied it in 1939. The original abbey survives only in the crypt of the eleventh-century church.

SELECT BIBLIOGRAPHY

Hibbert, Christopher. *Florence: The Biography of a City*. London: The Folio Society, 1997.

Istituto Geografico De Agostini. *Toscana*. 2 vols. Novara: Istituto Geografico De Agostini, 1980.

Levey, Michael. *Florence: A Portrait*. Cambridge, Mass.: Harvard University Press, 1996.

Mehling, Marianne, ed. *Florence and Tuscany: A Phaidon Cultural Guide*. New York: Prentice-Hall, 1986.

Mori, Giorgio, ed. *La Toscana*. Turin: Einaudi, 1986.

Tolaini, Emilio. *Pisa*. Rome: Laterza, 1992.

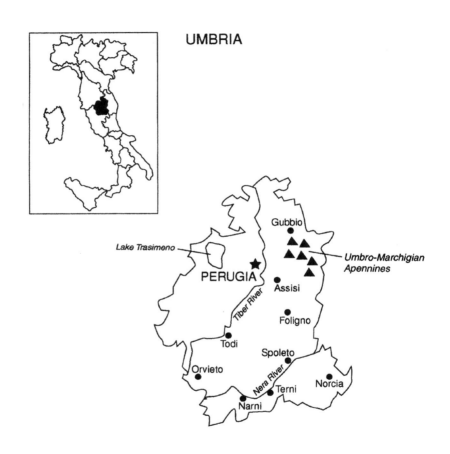

UMBRIA

Chapter 18

UMBRIA

REGIONAL CHARACTERISTICS. Area: 3,265 sq. mi. Population: 831,714. Capital: Perugia. Umbria ranks sixteenth among Italy's regions in terms of area and seventeenth in population. The Catholic metropolitan see is at Perugia/Cittá della Pieve.

Umbria is the only region in mainland Italy without a seacoast. Its shape is somewhat triangular, facing Lazio to the south, Tuscany to the northwest and Marche to the northeast. The Tiber and some other rivers provide a few flat valleys, but 70.7 percent of Umbria is officially hilly and 29.3 percent is mountainous. In Umbria's southeast corner is its highest peak, Monte Vettore (8,130 feet), which forms part of the Umbrio-Marchigian Apennines on the border with the Marche. The Tiber is Umbria's most important river. It rises north of Perugia and flows past Todi until it enters Lazio south of Orvieto. Another important waterway is the Nera, which rises in the highlands near the Marche border, then flows southwest past Terni until joining the Tiber near Orte. Umbria's ruggedness has long been the chief reason for its remoteness, a condition aggravated by bad train connections. Late twentieth-century road construction has, however, better integrated Umbria into the national economy. With only 67 percent of its people living in towns, it is Italy's most rural region.

ECONOMY. Of Umbria's 301,000 employed workers, 188,000 are men and 113,000 are women; 6.6 percent are in agriculture, 30.9 percent in industry, and 62.5 percent in the tertiary sector. In January 1998 Umbria's unemployment rate was 7.8 percent. The flat basins around Lake Trasimeno, Gubbio, and Todi are home to important wheat- and corn-growing areas, and livestock is also significant across Umbria. Key concentrations of steel production, chemicals, and petrochemicals are found at Narni, Terni, and Foligno. Terni is noted for arms manufacturing, and Perugia has gained a reputation for its textile and food industries, including the famous Perugina chocolates. Finished terra-cotta production distinguishes Deruta. Assisi is an important pilgrimage and tourist center.

CUISINE. Wine culture has long existed in Umbria. The Etruscans made wine at Orvieto before the Romans arrived there. Orvieto *classico* is made with local *grechetto* and other grapes, and is now more pale and dry than were its ancestors. It has been said that Pope Gregory XVI (1831–1846) ordered that his body be washed in Orvieto before his burial. Torgiano, near Perugia, produces Umbria's other noble wine. It is either red or white, although the red *riserva* is more distinguished. Umbria, furthermore, is known as a source of quality but unheralded and undiscovered local wines. Umbria's reputation for meat stems in part from Perugia's famous beef and from its pork, particularly around Norcia. Spaghetti *alla norcina* is made with a sausage and onion cream sauce. Also popular are cardoons, known as *gobbi* (cousins to artichokes). *Gobbi alla perugina* are fried and served with a red meat ragù. The black truffle (*tartufo*), a delicacy found in Umbria, is used as much as possible.

RIGATONI ALLA NORCINA

2 strips bacon, diced	Black pepper
½ lb. lean ground sausage	1 lb. rigatoni
4 Tbs. olive oil	Grated parmesan cheese
½ c. heavy cream	

Sauté bacon and sausage in oil over low heat until brown. Add cream and pepper to taste. Meanwhile, prepare rigatoni according to package directions. Drain pasta, combine with sauce, and add parmesan cheese.

HISTORY. Umbria does not have a cohesive history. Parts of it have been settled since Paleolithic times; traces of these settlements survive near Perugia in an arc between Lake Trasimeno and the Tiber headwaters. Many Neolithic and Bronze Age remains can be found in the south around Terni, Spoleto, and the Lazio border. Also near Spoleto are Iron Age tombs. In ancient times the Tiber separated two distinct cultures, Etruscan and Umbri. The Romans penetrated Umbria early, mostly at the end of the fourth and into the early third centuries B.C. In 220 they built the Flaminian Way across the region. But the road did not forge a lasting regional identity, in part because Emperor Augustus's later administrative reforms reemphasized the split along the Tiber with Regio VI, Umbria, to the east and

Regio VII, Etruria, to the west. Only in the fourth century A.D. did Diocletian unite the two as Tuscia et Umbria. The Flaminian Way, nevertheless, facilitated the spread of Christianity into Umbria. By the fourth century, twenty-two episcopal sees were located there, and by the fifth and sixth centuries, the areas near Norcia and Spoleto were the sites of intense monastic and hermetic activity.

Barbarian and Byzantine incursions destroyed Umbria's urban culture, and much of its cultivated land was left fallow, to languish as malarial marshland. Early medieval Umbria was contested by Lombards, the Carolingian Empire, the Church, and the Dukes of Spoleto. By the eleventh century, a demographic revival and increased cultivation of the land brought renewed prosperity to Umbria. Healthy medieval communes developed in Perugia, Gubbio, Assisi, Spoleto, Todi, Orvieto, and elsewhere.

At the same time the Church in Rome exerted more and more control, although effective rule was frequently disrupted. Roman sway lessened, for instance, when the king of France removed the Holy See to Avignon in the fourteenth century. By the 1350s and 1360s, however, Cardinal Egidio (Gil) Albornoz, the papal legate, came to central Italy to prepare the political field for the pope's return. Shortly afterward, Umbria was almost united briefly under the rebellious Perugino tyrant Braccio Fortebraccio, who was defeated at L'Aquila in 1424. At the end of the fifteenth and start of the sixteenth centuries, Cesare Borgia heralded the prospect of some kind of union while Popes Julius II (1503–1515) and Paul III (1534–1549) again struggled (separately) to keep Umbria in the papal fold.

By the middle of the sixteenth century, Umbria was considered a papal province. Its borders did not strictly correspond to the current ones: Rieti was included in Umbria but Orvieto was not, and Camerino was added later. Napoleon reorganized much of the area between 1809 and 1814 as the Departments of Trasimeno and Clitunno, with Perugia and Spoleto as their respective capitals. Papal restoration changed the province into the "legation" of Umbria with the "delegations" of Spoleto, Perugia, and Rieti. Risorgimento activity distinguished many Umbrian towns, particularly the Revolution of 1831 in Perugia, Gubbio, Foligno, and Spoleto. In June 1859, inspired by Piedmont's victorious war against Austria and the annexations of Tuscany and papal Romagna, Perugia rose in a tragic, aborted revolution. On September 11, 1860, Italian forces under Manfredo Fanti crossed into Umbria, and the region was absorbed into the new kingdom. A unified Umbria was resurrected the following year as one large province with Perugia its capital. In 1923 the Fascists detached the Sabina area around Rieti from Umbria and awarded it to Lazio. Four years later they created a separate province of Terni.

Nineteenth-century industrialization contributed to the growth of places like Foligno and Terni, one of Italy's most important steel centers in 1886. Such concentrations have been associated with the strong Marxist tradition in Umbria's politics. Consequently, Umbria was a frequent battleground between Socialists, Communists, and Fascists in the tumultuous years between the end of the First World War and the establishment of Mussolini's dictatorship in October 1922. Perugia, whose mayoral offices were bombed by the Fascists, was chosen by Mussolini as headquarters for the March on Rome when he assumed power. During the Second World War much of Umbria was spared damage by a rapid German retreat to the Apennines after the fall of Rome in June 1944. After the war the region reclaimed, along with Tuscany and Emilia Romagna, its Marxist heritage as part of Italy's "Red Belt" across the center of the peninsula. The Communists regularly secured about half of the region's vote until the party's collapse at the end of the 1980s.

RECENT POLITICS. Umbria votes as the thirteenth electoral district (*circoscrizione*). In the 1996 majoritarian election to the Chamber of Deputies, the leftist Ulivo coalition captured 50 percent of the tally. The Polo per le Libertà took 41.2 percent. In the proportional vote, the Democratic Party of the Left obtained 33.2 percent of the vote, the right-wing National Alliance took 19.9 percent, and Forza Italia claimed 16.5 percent. In the 1996 Senate vote the Ulivo took four seats with 47 percent; the Polo got none, based on its 40.6 percent of the overall total. The April 2000 regional elections did not alter Center-Left rule in Umbria. President Maria Rita Lorenzetti headed a coalition that earned 56.4 percent of the vote, versus 39.2 for the opposition center-right union.

PERUGIA

PROVINCIAL PROFILE. Area: 2,446 sq. mi. Population: 608,398 (province), 153,326 (city). The province contains 92 communes. Perugia is physically much larger than Terni, Umbria's other province, to its south. To its west is Tuscany, and to its east are the Marche. The province wedges between those two regions at its northern point. Perugia also touches Lazio to the southeast. Forty percent of the province is covered in woodlands. Some flatlands are along the Tiber River and around Spoleto, the Valle Umbra. Smaller basins are at Gubbio, Gualdo Tadino, and Norcia. West of Perugia city is Lake Trasimeno. At 49 square miles, it is the largest lake in peninsular Italy. It is also one of the shallowest; its maximum depth is only 15.6 feet.

HISTORY. Perugia began as an ancient Umbri center. By the sixth or fifth century B.C., however, the town had become Etruscan, and was later a member of the twelve-city Etruscan Confederation. The Romans took it in 310 B.C. and called it Perusia. The city remained loyal during Hannibal's invasion (217–216 B.C.), and it prospered. Benefits of Roman rule were not refused even after Augustus laid siege and burned it in 41–40 B.C. to defeat the forces of Lucius, brother of Mark Antony. Perusia then became Augusta Perusia. After periods of Lombard and Carolingian rule, Perugia became a semi-independent commune in the twelfth century. It changed hands from the fourteenth to the sixteenth centuries between the adventurer Braccio Fortebraccio, the Oddi and Baglioni families, and the popes. The city's power reached its apex around 1350. Fifteenth-century Perugia endured domination by the Visconti (1400–1402), Naples (1408–1414), and Braccio da Montone (1416–1424). Pope Paul III took it in 1540 and consolidated it into the papal territories, where it remained with few exceptions until the Risorgimento. In 1922 Perugia was the Fascist command center when the Blackshirts prepared to march on Rome unless their leader, Mussolini, was permitted to form a cabinet.

ARTS AND CULTURE. Perugia's hilltop setting is particularly striking. The city practically climbs the hills overlooking the Tiber, and weary pedestrians on their way up or down may find some help in long escalators. Down in the valleys the town spreads out in factories and modern neighborhoods; but on top of the hill, Perugia is one of Italy's finest medieval cities.

The center of Perugia is the cluster of structures around the Piazza IV Novembre with its thirteenth-century fountain, the Fontana Maggiore. The city's cathedral, dedicated to San Lorenzo, is an unfinished fifteenth-century Gothic structure. Fire damaged part of the interior around the choir in 1985. Nearby is the city hall, the Palazzo dei Priori. Constructed between 1293 and 1443, it contains the Umbrian National Gallery (Galleria) nazionale dell'Umbria), the region's most important art museum. Medieval and early Renaissance Umbrian art was dominated by Siena and Florence, although an independent style, based principally in Perugia, developed in the fifteenth century. Active in the Umbrian style were such figures as **Gentile Da Fabriano** (Ancona, c. 1370–1427), **Raphael** (Urbino, 1483–1520), and two Umbrians, **Perugino** (c. 1450–1523) and **Pinturicchio** (c. 1454–1513).

Behind the Palazzo dei Priori is the old exchange house, the Collegio del Cambio. Built in 1452, it contains frescoes by Perugino. Perugia's Renaissance masterpiece is the Oratorio of San Bernardino, built in 1457 by the Florentine artist **Agostino di Ducio** (1418–c. 1481). Underneath part of Perugia is a medieval neighborhood that was covered with a ceiling, the *rocca paolina*, on orders from Pope Paul III. The result is a strange underground place.

Perugia's patron is San Costanzo, an early bishop of the city who was jailed in the second century, during the persecutions of Marcus Aurelius. He converted his guards and fled Perugia; the Romans caught up with him near Foligno and decapitated him. His feast day is January 29.

Rebellious students from Bologna founded the University of Perugia in

1200. It was recognized by Pope Clement V in 1308 and acquired fame as a major academic center. When it joined the Kingdom of Italy, the university broke from papal control in 1860. Perugia is also home to the University for Foreigners.

Perugia is home to an important "Death Fair" (*Fiera dei Morti*) in early November. Umbria is home to a form of dialect poetry. **Ruggero Torelli** (1820–1894), for example, wrote pieces in the tongue of the Perugian countryside. **Giuseppe Prezzolini** (1882–1982), a leader of Italy's nationalist movement, was born in Perugia. Cultural issues were central to Prezzolini, who directed the Florentine review *La Voce* (The Voice) from 1908 until 1914. His early support of Mussolini and the Fascist regime withered after the Lateran Pacts, the conquest of Ethiopia, and the German alliance. From 1930 until 1950 he taught at Columbia University in New York and administered its Casa Italiana, one of the most important centers of Italian studies in the United States.

OTHER CENTERS. As one of Italy's largest provinces, Perugia embraces an extraordinary number of important centers besides its capital. The old city of **Assisi** sits on a spur of Monte Subasio. First an Umbri settlement (founded in myth by Dardanus in 865 B.C.), the city passed to the Romans, who called it Asisium and whose tenure is recalled by the Temple of Minerva in the middle of the city. Built in the first century A.D., it commands the central Piazza del Comune, not as a pagan temple but now as a Christian church.

After the barbarian invasions, Assisi was taken by the Dukes of Spoleto until the twelfth century, when it became an independent commune. The popes took control in the thirteenth century. In 1181 or 1182, Francesco Bernardone, who became Saint Francis (San Francesco), was born there. In 1205 Francis rejected the comfortable existence of his father, a prosperous merchant, and devoted himself to prayer, the ascetic life, and preaching. In 1208 he began his new life and gained a devoted following. The next year, after initial rejection, Pope Innocent III sanctioned Francis's order. During his wanderings, Francis composed what became known as the *Laudes Creaturarum*, the "Praises of God's Creatures" or "The Canticle of the Sun." It is one of the earliest tracts of substance in the Italian language. Upon his return to Italy from missions abroad, bickering among his followers disappointed Francis, and in 1223 he left the leadership of his order. He spent the next three years in solitude and received the stigmata while in prayer on Monte La Verna. He died in 1226, and two years later, Pope Honorius III canonized him. In 1939 Francis was proclaimed the patron saint of Italy by Pope Pius XII.

The thirteenth-century Franciscan revival spread to the rest of Italy from Umbria, and accounts in part for the diffusion of the Italian Gothic style. Assisi's Basilica of Saint Francis, begun by Brother Elia in 1228, was one of the first and finest of Italy's Gothic structures. The building houses two churches, almost wholly separated from one another. The lower church is dark and heavy, but brightened by magnificent frescoes by, among others, the Florentine Cimabue (c. 1240–c. 1302) and two Sienesi, Pietro Lorenzetti (c. 1280–c. 1348) and Simone Martini (c. 1285–1344). The tomb of Francis sits below this part of the church. Brother Elia placed his remains there, and Pope Eugenius IV sealed the site in the fifteenth century. It was rediscovered in 1818, and chapels were twice constructed around it. The current structure dates from 1932. The basilica's upper church is graced with works by Cimabue and Lorenzetti, and particularly by Giotto's (c. 1267/1276–1337) magnificent frescoes depicting the life of Saint Francis. Some of the works were damaged in the 1997 earthquake.

Another important example of the Gothic style is Assisi's Basilica of Saint Clare (Chiara), a rose and white structure begun in 1257 and joined to flying butresses at the end of the fourteenth century. Clare's body was entombed there in 1260; the ornamentation on the crypt dates from the nineteenth and twentieth centuries. Assisi's cathedral is dedicated to San Rufino, an early bishop and martyr. It was built between 1140 and 1228 over Roman foundations and a smaller eighth-century church which also honored the saint.

Assisi's immediate environs contain many places associated with the lives of Francis and Clare. Down a slope from the city is San Damiano, the convent where Christ is said to have urged Francis on his mission to "repair" his fallen home, the church, in 1205. Saint Clare and her followers, the "Poor Clares," occupied San Damiano until her death there in 1253. At another spot on the mountainside is the Hermitage, the *Eremo delle carceri*, a wooded glade where Francis and his followers retired from the world in caves and hovels. In the fifteenth century San Bernardino of Siena built a convent on the spot of the saint's cave which can still be seen. In medieval times the woods continued onto a lower plain that stretches from the mountain and embraced Francis's chapel, the Porziuncola, where he died. The wooded atmosphere is gone and the area has become Assisi's detached modern quarter, but the chapel remains within a larger structure, the rambling Basilica of Santa Maria degli Angeli. Begun in 1569 by Pope Pius V, it suffered extensive earthquake damage and underwent restorations that extended into the twentieth century. The basilica's dome, however, was unharmed and still protects the little chapel. The Benedictines presented the Porziuncola to Francis in 1211 in return for a bowl of fish from the Tescio River. Assisi also holds one of Italy's most noteworthy Calendimaggio festivals, based on medieval rituals.

The artist Pietro Vannucci, known as Perugino (c. 1450–1523), was born in **Città della Pieve**. Many of his works remain there, in the Duomo; in the churches of Santa Maria della Mercede and Sant'Antonio Abate; and in the Oratorio di Santa Maria dei Bianchi, which contains his *Adoration of* *the Magi* (1504). Perugino is considered one of the best Umbrian painters as well as an important teacher.

Foligno's origins are pre-Roman; the Romans took the city in 295 B.C. after the Battle of Sentino and named it Fulginiae. Later, Foligno suffered destruction at the hands of both Muslim and Hungarian raiders in the Dark Ages. In the thirteenth century it surfaced as a free Ghibelline commune but was absorbed by the papal domains in 1439. Foligno developed into an important industrial and transportation hub of Umbria. In the 1930s it was known for its Macchi airplane plants and flight school. Unfortunately, this fame caused the city to be targeted during the Second World War and it suffered intense bombardments. After Terni, Foligno received the worst attacks in Umbria; over 40 percent of the city was damaged. It nevertheless preserved many of its medieval and Renaissance structures, including its twelfth- and thirteenth-century Duomo, the twelfth-century Romanesque Church of Santa Maria Infraportas, and the Palazzo Trinci, which dates from 1407. Foligno was the birthplace of the architect Giuseppe Piermarini (1734–1808). After studying in Rome, Piermarini moved to Milan, where he became court architect and one of Lombardy's most noted builders of the late eighteenth century. Foligno boasts a Giostra della Quintana, a joust and race that dates from 1613.

Near Foligno is **Bevagna**, a town that has conserved much of its medieval look in its Piazza Silvestri and thirteenth-century Palazzo dei Consoli. Its remarkable Romanesque churches of San Silvestro and San Michele date from the twelfth century.

Gubbio possesses one of Umbria's principal artistic patrimonies. Its neighborhoods have retained much of their medieval essence as they tumble almost to the the foot of Monte Igino. A tribal village in the second or third century B.C., the Romans knew it as Iguvium. Gubbio eventually allied itself with Rome, into whose domain it was later absorbed. Evidence of Roman prosperity remains in a first-century A.D. theater outside of the city walls. After Gubbio's destruction at the hands of the Goth Totila in the sixth century, and later by the Hungarians, the city was reborn in the eleventh century as a medieval commune. It fell under Perugia's dominion in 1183 and became a possession of the Montefeltro dukes of Urbino in 1384. The Papal States annexed it in 1631.

Gubbio boasts some important structures, including the Gothic thirteenth-century Church of San Francesco and the Palazzo Ducale, built over Lombard ruins on the order of Federigo da Montefeltro in 1470. The city's most important structure is the Palazzo dei Consoli. Built in the fourteenth century, perhaps by Angelo da Orvieto (active 1334–1352), it is considered one of Italy's best medieval buildings. The palace houses the civic museum and art gallery. In the museum are the seven "Eugubine Tables," ancient bronze tablets discovered in the fifteenth century that bear incriptions in the Umbri and Etruscan tongues. Gubbio hosts a *palio "della Balestra"* and one of Umbria's most popular celebrations, the *Festa dei Ceri*, (Feast of Candles) on May 15, the feast day of Saint Ubaldo.

Known to the ancients as Nursia, **Norcia** was a Sabine town until Rome annexed it in 209 B.C. It suffered sacks by Goths, Lombards, and Muslims before it surfaced as an independent commune in the Middle Ages. Perugia took control of Norcia, followed by papal domination in the fourteenth century. A sixteenth-century papal castle protects Norcia, but its principal structure is a fourteenth-century church which honors its most famous son, Saint Benedict (San Benedetto). He and his twin sister, Saint Scolastica, were born about 480 in a house said to have been at or near the church grounds. Privileged children of the nobility, the siblings abandoned their comfortable lives to devote themselves to the Church. Benedict gained a following, and his "Rule" assumed fundamental importance as a model for the discipline of Latin (Western) monasticism. He and his Benedictine comrades went on to establish monasteries throughout central Italy, the most famous, according to tradition, being Monte Cassino in southern Lazio. In October 1964 Pope Paul VI declared Saint Benedict the patron of Europe.

Close to Foligno, on the southern slopes of Mount Subasio, is **Spello,** a town whose Roman heritage can still be seen in the remains of a first-century A.D. amphitheater and impressive walls. Spello later became a medieval commune, a papal territory, and part of the Duke of Spoleto's holdings before it returned to the Church in 1583. The town's primary fame stems from its Church of Santa Maria Maggiore. Built in the twelfth and thirteenth centuries, its Baglioni Chapel, with a floor of majolica from Deruta, contains outstanding frescoes by the Perugian artist Pinturicchio. His works, and those of Perugino, can be admired elsewhere in the church. Outside of Spello is the twelfth-century church of San Claudio, built on a Roman foundation.

At the southern end of the province, **Spoleto** became the Roman colony of Spoletium in 241 B.C. In 217 it earned a place in history after Hannibal devastated the Romans at the Battle of Lake Trasimeno and began a relentless march on Rome. The victorious Carthaginian pushed aside everything in his way until he reached Spoleto, which put up such a spirited defense that Hannibal was forced to detour and head farther south. Spoleto later prospered as an important link on the Flaminian Way. In the first century B.C., Augustus included it in his Regio VI, and in the fourth century Diocletian integrated it into his Tuscia et Umbria. Rome's dominion can still be recalled in the ruins of a 3,000-seat theater, a bridge, and the Arch of Drusus, which served as entrance to the ancient forum. Spoleto was an episcopal see as early as 353.

After the fall of Rome (476) the Byzantines took Spoleto in 537. But it is post-Byzantine Spoleto that is best remembered in history, as the seat of a powerful Lombard duchy established c. 570. Faroald, the first duke, established an autonomous state that stretched through central Italy from the

Tiber almost to the Adriatic. Duke Trasimondo (724–739) led the conversion of the Spoleto Lombards to Christianity, and the duchy served as protector of the important monasteries of Ferentillo and Farfa and the convent of San Giorgio near Rieti. Toward the end of the eighth century, however, Spoleto succumbed to Frankish rulers, lost much of its eastern and southern territories, and became an imperial satellite.

Nevertheless, Spoleto remained semi-independent to such an extent that it refused to pay tribute to Emperor Frederick Barbarossa in 1155 and rejected his demand to feed his troops. Barbarossa responded by razing the rebellious city with a wrath so vicious that little remains of Spoleto antedating the attack. Still, the city recovered to become a major commune in central Italy. Its cathedral, with an exterior mosaic of Christ, Mary, and Saint John, was rebuilt in 1175. Inside the church are frescoes depicting events in the life of the Madonna by the Florentine Filippo Lippi (c. 1406–1469). Lippi died at Spoleto and is buried in the cathedral. His son, Filippino (c. 1457–1504), designed the tomb. Although medieval Spoleto was still technically a duchy, no dukes remained, and the city came under the control of Pope Gregory IX and the Church by the mid-1200s. Papal control was reconfirmed in the fourteenth century by Cardinal Gil Albornoz, who ordered the construction of a massive fortress, the Rocca, which still dominates the city. It was begun by Todi's Ugolino di Montemarte and finished by another Umbrian architect, Matteo di Giovanello, known as Il Gattapone (Gubbio, active 1362–1376). Di Giovanello also built a spectacular aqueduct and pedestrian bridge, the Ponte delle Torri, that connects the town to the Monteluco.

Spoleto boasted a strong liberal tradition in the nineteenth century. Napoleon had designated it capital of his Department of Trasimeno, and the city later rose in the revolutions of 1831—the people expelled Archbishop Giovanni Maria Mastai Ferretti (the future Pope Pius IX). But the Risorgimento also signaled a decline for Spoleto. The city lost its traditional distinction as an administrative center when the Kingdom of Italy merged it into the new province of Umbria with its capital at Perugia.

Umbria's most renowned celebration of the arts is the Festival of Two Worlds in Spoleto. Launched by the Italo-American composer Gian Carlo Menotti in 1958, it has grown into one of Europe's major arts festivals and has spawned a twin in Charleston, South Carolina. Near Spoleto, **Genga** is the birthplace of Annibale della Genga, who in 1823 was elected pope and took the name Leo XII. One of the Holy See's leading *zelante* (zealot) reactionaries in Europe's "Age of Reaction," Leo reigned until 1829.

Marsciano is the birthplace of Luigi Salvatorelli (1886–1974), a historian at the University of Naples and a journalist. His opposition to Fascism, portrayed in his 1923 analysis *Nazionalfascismo* (National Fascism), caused his removal from Turin's *La Stampa* newspaper. Salvatorelli was among the founders of the Action Party in 1942.

Todi was an Umbrian settlement on a hill above where the Tiber River meets the Naia. It was later an Etruscan fortress town until the Romans took it in the fourth century B.C. and called it Tuder or Tutere. The Romans developed the city, and it became an important transportation hub, using the old Etruscan Veiense Road when the Flaminian Way fell into disrepair. Its hilltop location spared it from some of the worst barbarian destruction. Todi's golden age was the thirteenth century, when it maintained trade contacts with many of Tuscany's Guelph cities and its rule extended to include Terni. It was finally absorbed as a papal territory in 1503.

The city has retained a great deal of its medieval quality. A great proportion of its wall remains, as do impressive gates, particularly the Porta Perugina. Three of its most important structures are thirteenth-century secular buildings: the palazzi dei Priori, del Popolo, and del Capitano. The last contains a museum of Etruscan and Roman antiquities and the city's art gallery. Todi's Duomo was built between the twelfth and sixteenth centuries. Its Church of San Fortunato is an impressive Gothic structure begun in 1292, and contains the tomb of Todi's greatest literary figure, Jacopone da Todi (c. 1230–1306). A crusading Franciscan poet, Jacopone's attack on church corruption brought his excommunication by Pope Boniface VIII. The next pontiff, Benedict XI, reconsidered and lifted the interdict. The Church of Santa Maria della Consolazione is perhaps Todi's most artistically noteworthy. Lying just beyond the city walls, this sixteenth-century work of Cola di Matteuccio da Caprarola (active 1494–1518) is considered one of Umbria's Renaissance masterpieces.

One of Umbria's oldest Christian churches is the Temple of **Clitunno**, or San Salvatore, near **Trevi**. A fifth-century structure built with remnants of pagan buildings, it contains the most ancient Christian frescoes in Umbria. Umbria's churches are generally free of Norman and Byzantine adulteration, and stand on their own as Italian Romanesque structures. The territory from Spoleto to Assisi is rich in Romanesque churches.

TERNI

PROVINCIAL PROFILE. Area: 819 sq. mi. Population: 223,316 (province), 108,432 (city). Terni province contains 33 comunes. In Umbria's southwest corner, the province runs roughly from northwest to southeast. To its north and northeast is Perugia. To its west and south are Tuscany and Lazio. It is home to a mammoth hydroelectric concentration.

HISTORY. The Sabines founded Terni and called it *Interamna*, a name derived from its location "between two rivers," the Nera and the Serra. (Teramo in L'Aquila shares the same linguistic root.) The Romans absorbed Terni very early. One Latin inscription dates the union at 672 B.C. Later,

Terni's sympathy for Hannibal in the Second Punic War guaranteed that victorious Rome's grip on it in 205 B.C. would last. The city prospered under the Roman Empire and later, in the twelfth century, became a free commune under the Dukes of Spoleto. A series of local wars began in the fourteenth century and continued until Pope Alexander VI reintroduced a measure of stability when it became part of the papal lands at the end of the fifteenth century. Terni prospered until a general decline in the eighteenth century and the French invasions. Terni joined in riots in the uprising of 1831 and actively supported the Roman Republic in 1849. In the 1860s, after its union with the Kingdom of Italy, the city served as a base for Giuseppe Garibaldi's adventures against the Papal States.

Shortly after the Risorgimento, Terni's industrial development started, and brought it the reputation as the "Manchester of Italy." In 1875 a munitions plant opened, followed soon after by iron foundries and textile mills. In 1927 Terni became a province. Terni was an industrial target during the Second World War, and aerial bombardments severely damaged it. From August 1943 until June 1944, 101 air raids were inflicted on the city, destroying most of its northern end and causing the deaths of 1,500 people. The city nevertheless retooled and rebuilt, so well that Terni's postwar industries flourished as never before.

ARTS AND CULTURE. Saint Valentine is the patron of Terni as well as of lovers and engaged couples. According to tradition, he was a third-century bishop of the city and is buried there. Terni's cathedral is dedicated to the Assumption. It was rebuilt in 1653 on ancient foundations, and medieval influence is visible in some of the doorways. Other important churches are the Romanesque Sant'Alò, the twelfth-century San Salvatore, and San Francesco, which was built in 1265 and enlarged in 1437. The Florentine **Antonio Sangallo the Younger** (c. 1483–1546) died in Terni while working on the Palazzo Spada. The city boasts a Prehistoric Museum and a civic art gallery with works by **Benozzo Gozzoli** (1420–1497). In 1973 a group of Terni steel workers established an experimental theater, the Gruteater (Gruppo Teatro Terni).

OTHER CENTERS. In the eighth century, Duke Faroald II of Spoleto established the abbey of San Pietro in Valle outside of **Ferentillo**. Reconstructed in the tenth and eleventh centuries, it remains one of the duchy's principal legacies.

Narni's attractive situation on a verdant hill above the Nera River and its historical attractions have aided its tourist business in recent years. It was the Umbri city town of Nequinum before 299 B.C., when the Romans took it and dubbed it Narnia. Medieval Narni was a papal city until it broke from Rome and established itself as a free commune. Principal structures in the town's historic center include its twelfth-century Duomo, dedicated to San Giovenale; the Palazzo del Podestà (or Comunale), which contains a work by the Florentine artist Domenico Ghirlandaio (1449–1494); and the fourteenth-century Loggia dei Priori. Above Narni is the fourteenth-century fortress built by the ubiquitous advocate of papal control, Cardinal Gil Albornoz. Below the town are the remains of the Ponte di Augusto, a Roman bridge over the Nera that served as a link on the Flaminian Way. The area around Narni is home to many examples of Italian Romanesque structures including the Church of Santa Maria Assunta at Lugnano in Teverina.

Atop a dramatic rock, **Orvieto** assumes a defiant position typical of the Etruscan hilltop cities. Two important necropolises and a fifth-century B.C. temple recall the city's Etruscan phase, when it was known as Volsinii Veteres. The Romans took the town in 254 B.C., slaughtering or exiling the residents, and renaming it Urbs Vetus. The site was eventually abandoned, although its command of the surrounding area made it a military prize in the chaos following the fall of the Roman Empire (476). After occupations by Alaric and Odoacre in the fifth century, the Byzantine General Belisarius took the city following a long siege in A.D. 538. It became the seat of a Lombard duchy and then of a Tuscan county, and finally was a free commune in the eleventh century. By the middle of the next century, however, Orvieto had drawn so close to Rome that it had become one of central Italy's most important Guelph strongholds. In 1354 Cardinal Gil Albornoz gained Orvieto's loyalty to the Papal States and constructed a fortress there, although the city retained its self-governing status and administration. The papacy formally reannexed it in 1448 and made it the capital of the fifth province.

Orvieto's Duomo, one of Italy's most famous, dominates the city. Its colorful facade was begun, perhaps by the Tuscan Arnolfo di Cambio (c. 1245–1302) or, more probably, by the Sienese artist Lorenzo Maitani (c. 1270–1330); it was not finished until the seventeenth century. The church owes much to the work of Maitani, who headed its construction and labored on its ornamentation. He left remarkable bas-reliefs and bronze depictions of the Evangelists. The Duomo also contains works by the Marchigian Gentile Da Fabriano (c. 1370–1427), the Tuscans Beato Angelico (c. 1387–1455) and Benozzo Gozzoli (1420–1497), and the Veronese Michele Sanmicheli (1484–1559). The modern doors were added in 1970, the work of Emilio Greco. Pope Urban IV (1261–1264) intended the church to honor the miracle of Bolsena, a thirteenth-century event in which, during a Mass, the blood of Christ is reputed to have dripped from the Host onto the altar linen. The precious cloth is kept in the Duomo's Corporale Chapel. Orvieto stages a Corpus Domini (Body of the Lord) Festival on June 20 and an important commemoration of departed souls, the Fiera dei Morti (Fair of the Dead), at the beginning of November.

SELECT BIBLIOGRAPHY

Bracalente, Bruno. *Il Sistema industriale dell'Umbria*. Bologna: Il Mulino, 1986.

Covino, Renato, and Giampaolo Gallo, eds. *L'Umbria*. Turin: Einaudi, 1989.

Grohmann, Alberto, ed. *Perugia*. Rome: Laterza, 1990.

Istituto Geografico De Agostini. *Umbria*. Novara: Istituto Geografico De Agostini, 1982.

Chapter 19

VALLE D'AOSTA

REGIONAL CHARACTERISTICS. Area: 1,260 sq. mi. Population: 119,610. Capital: Aosta (pop. 35,098). The Valle d'Aosta is an autonomous region and Italy's smallest, ranking twentieth in area and population. It contains only one province, that of Aosta. Seventy-four communes dot the region.

In Italy's northwest corner, the Valle d'Aosta is wholly an Alpine land. The Italian Statistical Institute has determined that mountains occupy 100 percent of its terrain. The Valle d'Aosta is divided by the east-west flow of the Dora Baltea River, which rises at Monte Bianco (15,771 feet). Monte Bianco (or Mont Blanc) is Italy's tallest mountain and straddles the French border, serving as part of the watershed between the Po and the Rhone River networks. Bottled up in the mountains, the Valle d'Aosta might have been spared invaders had it not been for its crucially important Great and Little Saint Bernard Passes that link the Po valley to Europe beyond the Alps. At the Great Saint Bernard Pass sits a massive hospice (at 8,100 feet) that was founded, according to tradition, by Saint Bernard of Mentone (or Montjoux or Menthon), the archdeacon of Aosta. The region also boasts the Gran Paradiso National Park, the nation's first such reserve. The nucleus of its 173,000 acres was donated by the Italian royal house of Savoy (Savoia) in 1919. The region is bordered to the north by the Swiss canton of Valais, to the west by France, and to the south and east by Piedmont. Along the northern frontier, the Valle d'Aosta and Switzerland share Monte Cervino (or the Matterhorn, 14,690 feet) and Monte Rosa (15,203 feet).

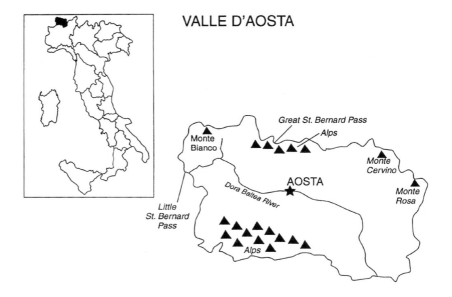

VALLE D'AOSTA

ECONOMY. Of the region's 52,000 employed workers, 31,000 are men and 21,000 are women. In January 1998 the unemployment rate was 5.7 percent. The tertiary sector accounts for 69.2 percent of workers, industry for 23.1 percent, and agriculture for 7.7 percent. Iron and steel account for much of the industrial employment. Most of the agricultural endeavors are devoted to cattle and dairy farming. Opportunities in agriculture, however, have always been limited, in that 20 percent of the Valle d'Aosta is covered with rock and ice, and 60 percent is heavily wooded or very secluded meadows. The bulk of the Valle d'Aosta's employment is in tourism, and success in that sector has more than made up for declines in the primary and secondary sectors.

CUISINE. The Valle d'Aosta's cuisine is noted for polenta and soups, such as *valpellinentze*, which is almost a combination of soup and fondue. Fontina cheese is very popular among the Valdostani, as is *toma*, made from ewe's milk. Honey is produced throughout the region. Spiced trout (*trotta spaccata*) is a local favorite. The *nebbiolo* grape, identified with Piedmont, is cultivated in trellised and terraced vineyards of the high Dora valley. From the Aosta nebbiolo come the Donnaz and Piedmontese Carema red wines. A local *moscato* grape produces the sweet white Chambave. In recent years the indigenous Blanc de Morgex (or Blanc de Valdigne or de La Salle) has enjoyed a successful revival. The vineyards of Morgex and La Salle in the region's northwest corner are said to be the highest ones in Europe.

ZUPPA ALLA VALPELLINENTZE

1 cabbage (preferably savoy cabbage)

Slices of white and wholemeal bread, toasted

7 oz. Fontina cheese, sliced

¾ c. beef broth, heated

2 Tbs. butter, chopped into small pieces

2 tsp. cinnamon

Preheat the oven to 375°. Stew the cabbage in a pot. Place a layer of toasted bread in the bottom of a casserole dish, then follow with a layer of stewed cabbage and a layer of cheese. Repeat the procedure until all the ingredients have been used. Pour the broth over the ingredients. Sprinkle butter and cinnamon on top of the casserole and bake for 15–20 minutes.

HISTORY. Neolithic tribes with ethnic ties to Swiss valley dwellers were the first to settle the Valle d'Aosta as early as the third millennium B.C. Between the eighth and the fifth centuries B.C. Celtic peoples invaded, and mixed with the local population, eventually forming the Salassi nation. The Romans subjugated the Salassi, and built an important road through the area which forked to the two mountain passes. In 25 B.C. they established their main colony at Augusta Praetoria (modern Aosta). The new masters devoted a great deal of their energies to building a city there. Much of the street plan of Aosta, for instance, still bears witness to the rectangular network conceived by the Romans. After the fall of the Roman Empire (A.D. 476), the valley was contested by Franks and Burgundians, then conquered by the Carolingians in 888.

In 1032 the Savoy Count Umberto I incorporated the Valle d'Aosta into his domain, the lands of Italy's future royal house. The Savoy favored the more southern Mount Cenis route to France rather than the Saint Bernard passes, and their participation in dynastic warfare brought invasions. During the Renaissance, the Valle d'Aosta's fortunes rose as trade between Italy and northern Europe produced a greater flow of commerce through the passes. The year 1630 was a particularly brutal one. France occupied the Valle d'Aosta and plague claimed two-thirds of its inhabitants. A catastrophic defeat of the Savoy at French hands in 1536 meant that their rule would be less intrusive, and allowed the Valdostani 200 years of self-government. Only in the eighteenth century was the Savoy presence reemphasized in earnest. The local Conseil des Commis (Parliament) was abolished by edicts of 1757 and 1758, and replaced with Savoy representatives. The Valdostano common law, the *Coutumier* was scrapped for Turin's system, and the local *donativo* (voluntary) tax was replaced with obligatory ones.

In 1796 the French invaded again, and annexed the Valle d'Aosta, which remained in their hands until the fall of Napoleon, when the Congress of Vienna (1815) returned it to the Savoys. In 1861 the Valle d'Aosta became part of the Kingdom of Italy as part of the province of Turin in the region of Piedmont. In 1927 Aosta became a province, but still was in Piedmont. The Valle d'Aosta's mixed Franco-Italian culture alarmed Mussolini's hypernationalist Fascist regime during the 1920s and 1930s, and the dictator enforced a policy of Italianization through education and heavy settlement by outsiders. After the Second World War, the Union Valdotaine worked for autonomy and, in some sectors, annexation to France. Some of its aims were achieved when the Valle d'Aosta separated from Piedmont and became an autonomous region in February 1948. The Valdostano historian and resistance leader, Federico Chabod (1901–1960), served as president of the first regional council in 1945–1946. The 35-member body meets in Aosta. Immigration into the region from southern Italy in the decades after the war reinforced the more Italian element in the ethnic mix.

In 1980 Valle d'Aosta was allowed to retain 90 percent of its taxation, and today the Valdostani enjoy one of Italy's highest per capita incomes. With autonomy came greater prosperity, particularly as the valley developed as a tourist destination. A flurry of cable-railway construction linked many of the mountain resorts, and the Casino at Saint-Vincent, one of Europe's largest, added to the lure. Traffic was facilitated by the completion of the Great Saint Bernard and Monte Bianco tunnels in 1964 and 1965.

RECENT POLITICS. Tiny Valle d'Aosta holds only a majoritarian vote in national elections. It constitutes Italy's twenty-seventh electoral district (*circoscrizione*). In the 1996 contest for the Chamber of Deputies, the Pour la Vallée d'Aoste took 48.6 percent of the votes, against 20.5 for the Polo per le Libertà. Tallies for the Senate election were about the same, 44.2 percent for the Pour la Vallée d'Aoste and 22.1 percent for the Polo. As an autonomous region, the Valle d'Aosta did not participate in the April 2000 regional elections.

ARTS AND CULTURE. Along with the street grid, Roman rule of Aosta remains visible in the impressive Praetorian Gate, in an Augustan arch, and in a well-preserved amphitheater. Medieval Aosta is recalled in the collegiate Church of Sant'Orso. Built in the eleventh century over the foundations of a paleo-Christian structure, it was renovated in the fifteenth. The church is dedicated to the region's popular patron, a protector from natural calamities, particularly drought. He was a presbyter who probably lived in Aosta between the fifth and the eighth centuries. Also dear to the Valdostani is Saint Anselm, who was born to a noble family of Aosta in 1033/1034. He left Italy in 1060 to live at the Benedictine monastery of Bec in France. He became Archbishop of Canterbury in 1093. Each September 7 the Valdostani celebrate the feast of San Grato, a fifth-century bishop and another protector of the region.

OTHER CENTERS. As an important avenue of conquest between

France and Italy, Valle d'Aosta is distinguished by its many castles. **Fenis** has an impressive one from the fourteenth century that was restored in the nineteenth and twentieth centuries. Its chapel contains frescoes by the Torinese artist **Giacomo Jaquerio** (1375–1453). Other important restored castles are at **Verres**, built in the fourteenth century and at **Issogne**, built in the late fifteenth century by Giorgio di Challant, prior of Sant'Orso in Aosta. Today the castle at Issogne is a museum. A twelfth-century stronghold, restored in the nineteenth, is at **Saint-Pierre**. Remains of castles are at **Arnad, Graines, Quart, Sarre,** and **Ussel,** which is under restoration near the industrial town of **Chatillon. Aymaville** boasts a third-century A.D. Roman bridge, the Pondel, as well as a medieval castle that was converted in the eighteenth century into a distinctive palace with four towers. Another Roman bridge is at **Pont-Saint-Martin.** The most impressive of the valley's bastions is the *forte* at **Bard,** built on a rocky point. Napoleon razed it, but it was rebuilt in the nineteenth century.

The Valle d'Aosta, known as the *petite patrie*, is home to one of Italy's most distinctive cultures. Although Italian is generally spoken in public discourse, most locals maintain their dialect, which is akin to Provencal. An exception is the town of **Gressoney,** which is home to a German dialect that probably descended from Switzerland. Local traditions include woodworking and athletic events such as *tsan, rebatta,* and *rouletta,* (which resembles a more vigorous bocce and is often played on festive occasions).

SELECT BIBLIOGRAPHY

Cuaz, Marco, ed. *Aosta: Progetto per una storia della città*. Quart, Valle d'Aosta: Musumeci Editore, 1987.
Gatto Chanu, Tersilla. *Leggende e racconti della Valle d'Aosta*. Rome: Newton Compton, 1992.
Istituto Geografico De Agostini. *Piemonte*. 2 vols. Novara: Istituto Geografico De Agostini, 1979.
Woolf, S. J., ed. *La Valle d'Aosta*. Turin: Einaudi, 1995.

VENETO

Cadore Range

Dolomite Range

Lake Garda

Feltre

Belluno

Bassano

Plave River

Verona

Vicenza

Treviso

Padua

VENICE

Gulf of Venice

Adige River

Adige River

Euganean Hills

Rovigo

Adria

Po River

Adriatic Sea

Chapter 20

VENETO

REGIONAL CHARACTERISTICS. Area: 7,096 sq. mi. Population: 4,469,156. Capital: Venice (Venezia). Veneto is Italy's eighth region in land area and its fifth in population. The region contains 580 communes. Venice is a Catholic patriarchal metropolitan see.

The Veneto region borders Friuli-Venezia Giulia to the east, Austria to the north and northeast, and Trentino-Alto Adige to the northwest. On the west, the Veneto is separated from Lombardy in part by Lake Garda, its southwest border is shared with Emilia Romagna, and it meets the Adriatic Sea on its south. The Veneto is a land of dramatic geographic contrasts, from rugged Dolomite Alps in the north to Piedmont and lowlands toward the shore. The northwest reaches of Belluno province contain peaks over 9,800 feet in the Tofane range; the region's highest mountain is Marmolada (10,965 feet), on the Veneto-Trentino border. Plains account for 56.4 percent of Veneto's land, 29.1 percent of it is hilly, and 14.5 percent is mountainous. Three of Italy's most important rivers—the Po, the Piave, and the Adige—flow through the Veneto and empty into the Adriatic.

ECONOMY. Of Veneto's 1,850,000 employed workers, 1,140,000 are men and 710,000 are women; 5.4 percent of the region's workers are in agriculture, 41.4 percent in industry, and 53.2 percent in the tertiary sector. The unemployment rate in January 1998 was 5.7 percent. The region's main industrial concentrations are in Padua and in Mestre and Marghera, along the coast facing Venice. Food processing occupies an important place in the industrial output of places like Rovigo. The lowlands of Padua and the delta area of Rovigo province yield wheat, beets, and rice. Corn is grown in Treviso province and southwest of Verona. Lead and zinc are mined in the region. Tourism is the Veneto's largest business. The Veneto hosts more foreign tourists and more tourists in general than does any other region.

CUISINE. Veneto's cuisine is diverse. Venice's tradition reflects its activity in the medieval spice trade and its location as a port. But the city's culinary reputation begins above all with *risi e bisi*, made with rice and peas, and a cross between a soup and a risotto. Rice is combined with fish or vegetables in countless other Venetian dishes. One of the more unusual is *risi co' la ua* (rice and grapes). *Risotto nero*, blackened with squid ink, is occasionally found. Pasta with beans, known as *pasta e fasioi*, is enjoyed across the region; but rice's status, and that of polenta, generally keep pasta off most of Veneto's stoves. An exception, however, is *bigoli*, a thick pasta common around Padua. A traditional meat dish is *pastissada di manzo*, beef or horsemeat in wine served with gnocchi or polenta. The Bassano area in Vicenza province is noted for white asparagus served with chopped hard-boiled eggs in vinegar and oil. Another mainland specialty, called *peará* in Verona and *pevarada* in Treviso, is a sauce of marrow, Parmesan cheese, and an abundance of pepper.

The Veneto produces more wine than any region outside of Sicily and Apulia, but none yields more DOC varieties. The center of the region's winemaking is Verona province, which produces two-thirds of the total (and more than the entire region of Piedmont). The Veneto's best and perhaps most famous wine, Soave, primarily comes from the hills between Vicenza and Verona. The southern foothills of the Lessini, northeast of Verona, yield Valpolicella, a variant of which is found in the Valpatena, running north out of the city. Wine-producing lands along Lake Garda's southeast shores and its hinterland offer the well-regarded Bardolinos and Bianco di Custoza. In the east, the plains along the Piave as it rolls toward the Adriatic is Italy's principal source of merlot. A popular local grape is the *raboso*, which is found in the flatter lands between the Piave and the Livenza rivers and near Padua, where it is referred to as the *raboso veronese*. It is usually mixed with Merlot, Cabernet, Italian Reisling, or local Tocai.

RISI E BISI

10 oz. fresh peas	2 Tbs. olive oil
3 c. water	2 c. Arborio rice
Salt to taste	1 Tbs. butter
½ medium onion, chopped	Grated Parmesan cheese, to taste
½ lb. pancetta (may substitute prosciutto)	

Boil peas in slightly salted water. In a separate pot sauté onion, pancetta, and oil until onion begins to brown. Add rice and cook for a few minutes, until the grains are coated. After a few minutes, slowly add water from peas into the sautéed mixture, stirring constantly. When about half of the water absorbed, add the peas. When the rice is fully cooked, mix in the butter and cheese.

HISTORY. Although the Veneto region is closely associated with its capital, Venice, the offshore city and the mainland had distinct histories until the 1400s. Under the Romans, in fact, Venice did not exist. The Veneti, who spoke a tongue akin to Illyrian, settled first in the area which the Romans incorporated in the 200s and 100s B.C. The Romans had called the region Venetia to honor the Veneti, with whom they were allied against their mutual enemy, the Boii Gauls. The major towns of the province were on the mainland: primarily Padua, which had been the Veneti capital, and Aquileia, on the Adriatic coast at the terminus of the Postumian Way from Genoa and the Annian (or Popilian) Way from Adria. Caesar Augustus incorporated most of the area into Region X, Venetia et Histria.

By the fourth century, Christianity had established a foothold, with episcopal sees at Padua, Altino, and Verona. The influence of the see at Aquileia, in Friuli, also reached far into the area. In 410 Alaric and the Goths invaded Venetia and launched the beginning of the end of Roman rule. Byzantine forces took Venetia in the 530s, but lost most of it to the Lombards within 100 years. Padua, for instance, fell in 601 or 602, and resistance at Oderzo, the last Byzantine territory on the mainland, collapsed in 667. The offshore islands, however, particularly the young city of Venice, technically remained under the Byzantines for much longer.

But Lombard rule was also brief. In the late 700s the Franks defeated them and made Venetia one of their marches. The region remained for the most part in Frankish hands until the late 800s, when the Kingdom of Italy briefly surfaced under King Berengar I of Friuli (888–924). The attempt failed under his grandson, Berengar II (950–952), when the Crown of Italy united with the Holy Roman Empire under the Carolingian Otto I (936–973). The Veneto continued to suffer barbarian invasions. Magyars charged through at the end of the ninth century, taking terrible tolls on Vicenza, Verona, Feltre, Asolo, Padua, and Chioggia until the Venetian Doge Pietro Tribuno beat them back in 900.

Medieval Venice established trade routes to the eastern Mediterranean and beyond without concerning itself with the mainland. The hinterland, on the other hand, involved itself more with Italian affairs. The first alliance against Emperor Frederick Barbarossa, for example, which led to the Lombard League (1167) was made by Verona, Vicenza, Padua, and Treviso in 1164. Thirteenth-century politics in the Veneto were dominated by the da

Romano clan. When Ezzelino III (1194–1259), a tyrant of legendary cruelty, joined the Ghibelline cause, imperial support enabled him to extend his family's power across the Veneto and into Lombardy. An alliance led by the pope and the Este family ended the da Romano ambitions at the battle of Cassano in 1259 and killed all members of the family.

By the early 1400s Venice became more of a factor on the mainland and annexed nearby towns in what are today the Veneto, Lombardy, and Friuli–Venezia Giulia. Allied to Florence in 1425, the Venetians reached as far inland as Como in 1427. Venetian sovereignty over Treviso, Feltre, Belluno, Ceneda, Padua, Brescia, Bergamo, Casalmaggiore, Soncino, and San Giovanni in Croce, along with much of the Cremonese and eastern Lombardy, was recognized by the Holy Roman Emperor in 1437 and confirmed in the Peace of Lodi in 1454. At the same time the city consolidated and expanded its Dalmatian territories. A free and strong Venice, however, proved too much for powers beyond the Alps, as well as for some jealous Italian cities and the fervidly anti-Venetian Pope Julius II. Consequently, in December 1508 the League of Cambrai was formed by Louis XII of France, Emperor Maximilian I, Aragon, England, Hungary, Savoy, Ferrara, Mantua, and Florence against Venice. Pope Julius formally added his hand to the mix and excommunicated the Venetian Republic. Venice had no chance against such an array, and succumbed near Cremona at the Battle of Agnadello on May 14, 1509. Almost immediately, Pope Julius reversed his policy and organized an alliance with Venice against France. The republic quickly regained a number of its holdings on the mainland, but it never again played a central role in Italian political affairs. Cultural affairs were another story, however, and Venice maintained its prestige as a capital of art and learning.

Napoleon's conquest ended Venice's authority on the mainland, and the Most Serene Republic itself. The Treaty of Campo Formio in October 1797 awarded the Veneto to France. In 1805, Napoleon reorganized the area, along with Lombardy and much of northern Italy, to form the Kingdom of Italy. Napoleon himself wore the crown. But French control eroded across Europe, and in October 1813 Austria invaded Italy. Vienna took possession of Lombardy and Venetia under the Convention of Schiarino-Rizzino of April 1814, and the Congress of Vienna (1815) affirmed its control. As half of the Lombard-Venetian Kingdom under an Austrian viceroy, the "Congregation" of Venetia encompassed today's Veneto and most of what is now Friuli–Venezia Giulia.

During the first days of April 1848, Piedmontese troops crossed the Mincio River, then the border with Lombardy, and entered Venetia. Small revolts against the Austrians spread across the region and into Friuli, and for a brief springtime, Venetia had achieved independence. But Vienna's soldiers descended from the Alps and reclaimed the territory. The Battle of Custoza (July 24–25) crippled Piedmont's forces. After that, only Venice, which had been proclaimed a republic under Daniele Manin, and the mountain stronghold of Osoppo held the line. But their resistance was doomed; Venice fell in August 1849, and Osoppo finally capitulated in October. Austria returned, and administered Venetia as a police state.

In the 1859 campaign Austria held on to Venetia but lost Lombardy to the Italians. Hapsburg troops retreated into the Quadrilateral, a network of fortifications of Verona, Peschiera, Mantua, and Legnago, and held the region until it finally passed to the Kingdom of Italy after the Seven Weeks (Austro-Prussian) War of 1866. Italy's performance on land during the war was at best lackluster; at Custoza the army received a second drubbing at Austrian hands. But at sea the war was a catastrophe. At the Battle of Lissa on July 20, the Austrians sent Admiral Carlo di Persano's flagship, the *Re d'Italia*, to the bottom of the Adriatic and delivered a devastating blow to the Italian navy. But Italy's ally Prussia crushed Austria at the Battle of Sadowa (Bohemia) and Rome found itself on the winning side, enabling it to annex Venetia. The region's western zone around Mantua was then incorporated into Lombardy, where it remains today.

Conflict with Austria erupted again in May 1915, when Italy entered the First World War on the side of Britain and France. The Veneto became a battleground, and much of the struggle took place in the area around Feltre and Vicenza (the Vicentino). The collapse of Russia in 1917 freed German troops, allied to the Austrians, and allowed the transfer of many of them to Italy. The front collapsed at Caporetto in October, and Italy's army endured a wild retreat until it reassembled and held on the banks of the Piave and on Monte Grappa. Italy's revenge came a year later when, at the end of October and beginning of November 1918, it launched its final victorious drive of the war, destroying the enemy forces at Vittorio Veneto. On November 3 an armistice was signed at the Villa Giusti, outside of Padua.

In 1944 the Germans occupied the area and detached Belluno province from the rest of the region. They merged it with the Trentino–Alto Adige and incorporated it into the Reich as Alpenvorland. With the rest of the Veneto, Belluno was liberated in the spring of 1945. After the war the province of Udine was shifted from Veneto to form part of Friuli-Venezia Giulia.

RECENT POLITICS. Postwar politics in the Veneto were dominated by the Christian Democrats (DC), who gained most of their support from the northern parts of the region. Although the Communists were strong in the city of Venice, the DC captured 50.6 percent of the total vote in 1979. Through the 1980s and 1990s, however, Christian Democratic popularity dwindled before the rightist League movement. In 1979 Franco Rocchetta's Liga Veneta was the first of the Northern Leagues to form, and by 1992 it controlled 17 percent of the vote. The Veneto votes in two electoral districts (*circoscrizioni*): the seventh, which occupies most of the western half of the region, and the eighth, which embraces Venice and the rest of the east.

In the 1996 majoritarian elections to the Chamber of Deputies, the Polo per le Libertà alliance captured a plurality of the seventh district's ballots with 33.2 percent. The Lega Nord took 31.8 percent, and the Ulivo took 31.6 percent. In the eighth district the Lega Nord captured 34.3 percent of the votes against the Ulivo's 32 percent and the Polo's 31 percent. In the seventh district's proportional vote the Lega Nord maintained its lead with 26.9 percent. Forza Italia took 16.2 percent, the Alleanza Nazionale took 13 percent, and the Partito Democratico Della Sinistra (PDS) registered 11 percent. The eighth district also gave the Lega a plurality with 32.8 percent. Forza Italia took 18.4 percent, the PDS tallied 13 percent, and the Alleanza Nazionale had 9.8. In the Veneto's 1996 Senate vote the Ulivo coalition acquired eight seats (33.9 percent), as did the Lega Nord (30.3 percent). The April 2000 regional elections reaffirmed Center-Right leadership of the Veneto, with Giancarlo Galan's election as president at the head of a co-alition with 54.9 percent of the vote. The Center-Left captured 38.2 percent.

VENICE (VENEZIA)

PROVINCIAL PROFILE: Area: 2,950 sq. km. Population: 815,807 (province), 296,422 (city). Venice contains forty-three communes. Venice province curves around the northwest corner of the Adriatic Sea, stretching from Friulia–Venezia Giulia to its northeast, past Treviso to its north, Padua to its west and Rovigo to its south.

HISTORY. Venice began as an offshore place of refuge for those fleeing the barbarian invasions at the end of the Roman Empire. In the 400s A.D. small shelter communities sprang up along the coastline of the northern Adriatic, or just off it. The historic appearance of these villages coincides with the legendary date for the establishment of Venice (421). By the early 500s Venice had become one of the most important of these makeshift towns, significant enough to entice the Byzantines to annex it and rely on its port. From their capital at Ravenna, they appointed tribunes to rule Venice, which by 697 was strong enough to lead a confederation under its own *dux*, or doge. In 811, after repelling an attack by King Pepin and the Franks, the seat of a united Venetian government was established at Rivus Altus, or Rialto, the center of the city, which had moved into the lagoon from the outlying Lido.

Venice maintained a tenuous attachment to the Byzantines but obedience to the emperor eroded more and more into a fiction. In 841 Constantinople courted the Venetians for assistance in its naval war with the Muslims.

This aid, however, brought disaster on the city. Much of Venice's fleet was sunk off Crotone in Calabria, and the victorious Muslims chased the rest of it up the Adriatic almost to the Venetian lagoon. They turned back only when the dangerous currents around the Po delta hampered navigation. The Magyars turned to Venice in 899, after sweeping through the mainland. They reached the Lido from Chioggia but were stopped there. Venice's greatest calamity, however, came from within. An uprising in 976 against the wildly unpopular Doge Pietro Candiano led to destruction of the doge's the palace and the burning down of the center of the city; the doge and his infant child were hacked to death. Despite such troubles, Venice, *la Serenissima* or "Most Serene Republic," recovered and prospered. Under Candiano's capable successors, particularly Pietro Orseolo (whom the Catholic Church beatified), the city assumed a place of central importance in the Mediterranean.

Of inestimable help in Venice's triumph were the Crusades, which began in 1095 and which the Republic joined in 1099. For the next 200 years, the city's fleet shuttled Christian warriors and pilgrims back and forth to the Holy Land. The Fourth Crusade (which departed from Venice in November 1202) served the doge and his merchant aristocracy most of all. They directed the ships and their cargoes of knights to stop on the Dalmatian coast in order to crush Zara, a town of pesky rival merchants and pirates. At this point, alarmed by Venice's dereliction, Pope Innocent III excommunicated the Crusaders. The Crusade continued, however, not to the Holy Land as planned, but to Christian Constantinople. There the Venetians directed one of the greatest sacks of history, channeling treasures of inestimable worth back to their city. Throughout this epoch audacious Venice established an empire whose influence and colonies cascaded down the Dalmatian coast to Greece, through the Aegean to Constantinople and to the Black Sea. Its larger possessions included Crete, the Peloponnesus, and Cyprus.

Venice's ambition brought frequent conflict with Italian states. During the First Crusade (1095–1099), for instance, the Venetians took the opportunity to defeat their Pisan rivals at Rhodes before they sailed on to the Holy Land. Genoa was Venice's foe through most of the later Middle Ages. A great act in the drama began in 1293 when fighting erupted between the two that reached from Dalmatia to the shores of Armenia. In 1298 the Genoese scored a great victory over their rivals at Curzola in the Adriatic, but the war ended inconclusively the next year. The Venetians finally settled the question with their victory over Genoa at Chioggia in 1379–1380.

In the fourteenth and fifteenth centuries, Venice extended its reach into the mainland territories and encountering Milan as a frequent rival and enemy. The domain stretched past Veneto, deep into both Friuli and Lombardy before Venice was decisively defeated at Agnadello in 1509. Its role thereafter was greatly restricted.

After the encroaching Turks took Constantinople in 1453, they began to gnaw at Venice's empire. In 1470 they took Euboea in the Aegean Sea and, step by step, annexed all of the republic's possessions east of the Adriatic. Cyprus fell in 1571, and Crete did so in 1669, after a 20-year seige. Francesco Morosini staged a last hurrah when he reconquered the Peloponnesus and Athens in 1687. The Treaty of Passarowitz (1718) surrendered all of Venice's Aegean holdings to the Turks, ending the city's empire in the east.

The Most Serene Republic was drawing to an end as well. Napoleon took Venice in May 1797, ending the independence it had enjoyed for a thousand years. His initial occupation was brief, and the Austrians took the city from him, holding it until 1805. Napoleon returned that year and administered Venice until the Austrians retook it in 1814.

Austrian rule was unenlightened, and the city suffered a general decline. A strong sentiment for union with a united Italy, led by Daniele Manin (1804–1857), developed. As the revolutions of 1848 were brewing in Vienna and Milan, Manin was arrested in Venice; the popular furor that demanded his release sparked an uprising.

Out of prison, he led the people in the expulsion of the Austrians and proclaimed the Republic of San Marco. The rebellion spread to the mainland, then collapsed (except for Osoppo) before the Austrians took the city in August 1849.

Prime Minister Luigi Luzzatti (1841–1927) came from a Venetian Jewish family. He served as treasury minister five times before becoming head of the government in 1910–1911.

During the 1920s and 1930s Venice's industry and politics were dominated by Giuseppe Volpi. Volpi was active in Italian trade in the Balkans and in power companies in the Veneto and the northeast. He negotiated the end of the Italo-Turkish War in 1912, was a delegate to the Paris Peace Conference in 1919, and served as governor of Tripolitania in North Africa in the years before the Fascist regime. Volpi joined the Fascist Party, and Mussolini utilized his talents as an international agent for Italy and as minister of finance. During the 1930s Volpi returned to Venice to chair the Biennale art exhibition and manage his enormous industrial and financial holdings. He was the president of the Italian large manufacturers' association, Confindustria, until 1943, when the Fascists, unsure of his continued loyalty, forced his resignation.

Venice suffered little damage during the Second World War. The Germans surrendered it to the Partisans and evacuated in 1945 without incident. The city quickly revived as a center of culture and tourism. A serious flood in 1966 mobilized friends of the city in Italy, around the world, and at the United Nations on a crusade to save Venice from further damage. Unfortunately, the city continues its slide into the lagoon.

ARTS AND CULTURE. At the heart of Venice is the Piazza San Marco with the city's magnificent cathedral that honors the saint. The structure served as the doges' chapel, and became the cathedral only in 1807. Before that, Venice's cathedral stood at the site of San Pietro in Castello at Olivolo, an island at the city's eastern end. The first church on the site (seventh century) was dedicated to Saints Sergius and Bacchus followed by a ninth-century structure that honored Peter the Apostle. As the name implies, the city's chief fortress once stood nearby. The current San Pietro di Castello was built in the seventeenth century based partly on a design by Andrea Palladio and includes a high altar and impressive Vendramin Chapel by **Baldassarre Longhena** (1598–1682).

Venice's greatest church dates from 829, when Doge Giustiniano Partecipazio ordered the construction of a basilica to honor Saint Mark the Evangelist. That first structure was destroyed in the tenth-century riots against Doge Pietro Candiano and had to be rebuilt. Doge Pietro Contarini undertook its reconstruction in 1063. Venice's identification with its patron, Saint Mark, stems from the decline of what had been larger communities on the shore, Aquileia and Grado. Aquileia had been founded (in tradition) by that saint, and thus, in the late Roman Empire, its bishop enjoyed the status of patriarch. The rival city of Grado soon claimed the title, and attained it in the 600s after a schism. As Grado declined, Venice took the honor by dint of its possession of Saint Mark's body. According to legend, in 827 two merchants, Buono da Malamocco and Rustico da Torcello, removed the body of Saint Mark from its resting place in Alexandria, Egypt, and transported it to Venice. Saint Mark was finally named the city's patron in the eleventh century, replacing Saint Theodore of Amansea, whose statue still stands (in replica; the original is in the Doge's Palace), with one foot on a crocodile-like dragon, atop a pillar that Doge Sebastiano Ziani (reigned c.1102–c. 1180) placed in the piazzetta facing the lagoon.

Part of San Marco's incredibly rich decoration stems from a medieval law that required ships to bring back from their travels some adornment for the church. The structure, both inside and out, is distinguished by one of the greatest arrays of mosaic art found anywhere. Most of the interior works were completed between 1067 and 1277. On the facade only one of the original mosaics remains, that depicting the translation of Saint Mark's body to the basilica. The last external mosaics were completed in the 1830s. Above the central doorway are replicas of four magnificent bronze horses; the originals have been moved inside to protect them from pollution. The quartet dates from ancient times and was carted to Venice from Constantinople after the sack of 1204. Napoleon stole the horses from the Venetians in 1797; they were returned in 1814. The remains of many doges rest in the basilica, as does the body of Saint Pius X. From Treviso province, he served as patriarch of Venice before he became pope in 1903.

He promised to return to the city and his wish was finally granted through his burial there in 1958, over forty years after his death.

The Greek icon of the Madonna of Nicopeia, among Venice's greatest religious treasures, is in a chapel that bears her name. She is revered as Venice's protector; the image, carried by Byzantine emperors into battle, was taken during the sack of Constantinople in 1204. Next to her chapel is one that honors Saint Isidore. By some accounts, it is on the spot where the Byzantines dedicated one of Venice's first churches to Saint Theodore. Behind the high altar is the remarkable *pala d'oro*. Crafted in Constantinople and Venice between the tenth and fourteenth centuries, it is an amalgam of depictions from the Bible and the lives of the apostles in gold, and is set with precious stones.

San Marco faces onto its elegant piazza, which Napoleon labeled the "finest drawing room of Europe." A creek, the Rio Batario, ran through the square until Doge Ziani filled it in and paved it in the twelfth century.

Next to the basilica is the Doge's Palace, the Palazzo Ducale, which was the residence of the ruler as well as the seat of the government and the courts. A castle was built on the spot in the early ninth century, and the present palace dates from an extensive reconstruction begun in the mid-1300s. The central endeavor in the rebuilding was an expansion of the structure to accommodate the great hall, the *sala del maggior consiglio* (Hall of the Great Council). Fifteenth- and sixteenth-century modifications were made by a number of Venetian artists, particularly **Bartolomeo** (1374–1467) and **Giovanni** (1382–1443) **Bon**, and **Giorgio Spavento** (active 1468–1509), as well as the Veronese **Antonio Rizzo** (c. 1430–c. 1499).

Gothic Venice is distinguished by two of the city's largest churches, the thirteenth- and fourteenth-century Dominican basilica of Santi Giovanni e Paolo (or San Zanipolo) and an almost identical Franciscan structure from the fourteenth and fifteenth centuries, Santa Maria Gloriosa dei Frari. In the piazza facing Santi Giovanni e Paolo is the bold equestrian statue of Bartolomeo Colleoni, finished in 1488 by the Florentine artist **Verrocchio** (1435–1488). Colleoni was a prominent soldier who bequeathed a fortune to Venice if it would erect a monument to him in the Piazza San Marco. Venice accepted the inheritance but could not quite bear its end of the deal. The city cheated the dead warrior by placing his monument, Verrocchio's masterpiece, in its more secluded location.

The cavernous Frari contains some outstanding works, particularly the *Madonna and Child with Saints Nicholas, Peter, Benedict, and Paul* by Giovanni Bellini (Venice, 1430–1516) and *The Assumption* by **Titian** (Tiziano Vecelli, 1488/1490–1576), a native of Belluno province. San Zanipolo contains some noteworthy works of art as well, including Bellini's polyptych on the life of Saint Vincent Ferrer and a collection of doge's tombs, particularly Pietro Mocenigo's sepulchre by the Swiss artist **Pietro Lombardo** (c. 1435–c. 1515). Lombardo is buried in the Frari. San Zanipolo houses the remains of Doge Giacomo Tiepolo, who donated the land for both churches.

Another school of thought holds that Venice's premier Gothic church is the fourteenth-century Madonna dell'Orto. A large statue of Saint Christopher reputedly by Bartolomeo Bon recalls that the church was first dedicated to him. The church also has a number of works by a son of Venice and one of its greatest artists, **Tintoretto** (Jacopo Robusti, c. 1518–1594), who worshiped and was buried at the Madonna dell'Orto.

Venice's great age of economic power is recalled in many places throughout the city. Some of the secret to the city's success can be considered at the Arsenale (Arsenal), where Venice made its ships. Its efficiency and production made it one of the wonders of medieval Christendom. Foreigners and non-Christians lived and worked in designated areas of Venice, some of which can still be observed. Beginning at least in the thirteenth century, Germans gathered at or near the *fondaco dei tedeschi* near the Rialto Bridge. They occupied it until 1812; today it is Venice's post office. Until 1838 the Ottomans rented a palace that came to be known as the *fondaco dei turchi*. The Venetian Senate gave permission for such a place in 1575, although only Bosnian and Albanian Muslims were allowed. The Jews lived at the "new foundry," or *ghetto nuovo*, a name derived from a cannon factory that stood there at one time. During the Middle Ages, Venice's Jews had lived mainly on the outlying Giudecca island or on the coastline at Mestre; a few were allowed into the city proper. The ghetto was created in 1516 and expanded in 1663 with only one secured entrance. Napoleon's soldiers ended restrictions that limited Venice's Jews to the ghetto, but with five synagogues it remained Venice's primary Jewish neighborhood.

The wealth of Venice is also revealed in its palaces. The Ca'd'Oro may be the most splendid of these structures. Built in fifteenth century on the site of a Byzantine palace, it was rescued from ruin by Baron Giorgio Franchetti, who gave it to the city in 1916 as a museum. Other palaces that have become museums include the sumptuous Ca'Rezzonico, which was begun in 1667 by **Baldassare Longhena** (1598–1682) and completed in 1756 by another Venetian, **Giorgio Massari** (c. 1686–1766).

Longhena was the most Baroque architect in a very Baroque city. His works left a mark on Venice almost as great as Bernini's did on Rome. The city's outstanding Baroque structure is Longhena's Santa Maria della Salute, begun in 1631 and completed in 1687. Situated in one of the city's choicest spots, where the Grand Canal widens into the lagoon and across from Piazza San Marco, it was built in gratitude for the Madonna's protection during a plague.

The Church of San Rocco was begun in 1489 by Bartolomeo Bon and rebuilt in the eighteenth century. Born in the Languedoc region of France, Rocco died in Italy, where he is greatly venerated as the protector of small animals and is felt to help in case of plague. He is buried in the magnificent church named for him. The church houses an impressive series of paintings celebrating his life. Next to the Church of San Rocco is the Scuola Grande di San Rocco (1478). The *scuole* (schools) of Venice date from the Middle Ages and are devotional organizations reminiscent of guilds. The larger ones, like that of San Rocco, became famous for their assistance to the arts and for civic beautification. The Scuola Grande di San Rocco contains a cycle of Mannerist paintings on the life of Christ, the glory of Tintoretto's career. His works can also be seen in the Doge's Palace (Palazzo Ducale), particularly the enormous paintings *Venice, Queen of the Sea* and *Paradise*.

Tintoretto's contemporary, Paolo Caliari, known as **Veronese** (1528–1588), was also active in the city. He, too, enhanced the Doge's Palace with his monumental *Triumph of Venice* in the great hall. Veronese worked on the decorations of his favorite church, dedicated to San Sebastiano, where he is buried.

Napoleon launched a number of changes in the city's landscape at the end of the eighteenth and the beginning of the nineteenth centuries. In 1807 he demolished the Church of San Gemigniano, which faced the cathedral from the opposite end of the piazza, and replaced it with the Ala Napoleonica, a palace that today houses the Correr Museum, which is devoted to the history of the city. Napoleon tore down a number of monasteries as well, to make way for public gardens near the eastern end of the city.

Figures such as **Ermolao Barbaro the Younger** and **Pietro Bembo** made Venice an important city of Renaissance humanist literature. A Venetian aristocrat who studied at the University of Padua, Barbaro (1453–1492) was a key translator of Greek texts. Bembo, born to a noble Venetian family in 1470, benefited from his father's diplomatic positions by growing up close to two of the chief Renaissance courts, those of Florence and Ferrara. He was greatly influenced by Petrarch, and his *Gli Asolani* (1505) was a discussion of the nature of love. In 1530 he became the official historian of Venice and wrote a narrative of the Republic from 1487 until 1513. Bembo became a cardinal of the Catholic Church in 1539 and died at Rome in 1547. A friend of Bembo, a humanist, and one of Europe's first important publishers was **Aldo Mannucci** (or Minuzio), known as Aldus Manutius (1449–1515). He printed his first book at Venice in 1495. Another Venetian humanist was **Cassandra Fedele** (1465–1558), the most accomplished woman author of the age, who wrote a defense of female education in 1488.

Venice boasts important contributions to music. **Giovanni Gabrieli** (c. 1556–1612) was born in Venice (as was his uncle, the musician **Andrea Gabrieli** [c. 1510–1586]) and was the organist at San Marco and at the Scuola Grande di San Rocco. His sacred works, madrigals, and music for wind ensembles are worthy examples of the late Italian Renaissance. Another Venetian was **Antonio Vivaldi** (1678–1741). In 1703 he was ordained as a priest and became the choirmaster at a girls' orphanage with which he enjoyed a long association. Although Vivaldi wrote for voice as well, he is best remembered for the refinements he brought to the concerto form. Venetian opera was enriched by **Claudio Monteverdi**. Although born at Cremona 1567, Monteverdi spent much of his career in Venice, beginning in 1613 as choirmaster of San Marco. Particularly through his operas, including *L'incoronazione di Poppea* (The Coronation of Poppea), Monteverdi exerted enormous influence on Venice's musical life until his death there in 1643. **Tomaso Albinoni** (1671–1751) was born in Venice and is remembered for operas, such as *Zenobia* (1694), cantatas, and works for strings. **Francesco Algarotti** (1712–1764) was a theoretician of music whose work *Saggio sopra l'opera in musica* (Essay on Opera) is said to have influenced Christoph Gluck. He also wrote travel literature and served as chamberlain in the court of Frederick II of Prussia.

Seventeenth- and eighteenth-century Venetian intellectual life revolved around the Academy of the Ignoti (Unknowns), established by the patron and novelist **Giovan Francesco Loredano** (1607–1661), and around local representatives of the "Arcadians," established at Rome by the exiled Queen Christina of Sweden in 1656. Two Venetian Arcadians, **Apostolo Zeno** (1668–1750) and the Veronese nobleman **Francesco Scipione Maffei** (1675–1755), established the influential *Giornale de' letterati d'Italia* (Italian Journal for "Men of Letters") in 1710. Maffei, in particular, became a key figure in the Italian Enlightenment who developed close ties with many like-minded persons in France and northern Europe.

No single figure exemplifies literary Venice of the eighteenth century. Perhaps its most famous Enlightenment figure was the notorious **Giovanni Giacomo Casanova** (1725–1798), who left impressive memoirs. Nevertheless, the works of **Carlo Goldoni** (1707–1793), usually in dialect, best conjure the spirit of the city. The young Goldoni left Venice for school in Pavia and launched his own saga of wandering, which included a long term in Pisa as a lawyer and a member of the local Arcadian group before returning to Venice in 1748. There, Goldoni wrote plays about everyday Venetian life with the intent of replacing the traditional commedia dell'arte form with a more refined style, and joined a lively and testy rivalry with an abbot born in Brescia, **Pietro Chiari** (1712–1785) and the Venetian **Carlo Gozzi** (1720–1806). In 1762 Goldoni went to Paris to work with the Comedie Italienne, and stayed there until his death. Of Goldoni's two rivals, Gozzi was the more talented. He represented a more conservative Venetian theater in his defense of the *commedia dell'arte*, and his works are often ranked at least as high as Goldoni's. He staged a number of fantasies, (*fiabe*), such as *L'amore delle tre melarance* (Love for Three Oranges, 1761) and *Turandot* (1762), which were later turned into operas by, respectively, Sergei Prokofiev and Giacomo Puccini.

One of the chief authors and poets of the Risorgimento, **Ugo Foscolo**, was born in 1778 as a Venetian citizen on the Greek island of Zante. As a boy, he and his widowed mother moved to Venice. He left for Milan in 1799 and joined Napoleon's forces. During this time he began his *Ultime lettere di Jacopo Ortis* (Last Letters of Jacopo Ortis), credited by some as the first modern Italian novel. In 1806 Foscolo wrote his masterpiece of poetry, *Dei sepolcri* (Tombs). When Napoleon's empire fell, Foscolo fled to England, where he died in 1827.

On Ascension Day, Venice celebrates the Feast and Regatta of the Sensa, an important civic holiday which commemorates the departure in A.D. 1000 of Doge Pietro Orseolo II's fleet. One of Venice's greatest leaders, Orseolo proceeded down the Dalmatian coast to defeat some of the republic's most irritating enemies, the Croatian pirates. The departure is recalled by the appearance of the doge on his flagship, the *Bucintoro*, and Venice's symbolic "marriage to the sea," the *sposalizio col mare*. He performs the ceremony by tossing a wedding ring into the lagoon, to the accompaniment of choruses and colorful displays of flags and decorations. The "marriage" was added some years after the reign of Orseolo, who, on that Ascension Day in 1000, was anointed with oil and received a consecrated battle standard from the Bishop of Olivolo. A similar celebration, the *Regata Storica*, occurs in September; it dates from the second half of the fourteenth century.

Many important museums are *found* in Venice. Along with those mentioned above, the Accademia is one of the most important in Italy. It boasts works by such Renaissance masters as **Giorgione** (c. 1477–1511), Giovanni and **Gentile Bellini** (Venice, c. 1429–1507), Tintoretto, Veronese, and Titian. It also contains works by native Venetian masters of the eighteenth century, **Giovanni Battista Tiepolo** (1696–1770), **Canaletto** (Giovanni Antonio Canal, 1697–1768), and **Francesco Guardi** (1712–1793). The Peggy Guggenheim Collection has one of Italy's finest displays of modern and contemporary art.

Venice's Carnival before Lent is well known as one of the most important in Italy. It is a tradition celebrated across the Veneto.

One of the world's chief art festivals is the Venice Biennale. It began as an international arts festival in 1895 and greatly expanded its scope in the 1930s to include music (1930) and cinema (1932). In 1975 architecture was added.

OTHER CENTERS. An early rival to Venice was **Caorle**. On the coast at the head of its own lagoon, the Laguna di Caorle, the town grew, as Venice did, when Roman refugees chose it as a safe haven from barbarians. It was an early episcopal see and, although this status has been lost, Caorle retains its cathedral dedicated to Santo Stefano. The Romanesque structure was rebuilt in the eleventh century and is distinguished by Byzantine artwork and a cylindrical campanile. Caorle's founders fled from their mainland home of **Concordia Sagittaria** (at that time Julia Concordia), a place that survived despite their fears. It still contains some traces of its Roman past—a military necropolis and a three-arched bridge, for example—as well as an exemplary eleventh century baptistery.

Chioggia sits on the mainland at the southern tip of the Venetian lagoon and the mouth of the Brenta River. Its medieval importance stemmed from its role as a port and as a center of salt production. Chioggia is the place where Venice's rivalry with Genoa was settled. On August 16, 1379, a Genoese naval squadron under Pietro Doria took Chioggia and launched a blockade of Venice. In December the octogenarian doge, Andrea Contarini, retaliated and sealed the Genoese in Chioggia. Their surrender the following June assured Venice's primacy.

Near Mestre, **Mogliano Veneto** is the birthplace of the engraver and designer Giovanni Battista Piranesi (1720–1778). Piranesi's fascination with ancient structures manifested itself early on, but it flowered when he relocated to Rome and published his four-volume *Le antichità Romane* (Roman Antiquities) in 1756. He published a number of other works on Roman ruins in the city and elsewhere. Piranesi's fantastic etchings, collected in *Carceri d'Invenzione* (Fantastic Prisons, 1761, reworked from a 1749–1750 work), had a great impact at the dawn of the Romantic era.

Murano is an island in the Venetian Lagoon famous since the thirteenth century for the production of glass. Also notable are the Romanesque Church of Santi Maria e Donato with its twelfth-century mosaic floor, and the fifteenth-century Dominican Church of San Pietro Martire. The latter contains two works by the Venetian artist Giovanni Bellini, as well as a depiction of Saint Jerome by Veronese.

Another island in the lagoon with a long history is **Torcello**. It had an early concentration of settlers from the mainland, and the Bishop of Altino fled there in 638. He began Torcello's cathedral the following year. Dedicated to Maria Assunta, it was extensively rebuilt in 824 and 1008. Next to the cathedral is the smaller twelfth-century Church of Santa Fosca. Both are leading examples of Venetian Romanesque with arched porticoes that betray Arab influence.

The Venetian aristocracy built villas along the Brenta Canal. Some of these are concentrated at **Mira**. Among the most noteworthy are the Villa Widmann (1719) and, at nearby **Gambarare di Mira**, Andrea Palladio's Villa Foscari (1560). Other villas are at **Stra**, where Hitler and Mussolini stayed during their first meeting in 1934. Most important is the sumptuous Villa Pisani, built by the Padovano Gerolamo Frigimelica (1653–1732), with additions by Francesco Maria Preti (1701–1774), an artist from Castelfranco Veneto.

BELLUNO

PROVINCIAL PROFILE. Area: 1,420 sq. mi. Population: 211,458 (province), 35,336 (city). Belluno province contains 69 communes. Belluno province juts north from the Veneto all the way to the Austrian border. To the east of the province is Friuli–Venezia Giulia, and to its west is Trentino–Alto Adige. South of Belluno are Treviso and Vicenza. The capital, Belluno city, is in the southern part of the province, where the Adige meets the Ardo River. Most of the province is in the Dolomite Alps, reaching to the peaks of the massive Cadore Alps in the north. It includes the Dolomiti Bellunesi National Park and the Dolomiti d'Ampezzo Regional Park.

HISTORY. The Romans knew Belluno as Bellunum, but a settlement existed there long before their arrival. It was later a Frankish county and a medieval free commune. In the 1320s Belluno and Feltre were captured by the Veronese adventurer Cangrande della Scala. Belluno voluntarily surrendered its sovereignty to Venice in 1405.

Much of the First World War in Italy was fought in Belluno's mountains, and in 1917 the Italians stopped the Austrian advance on the Piave River, which flows through much of the province. After the fall of Benito Mussolini and the German invasion of Italy in 1943, Belluno was annexed to the Third Reich along with the provinces of Trento and the Alto Adige as Alpenvorland. It was liberated at the end of April 1945.

ARTS AND CULTURE. Belluno's Church of Santo Stefano (1468) contains an impressive altar by local artists, **Antonio, Francesco,** and **Matteo Cesa,** who were active at the end of the fifteenth century. The early sixteenth-century Duomo is dedicated to San Martino di Tours (Martin of Tours), the city's patron. The campanile was built by the Sicilian architect **Filippo Juvara.** Bellunesi throughout the province enjoy drifting down the Piave on rafts (*zattere*). Usually undertaken in traditional garb, the trips are in part reenactments of barge traffic that has existed on the Piave since prehistoric times.

Pope Gregory XVI (1765–1846) was born Bartolomeo Cappellari in Belluno. He was elected to the Throne of Saint Peter in 1831, and his fifteen-year pontificate extended through tumultuous years of nationalist agitation, liberalism, and the beginnings of industrialism. He condemned most of these developments in his 1832 encyclical, *Mirari Vos*.

The writer **Dino Buzzati** (1906–1972) was born in Belluno. He was a journalist and wrote novels, of which his *Il Deserto dei Tartari* (The Tartar Steppe, 1940) is considered the best. His short stories are particularly well regarded. A collection of them, *Sessanta racconti* (Sixty Stories) received the 1958 Strega Prize.

OTHER CENTERS. West of Belluno is **Feltre,** a town with pre-Roman roots. It was annexed to Rome in 140 B.C. After barbarian sacks, Feltre reemerged as a free city at the end of the tenth century. It changed masters a number of times, from the Veronese della Scala (Scaligeri) family, to the Dukes of Austria and Carinthia, and the King of Bohemia, until 1405, when it passed, along with Belluno, to the Venetians. Between 1509 and

1511 Feltre was caught in the League of Cambrai's wars against Venice. Emperor Maximilian I laid siege to the city and burned it to the ground. Feltre was the home of a significant Renaissance humanist, Vittorino da Feltre (1378–1446), one of the fathers of physical education. Between Feltre and Belluno is the Villa Pagani-Gaggia, where Mussolini met Hitler for the last time before he was deposed in July 1943. The Duce's humiliated silence before the Fuhrer disappointed many of his lieutenants, who were convinced that he was no longer capable of governing Italy. Days later Mussolini fell from power. To commemorate the city's annexation by Venice in the fifteenth century, Feltre stages an annual *palio*. It is marked by parades in period costume and horse races through its historic center.

Albino Luciani (1912–1978), who became Pope John Paul I in 1978, was born in **Canale d'Agordo**. After working in the diocese of Belluno and becoming Bishop of Vittorio Veneto, he was appointed Patriarch of Venice by Pope Paul VI in 1969. Luciani succeeded Paul on the Throne of Saint Peter, but served for barely a month before he succumbed to a heart attack.

Cortina d'Ampezzo, a noted center of winter sports, was the site of the 1956 winter Olympic Games. It is situated along the Boite and Bigontina rivers between spectacular Dolomite Alpine peaks. The people of the valley have retained elements of their Ladino language.

Pieve di Cadore, a city of Roman origin, is the birthplace of Titian (Tiziano Vecelli, 1488/1490–1576). His painting *The Madonna and Child with Saints Tiziano and Andrea* is in the parish Church of Santa Maria Nascente. The town has a museum dedicated to the painter.

—————— *PADUA (PADOVA)* ——————

PROVINCIAL PROFILE. Area: 827 sq. mi. Population: 842,091 (province), 212,542 (city). Padua province contains 104 communes. Padua is the crossroads of the Veneto, with Venice to its east, Rovigo across the Adige to its south, Verona to its west, Vicenza to its northwest, and Treviso to its northeast. Southwest of Padua city is the Euganean Hills Regional Natural Park, an area distinguished by cone-shaped hills that pop up dramatically from the Po flatlands. Among the hills are a number of hot-water baths, such as Battaglia Terme, Abano Terme, and Montegrotto Terme, as well as the eleventh-century Benedictine monastery of Praglia.

HISTORY. In legend, Padua was founded by the Trojan hero Antenor, who left his city after having been falsely accused of betraying it to the Greeks. The Romans annexed Padua as a colony in 89 B.C. and sanctioned its status as a *municipium* (free town) in 45 B.C. They called it *Patavium*, and their rule blessed the city with great prosperity. The census of A.D. 14, for example, listed Padua's wealth as second only to Rome's. The Middle Ages brought physical hardship to the city; it was sacked by the Lombards in the sixth century and by the Magyars in the tenth, and was leveled by an earthquake in 1117. Padua was a free commune by 1164, the first to declare its independence from the Holy Roman Empire. In 1237 the Veronese adventurer and tyrant Ezzelino III da Romano acquired it. In 1328 the Della Scala (Scaligeri) family held Padua, and in 1337 it passed to the Carrara, thanks to the treachery of Marsilio da Carrara, who betrayed his Scaligeri allies. The Carrara earned Venice's everlasting enmity in frequent hostilities and for their support of Genoa's attack on Chioggia. The clan, nevertheless, joined forces with the Venetians against the greater threat from Milan's Gian Galeazzo Visconti. But when Visconti died in 1402, so did the alliance, and Venice opted once and for all to move against the Carrara. Venice took Padua in November 1405 and threw Francesco "il vecchio" Carrara and his son, Francesco Novello, into a dungeon. The two were hastily condemned to death and strangled.

Imperial forces took Padua after the Battle of Agnadello in 1509, but a Venetian force recaptured it soon after and successfully resisted a siege by Emperor Maximilian I. The city remained in Venice's hands until the Napoleonic conquest in 1797. After the Austrian occupation of 1814–1866, it was annexed to Italy. As part of Mussolini's puppet Salò regime toward the end of the Second World War, Padua was the seat of the Ministry of National Education.

ARTS AND CULTURE. Padua boasts a rich cultural heritage. The historian **Livy** was born there in 59 B.C. His study of Rome ran to 142 books, only a fraction of which remains today. Livy died at Padua in A.D. 17.

Padua is the seat of one of Europe's great universities, with roots in the Middle Ages. Established in 1222 by a group of disgruntled students from the University of Bologna, it was one of the Italy's first centers of humanist thought. The university was distinguished by such early classical scholars as **Lovato Lovato** (1241–1309), who studied Livy and Seneca, and the poet **Albertino Mussato** (1261–1329), whose *The Ecerinis* was an indictment of tyranny (and of Ezzelino III da Romano) and one of the first humanist tragedies. Others who studied at Padua include **Dante, Petrarch, Copernicus, Galileo,** and **William Harvey. Elena Cornaro Piscopia** (1646–1684) became the first woman to earn a doctorate at Padua—or anywhere else. Hers was in philosophy.

Padua has retained many important medieval structures. The ninth-century Church of Santa Sofia, renovated in the twelfth and thirteenth centuries, shows some influence of Ravenna; the twelfth-century baptistery next to the Duomo contains frescoes completed by the Florentine **Giusto de' Menabuoi** (c. 1320–1397) in 1378. The remarkable Palazzo della Ragione, also called the Salone, was built as a law court in the thirteenth century and is now used for exhibitions. Later buildings include the massive sixteenth-century Basilica of Santa Giustina, which faces a charming eighteenth-century park, the Prato della Valle.

The city's most renowned structure is probably the Santo, the thirteenth-and fourteenth-century basilica which honors the city's patron, Sant'Antonio di Padova (Saint Anthony of Padua). The Santo is one of the most popular shrines in Italy and hosts a seemingly endless procession of pilgrims. Sant'Antonio was a Portuguese nobleman, born in 1195, who became a follower of Saint Francis in 1220 and, nine years later, moved to Padua. He died in Vercelli in 1231. His *Sermons* earned him the title Doctor of the Church; the many miracles attributed to him and his reputation as a saint of lost causes have given him a large and devoted following. Many important artists contributed their labors to the basilica, which has works by the Florentine **Donatello** (c. 1386–1466) and frescoes of the life of Sant'Antonio by, in part, the young **Titian** (1488/1490–1576).

In the piazza in front of the "Santo" is Donatello's bold, free-standing equestrian statue *Gattamelata*, which depicts the Renaissance condottiere. The monument is said to have been inspired by the statue of the Roman Emperor Marcus Aurelius.

The arrival of **Giotto** (1266/1267 or 1276–1337) was an important cultural event for Padua. His frescoes in the Scrovegni Chapel formed an extraordinary display and inspired an entire school of followers. The merchant Enrico Scrovegni commissioned the frescoes in 1304 to atone for his father's greed. Giotto's work, which fills most of the chapel, is considered a landmark break from rigid medieval forms toward the more human visions of the Renaissance. The Scrovegni Chapel forms part of a complex which includes the thirteenth-century Church of the Eremitani. Many of the Carrara are buried there. The church is chiefly remembered because it suffered heavy bomb damage in the Second World War and lost frecoes by the Padua (Isola di Carturo) native **Andrea Mantegna** (1431–1506). Padua's civic museum also forms part of the complex. It contains works by **Giorgione** (c. 1477–1511), Titian, **Giovanni Bellini** (c. 1430–1516), and Giotto the *Crucifixion* from the Scrovegni Chapel).

Carlo de' Dottori (1618–1685), an important Baroque Padovano author, is best remembered for his tragedy *Aristodemo* and his *Confessioni*, one of the seventeenth century's best autobiographies.

Padua was the birthplace of the writer **Ippolito Nievo** (1831–1861). Nievo identified with the Friuli area and also lived in Milan. A Risorgimento patriot, he fought under Giuseppe Garibaldi in the 1859 campaign and in Sicily a year later. Nievo finished his novel, *Le Confessioni d'un Italiano* (Confessions of an Italian; also titled Confessions of an Octogenarian and The Castle of Fratta), in 1858. The central figure of the novel is a Venetian born in 1775 whose wish is to die as an Italian. Nievo died in a shipwreck; his *Confessioni* was published posthumously in 1867.

The composer and librettist **Arrigo Boito** (1842–1918) was born in Padua but lived primarily in Milan. Besides his work as librettist for Giuseppe Verdi and the Lombard Amilcare Ponchielli (Paderno, 1834–1886),

Boito composed operas of his own, particularly an Italian *Faust* (*Mefisto-fele*) which had a disastrous premier in 1868 but was revised and restaged until it met with success in Milan at La Scala in 1881. His brother, **Camillo Boito** (1836–1914), was a writer of the *verista* (realist) school whose most important work was *Senso* (1882).

OTHER CENTERS. Este was a Veneti settlement before it became the Roman town of Ateste. Venice took it in 1405. The town is the seat of the Este family, members of which moved on to become the Dukes of Ferrara. Este is dominated by an imposing fourteenth-century castle built on the ruins of an eleventh-century one. In the Duomo, rebuilt between 1690 and 1708, is Giovanni Battista Tiepolo's painting *Santa Tecla Frees Este from the Plague*. The Duomo is dedicated to Santa Tecla.

Monselice was the Roman Mons Selicis and, later, a Lombard stronghold in the Euganian Hills before Venice incorporated it into its territories. Monselice boasts a thirteenth-century castle, sometimes called Ca Marcello, and the remains of a fortress built by Frederick II. Its Romanesque-Gothic Duomo is dedicated to Santa Giustina.

Montagnana is a stronghold with prehistoric roots. Most of its medieval walls are still intact, as are the gate of the Castello San Zeno and the powerful Porta Legnago (or Rocca degli Alberi). Outside the walls is the Villa Pisani, built in 1553 from a design by Andrea Palladio.

ROVIGO

PROVINCIAL PROFILE. Area: 696 sq. mi. Population: 244,595 (province), 50,962 (city). Rovigo province contains 50 communes. The province is a long and thin, east-west unit that occupies the Veneto's southernmost tier. The Po forms its southern border with Emilia Romagna. At Rovigo's eastern end, the Po empties into the Adriatic Sea through a complex delta, much of which is protected as the Bocche di Po nature reserve. The Adige River forms most of the province's northern border, which is shared, from west to east, with Verona, Padua, and Venice. At its western end, Rovigo touches Lombardy.

HISTORY. The province of Rovigo, mostly known as the Polesine, has suffered invasions throughout history. Being at the mouth of the Po, it could control most of northern Italy's river ports and their hinterlands. The Po, furthermore, changed course on occasion and further hampered the development of the Polesine. Venice understood the area's value, and annexed most of it in the 1480s after a long contest with Ferrara. Rovigo remained mostly in the Venetian grip until Napoleon's conquest in 1797 and the end of the Most Serene Republic. Upon the defeat of the French, Rovigo passed to the Austrians and then to Italy in 1866.

ARTS AND CULTURE. The tenth-century Donà and Mozza towers, remnants of a medieval castle, are in Rovigo. The city's Duomo, dedicated to the Saint Stephen, (Pope Stephen I), was constructed in the tenth century and renovated in 1461 and 1696, the last time following the design of the Padovano artist **Girolamo Frigimelica** (1653–1732). Rovigo's patron is San Bellino di Padova. As Bishop of Padua, he was caught in the struggles between pope and emperor, and was murdered in 1147. Some rely on Bellino for protection from rabies. Rovigo's most distinctive structure is the octagonal Baroque Church of the Beata Vergine del Soccorso, also known as the Rotonda. Completed in 1602, it contains an impressive collection of paintings, many by the Vicentino **Francesco Maffei** (1600–c. 1660). Rovigo also boasts a collection of Veneto masters in its Pinacoteca dell'Accademia dei Concordi (Art Gallery of the Peace Academy).

OTHER CENTERS. Much older than Rovigo city is **Adria**, the second town of the province. Adria's known history begins in the sixth century B.C. as a Veneti (or proto-Veneti) settlement, and then as an Etruscan river port off the Adriatic, the sea for which the town is named. The Romans appreciated Adria's commercial and transportation value, and put it on their Popilian and Annian Ways. The town lost some status after silting removed it from the coast and after the Romans built and favored the port of Classe outside of Ravenna. Venice took Adria in 1511, and many of its buildings reflect Venetian or post-Venetian rule, although some Byzantine mosaics survive. Adria contains an important National Archeological Museum.

The province contains a number of monasteries and abbeys. **Badia Polesine** is home to the tenth-century abbey of Santa Maria della Vangadizza. It was later incorporated into the Palazzo d'Espignac, although much of the original cloisters, refectory, and parts of the church remain.

TREVISO

PROVINCIAL PROFILE. Area: 956 sq. mi. Population: 769,365 (province), 81,250 (city). Treviso province contains 95 communes. The province of Treviso borders Belluno on its north, Vicenza on its west, Padua on its southwest, Venice on its southeast, and the region of Friuli–Venezia Giulia on its east. The Piave River cuts across the region from northwest to southeast. The city of Treviso sits on the Sila and Cagnan rivers, as well as on a number of canals.

HISTORY. The Celts established Treviso, and it prospered under the Romans as Tarvisium until the barbarian invasions. The devastation, however, was not as bad as that of other towns because Treviso was not directly on the invasion route, the Postumian Way. After Rome's collapse in 476,

Treviso was an important episcopal see and a Lombard duchy. The city was incorporated into the Holy Roman Empire (776) as capital of the Trevisan march and served Charlemagne as a mint. It suffered an extensive sack by the Magyars in 899. As the chief city of the march, Treviso evolved into a self-governing commune with privileges granted by Emperor Frederick Barbarossa. As a commune and then under the da Camino family in the thirteenth century, Treviso reached the height of its power. Sometimes allied with Venice, it extended its power to Feltre and Belluno. A university was established in the city in 1263.

After a brief rule by Cangrande della Scala in 1329, Treviso joined the Venetian Republic in 1339, and again in 1388, remaining, with some brief exceptions, until the French invasion of 1797. Treviso proved to be a loyal satellite and held firm after Venice's catastrophe at Agnadello in 1509, one of the few places west of Friuli to do so. In 1813 Austria established its rule after Napoleon's empire fell. Treviso rebelled in 1848, and on March 19 declared a provisional government which lasted until Austria's victory on June 14. The city's incorporation into the Italian Kingdom occurred in 1866.

The First World War reached Treviso in 1917, when the Italian line collapsed at Caporetto. The Austrian army overran and devastated part of the province, and the city suffered enormous damage. However, it never fell to the enemy. Treviso again suffered extensive damage in the Second World War, but it recovered. Its old center has not experienced further ruin at the hands of zealous urban planners.

ARTS AND CULTURE. Amid the many arcaded streets of central Treviso is its twelfth-century cathedral, dedicated to Saints Peter and Paul. Treviso's patron, however, is the late fourth-century San Liberale, who is buried in the church's crypt. The church contains an *Annunciation* by **Titian** (1488/1490–1576), a native of Belluno province, and many works by the Swiss artist **Tullio Lombardo** (c. 1455–1532). The cathedral has been altered often; a west portico was added in the nineteenth century, and repairs followed World War Two damage. Treviso's principal Gothic structure is the thirteenth- and fourteenth-century church of San Nicolò. Much of the church is adorned with frescoes by **Tommaso da Modena** (1326–1379) and his students. The artist made a number of contributions to other churches in Treviso, particularly a series of frescoes depicting Dominican worthies at the former convent of San Nicolò, which is now the diocesan seminary. Treviso is home to the Luigi Bailo Civic Museum, which has works by **Giovanni Bellini** (c. 1430–1516), Titian, **Lorenzo Lotto** (c. 1480–1556), **Antonio Canova** (1757–1822), and a native of Treviso, **Arturo Martini** (1889–1947).

Treviso was the birthplace of the Catholic social philosopher and economist **Giuseppe Toniolo** (1845–1918). Inspired by a Romantic vision of the Middle Ages, he considered the Church as the vehicle to elevate the status and conditions of working people.

OTHER CENTERS. Asolo boasts prehistoric roots and was known to the Romans as Acelum. It achieved some fame in the Renaissance as the site of a court under Caterina Cornaro (1489–1510) which Pietro Bembo immortalized in his work *The Asolani* (1505). Toward the end of the Second World War, Asolo served Mussolini's Salò regime as the site of the Ministry of War. The town has maintained an attractive historic center and most of Cornaro's castle.

The Trevisani built **Castelfranco Veneto** in 1199 as a fortress against Padua. Venice absorbed the town into its domains in 1139. Much of the old town has been preserved within its twelfth-century walls. It is the birthplace of the Venetian painter Giorgio Zorzi, known as "Giorgione" (c. 1478–1511). His house, the Casa Pellizzari, has been preserved as the civic museum. Giorgione's altar painting *The Madonna Enthroned Between Saints Francis and Liberale* is preserved in the eighteenth-century cathedral. The church honors San Liberale, patron of both Castelfranco Veneto and Treviso city. The saint was a hermit; but because he lived in a violent age at the start of the barbarian invasions, many artists, like Giorgione, made a leap of faith to depict him as a warrior in full armor. Southeast of the town is a country villa built by Andrea Palladio between 1566 and 1576 for the Venetian Doge Giorgio Cornaro.

The well-preserved twelfth-century abbey of Santa Maria was first a Benedictine place and then Cistercian. It is in the Soligo valley at **Follina**.

The writer Giuseppe Berto (1914–1978) was born in **Mogliana Veneto**. During the Second World War, Berto served in the Italian North African campaign until he was captured and sent to a prisoner of war camp in Texas. There he began to write works including an acclaimed account of his wartime experiences, *Guerra in Camicia Nera* (War in Black Shirt, 1955), and his psychological study, *Il Male Oscuro* (Incubus), which won the 1964 Viareggio Prize.

Perhaps Italy's most important neoclassical sculptor, Antonio Canova (1757–1822), was born in **Possagno**. The town contains his Tempio Canoviano, modeled on the Pantheon in Rome, and the Gipsoteca Canoviana, a museum of his work, noted particularly for its collection of gesso models of his creations.

Pope Pius X (1835–1914) was born in **Riese** as Giuseppe Sarto. When he was elected to pilot the Catholic Church in 1903, he chose the name Pius to honor his reactionary predecessor, Pius IX. Sarto's pontificate, too, was conservative in its attack on the "modernist" movement and curtailment of the lay activist organization Opere dei Congressi (Works of the Congresses). However, Pius relaxed the Holy See's insistence that Italian Catholics not participate in politics.

The poet Andrea Zanzotto was born near Treviso at **Pieve di Soligo** in

1921. Active in the anti-Fascist resistance during the Second World War, he began his work in the hermetic tradition but moved on to experimental forms, and was later influenced by ancient Greek, Hebrew, and Latin styles.

Vittorio Veneto was the site of Italy's crucial First World War victory over the Austrians. It was formed in 1866 by the union of a lower town, Ceneda, and its highland neighbor, Serravalle. Both parts of the town boast impressive heritages. Ceneda contains the museum that commemorates the battle. Vittorio Veneto was the birthplace of the librettist Emanuele Conegliano (1749–1838), who became known as Lorenzo Da Ponte. Da Ponte was a Jew who converted to Catholicism and became a priest. He moved to Vienna and worked with Mozart on the lyrics for *Le Nozze di Figaro* (The Marriage of Figaro, 1786), *Don Giovanni* (1787), and *Così Fan Tutte* (1790). After a period in London (1793–1805), Da Ponte moved to New York, where he taught Italian and was active in the production of operas.

VERONA

PROVINCIAL PROFILE. Area: 1,196 sq. mi. Population: 810,686 (province), 254,520 (city). Verona contains 98 communes. Verona is the Veneto's westernmost province. On its east are Vicenza, Padua and Rovigo; Lombardy is to its west and southwest; and Trentino–Alto Adige shares its northern border. The northern stretch of the Lombardy border is Lake Garda. The Adige River flows into Verona from the Trentino and cuts the province on a northwest to southeast diagonal until it forms the border between Padua and Rovigo.

HISTORY. Verona sits on one of Europe's oldest roads, a link since prehistoric times that today parallels the A22/E45 autostrada and connects Italy and the Mediterranean, through the Brenner Pass, with Germany and central Europe. Thanks in large part to its strategic location, Verona has been a frequent prize for conquerors. It was first a prehistoric settlement; later the Etruscans and then the Gauls occupied the site; the Romans established a colony in 89 B.C.

After the fall of the Roman Empire (476), Verona was occupied by the Ostrogoths and the Lombards; the latter made their last stand there in 774 when their leader, Adelchis, collapsed before the victorious Franks. The son of the last Lombard king, Adelchis had fled to Verona after his father, Desiderius, failed to hold at Pavia. The beaten Adelchis then escaped to Constantinople. By the twelfth century Verona was an independent commune and a member of the Lombard League. In the thirteenth century a pact with local factions that included the "Party of Eighty" brought Verona the rule of Ezzelino III da Romano, who used the city as his base. After the collapse of da Romano power in the 1260s, the Veronesi turned quickly to the della Scala family. In the 1320s and 1330s, Verona was ruled by the despot adventurer Cangrande della Scala and his nephews, Alberto and Mastino II, who embarked on a remarkable path of conquest. In 1328 Cangrande captured Padua, and the following year, Treviso, where he died of a fever. In 1332 Brescia fell to Mastino, as did Parma and Lucca in 1335. The aggressive della Scala (or Scaligeri) had angered so many states that Venice found it easy to assemble a league against them. The usurpers were defeated by Venice's alliance in 1338, and the della Scala fell in 1387. Venice then held Verona from 1405 until Napoleon's conquest in 1797.

After Napoleon's empire crumbled in 1814, the city passed to the Austrians, who fortified it as part of their "quadrilateral" network. Verona and the other three fortresses successfully protected the Austrians during the wars of 1848 and 1859. After the Seven Weeks War in 1866, Verona became an Italian city. In late 1943, Benito Mussolini's deposed Fascists formed a new government at a congress held at Verona. Dubbed the Salò Republic, it enjoyed German backing although it met with widespread indifference or opposition from the Italian people.

ARTS AND CULTURE. Verona's cultural heritage is one of the most impressive in Italy. Roman rule is recalled in the impressive arena in the central Piazza Brà. Built in the first century A.D., the structure is now the setting for both operas and rock concerts. Near the Adige River, a Roman theater of about the same date has been extensively restored, and a few noteworthy gates remain throughout the city. The Church of San Zeno Maggiore honors the patron of Verona, a figure who left North Africa for Italy during the fourth century. He became the city's eighth bishop and is also considered the patron of freshwater fishermen. Largely completed in the twelfth and thirteenth centuries, the church is a Romanesque masterpiece, one of the finest in Italy. Inside, at the high altar, is a triptych by **Andrea Mantegna** (1431–1506), a native of the province of Padua. Below, San Zeno is buried in the church's crypt.

Near the charming Piazza delle Erbe and the Palazzo della Ragione (city hall) are the tombs of the della Scala rulers, the Arche Scaligere. Clustered in and around the Church of Santa Maria Antica, the monuments include fourteenth-century equestrian statues of Mastino II and Cansignorio. Verona's largest church is that of Sant'Anastasia, an impressive Gothic structure begun in 1290 for the Dominican order. The city's cathedral, dedicated to Santa Maria Matricolare, was begun in 1139 and expanded after 1440. The Della Scala fortress, the Castelvecchio, sits on the Adige and connects to a bridge, the Ponte Scaligero or Ponte Merlato, which crosses the river. Built for Cangrande II between 1354 and 1375, it was later a barracks and military college. In the Second World War it housed the neo-Fascist congress that established the Salò Republic. Today it contains Verona's principal museum. **Jacopo Bellini** (Venice, c. 1400–c. 1471), the father of Giovanni and Gentile, is well represented in its collection, as is the work

of Mantegna and Paolo Caliari, or **Veronese** (1528–1588) who was born
in the city. In April, Verona hosts Italy's principal wine and spirits fair,
"Vinitaly."

OTHER CENTERS. **Bardolino,** noteworthy as a tourist center on the
eastern shore of Lake Garda and as home to Bardolino wine, also boasts
the small ninth-century church of San Zeno, an important and well-
preserved reminder of Carolingian influence in Italy. Nearby is San Severo,
another ancient church from the ninth century, which was rebuilt with
frescoes in the twelfth.

VICENZA

PROVINCIAL PROFILE. Area: 1,051 sq. mi. Population: 775,064 (province), 108,281. Vicenza province contains 121 communes. Vicenza is bordered on its southwest by Verona, on its north and northwest by the region
of Trentino–Alto Adige, on its northeast by Belluno, on the east by Treviso,
and on the southeast by Padua. The city of Vicenza sits in a valley formed
by the Retrone and Bacchiglione rivers, which separate Berici and the Lessini Mountains.

HISTORY. Vicenza was a Veneti settlement before the Romans took it
and named it Vicentia. After the Roman Empire fell (476), the town became
the seat of a Lombard duchy, and was later caught in local struggles between Verona and Padua. After a period of subjugation under the Veronese
della Scala (Scaligeri) beginning in 1311 and the Milanese Visconti beginning in 1387, Vicenza joined with Venice in 1404. It developed as a rice-
growing area and as the site of healthy silk and wool industries. Vicenza
remained in the Venetian orbit until Napoleon's conquest (1797) and the
subsequent introduction of Austrian rule in 1814. With the rest of the
Venetian lands, Vicenza was incorporated into Italy in 1866.

In the twentieth century Vicenza was a center of lay Catholic organization. The efforts of Giacomo Rumor to establish the Banca Cattolica Vi-
centina illustrated this activism early in the century. Following the First
World War, much of the clergy assumed the leadership of a progressive
land reform movement after the landlords fled before the advancing Austrians. Later, upon the fall of Fascism, the city turned consistently to the
Christian Democrats and was considered one of Italy's "whitest" (most
politically Catholic) cities. In the 1990s, however, Vicenza's voters swung
more and more to the Northern Leagues.

ARTS AND CULTURE. Vicenza's basilica of Saints Felice and Fortunato is a treasure with fourth- and fifth-century roots. Much of the current
structure was built in the twelfth century and modified in the fourteenth.
It honors a group of saints led by Vincent of Saragossa. Felice was a native

of Vicenza and Fortunato came from Aquileia; Vincent was a Spaniard martyred during Diocletian's persecutions in the early fourth century. The Vicentini chose Vincent and his companions as their patrons in the late fourteenth century; the reason for the choice is something of a puzzle. The city's cathedral built between the fourteenth and sixteenth centuries, suffered almost total destruction from bombardments in 1944. The building was restored, however, and still contains important art such as a *Madonna* by **Bartolommeo Montagna** (1450–c. 1523). A native of Brescia, Montagna produced most of his work in Vicenza. He also contributed to the Dominican Church of the Santa Corona, a structure begun in the thirteenth century which holds **Veronese's** *Adoration of the Magi* and **Giovanni Bellini's** masterpiece, *Baptism of Christ.*

Vicenza's most renowned artist was the late Renaissance architect Andrea di Pietro della Gondola, known as **Andrea Palladio** (1508–1580). Although born in Padua, the artist is jealously identified with Vicenza, the city and region where he accomplished most of his work. His basilica, in the center of Vicenza, is one of his greatest individual works. The title "basilica" may be misleading, however, because the building was intended as a courthouse, an administrative structure, and a market rather than as a place of worship. His last project was Vicenza's Teatro Olimpico, Europe's oldest theater. After researching ancient models at Verona, Orange in France, and elsewhere, Palladio produced a remarkable design for the wood and stucco Olimpico with a fixed stage that resembles a Roman arch and street scene. He died before it was completed, but **Silla Palladio** (his son) and **Vincenzo Scamozzi** (1552–c. 1616) finished it.

Palladio's singular achievement was the construction of a collection of palaces in the city and villas throughout the countryside, the Vicentino. In Vicenza, there are the Palazzo Thiene (1552) and Palazzo Valmarana (1566), as well as the Palazzo Chiericati (1550), which houses the civic museum. Many of the country places were designed for the Venetian elite. Their style inspired centuries of builders in Europe and America, including Thomas Jefferson, who based his design for Monticello on Palladian principles. Palladio's most famous villa, however, is in the city, the Rotonda (Villa Almerico, begun in 1550).

Luigi da Porto (1486–1529) was a writer from Vicenza whose novella of star-crossed lovers inspired William Shakespeare to write *Romeo and Juliet.* Da Porto took an older tale set in Siena and shifted it to Verona.

The Veneto's most significant Romantic writer, **Antonio Fogazzaro**, was born at Vicenza in 1842. His novels, such as *Daniele Cortis* (1885), attempted to reconcile the modern scientific world with traditional culture based in faith. His novel *Il Santo* (The Saint, 1906), led Rome to condemn his work. Fogazzaro achieved his greatest fame with his sentimental masterpiece, *Piccolo mondo antico* (Small Old World, 1896), considered a classic nineteenth-century Italian novel. He died in 1911. Vicenza gave Italy another noteworthy writer in **Guido Piovene** (1907–1975). He began as a Fascist journalist but moved on to Marxism and a series of literary successes which included his commentary on the United States, *De America* (1953), and his last major novel, *Le stelle fredde* (The Cold Stars, 1970), which won the Strega Prize.

Vicenza is known as a goldworking center, and every January, June, and September, it hosts major international fairs which deal with the trade.

OTHER CENTERS. Northeast of Vicenza is **Bassano**, on the Brenta River, below Mount Grappa. The mountain is at the junction of Vicenza, Treviso, and Belluno provinces. Bassano was the site of one of Napoleon's key victories over the Austrians (1796) and of some of the worst fighting of the First World War. At the Battle of the Grappa, between November 13 and 26, 1917, the Italian army halted the Austrian advance after the catastrophe at Caporetto the previous month. The tragic bloodletting is commemorated in a colossal ossuary, the Ossario Monumentale, on Mount Grappa. Toward the end of the Second World War, Mussolini's puppet Salò regime located its Air Ministry in Bassano.

The city is not, however, known simply for its place in war. It boasts many medieval structures, including two castles from the tenth and fourteenth centuries, a Duomo begun in 998, and a thirteenth-century wooden covered bridge over the Brenta. It is also regarded as the center of the grappa industry—its Nardini distillery was opened in 1779—and as an important ceramics and mushroom-growing area. Bassano has a significant civic museum.

The Da Ponte family of painters came from the town and are more generally known by their adopted name, Bassano. Francesco the Younger (1549–1592), Jacopo (c. 1515–1592), and Leandro (1557–1622) Bassano were all born in the town and worked there. Francesco the Elder (c. 1470–1540), however, though he assumed the name, was born in Vicenza. The lyric baritone Tito Gobbi (1913–1984) was a native of Bassano.

Palladio's villas dot the Vicentino. Among the most important are his first, the Villa Godi Valmarana (or Malinverni, 1542) at **Lugo di Vicenza,** the Villa Pisani (1576) at **Lonigo,** and the Villa Barbaro (1557) at **Maser,** which also contains some of the finest works of Veronese. Palladio's influence can also be seen in the Villa Cordellina Lombardi, built from a design by the Venetian architect Giorgio Massari (c. 1686–1766). Built between 1735 and 1760 at **Montecchio Maggiore,** it also contains frescoes by Giovanni Battista Tiepolo.

SELECT BIBLIOGRAPHY

Franzina, Emilio, ed. *Venezia*. Rome: Laterza, 1986.
Hibbert, Christopher. *Venice: The Biography of a City*. London: The Folio Society, 1997.

Istituto Geografico De Agostini. *Veneto*. 2 vols. Novara: Istituto Geografico De Agostini, 1981.

Lanaro, Silvio, ed. *Il Veneto*. Turin: Einaudi, 1984.

Lane, Frederic C. *Venice: A Maritime Republic*. Baltimore: Johns Hopkins University Press, 1973.

Norwich, John Julius. *A History of Venice*. New York: Vintage Books, 1989.

Puppi, Lionello, and Mario Universo. *Padova*. Rome: Laterza, 1982.

Touring Club Italiano. *Veneto (esclusa Venezia)*. Milan: Touring Club Italiano, 1992.

GLOSSARY

abbadia/abbazia (badia): abbey

Alt'Italia: northern Italy

Autostrada: expressway, motorway

Blackshirt: Fascist follower of Benito Mussolini

borgo: suburb or quarter

bracciante: landless field hand

campanile: bell tower

certosa: Carthusian monastery

cima: mountain peak

Cinquecento: the 1500s (sixteenth century)

circoscrizione: electoral district

colle (collina): hill (small hill)

collegiata: collegiate church

commune: municipality: town or city

crepuscolare: late-nineteenth-century poetry movement

D.O.C.: government-regulated verification of wine quality

Duecento: the 1200s (thirteenth century)

Duomo: literally "dome"; usually refers to cathedral

eremo: hermitage

fabbrica: factory

fattoria: large farm (typically in Tuscany)

fiume: river

galleria: tunnel

Ghibelline: term for those who supported the Holy Roman Empire against the popes during the Middle Ages

Guelph: term for those who supported the popes against the Holy Roman Empire during the Middle Ages; during the nineteenth-century Risorgimento, it referred to those who supported a role for the papacy in united Italy

lago: lake

liceo: roughly equivalent to American high school

macchiaioli: mid- to late-nineteenth-century painting movement based in Tuscany

majoritarian elections: The result of a 1993 electoral reform in which three-quarters of deputies and senators win their seats based on simple majority votes. The other 25 percent continue to be elected on variations of the older proportional system.

mani pulite: enormous scandal uncovered in 1992 that ended the political system that had been in place since the Second World War

mare (mar): sea

Meridione (Italia Meridionale): southern Italy

mezzadro: sharecropper

Mezzogiorno: southern Italy

montagna (monte): mountain

Novecento: the 1900s (twentieth century)

Ottocento: the 1800s (nineteenth century)

passo: mountain pass

piano (piana, pianura): plain

pizzo: mountain peak

punta/punto: cape

Quattrocento: the 1400s (fifteenth century)

Risorgimento: Italy's nineteenth-century struggle for independence and union; the Kingdom of Italy was created after the wars of 1859–1860, and Rome was made its capital in 1871.

Seicento: the 1600s (seventeenth century)

Settecento: the 1700s (eighteenth century)

Settentrione (Italia Settentrionale): northern Italy

traforo: tunnel

Trecento: the 1300s (fourteenth century)

val (valle): valley

valico: mountain pass

CHRONOLOGY

c. 3000 B.C.	Early settlements in Po valley
1500–1400 B.C.	Mycenaean settlements in southern Italy
1200 B.C.	Early Etruscan culture in Tuscany
8th century B.C.	Establishment of Etruscan Confederation
753 B.C.	Mythic date of founding of Rome
c. 730–700 B.C.	Greek settlements in southern Italy
6th century B.C.	Paestum: Basilica and Temple of Caeres built
c. 550 B.C.	Etruscans establish Felsina (Bologna)
c. 509 B.C.	Etruscan Tarquin kings expelled from Rome, establishment of Roman Republic
484 B.C.	Roman forum: Temple of Castor and Pollux built
471 B.C.	Etruscans found Capua
450–420 B.C.	Paestum: Temple of Neptune built
c. 380 B.C.	Gauls sack Rome
282–270 B.C.	Roman conquest of southern Italy from Greeks
275 B.C.	Romans defeat Greeks at Battle of Beneventum (Benevento)

264–241, 218–201, 149–146 B.C.	Rome's Punic Wars against Carthage
241 B.C.	Rome annexes Sicily
236 B.C.	Rome repulses invasion of Boii Gauls at Rimini
222 B.C.	Rome takes Milan from the Insubri Gauls
216 B.C.	Carthaginians defeat Romans in Apulia at Battle of Cannae
202 B.C.	Battle of Zama, defeat of the Carthaginian general Hannibal
91–87 B.C.	Social War between Romans and other Italian peoples
89 B.C.	Verona becomes Roman colony
44 B.C.	Roman Emperor Julius Caesar murdered
31 B.C.–27 B.C.	Battle of Actium; Empire established under Caesar Augustus
A.D. 64.	Rome burns
c. 72–80	Rome: Colosseum built
81	Roman forum: Arch of Titus built
c. 100	Verona: amphitheater built
118	Under Emperor Hadrian, greatest extent of Roman Empire
203	Roman Forum: Arch of Septimius Severus built
c. 300	Rome: construction of Baths of Diocletian (later, parts incorporated into Santa Maria degli Angeli)
313	Emperor Constantine issues Edict of Milan, recognizing Christianity as religion of Roman Empire
315	Rome: Arch of Constantine constructed
354	Capital transferred from Rome to Milan
395	Death of Emperor Theodosius; Roman Empire formally divided into Eastern and Western Empires
397	Death of Saint Ambrose, Bishop of Milan
402	Emperor Honorius moves Roman court to Ravenna

410	Rome sacked by Goth King Alaric
421	Legendary founding of Venice
422	Rome: Church of Saint Peter in Chains built
c. 430	Rome: Church of Santa Sabina built
476	Rome falls to German mercenary Odoacer, who proclaims himself king; formal end of Roman Empire
488	Invasion of Italy by Theodoric and Ostrogoths
493	Odoacer defeated and killed by Theodoric at Ravenna
c. 510	Saint Benedict establishes his first monastery at Subiaco, the Sacro Speco
530s	Byzantine reconquest of Italy; Ravenna reestablished as capital
547	Ravenna: Consecration of Church of San Vitale.
549	Ravenna: Consecration of Sant'Apollinare in Classe
early 700s	End of real Byzantine control of Italy
751	Lombard destruction of Greek Exarchate of Ravenna
800	Pope Leo III crowns Charlemagne Holy Roman Emperor; most of Italy north of Rome included in that empire
827	Muslim conquest of Sicily
c. 832	Venice: Foundation of Church of San Marco
800s and 900s	Golden Age of Amalfi
1000s	Norman kingdoms in south; rise of city-states (*comunes*) in north
1060–1091	Muslims lose Sicily to the Normans
1100s	Rome: completion of Santa Maria in Cosmedin (begun in 500s)
1115	Death of Countess Matilda of Tuscany
1150	Florence: completion of Baptistery
1152	Frederick I Barbarossa, of the house of Hohenstau-

fen (Swabia), succeeds his uncle, Conrad III, as Holy Roman Emperor

1176	Battle of Legnano; Italian communes beat back imperial German forces
1190	Death of Frederick I Barbarossa
1202–1204	Fourth Crusade; sack of Constantinople, with enormous gains by Venice
1209	Franciscan order founded
1215	Dominican order founded
1225	Verona: completion of Santo Zeno Maggiore
1226	Death of Saint Francis of Assisi at the Porziuncola, near Assisi
1232–1300s	Padua: construction of Il Santo, the shrine of Saint Anthony
1250	Death of Emperor Frederick II
1253	Assisi: Basilica of Saint Francis consecrated by Pope Innocent IV
1254	Death of Emperor Conrad IV, son of Frederick II
1257–1265	Assisi: construction of Church of Saint Clare
1266	Death of Manfred, son of Frederick II
1268	Death of Conradin, son of Conrad IV
1296–1436	Florence: construction of Santa Maria del Fiore
c. 1302	Poet Dante Alighieri expelled from Florence
1303	Imprisonment and death of Pope Boniface VIII
1303–1308	Padua: Construction of Scrovegni Chapel (with frescoes by Giotto)
1307–1321	Dante writes *The Divine Comedy*
1309	Venice: start of construction of Doge's Palace
1309–1377	Holy See, under French influence, is moved to Avignon, France
1334–1359	Florence: construction of "Giotto's" bell tower
1347–1350	The Black Death (bubonic plague)

1348–1353	Giovanni Boccaccio writes *The Decameron*
1374	Death of the poet Francesco Petrarch (Petrarca)
1378–1417	"Great Schism" creates at least two (Avignon and Italy) rival popes
1382	Siena: Completion of cathedral
1401	The painter Masaccio is born
1415	Council of Constance resolves "Great Schism" and confirms the Holy See in Rome
1434–1464	Rule of Cosimo de' Medici (the Elder) in Florence
1469–1492	Rule of Lorenzo de' Medici (the "Magnificent") in Florence
August 1494	King Charles VIII of France launches his invasion of Italy
November 9, 1494	Medici expelled from Florence after humiliating peace treaty with Charles VIII
February 22, 1495	King Charles VIII of France enters Naples
March 31, 1495	Pope Alexander VI, Venice, Milan, Spain, and the Holy Roman Empire form the Holy League to oppose the French in Italy
1495–1498	Milan: Leonardo Da Vinci paints *The Last Supper*.
1506	Rome: Pope Julius II orders reconstruction of Saint Peter's Basilica
1508–1512	Rome: Michelangelo works on Sistine Chapel frescoes.
1509	League of Cambrai defeats Venice
1517	Rome: Construction of Palazzo Farnese begins
	Reformation launched by Martin Luther
1519	Death of Leonardo Da Vinci
1525	Emperor Charles V defeats the French at Pavia
1527	Death of Niccolò Machiavelli; sack of Rome by forces of Emperor Charles V

1545–1563	Council of Trent launches the Catholic Reformation (Counter-Reformation)
1547–1564	Rome: Michelangelo works as chief architect on Saint Peter's Basilica
1559	Treaty of Cateau-Cambrésis effectively ends Italian independence and recognizes Spanish hegemeony
1560	Florence: work begun on Uffizi Palace
1564	Death of Michelangelo
1568	Rome: work begun on Church of Gesù
1600	Giordano Bruno burned for heresy in Rome's Campo de Fiori
1626	Rome: completion of St. Peter's Basilica
1633	Galileo recants before Roman Inquisition his statement that Earth revolves around Sun
1656	Rome: Giovanni Bernini's Fountain of the Four Rivers completed in Piazza Navona
1713	Treaty of Utrecht awards Spain's Italian possessions to Austria
1725–1726	Rome: Spanish Steps completed
1735	Bourbon rule established in Naples
1762	Rome: Trevi Fountain completed
1793	Venetian writer Carlo Goldoni dies in Paris
1796	Napoleon leads first French invasion of Italy
1797	Genoese and Venetian republics dissolve
1812	King Ferdinand IV of Naples (Ferdinand I of Two Sicilies) grants Sicily a constitution
1813–1814	End of French rule in Italy
1815	Congress of Vienna confirms Austrian hegemony in Italy
1820–1821	Conspiracies and revolutions across Italy
1830–1831	More revolts in Piedmont and Papal States
1848–1849	First War of the Risorgimento

1849	Roman Republic declared under Giuseppe Mazzini and Giuseppe Garibaldi; defeated by French, Spanish, and Neapolitan troops
1859–1865	Turin capital of Italy
1859–1870	Italian unification under King Victor Emmanuel II of Piedmont
1865–1871	Florence capital of Italy
1866	Italy takes Veneto from Austria
1870	Rome conquered from Pope Pius IX
1871–present	Rome capital of Italy
1872	Nationalist leader Giuseppe Mazzini dies
1882	Nationalist leader Giuseppe Garibaldi dies
1901	Composer Giuseppe Verdi dies
1911	Rome: Victor Emmanuel Monument completed
1915–1918	Italy participates in First World War
1918–1919	After First World War, the Austrian Sud Tirol region is transferred to Italy and renamed Alto Adige
1922–1943	Fascist regime of Benito Mussolini
1924	Composer Giacomo Puccini dies
1929	Lateran Accords between Italy and the Holy See recognize Catholicism as Italy's official religion and establish an independent Vatican State
1934	Italy hosts and wins soccer's World Cup
1935–1936	Italy invades and conquers Ethiopia; unites it with Somalia and Eritrea to form Italian East Africa (Italian Somaliland)
1936	Italy wins Olympic gold medal in soccer at Berlin
1937	Florence: Santa Maria Novella train station completed
1938	Italy wins soccer's World Cup
1938	In September, Mussolini decrees racial legislation against Jews

February 1939	Death of Pope Pius XI and election of Pius XII to the Throne of Saint Peter.
May 1939	Italy signs Pact of Steel with Germany.
1940	Mussolini declares war on Britain and France; invasions of France, Greece, and Egypt fail
1941	Mussolini declares war on the Soviet Union and the United States; end of Italian East Africa
1942	Rome: Planned World's Fair results in construction of EUR
1943–1945	Mussolini overthrown; German and Allied invasions; Mussolini launches puppet state (Italian Social Republic, or Salò Republic) in north; civil war
April–May 1945	Death of Mussolini; end of Second World War in Italy
1946	Establishment of Italian Republic
1948	Italian constitution ratified and Christian Democratic control of government confirmed in April elections
1956	Inauguration of first link of Italian expressway system
1956	Cortina D'Ampezzo hosts winter Olympic Games
1960	Rome: construction of Pier Luigi Nervi's stadia
1960	Rome hosts summer Olympic Games
1978	Murder of Christian Democratic leader and former Prime Minister Aldo Moro by Red Brigades; deaths of Popes Paul VI and his successor, John Paul I; Polish Karol Wojtyla becomes Pope John Paul II, first non-Italian pope since the sixteenth century
1981	Assassination attempt on Pope John Paul II in Saint Peter's Square.
1989	Italian Communist Party unravels
1990	Italy hosts Soccer's World Cup competition
1992	*Mani pulite* (clean hands) scandal uncovered
1992–1994	National elections trigger collapse of Christian Dem-

ocratic Party, Socialist Party, and Italian political system

1994 Silvio Berlusconi and *Forza Italia* lead Center-Right coalition in Parliament

1996 Center-Left *Ulivo* coalition under Romano Prodi takes power

1998 Italy is a charter member of the European Union's monetary group

BIBLIOGRAPHY

Anderson, Burton. *The Simon and Schuster Guide to the Wines of Italy*. New York: Simon and Schuster, 1992.

——. *The Wine Atlas of Italy and Traveller's Guide to the Vineyards*. Edited by Mitchell Beazeley. London: Reed Consumer Books, 1990.

Arnold, Denis, ed. *The New Oxford Companion to Music*. Oxford: Oxford University Press, 1984.

Avagliano, Lucio, ed. *L'Italia industriale nelle sue regioni: Bilancio storiografico*. Naples: Edizioni Scientifiche Italiane, 1988.

Avery, Catherine B., ed. *The New Century Italian Renaissance Encyclopedia*. New York: Meredith, 1972.

Bellotta, Ireneo. *I Santi patroni d'Italia*. Rome: Newton Compton, 1988.

Bobbio, Norberto. *Ideological Profile of Twentieth-Century Italy*. Translated by Lydia Cochrane. Princeton, N.J.: Princeton University Press, 1995.

Bondanella, Peter, and Julia Conaway Bondanella, eds. *Dictionary of Italian Literature*. Rev., enl. ed. Westport, Conn.: Greenwood Press, 1996.

Caesar, Michael, and Peter Hainsworth, eds. *Writers and Society in Contemporary Italy*. New York: St. Martin's Press, 1984.

Carpanetto, Dino, and Giuseppe Ricuperati. *Italy in the Age of Reason*. Translated by Caroline Higgit. London: Longman, 1987.

Cattabiani, Alfredo. *Calendario: Le feste, i miti, le leggende e i Riti dell'Anno*. Milan: Rusconi, 1994.

——. *Santi d'Italia*. Milan: Rizzoli, 1993.

Chastel André. *Italian Art, Architecture, Painting and Sculpture from the Early Christian Period to the Present Day*. Translated by Peter Murray and Lindsay Murray. New York: Harper & Row, 1963.

Chilver, G. E. F. *Cisalpine Gaul: Social and Economic History from 49 B.C. to the Death of Trajan.* Oxford: Oxford University Press, 1941.

Clark, Martin. *Modern Italy 1871–1995.* London: Longman, 1996.

Contini, Gianfranco. *La Letteratura italiana, otto–novecento.* Milan: Rizzoli, 1992.

Coppa, Frank. *The Italian Wars of Independence.* New York: Longman, 1992.

———, ed. *Dictionary of Modern Italian History.* Westport, Conn.: Greenwood Press, 1985.

David, Jean-Michel. *The Roman Conquest of Italy.* Translated by Antonia Nevill. Malden, Mass.: Blackwell, 1996.

Di Scala, Spencer M. *Italy from Revolution to Republic, 1700 to the Present.* Boulder, Colo.: Westview Press, 1998.

Duggan, Christopher. *A Concise History of Italy.* Cambridge: Cambridge University Press, 1994.

Enciclopedia Italiana di science, letteri ed arti. 35 vols. Rome: Instituto della Enciclopedia Italiana 1949.

Encyclopedia of World Art. 16 vols. New York: McGraw-Hill, 1959–1983.

Ferrero, Guglielmo, and Corrado Barbaglio. *A Short History of Rome.* 2 vols. New York: Capricorn Books, 1964.

Ginsborg, Paul. *A History of Contemporary Italy: Society and Politics 1943–1988.* London: Penguin, 1990.

———, ed. *Stato d'Italia.* Milan: Bruno Mondadori, 1994.

Giovannini, Giovanni. *Italia Regioni.* Turin: Autori Editori Associati, 1971.

Gosetti, Fernanda, and Giovanni Righi Parenti. *Il vino a tavola e in cucina: Vini e ricette regionali di Val d'Aosta, Piemonte, Liguria, Lombardia, Veneto, Trentino, Alto Adige, Friuli-Venezia Giulia.* Milan: AMZ, 1980.

Gottardo, Giuseppe, and Ulderico Gamba. *Monasteri e santuari d'Italia.* Rome: Newton Compton, 1994.

Grant, Michael. *Greek and Latin Authors, 800 B.C.–1000 A.D.* New York: H. W. Wilson, 1980.

Hauser, Ernest O. *Italy: A Cultural Guide.* New York: Atheneum, 1981.

Hearder, Harry. *Italy in the Age of the Risorgimento, 1790–1870.* London: Longman, 1983.

Homo, Leon. *Primitive Italy and the Beginnings of Roman Imperialism.* Translated by V. Gordon Childe. New York: Alfred A. Knopf, 1926.

Jones, Philip. *The Italian City-State: From Commune to Signoria.* Oxford: Oxford University Press, 1997.

Kreutz, Barbara. *Before the Normans: Southern Italy in the Ninth and Tenth Centuries.* Philadelphia: University of Pennsylvania Press, 1996.

Lacoste, Yves, ed. *Dictionnaire de Géopolitique.* Paris: Flammarion, 1995.

Larner, John. *Italy in the Age of Dante and Petrarch, 1216–1380.* London: Longman, 1985.

Leprohon, Pierre. *The Italian Cinema.* New York: Praeger, 1972.

Levy, Carl, ed. *Italian Regionalism: History, Identity and Politics.* Oxford: Berg, 1996.

Macadam, Alta, ed. *Blue Guide. Northern Italy from Rome to the Alps.* New York. W. W. Norton, 1991.

Mack Smith, Denis. *Modern Italy: A Political History.* Ann Arbor: University of Michigan Press, 1997.

Martines, Lauro. *Power and Imagination: City-States in Renaissance Italy*. Baltimore: Johns Hopkins University Press, 1988.

Ministero dell'Interno. *Elezioni politiche, 21 Aprile 1996*. Vol. 1, *Camera dei Deputati*. Vol. 2, *Senato*. Rome: Istituto Poligrafico e Zecca dello Stato, 1996.

The New Catholic Encyclopedia. 15 vols. Washington, D.C.: Catholic University of America, 1967, 1981.

The New Enyclopedia Britannica. Chicago: Encyclopaedia Britannica, 1998.

Picchione, John, and Lawrence R. Smith, eds. *Twentieth Century Italian Poetry: An Anthology*. Toronto: University of Toronto Press, 1993.

Procacci, Giuliano. *History of the Italian People*. New York: Harper & Row, 1970.

Rice, Timothy, James Porter, and Chris Goertzen. *Europe*. Vol. 8 of *The Garland Encyclopedia of World Music*. New York: Garland, 2000.

Ring, Trudy, and Robert Salkin, eds. *International Dictionary of Historic Places*. Vol. 3, *Southern Europe*. Chicago: Fitzroy Dearborn, 1995.

Root, Waverley. *The Food of Italy*. New York: Vintage Books, 1977.

Sadie, Stanley, ed. *The New Grove Dictionary of Music and Musicians*. Washington, D.C.: Grove Dictionaries of Music, 1980.

Salvatorelli, Luigi. *A Concise History of Italy, from Prehistoric Times to Our Own Day*. Translated by Bernard Miall. New York: Oxford University Press, 1940.

Sella, Domenico. *Italy in the Seventeenth Century*. London: Longman, 1997.

Sinnigen, William G., and Arthur E. R. Boak. *A History of Rome to A.D. 565*. New York: Macmillan, 1977.

Thomsen, Rudi. *The Italic Regions from Augustus to the Lombard Invasions*. Rome: "L'Erma" di Bretschneider, 1966.

Tobacco, Giovanni. *The Struggle for Power in Medieval Italy: Structures of Political Rule*. Cambridge: Cambridge University Press, 1989.

Turner, Jane, ed. *The Dictionary of Art*. New York: Grove's Dictionaries, 1996.

Wickham, Chris. *Early Medieval Italy: Central Power and Local Society 400–1000*. Totowa, N.J.: Barnes and Noble, 1981.

Wilkins, Ernest Hatch. *A History of Italian Literature*. Revised by Thomas G. Bergin. Cambridge, Mass.: Harvard University Press, 1974.

Woolf, Stuart. *A History of Italy, 1700–1860: The Social Constraints of Political Change*. London: Methuen, 1986.

Zuffi, Stefano, ed. *Italia centrale: Toscana, Marche, Umbria, Lazio*. Milan: Electa, 1994.

———. *Italia meridionale: Abruzzo, Molise, Campania, Puglia, Basilicata, Calabria, Sicilia, Sardegna*. Milan: Electa, 1994.

———. *Italia settentrionale: Valle d'Aosta, Piemonte, Lombardia, Trentino–Alto Adige, Veneto, Friuli–Venezia Giulia, Liguria, Emilia Romagna*. Milan: Electa, 1994.

WEB SITES

www.camera.it. Web site of the Italian Chamber of Deputies.

www.istat.it. Web site of the Italian State Statistical Institute.

www.italyemb.org. Web site of the Italian Embassy in the United States.

www.repubblica.it. Web site of *La Repubblica*, one of the nation's leading newspapers.
www.senato.it. Web site of the Italian Senate.
www.vatican.va. Web site of the Holy See.

INDEX

Agathocles of Syracuse, 50
Agnadello, Battle of, 370, 373, 384, 388
Agnelli, Giovanni, 236
Agnes of Montepulciano, Saint, 344
Agnolo, Donato di. *See* Bramante (Donato di Agnolo)
Agnone, 227
Agrate Conturbia, 250
Agriculture: and Abruzzo, 2, 3; and Apulia, 15, 17, 19; and Basilicata, 31–32; and Calabria, 40–41, 44; and Campania, 54; and Emilia Romagna, 75–76, 86; and Friuli–Venezia Giulia, 104; and Lazio, 121–22; and Liguria, 155–56; and Lombardy, 174; and Marche, 205–6; and Molise, 221–22; and Piedmont, 229; and Sardinia, 255–56, 258–59; and Sicily, 270, 283; and Trentino–Alto Adige, 298; and Tuscany, 310–11; and Umbria, 347–48; and Valle d'Aosta, 362; and Veneto, 367–68, 392
Agrigento, 280–82
Aistulf, 92, 106, 128, 231
Alaric, 13, 42, 46, 105, 115, 128, 175, 215, 231, 359, 369
Alaric II, 243
Alassio, 166–67
Alatri, 145, 150
Alba, 230, 247
Alba Longa, 126
Albanians, 47, 223
Albano Laziale, 141
Albano Terme, 383
Albe, 8
Albegna, 158, 167, 169
Alberobello, 22
Albertario, Don Davide, 201
Alberti family, 339
Alberti, Leon Battista, 101, 163, 198, 319, 326
Albertini, Luigi, 211
Alberto "the Wise," 92
Albertolli, Giocondo, 192
Albinoni, Tomaso, 379
Alboin, 106

Albornoz, Cardinal Gil (Egidio), 88, 124, 129–30, 207, 210, 212, 349, 356, 359
Albugnano, 244
Alcuin, 179
Alczeco, King of the Bulgars, 225, 226
Aldobrandeschi family, 328
Aldobrandini family, 138, 142
Aleramici, 242
Aleramo, 242
Ales, 263
Alessandria, 230, 232, 240–43, 244
Alessi, Galeazzo, 162, 253
Alexandria, Egypt, 159, 209, 375
Alfano, Franco, 65, 333
Alfieri, Vittorio, 233, 244
Alfonso of Aragon, 58–59
Alfonso II, 59
Algarotti, Francesco, 379
Alghero, 257, 266
Alighieri, Dante. *See* Dante Alighieri
Alleanza Nazionale (National Alliance), 5, 19, 34, 44, 45, 57, 79, 125, 177, 208, 224, 234, 275, 313, 350, 372
Allegri, Antonio. *See* Correggio (Antonio Allegri)
Allori, Agnolo. *See* Bronzino, il (Agnolo Allori)
Alpenvorland, 301, 302, 371, 382
Alpini troops, 307
Altamura, 22
Altare della Patria, 138
Altavilla. *See* Hauteville, d'(Altavilla) family
Altino, 369, 381
Altomonte, 47
Alvaro, Corrado, 50
Alviano, d', family, 115
Amalfi and Amalfi Coast, 54, 55, 73–74
Amalusuntha, Queen, 98
Amati family: Andrea, Antonio, Girolamo and Nicolo, 194
Amato, Antonio, 285
Amato, Giacomo, 278–79
Amatrice, Cola d', 7, 214
Ambrogi, Melozzo degli. *See* Forlì,

432

INDEX

and Piedmont, 238; and Umbria, 352
Dialect theater: and Campania, 66; and Friuli–Venezia Giulia, 112, 118; and Veneto, 379
Diaz, Armando, 62, 250
Diocletian, Roman emperor, 33, 55, 127, 128, 133, 214, 260, 314, 349, 355, 392
Diomedes, 18, 23, 24
Dionysius the Elder, 42, 50, 290, 291
Dionysius the Younger, 42, 49
Disraeli, Benjamin, 87
Dolcebuono, Gian Giacomo, 200
Dolianova, 261
Domenichino, il (Domenico Zampieri), 63
Domenico di Sora, Saint, 8
Dominican Order, 64, 134, 183, 315, 316, 317, 333, 376, 381, 388, 391, 393
Domitian, Roman emperor, 133, 138
Donatelli, Carmine, 34
Donatello (Donato de Betto di Bardi), 317, 318, 340, 385
Dongo, 192
Donizetti, Gaetano, 187–88
Dono, Paolo di. *See* Uccello, Paolo (Paolo di Dono)
Dorelli, Johnny (Giorgio Guidi), 185
Dorgali, 262
Doria, Andrea, 159–60, 162, 165
Doria, Percivalle, 216
Doria, Pietro, 381
Doria family, 165, 266–67
Dossetti, Giuseppe, 161
Dossi, Carlo, 184
Dossi, Dosso (Giovanni Luteri), 86, 219
Dottori, Carlo de', 385
Doxapatres, Neilos, 278
Drusus (adopted son of Augustus), 299
Ducio, Agostino di, 351
Duino, 112
Duphot, General Leonard, 130

Earthquakes: and Abruzzo, 7; and Apulia, 25; and Basilicata, 35; and Calabria, 43, 44, 45, 46, 48, 49, 51; and Campania, 54, 63, 68; and Friuli–Venezia Giulia, 117, 119; and Lazio, 152; and Marche, 210, 214, 219; and Molise, 226; and Sicily, 23, 284, 288, 290, 292, 294; and Umbria, 353; and Veneto, 384
Ecclesius, Bishop, 98
Eco, Umberto, 241
Education: and Abruzzo, 1, 2; and Apulia, 21, 27; and Basilicata, 35, 38; and Calabria, 45; and Campania, 60, 64, 73; and Emilia Romagna, 82–83, 90, 91; and Friuli–Venezia Giulia, 110, 118; and Lazio, 139–40, 151; and Lombardy, 183–84, 200; and Marche, 211, 214, 216, 219; and Molise, 225; and Piedmont, 237–38, 241; and Sardinia, 265; and Sicily, 284, 285; and Trentino–Alto Adige, 303, 306; and Tuscany, 314, 321, 323, 330, 335, 336; and Umbria, 351–52; and Veneto, 378, 384, 388
Efisio, Sant', 260
Egadi Islands, 269, 271, 295
Egidian Constitutions, 124
Einaudi, Luigi, 247
Elba, 330–31
Eleonora of Sardinia, 263
Elia, Antonio Sant', 191–92
Elymi people, 293, 294
Emidio, Saint, 214
Emilia Romagna, 75–102; agriculture, 75–76, 86; and Austrians, 85–86, 88, 91, 93; and Byzantines, 78, 85, 93, 97–98, 101; and Christian Democratic Party, 99; and Communist Party, 79, 81; and dialect literature, 101–2; education, 82–83, 90, 91; and Etruscans, 78, 80, 84; and Fascism, 79, 81, 87, 89–90, 95; festivals and fairs, 77, 100; food, 77–78; and France, 78, 93, 94, 97, 99; and Hungarians, 99; industry, 75–76, 81; and Lombards, 78, 84, 85, 93, 97; moun-

Veneto, 377, 378, 380, 383, 385, 387, 388, 389, 391, 393, 394

Muslims: and Abruzzo, 4; and Apulia, 18, 19, 23, 26, 28, 29, 74; and Basilicata, 33, 35, 37; and Calabria, 42, 43, 46, 48, 49, 51; and Campania, 55, 58, 70, 72; and Lazio, 128, 143, 148, 150; and Liguria, 157, 159, 165, 167, 168; and Marche, 207, 209; and Molise, 225, 226, 227; and Piedmont, 243; and Sardinia, 257, 261, 264, 265; and Sicily, 271–72, 276, 277, 278, 281, 283, 284, 286, 287, 288, 290, 292, 293, 294; and Tuscany, 331, 335; and Umbria, 354, 355; and Veneto, 372–73. *See also* Turks

Mussato, Albertino, 384

Mussolini, Benito, 12–13, 21, 26, 27–28, 65, 70–71, 79, 81, 89–90, 107, 113, 131, 132, 135, 138–39, 140, 147, 149, 168, 171, 181, 185, 186, 190, 192, 198, 211, 234, 245, 248, 251, 258, 264, 274, 275, 289, 294–95, 329–30, 350, 351, 364, 374, 381, 383, 384, 389, 391, 394

Naples (Napoli), 53, 54, 55, 56, 57–67, 68, 72, 74; and Abruzzo, 4; and Apulia, 19, 25, 28, 29; and Calabria, 43; and Lazio, 131, 150; and Marche, 213; and Molise, 222, 223, 224; and Sicily, 276; and Tuscany, 339; and Umbria, 351

Napoleon Bonaparte, 25, 33, 37, 43, 60–61, 62, 78, 89, 99, 106, 117, 124–25, 130–31, 145, 157, 160, 165, 166, 168, 170, 176, 181, 187, 191, 192, 195, 196, 198, 202, 208, 212, 216, 223, 232, 240, 242, 244, 246, 252, 258, 273, 300, 305, 313, 316, 321, 331, 332, 334, 342, 349, 356, 364, 365, 370, 374, 375, 377, 378, 380, 384, 388, 391, 394

Narni, 348, 358

National Alliance. *See* Alleanza Nazionale (National Alliance)

Nature Reserves. *See* Parks (nature reserves)

Naturno, 305

Nazzari, Amedeo, 260

Neapolitan Bourbons, 4, 10, 11–12, 19, 21, 43, 56, 60–64, 70, 71, 93, 137, 148, 223, 273

Negri, Ada, 197

Nelson, Horatio, 273

Nenni, Pietro, 98–99

Neon, Bishop, 97

Neorealism, 141, 166, 185

Nepi, 152

Neri, Pompeo, 313

Nero, Roman emperor, 114, 133

Nervi, Pier Luigi, 183, 202, 237

Nettuno, 143

Newspapers: *Avanti!*, 199; *Corriere della Sera*, 50, 211, 247, 280; *Diario Ordinario*, 139; *Gazzetta del Mantova*, 199; *l'Indipendente*, 110; *il Mondo*, 50, 65; *il Piccolo*, 110; *il Resto del Carlino*, 50; *Stampa, la*, 247, 280, 356

Niccolini, Antonio, 63

Nice, 233

Nicholas, Saint (San Nicolo), 21, 27

Nicholas of Tolentino, Saint, 216

Nievo, Ippolito, 385

Nigetti, Matteo, 321

Nilo, Saint, 141

Ninfa, 147

Nitti, Francesco Saverio, 36

Nittis, Giuseppe De, 22

Nogaret, Guillaume de, 146

Nola, 61

Noli, 170–71

Nonantola, 75, 92

Nora, 261

Norcia, 142, 348, 355

Normans: and Abruzzo, 4, 10; and Apulia, 18, 27, 28; and Basilicata, 33, 35, 36; and Calabria, 43, 46, 48, 50; and Campania, 55, 56, 58, 71; and Lazio, 128, 129; and

Pontecorvo, 55
Pontedera, 337
Pontelli, Baccio, 136
Ponti, Gio, 183
Pontine Islands, 148
Pontinia, 147
Pontormo (Jacopo Carrucci), 324, 327
Ponza, 147, 149
Ponzio, Flaminio, 137
Popes: Adrian I, 176; Alexander II, 25; Alexander III, 241; Alexander VI, 6, 59, 80, 88, 143, 152, 358; Alexander VII, 64, 130, 136, 137; Benedict XI, 357; Benedict XIV, 119; Benedict XV, 161, 216; Boniface IV, 133; Boniface VIII, 129, 139, 146, 257, 357; Celestine V, 6–7, 226; Clement IV, 69; Clement V, 352; Clement VI, 336; Clement VII, 81, 130, 133, 210, 314; Clement XII, 138, 210, 211; Eugenius III, 129, 151; Eugenius IV, 163, 317; Formosus, 129; Gregory the Great, 4, 168; Gregory II, 128; Gregory VII, 55, 73, 100, 129, 193; Gregory IX, 356; Gregory XVI, 206, 348, 382; Honorius III, 352; Innocent III, 74, 272, 352, 373; Innocent IV, 25; Innocent X, 130, 138, 339; Innocent XI, 192; Innocent XII, 143; John XXIII, 188; John Paul I, 383; Julius II, 78, 81, 97, 134, 135, 136, 141, 152, 170, 349, 370; Julius III, 137, 144; Leo the Great, 128; Leo X, 134, 319, 339; Leo XII, 356; Leo XIII, 145; Liberius, 262; Lucius II, 129; Marcellus, 214; Nicholas II, 18; Nicholas V, 136; Paul III, 93, 96, 135, 151, 208, 216, 249, 305, 349, 351; Paul IV, 9; Paul V, 130; Paul VI, 190, 355, 383; Pius II, 109, 212, 342–43, 345; Pius III, 345; Pius IV, 180, 211; Pius V, 242; Pius VI, 89, 130–31; Pius VII, 89, 92, 131, 133, 170; Pius IX, 86, 131, 148, 212, 307, 356; Pius X, 375–76, 389;

Pius XI, 131, 142, 186, 214, 216; Pius XII, 132, 214, 352; Sergius I, 118; Sixtus IV, 134, 170, 218, 315; Sixtus V, 130; Stephen I, 387; Stephen III, 128; Sylvester I, 142; Urban II, 20; Urban IV, 33, 359; Urban VIII, 130, 136, 142
Popolari, 286, 337
Poppone, Patriarch, 114, 119
Pordenone, 103, 106, 108, 115–16
Pordenone, il (Giovanni Antonio de'Sacchis), 116
Porta, Giacomo della, 136, 137, 140
Porto, Luigi da, 393
Porto Empedocle, 281
Porto Garibaldi, 88
Porto Maurizio, 165
Porto Torres (Torres), 257, 265, 266, 267
Portoferraio, 331
Portovenere, 168
Posilippo, 65
Positano, 73
Possagno, 389
Potenza, 31, 35–36
Poverty: in Basilicata, 34, 36, 37; in Calabria, 44; in Tuscany, 342
Pozzallo, 291
Pozzo, Andrea, 111, 137, 248, 307
Pozzomaggiore, 266
Pozzuoli, 63, 67
Praetutii people, 4, 13
Prampolini, Enrico, 91
Prato, 339–40
Pratolini, Vasco, 322
Pratomagno, 324
Predappio, 89–90
Predappio Alta, 77
Preti, Francesco Maria, 381
Prezzolini, Giuseppe, 321, 352
Priamar Fortress, 170
Principato Citra (Citeriore), 56, 69, 72
Principato Ultra (Ulteriore), 56, 68, 69
Procida, Giovanni da, 72
Prodi, Romano, 224
Prokofiev, Sergei, 379
Prospero, Saint, 100
Proto, Saint, 265

Sforza family, 93, 166, 193, 196, 201, 217, 219, 241, 242, 332
Shakespeare, William, 393
Shelley, Mary and Percy Bysshe, 169
Shroud of Turin, 236–37
Sibari, 46, 55
Sica, Vittorio De, 140, 141, 144, 146
Sicani people, 271, 287, 293
Sicilian Vespers, 272, 276
Sicily, Kingdom of, 4, 56, 272
Sicily (Sicilia), 268–95; agriculture, 270, 283; and Apulia, 272; and Austrians, 273; and Byzantines, 271, 272, 276, 281–82, 284, 287, 288, 289, 290, 291–92, 293; and Calabria, 43, 272; and Campania, 58; and Christian Democratic Party, 275, 286, 291; and Communist Party, 282, 292; earthquakes, 23, 284, 288, 290, 292, 294; education, 284, 285; and Fascism, 274–75, 277, 279, 280, 281, 283, 286, 287, 290, 294–95; festivals and fairs, 278, 287; and Florence, 291; food, 270–71; and France, 273, 276; and Frederick II Hohenstaufen, 272, 278, 283, 284, 285, 287, 289; and Genoa, 292; and Goths, 276, 281, 284; and Greeks, 271, 279, 280–82, 283, 284, 287, 288, 289, 290, 291, 293, 294; industry, 270, 281, 283, 292; mountains, 275–76, 283, 288; museums, 277–79, 280, 282, 284, 286, 289, 293, 294; and Muslims, 271–72, 276, 277, 278, 281, 283, 284, 286, 287, 288, 290, 292, 293, 294; and Naples, 276; and Normans, 272, 276, 278, 279, 280, 281, 283, 286, 293; parks (nature reserves), 276, 284, 288, 293; and Piedmont, 273; recent politics in, 275; and Risorgimento, 273–74, 277, 282; rivers, 276, 282, 283, 285, 290, 291, 292, 294; and Rome, Ancient Republic and Empire, 269, 271, 276, 279, 281, 284,

287, 288, 289, 291, 293, 294; and Sardinia, 257; and Spain, 272–73, 288, 289; tourism, 280, 285–86, 289–90, 295; wine, 270; and World War One, 277; and World War Two, 274–75, 277, 283, 288, 292, 293
Siculan people (Siculi or Sicels), 49, 50, 271, 287, 289, 290
Siena, 309, 312, 328, 341–45
Sigismund, King of Hungary, 106, 113
Signorelli, Luca, 327, 340, 343, 344
Signorini, Telemaco, 321
Sigonella, 291
Sila Law, 44
Silanus, 262
Sile (Sila), 39, 41
Silone, Ignazio (Secondo Tranquilli), 9
Sinisgalli, Leonardo, 36
Sion, Bishop of, 239
Siracusa, 42, 49, 50, 208
Sirai, 261
Siri, 33
Sironi, Mario, 256
Skanderbeg, George Kastrioti, 223
Slapater, Scipio, 111–12
Slovenia, 103, 109, 111, 113
Sluderno (Schluderns), 305
Soccer, 163
Social War, 4, 213
Socialism and Socialist Party, 28, 81, 84, 94, 99, 161, 171, 192, 193–94, 199, 234, 236, 238, 246, 248, 259, 284, 326, 350
Socrate, Virgilio (Achille Funi), 87
Sodoma, il (Giovanni Antonio Bazzi), 252, 342, 344
Soffici, Ardegno, 321
Solari, Giovanni, 200
Solari, Guiniforte, 200
Soldati, Mario, 185, 238
Solimena, Francesco, 62–63
Sondrio, 201–2
Sonnino, Sidney, 336
Sora, 146
Sorbara, 77
Sordi, Alberto, 140
Sormano, Pace, 170

About the Author

ROY DOMENICO is an associate professor of history at the University of Scranton, Pennsylvania. He has written frequently on Italy and the Vatican.